D1607861

· THE ·

International

ENCYCLOPEDIA

OF SEXUALITY

Editor

ROBERT T. FRANCOEUR

Associate Editor

RAYMOND J. NOONAN

· THE ·

International

ENCYCLOPEDIA

OF SEXUALITY

VOLUME IV

Including New Countries

CONTINUUM
NEW YORK · LONDON

2001

The Continuum International Publishing Group Inc
370 Lexington Avenue, New York, NY 10017

The Continuum International Publishing Group Ltd
The Tower Building, 11 York Road, London SE1 7NX

Copyright © 2001 by Robert T. Francoeur

Typography, Design Coordination, and Computer Graphics by
Ray Noonan, ParaGraphic Artists, NYC http://www.paragraphics.com/

Printed in the United States of America

Library of Congress Cataloging-in-Publication Data

The international encyclopedia of sexuality / edited by Robert T.
  Francoeur ; foreword by Timothy Perper ; preface by Ira L. Reiss.
Raymond J. Noonan, Associate Editor vol. 4
    v. cm.
    Includes bibliographical references and index.
    ISBN 0-8264-0838-9 (v. 1 : alk. paper)
    1. Sex—Encyclopedias.   2. Sex customs—Encyclopedias.
I. Francoeur, Robert T. II. Noonan, Raymond J.
HQ21.I68   1997
306.7'03—dc20   95-16481
                                                           CIP

Vols. 1-3 ISBN 0-8264-0841-9

Vol. 4 ISBN 0-8264-1274-2

CONTENTS

VOLUME FOUR

The International Encyclopedia of Sexuality, Volume 4: An Introduction

Robert T. Francoeur, Ph.D., A.C.S., Editor

Ten years ago, I was seduced by a fascinating, irresistible, and seemingly simple idea for a unique and much-needed human sexuality reference book, an *International Encyclopedia of Sexuality*, describing sexual attitudes and behavior in 20 countries around the world. I created an outline covering basic premises of sex, love, and gender roles, ethnic and religious influences, sex education, heterosexual relations, homosexuality and bisexuality, contraception and abortion, teen pregnancy and population control, coercive sexual behavior, pornography, prostitution, STDs, HIV/AIDS, and the like. As I spoke with a dozen or more leading sexologists outside the United States and colleagues in the Society for the Scientific Study of Sexuality, I found a small group of colleagues who were experts on sexuality in their own cultures or who had done extensive research in another culture. These I invited to write a chapter of 20 to 25 pages describing sexual attitudes and behaviors in their chosen culture. My volunteers came from a variety of disciplines. Beyond their interest in sexology, each had professional training in an orthodox discipline, such as psychology, sociology, medicine, biology, history, anthropology, or health education. Together we planned a unique reference and resource volume that would let scholars, public health professionals, counselors, and educators compare contraception attitudes and behavior, marital patterns, or any other sexual issue or topic in 20 different countries.

My volunteers were prominent and respected scholars, and very busy. Fortunately, they quickly recognized the need for this kind of in-depth cross-cultural reference. They were eager to write, even without any financial compensation for their labor beyond the customary complimentary copy. As e-mail replaced much slower and far-less-reliable postal mail, my life as editor became far less difficult and frustrating, and much more interesting and demanding than I could ever have expected.

What was supposed to be a single-volume, 400-page encyclopedia mushroomed. By 1996, the passion, zeal, and expertise of my international team of experts had resulted in three volumes instead of one volume, 32 countries instead of 20 countries, and 1,737 pages instead of 400 pages. Instead of 25 or 30 colleagues, I ended up with 40 team leaders and 130 co-authors and contributors. All that was too much for the original publisher, who still wanted 20 countries in a single 400-page volume. I refused to amputate the incredible chapters and fortunately found Continuum International willing to publish the whole three volumes.

When the first three volumes of *The International Encyclopedia of Sexuality* (*IES*) were presented in 1997 at the World Congress of Sexology in Valencia, Spain, the response was more than enthusiastic. The World Association of Sexology, an international society of leading scholars and eighty professional organizations devoted to the study of human sexual behavior, endorsed the *Encyclopedia* "as an important and unique contribution to our understanding and appreciation of the rich variety of human sexual attitudes, values, and behavior in cultures around the world." The *Encyclopedia* also received the "1997 Citation of Excellence for an outstanding reference work in the field of sexology" from the American Foundation for Gender and Genital Medicine and Science.

Library Journal described *IES* as "an extraordinary, highly valuable synthesis of information not available elsewhere . . ., one of the most ambitious cross-cultural sex surveys ever undertaken." *Choice* picked the three volumes as the "Best Reference Work of 1997." *Contemporary Psychology* said *IES* is "an invaluable, unique scholarly work that no library should be without." The British journal *Sexual and Marital Therapy* said that *IES* "enables us to make transcultural comparisons of sexual attitudes and behaviours in a way no other modern book does." Lengthy favorable notices appeared in Austria's *Focus das Moderne Nachrichtenmagazin* and Spain's *Camb16*.

Very soon after this, with the first three volumes moving toward a fourth printing, my editor at Continuum suggested that we move ahead with a fourth volume. The chapters in this volume were written by 60 sexologists, who fill in gaps in our earlier coverage of Europe, with chapters on Italy, Iceland, Portugal, Croatia, Cyprus, Norway, and Turkey. To our African coverage, we add very interesting contrasts in Islamic Arab Egypt and Morocco, and a finely nuanced emic view of sexuality in Nigeria. Colombia is added to our South American picture. In the Far East and Southeast Asia, volume 4 offers Korea, the Philippines, Hong Kong, Indonesia, Papua New Guinea, and Vietnam, with important discussions of the indigenous tribal cultures in several of these societies. Because this fourth volume appears early in the twenty-first century, we have included an entry on "Outer Space" by Raymond J. Noonan, associate editor for this volume. This chapter highlights many of the special issues and concerns that are coming to light in the realm of sexology and space psychology as multinational crews begin to inhabit the new International Space Station.

Despite our concentrated efforts, we were not able to solve two major frustrations in gathering the material for volume 4. In spite of persistent efforts and the helpful suggestions and negotiations of colleagues, including

Marc Ganem, president of the French Sexological Association, and Evelyne S. Schreier, we were unable to obtain a chapter on France. Our other major disappointment was not being able to complete a chapter on Cuba in time to include it in this volume. Before the first three volumes were published in 1997, we started working with key persons in Cuba's Centro Nacional de Educacion Sexual. That three-year effort failed for a variety of reasons, but what we learned about Cuban sexual attitudes and behavior, and the outstanding progress Cuba has made in sexuality education, made a chapter on Cuba very desirable. In late 1999, serendipitous connections led us to a South American health educator doing fieldwork in Cuba. Her several field trips to Cuba provided enough material for a very interesting field report, but our deadline for this fourth volume did not allow completion of a full chapter. In volume 5, we plan to include Norway and Hong Kong (updated), France and Denmark, Cuba and Peru or Chile, Tanzania or another sub-Saharan African nation, a Baltic state or a former member of the USSR, Pakinstan or Bangladesh, and Sri Lanka or New Zealand.

The International Encyclopedia on the World Wide Web

Thanks to Professor Erwin Haeberle, Germany's leading sexologist and an international scholar, you can view the first three volumes of *The International Encyclopedia of Sexuality* (*IES*) on the World Wide Web. Go to http:// www.sexology.cjb.net. This will bring up Humboldt University in Berlin, the Archive for Sexology (*Archiv fur Sexualwissenschaft*) home page. Scroll down the left column to Sexual Behavior Around the World. Select the *International Encyclopedia of Sexuality* in the Sexual Behavior contents. Click on GO, and the *IES* home page will come up. While this is not a substitute for the convenience and usability of the printed volumes, it does allow us to share it with our colleagues in third world countries.

Supplemental Notes for IES

For this fourth volume, we asked the contributors to volumes 1 through 3 to prepare a few pages describing three or four significant developments in their country since 1996 for an updating supplement. Unexpectedly, their enthusiasm went far beyond our expectations. In the United Kingdom, Kevan Wylie and his colleagues responded enthusiastically with a 35,000-word "Supplement"—practically a whole new chapter. Jakob Pastoetter provided a similar in-depth expansion for Germany, as did Fang-fu Ruan for China, Anne Bolin for French Polynesia, and Igor Kon for Russia. The unexpected length of these and other not-so-brief Supplemental Notes made their inclusion in this volume impossible. This forced an editorial decision we had no way of anticipating. Our only alternative was to shift the 40 pages of Supplemental Notes from volume 4 to our SexQuest Web site at http://www.SexQuest.com/IES4/.

At the same time, the translations of two key chapters, Colombia and South Korea, produced chapters much longer than expected. Because these translations were completed only a few weeks before our final deadline, we faced another difficult decision with our publisher. This required shifting two chapters to our SexQuest Web site. We sincerely apologize to Emil M. L. Ng and Joyce L. C. Ma, our Hong Kong authors, and to Elsa Almas and Esben Esther Pirelli Benestad, our Norwegian authors, but we had no alternative. We invite our readers to consult the chapters on Hong Kong and Norway, as well as the Supplemental Notes at http://www.SexQuest.com/IES4/. Both chapters and the full Supplemental Notes are included in the index at the end of this fourth volume.

Acknowledgments from the Editors

As editors of this fourth volume of *The International Encyclopedia*, we are happy to acknowledge the dedicated and passionate commitment of the 60 authors who researched and wrote the chapters in this volume. We thank each of them. We also want to thank the 21 sexologists who contributed Supplementary Notes to update the chapters in our first three volumes. The 250 sexologists on 6 continents who helped create this unique and "herculean" four-volume resource can take great pride in our labor of love. We also appreciate the support of Evander Lomke, our editor at Continuum International. The editor is also grateful to his new associate editor, Raymond J. Noonan, a long-time friend and colleague, for his invaluable work in copyediting, graphic design, and problem solving. I also thank Luciane Raibin for her patient work as my point person for communications with our Latino and Portuguese contributors.

Readers of *The International Encyclopedia of Sexuality* are invited to submit important news items or reports of findings of new sex research being done in any of the countries covered here, or any other country in the world. We will try to keep the SexQuest Web site updated with your help. Send items in English if possible, with appropriate citations, to Raymond J. Noonan, Ph.D., IES Associate Editor, Health and Physical Education Department, Fashion Institute of Technology, 27th Street and 7th Avenue, New York, NY 10001 USA, or by e-mail to rjnoonan@SexQuest.com.

Austria
(*Republik Österreich*)

Dr. Rotraud A. Perner, L.L.D.* **

Contents

Demographics and a Historical Perspective

A. Demographics

Located in south central Europe, Austria had a population of slightly over eight million in 2000. With a landmass of 32,378 square miles, Austria is smaller than the state of South Carolina and larger than Maine. Austria's

Communications: Mag. Dr. Rotraud A. Perner, Postfach 23 A-1013, Vienna, Austria; perner.perner@magnet.at, perner.perner@nextra.at, rotraud.a.perner@chello.at.

**The General Editor gratefully acknowledges Linda Kneucker's able translation of Dr. Perner's German text and her gracious service as an intermediary between Dr. Perner and myself. I also greatly appreciate the review of this chapter and additional comments by Martin Voracek, Ph.D., M.Sc., of the Medical Faculty at Vienna General Hospital at the University of Vienna. His comments are indicated by [. . . (Voracek)].

neighbors include Switzerland and Liechtenstein on the west, Germany and the Czech Republic on the north, Slovakia and Hungary on the east, and Slovenia and Italy on the south. Austria is very mountainous, with the Alps and their foothills covering the western and southern parts of the nation. The eastern provinces and the capital, Vienna (1999 estimated population 1.7 million), are in the Danube River basin.

Since the collapse of the Habsburg (or often spelled Hapsburg in English) Empire in 1918 after the end of World War I, Austria comprises only nine states (or provinces). Clockwise, they are: Lower Austria, Vienna, Burgenland, Styria, Carinthia, Upper Austria, Salzburg, Tyrol, and Vorarlberg. In Burgenland, the smallest and farthest east, Hungarian and Croatian influences are noticeable, whereas Voralberg, lying farthest west, tends strongly towards Switzerland.

Twenty percent of Austria's entire population lives in Vienna. Eighteen percent of the eight million Austrians are under the age of 15, 67 percent are between age 15 and 65, and 15 percent are 65 and older. Fifty-four percent live in the cities. Ethnic distribution is 99 percent German, with Slovene and Croatian minorities. Eighty-five percent of Austrians are Roman Catholic and 6 percent are Protestant. The average life expectancy at birth in 1999 was 74 for males and 81 for females. The 1999 birthrate was 9.6 per 1,000, the infant mortality rate was 5.1 per 1,000 live births, and the death rate was 10 per 1,000, for a negative annual natural increase of 0.042 percent. The Total Fertility Rate (TFR) in 1995 was 1.4 births per fertile woman, ranking Austria 209 among 227 nations of the world in total fertility. Austria has one hospital bed per 117 persons and one physician per 289 persons. The literacy rate in 1993 was 100 percent, with 95 percent attendance for nine years of compulsory school. Education is free and compulsory from age 6 to 15. The estimated per capita gross domestic product in 1997 was $21,400.

B. A Brief Historical Perspective

The Romans conquered Austrian lands from Celtic tribes around 15 B.C.E. In 788 of the Common Era, the territory was incorporated into Charlemagne's Holy Roman Empire. By 1300, the House of Habsburg had gained control of the land. In the next few hundred years, they added to their realm vast territories in all parts of Europe.

Austria's dominance of Germany was undermined in the eighteenth century and ended with the rise of Prussia in 1866. However, the 1815 Congress of Vienna confirmed Austria's control of a large empire in southeast Europe, consisting of Germans, Hungarians, Slavs, Italians, and others. The Austro-Hungarian dual monarchy was established in 1867, when Hungary was given some autonomy. Fifty years of peace followed.

The 1914 assassination of Archduke Franz Ferdinand, the Habsburg heir, by a Serbian nationalist, led to World War I and dissolution of the Habsburg Empire when Austria, Germany, and the Ottoman Empire were defeated.

Austria was then reduced to a small republic with the borders it has today. Nazi Germany invaded Austria in 1938; the republic was reestablished in 1945 under Allied occupation. Full independence and neutrality were restored in 1955.

Politically, Austria is a democratic federal republic. After the national elections in 1995, the 183 seats in Parliament were distributed to the following political parties: 71 mandates for the Social Democrats; 52 for the conservative People's Party; 41 for the Freedom Party, and 9 each for the Liberal Forum and the (environmentalist) Greens, and one without party affiliation. The Social Democrats and the People's Party formed a coalition government. The Social Democrats were often ideologically supported by the Greens and the Liberal Forum. The nationalistic anti-immigration Freedom Party presented the only real opposition.

There has been a radical change in Austria's political situation since October 3, 1999. The Parliamentary mandates in early 2000 were: 65 for the Social Democrats, 52 for both the People's Party and the Freedom Party (with clear self-acknowledged fascist tendencies). The environmentalist Greens held 14 seats, and the Liberal Forum was no longer represented. There is now a coalition government between the conservatives and the Freedom Party. Observers expect this alliance to bring a distinct increase of conservative, restrictive, and xenophobic ideas. The first sign of this conservative swing was seen in the abolishment of the Federal Ministry for Women's Affairs, which had, in its ten-year existence, been strongly engaged in combating violence against women and enacting harsher punishment for sexual offenses.

1. Basic Sexological Premises

A. Character of Gender Roles

At the end of the 1960s, a kind of "velvet" cultural revolution began. Austria's women became conscious of the discrimination they experienced as women, their reduced roles as reproducers, and discrimination in the labor market. Social politics, activated by women in the new feminist movement, brought considerable social change, especially in the first years of the Socialist Government, between 1970 and 1983. Two signals of this revolution were the appointment of a State Secretary for Women's Rights in 1979 and, in 1990, establishment of a Ministry for Women's Affairs.

Women benefited most from the educational reforms of the 1960s and 1970s, even if there is still a difference in educational levels between men and women. The employment of women increased at the beginning of the 1970s and, in 1992, 62 percent of all women between the ages of 15 and 59 were gainfully employed. Improved training and the more skilled qualifications of women had, however, little influence on their salaries and positions. The average gross income of men was 43 percent higher than that earned by women.

In the course of the Family Law Reform of 1978, the marriage laws were changed from the legally incapacitating discriminatory laws against women to an emphasis on marriages based on partnership. Before this reform, the man was the "head of the family," and the woman had to take on his name. The man decided the place of residence. He could forbid his wife to work and could make all decisions concerning the children. His wife had to obey his "orders."

The practically unchanged sole responsibility of women for the care of children, the lack of institutions, such as day care centers and kindergartens, a shortage of qualified part-time jobs, as well as potential motherhood, still greatly lessen the possibilities for women in the labor market. Women are subject to certain work prohibitions that are supposed to protect them, e.g., night shifts, but actually make entering certain occupations more difficult. Women who want both children and careers, something that is a matter of course for men, can often fulfill this only with double or triple burdens. Although it has been legally possible since January 1, 1990, for fathers to take leaves of absence from work for childcare (*Karenzurlaub*) until the child's second birthday, few men take such leaves. Many men also have difficulties with the legally established partnership in running a household, dividing the responsibilities of earnings, running the household, and raising children.

B. Sociolegal Status of Males and Females

According to the equality principles of the Austrian constitution, all citizens (written in masculine form) are equal before the law (Article VII). Nevertheless, there are gender-specific differences in some laws that cannot be biologically justified, such as the legal protection for pregnant women and mothers.

Women and men are considered sexually mature when they are 14 years of age, i.e., they are seen as adult enough to be able to accept desired sexual contacts and refuse those they do not want (Perner 1994). In the case of homosexual contacts, however, the lawmakers believe that young men are not able to decide independently for or against them until they are 18. Women and men who are 19 are both considered to be of full legal age, but the marriageable age for women is 16, and for men 19 years. Women can retire with pension at age 60, five years earlier than men, but, as of 2019, the age will be successively raised for women who were born after 1962 and eventually the pension age for men and women will be the same—65 years. There is no military conscription for women.

C. General Concepts of Sexuality and Love

The general sexual concept of love is within a heterosexual relationship. It is based on love and should be realized, preferably, in a life-long marriage, or at least as a partnership for life or a stable partnership. As a result of this attitude, practically all young Austrian women were married in the early 1960s. Since the 1970s, there has been a change to more pluralism: The age for marriage and for bearing the first child has risen; the number of those who marry and have children has fallen. The number of extra-marital births has risen, as well as the possibility of divorce and remarriage of those who have divorced. Still, the wish to marry is prevalent among 70 to 80 percent of youth.

Norms and attitudes relating to sexuality have also changed since the end of the 1960s. The availability of different methods of birth control and the possibility for legal abortion within the first three months (trimester) have given many women their first feelings of freedom regarding sexuality. Considering the frequent occurrence of sexual violence against women, it is, however, only possible in a limited way to talk about the sexual liberation of women.

Except in a few ethnic groups and religious minorities, virginity is not given any special value at the time of marriage. Although "wild" marriages and unmarried mothers and their children were stigmatized and legally discriminated against in the 1960s, life partnerships, "illegitimate" children, and single mothers are increasingly accepted in society. Likewise, relation-ships before marriage that include sexual intercourse and a series of monogamous relationships are accepted, and not only the ideal of "one great love." Despite the Church's opposition (e.g., by forbidding the use of most birth control methods), sexual desire and procreation are seen as separate from one another; as proven by the low fertility rate of 1.5 children per woman.

The norm for sexual intercourse is still the "complete" face-to-face heterosexual coitus with ejaculation. The attitude towards homosexuality is still negative, socially excluding, and, in traditional Catholic circles, openly hostile. Its impact can be seen in attempts to maintain legal dis-crimination against homosexual lovers. However, in recent years in Austria, the discussion in favor of recognition of homosexual partners is no longer taboo, and is in fact increasing.

2. Religious and Ethnic Factors Affecting Sexuality

A. Source and Character of Religious Values

To be religious in Austria is a sort of "social-cultural matter of course" accompanied by a certain amount of social pressure. The majority of Austrians are members of the Roman Catholic Church, which exerts a traditionally dominant role in comparison to other religious communities. Especially during the time of Austrian Fascism, 1934-1938, the cultural and political life was determined by the Catholic Church. Austria was organized as a so-called corporate country that met the Catholic concept of a corporate system (Encyclical, *Quadragesimo Anno* of Pius XI: 15.5.1931). It was seen as the responsibility of the State to guard moral life. In this model, according to the Constitution of 1934, women were only considered equal to men if laws did not determine otherwise. In 1929 and in 1930, Pope Pius XI had confirmed the subordinate role of the woman in marriage in two encyclicals.

Since 1970, the number of withdrawals from the Catholic Church has increased dramatically, especially because of the sexual morals of the Church that are no longer accepted by many of its believers (above all, because of the prohibition of the pill in the encyclical, *Humanae Vitae*, by Pope Paul VI in 1968). These teachings define the Catholic view regarding the rigid regulations of the sexes: Mary, the Mother of God, as childbearing without sexuality (on the basis of the virgin birth) as a model for women was emphasized. Virginity was given the highest value, and a motherhood of sacrifice was propagated as the essential duty of women. During the period of National Socialism, the veneration of Mary and the ideal of chastity were mixed with ideas of "racial purity" and therefore fit into the National Socialist regime.

Sexuality in Catholicism is only permitted in the insoluble state of marriage, since for hundreds of years biological reproduction was considered the one purpose of marriage. The encyclicals of Pope Pius XI (1930) dealing with marriage underlined the value of love in marriage that was especially confirmed later by the Second Vatican Council (1962-1965): The value of this love exists, even without reference to procreation. It is bound to marriage, with sexual intercourse, as a permanent unity. The moral system, according to the teachings of the Church, requires that heterosexual coitus must not interfere with the possibility of procreation. However, intercourse is also permitted when procreation is not possible (during the woman's monthly infertile period) or no longer possible (after menopause).

Marriage in Catholic teaching is the replica of the love of God for human beings: Christ is the bridegroom, the Church is the bride, and the Catholic family is the smallest church community, the "home church." The love relationship of the responsible couple, according to this concept, includes "natural birth control" (measurement of the infertile days of the woman).

According to the encyclical *Humanae Vitae* (1968), every form of active birth control is forbidden by the Church. However, this opinion does not require absolute obedience, as it is not a question of infallible dogma, but a writing of the pope. Because of the acceptance of the theological concept of "immediate animation," the presence of the soul at the moment of conception, abortion was (and is) considered murder. In 1991, one third of all Austrians and 40 percent of the female population stated that religion was meaningful for conducting their life. Forty percent of those who were religious thought that sex education in schools was damaging. A third of the religious wished that homosexuality would be again legally punishable (of the non-believers, one fourth wanted this).

The 1995 encyclical *Evangelium Vitae* (John Paul II) condemned abortion as well as birth control as generally being enemies of "life." Masturbation was seen as a terrible sin, or, at least, as against the rules. In the same way, practiced homosexuality was condemned as immoral.

Mostly it is the rural and farming population that lives according to Catholic norms. However, the majority of Austrians do not think highly of the ever-increasingly authoritarian path the Vatican has been taking. The comments of the official Church regarding sexual themes are reacted to with resistance.

In 1995, a Church referendum was initiated, calling for a "sisterly church," i.e., demanding that women be admitted to Church offices. It opposed the compulsory celibacy of priests, protested against the equating of birth control with abortion, and pleaded that questions of sexual morals be the responsibility of the individual's personal conscience.

In the minority Protestant churches, heterosexuality and one life-long marriage are seen as values that in a specific way correspond to the will of God. Marriage is, however, a worldly concern and therefore does not have a sacramental character as in the Catholic Church. For unborn life, the same rights of protection are given as for persons; but abortion is not categorically considered murder.

Discussion of homosexuality is still controversial in the Protestant church. In 1992, the theological commission published a statement declaring:

- the right of people to determine their own lifestyles;
- homosexuals must be respected and accepted in Christian communities;
- an ethical judgment on homosexuality in today's humanistic understanding cannot be found in the Bible; and
- a homosexual identity cannot be "turned around" or cured.

In Austria's Protestant churches today, those who identify themselves as homosexuals can be employees as well as pastors. The blessing of homosexual couples is not yet officially possible in the Protestant churches. However, an agenda for a concept for blessings is being worked out and will probably be accepted at the next synod.

In contrast, the "Invocavit" declaration of 1995, which was signed by 150 Protestant theologians and church employees as a reaction to the General Synod, rejected homosexuality, considering it contradictory to the will of God, the creator. It was considered a "destructive aberration of emotional life." In the view of the authors, homosexuals may not be employees in the church, and church blessings for homosexual couples are rejected as well.

The synod of the Neo-Catholic Church of Austria resolved that homosexuals are to be respected in their personalities, beliefs, and their cooperation in their communities. For homosexual life companions who intend their relationships to be permanent, church blessings were made possible at the synod of October 18, 1997.

3. Sexual Knowledge and Education

A. Government Policies and Programs

In the nineteenth century and earlier, sex education was part of the Catholic educational instructions. The emphasis was on what was forbidden, and on remaining caste and faithful before and in marriage. Masturbation was forbidden as a sin. Sexual intercourse before marriage, with or without force, was taboo and therefore not talked about. Nevertheless, the first sexual intercourse of aristocratic young men was often arranged by their fathers, when it was clear they had completed puberty. They were taken to a brothel for their first sexual experiences. In the upper-middle class or among prosperous farmers, sexual availability was expected from the female servants. If one became pregnant, she was sent away.

After the establishment of the Republic in 1918 and the election of the first female representatives, the female pioneers of the Social Democratic Party continually demanded institutions for sex education and counseling, and their priority was to increase help with questions about birth control. The first attempts were made when the Social Democrats took over the government in the capital, Vienna, through the work of the legendary City Councilman Julius Tandler. At the same time, Wilhelm Reich, a student of Freud, established the first outpatient sex clinics. With the growing strength of National Socialism and the emigration of the leading Jewish doctors, the initiative came to a standstill. After the end of World War II, it took about twenty-five years until the women's movement could push for a new abortion law and address questions of sex education. At practically the same time, at the suggestion of the parents' council of the Education Ministry, a seminar conducted by experts in September 1969 provided the push, making possible the decree, *Sex Education in the Schools* (November 24, 1970), in which sex education was introduced as an interdisciplinary principle of instruction.

A *Media Package* was prepared by the Federal Ministry of Education and the Federal Ministry for Family Affairs (now known as the Federal Ministry for the Environment, Youth, and Family) as the main teaching tool from 1984 to 1989. This production produced a vehement argument between the Marxist-oriented progressive psychoanalysts and Christian-conservative repressive-oriented sex educators. In the final edition that came out with the title, *Love with Responsibility*, basic sexology was emphasized, and in the didactic part a wealth of suggestions for exercises and games for the classroom was given.

The Catholic-oriented Institute for Marriage and Family, with the support of the Education and Family Ministries, developed a program, *Working Group: Parents, Students and Teachers—Partners in Sex Education*. For this, specially trained moderators in the schools offered general help in establishing communication between the groups and in working out concrete sex education projects for specific schools. This was done at no cost to the schools. (For additional information on sexuality education in the schools and at home, see Section 5B below).

In addition, both ministries offered special booklets. *Gynnie*, cosponsored by the Austrian Medical Association, provided answers to relevant gynecological questions, as well as questions about relationships. Brochures were also published for non-students; for example, the Family Ministry offered *So That Love Can Grow*, along with accompanying group discussions and help in seminars concerning topics of sexuality. Austrians seeking counseling and advice can turn to 220 family and partner counseling centers that have been established all over Austria and are financially supported by the Family Ministry. Four of these centers are explicitly declared as counseling centers for sex and sexuality. The Austrian Society for Planned Parenthood, founded in 1966, has established six counseling centers with an emphasis on birth control. These centers are in hospitals, and one is especially for young people. There, examinations can be carried out and contraception prescribed and distributed. Another initiative of this group is *Herzklopfen* (*Heart Throbbing*), which offers confidential telephone counseling especially for young people, and is therefore available on Saturday afternoons.

B. Informal Sources of Sexual Knowledge

Bravo, a German magazine for young people, is widely read in Austria, mainly, however, by less educated youngsters. In the late 1980s and early 1990s, *Rennbahn Express* (*Racetrack Express*) was quite popular and widely read by educated young people. Although it offers sexual information on two full pages eleven times a year, answers letters to the editor about sex, carries regular columns on health relating to sexuality, and has an Internet Web page offering counseling, the magazine is now decidedly out-of-fashion among young people, leaving the field open for new magazines to move in.

The media offers popular, if not always serious sexual information. The *Kronen Zeitung*, a daily newspaper in small format published in Vienna, offers "the man in the street" flowery-formulated but simply expressed answers to questions related to sex, and every Tuesday publishes letters from readers. Some newspapers in the provinces copy these letters. The original radio program, *Sex Hotline*, appreciated by many older listeners, was offered by ORF, the Austrian Radio, every two weeks on Fridays for two hours beginning at midnight. After 5 years, the program was given a new name, *Love Line*, and a year later was taken off the air, because the public was no longer as interested as in earlier years. *Zick Zack*, a program for youth that also offered young people the opportunity to call up and ask for advice, was a success, but was no longer aired after January 1995. Until 1997, there was a radio talk show that was replaced by *Joe's Nachtclub* (*Joe's Nightclub*) every Saturday from midnight until 2 a.m. While these informal sources of sexuality information come and go, Austrian media consistently provides some popular sources of information on sexuality.

4. Autoerotic Behaviors and Patterns

A. Children and Adolescents

Austria is a country without any tradition in sex education and pedagogy. To a large extent, moral values are stamped "Repress the bodily functions" by the Catholic Church as well as by the Puritanism of the *petite bourgeoisie*. Masturbation may be still tainted as sinful and forbidden for many older Austrians, who view it as "tainting your soul" ("*schwarze Pädagogic*") or still believe the myth that the number of ejaculations in their lives will be limited to 1000—"*1000 Schuß, dann ist Schluß*" ("1000 shots poured and then there is nothing more").

Nevertheless, masturbation is widespread among young people, and aside from traumatic sexual experiences, autoeroticism is among their very first conscious sexual experiences. Among boys, 60 percent of the 13-year-olds and 80 percent of the 14-year-olds have experience in masturbation, and 100 percent of the 16-year-olds. According to Nöstlinger and Wimmer-Puchinger (1994), girls have less experience with masturbation than boys: 25 percent of the 13-year-olds and 50 percent of the 17-year-olds. European studies indicate that masturbation is experienced earlier than it was in the 1960s, especially for girls. There are no comparative figures for Austria, but it can be assumed that the tendency is similar.

B. Adults

In Austrian studies, questions about masturbation are either not asked or are peripheral questions. Langbein and Fritsch (1991) remarked that masturbation was not thematically included in the basic Institut für Empirische Sozialforschung (IFES, Institute for Empirical Social Research) study, since international studies would in any case show that around 90 percent of all adults practice masturbation. A study by Senger and Hoffmann (1993) reported that about three quarters of all men and less than two thirds of all women masturbate, whereas the frequency of men, 1.6 times weekly, is twice that of women. Single people masturbate above the average, 2.2 times each week, and persons under the age of 40 masturbate more often than older people.

Adult heterosexuals who consult clinicians on the issue of masturbation usually do so because they view masturbation as taboo and something that is done in secret with a bad conscience. Many ask if it is "normal" to have the need to masturbate parallel to sexual intercourse.

The problem hardly affects homosexual men, because they view mutual masturbation as a favored sexual outlet. When AIDS emerged, "jack-off parties" became just as popular in Austria's gay communities as in other countries. These parties were held in private circles where community masturbation as a safer-sex method was practiced. Verified information from lesbians is not available, although the tendency is probably rising, as it is for women in general. Stronger self-determination in sexuality and more confident attitudes about their own bodies "My body belongs to me!"—have probably contributed positively to the frequency of masturbation for both heterosexual and lesbian women.

Altogether, the viewpoint that masturbation is by all means an enrichment and not only a substitute for one's sex life in a partnership is gaining recognition, even if slowly and still unmentionable in public.

Masturbation does not cease when Austrians get older. Although there are no statistics available for Austria, the experiences in supervised residential situations reveal that, just as seen in international studies, masturbation in old-age homes or nursing homes are part of daily life.

5. Interpersonal Heterosexual Behaviors

A. Children

The uncontested right of children to their individual forms of sexuality, as recognized by sexual researchers, is acknowledged only hesitantly by the general public. The only context in which children's sexuality is usually mentioned or discussed is in the context of sexual abuse.

When observed, any form of children's sexual activities—masturbation, "playing doctor," father-mother games—are often repressed and denied, because "what is not permitted, does not exist." A still-restrictive sex education concept tries to condemn children's sexual behavior with "black pedagogical" sanctions, or to keep it a secret. Rethinking these questions began slowly in the early 1990s.

B. Adolescents

Young people enter puberty earlier than they did a few generations ago. The first menstruation also takes place earlier. Eleven-year-olds who have their first periods are now the rule rather than the exception.

Based on law, a decree known as the "Sex Education Decree" was issued by the Ministry for Education about fifteen years ago. Sex education was to be given at schools as an interdisciplinary subject, with the strong participation of parents. In the middle of the 1980s, the Austrian Institute for Family Research undertook a study to find out how far the program had actually been put into practice. The first finding of this study was that when sex education is taught, it was in two subject areas: in biology classes, where information is emphasized, and in religion classes, where values are emphasized. Thereupon, the Institute developed a model that is called *Love Talks* to coordinate the two. It is the only model for sex education in Austrian schools, and has been adopted for use in South Tyrol, Germany, and the Czech Republic. The second finding showed that sex education is not a question of knowledge, but rather a communication problem. This information was incorporated into *Love Talks*. A moderator, who comes from outside the school, works to bring parents, teachers, and students together at one table to discuss pertinent topics. In addition, a sex education program for the school (workshops, field trips, etc.) is planned for different levels and classes. How this is concretely carried out depends on the individual interests of the school. The cost of the moderator is covered by the Ministry for Education, and therefore, the model can be offered to the schools at no additional cost.

Meanwhile, time and again, there are discussions about including sex education as a regular school subject in the curriculum. Up to the present, however, sex education as an educational means to support the capability of entering and experiencing relationships in all of their complexity is only available through *Love Talks*.

Sex education is not necessarily keeping pace with the personal experiences of youth. Although sex education in schools has been established as an educational principle for more than two generations, only half of the young people are actually given sex education in schools. At home the situation is the same. In a large-scale study about the sexuality of youth in 1994, 1,108 young people between the ages of 15 and 18 were questioned. The responses were: 94 percent of all young people had been in love once—on average, at 12.9 years old the first time, with 14 years old most often reported as the age. By age 14, 91 percent had had a date, and 89 percent had already "put their first kiss behind them" (with the average age for their first kiss at about 13). For male students, the percentages were clearly lower.

Young people reported their first romantic friendships, on average, at the age of 14, when 72 percent of the 1,108 students sampled had already had a steady partner. On average, at age 15, the first petting took place, for 62 percent of those surveyed. The least experienced with petting were male students who lived in the country, 44 percent; the most experienced were female apprentices living in the cities, 91 percent. Forty-three percent of the young people reported that they already had had their first heterosexual experiences other than petting at age 15. The highest percentage was among male apprentices in cities, where 85 percent reported having had their first heterosexual [oral sex] experience, clearly above the average. The average young person was 15.5 years old the "first time", with the first sexual intercourse taking place at the age of 16: girls 33 percent and boys 36 percent. Among the girls, 4 percent were less than 13 years old; 3 percent of the boys were under age 13. In the 14-to-15 age group, more girls have had sexual intercourse than boys.

The sexually experienced young people reported having had sexual intercourse a number of times. The most frequent sexual intercourse took place with a steady partner (40 percent); and 39 percent reported that they had had two or three partners. Only 4.5 percent of the girls and 11 percent of the boys had had sexual experience with more than five partners. At the time of the study, 72 percent had a steady boy- or girlfriend. The average duration of a friendship for young people was eleven months; the response most often given was sixty days.

Kissing and cuddling are the sexual activities most often indulged in, reported by 98.5 percent. Eighty-five percent reported "petting" and 66 percent sexual intercourse. Their emotional level and sense of sexual faithfulness play an important role for young people. Only 6 percent reported that they had been "unfaithful" to their partners.

A lasting relationship is an ideal for 79 percent of young people. Almost two thirds emphasized the wish to marry, and three fourths expressed the desire to have children. There was no significant difference between boys and girls. The figures from the study coincide with information from counseling and work with young people, where the expectation of traditional values, such as partnership, faithfulness, family, etc., are clearly articulated.

C. Adults

The legal regulations on the protection of minors generally set the "age of consent" at 14 years for consensual sexual relationships. This applies to both heterosexual and lesbian relationships. For male homosexual relationships, the age of consent is 18. Sexual relationships between adults and minors over 15, with the exception of gay male relationships, are legally permitted, as long as force or coercion is not used, and there is no exploitation of a dependent relationship.

About 18 percent of the adult Austrians between the ages of 17 and 70 live as "singles." The trend towards living alone is quickly rising. In 1993, about 900,000 people lived on their own; two years later, the figure was 1.2 million, an increase of 33 percent..

"Typical" singles are women over 50 years of age. Twenty-five percent of this age group lives alone, although whether they are divorced, widowed, or simply without partners is not known. Other singles include young men—38 percent of all those under the age of 30—as well as young women in school, about 40 percent, and farmers, 20 percent. Females in colleges and universities are more likely to live along than their non-academics peers.

The incidence of sexual intercourse among singles is low. More than half have no sexual partner, and only one in ten have intercourse once a week (Langbein and Fritsch 1991). Only 5 percent live as "swinging singles," i.e., have several sex partners at the same time. Of these, 42 percent want a steady relationship.

Another trend is a steady relationship without a common household, currently about 16 percent. A third of the young couples under the age of 30 and practically half of all divorced persons have such relationships. Of those, 68 percent said that they have sexual intercourse at least once a week. Only 6 percent do without sexual activities completely. Of those couples, who live separately, two thirds stated that they had happy and intensive love relationships, whereas of those pairs living together, only 56 percent expressed this view. Altogether, sex is more important to those who do not live together than it is to those who do live together. Nineteen percent had the opinion that sex was the strongest bond to their partners, and 59 percent are satisfied with their sex lives. Of those who live together, 8 percent felt that sex was the strongest bond, and 49 percent are satisfied with their sex lives.

About one third of all Austrian women between the ages of 16 and 70 live in a common household with their partners. The reference to the age limit of 70 is important, because in the study cited here, people over 70 were not included. If they are added to the figures, then the number of single households rises, and the number of pairs sharing a household becomes smaller. Higher life expectancy and lower birthrates lead to a constantly rising proportion of single older women. Senger and Hoffmann (1993) point out in their study that 22 percent live alone, 22 percent live in a partnership without children, and 56 percent live in a traditional family with children. The trend points clearly to families with one child.

Every third marriage does not last. In large cities, every second marriage ends in divorce. In the country, where traditional values and social controls have a stronger influence, the rate of divorce is clearly lower.

The average number of acts of sexual intercourse among adult Austrians is 2.4 times a week. The modal value is, however, once a week (21.1 percent). Twenty percent have intercourse up to twice a week, and just as high is the share of those who have intercourse less than once a month or never. This tendency is sinking. In 1980, only 11 percent of those asked answered that they had less sexual intercourse than once a month or never, and at least 63 percent responded with at least once a week, and in 1991 it was only 53 percent. Men are somewhat more active than women—2.6 times a week for men, and 2.1 times a week for women. This indicates that women are "more faithful" than men.

As varying as the survey data is for "faithfulness," the proportion has stayed the same. For every unfaithful woman there are two unfaithful men (12 percent to 20.7 percent in contrast to 29 percent to 40.1 percent, respectively). Compared to these figures, nine out of ten Austrians responded that faithfulness in a relationship is especially important.

The satisfaction with the extent and quality of one's sex life is relatively high. Sixty-seven percent (men, 63 percent, women, 71 percent) indicated that they did not wish for more sex. Only 16 percent (24 percent men, 8 percent women) were not satisfied. The sexually most active is the group of 30- to 49-year-olds (at least once a week—60 percent), and satisfaction is here somewhat higher than the average (men, 65 percent; women, 8 percent). The majority of Austrians are satisfied with the length of intercourse: 28 percent said that the average sexual act lasted more than half an hour, and around half spend ten to thirty minutes. There is a significant difference between housewives and working women: 70 percent of the housewives are content with their sexual lives, as opposed to 53 percent of working women. That women are, in general, more sexually contented than men is certainly linked with the still prevailing Catholic image of the woman who is to remain passive and take the place to which she is directed. The growing employment of women appears to allow a slow but certain emancipation process to develop.

For unconventional sexual practices there are no legal restrictions, as long as they are carried out with mutual consent and injuries do not result. There are practically no statistics about the societal acceptance of fetishes, sadomasochism, or other unconventional sex games. What pleases both is permitted, as long as this is not spoken about too publicly. Advertisements are permitted.

About 60 percent of Austrians practice oral sex (men, 70 percent, women, 52 percent). Heterosexual anal intercourse is acknowledged as a possibility by about one third (40 percent of the men, but less than 20 percent of the women).

The wish for group sex is felt by a third of Austrians. Around 1,000 persons actually look for appropriate saunas and clubs so that they can practice group sex and partner exchange, and this is done by, above all, the educated, independently employed, and freelancers. Interest is highest among young men between the ages of 16 and 29. Seven percent of the men enjoy this, but only 1 percent of the women.

The sexuality of the aging is an area that has undergone very little research, because the issue is largely suppressed in public. "Love," as the most important element in a relationship with a partner, is mentioned by only one quarter of the women and one third of the men, and only 4 percent mention sexuality as the element that binds one partner to the other. That does not mean that sexuality no longer plays a role: 45 percent of the men and 21 percent of the women between the ages of 50 and 60 stated that they had sexual intercourse at least once a week. International studies reveal regular sexual contact also by those who are over 70. In Austria there are no figures available. Observations and experience working with aging people show, however, that sexuality in old age is not passé, only the quality changes. As with young people, manual practices have an important place, although they are often discriminated against as "senile disinhibition." A serious consideration of sex in old age has only begun, and this, slowly. Those studying this question are usually people who work in health professions.

Similarly not discussed is the sexuality of handicapped persons. The legal regulations of protection against encroachment, abuse, and exploitation of dependency are also supposed to apply to the mentally handicapped.

Within these regulations is the controversy about the sterilization of mentally handicapped persons. Until 1974, compulsory sterilization was carried out on mentally handicapped persons. The basis for this was the *Reichsüberleitungsgesetze* of the National Socialist legal system. Such regulations did not exist in the Austrian penal code before 1938. Still today, the sterilization of mentally handicapped persons can be carried out against the will of the affected person, if the parents or the guardian and the responsible court give their permissions for the operation. The question does arise whether or not a mentally retarded individual has the possibility to understand the operation. According to reliable reports, this permission is given less and less in recent years, partly because of strong protests from human rights activists.

Until recently, the sexual needs and rights of handicapped persons are often ignored or denied in public discussion. Now at least, thanks to the initiative of the handicapped themselves and organizations for the handicapped, a serious discussion has begun, albeit slowly. One of the major reasons, and goals, of the discussion is so that institutions, such as homes or nursing hospitals, can create the necessary basic conditions that permit and safeguard intimacy, as well as allow physical contact between those who live and work there.

6. Homoerotic, Homosexual, and Ambisexual Behaviors

Data that would allow reliable conclusions about how many Austrian women and men are homosexual is scanty, and until now was only available as a "by-product" of two empirical studies about the sexual behavior of Austrians. Langbein and Fritsch reported in 1991 that 200,000 Austrians identified themselves as homosexual or bisexual, i.e., about 3 percent according to a representative study by Weiss and Perner 1991 for Institut für Empirische Sozialforschung. In a study done by Senger and Hoffmann (1993) based on a questionnaire distributed by the popular newspaper, *Neue Kronenzeitung*, 6.2 percent of the men and 9.6 percent of the women who answered declared themselves homosexual. Seven percent of the women responded as bisexual. [It was not clear from the newspaper report whether the 7 percent of the women who responded as bisexual were part of the 9.6 percent or in addition to it. (Editor)] However, the author assumes that the differences between this Austrian data and data from other countries is not significant.

Studies concerning how many young people have homosexual experiences during adolescence, or about a "coming-out" phase do not exist. The comparison of data from other countries with testimony from those affected lead to the conclusion that the coming out of homosexual Austrians does not differ from other white Europeans or North Americans: Most of them define themselves as definitely homosexual by the ages of 19 to 21. The length of time for the coming out of girls is increasingly similar to that of boys. The differences between city dweller and those who live in the country play a large role for both sexes. Comparatively, however, few young Austrians are without prejudices. And few have access to positive information about homosexuality. Those who do have this information are mostly homosexuals and lesbians, and most of these are in Vienna.

Gay male adolescents seeking to establish personal contact with peer or older homosexuals, or wrestling with the decision of whether or not to come out face two obstacles. Gay males over age 19 face the risk of legal charges if they develop a personal relationship with another gay under age 18. In addition, the societal reaction to AIDS resulting in negative attitudes toward homosexuals has also made coming out more difficult. In comparison, young women have an easier time coming out, since the silence about lesbians and a lesbian way of life has been broken, and consequently models of behavior have become socially visible.

However, the societal, legal, social, and political situation is, as mentioned above, typified by numerous discriminations. Basically, it has been observed and established that brutal forms of discrimination are employed against male homosexuals (in the penal code and in working situations, while lesbians are more likely to encounter silence, ridicule, or put-downs in the popular media and in the health care community. Anti-pornography laws are seldom if ever invoked to restrict portrayals of lesbian sexuality used by the pornography industry for their erotic appeal to heterosexual men, but erotic videos made by lesbians for lesbians are very often confiscated and forbidden.

With respect to the legal situation of homosexuality, prior to the "small reform" of Austrian criminal laws in 1975, sexual acts between members of the same sex were punishable. This was a tradition that goes back to the Empress Maria Theresia in Article 74 of the "Constitutio Criminalis Theresiana" (1768), a criminal code issued for the Habsburg countries, where the death penalty was permitted. In 1852, Article 129 of the Austrian Penal Code stipulated hard prison sentences between one and five years for "unnatural fornication" for both sexes. The resistance of Catholic organizations prevented removing female homosexuality from the realm of the criminal in 1930.

During the time of the National Socialist occupation, Article 129 still applied and Austrian laws concerning homosexuality remained in effect. From 1938 until 1945, an unknown number of homosexual Austrians, who were identified with a pink triangle that they were forced to sew on their clothing, were sent to concentration camps and murdered. Lesbians were persecuted as "anti-social" and sent to work and penal camps. The number of trials involving homosexuals of both sexes and the number of those condemned to prison multiplied. However, basic historiographic research has not yet been done.

Unlike other groups, who have been officially recognized as victims and, as such, have received some indemnity and some compensation from the Republic of Austria, homosexuals have not been compensated, not only because of the objections of the interest groups of survivors of the concentration camps, but also because the responsible federal ministers for social affairs have refused to recognize homosexuals as political victims.

Until the "small reform" of the criminal code removed "simple homosexuality" from the criminal code in 1975, about 13,000 Austrians were convicted of "unnatural fornication" between 1950 and 1971, of which 5 percent were women. After 1971, because of special pressure from the Catholic Church, conservative circles, and government advisors, four articles discriminatory against homosexuals were introduced into the Austrian Criminal Code:

- Article 209 states that a sexual relationship between someone over the age of 19 with someone who is younger than 18—the "age of consent"—is a criminal act.
- Article 210, which made prostitution between men punishable and therefore forced it into the underground, was removed in 1989, based on arguments pertaining to AIDS prevention.
- Article 220 forbids both sexes to advertise fornication with animals or persons of the same sex.
- Article 221 forbids both sexes to establish associations with the same goals.

On November 26, 1996, Article 220 forbidding advertising and Article 221 forbidding the establishment of associations were eliminated from the criminal code. However, the age of consent for boys (Article 209) remains in effect. In Austria, the age of consent for male homosexuals is 18; for female homosexuals and heterosexuals, however, it is 14 years of age.

Other forms of discrimination can also be found in civil law, especially in rental laws vis-à-vis life partnerships of homosexuals, and even stronger regarding laws regarding marriage, employment, and social insurance. Central to this discrimination is the definition of "relatives," which includes marriage partners, parents, children, and in certain instances heterosexual partners. Only those mentioned, for example, have the right to be party to contracts. In 1998, the definition of "relationships" was extended to include homosexual partnerships.

Because of its important social and political position and as a regular advisor in questions of legal reforms, the Catholic Church, with its strong discriminatory policy against homosexuals, has the possibility to act in far more cases than in those involving only religious questions. In comparison, the Protestant and Neo-Catholic churches in Austria play an insignificant political role.

In the fields of medicine, psychiatry, psychology, psychotherapy, and health institutions, there are at least no official attempts to force people to be heterosexual. In Vienna, lesbians and gay men can turn to a few homosexual or unprejudiced doctors and psychotherapists.

Although in the pedagogical professions there are no official prohibitions against the employment of homosexual educators, in practically all occupations unconventional sexual preferences are kept secret. Individual cases of firing are known. Information about homosexuality is not made available in the teacher training. However, in the last few years, students in Vienna's Academy for Social Professions have been permitted to do internships at homosexual associations.

In scientific research, only one study of lesbians and gay men has been financially supported by the government. At Austrian universities, the personal initiative of a few dedicated scholars has introduced some lectures on lesbian and gay studies in the areas of sociology, psychology, and political science. Notice was given to self-acknowledged lesbians at the University of Vienna at the beginning in the early 1990s that lesbian and other homosexual research is not considered among the mainstream disciplines. Supporters of this research are always under pressure to scientifically prove the legitimacy of their studies.

The possibility for an undisguised and self-determined homosexual way of life depends strongly on geographical and social conditions. By and large, Austria is a country with small-town structures, and social and sociosexual control mechanisms, which have remained intact despite tourism. Hence, homosexuals avoid the cultural difficulties of living in the country and towns and move to the larger cities, especially Vienna, where there is a certain protection, on the one hand, and on the other, better opportunities for contacts. The question of "How do I tell my parents?" is much more difficult in rural villages, not only because of the possible ostracism of the person affected, but also for the family from which he or she comes.

In the past few years the trend among homosexual men to establish permanent relationships has become apparent, on the one hand, because of the influence of AIDS, but, on the other hand, because of increasing socialization opportunities. How many lesbians or gays live in partnership is unknown. How far these structures differ from those in heterosexual partnerships is now (in late 2000) being studied for a dissertation at the Department of Psychology at the University of Vienna.

Sexual practices made a striking shift in the 1980s because of AIDS. Austria was the first country in Europe with a sex education brochure about AIDS. The brochure was done through an initiative of the gay movement. The social pressure to use protection in anal and oral intercourse is very strong, especially in towns where activist groups exist. According to Senger and Hoffmann, oral intercourse is the most frequent practice among homosexuals, followed by anal intercourse. (However, since the study is based on responses to a questionnaire in a popular newspaper to which Senger has contributed a popularly written column for years, the representativeness and lack of bias in the sample is certainly questionable). There are no researched statistics on the sexual practices of lesbians. Based on the work of Shere Hite and the Kinsey Institute, one can assume that in

Austria, as elsewhere in Europe and North America, oral intercourse and digital stimulation are the most frequent sexual lesbian practices.

Lesbians and gay men have organized themselves, although rather late, because of rigorous criminal laws as well as everyday persecution, even though Vienna, at the time of the First Republic (1918-1934) was one of the European centers of homosexual subculture and a very differentiated homosexual movement existed. These early traditions were completely destroyed by Austrian fascism (1934-1938) and National Socialism (1938-1945), both in substance, in organization, and in persons.

The first modern organizations for lesbians grew out of the autonomous feminist movement in the 1970s. Today, independent lesbian separatist feminist groups exist in Vienna as well as in some other provincial capitals. Their members are usually active in various areas of the independent feminist movement. Gays began to organize themselves only at the end of the 1970s. The first institution was the Homosexual Initiative (HOSI) Vienna, which is also active in various international homosexual associations (ILGA—International Lesbian and Gay Association, ILIS—the International Lesbian Information Service, and IGLYO—International Gay and Lesbian Youth Organization). In Church circles, Homosexuality and Church, an ecumenical working group, is significant, as well as the Ecumenical Platform of Homosexual Clergymen (ÖPSSÖ). At present, there are a number of lesbian and gay pressure groups that are also active in international homosexual associations. The high point on the lesbian–gay calendar is the Gay Pride Day at the end of June that usually includes a demonstration. For lesbians, March 8, the International Women's Day is a "must." In 1984 and 1989, Vienna was the venue for the Annual Conference of the International Lesbian and Gay Association (ILGA), and was organized by HOSI, Vienna.

In June 2001, Vienna will be the venue for "Europride," a month-long festival of activities and a parade with participants from all over Europe. This congress is being organized in Vienna by the European Pride Association.

7. Gender Conflicted Persons

Estimates put the number of transgendered persons in Austria between one and two thousand, but the figure might be closer to five thousand.

Austria at present has no laws dealing with transsexuality. In 1983, the Federal Ministry of Internal Affairs ascertained that there were too few cases for such laws. Nevertheless, the Federal Ministry for Work, Health, and Social Matters has published recommendations for the treatment of transsexuals. Before medical treatment, there must be an ongoing psychotherapeutic accompaniment that lasts at least one year, i.e., a minimum of fifty hours. After the psychotherapeutic findings have been established, hormone treatment and the so-called "everyday test" can be carried out.

When transsexuality is established, a doctor's verification can be demanded, in which the diagnostic assignment to the opposite sex, as well as the correlation between the treatment and the outward appearance is presented, with the maximum validity of two years. The high costs for the treatment are only partly covered by public health insurance.

In Austria, relatively few doctors perform sex change operations (in Vienna, Salzburg, and Innsbruck) and they are considered comparatively less experienced than their foreign colleagues.

After the operation, it is possible to change the first name in the personal status in all documents, although the authorities may show resistance. Before, transsexuals could only choose a gender-neutral name. In this connection, the transgender movement advocates not having the gender recorded in the birth registry as well as all other documents. The position expressed in the movement is that many operations would be superfluous if society did not demand a strictly known identification with one of the two sexes.

Marriages of those who have undergone an operation are considered dissolved with the change of sex. Here, apparently, in the course of the acceptance of such marriages lies the fear that, as a consequence, homosexual marriages may no longer be forbidden. There is official pressure for divorce. Government officials can also make contact with the person's own children difficult. As for employers, the pressure for agreed-upon severance is the normal practice. Many transsexual (transgendered) persons do not find new employment after they have changed their names and legal status. Prostitution is sometimes their only means of supporting themselves.

In June 1995, a four-day international human rights tribunal took place in Vienna that dealt with the discrimination against lesbians, gays, and transgendered persons. The indictment ascertained that lesbians, gays, and transsexual persons are discriminated against in various ways and that there is in no way legal protection. Accordingly, the government and Parliament were asked to initiate activities to counteract the situation. In February 1999, the first Austrian interdisciplinary symposium on transsexuality was held. As of early 2000, there were two self-help groups for transgendered persons, both in Vienna.

8. Significant Unconventional Sexual Behaviors

A. Coercive Sex

Child Sexual Abuse, Incest, and Pedophilia

In 1995, when the chairman of the Bishop's Conference of the Catholic Church in Austria was accused by a former pupil of sexual abuse when he was a pupil, the theme of sexual abuse of children was brought sharply to the attention of the public, both in Austria and internationally. The Austrian Church's governing body and the Vatican refused to investigate the case and at the same time defamed the accusing victim in the media, making it clear that a fundamental taboo had been touched upon.

The Austrian criminal code states that the sexual abuse of children—defined as sleeping with, or fornication with minors—will be punished with up to ten years in prison.

About 500 cases of sexual abuse a year are reported to the authorities, but the actual frequency is estimated at from ten to twenty-five thousand. In 1997, 848 cases were reported, involving 231 male and 617 female victims (Federal Ministry of the Interior, Statistics on Victims, 1997). The unusually high level of unreported cases that do not appear in statistics (*graue Zone*) can be understood because the perpetrator is usually closely associated with the close social circles of the victim—24 percent occur within the family, and the probability of bringing charges against someone in such a close relationship diminishes.

Eighty to 90 percent of the victims are girls, mostly between the ages of 6 and 11 years of age. The perpetrators are up to 80 percent men from all social levels. According to the Federal Ministry for Environment, Youth, and Family, every third to fourth girl and every eighth to ninth boy will be sexually abused.

To fight the sexual abuse of children, literature on the subject asks for an emancipating education and a change from gender-specific power structures. To this end, various institutions and places for maltreated and abused children have been established, including emergency telephone hotlines for children and child protection centers.

Austria has no pedophilia movement in favor of the legalization of sex with minors such as exists, for example, in the United States.

Sexual Violence Against Women

The women's movement removed the taboo from the subject of sexual violence against women in the 1970s. It was pointed out that forced sex has less to do with sexuality than with power, conditioned by the differences between the social positions of men and women.

The first "women's house" in Austria was built in 1978. In a short time, it was overfilled. Today, in Vienna there are three such houses, and in the other provinces another fifteen, where women threatened with domestic or marital violence can seek refuge. In 1982, women set up the first emergency telephone for raped women and girls. At present, there are seven emergency telephone services in the larger towns. These refuges have been initiated for the most part by autonomous women's groups and they experience great financial difficulties, because there is very little financial support from government agencies.

Sexual Harassment

The public debate about sexual harassment at the workplace began in the late 1980s. In a study conducted in 1981, 81 percent of the women surveyed indicated that once, or more than once, they had experienced sexual advances by men against their will at work (Federal Ministry for Work, Health, and Social Affairs). Those affected are more often single women, frequently in insecure positions, and relatively often in typical occupations for females, especially secretaries. The perpetrators are frequently substantially older than their victims and, over-proportionally, their supervisor or manager (Federal Ministry for Work, Health, and Social Affairs, 1993).

A law was enacted in 1993 that not only declared sexual harassment itself punishable, but also addressed negligence on the part of the employer in dealing effectively with the complaint. In the same way, the creation of a hostile and humiliating work environment at the workplace is forbidden. The person discriminated against has the right to demand reasonable damages, at least a minimum of ATS 50,000.

Since then, it is possible to start a legal procedure, but all women who, up to now, have sought legal process, were forced to leave their jobs while pursuing legal remedy. The official responsible for equal treatment questions has demanded protection against dismissal for victims.

Rape

The crime of rape is treated in the criminal code as "punishable acts against morals." On the contrary, it would be more appropriate, at the present time, not to choose an abstract morality as a basis for protection, but rather the violation of sexual self-determination, i.e., the sexual integrity of the person. With the reform of the penal laws in 1989, rape within marriage or common-law marriage became punishable, but only upon application of the woman. In the past, the woman's inability to resist determined possible conviction as well as the extent of punishment. Today, the extent of the violence by the aggressor is decisive. Punishment for graver cases of rape is between one and ten years, for less violent assaults between six months and five years. The provisions of the law are formulated in gender-neutral language; men as rape victims are acknowledged. Still needed are improved counseling and support for women by the police and courts, help during the investigations, as well as increased claims for damages and psychological injuries suffered.

In connection with rape, old prejudices are still commonly held, such as the overpowering sexual drive of men or the alleged yearning of women for brutal sexual intercourse. The guilt is often assigned to the woman or shared guilt is assumed, as she is accused of having sexually provoked the perpetrator. Because she agreed to a meeting, the American notion of "date rape" is played down even in legal proceedings, since the woman's agreement is assumed. Rape within marriage is still represented by the notion that the husband has sexual control over his wife. It is therefore not surprising that affected women, whether out of a sense of resignation or shame, seldom report marital rapes.

According to police statistics, 507 rapes were known in 1997, of which 35 took place within marriages. Trials often end in acquittals. In 1990, one third of the accused were found "not guilty."

B. Prostitution

Provincial governments regulate prostitution in Austria and only one of the nine states outlaws it. Pimping is forbidden and punishable, but it obviously exists. Until 1989, male prostitution was a criminal offense. Prohibition was lifted especially in the interest of AIDS prevention. Officially recognized prostitutes are registered with the police, and must undergo examinations for sexually transmitted illnesses once a week. Since 1984, prostitutes must pay income tax. However, tax estimates are often too high and arbitrary to be paid, forcing many prostitutes into the underground. Although prostitution was put on an equal footing with other occupations, social and pension rights are not included. Prostitutes can voluntarily pay for health insurance, but have no rights to a pension or to the same protection as pregnant women—they fall through the loopholes of the social system.

There are hardly any studies concerning prostitution and the social situation of prostitutes. According to the Health Office of the City of Vienna, there are 630 female and 5 male prostitutes officially registered. Illegal prostitution is many times higher; many women who are registered as bartenders and hostesses work as prostitutes. In Vienna, about 5,000 prostitutes work each day. There are no figures for the whole of Austria.

The appearance of AIDS and the opening of Eastern European borders had a far-reaching influence on prostitution. HIV tests are required on a regular basis for prostitutes. As a result of the opening of the borders to the former Eastern countries (Czech Republic and Slovakia) in 1989, there was a rise in competition, and an increase of "secret" prostitution. It is known that international organizations are involved in the traffic of women. In Austria, many prostitutes come from Eastern Europe, Brazil, the Dominican Republic, Thailand, and the Philippines.

C. Pornography and Erotica

Pornography is regulated through a federal law passed in 1990, "The Federal Act Against Obscene Publications and for the Protection of Youth Morally Endangered." Because this law is considered completely out-of-date in progressive circles, its total reform was begun in 1992, two years after its enactment. The reform is still being worked on in the Federal Ministry of

Justice. A new version of the law has already failed to pass, because of pressure by conservatives and church groups.

The immediate cause for seeking a reform was a study initiated by the Federal Ministry of Environmental, Youth, and Family Issues about the existence and distribution of video films showing violent acts against children. The goal was to stop the production and dissemination of such films. A broad discussion began about whether punishment should be limited to trade in such videos, or extended to include ownership or possession as well. In addition, punishment was aimed at the presentation of violence; however, pornography without violence and presentations of sexual acts between members of the same sex were to be liberalized. But since no agreement could be reached with the People's Party coalition partner, the Social Democrats, who had been working for this reform, they could not carry it through. In 1994, punishment for producing, selling, and possessing child pornography was written into law.

[A trichotomy of pornographic material is widely accepted in Austria, namely soft pornography or erotica with limited or no explicit sex acts (e.g., *Playboy* magazine, and the like), hardcore pornography with explicit sex acts, and hardcore pornography with legally prohibited "violent" content. The minimum age for a person buying soft porn/erotica, a *Playboy* magazine for instance, is 16 years. The minimum age for buying porn or entering an adult video store where hardcore pornography is available for rental or sale is 18 years. Violent content, including bestiality, sexual acts involving minors, and violent sexual acts is, of course, legally forbidden in Austria.

[Gay pornography is not forbidden in Austria and almost every adult shop has a section featuring gay porn. Furthermore, in recent years a few gay adult stores have opened in Vienna. (Vorachek)]

Punishment is limited to those who produce or distribute obscene texts, pictures, or films or other obscene objects for profit (Paragraph 1, Pornography Law). Possession or non-commercial exchanges of violent pornography is still permitted.

9. Contraception, Abortion, and Population Planning

A. Contraception

The attitude of the Austrian population to questions of family planning is influenced by the Catholic sexual dogma, based on the "Pill Encyclical" (*Humanae Vitae*) of 1968, in which contraception and abortion were equally condemned.

Results from surveys show contradictory attitudes. The belief of most women in the effectiveness of family planning is confronted by the reality of unwanted pregnancies. Being relatively well informed about contraception is not borne out by the use of contraceptives. Thirty-nine percent of first live births and far more pregnancies were generated despite the use of contraceptives. Women with higher educational achievements, fewer religious bonds, and who live in cities have more faith in the planning of pregnancies. The higher the job qualifications, the fewer unwanted pregnancies occur. The same is true in cities, as compared to rural areas. In all of Austria there are more than 200 publicly supported family and partnership counseling centers, whose responsibilities include counseling about pregnancy and informing clients about birth control methods.

Contraceptive preference and use changed drastically in the 1970s. After the rapid spread of the use of hormonal contraceptives, there followed, at the end of the decade, again a gradual turning away from the pill and turning to the coil IUD and sterilization, as well as to natural methods of contraception. The pill, however, remained the most-used contraceptive, being used by one third of all women at risk for pregnancy. Seen internationally, Austria is a "pill stronghold." Those who use the pill but are anxious that it may be detrimental to their health have two more reasons for using it anyway: reliability and convenience. Birth control is still something left to women, although, since the appearance of AIDS, contraceptives are advertised by public authorities.

Forty-two percent of all sexually active and fertile women between the ages of 15 and 44 take the pill. This rate declines as women get older. Students and religious women take the pill less often. Women who use no contraceptive constitute the next largest group, at 18 percent. Twelve percent use unreliable contraceptive methods, mainly withdrawal or coitus interruptus. In fourth place on the frequency scale is the condom, followed by the coil IUD, and then spermicides. The diaphragm is only marginally used.

The choice of contraceptive method depends on the level of education, the importance of religion, the size of the hometown, and the age of the woman. In groups with lower incomes, unreliable methods are often used. The higher the education, the more the pill is taken and the less coitus interruptus is employed.

In terms of convenient availability, the pill is made more difficult, because a doctor must prescribe it, whereas condoms are readily available in apothecaries, drugstores, and in machines in men's toilets of almost all bars, restaurants, cafes, clubs, discos, and the like.

B. Teenage (Unmarried) Pregnancies

Among nations for which out-of-wedlock pregnancy statistics are available, Austria has one of the highest rates of out-of-wedlock births. Since the 1960s, the number of illegitimate births has been rising while the rate of children born to married couples has declined. In 1998, the number of births was 80,321, of which 23,588 were born out-of-wedlock. Currently, one quarter of all live births are out-of-wedlock, double or triple the rates in the neighboring countries. This appears to be a continuing trend. Within Austria, however, there are large regional differences, with the large cities having especially high rates. [With regard to these regional-level differentials, apart from the urban/rural differential, it is also noteworthy, that some areas within Austria, independently from the urban/rural differential, consistently experience high out-of-wedlock birthrates. The most prominent case for this observation is Carinthia, the southernmost of Austria's nine states, which traditionally, for centuries, has had the highest out-of-wedlock birthrates within Austria. (Voracek)]

Still higher than the rate of illegitimate births altogether is the rate of out-of-wedlock first-born children. At the end of the 1980s, about every third first-born was born to unwed parents; 60 percent of all women did not have their first babies conceived within marriages. From this it follows that in many regions of Austria, the out-of-wedlock birth of the first child is the rule, rather than the exception.

Since 1989, single mothers are automatically given guardianship over their children; prior to 1989, the mother had to apply for custody.

C. Abortion

In 1787, as a result of the Enlightenment, the death penalty for abortions was removed from the "*Josephinisches Strafgesetzbuch*" (Penal Code of Emperor Joseph II), and replaced with a long prison sentence. This law is the basis for the current abortion paragraphs, which, with the exception of the era of National Socialism, was in effect until 1974. Under this law, abortion, in every case, even those carried out for medical indications, was punishable. Since 1869, according to the Roman Catholic Church, every abortion from the time of fertilization incurs an automatic penalty of excommunication.

In the 1960s, only a small percentage of abortions were actually punished by law. It was also clear that only those persons who were poor where prosecuted. Estimates from that time assume from 30,000 to 100,000 abortions per year. In addition to the illegal abortions carried out within Austria, "abortion tourism" began to countries with more liberal laws, above all, to Great Britain and Holland.

With the votes of the Social Democrats, the abortion articles were abolished as part of the amendments of the Criminal Code in 1975. Instead, time-limited permission (*Fristenlösung*) went into effect. According to the law, which is still binding, abortion is basically punishable, but will not be punished when the abortion is carried out within the first three months after implantation (nidation) or after the fourth month if a medical or eugenic indication is presented, or the person is still a minor. In order not to be punishable, the following prerequisites must be met:

- permission of the pregnant person;
- strict adherence to the three-month limit;
- counseling beforehand by a doctor; and

- neither doctors nor other medical personnel can be forced to participate.

The operation must take place in a public hospital, clinic, or private practice, normally under anesthesia by aspiration. The costs are only carried by the national health system if there is a medical necessity. In Austria, no records of abortions are kept.

If the pregnant woman is below the age of consent (i.e., has not yet completed her fourteenth year of age), abortions are not punishable even after the fourth month, but they require the permission of her legal representatives, usually her parents. There is no unanimous opinion in the legal literature on this question if the pregnant woman is still a minor and has not yet completed her nineteenth year of age.

In recent years the discussion about abortion has again flamed up. Kindled mainly by the leading members of the Catholic Church, the discussion ostensibly circles around the emphasis on the "right to life" based on the European Convention on Human Rights and Fundamental Freedoms, 1958, and the connected question: When does human life begin? In addition, the function of required counseling has become an important issue, since those who demand that abortion be punished also oppose sex education for the purpose of avoiding unwanted pregnancies. It appears obvious that opposition to the right of women to self-determination about their own bodies is the real motivation of those who oppose abortion. The opposition of these political factions delayed the government's efforts to allow distribution of Mifegyne (RU-486, the abortion pill) in Austria.

As in some other Western industrial nations, Austria has liberal abortion laws accompanied by a high degree of tabooing and insufficient infrastructure to carry out the operations. Even today, hospitals in the provinces dominated by the conservative People's Party refuse to perform abortions.

D. Populations Programs

By international comparison, Austria is distinguished by noticeably low birthrates. In the 1980s, Austria had the third lowest birthrate in the world after Italy and Germany; in the 1930s, it was the lowest in the world.

Despite continually pessimistic voices from the press since the 1970s that speak about a threatening situation, Austrians have very reserved attitudes towards the intervention of the state. There is no openly declared policy for a planned population. The influence of the State on reproductive behavior occurs indirectly, through establishment of financial and institutional incentives.

The population policies of the National Socialist dictatorship, the goal of which was to eliminate life that was unworthy of reproduction and to increase the "German race," led to an economic boom and a temporary increase in births, beginning in 1938. After the war, a family support policy was developed that provided both tax relief and other social support. These have been in effect since the 1950s as a permanent part of Austrian social policies.

In 1954 and 1955, a Family Support Fund was established to affect the distribution of money for family support as well as to influence pronatalist attitudes. And, indeed, there was a temporary baby boom at the end of the 1950s and beginning of the 1960s.

The decrease of births in the late 1960s and 1970s brought about a discussion about population policy measures, in which the Social Democratic Party and the labor unions participated, in order to achieve more financial support for births, etc. The People's Party and the Catholic Family Organization wanted to introduce more tax incentives for families with children. Altogether, Austria is one of the countries with the highest rates of family support.

In the 1980s, a program was initiated to combat sterility among women that included the possibility for artificial insemination. The "Medical Reproduction Law" of 1992 permitted in vitro fertilization (IVF) for heterosexual infertile couples who lived together. Surrogate motherhood and ovum donation, however, are forbidden. The first Austrian test-tube baby was born in 1982. Every year, about 2,000 IVF attempts are made. The success quota is very small, among other reasons, because the majority of women give up before the completion of the very burdensome program required.

10. Sexually Transmitted Diseases

Since the 1920s, it has been compulsory to report diseases transmitted through sexual intercourse. The current law, the AIDS Act of 1986, requires reporting of: syphilis, gonorrhea, ulcus molle (soft ulcer, soft chancre), lymphphogranuloma venerum (pudendal ulcer), granuloma inguinale (groin ulcer or ulcerating granuloma of the pudendum), as well as full-blown cases of AIDS. Registered prostitutes are also legally required to be examined at regular intervals (weekly) for venereal diseases. These statistics are maintained by the Health Office of the City of Vienna. The available statistics published in medical journals are still not reliable, because it can be presumed that only an estimated 20 percent of the actual cases are reported to the health authorities. Nevertheless, it is possible to understand the trend from these figures: Reported cases of syphilis and gonorrhea are diminishing while non-reportable diseases, such as chlamydia and Trichomonas infections, are clearly increasing.

In Vienna, a little under 1,000 cases of syphilis and gonorrhea were reported in both 1993 and 1994, the last year for which data has been published. A slight rise in cases of syphilis can be explained by the registration of persons from former Yugoslavia, for whom genital scarring was reported but treatment could not be ascertained. In the Health Office of Vienna, from which about one fifth of all the figures in Vienna come, a tendency towards a decrease in cases of gonorrhea became apparent after the high point had been reached right after the borders to the Czech Republic and Slovakia were opened at the beginning of the 1990s.

The treatment of STDs as well as counseling takes place in clinics with the appropriate professional departments and with established doctors, mainly dermatologists, and less frequently urologists and gynecologists. Vienna has a special outpatient clinic where poor people can receive counseling, examinations, and treatment at no cost.

Programs in education and prevention practically do not exist. With the exception of AIDS, sexually transmitted disease is not a topic spoken about in public. The public campaigns, such as the one carried out by the company that produces Acyclovir, are the exceptions. The manufacturing firm advertised its product, and at the same time promoted the use of condoms as protection against the contagious contraction of herpes.

11. HIV/AIDS

A. Government Regulations

As early as 1986, Austria had its own AIDS law, since it could not be sensibly included either in the laws concerning epidemics nor venereal diseases. As a result, clear cases of AIDS, according to the American CDC classification, as well as cases of death, must reported to the Federal Ministry for Health; reports include the sex, date of birth, and the initials of the person, but not his or her name. HIV infections are not reported, to guarantee the anonymity of persons infected with HIV and to prevent possible discrimination in schools, at the workplace, etc.

Commercial sexual activities are forbidden to those infected with HIV, and this is anchored in law. Registered prostitutes are, in addition, required every three months to undergo an HIV antibody test. Also regulated by law is the right of an HIV-infected person to attend school, as long as the affected person is able to physically meet the demands. The same is true, *de jure*, for the carrying on of other occupations. An HIV infection is a reason for ineligibility for military service.

While HIV tests are not carried out in the standard procedure when blood tests are made, the law does not prohibit testing for HIV without the permission of the person involved. In hospitals, especially in Vienna, mass screenings were made without the permission of the patients. This doubtful procedure, which caused vehement discussion, was made legitimate in a directive issued at the beginning of the 1990s by the City Council member responsible for such matters.

Austria's health insurance regulates that those who are infected with HIV, and people ill with AIDS, may use the national insurance the same as anyone else. Private insurance companies, (e.g., organizations offering life insurance, are increasingly demanding HIV antibody tests and/or excluding those with HIV infections and those with AIDS.

B. Statistics for HIV Infections and AIDS

Since the beginning of the AIDS pandemic in the early 1980s, the registered (cumulative) numbers for Austria are:

- 7,609 people currently infected with HIV;
- 2,036 people currently living with AIDS; and
- 1,243 Austrians who have died of AIDS.

Although these statistics from the Department of Virology of the University of Vienna Medical School, as of October 30, 2000, and published December 1, 2000, are highly reliable, the AIDS-Help organization in Vienna claims that the realistic number is 15,000 to 18,000 infections. [Martin Voracek, at the University of Vienna General Hospital Department of Documentation and Research, has challenged this estimate from AIDS-Help as exaggerated:

> [Where are these additional cumulative 7,000 to 9,000 people? Certainly, they are not under medical treatment. Sooner or later these unreported persons infected with HIV or AIDS will die. Then, because Austria has a very high autopsy rate and therefore one of the most accurate mortality statistics worldwide, such cases would be detected at least postmortem. But the autopsy and causes-of-death statistics give no evidence for the alleged unreported cases of HIV infections and AIDS cases. (personal communication to the Editor, October 2000)]

The number of new infections was 92 in 1998 and 18 in 1999. Between January 1 and October 30, 2000, 366 new HIV-infections were registered. Austria's current population is about 8.1 million.

Homosexual and bisexual men were the main affected group, but recently, the number of new infections in this group has declined steadily. This can most likely be attributed to a change in behavior, based on the increased information available to the public. In the case of intravenous drug users, the number of new infections is stable. However, the number of cases of new infections by way of heterosexual sexual intercourse is rising drastically. In this trend, women are especially affected.

At the end of May 1999, the number of AIDS illnesses recorded cumulatively since 1983 was 1,905. Of this number, 1,198 had already died; 738 were homosexual or bisexual persons, 476 were drug-users, 258 became ill through heterosexual contact, 281 persons became ill for other or not-known reasons: 74 hemophiliacs, 38 as a result of blood transfusions, 25 maternal transmission to children, and 15 homosexual or bisexual persons plus IV-drug users. The overall gender ratio was: men 1,547 (994 died), and women 358 (204 died).

C. Treatment and Research

HIV tests can be administered in hospitals, clinics, and numerous doctors' offices. Anonymous and free-of-charge tests can only be given at privately supported AIDS-help organizations. Treatment is possible at all university clinics and some larger hospitals. In Vienna, two wards for AIDS patients were set up, where stationary as well as day-care medical attention is possible. Extramural care causes personnel and financial problems and is largely limited to private nursing activities. However, people ill with AIDS can have the same social services, help at home, home food delivery, etc., as others who are either ill or need care.

Since Austria has a very strict drug law, the treatment of AIDS is limited to traditional orthodox medicine and proven methods. The medical profession is generally skeptical about alternative ways of treatment; they are not financially supported and are exclusively available only through private initiative and payments.

In research, Immuno, a pharmaceutical company with laboratories in Austria, leads worldwide in the development of vaccines. The use of gene technology is followed by the public with skepticism. Militants active in animal protection are leading a vehement discussion about the experimentation with animals.

D. Prevention

Despite legal requirements, there is no national policy regarding AIDS in Austria.

Homosexual and bisexual men were those most affected by AIDS at the beginning of the 1980s. Information and explanations were offered first by lesbian and gay organizations exclusively. In 1985, HOSI Vienna (Homosexual Initiative Vienna) played a decisive role in the founding of the Austrian AIDS Help organization, a private organization, but financed with help from the Federal Ministry for Health. Information, availability of tests, and the support of social workers lay mainly in the hands of this non-governmental organization. In 1991, the Austrian-wide organization was split into several regional AIDS Help organizations that are subsidized by the government.

In recent years, a number of other non-governmental organizations have been established: the "Buddy" association, the Names Project, and other groups providing information. These groups have taken on different tasks, especially in prevention, education, and support services, but receive absolutely no governmental or public subsidy.

Information and educational campaigns are only offered sporadically by the health authorities. HIV/AIDS as a theme appears about every two years for a few weeks on billboards and in TV spot announcements. Such campaigns are usually directed to the whole population ("AIDS Affects Us All") or to young people. Only in recent years has it been possible to talk about condoms publicly. Certain areas, for example, the theme of lesbians and AIDS, do not even appear in public discussions. Recommendations do exist that an educational campaign regarding information about AIDS be held at schools, but the means to carry out this campaign either do not exist, or the funding is inadequate.

With respect to behavior among young people, although less than 10 percent of sexually active girls and boys see a real danger of HIV infection, 28 percent—in rural areas as high as 40 percent—thought about AIDS at the time of their first sexual intercourse. For 31 percent of the young people, AIDS is a subject that they have never thought about; 13 percent are very concerned, and 39 percent reported that they never restricted their sexual lives because of AIDS; but, after all, more than half used a condom most of the time.

The amount of information known to homosexuals is especially high. In one study, 74 percent of the gays interviewed said that they had changed their sexual habits when AIDS appeared. Forty-one percent reduced the number of partners they had; 87 percent practiced "safer sex" from then on; 74 percent used condoms; 64 percent avoided ejaculation in the mouth of their partners; 22 percent gave up anal intercourse; 21 percent said that they now live in a monogamous partnership, and 36 percent are in a lasting relationship.

12. Sexual Dysfunctions, Counseling, and Therapies

Traditionally, in "silent Catholic Austria," sexual dysfunctions are only treated, if at all, in the offices of urologists, gynecologists, or in the four specialized sexual counseling centers. [Andrology, according to Martin Voracek, is an emerging medical specialization, as it is in other developed countries. (Editor)]

People who do not "function" sexually, or who suffer from failure anxieties, usually define themselves as ill. They are often treated as fools or insulted, and are often accused of deliberately refusing to have sex. There have been cases of men murdering their sexual partners because they were laughed at or belittled by them.

There are hardly any statistical records on the incidence of various sexual dysfunctions. In a survey carried out in a newspaper by Senger and Hoffmann (1993), 5 percent of the women identified failure to experience orgasm, 8 percent had pain during sexual intercourse, and 15 percent had cessation of sexual arousal. Of the men who replied, the researchers found that 10.4 percent had erection disorders, 27.3 percent had premature ejaculation, and 4.7 percent stated that they did not achieve erection. The investigators ascertained that 36.2 percent of the men, but only 22.3 percent of the women who responded, said they had problems with sex.

In June 1991, a study was made by an institute that carries out empirical research (IFES—Institut für Empirische Sozialforschung) of various areas of sexuality. Altogether, 1,667 persons (800 men, 867 women) between the ages of 16 and 69 were surveyed. Of these, 591 (35 percent) answered that religion was of great importance to them, and 276 (17 percent) found absolutely no influence from religion. In response to the question of whether or not discussions about sexuality had taken place at home, 913 (55 percent) said "no," 427 (26 percent) said "yes," and 84 (5 percent) answered "yes, often." Sixty-seven percent of those asked lived together with their partners in one household, and 17 percent lived alone without partners. Questions about partners received the following answers: 68 percent of those who lived in separate households had sex with their partners at least once a week, compared to 56 percent of those who lived together; 4 percent had no sex (6 percent of those living together); 19 percent felt that sex was the strongest binding element to their partners (8 percent of those living together); 29 percent had already experienced "extramarital" affairs (18 percent of those living together); 78 percent were able to talk to their partners about sexual problems (69 percent of those living together); and 59 percent were very satisfied with the sex in their partnership (49 percent of those living together).

Since sexual dysfunctions are still primarily looked at as organic illnesses, patients go to their family doctors or specialists and are usually sent, only if the doctors are younger and informed, to specialized counseling centers, i.e., psychologists or therapists, after unsuccessful treatment with orthodox medicine. Full payment by the public health plan is only made, however, if the therapist is a doctor; if not, partial subsidy is available. In cases where clinical psychologists have contracts with the public health insurance authorities, the psychological diagnosis is financially covered.

[The Vienna General Hospital, where the Medical Faculty of the University of Vienna is located, is the largest hospital facility in Middle Europe, with forty-some departments, institutes, and divisions, including psychoanalysis and psychotherapy. Sexual research, counseling, and treatment occur in these divisions even though there is not a distinct sex clinic as such. (Voracek)]

13. Research and Advanced Education

A. Graduate Programs and Sexological Research

Only one working group exists in all of Austria for reproductive biology and sexual medicine, and that is located in the Department of Medical

Biology and Human Genetics at the University of Innsbruck. There is no university chair (professorship) for sexology, sexual psychology, or sex education in Austria. The only postgraduate training for physicians is offered at the Vienna International Academy for Holistic Medicine (Wiener Internationale Akademie für Ganzheitsmedizin), with educational programs in sexual pedagogy, counseling, and therapy.

Continuing education in various sexual therapy aspects are offered by some psychotherapeutic organizations. For this, the Austrian Professional Association of Psychotherapists has set up its own working group

Because there is no university professorship in sexology, there is no openly declared research on questions of sexuality. But, indeed, in the context of psychological, sociological, and medical institutes, sexual themes are researched. In addition, research on sexual topics is carried out in some of the 128 state-sponsored and non-university research institutes and facilities. Until now, individual research projects have been generously supported by certain government ministries, above all, the Federal Ministry for Women's Affairs, Family, and for Education.

The Austrian Society for Research in Sexology (Österreichische Gesellschaft für Sexualforschung, ÖGS, (Postfach 23. A-1013 Wien, Austria), founded in 1979 in Vienna, has been especially active since 1996, and wrote into its statutes the responsibility for the compilation and dissemination of research findings. The organization also reviews relevant drafts of laws and is politically active.

Up to now, private research work in sexology has been financed by daily or weekly publications. Sexual researchers have financed their studies partly through grants from the pharmaceutical industry, their own resources, and partly from their sponsoring media.

Since 1991, the main author of this chapter and chairperson of the Austrian Society for Research in Sexology, Dr. Rotraud A. Perner, has been conducting a three-year training program in sexual counseling and sexual pedagogy at the Vienna Academy for Holistic Medicine. This advanced education program has also been offered since 1999 at the Association for Prophylactic Health Work in Linz. The Austrian Institute for Family Research (Österreichisches Institut für Familienforschung, ÖIF) trains moderators for *Love Talks* that are given in the elementary and secondary schools. Within the framework of the Austrian Professional Association of Psychotherapists, continuing educational courses are offered for some branches of sexual phenomena, for example, sexual abuse of children and sexual dysfunctions.

B. Sexological Organization and Publications

Sexus, the quarterly magazine of the Austrian Society for Research in Sexology (Österreichische Gesellschaft für Sexualforschung, ÖGS), was first published in 1989, and began to appear with regularity in 1996.

The main sexological organizations in Austria are:

Austrian Planned Parenthood Society (Österreichisches Gesellschaft für Familienplanung, ÖGF), Bastiengasse 36-38, A-1180 Vienna, Austria.

Austrian Society for Research in Sexology. (Österreichische Gesellschaft für Sexualforschung, ÖGS), Postfach 23. A-1013 Vienna, Austria

Austrian Institute for Family Research (Österreichisches Institut für Familienforschung, ÖIF), Gonzagagasse 19, A-1010 Vienna, Austria.

14. Important Ethnic and Religious Minorities

In Austria, Croatians, Slovenes, Sinti, and Roma ("Gypsies") are considered minority groups. The majority of the guest workers, those who came to Austria for jobs, the second generation of whom live here, are citizens of former Yugoslavia and Turkey. Those who work without permits are mostly from Eastern Europe. Africans and African-Americans are mostly students or United Nations employees. The largest non-Christian religious group is Islamic. Data about the sexual attitudes and behavior of these ethnic groups have not been gathered.

However, it is known that family members in the second generation of Moslem guest workers live in a cultural conflict that affects girls more than boys, although the fundamentalist movement has not been noticed in public until recently. The sexuality of girls is more intensely controlled than that of boys in Islamic families that defend themselves against assimilation. A double moral standard is evident. Female virginity plays a large role and homosexuality is a great taboo. According to social workers, the reconstruction of the hymen is carried out in operations in Viennese hospitals. Whether, and how often, female circumcision is carried out cannot be determined.

[The Department of Gynecology and Obstetrics at the Vienna General Hospital/Medical Faculty, University of Vienna, has all patient information forms, including information on sexuality, family planning, birth control, AIDS, and homosexuality, in German, Turkish, and Serbocroatian. Most likely other hospital facilities and counseling centers have similar patient information materials. (Voracek)]

Conclusion

As the new millennium begins in Austria, several trends become clear. Religious and cultural minorities who have settled here lose their specific identities as the children are integrated into general Austrian cultural traditions, but parents within these minorities try to enforce their sexual norms as long as their influence is possible.

Sexual violence in the home is receiving more and more attention and is increasingly discussed in public. The activities connected to the Internet and child pornography do not go unnoticed here, and both the private associations of the Internet providers in Austria and the Federal Ministry of the Interior have provided "hotlines" so that people can report what they find or receive. Organizations have set up emergency telephone numbers for battered women, and children subject to abuse, as well as for young people who have questions about sex or fear that they are pregnant. The first seminar to train professionals in crisis intervention for children, especially in cases of sexual abuse, was held on the campus of the University of Vienna in the summer of 1999, set up by a private association that works to combat abuse, and financially supported by the European Union. Even though basic sexual "morals" have not changed, the public is better informed, and much work is being done to give women and victims empowerment and the feeling of confidence so that they can speak up about problems that were, not so long ago, kept secret as if they did not exist.

References and Suggested Readings

Hite, S. 1976. *The Hite report on female sexuality.* New York: Macmillan.

Hite, S. 1978. *The Hite report on male sexuality.* New York: Alfred A. Knopf.

Institut Für Empirische Sozialforschung (IFES, Institute for Empirical Social Research). 1991. *A representative study by Weiss and Perner.* Vienna: Österreichische Gesellschaft für Familien Plannung (Planned Parenthood Association of Austria).

Kinsey, A. C., et al. 1948. *Sexual behavior in the human male.* Philadelphia: Saunders.

Kinsey, A. C., et al. 1953. *Sexual behavior in the human female.* Philadelphia: Saunders.

Langbein, K., & Fritsch, S. 1991. *Land der sinne* [*Land of senses*]. Vienna: ORAC Publishers.

Nöestlinger, C., & Wimmer-Puchinger, B. 1994. *Geschuetze liebe—Jugendsexualitaet und AIDS* [*Protected love: The sexuality of youth and AIDS*]. Vienna: Jugend & Völk Verlag.

Perner, R. 1998. *Scham macht krank* [*Shame leads to sickness*]. Vienna: Aaptos Verlag.

Perner, R. 1994. *Ungeduld des leibes—Die zeitrhythmen der liebe* [*The impatience of the body—Love's time rhythm*]. Vienna/Munich: ORAC Publishers.

Senger, G., & Hoffmann, W. 1993. *Oesterreichische intim* [*Intimate Austria*]. Vienna/Munich: Amalthea Verlag.

Weiss, F., & Perner, R. 1991. *A representative study for IFES, the Institut für Empirische Sozialforschung (Institute for Empirical Social Research).* Vienna: Österreichische Gesellschaft für Familien Plannung (Planned Parenthood Association of Austria).

Colombia

José Manuel Gonzáles, M.A.,* Rubén Ardila, Ph.D.,**
Pedro Guerrero, M.D., Gloria Penagos, M.D., and
Bernardo Useche, Ph.D.***
Translated by Claudia Rockmaker, M.S.W., and Luciane Raibin, M.S.

Contents

Demographics and a Historical Perspective

A. Demographics

Located in the northwest corner of South America, Colombia is bordered by the Caribbean Sea on the north, Panama on the northwest, the Pacific Ocean on the west, Ecuador and Peru on the south, and Brazil and Venezuela on the east. Its 440,762 square miles (1,138,910 square kilome-

Communications: Mtro. José Manuel González, M.A., Apartao Aereo 1190, Barranquilla, Colombia; jmgonzalez@playnet.net.co.

**Rubén Ardila: psycholo@latino.net.co.

***Bernardo Useche: busechea@aol.com.

ters) places it in size between the states of Texas and Alaska. Three mountain ranges, the Andes, the Western, and the Central and Eastern Cordilleras, run through the country from north to south. The eastern range is mostly high tablelands and is densely populated. The Magdalena River rises in the Andes and flows north to the Caribbean Sea through a rich alluvial plain. The sparsely settled eastern plains are drained by the Oronoco and Amazon Rivers. Four percent of the land is arable and capable of producing crops, 29 percent is pasture and meadowlands, 49 percent is forest and woodland, and 2 percent is devoted to permanent crops.

In the 1999 estimated 39.3 million Colombians, the age distribution was 33 percent under age 15 years, 62.4 percent between ages 15 and 64, and 4.6 percent age 65 or older. Ethnically, 58 percent of Colombians are *mestizo* Spanish and Amerindian mix, 20 percent white, 14 percent *mulatto* Caucasian and black mix, 4 percent black, and 4 percent other. Seventy-three percent live in the cities. Ninety-five percent of Colombians are Roman Catholic. Spanish is the official language. Life expectancy at birth in 1997 was 66.2 for males and 74.1 for females. The 1999 birthrate was 24.5 per 1,000 persons, the infant mortality rate 24.3 per 1,000 life births, and the death rate 6 per 1,000 persons, for an annual natural increase of 1.89 percent. The Total Fertility Rate (TFR) in 1997 was 2.7 births per fertile woman, placing Colombia 134 out of 227 nations. In 1992, Colombia had one physician per 1,078 persons. Education is free and compulsory for five years between the ages of 6 and 12. Eighty-seven percent of Colombians are literate. The 1997 estimated per capita Gross Domestic Product was $6,200.

B. A Brief Historical Perspective

Prior to the arrival of Europeans, the area that is now Colombia was home to various sedentary and semisedentary cultures, including the kingdoms of Funza and Tunja and the semisedentary Chibcha, who might have numbered about a million. Some of the area was part of the Inca Empire. By the 1530s, Spain had conquered the area and in 1538 established the colony of New Granada, with its capital in Bogatá, within the jurisdiction of the Viceroyalty of Peru. In 1740, a new Viceroyalty was established that included modern-day Colombia, Ecuador, Panama, and Venezuela. In 1819, forces under Simon Bolívar defeated the Spanish at the Battle of Boyacá, and the area gained its independence in 1821.

Colombia then became part of the Federation of New Granada. Venezuela and Ecuador broke away from this federation in 1829. By the 1850s, Colombia and Panama had adopted a federal system, but the system quickly deteriorated with the semi-sovereign states locked in a constant struggle with the central government for autonomy. In 1903, when the Colombian government rejected an offer by the United States for construction of a canal in Panama, the United States supported a revolt by Panama, which then declared its independence from Colombia.

Since the 1850s, Colombian politics have been characterized by a struggle between two groups that early on coalesced into the Liberal and Conservative parties. The on-going Liberal-Conservative struggle has led to at least six civil wars, usually ending in interparty compromise. For most of the last century, the Roman Catholic Church played a major role in Colombia's social life and political struggles. The 1987-1988 Concordat gave the Church "official protection," while the state assumed authority over public education. The Church's central position in Colombian society was not substantially affected by the Concordat of 1942.

The worldwide depression of the 1930s seriously disrupted both the economy and the politics of Colombia. The overall economic collapse, coupled with the Conservative Party's brutal repression of the labor movement, led to a Liberal victory in 1930, followed by a new civil war between peasants loyal to the two parties. By 1934, Liberal president Alfonso López had inaugurated his "Revolution on the March" program of socioeconomic reform.

During the 1946 elections, Conservatives won the presidency with a minority of the overall vote, defeating a split Liberal Party. Armed conflict instigated by leaders of the two parties erupted to start La Violencia, from 1948 to 1957, during which more than 200,000 people died. In the summer of 1957, the two parties reached an agreement on constitutional reform that was designed to last 16 years and allow for regular alternation of the presidency between the two parties. This agreement lasted 11 years, until 1968, when constitutional revisions allowed official recognition of other political parties.

The 1960s and 1970s were marked by the emergence of terrorist and paramilitary groups on both the right and left, some with ties to the drug trade. This violence greatly reduced the power-sharing monopoly of the two parties. Since 1989, political violence has claimed over 35,000 lives. In March 1990, one of the most notorious left-wing groups, M-19, laid down its arms, entered the political mainstream, and won 19 of the 70 seats in a constitutional convention called to rewrite the Constitution. Other left-wing groups soon followed suit.

Colombia has also had to cope with a thriving and growing narcotics trade. Throughout the 1980s, narco-terrorists murdered and kidnapped government officials, journalists, and innocent bystanders with impunity. Despite the assassination of four presidential candidates prior to the 1990 election, the Liberal Party won with a vigorous campaign against the narcotics trade. In 1994, another Liberal president was elected on the promise to invest billions of dollars to improve Colombia's infrastructure using money from newly discovered oil fields. Between the summer of 1995 and September 1996, the government arrested the seven top members of the Cali drug cartel.

1. Basic Sexological Premises

BERNARDO USECHE

A. The Cultural Legacy

Observing pieces of Pre-Colombian art and the descriptions of the historians of the Indies (when the colonists arrived), one finds strong evidence that the majority of the aboriginal tribes inhabiting the Colombian territory freely practiced the pleasurable side of sexuality. Among the art pieces of the time, one encounters representations of all possible sexual attitudes: masturbation, heterosexual activity, oral sex, homosexual activity, and bestiality. With the arrival of the Spaniards in the sixteenth century, the sexual interests of the conquistadors towards the Indian women made interracial marriages very popular. The evidence of interracial marriage is evident in the fact that 58 percent of Colombians today are *mestizo* Spanish/Amerindian and 14 percent *mulatto* black/Caucasian. At the same time, the Spaniards brought the Catholic religion and the repression of eroticism. The arrival of the African slaves during the seventeenth and eighteenth centuries signified a new miscegenation and the integration of new cultural elements favorable to pleasure rather than procreative sexuality. At the time of independence from Spain and the birth of the republic in the nineteenth century, a nation had been forged that, with respect to sexuality, was somewhere between the exalted libido of the macho population and the erotophobic restrictions of their profoundly religious culture. During the twentieth century, especially in recent decades, the progressive influences of North American culture have been added to Colombian culture. Profound transformations to the family structure and the traditional ideology are being generated by the changes in the Colombian economy at the end of the twentieth century. This has opened a new sexual panorama that is much more complex than in colonial times.

Even though there are important urban, rural, and regional differences, today's sexual attitudes in Colombia are characterized by a double standard, where men are permitted all types of sexual activities while "decent" women are limited to sexual activities within the confines of marriage for reproduction purposes. There is, however, the beginning of a more permissive attitude towards a woman's sexual pleasures if she is in a serious relationship, because the impoverished situation of the majority of Colombians makes it very hard for couples to maintain stable ties.

Colombia continues to be a country where the majority of the population is Catholic, with traditions deeply rooted in the cultural values of Spain. But the few studies that have been done on this issue indicate that the sexual conduct of the people frequently does not conform with the Church's religious norms. This implies that machismo has played an important role in Colombian society. It has perpetuated discrimination towards women in family life, the work environment, and throughout society as a whole. Machismo places great value on female virginity, emphasizes the importance of the extended family, and supports the underlying concept of sin and guilt as it pertains to sexuality.

The modernization of Colombia, beginning in the 1930s and continuing well into the 1980s, changed many of these societal values. Colombia was transformed from a rural country to an urban country. No longer was religion the focal point of education. In spite of opposition from the Catholic Church, couples were having fewer children and birth control was more widely used. The status of women improved considerably. Employment of women outside the home has led to changes in the family structure. It allowed women to make choices, including how many children they bear, as well as changed their societal status. These societal changes, brought about by the modernization, industrialization, and urbanization of Colombia, continues into the start of the twenty-first century.

B. Sexual Roles

Machismo, with its horrible discrimination against woman, is still present in Colombian family life, the work environment, and society. There are few men, even those in the lower socioeconomic bracket, who help with the housework or the raising of the children. With the impoverishment of the country, the number of single mothers who are head of the household increases constantly, but they are still not given the basics: same work, same salary, or even a job. This situation has driven many women and their daughters to prostitution. Politically, women were given equal rights under the law in the 1950s, but they are still the minority in positions of power or in government jobs. Only in the last decade has it been possible for Catholic couples to get a divorce. Abortion is still illegal in Colombia, even though there are estimates that over 300,000 illegal abortions are performed each year. A growing sexual liberation of women has been observed in the past 30 years, but the differences in the sexual conduct of young people of both sexes are still very significant, as seen in Table 1.

Table 1
General Differences of Sexual Conduct

Sexual Activity	Men Percent	Number Responding	Women Percent	Number Responding
Masturbation	92.3%	379	43.2%	604
Vaginal Coitus	62.2	379	30.8	604
Oral Sex	44.8	353	23.1	566
Anal Sex	20.6	355	7.7	560
Group Sex	21.6	310	1.6	492
Same Sex	17.1	346	9.3	572
Victim of Rape or Sexual Abuse	6.4	345	13.9	583

(Useche 1999)

In the movement toward gender/sexual equality in Colombia, we find sexologists like Helí Alzate, who was one of the first to vehemently refute the assumed physical, intellectual, and emotional inferiority of women. Also, intellectuals like Maria Lay Londoño and Florence Thomas, pioneers of the feminist movement since the 1970s, have dedicated enormous efforts to the study of couples and the promotion of sexual equality. The ground won by women in respect to their sexuality has not yet had an impact on the machismo attitudes of men. When it does, as it likely will in the near future, one can expect a crisis in the current model of masculinity.

2. Religious and Ethnic Factors Affecting Sexuality
JOSÉ MANUEL GONZÁLES

Recent studies (Bodnar et al. 1999; Gonzáles 1999a) show the presence of important religious beliefs related to sexuality. The concept of sin related to pleasure in sex, birth control, and some religious concepts that emphasize feminine resignation are important in the sexual life and relationship of couples in Colombia. According to Paulo Romeo, Apostolic Nuncio in Colombia, the Catholic Church is losing 200 practitioners daily (*El Tiempo* 1997). According to the calculation presented at the Assembly of Bishops, only 60 of every 100 people baptized will take their first communion. According to Carlos Alzate of the Episcopal Conference of Colombia, only 15 out of a 100 people who consider themselves Catholics on surveys go to Mass (*El Tiempo* 1997).

To better understand our sexuality, it is necessary to understand the influences of the three biggest ethnic groups in our heritage: the Spanish culture, the African Culture, and the Indian culture (González 2000).

- The Spanish cultural influence, which is a mix between the Arab-Andaluzian influences, mixes the glorification of sensuality and eroticism in its most beautiful form with the Spanish Catholic Inquisition's very strong repressive ideas. This is a major influence in much of what is known about sexuality in Latin America.
- The African culture looked at sexuality, eroticism, and sexual vigor as natural phenomena. Much is known about this influence on contemporary Colombian culture.
- The sexuality of the local aborigines was quite varied, but there is not much information about their common features and differences. When the conquistadors arrived in Colombia, they encountered a wide variety of indigenous cultural attitudes regarding sex, a sample of which follows:

  - The Panches, a Caribbean culture, practiced female infanticide and clitorectomies eight days after birth. If the child survived the sexual mutilation, its marriage was immediately arranged. If the firstborn was a female, she was immediately killed.

- Among the Lanches in the Boyacá region, if a women had five consecutive boys, the youngest would get special attention and was expected to take on the female role. They were brought up as females and were married off to a male.
- The Pamtagoros of Caldas were very puritanical and disapproved of any nudity. Their women were covered up to their ankles and were very careful when sitting not to show their legs. On the other hand, the Pijaos from Tolima would proudly show off their genitals.
- Both male and female Quimbayas from the western side of the central Andes were very sexually active. Among the Muiscas, from Cundinamarca and Boyacá, there was total freedom with respect to premarital sex, whereas among the Pijaos, it was common for the husband to kill his bride if she was not a virgin. The Pantagoros accepted infidelity, whereas the Pijaos punished infidelity very severely. An unfaithful Pijaos woman would be given to the single men of the village for their pleasure, after which she would be buried up to her waist in a public place where she would be whipped to death. The Muiscas had similar punishments for female infidelity.
- Both the Muiscas and the Quimbayas celebrated fertility festivals where they would get drunk and have sexual relations without restrictions. The Liles from the Valle would marry their sisters and nieces. The female Guane, from Santander del Sur, were very involved with the conquistadors. They were described as being the prettiest, the whitest, the cleanest, and the ones with the greatest ability to learn Spanish.
- Among the Noanamas and the Taso, from Choco, anal sex between men was very common. Sexual relations with women were only for reproductive purposes. Most female infants were drowned at birth.

3. Sexual Knowledge and Education
PEDRO GUERRERO

A. Government Policies and Programs

We can affirm with full accuracy that from the Spanish Conquest to the passing of Resolution 03353 by the Ministry of Education in July 1993, sexuality education in Colombia has functioned according to the guidelines set forth by the Catholic Church. Accordingly, sermons originating from the scriptures and dictated from the pulpit were obligingly echoed in all educational institutions.

Our medical students receive their sexological training via lectures in gynecology, urology, and psychology. However, this coursework does not include the erotic aspects of sexuality. It only deals with biological reproduction and the pathologies found in the genital organs. Sexually transmitted diseases are generally discussed with apprehension. At the same time, therapy for sexual dysfunctions remains unknown and the concept of the woman and the family is rooted in the old patriarchal ideology.

National Program on Sexual Education

The National Program on Sexual Education is best described as a set of principals and guidelines that collectively form the knowledge base, attitudes, behaviors, and values of sexuality. Its purpose is to meet the needs of Colombians in living a healthy, responsible, and gratifying sexual lifestyle, while promoting gender equality. Furthermore, it encourages the people to redefine the traditional roles of men and women, as well as the patriarchal family structure, thus attaining greater equality between marital couples and parents and their children. In addition, the National Program on Sexual Education encourages men and women, without coercion or pressure, to choose the appropriate time at which to bear children. As a result, they need to learn to adequately utilize effective birth control methods. The guidelines proposed by the National Program on Sexual Education should be viewed as a framework for the formation and pedagogical organization of sexual education programs in Colombian schools. Therefore, this proposal is optional and not mandatory.

The following items should be taken into consideration while reviewing these guidelines:

1. We must acknowledge the importance that culture plays in sexual education. Culture holds ethical values, morals, and spiritual and religious convictions. These not only determine the significance of the multiple dimensions of human existence, but also determine the people's level of acceptance of the academic proposals.
2. We must understand that sexuality is a fundamental dimension of humanity, which is ever-present in the lives of all men and women.
3. It is suggested that sexual education be integrated into the curriculum from a science and humanities context. This would then serve as an introduction to self-esteem, independence, interpersonal relationships, and health.
4. Sexual education is thought to be the responsibility of the educational community, including all educational institutes in both the public and private sectors, teachers and administrative staff, and parents and students.
5. The family is considered to be the primary source of education for children, as stated in Article 68 of the National Constitution of Colombia. In accordance with Article 68, the family reserves the right to choose the quality of education for their children. It is noted that the family unit serves as a model for the child's future perspectives on sexuality. It is in the family where children of both sexes learn their first lessons on solidarity, sensitivity, and gratitude. It is where a child

learns to love and be loved, to tolerate and be tolerated, to hold a dialogue, to share, and to respect and value life. By the same token, it can also be the place where a child can experience and later repeat child abuse, sexual abuse, gender discrimination, and other types of domestic violence.

6. The importance of *etiquette* in sexual education is evident. The National Constitution of Colombia addresses the issue of the rights and responsibilities as they pertain to the concept of sexuality. Among other rights, the Constitution stipulates the rights of all to personal development, the equality of rights and responsibility of a couple, and the right to choose the number of children they are to bear, among other rights.

7. It is suggested that sexual education should be a pedagogical program that forms the basis of all fundamental studies. That being said, all educational institutions are left with the task of creating their own sexual education programs.

8. The proposed curriculum consists of developing programs that focus on basic sexual education themes, as they relate to the individual student, the couple, the family, and society as a whole. Each fundamental objective is to be modified to the age and grade level, the developmental level, and the specific needs of the target audience. The proposed programs target primary through secondary grade levels. Suggested topics include: identity, tolerance, reciprocity, life in general, affection, communication, love–sexuality, responsibility, imagination, and critical thinking skills.

9. Workshops for educators are a suggested method of sharing information, as opposed to traditional methods like didactic lectures. In workshops, individuals can share information with the group in an open forum.

In order to test the effectiveness of the National Sexual Education Programs, two studies were initiated. The first case study, conducted by the Ministry of National Education, investigated 332 schools in 155 school districts in Colombia. Using quantitative methods, it was found that 92 percent of the schools utilized the sex education programs. These schools reported a marked improvement in school morale, as related to sexuality themes.

The second case study, also conducted by the Ministry of National Education, complimented the previous study in that it investigated the pedagogical process of the National Sex Education Programs in academic institutions. Utilizing qualitative methods to examine 16 subjects at different developmental stages in four different regions of Colombia, this study indicates that the sex education programs are at a critical phase of development. They have been introduced to the school system, and opened up avenues of employment and a new view on sexuality, but they have also identified four areas where further effort and development are needed:

1. Restructuring the aspects of human sexuality taught;
2. Promoting policies and other movements geared towards sexual well-being and reproduction with youth, both within and outside the educational system;
3. Increased utilization of sex education programs in academic institutions and successful replication of studies indicating their effectiveness; and
4. Participation and support from the congressional body, the judicial system, and educational institutions at both the national and international levels, for human sexuality, sex education, sexual health, and reproduction.

B. Informal Sources of Sexual Knowledge   JOSÉ MANUEL GONZÁLES

Investigations conducted by a variety of groups that strongly support sex education have found that parents are reclaiming their roles as the primary informants of sex education. Mantilla (1993) reported that men's primary sources of information on sexuality were: friends, mother, father, and school. Women reported that their primary sources of information on sexuality were: friends, mother, school, and father. Gutierrez and Franco (1989) found that women reported that their primary sources of information on sexuality were: school, mother, friends, and the general media. Men reported that their primary sources of information were: friends, school, the general media, and father. The Institute of Social Securities (Instituto de Seguros Sociales 1994) found that adolescents posed questions regarding sexuality primarily to their mothers, 47 percent of females and 20 percent of males, whereas only 16 percent questioned their friends and 11 percent questioned their fathers.

Everyday the Colombian mass media discusses sexuality more freely. Several related programs have surfaced. Maria Ladi Londoño-Cali, was one of the first pioneers in this area. Lucia Nader and Marta Lucia Palacio joined in on two major networks, Caracol and RCN (Palacio 1999), and presented a compilation of the most frequently asked questions by her viewers. In print, the pioneering column on sexuality was "Window to Sexuality" (González 1998, 1999b). This column was originated by José Manuel Gonzáles and is presently written by Fernando Bohorquez, Ph.D. The *Herald* (Barranquilla) has published an entire page dedicated to human sexuality since 1999, titled *Love and Intimacy* (González 2000). The pioneering television program was *Sexology on Television*, hosted by Elkin Mesa (August, 1979). Lucia Nader, Marta Lucia Palacio, Alonso Acuña, and Pedro Guerrero initiated another program, titled *It's Time to Live*. This program touched on all aspects of human sexuality. It was a popular program that also served as a basis for a book by the same name. Lucia Nader developed a magazine titled *In Private* (1996). Its theme was fundamentally sexuality. *Accent* was a magazine geared towards the gay community, published in 1997. Both publications have since gone off the market, because of financial difficulties.

4. Autoerotic Behaviors and Patterns

A. Children and Adolescents

Erotic autostimulation is rather common among children. Ardila (1986a) interviewed 700 mothers, pertaining to different Colombian subcultures, and found that three out of four mothers reported masturbatory behavior among children of 4 years of age. Acuña and associates (1986) explored the existence of this behavior and the anxiety that it causes for parents. In general, this type of autoexploratory and sexual gratification behavior is repressed by the adults.

Autoerotic behaviors are also common among adolescents. Masturbation generally starts between the ages of 13 and 15 (Alzate 1989; Domínguez et al. 1988; González 1995; Giraldo 1981; Gutiérrez & Franco 1989; Useche 1999). Among the adolescents, between 60 and 95 percent of men and 14 and 68 percent of women have masturbated at least once in their lives (Alzate 1989; Domínguez et al. 1988; González 1995; Giraldo 1981; Gutiérrez & Franco 1989; Useche 1999). In general, feelings of guilt and anxiety are reported with respect to masturbation (Domínguez et al. 1988; González 2000; Gutiérrez & Franco 1989).

B. Adults

Sexual autostimulation is also very common among adults. About 90 percent of men and 70 percent of women report having masturbated at least once in their lives (Alzate 1989; Elijaike et al. 1987; González 1979, 1985, 1995, 2000). The majority of those studies report a greater incidence of masturbatory behavior in those who are less religious.

A relationship between the personality, as measured by Eysenck's MPI test, and masturbation has been detected by González (1979). Men with high scores in introversion have confirmed a higher frequency of masturbatory behavior. Women with high scores for neuroticism have demonstrated a lower frequency of masturbatory behavior as compared to woman with normal scores. With relation to age, it has been reported that in people over 60 years of age, single women masturbate more than men (Bardugo & Segura 1988, González & González in press).

Sexual autostimulation generates many negative feelings. There are many myths and misinformed beliefs on the subject (Giraldo 1981; González 2000). In a recent survey done in the four biggest cities of Colombia, it was found that only 32 percent of women and 53 percent of men find masturbation to be a healthy sexual behavior. The rest believe that it is a crazy conduct that should be avoided, because it is a sexual deviance and a sin (*Semana* 1999).

5. Interpersonal Heterosexual Behaviors
JOSÉ MANUEL GONZÁLES

A. Children

Childhood sexual rehearsal play and sexual exploration are quite common. One out of every two mothers reported observing sexual rehearsal play in their 4-year-old children (Ardila 1986). Still, childhood sexuality is a theme that produces great anxiety in adults (Acuña et al. 1986; González 2000).

B. Adolescents

There are no widespread rituals of initiation to puberty. In some rural areas on the Caribbean coast of Colombia, it is common for adolescents to engage in sexual acts with animals, namely mules (González 2000).

Sexual activity among adolescents occurs frequently and functions according to the traditional male-dominant cultural pattern. Forty-four percent of Colombians initiate sexual interactions between the ages of 11 and 18. By 18 years of age, 72 percent of males and 40 percent of females have had sexual intercourse, according to Ministry of Health of Colombia (Ministerio de Salud 1994). Generally, female adolescents' first sexual encounter occurs with their boyfriends. Often, sexual relations between Colombian adolescents stem from an intimate relationship and not from an encounter with a prostitute (Bonder et al. 1999; González 1995; González et al. 2000; Useche 1999).

C. Adults

Premarital Relations, Courtship, and Dating

Premarital sex is quite common in Colombia. In recent studies, it was found that 90.4 percent of males and 62.8 percent of females have engaged in premarital sex prior to starting college life (González et al. 2000). Love is usually on the forefront. It is a fundamental part of Colombian culture: music, magazine articles, soap operas, and movies (Bodnar et al. 1999; González 1998; Guerrero 1996a, 1996b). In recent years, initiating friendships and intimate relationships has become easier. Formal introductions are no longer required. People have become more direct in their approach.

In recent studies, González (2000) found that men experience difficulties in expressing love and affection. It is common that people have unrealistic expectations regarding love, and, as a consequence, great frustrations and clashes between fantasy and reality in relationships. Frequently, the expectation is that the lover will satisfy all of their needs, provide unconditional love, and be who they want them to be and not who they actually are. They believe that pain, suffering, and jealousy are essential parts of a relationship. Generally, the woman is expected to be responsible for the affective part of the relationship. She is often expected to prove her love by engaging in sex with her partner. It is also believed that a sure way of keeping a man, or winning him back, is through sex. All the conditions aforementioned make choosing an appropriate mate difficult. Frequently, a partner is not chosen on reality-based merits. Instead he or she is chosen on unrealistic expectations, which inevitably will lead to a failed relationship.

Sexual Behavior and Relationships of Single Adults

Among adults, there exists a misconception of what sexual pleasure is. Generally, they do not understand the physiological and/or psychological concepts of eroticism. As a result, there exist irrational and unhealthy beliefs (González et al. 2000). Sex is commonly seen as bad, dirty, ugly, and degrading. This sex-phobic mindset distorts and impedes a healthy sexual lifestyle (González 1981). Often egotism is perceived as a process leading towards reproduction. Anything else is seemingly considered illegal, promiscuous, and guilt-ridden (González 1999a).

According to the *machismo* ideology, males tend to initiate sexual activity earlier than females. It tends to be more intense and promiscuous (Alzate 1989; Bodnar et al. 1999; González et al. 2000; Institute of Social Securities 1993; Useche 1999). Adult males will have more sexual partners than their female counterparts: One out of every three males reported having two or more sexual partners in the last twelve months, whereas only three out of every one hundred females reported multiple partners (Institute of Social Securities 1993). Generally, the male initiates sexual interactions within the relationship. Couples engage in sex frequently: 2 percent reported daily sexual activity, 19 percent reported sexual activity several times a week, 41 percent reported weekly sexual activity, and 16 percent reported monthly sexual activity (Ministerio de Salud 1994). The sexual positions most frequently practiced were the missionary man-on-top/woman-on-bottom position, the straddle where the woman sits on top of the man, and the rear-entry position with the man behind the woman (González 1994).

Eljaiek et al. (1987) found that almost 50 percent of the couples surveyed did not engage in sexual relations during menses, and almost 10 percent discontinued sexual activity during pregnancy. There also exists a great irresponsibility, for both men and women, in practicing safe sex and using some form of contraception. There is a high rate of sexual dissatisfaction for both genders (González 1998).

Marriage and Family

Colombians place a great importance on feeling as though one is "in love." Love is the primary motivating factor for matrimony, as reported by 87 percent women and 69 percent men (Eljaiek et al. 1987).

The marriage rate has decreased while the rate of cohabitation has increased, especially in the younger population. Mature couples in their mid-80s reported that 84 percent were married through the Catholic Church, while 15 percent cohabitated. Married couples in their mid-30s reported that 44 percent were married through the Catholic Church, while 54 percent cohabitated (Rojas 1997). The average age for matrimony or cohabitation has decreased for males and has increased for women (Presidential Council for Youth, Women, and Their Families 1994).

Rojas (1998) found that couples feel unfulfilled in their relationships. They feel that their counterparts do not demonstrate affection both physically and verbally, that they do not support their efforts, and that they do not make them feel valued. Additionally, they feel that there is a lack of communication with regards to problems, misunderstandings, and resolutions. Rojas also noted that of the couples surveyed, 50 percent did not have a set time in which to communicate.

The marital union in Colombia tends to be non-democratic and lacks equality between the partners. Often women seek gender equity, only to be met with violence from their counterparts. There also exist religious beliefs that support submissiveness and perpetuate this unjust marital relationship (González 2000). Misinformation pertaining to masculinity, femininity, and their interrelatedness permeates societal expectations. Men are perceived in terms of money, power, bravery, and freedom. Women, on the other hand, are perceived as tender, submissive, tolerant, able to bear suffering, and having a need to sexually satisfy their partner at the expense of her own sexual needs. These machismo-based values are believed to be biological in nature, disregarding educational, physiological, and/or psychological cultural factors (González 1998, 2000).

There has been an increase in separations and multiple sequential marriages in Colombia: 35 percent of all couples surveyed have been separated at least once (Presidential Council for Youth, Women and Their Families 1994). Zamudio and Rubiano (1991b) found that the primary causes for separations among Colombian couples were: infidelity, jealousy, or falling in love with another person, falling out of love or falling into a rut, and financial difficulties, in that order.

According to Gutierrez de Pineda (1975), there are four types of family structures: Andino, Santandereano, Negroide, and Antioqueno. These are characterized by the following factors:

- *Andino Family Structure* in the Cundinamarca and Boyaca regions. The dominant feature in this region is the patriarchal structure in which the father is the head of the household. The mother and children are viewed as subordinates. The male children imitate the father while the girls imitate the mother. Initially, the mother is the disciplinarian. However, as the boys grow older, the father tends to intervene more frequently.
- *Santandereano Family Structure* in the Santanderes. Here, the power of the male over the female is evident. His aggressiveness and physical dominance characterize the male. He takes great pride in his sons; however, he withholds any type of affection. Great emphasis is placed on the rift between social classes.

- *Negroide Family Structure* on the Atlantic Coast, in the regions of Chocco and Magdalena, Cauca, and the lower region of Antioquia. The basic characteristic of this family structure is the incidence of cohabitation. For men, it is considered prestigious to have multiple partners. Much attention is focused on the male genitals. The man is determined to father a vast number of children without regard for the childrearing responsibilities. Usually, the mother raises the children with the almost complete absence of the father.
- *Antioqueno Family Structure* in the regions of Antioquia, Caldas, Risaralda, Quindio, El Valle, Tolima, and parts of El Chocco. Here, religion has a great impact on the family structure. Catholic matrimonies are a dominant feature. The traditional gender roles are practiced. The man is the head of the household, but the woman rules in the home. The mother is strict with her daughters, especially as it pertains to sexuality. She is compliant with her sons, especially the youngest one.

Although these discrepancies are no longer as rigid as they once were, the general tendency continues to follow these traditional patterns (Gutierrez de Pineda 1975).

Extramarital Sex

Infidelity is an important element in a Colombian marriage (González 1998). Murillo (1993) found that there were three males for every one female who engaged in extramarital sexual relationships. Nadar and Palacio (1989) found the same results. Nadar and Palacio also found that 30 percent of separations were a result of infidelity. Findings indicate that there is a greater incidence of infidelity for men as the socioeconomic levels rise higher. For women, infidelity is more common at the upper-middle-class levels (Rojas 1997). A common misconception is that a man's infidelity is less serious because he is biologically driven, whereas women's infidelity is not.

Sexuality and Physically Disabled and Elderly Persons

Colombian sexology has little literature regarding disabled and elderly persons. The prevailing attitude is that this population is nonsexual and has no need for sexual intimacy. In a recent study of adults over the age of 60, González and González (in press) found that 94 percent of the men and 24 percent of the women maintain sexual interactions with their mates; males engaged in sex every two weeks, whereas women engaged in sex on a monthly basis. Seventy-six percent of men and 36 percent of women reported that there was a decrease in gratifying sexual intercourse after the age of 60. It was reported that 88 percent of these older men and 30 percent of the women are satisfied with their sex life. Eighty-two percent of the men and 18 percent of the women reported that they continue to seek out their partners for sexual activity. Forty percent of the men surveyed reported having sexual relations with someone other than their regular partner. Eighty percent of men and 52 percent of women reported that relations with their partners are at least cordial. Forty percent of all women surveyed reported that they do not have a good relationship with their partners. Seventy-two percent of men and 50 percent of women reported that they continue to be affectionate with their partners. The authors believe that the predominant machismo values distort a couple's lifestyle, resulting in resentful women.

Incidence of Anal and Oral Sex

Although there are no laws prohibiting anal sex and oral sex, they continue to be highly criticized in public and frequently practiced in private. Almost 80 percent of men and 70 percent of women have engaged in oral sex, now a regular part of foreplay (Eljaiek et al. 1987; González 1994, 1998).

6. *Homoerotic, Homosexual, and Ambisexual Behaviors*
RUBEN ARDILA

There has long been an interest in homosexuality in Colombia. Behaviors that can be categorized as homosexual have been noted within the cultures that existed in Colombia during the arrival of the Europeans. However, the study of homosexuality is filled with methodological ambiguities. There are certain behaviors that may or may not be considered *homosexual* by today's societal standards. Even so, these behaviors existed long before the arrival of the Spaniards. As in other cultures, homosexual behaviors were found more frequently among men than women.

From the onset of studies on sexuality amongst Colombians, homosexuality was always an interest (Alzate 1978, 1982; Botero 1980; González 1985). It was found that there were differences in homosexual activity between men and women. In Bogotá, 28 percent of the men and 13 percent of the women reported having had same-sex relationships. Interestingly, there was a marked difference between the various cities in Colombia. These ratios are not limited to homosexual activities exclusively. It reflects the number of individuals who engaged in some type of sexual activity with someone of the same sex. It could have been an isolated incident and/or the regular practice of homosexual or bisexual behaviors.

Anthropological and Social Aspects

José Fernando Serrano (1997, 1998), an anthropologist, has pointed out that the formation of the homosexual identity, as described by societal constructs, has been a long process. He reviewed sociological studies originating in Colombia and indicated which ones supported the argument of sexual orientation. He also argued the problem of collective identities at the international level.

The modernization of Colombia, which took place in the latter half of the twentieth century, enabled people to look outside their immediate society and expand their provincial traditions. It enabled them to study ideas from other countries, primarily from France and other regions of Europe, and the United States. The gay and lesbian liberation movements of Germany, several other European nations, and later from the United States slowly made their way to Colombia. Nevertheless, they had a great impact on the organization of the gay and lesbian movements. Modernization gradually brought about internationalization, globalization, and societal changes that influenced people's private lives.

Homosexual Identity

The beginnings of organized homosexual groups in Colombia began in 1970. Manuel Antonio Velandia, a sociologist and philosopher, initiated them. He associated with people who were interested in human rights, social change, and the general counterculture of the 1960s and 1970s on an international level. These gay and lesbian movements were difficult to organize, and were at times very short lived. Finally, in the late 1980s and 1990s, gay and lesbian groups succeeded in uniting and achieving their goals (Velandia 1999).

Velandia founded the Gay Liberation Group and the Homosexual Liberation Movement of Colombia in 1976. He also organized the first Gay Pride March in 1983 in Bogotá. These movements gained importance in 1998 and 1999 and included weeklong lectures on sexual diversity, collective identity, human rights, legislation, and other related topics. However, gay and lesbian communities are slow in coming. Although gay meeting places have been established since the 1970s, homosexual literature remains unseen. The first writings pertaining to the gay lifestyle—poetry, novels, theater, and soap operas—surfaced in the 1980s. This is not to discount earlier works by P. Barba Jacob. Today, soap operas and movies frequently touch on homosexuality.

The Constitution of Colombia, passed in 1991, prohibits discrimination in any form or manner. It recognizes that all people have the right to free personal development. The Constitution stipulates that homosexuals may not be discriminated against based on their sexual orientation. Sexual orientation that is not shared by the majority does not justify unequal treatment.

The rights given by the Colombian Constitution pertaining to sexual orientation during the 1990s have been favorable for homosexuals and bisexuals. For example, in April 1991, a law was passed that protects an individual's rights to free sexual identity. It affirms that homosexuality should be considered valid and legitimate. The Colombian Constitution also addressed the debate regarding homosexual educators. They determined that homosexuality has no bearing on an individual's ability to teach (in September 1998). Additionally, in July 1999, the Colombian legislature passed a law protecting homosexuals in the military. It states that individuals may reveal their status as homosexuals and continue to be held to the same norms and expectations as heterosexuals.

The Colombian legislature has defined the family as a union of a man and a woman (March 7, 1996). However, it went on to acknowledge the rights of partners, including same-sex couples, in terms of inheritance, transfer of assets, and financial support, among other things. There have been several attempts to legalize homosexual marriages, as has been done in several other areas, e.g., Denmark since 1989, Norway since 1993, Sweden since 1995, Iceland since 1996, Hungary since 1996, and Holland since 1997. In some cases, there exist legal sanctions against same-sex marriages because of the possibility of adoption. There are, however, gay activist groups who support the legalization of the *gay family* in all aspects, including adoption. The Family Pride coalition is one of the most important advocates of this movement.

One of the most recent proposals, in September 1999, sought to equalize the rights of homosexual couples with those of heterosexual couples. For instance, after two years of cohabitation, the couple may apply for Social Security benefits. Additionally, should the relationship end because of death, one partner may inherit the assets of the other. There already are companies in the private and public sectors that will allow an employee's partner of the same sex to register for benefits.

Psychological Investigations

Psychological studies regarding homosexuality, bisexuality, and homoeroticism have been conducted by Octavio Giraldo and his team (1979, 1981, 1982) at the University of "El Valle." Similar studies have been lead by Ruben Ardila (1985, 1986, 1995, 1998) at the National University of Colombia.

Ruben Ardila has focused on sexual orientation in the studies he has conducted for the past 15 years. Some of the issues he has researched have been: adaptation of homosexual males, lesbianism, sexual orientation, heterosexual attitudes towards homosexuals, stability of the homosexual couple, the life cycle of homosexuals and lesbians, the biological aspects of homosexuality, politics as they pertain to homosexuality, and other related topics.

One such study looked at the adaptation of male homosexuals (Ardial, 1998). There were 100 subjects, between the ages of 18 and 52 years of age. They all scored a five or six on the Kinsey Scale (indicating predominantly or exclusively homosexual). The following factors were studied: depression, solitude, timidity, social alienation, interrelations with heterosexuals, interrelations with homosexuals, sexual practices, traditional values, religion, morals, conformity, acceptance of homosexuality, emotional stability, guilt, concept of homosexuality as a mental illness, effeminacy, responsibility, interrelations with the opposite sex, secretiveness of homosexuality, personal adjustment, and psychosomatic symptoms.

The results indicate that Colombian homosexuals are well adapted and do not present any pathological qualities. However, 10 percent manifested signs of severe depression, while 44 percent were highly stable. Only 4 percent reported feeling guilty about their homosexuality. Fifty-nine percent stated that they had positive interpersonal relations, and 48 percent accepted their homosexuality. For further material on diverse aspects of sexual orientation for both women and men, see the References and Suggested Readings section.

Sexual Orientation in Colombian Society

Our society, based on the Judeo-Christian faith, has a very negative attitude towards homosexuality. Homosexuality is viewed as a violation, an illness, or a deviation from the norm that threatens normal behaviors and society. This homophobic view has permeated Colombian society throughout its history, although, there have been different levels of acceptance, depending on the individual's level of education, rural-versus-urban setting, age, and their affiliation with the Catholic Church. There is a deeply rooted belief that homosexuals are a threat to society, good upbringing, and family values. Similarly, homosexuality is thought to be related to child sexual abuse, AIDS, substance abuse, delinquency, and other serious social problems.

Homosexuals are discriminated against in education, in the workplace, in housing, in the mass media, and generally in daily living. This homophobia has its origins in the Latin-American cultures, which practice machismo, emphasize the importance of the family unit, and are highly influenced by the Catholic Church. In spite of this, the situation has considerably improved in recent years, from the homosexual liberation movements in the 1970s to the legislative, medical, and psychological advances that occurred later. In the larger cities of Colombia, especially those with higher levels of education, homosexuals are accepted. They are respected and are considered equal to heterosexuals. In these areas, discrimination is hardly noticeable. It is no longer believed that male homosexuals are less masculine than heterosexual males or that lesbians are any less feminine than female heterosexuals are. Additionally, there are certain groups within the Church who have worked towards improving the quality of life for gays and lesbians. Social support has shown improvement, which will then lead to a more pluralistic, diversified, and egalitarian society.

7. Gender Conflicted Persons
BERNARDO USECHE

As in most of the Latin-American countries, Colombia also does not have serious studies or reliable statistics on the frequency or psychological evolution of those people whose sexual identity is not well-defined or is confused. But, based on clinical exams and interviews with those people, it is possible to differentiate two large groups.

In the first group, one encounters heterosexual and homosexual transvestites and a few male-to-female transsexuals who were born and raised in lower-class environments and have socially isolated themselves in areas dedicated mostly to prostitution. Because of the almost non-existent control over the sale of hormones in the country, it is quite easy for such people to seek physical changes through auto-medication with estrogen. This type of hormonal auto-medication normally starts during adolescence and has the effect of changing the body type to the feminine phenotype, even though the vast majority of this group will not seek surgical sex reassignment.

Given the context of the social problems encountered by people living in poverty, members of this first group become sexually active at a very early age and soon transition to promiscuity and prostitution. A few work as strippers in the clubs that are very common in the prostitution areas of the big cities. A few others, under the auspices of "transformists," work as singers or actresses in nightclub shows. Very seldom, and only if sex-reassignment surgery is involved, will someone from this group obtain some type of professional therapy through the almost non-existent public health system. Members of this group also have received some help and orientation from non-governmental agencies involved in the prevention of HIV infection.

The following quote perfectly demonstrates what happens to members of this group:

> I began to dress permanently as a woman and take hormones when I was 18, and that provoked adverse emotional reaction from my parents who kicked me out of the house. They accepted me as a homosexual but not as a transsexual. The only place that accepts me as I am is the brothel where I go to work when I need money. (Author's clinical notes)

The second group is composed of those who belong to the upper classes, many of whom have college degrees and work as professionals. This group is currently composed of transvestites, fetishist transvestites, and some transsexuals who have access to information regarding their sexual identity, especially through the Internet. Some have their own Web pages and communicate among themselves, taking advantage on the initial anonymity of cyberspace to better understand themselves. Even though this group has the means to obtain professional help and counseling through private practice, they seldom do so. This is because of the fact that many therapists have no knowledge on the subject, and some even have a negative attitude to those who approach them with these problems. In the words of one client in this group:

> In the anguish of my situation I went to a psychiatrist who referred me to the best sex therapist in this city. In our first meeting, the sexologist was very frustrating and I felt offended and attacked. I never returned. (Author's clinical notes)

In recent years, sex-reassignment surgery has been performed in large cities like Bogotá, Cali, and Medellín.

8. Significant Unconventional Sexual Behaviors
JOSÉ MANUEL GONZÁLES

A. Coercive Sex

Child Sexual Abuse and Incest

Colombian law considers child sexual abuse a crime under Articles 303, 304, and 305 of the Penal Code. It is calculated that one Colombian child is sexually molested every six hours (Afecto Foundation 1999). In the great majority of cases, the aggressor is a person the victim knows (Florez & Consuegra 1998). These authors studied the cases of 80 girls under the age of 15 in the urban area of Barranquilla. In 53 percent of the cases, the aggressor was someone the victim knew but was not a family member, 41 percent of the perpetrators were family members, and only 6 percent were complete strangers. In 1.25 percent of the cases, pregnancy was a consequence.

Incest is also considered a crime under Article 259 of the Penal Code. Even though there are no reliable statistics, it is widely calculated that incest is a common phenomenon. In a recent survey conducted in the four largest cities, *Semana* (1999) found that 3 percent of males and 1 percent of females had had sexual relations with the father, mother, or a sibling.

In Colombia, 2 million children are victims of abuse, 850 of whom were in critical condition at the time of the Afecto Foundation survey (1999). In Colombia, an estimated 148 of every 1,000 Colombian children are abused in some way. Of these 148, 100 are verbally abused, 40 are physically abused, and 8 are sexually abused (*El Tiempo* 1999).

Sexual Harassment

Sexual harassment is not considered a crime in Colombia. Even though there are no reliable statistics, it is a very common phenomenon in academic and work environments. The machismo cultural pattern makes many man think it is their God-given right to sexually harass their female employees and co-workers.

Rape

Rape is considered a crime under Article 298 of the Penal Code and does happen with some frequency. Profamilia (Planned Parenthood of Colombia; 1995) found that 5.3 percent of women in the fertile age group have been forced to have sexual relations. Before 1996, forced sexual relations within married couples were not considered a crime. With the creation of Law 294 under Article 25, forced sexual relations within married couples are now a crime.

Spousal abuse is a very common phenomenon. In 1996, of the 42,963 cases seen by the Legal Medicine group, 71 percent involved spousal abuse. Of those cases, 95 percent of the victims were women, with a ratio of 18 women for every man. The group at most risk of abuse are women between the ages of 25 and 34. In a 1998 study in several Colombian cities, 14.3 percent of the persons interviewed said that they had been attacked by their spouses (*El Tiempo* 1998). Further interviews showed that 60 percent of the women had been verbally, physically, psychologically, or sexually attacked by their husbands or partners. Twenty percent were physically attacked and 10 percent were forced to have sexual relations with their husbands (Profamilia 1995). Most of these women tried to solve their problems without the intervention of the police or other governmental agencies. Most of these women were completely passive regarding the attacks of their partner. Most battered women say that the main causes of the aggression are drunkenness and jealousy on the part of their partners. The most common physical abuses are punches 88 percent, kicks 27 percent, and shoves and pushes 24 percent. In 35 percent of the cases, the episode is observed by a child (Profamilia 1995).

B. Prostitution

Prostitution is considered a crime under Articles 308, 309, 311, and 312 of the Penal Code. In 1998, the Renacer Foundation estimated 30,000 Colombian boys and girls were engaged in prostitution. At the same time, the Foundation estimated that there were 90,000 sex workers in the country. The sex trade seems to be increasing in the past five years, particularly in the tourist areas and with minors. In the most recent government administrations, there has been a greater emphasis on efforts to combat situations, such as the sex trade, that are problematic to the community.

C. Pornography and Erotica

Pornography possession and its use among adults are not crimes. Article 312 of the Penal Code does limit and penalize the circulation of pornographic material for minors under age 18 years. Pornographic movies can be seen or rented with great ease in the cities. Pornographic magazines circulate all over the country. A 1999 survey by *Semana* shows that 48 percent of men and 35 percent of women think that pornographic movies and magazines make their sexual life more interesting. Regarding pornographic magazines, 13 percent of men and 3 percent of women reported having read one in the previous 30 days. It is also interesting to note that 16 percent of men and 44 percent of women had never read a pornographic magazine in their lives. As for pornographic movies, 21 percent of men and 6 percent of women confirmed having had seen a pornographic movie in the previous 30 days. Also, 14 percent of men and 39 percent of women stated that they had never seen a pornographic movie in their lives. In the large cities, live sexual shows are performed, but 65 percent of men and 85 percent of women claimed they had never seen one (*Semana* 1999).

The new digital media, Internet, and World Wide Web have also been affecting sexual relationships: 17 percent of men and 4 percent of women affirmed having visited a pornographic site on the Internet. Also, 14 percent of men and 4 percent of women admitted to having engaged in phone sex.

9. Contraception, Abortion, and Population Planning
GLORIA PENAGOS

A. Contraception

Birth control, more commonly known as family planning, was introduced in Colombia in 1964. It was managed under the sponsorship of population and medical specialists. The objective was to improve the health of women and their children, to facilitate the growth of women in areas related to motherhood, and population control.

Although the majority of Colombians practice Catholicism, which prohibits the use of any type of artificial birth control, economic and social needs, marital instability, and constant changes in the family structure have led to the acknowledgment of the civil rights of all couples and their children. Thus, the contradiction between what is forbidden by the Catholic Church and what is practiced by the general public has led to an appreciation of the right to the enjoyment of sexuality without the burden of pregnancy. The majority of people continue to practice Catholicism without feeling the guilt put upon them by the Church regarding birth control. Close to three quarters of all women in a relationship, 72.2 percent, utilize some method of birth control. However, for every six women using birth control, only one man uses a contraceptive (Profamilia 1995). Table 2 shows a comparison of the use of birth control worldwide and the usage in Colombia in 1995.

Table 2
**A Comparison of Birth Control Methods Used
Worldwide and in Colombia (1995)**

Contraceptive Method	Worldwide Usage	Colombian Usage
Tubal ligation	13.0%	16.9%
Vasectomy	5.9	0.7
Vaginal suppository	1.0	1.0
Oral contraceptives	8.0	8.5
Intrauterine device (IUD)	9.0	7.4
Injectable contraceptives	1.0	1.8
Coitus interruptus	4.0	6.0
Rhythm	4.0	5.3
Condom	5.0	4.3

The most commonly used methods of birth control are tubal ligation and vasectomy. Recently, Colombia's Social Security System and medical service providers, the equivalent of Medicaid in the United States, now fund these procedures. In the past, they may not have been funded by the government out of deference to religious authorities rather than for economic reasons. Nonetheless, the cost of unwanted pregnancies and abortions reinforces the current position.

Oral contraceptives are the second most frequently used contraceptive method. According to Article 100 of the Social Security act, provision of oral contraception is mandatory. However, 70 percent of Colombians who use oral contraceptives obtained them through the private sector, whereas 30 percent obtained them through the public sector. This evident lack of active participation by the state would suggest that most families prefer to incorporate the cost of oral contraceptives into the family budget rather than rely on the government.

Colombia has several laws that protect the rights of women and children; however, implementation is often lacking. Family planning is viewed as an individual's right and an obligation of the state. The Constitution of 1991, Articles 17 through 30, denounces all forms of discrimination against women: "Women have civil rights as they pertain to reproduction and the judicial system equal to men in education, nationality, employment, health, matrimony and family." Two other articles deal with pregnancy and children:

- Article 42 stipulates that a couple has the right to freely and responsibly choose the number of children they will bear. They will provide and educate them while they are minors unable to provide for themselves.
- Article 43 states that men and women have equal rights and opportunities. A woman can not be discriminated against. The law also protects a woman while pregnant and post-partum, and the state will provide financial assistance and food supplements should she be unemployed and/or homeless. The state will assist women who are heads of households.

The aforementioned legal structure allows us to reflect on how little the state is actually doing to defend the rights of individuals, and, in failing to acknowledge the discrimination, women suffer within Colombia's poorly organized health system.

B. Teenage (Unmarried) Pregnancies

One out of every ten adolescents has had sexual relations between the ages of 13 and 14 years. Four out of every ten adolescents have had sexual relations between the ages of 15 and 17 years. Seven out of ten have had sexual relations by the time they reach the age of 18.

One out of every three adolescents believes that abortion is unacceptable; however, 70 percent feel that it may be necessary in certain situations.

Sixty-two percent have had some discussion on sexually transmitted diseases and 95 percent understand that anyone can contract AIDS. The contraceptive methods most commonly used by adolescents are: the condom (94 percent), oral contraceptives (77 percent), and contraceptive suppositories (60 percent). The rhythm method is the least-used method (42 percent), which coincides with women's lack of awareness of their menstrual cycle (Profamilia 1995).

There has been an increase in birth rates among adolescents. This may be because of several factors: earlier onset of puberty, earlier onset of sexual activities, low socioeconomic levels, low levels of education, increased age for marriage, changes in value system because of urbanization, and the increased ability of communication.

According to a study conducted by the University of Colombia (Universidad Externado de Colombia 1992), one third of all women between the ages of 15 and 19 years, of low educational level, and who had at least one child, were single, lived in an urban area, and were more fertile than their counterparts living in rural areas.

Profamilia (1995) reported that 17 percent of women between the ages of 15 and 19 years were mothers or were pregnant at the time of the study. At the age of 19, four out of every ten women surveyed were mothers and 9 percent already had at least one child. It was also reported that 33.6 percent did not utilize birth control because they believed that they were infertile. Ten percent of these women and 2.8 percent of their contemporaries are opposed to the use of birth control. Three percent were unfamiliar with birth control methods and 7.9 percent were afraid of the side effects. These results reflect the lack of adequate information, existing myths, unawareness, and a lack of responsibility in spite of knowing the consequences.

Pregnancy in adolescents brings with it many consequences, including compromised physical and mental health and both economic and social challenges, which affect the mother, father, and child, as well as the family and society as a whole. The education dropout rate in this population is very high, leading to limited employment opportunities. Children born of adolescents show a higher incidence of prematurity, lower birthweight, more congenital diseases, and a higher incidence of abandonment and abuse. It is estimated that about 10 percent of children of teenage mothers are given up for adoption (Pardo & Uriza 1991).

C. Abortion

The actual incidence of abortion in Colombia is unknown. It is estimated that 24 percent of all pregnancies end in abortion and 26 percent result in unwanted pregnancies (Profamilia 1995). In a 1992 study, *The Incidence of Abortion in Colombia*, researchers at the Universidad Externado de Colombia found that 30 percent of urban women between the ages of 15 and

49 years had had at least one abortion, with the highest incidence among women between ages 20 and 29 years. In at least 78 percent of those cases, no birth control was utilized; the remaining 22 percent had used a birth control method that failed and resulted in pregnancy. There is a 22-percent incidence of abortion among women ages 45 to 49 years of age, and a 19.4-percent incidence of abortion among women ages 50 to 55. A third of the women surveyed reported that they had been pressured by their partners to abort.

Abortion is illegal in Colombia, and women go to health clinics much too late in the pregnancy when they show complications that cannot be resolved on their own. Complications are the most common reason for aborting, and abortion is the leading cause of death for Colombian women. There is an estimated 300,000 illegal abortions yearly. In other words, for every 10 births, there are four illegal abortions, and one out of every 100 women between the ages of 15 and 49 years old has had at least one abortion. The women most likely to abort are those who failed to use contraceptives.

The majority of families in Colombia are rooted in the traditional patriarchal family structure, based on economic, political, and religious power, which conditions women to utilize family planning methods. However, contraception should not be limited only to birth control. The meaning and implications of contraception should also include the significance, attitudes, and values people place on relationships, affection, and sexuality. These factors should take us beyond the stereotypes created by patriarchal gender roles, thus facilitating a better understanding of the individual, their health, and their relationships (Londoño 1996). In this extended meaning of contraception, it is necessary for women to acquire higher educational levels to attain better employment opportunities. They should be able to access better social security and health systems. The medical assistance model should not be solely based on doctors and technology, but also on the premise of caring for one's self and gaining the knowledge women need to balance, preserve, and improve their health.

D. Population Programs

Since the introduction of contraceptives in the mid-1960s, Colombia's population growth rate has decreased steadily. Between 1980 and 1995, Profamilia estimates the population growth rate decreased by 23 percent. On average, there were 7 children born per family in the 1960s. In early 2001, the average Colombian family has 2.8 children per family. However, the averages vary from region to region. In the mountainous regions, the average family size is 4.3 children. Education level also plays an important role in determining the number of children per family. On average, there are 5 children per family for women with no formal education versus 1.8 children per family for women with higher levels of education (Profamilia 1995).

10. Sexually Transmitted Diseases
JOSÉ MANUEL GONZÁLEZ AND GLORIA PEGANOS

A. Incidence

A true evaluation of the incidence of sexually transmitted diseases (STDs) is very difficult in any country, because the percentage of actual cases is considerably higher than the number of cases reported to health officials. In 1994, the Institute of Social Security found that 2 percent of Colombian males and 1.1 percent of females had some type of STD. The most common infections were gonorrhea, condylomas (warts), genital herpes, and syphilis. The majority of cases occurred in people between the ages of 15 and 44. Useche (1999) found that 4 percent of male students in high school reported some type of STD. Zuluaga and contributors (1991) found that 16.4 percent of male and 2.4 percent of female Mendellin University students had had some type of STD, the most common being gonorrhea and condylomas. Among university students from Baranquilla, González (1985) found that 13 percent of males and 1 percent of females had had some type of STD. In a follow-up study ten years later, González (1995) found that 12 percent of males and 2 percent of females had had some type of STD, with gonorrhea being the most prevalent. In the last few years, the incidence of STD cases has grown considerably. This is in part because of teenagers having sexual relations earlier that in previous times, teenagers having sex without protection, and cultural stereotypes that only sex workers can get STDs and not promiscuous men. When the increase in STDs is compared to the increase in the population, however, one can actually see a slight decrease in the overall percentage of STDs in the population.

Papilloma and Condyloma Infections

Although the actual incidence of STD infections is not known, there has been a large increase in the number of new diagnosed cases, in conjunction with other infections like gonorrhea, syphilis, non-gonococcal urinary tract infections, trichomonas, and HIV. Ninety percent of the pre-cancerous lesions in the uterine matrix test positive for the papilloma virus. Between 75 and 80 percent of the atypical cell cultures in women between the ages of 15 to 25 show infections of the human papilloma virus. Based on this, when tested, 40 percent of their partners are also infected by the disease.

Gonococcal Infections

Only 33 percent of acute cases of inflammatory pelvic disease (IPD or PID) test positive on the Tayler Martin test, but this result is in direct relationship to the beginning of the infection and when the sample was taken. Half of the gonococcus-infected patients are asymptomatic and therefore can present the following complications: Asymptomatic tuboperitoneal factors result in infertility in 20 to 30 percent of patients, chronic pelvic inflammatory disease in 20 to 25 percent, chronic pelvic pain in 5 to 15 percent, ectopic pregnancies in 7 percent, and irregular menstrual cycles in 5 percent.

Syphilis

The number of congenital syphilis cases has decreased in Colombia. In 1998, the following number of cases were reported in Colombia by region. Costa Altántica, 64; Amazonia, 25; Orinoquia, 21; Oriente, 193, including Boyacá, Cundinamarca, Satanderes, Tomolina, and Bogotá; and Occidente, 347, including Caldas, Antioquia, Chocó, Quindío, and Valle. Two cities in the Occidente must be highlighted: Antioquia with 99 cases and Valle with 149 cases. The incidence of reported cases of congenital syphilis is 36.6 cases per 100,000 live newborns (Ministerio de Salud 1998, 1999).

B. Treatment

There are some formal programs available for the treatment of STDs. However, they are poorly organized and not fully developed as of early 2001.

11. HIV/AIDS
JOSÉ MANUEL GONZÁLES AND GLORIA PENAGOS

On January 5, 1983, a 23-year-old woman, a known prostitute, was hospitalized at the University Hospital of Cartagena. She died four months later. She was the first person to be officially diagnosed with AIDS in Colombia (González 2000). According to the Colombian Coalition Against AIDS, there are 200,000 people living with HIV (González et al. 2000). Every hour someone new is infected.

In 1997 and 1998, 81 percent of all reported cases were between the ages of 15 and 44 years (Ministerio de Salud 1998). Even though the group most at risk for contracting AIDS are adolescents, the general public continues to remain unaware of the dangers involved. Of households with children under the age of 18 years, 63.3 percent believe that they were not at risk of contracting HIV/AIDS. There was no discussion on AIDS prevention in 39 percent of households where there were minors under the age of 18 years.

According to the Colombian Ministry of Health, in 1986, there was one woman for every forty-seven men infected with HIV. In 1997, the ratio was one woman to four males. It is estimated that in 2001, the ratio will be 1:1. The risk among women is quite high and is believed to be related to the social inequity between men and woman. Women are kept at the subordinate level socially, by marital status, and economically, which contributes to their inability to adequately protect themselves. Consequently, religious beliefs that reject the use of condoms, anal sex at the insistence of the male, failing to acknowledge adultery for fear of being accused of infidelity, all these factors and other similar ones lead to an increase in HIV/AIDS-positive women (Penagos 1997).

Sexual contact constitutes the primary mode of transmitting HIV/AIDS (Ministerio de Salud, 1998). For females, heterosexual contact accounted for 91.5 percent of cases of HIV infection, blood transfusions for 1.7 percent, and 6.8 percent became infected during delivery or perinatally. (No percentage was given for other modes of transmission, notably intravenous drug usage.) In men, 56.1 percent contracted HIV through heterosexual relations, 41.8 percent through homosexual/bisexual contact, perinatal transmission was 0.7 percent, and by transfusions were 1.4 percent.

One of the most important factors contributing towards the transmission of AIDS is the lack of adequate information. González (2000) conducted a study with university students, in which the following information was found:

- 95 percent of the students were unaware that anal penetration is the most high-risk sexual activity that may lead to the transmission of AIDS;
- 78.9 percent were unaware that it may take three months or more for an AIDS test to come up positive once a person is infected;
- 66.4 percent were unaware that it may take five to ten years to develop any AIDS-related symptoms;
- 48.1 percent were unaware that individuals may transmit HIV as quickly as they have acquired it; and
- 41.2 percent were unaware that semen is the body fluid that carries the highest concentration of HIV.

The study also found that 80.2 percent of men and 88.5 percent of women believe that there is a high risk of contracting AIDS while having unprotected sex with someone you do not know. Fifty-six percent of men and 66.9 percent of women believe that there is a high risk of contracting AIDS while having unprotected sex with an occasional partner; 14.8 percent of men and 16.1 percent of women believe that there is a high risk of contracting AIDS while having unprotected sex with a regular partner. As is evident, there is a popular misconception that AIDS can only be transmitted through unprotected sex with a one-time partner or an occasional partner. Consequently, people who are in new (exclusive) sexual relationships fail to practice safe sex. They do not take into account previous sexual partners nor have they taken an AIDS test (González et al. 2000).

Generally, there is minimal use of condoms. González and colleagues (2000) found that 33 percent of males and 53 percent of females have never used condoms during vaginal penetration. It was also reported that 48.4 percent of men and 63.2 percent of women never used condoms during anal sex.

The Colombian Constitution of 1991 enacted laws that protects the rights of all citizens. These laws stipulate that anyone living with HIV/AIDS, with or without financial means, can receive social security benefits. Although there exists budgeting and administrative problems that may delay the process, everyone has the fundamental right to medical care, psychological care, and pharmacological care. Generally, those individuals living with HIV/AIDS have access to antiviral medication.

On June 12, 1997, the Colombian Ministry of Health passed Decree #1543. It provides a standardized protocol for people with AIDS that indicates their rights and obligations. The protocol is as follows:

- Written consent from an individual is required in order to obtain an AIDS test.
- A health care provider or institution cannot deny care to someone diagnosed with the HIV/AIDS.
- Comprehensive care must be provided: psychological, biological, and social.
- All records pertaining to patient care must remain confidential.
- Requesting an AIDS test to secure or maintain access in an educational facility, religious center, political group, cultural center, rehabilitation center, workplace, or health-related services, or to gain entry to a country is strictly prohibited.
- AIDS-test results may only be exchanged between patient and a qualified caregiver.
- Guaranteed job relocation when needed.

The decree also created CONASIDA (National Council on AIDS). It is comprised of the Ministry of Health, Ministry of Education, Ministry of Communication, Ministry of Employment, Colombian Institute of Family Wellness, National Institute of Health, Public Defendants, the Institute of Drug Administration and Regulations, ONUSIDA (AIDS Organization of the United Nations), representatives from non-governmental organizations (ONGs), and advocates for AIDS victims. Generally, people who are living with AIDS are involved in political development and decision-making processes, as recommended by ONUSIDA. Presently, the ONGs are changing the image of AIDS from a "terminal disease" to a "treatable chronic disease."

AIDS-prevention programs and assistance to victims of AIDS are faced with serious financial problems. There have been government budget cuts since 1998. Additionally, discrimination and rejection of AIDS victims are two problems that must be addressed in health and sexuality.

12. Sexual Dysfunctions, Counseling, and Therapies
JOSÉ MANUEL GONZÁLES

Until the 1980s, sexual dysfunction was unknown as a health-related problem. Traditionally, treatments for sexual problems were seen as something unnecessary and even excessive. Generally, people who suffered from sexual dysfunctions failed to seek professional help because of embarrassment or guilt, even though, for more than 50 years, there have been private institutions in Colombia that provided sex therapy (González 1999c).

In the last five years, there has been an important change in the outlook on sexual dysfunction. The National Program on Sexual Education has generated a change in attitude towards sexuality and sexual health. There are now a few professionals who specialize in clinical sexology. An association of professional sex therapists has yet to be organized. In the next few years, there will be an increase in the quantity and quality of sex therapists because of the high demand for their services.

Dr. Rodriguez A. (*sic*) was the pioneer in sexual therapy in Colombia (González 1999c). He studied abroad in France, where he specialized in reflexology. In the late 1940s, he returned to Santafé de Bogotá, where he founded a clinic for sexual dysfunctions. He trained prostitutes in collaboratively assisting in his patients' treatments. This is what is now called sexual surrogates, or bodywork therapists. However, an animosity developed between Dr. Rodriguez A. and his colleagues that resulted in lawsuits and other legal problems. Consequently, Dr. Rodriguez A. closed his institute in Santafé de Bogotá (Guerrero 1997) and shortly thereafter opened a sexual therapy clinic in Fusagasuga. He died in the late 1970s.

In the late 1960s, a group of doctors and psychologists, including Heli Alzate, Cecilia Cardinal de Martin, Octavio Giraldo, and German Ortiz Umana, developed an interest in sexology and sexual therapy. In 1968, Heli Alzate offered the first formal courses in sexology to medical students attending the University of Caldas in Manizales. Octavio Giraldo offered courses in sexology to medical students at the University of El Valle. In 1971, Celcilia Cardinal de Martin and German Ortiz Umana offered coursework in sexology at the University of Rosario de Bogotá. José Manuel Gonzáles initiated the coursework in sexology in the Metropolitan University of Barranquilla in 1976. Luis Dragunsky offered coursework on sexology at the University of Santo Tomas in Bogotá in 1977. During this time, the first texts on sexology were published: *Medical Sexology in Summation* (Alzate 1978), *Lectures in Sexology* (Dragunsky & González 1979), and *Exploration of Human Sexuality* (Giraldo 1981).

In May 1978, the Colombian Institute on the Development of Advanced Studies (ICFES) brought together a group of specialists to discuss and evaluate the state of sexology as a science: Heli Alzate, Cecilia Cardinal de Martin, Octavio Giraldo, José Manuel Gonzáles, and German Ortiz Umana. They generated an important document, which stated specific recommendations (ICFES 1978). As a result of this meeting, the participants felt a need to develop a committee that would coordinate the efforts and publicize the findings of studies that would support the development of sexology in Colombia.

One year later, the Colombian Association of Sexology was founded in June 1979. The original founders were: Heli Alzate, Maria Clara Arango, Mario Bedoya, Cecilia Cardinal de Martin, Luis Dragunsky, Mario Gartner, Octavio Giraldo, José Manuel Gonzáles, Maria Ladi Londoño, Saulo Munoz, German Ortiz Umana, Francisco Sanchez, and Jorge Villarreal Mejia. The elected president was Heli Alzate. As a consequence, sex therapy has developed its own niche in the larger cities. The group in Manizales has generated the most investigations and published internationally. The Cali group, with Octavio Giraldo, Mari Ladi Londoño, Javier Murillo, Diego Arbelaez, Nelssy Bonilla, Monica Lozada, and other colleagues, has been most active in advocating for the rights of minorities and the oppressed: women and homosexuals. Two other active groups, in Bogotá, Medellín, have pioneered in the treatment of premature ejaculation, erectile problems, patients suffering from various psychosexual dysfunctions, prolonging the pleasure phase, transsexuals, and interesting ways of dealing with infertile couples (Acuña et al. 1997).

Sex therapy in Colombia is marked by several characteristics (González 1999c):

- It is interdisciplinary, although most of the professionals in the field are also trained in the medical or psychological fields.
- It originates mostly from behavioral psychology, cognitive psychology, and human development, with little basis in psychotherapy.
- It provides advocacy for the rights of minority groups and oppressed groups, specifically homosexuals and lesbians.
- Private practice and college coursework solely dedicated to sex therapy is non-existent. Most sex therapists have maintained their origins in psychology and/or medicine.
- There is an absence of formal training for sex therapists. In 1983, Luis Dragunsky and José Manuel Gonzáles founded the first accrediting committee, the Colombian Association of Sexology (CAS). Only five sex therapists have been accredited by CAS and very few Colombian sex therapists are accredited by the Latin American Federation of Sexological Societies and Sexual Education (FLASSES).
- There is extensive coverage by the mass media.

There has been active participation by most sex therapists in the events sponsored by the Colombian Association of Sexology.

13. Research and Advanced Education
BERNARDO USECHE

Generally, scientific studies in Colombia are very scarce and poorly funded. In 1999, the total budget earmarked by "Colciencias," a government body responsible for all studies conducted in Colombia, was approximately US$6,000,000. Only recently have there been doctoral programs in the basic sciences. However, there are no doctoral programs offered in disciplines that could directly contribute towards the study of sexology, such as physiology, anthropology, psychology, or sociology. It is in this context that we must understand the limited development of the study of human sexuality in Colombia.

In recent years, Abel Martinez of the University of Pedagogy and Technology of Tunja has specialized in the study of *Colombian Sexual Archeology* (unpublished). He presents a poetic description of sexuality during the Spanish Conquest, colonization, independence, and the beginning of the Republic. The study of the mythology of the aborigines and the key role the erotic played in the blending of the races is evident throughout his work. In *Daughters, Wives and Lovers*, anthropologist Suzy Bermudez discusses the same time frame covered by Abel Martinez, the Spanish Conquest to the Republic. However, she took a feminist perspective, dealing with native women, European women, African slave women, married women, widows, and single women. Although it was not her main objective, Bermudez attempted to clarify how social class, ethnicity, and age play an important role in understanding the history of women's sexuality in Colombia.

In the second half of the twentieth century, Virginia Gutierrez de Pineda (1975) led an important anthropological investigation that set the foundation for the comprehension of human sexuality for Colombians. In her analysis and classification of the various cultural elements that correspond to the different regions of Colombia, Gutierrez explained the logic behind the different types of marriages and polygamy, and the significance of prostitution and homosexuality thought to be tolerated but tacitly encouraged by religious subcultures in hopes of preserving young women's virginity and protecting the institution of matrimony. Her description of families in the second half of the twentieth century is considered to be a key reference for anyone wanting to study the changes in the sexuality of Colombians at the end of the century.

Heli Alzate, another pioneer of sexology in Latin America, developed an extensive and rigorous curriculum for the School of Medicine at the University of Caldas. He also published four books and numerous scientific articles in North American and European publications. A member of the editorial committee of the *Archives of Sexual Behavior* for a quarter-century, Alzate has theorized a conceptual model of the function of erotica and completed three studies pertaining to sexuality:

1. Evaluation of a curriculum pertaining to sexuality (Alzate 1990);
2. Sexual behavior of secondary-level students and university-level students (Alzate 1989; Useche, Alzate, & Villegas 1990; Alzate & Villegas 1994); and
3. Studies pertaining to vaginal erogeneity (Alzate 1985; Alzate & Hoch 1986; Alzate, Useche, & Villegas 1989).

Alzate also evaluated the knowledge and sexual attitudes of his medical students with an adapted version of the Sexual Knowledge and Attitude Test, or SKAT, originally formulated by Harold Lief. Later results from his modified SKAT, or ACSEX, indicated that it is possible to impart scientific knowledge and achieve a positive attitude towards sexuality utilizing coursework in sexology, audiovisual media, and active class participation from medical students.

The studies of the sexual behavior of the younger generation with secondary- or university-level education in one of the most traditional and conservative areas of Colombian culture give a fair picture of the evolution of Colombian sexuality in the past quarter-century, the incidence of first sexual encounters, the motives behind sexual activity, the types of couples, and above all the differences in sexual behaviors between genders.

Of particular interest, in view of the significant growth of the women's liberation movement in recent years in Colombia, are several studies on the erogenous zones of the vagina. According to these studies, the majority of women, if not all, have vaginal erogenous zones, frequently located in the anterior vaginal wall, which, if stimulated appropriately, will culminate in orgasm. Colombian researchers consider this a vital factor in the context of normal sexuality of the woman and also as important in the treatment of coital dysfunctions of women. Alzate believes that the theories, that have thus far been conceptualized to explain these sexual dysfunctions, should be revised. He also believes that sex therapists who are confronted with these issues should recognize the necessity of referring clients for gynecological exams so as to locate their erogenous zones (Alzate 1997b). Alzate also introduced modifications of the human sexuality functioning model originally proposed by William Masters and Virginia Johnson and later enriched by Helen Singer Kaplan. Alzate's premise was to "seek out and responsibly enjoy pleasure." Presently, there are no other systemic studies by Colombians in the field of sexology other than those provided by Alzate.

At the international level, publications by Colombians in the area of human sexuality are very scarce, almost non-existent. However, there have been other unpublished works that originated in Colombia. Florence Thomas's 1994 *Dissertation on Love and Communication* analyzed communications from a gender perspective, and Guillermo Carvajal (1993) completed a psychoanalytic vision of the adolescent. Pedro Guerrero (1985) led a study on the use of erotica in literature by some of the most prominent writers in Colombia, and Maria Ladi Londoño has published numerous articles dealing with sexuality and reproductive rights. In a recent study, also of note, is Ruben Ardila's 1998 study of 100 male homosexuals, which found that generally these individuals did not have serious adaptation problems, nor did they seem to suffer from adjustment issues.

The *Latin American Journal on Sexology of Colombia* (ISSN 0120-7458), with a base in Colombia, serves as the medium for the Latin American Federation of Sexological Societies and Sexual Education (FLASSES).

The Colombian Society of Sexology, founded in 1979, has organized ten congress meetings, several seminars, and other academic events. These have involved world-renowned researchers, among others, Eli Coleman, John Money, Ira Reiss, Eusebio Rubio, Luis Dragunsky, Joseph LoPiccolo, Andres Flores Colombino, and Ruben Hernandez.

Other sexological studies in Colombia have been conducted by students in their post-graduate studies. These are generally non-funded and usually remain unpublished. Some of these studies have originated from the University of Bogotá (Bodner et al. 1999), University Simon Bolivar of Barranquilla (González 1999b; González et al. 2000), and the University of Caldas in Manizales (Useche 1999). Since the Ministry of Education established the National Project on Sexual Education in 1993, there has been a significant increase in the need for these studies. Private universities have thus developed them.

In terms of the future, we hope that the small group of dedicated and diverse Colombian professionals interested in sexological issues will be able to continue their work with sexological organizations and individuals around the world, and thereby contribute to a more solid and in-depth understanding of human sexuality, if the economic crisis in Colombia allows.

References and Suggested Readings

Acuña, A. 1987. *Tercera edad y sexualidad.* IV Congreso Colombiano de Sexología. Medellín, 9-12 de octubre.

Acuña, A., Nader, L., Palacio, M., & Guerrero, P. 1993. *Sexo al día: Es tiempo de vivir.* Bogotá: Unidad de Psicoterapia y Sexualidad Humana.

Acuña, A., Palacio, M., & Guerrero, P. 1986. *Sexo: En los niños.* Santafé de Bogotá: Editora Cinco.

Alzate, H. 1977. Comportamiento sexual de los estudiantes de Medicina. *Acta Médica Colombiana, 22*:111-118.

Alzate, H. 1978. *Compendio de sexología medica.* Santafé de Bogotá: Temis.

Alzate, H. 1985. Vaginal eroticism. *Archives of Sexual Behavior, 14*:529-537.

Alzate, H. 1987. *Sexualidad humana* (2 edición). Bogotá: Editorial Temis.

Alzate, H. 1989. Sexual behavior of unmarried Colombian university students: A follow-up. *Archives of Sexual Behavior, 18*:239-250.

Alzate, H. 1990. Effectiveness of an independent sexology course for Colombian medical students. *Medical Teacher, 12*:69-75.

Alzate, H. 1997a. *Sexualidad humana* (Reimpresión de la 2ª edición). Bogotá: Temis.

Alzate, H. 1997b. *La sexologie a l université de Caldas, Manizales, Colombie. Panoramiques.* Paris: Arléa-Corlet.

Alzate, H., & Hoch, Z. 1986. The 'G spot' and 'female ejaculation': A current appraisal. *Journal of Sexual & Marital Therapy, 12*:211-220.

Alzate, H., Useche, B., & Villegas, M. 1989. Heart rate change as evidence for vaginally elicited orgasm intensity. *Annual of Sex Research, 2*:345-357.

Alzate, H., & Villegas, M. 1994. Sexual behavior of unmarried Colombian university students in 1990. *Journal of Sex Education and Therapy, 20*:287-298.

Ardila, R. 1985. La homosexualidad en Colombia. *Acta Psiquiátrica y Psicológica de América Latina* [Buenos Aires], *31*:191-210.

Ardila, R. 1986a. *Psicología del hombre colombiano.* Santafé de Bogotá: Planeta.

Ardila, R. 1986b. Homosexualidad y aprendizaje. *Revista Latinoamericana de Sexología, 1*:45-54.

Ardila, R. 1995 (26 de Noviembre). Nuevos hallazgos sobre homosexualidad. ¿Fatalidad biológica o deformidad cultural? *El Tiempo Lecturas Dominicales,* pp. 2-4.

Ardila, R. 1998. *Homosexualidad y psicología.* México: El Manual Moderno.

Berdugo, E., & Segura, A. 1988. *Estudio descriptivo del comportamiento sexual de las personas mayores de 60 años en Barranquilla* (Tesis de grado). Barranquilla: Facultad de Psicología, Universidad del Norte.

Bodnar, Y., Tovar, E., Arias, R , Bogoya, N., Bricño, P., Murillo, J., & Rodriguez, E. 1999. *Cultura y Sexualidad en Colombia.* Bogotá: Universidad Distrital Francisco José de Caldas.

Botero, E. 1980. *Homofobia y homofilia. Estudios sobre la homosexualidad, la bisexualidad y la represión de la conducta homosexual.* Medellín, Colombia: Editorial Laelon.

Caballero, M. C. 1996. Conocimiento y comportamiento de riesgo de infección por VIH en estudiantes universitarios. Un caso: Universidad Industrial de Santander. *Revista Latinoamericana de Sexología,* 11(1):41-56.

Colombia. Consejería Presidencial para la juventud, la mujer y la familia. 1994. *Año Internacional de la Familia. 1994,* 1(2).

Colombia. *Instituto Nacional de Medicina Legal y Ciencias Forenses. Regional Norte.* 1996. Primer semestre (Boletín informativo).

Domínguez, E., Mendoza, A., Merlano, L., & Navas, M. 1988. *Estudio descriptivo del comportamiento sexual del estudiante de Bachillerato de Barranquilla* (Tesis de grado). Barranquilla: Facultad de Psicología, Universidad del Norte.

Dragunsky, L. 1977. *El mito del sexo.* Bogotá: Editorial Pluma.

Dragunsky, L., & Gonzales, J. 1979. *Lecciones de sexología.* Santafé de Bogotá: Editorial Pluma.

El Tiempo. El Catolicismo pierde clientela. 1997 (13 de Julio). p. 17A.

Eljaiek, L., Saade, M., & Vargas, P. 1987. *Estudio descriptivo del comportamiento sexual de hombres y mujeres que mantienen relación de pareja* (Tesis de grado). Barranquilla: Facultad de Psicología, Universidad del Norte.

Florez, P., & Consuegra, E. 1998 (16 de Octubre). *Abuso sexual en adolescentes. IX Jornada Científica de Ginecoobstetricia.* Barranquilla: Universidad Libre.

Fuscaldo, M., Mercado, R., & Rolong, M. 1987. *Estudio descriptivo del comportamiento sexual del estudiante universitario en Barranquilla* (Tesis de grado). Barranquilla: Facultad de Psicología, Universidad del Norte.

Giraldo, O. 1979. La homosexualidad masculina: Una revisión. *Revista Latinoamericana de Psicología,* 9:81-100.

Giraldo, O. 1981. *Explorando las sexualidades humanas.* México: Trillas.

Giraldo, O. 1982. Más allá de la heterosexualidad. *Avances en Psicología Clínica Latinoamericana,* 1:79-94.

González, J. M. 1979. Masturbación: Un proyecto de investigación. *Revista Sexualidad Humana y Educación Sexual,* 2(1):11-17.

González, J. M. 1985. *El comportamiento sexual del universitario.* Santafé de Bogotá: Fundación para el Avance de la Psicología.

González, J. M. 1993. SIDA: Síndrome de inmunodeficiencia adquirida. *Serenidad. Revista del Programa de Alcoholismo y Drogadicción,* 1(3):8-10.

González, J. M. 1994. *Educación de la sexualidad.* Barranquilla: Club del Libro.

González, J. M. 1995. Diferencias genéricas en el comportamiento sexual de estudiantes universitarios solteros de Barranquilla. *Revista Latinoamericana de Sexología,* (2):161-76.

González, J. M. 1996. El aporte de la Sociedad Colombiana de Sexología. *Revista Latinoamericana de Sexología,* Separata 1, 166-192.

González, J. M. 1997. *Eyaculación precoz: Evaluación y tratamiento.* X Seminario Colombiano de Sexología, Barranquilla, 1-3 de Noviembre.

González, J. M. 1998. *Sexología y periodismo: Una columna de preguntas sobre temas sexuales en un periódico colombiano.* 8 Congreso Colombiano de Psicología, Santafé de Bogotá, Abril 30-Mayo 3.

González, J. M. 1999. Abuso sexual infantil en mujeres alcohólicas y drogadictas de Barranquilla. *Revista Terapia Sexual* [Brasil], 2(1):37-43.

González, J. M. 1999a. Pobreza, valores humanos y sexualidad. *Revista Encuentro Bolivariano, Barranquilla,* 2(2):121-126.

González, J. M. 1999b. Sexualidad y sesarrollo. *Revista Investigación Bolivariana, Barranquilla,* 2(2):195-199.

González, J. M. 1999c. La terapia sexual en Colombia: 1948-1998. *Revista Terapia Sexual,* 2(1):33-36.

González, J. M. 1999d. Pobreza, salud sexual y desarrollo. *Revista Salud Sexual,* 2(1):25-30.

González, J. M. 2000. *Amor & intimidad en el caribe colombiano.* Barranquilla: Editorial Antillas.

González, J. M., Alonso, M., & Pinto, I. 1991. Sexualidad y farmacodependencia en pacientes de dos clínicas de Barranquilla, Colombia. *Revista Latinoamericana de Sexología,* 6(3):235-246.

González, J. M., Cepeda, J., Fonseca, L., Burgos, N., Pinto, I., & Sanchez, L. 1996. Estudio descriptivo de la sexualidad en 30 mujeres farmacodependientes de Barranquilla, Colombia. *Archivos Hispanoamericanos de Sexología, 3*(1): 79-91.

González, J. M., Gomez, I., & de Cortes, T. 1977. Comportamiento sexual: Un estudio exploratorio. *Revista Latinoamericana de Psicología, 9*(1):13-20.

González, J. M., & Gonzales, J. en prensa. *Sexualidad en el adulto mayor.*

González, J. M., Marin, J. C., Chala, D., Schmalbach Fruto, R., & de Albade Alba, N. 2000. *Juventud y VIH/SIDA: Una experiencia universitaria en el caribe colombiano.* Barranquilla: Editorial Antillas.

González, J. M., Rosado, M. C., Bernal, M., & Marin, J. C. 2000. *Pobreza, salud sexual y desarrollo.* Bogotá: Plaza & Jane.

Guerrero, P. 1985. *El miedo al sexo.* Bogotá: Antares.

Guerrero, P. 1996a. Amor, sexualidad y matrimonio en los medios de comunicación. *Revista Latinoamericana de Sexología,* Separata 1, 129-135.

Guerrero, P. 1996b. Amor, sexualidad y matrimonio en los graffiti. *Revista Latinoamericana de Sexología,* Separata 1, 136-139.

Guerrero, P. 1997. Comunicación personal.

Gutierrez de Pineda, V. 1975. *Familia y cultura en Colombia.* Santafé de Bogotá: Instituto Colombiano de Cultura.

Gutierrez, M. de, & Franco, G. 1989. Encuesta sobre sexualidad en adolescentes. *CAFAM. II Curso de atención integral al adolescente.* Santafé de Bogotá: CAFAM.

Instituto de Seguros Sociales (ISS) [Institute of Social Securities]. 1994. *Encuesta nacional sobre conocimientos, actitudes y practicas relacionadas con las enfermedades de transmisión sexual, SIDA, enfermedades cardiovasculares, cáncer y accidentes.* Santafé de Bogotá: ISS.

Londoño, M. L. 1991. *Prácticas de libertad.* Cali: Impresor Feriva.

Londoño, M. L. 1996. *Memorias Congreso Sexualidad y Género . . . Un proceso cultural.* VII Congreso Colombiano de Sexología, Medellín, Mayo 23 al 25, 1996.

Mantilla, A. 1993. El modelo Gamma de educación sexual. En: , *Asociación salud con prevención. Sexualidad en la adolescencia.* Santafé de Bogotá: Editorial Presencia.

Ministerio de Salud. 1994. *Estudio nacional de salud mental y consumo de sustancias psicoactivas.* Santafé de Bogotá: Ministerio de Salud de Colombia.

Ministerio de Salud. 1995. *Boletín epidemiológico nacional, Enero-Marzo.*

Ministerio de Salud. 1997 (15 de Marzo). *Boletín epidemiológico nacional, 2*(5).

Ministerio de Salud. 1997. *Medicina legal en cifras. Enero-diciembre 1996-1997.* Bogotá: Instituto Nacional de Medicina Legal y Ciencias Forenses.

Ministerio de Salud. 1998 (30 de Noviembre). *Boletín epidemiológico nacional, 3*(22).

Ministerio de Salud 1998. *Lineamientos para la política de salud sexual y reproductiva.* Santafé de Bogotá: Dirección General de Promoción y Prevención.

Ministerio de Salud, Oficina de Epidemiología. Informe Quincenal Epidemiológico Nacional. (Enero 15) *Dirección general de promoción y prevención, 4*(1).

Murillo, J. 1993. Relaciones extramatrimoniales, celos y familia. *Revista Latinoamericana de Sexología, 8*(1):56-65.

Murillo, J. 1996. *Trabajadoras sexuales.* Palmira: CORPICH.

Nader, L., & Palacio, M. L. 1989. Relaciones extramaritales. En: *Es tiempo de vivir. Unidad de Psicoterapia y Sexualidad humana.* Santafé de Bogotá.

Nader, L., Palacio, M. L., & Acuña, A. 1997. *Modelo terapéutico en disfunciones sexuales.* X Seminario Colombiano de Sexología, Barranquilla, 1-3 de Noviembre.

OPS/OMS, Programa Regional de SIDA/ETS. *Vigilancia del SIDA en las Américas. Informe trimestral 10 de junio de 1997,* OPS/HCA/97.006.

Organización Panamericana de la Salud 1985. *La salud del adolescente y el joven en las Américas* (Publicación científica N. 489). Washington, DC: .

Ortiz, G. 1993. El sexo de asignación, el de crianza y los papeles sexuales en la familia. *Revista Latinoamericana de Sexología, 8*(1):38-45.

Palacio, M. L. 1999. *Hablemos de sexo con Marta Lucía Palacio.* Bogotá: Intermedio.

Pardo, F., & Uriza, G. 1991 (Abril-Junio). Estudio de embarazo en adolescente en 11 instituciones Colombianas. *Revista Colombiana de Obstetricia y Ginecología* (Bogotá), *42*(2):109-121.

Penagos, G. S. 1997. *Mujer, género y SIDA.* Memorias Congreso Internacional de ETS, SIDA. Medellín.

PNUD—Programa de las Naciones Unidas para el Desarrollo. 1995. *Informe sobre desarrollo humano 1995.* New York: Naciones Unidas.

Profamilia. 1995. *Encuesta nacional de demografía y salud 1995.* Santafé de Bogotá: Profamilia (Planned Parenthood of Colombia).

Riso, W. 1996. *Deshojando margaritas. Acerca del amor tradicional y otras malas costumbres.* Santafé de Bogotá: Norma.

Rojas, N. 1997. *La pareja* (7ª edición). Santafé de Bogotá: Planeta.

Rojas, N. 1998. *Qué nos une. Qué nos separa.* Santafé de Bogota: Planeta.

Ruiz, M. 1996. *Conocimientos, actitudes y comportamiento sexual de los adolescentes.* Memorias XX Congreso Colombiano de Obstetricia y Ginecología, Medellín.

Semana. 1996 (9 de Enero). "La gran encuesta del 96" (Edición 714).

Semana. 1997 (28 de Julio). "Sexo: Informe especial" (Edición 795).

Semana. 1999 (30 de Agosto). "Sexo 99" (Edición 904).

Serrano, J. F. 1997. Entre negación y reconocimiento. Estudios sobre "homosexualidad" en Colombia. *Nómadas Universidad Central* (Bogotá), *6*:67-79.

Serrano, J. F. 1998. Igualdad, diferencia y equidad en la diversidad de la experiencia sexual. Una mirada a las discusiones sobre los derechos sexuales de lesbianas y gays. *Memorias del Tercer Seminario Nacional sobre Ética, Sexualidad y Derechos Reproductivos* (pp. 25-54), CERFAMI, Medellín, Colombia, agosto 13 y 14 de 1998.

Servicio Seccional de Salud de Risaralda. 1997. *Plan de información y educación sexual a la mujer y a la familia.*

Universidad Externado de Colombia. 1992. *La incidencia del aborto en Colombia* [*The incidence of abortion in Colombia*] Bogotá: Universidad Externado de Colombia.

Useche, B. 1999. *5 Estudios de sexología.* Manizales: ARS Ediciones.

Useche, B., Villegas, M., & Alzate, H. 1990. Sexual behavior of Colombian high school students. *Adolescence, 25*(98):291-304.

Velandia, M. A. 1999. *Y si el cuerpo grita . . .* Bogotá: Equiláteros. Proyecto de Diversidad y Minorías Sexuales de Colombia.

Zamudio, L., & Rubiano, N. 1991a. *La nupcialidad en Colombia.* Santafé de Bogotá: Universidad Externado de Colombia.

Zamudio, L., & Rubiano, N. 1991b. *Las separaciones conyugales en Colombia.* Santafé de Bogotá: Universidad Externado de Colombia.

Zuluaga, L., Soto, C., & Jaramillo, D. 1991 *Problemas de salud asociados al comportamiento sexual en estudiantes de ultimo año.* Medellín: Universidad de Antioquia.

Croatia
(The Republic of Croatia)

Aleksandar Štulhofer, Ph.D.,* Vlasta Hiršl-Hecej, M.D., M.A.,
Zeljko Mrkšic, Aleksandra Korac, Ph.D., Petra Hoblaj,
Ivanka Ivkanec, Maja Mamula, M.A.,
Hrvoje Tiljak, M.D., Ph.D., Gordana Buljan-Flander, M.A.,
Sanja Sagasta, and Gordan Bosanac

Contents

Demographics and a Historical Perspective

A. Demographics

Croatia is a former Yugoslav republic east of the Adriatic Sea and opposite
the eastern coast of Italy. With approximately 22,000 square miles, Croatia
is about size of the state of West Virginia in the United States. The Dinaric
Mountains, which run from northwest to southeast mark a barren rocky
region, while the Zagorje region in the north, around the capital Zagreb, is

Communications: Dr. Aleksandar Štulhofer, University of Zagreb, Department of Sociology,
Faculty of Philosophy, I. Lucica 3, 10 000 Zagreb, Croatia; fax: 385-1-615-6879; astulhof@ffzg.hr.

a land of rolling hills. The Drava, Danube, and Sava Rivers border the eastern fertile agricultural region of the Pannonian plain, Slavonia. The northern part of Croatia stretches about 270 miles from the Istrian peninsula in the northwest on the Adriatic Sea to the Vojvodina region of Yugoslavia on the east. Croatia's neighbors are Slovenia and Hungary on the north, Yugoslavia on the east, and Bosnia and Herzegovina on the southeast. In the far south, Croatia shares a small border, south of Dubrovnik, with Montenegro. Croatia's western coastline, which includes many islands, stretches about 300 miles from Slovenia at the northern end of the Adriatic Sea to Montenegro at the Adriatic's southern end, opposite the boot of Italy.

Croatia had an estimated 1999 population of approximately 4.7 million. The age distribution was 17.5 percent under age 15, 67 percent between ages 15 and 65, and 15.5 percent 65 years and older. Ethnically, in 1991, before the total breakup of Yugoslavia, 78 percent of the people were Croat, 12 percent Serb, 0.9 percent Muslim, 0.5 percent each for Hungarian and Slovenian, and 8.1 percent other. Similarly, 77 percent were Catholic, 11 percent Serbian Orthodox, 1.2 percent Slavic Muslims, 0.4 Protestant, and 10.8 percent other. A slight majority of the people, 56 percent, lived in the cities. The average life expectancy in 2000 was 70.7 years for men and 77.5 for women. The birthrate in 1998 was 10.5 births per 1,000 population, the infant mortality rate was 7.84 per 1,000 live births, and the death rate was 11.6 per 1,000 population, giving Croatia an annual natural increase of negative 1.2 percent. Croatia's Total Fertility Rate (TFR) in 1998 was 1.45 children per fertile woman. Education is free and compulsory from ages 7 to 15. In 1991, 9 percent of the population age 15 years and older had a college or university education. Literacy reported in 1993 was 97 percent. The Gross Domestic Product per capita in 1999 was around $4,500.

B. A Brief Historical Perspective

Most probably, the Slavic Croats originally came from the region around the Polish city of Krakow. In several waves during the sixth century, Croatian tribes arrived in the region that is now Croatia, but was then the Roman provinces of Pannonia and Dalmatia. The Croats converted to Christianity between the seventh and ninth centuries and adopted the Roman alphabet under the rule of Charlemagne. In 879, Pope John XIII proclaimed the Croats independent from Byzantine and Frankish invaders. An independent kingdom was established, which reached its peak in the eleventh century. Following a defeat in a war with the Hungarians in 1097, the Croatian chiefs and Hungarian king politically united the two nations under the Hungarian king in 1102, although Croatia retained its autonomy.

When the Turks defeated the Hungarians in 1526, more than two thirds of Croatia fell under Ottoman rule until the end of the seventeenth century. Unlike other Balkan states whose religious affiliations shifted under Muslim Ottoman rule, Catholicism remained strong in Croatia, becoming in effect one of the defining traits of the Croatian identity. The rest of Croatia chose

Ferdinand of Austria as its king, entering the Habsburg domain. With the 1867 establishment of the Austro-Hungarian kingdom, Croatia and Slavonia came under Hungarian jurisdiction and remained part of the Austro-Hungarian Empire until it was defeated in 1918 at the end of World War I. In October 1918, Croatia declared its independence, and on December 1, joined Montenegro, Vojvodina, Serbia, and Slovenia to become a part of the Kingdom of Serbs, Croats, and Slovenes. In 1929, the nation changed its name to the Kingdom of Yugoslavia.

When Germany invaded Yugoslavia in 1941, Croatia became a Nazi puppet state. Croatian Fascists, the Ustashe, launched a purge of Serbs and Jews. Already in June 1941, the first antifascist guerilla units, the Partisans, were organized. After Germany was defeated in 1945, Croatia became a republic in the new Socialist Republic of Yugoslavia. Unlike other communist countries in Europe, Yugoslavia was never a member of the Warsaw pact, but one of the founders of the Non-Alignment movement. On June 25, 1991, the Croatian Parliament declared its independence from Yugoslavia. A devastating six-month civil war followed, with great destruction and the loss of thousands of lives, before the advance of the Serb-dominated Yugoslav military was halted and a United Nations cease-fire signed on January 2, 1992. In May and August of 1995, the Croatian army finally returned western Slavonia and the central region of Krajina to Zagreb's control. The last Serb-held enclave, East Slavonia, was peacefully returned to Croatian control on January 15, 1998, after being a United Nations' protected zone for several years.

1. Basic Sexological Premises

A. Character of Gender Roles

Unlike other European communist countries, Tito's Yugoslavia (1945-1990), independent from Soviet influence, has been extremely open towards Western cultural production, both in terms of high and popular cultures. This influence was amplified by the fact that from the 1960s on, Croats traveled and worked extensively in the West. In addition, throughout the 1970s and 1980s, the Croatian coast on the Adriatic was a major European tourist destination. This influence changed attitudes and lifestyles in the Mediterranean part of Croatia considerably, affecting even the small island communities. As a result, contemporary Croatian culture is deeply marked by permissiveness and liberal attitudes regarding gender and sexuality. Premarital sex is an unquestionable rule, as well as the right to sexual pleasure. This is especially true for the younger generations, brought up on Hollywood movies and teen sequels, MTV, and, recently, a local edition of *Cosmopolitan* magazine.

The adult world represents a more complicated picture. In the context of sexuality, there are several lines of division within the general population. These divisions are: sex/gender, education, religiousness, and place of residence. As elsewhere, the more educated people are the more permissive and tolerant of diversity and variety. This was confirmed in numerous public-opinion surveys carried out in the last decade. Older people, who tend to be less educated, place more importance on their religious identity, and are, consequently, less permissive and tolerant. Their attitudes toward sexuality and gender roles follow the traditional Catholic pattern of the Central European past, emphasizing a rigid division of gender roles, the sexual double standard, and the rejection of all non-standard sexual choices, particularly homosexuality.

It should be noted that the majority of Croatian men and women define themselves as religious. However, the nature of this identity is largely generation-specific. Younger generations express their religiousness both as a part of the national tradition, a marker of ethnonational identity, and as an individualized faith. Their religious identity is secularized and oblivious to the sexual moralities of the Church. According to the World Value Survey Croatia (1995), over 70 percent of the respondents in a nationally representative sample disagreed with the statement that religion offers the best guidance in sexual matters.

Whereas the rural areas in Croatia still exhibit elements of Catholic patriarchy, particularly in the older generations, urban places are generators of permissiveness and, somewhat less often, gender equality. It seems that Croatian public opinion is at the moment almost equally divided between non-traditional and permissive (more educated, younger, and urban) residents and religiously traditional men and women. This can be illustrated by a result from the 1996 Social Capital survey (Štulhofer, Karajic, & Meštrovic 1996) carried out on a representative national sample. When asked whether women and men should have equal rights to sexual expression, 57 percent of respondents agreed. In general, women are less supportive of the traditional gender-role division.

B. Sociolegal Status of Males and Females

The Titoist version of "socialist" transformation stressed the importance of gender equality. This was one of the departing points for the new society in leaving behind the decaying bourgeois society. Because of this ideological stance, women and men were granted equal rights since the end of World War II, especially in education and the labor market. Sex discrimination was officially discouraged and equal salaries were guaranteed, although in reality little has been done to change the prevailing male-dominated culture. Because the feminist movement was regarded as liberal, middle-class Western reformism, and therefore politically suspicious, the criticism of communist gender policy was severely limited. After 1990, the process of post-communist transition, especially the economic transformation, significantly affected certain privileges, such as long maternity leaves, and social services, such as preventive health services and free kindergartens, designed to improve women's social position.

Women composed 46 percent of the labor force in 1997, but their average salary was lower than men's. In addition, they were over-represented among the unemployed in the age cohorts 25 to 34 and 35 to 44 in 1999. On the other hand, women are becoming more visible in politics. They occupy slightly more than one fifth of all parliamentary seats (7 percent in 1997), and have positions in higher education, the sciences, and top management. During the first half of the 1990s, a significant number of female professionals became entrepreneurs, helping in the development of the market economy and changing the old image of male-dominated industry. Still, women are far from similar representation and prominence in all the sectors mentioned.

Abortion has been legal in Croatia since the early 1970s. The secularized version of Catholicism discussed above is evident in the stability of attitudes and public perception regarding abortion. During the last decade, according to studies carried out in 1990, 1992, 1995, and 2000 by the Faculty of Political Science in Zagreb, the percentage of pro-choice respondents was constantly over 70 percent. This was the reason why the previous nationalist and pro-populationist government (1990-2000), which often sought and received support from the Catholic Church, refrained from changing the abortion law, in spite of frequent appeals from Church authorities.

The legal rights of children stem from the *Convention on the Rights of the Child* ratified in the early 1990s. Although real-life situations are different, especially in the rural areas, the new Family Law (of 1998) prohibits corporal punishment. Primary education, the first eight years of schooling, is compulsory. The legal age in Croatia is set at 18, but because of meager salaries, a housing shortage, and high rents, young people rarely leave the parental home before starting a professional career. Actually, a significant number of people continue to live with their parents, even after they have married.

C. General Concepts of Sexuality and Love

Contemporary Croatia is a relatively permissive society, especially in the large urban centers. From the 1970s on, the traditional Catholic culture has been gradually replaced with sexual permissiveness, i.e., tolerance toward premarital, non-reproductive, and even extramarital sex. For most urbanites, sexuality equals love and pleasure. However, the relationship between these two dimensions, romantic love and erotic pleasure, is often perceived as confusingly inconsistent. Apart from the intimate dilemmas and/or rebellion it causes within younger generations, the still-dominant societal script of the unity of love and pleasure supports the continuation of the double standard. Based on the popular conviction that love is more important for women than for men, sexual capital (defined as the aggregate of individual sexual experience) is almost never evaluated in a gender-neutral way. Unlike male sexual capital, female sexual capital tends to be negatively correlated with social respectability. This remains true even for Croatian teenagers.

Regardless of the fact that most people agree that there should be no gender difference in the pursuit of sexual happiness, men and women often differ in their attitudes regarding the preferred path. According to a 1998-1999 study of urban sexual styles (Štulhofer 2000), 56 percent of female respondents and 33 percent of male respondents agreed that "sex is enjoyable only with the loved one," whereas 26 percent and 44 percent, respectively, disagreed. Interestingly, the gender gap was far less pronounced in the case of romantic love. Almost 50 percent of women and over 40 percent of men did not feel that "romantic love is overrated." Of the opposite opinion were 29 percent of women and 25 percent of men. The prevalence of the *relational concept* of female sexuality, in which love (emotions) provides justification for sexual pleasure, demands the perfect match between sexual and relationship needs. As one recent study pointed out (Štulhofer 1999a), it is precisely the women with the most active sexual lives who reported the most frequent guilty feelings about sex.

In general, it can be safely said that the majority of Croats, at least at one point in their lives, firmly believe in romantic or "true love." Notions of an ideal partner and long-lasting erotic happiness are still the essence of the prevailing image of intimate life. On the other hand, there seems to be a growing number of media suggestions, recently also found in women's magazines, stressing that, if or when love fails, one should go after the pleasure.

2. Religious and Ethnic Factors Affecting Sexuality

Patriarchal characteristics of traditional cultural patterns in Croatian villages and small towns used to permeate all sexual habits. The inherited moralities are still influential in the less urbanized parts of the country, especially in the cultural reproduction of female gender/sexuality. During the last two decades, however, traditional moral codes have been continuously losing their grip, especially in younger rural generations, and have been partially replaced by recognition of sexuality as an essential need.

A. Source and Character of Religious Values

Traditionally, the Roman Catholic Church has held a central role in the culture and worldview of the majority of Croats. Throughout the centuries, Catholic faith has served as an ethnic marker and common interpretative denominator, and as such, it became an integral part of all the dimensions of individual and social life. Church institutions, with their educational, cultural, and legal impact, provided a general framework of life. Naturally, this included both legal and conceptual (discursive) power over sexual meanings and practices, which is probably most transparent in the case of "unfaithfulness" and related collective sanctions. In a historical perspective, it should be noted that the Catholic Church in Croatia combined the laws of the Bible and other religious norms with elements of local pagan beliefs and traditions, bringing its teaching as close as possible to the life reality of a poor rural population.

According to Catholic teachings, everything that deviates from the religious norms had to be publicly sanctioned. In essence, the aberrations were dealt with in a gender-specific manner. Two sets of rules were tacitly developed. The first, based on the symbols of female impurity, provided concepts and methods of punishment that were utilized to control women. The second, organized around the images of almighty father, a breadwinner and the head of the family, was instrumental in tolerating heterosexual transgressions of men. This double standard is clearly visible in the Church practice regarding confession. In the case of female sexual transgressions (premarital or extramarital sex), the institution of confessional secrecy was annulled. That has often resulted in public "trials" led by a priest in which "deviant" women were punished both socially (being expelled from home, ostracized, or isolated) and symbolically—usually by stripping off her maiden symbols (cap, scarf, sash, or apron, depending on the region). The Church was notably less vigilant in cases of polygyny, when the second woman was brought into the house after the first one, the legal wife, was announced infertile. This Church control over everyday eroticism and sexuality can still be found in some remote and underdeveloped areas.

B. Character of Ethnic Values

The cultural tradition of Croatia is a product of various regional and ethnic influences (Stein Erlich 1971/1966). Although predominantly formed by the Croatian ethnic group, its symbols and values were profoundly influenced by historic ties—primarily of an economic, military, and marital nature—with the Serbs, Muslims, and Bosnians, and the Slovenes, Italians, Austrians and Hungarians. However, this diversity of ethnic cultural influences has a strong common denominator—religious control of sexuality, as described in the previous section. Occasional aberrations from religious codes can be found in magical rituals and practices specific for a certain locality and time.

Often a substitute for the socially proscribed "real thing," erotic and sexual fantasies and longings are expressed through folk songs and popular sayings, male vulgarities and female curses, geographical names, and nicknames. In some regions (e.g., Slavonia), where it is freely used at collective celebrations such as marriages, obscene language is much more than a subversion. Many festivities, especially those that take place in spring (Carnival) or summer, are rich with rituals that include sexual innuendoes. In spite of modern permissiveness and erotic saturation in the mass media, they enjoy popularity even nowadays.

Sexual codes and messages are also notable in folk dresses and their ornaments. Most often, one finds symbols or "simulations" of fertility, such as *guzalo*, a device that a woman would use to make her buttocks look fuller.

Also, village women would use various techniques of deception to make their breasts look bigger while men would use a codpiece or stuff their crotch with various objects to appear better endowed. Sometimes the clothing ornaments would take the shape of a vulva or penis, or they would include images of sexually vigorous animals (a cock, rabbit, or horse). Pieces, like sash, aprons, or maiden caps (and specific ornamentation or coloring) were frequently employed to signal female sexual status, i.e., virginity or marital commitment.

3. Sexual Knowledge and Education

A. Government Policies and Programs

Croatia has never had a systematic, school-based sex education program and is still waiting for one. Although there were some efforts as early as the mid-1960s aimed at introducing some kind of educational program in primary and secondary education (Košicek 1965), they did not accomplish much. For the last 30 years, sex education in Croatian schools amounts to infrequent STD and HIV/AIDS one-hour medical lectures in secondary schools. Not even those minimal, non-comprehensive, and non-interactive interventions are formally organized. In most cases, they are left to the initiative of a local physician, teacher, or schoolmaster. As a consequence, most teenagers outside of the big cities receive only the most elementary information on human reproduction offered in biology class.

Recently, a small network of social scientists, medical doctors, and feminists started coordinating their efforts and pushing forward an introduction of a comprehensive sex education curriculum in Croatian primary and secondary schools. Adolescents seem to be fully supportive of such an initiative. Almost 90 percent are in favor of school-based sex education. Public opinion is similarly favorable. In a recent national poll (Štulhofer, Karajic, & Meštrovic 1996), more than 70 percent of respondents agreed with a compulsory sex education program.

Interestingly, during the last decade, there might have been a peculiar form of (anti)sex education in Croatian schools. Namely, one quarter of students interviewed in a study claimed that the religious education class offered in primary schools had significantly influenced their sex lives (Štulhofer, Jureša, & Mamula 1999).

B. Informal Sources of Sexual Knowledge

According to recent surveys (Hiršl-Hecej, Šikanic-Dugic, & Dobravc-Poljak 1998; Štulhofer, Jureša, & Mamula 1999), Croatian adolescents learn about sexuality primarily through youth magazines, television, and peers. The magazines, including the very popular Croatian edition of *Cosmopolitan*, extensively discuss sex, often sending conflicting messages. More precisely, they emphasize both sexual liberation and equality of young women, and the "naturally given" relational concept of female sexuality. In addition, media images often stress female beauty and erotic appeal as the central personal quality.

As elsewhere, peer pressure is one of the central aspects of adolescent sexual development. In Croatia, peers are important for the timing of the first intercourse, contraceptive choices, and the formation of sexual attitudes. However, peer influence is perceived by adolescents as moderate in effect. Less than 10 percent of surveyed freshmen acknowledge substantial influence of friends on their sexual behavior.

A recent study pointed out intergenerational differences in the mother–daughter conversation about sexuality. According to the results, younger generations of mothers are significantly more likely to discuss sex with their pre-teen and teenage daughters. These conversations seem to have an effect on the daughters' satisfaction with their first coital experience.

Although the effects are unexplored, pornography, especially explicit videotapes, is an additional source of sexual knowledge. According to a study (Štulhofer, Jureša, & Mamula 1999), 80 percent of female students and 98 percent of male students (all freshmen) are familiar with explicit movies. On average, they had their first exposure at the age of 13.

4. Autoerotic Behaviors and Patterns

A. Children and Adolescents

In the past, the autoerotic behavior of children and adolescents had an extremely negative connotation, derived both from Catholic tradition and nineteenth-century medical concepts. If discovered, children were punished for masturbation. Masturbatory practice, especially in preschool children, was viewed by the parents either as their own failure in child rearing or as the child's developmental disorder. As a result, numerous adolescents grew up troubled by guilt feelings.

During the 1980s, adolescent masturbation was gradually normalized. A similar thing happened with the autoerotic behavior of children in the 1990s, at least within urban culture and educated circles. Nowadays, parents generally accept the fact that masturbation is a universal practice of children of both sexes. More and more, it is regarded as a normal expression of children's curiosity and body explorations. However, if a child masturbates excessively (seven to eight times a day), experts suggest that parents should pay close attention, because this can be a sign of urogenital infection, neglect, or child abuse.

In a survey carried out on a large sample of urban adolescents, ages 18 to 20 just starting college, 52 percent of female students and 7 percent of male students reported that they never masturbate. One-in-two males masturbate once a week or more frequently; among female students, this is the case with one in every ten (Štulhofer, Jureša, & Mamula 1999).

B. Adults

According to a study on sexual attitudes and behavior in the five largest Croatian cities (Štulhofer 1999b), 3 percent of men between 18 and 48 years of age and more than one fourth (28 percent) of women of the same age have never masturbated. Interestingly, a significant number of respondents of both sexes (23 percent of women and 19 percent of men) stated that they ceased to masturbate. Among this group of respondents, the married ones are over-represented, which might suggest certain moral tension between masturbation and marital sexual life.

In general, masturbation is regarded as a pleasurable and completely normal erotic activity. However, most people are extremely secretive about it, not the least because masturbation can be perceived as a sign of an inability to attract sexual partners.

5. Interpersonal Heterosexual Behaviors

A. Children

Sexual Exploration and Sex Rehearsal Play

No data exist on the sexual activities of Croatian children. In the 1990s, child sex abuse erupted, both as a moral panic and as a public recognition of a grave, long-suppressed, and overlooked problem. As an unfortunate result, systematic research on childhood sexuality is currently regarded as far too controversial.

B. Adolescents

Puberty Rituals and Premarital Relationships

According to the research on the sexual behavior of adolescents in Croatia carried out from 1971 to the present, the proportion of adolescents with sexual experience is increasing and the age of sexual debut has decreased somewhat. In 1971, 16 percent of adolescent girls and 30 percent of adolescent boys between 15 and 19 years of age had experienced coitus (Trenc & Beluhan 1973). Twenty years later, the proportion had increased to 22.1 percent of girls and 48.9 percent of boys (Stampar & Beluhan 1991). The latest studies point out that 24.3 percent of girls and 46.3 percent of boys, high-school students between 15 and 19 years of age, have experienced coitus (Hiršl-Hecej, Šikanic-Dugic, & Dobravc-Poljak 1998). Living with both parents and attendance at grammar school, which is an indicator of family socioeconomic status, decrease the probability of sexual experience in urban adolescents.

On average, young people in Croatia have their first sexual intercourse at 17, but more than a third of sexually active adolescents have their sexual debut at the age of 15 or earlier (Štulhofer, Jureša, & Mamula 1999).

Adolescent girls in Croatia report fewer sexual partners than their male peers; almost 40 percent of girls and 65 percent of boys between 15 and 19 years of age have had two or more lifetime sexual partners, and 22 percent of girls and 44 percent of boys have had three or more. The pattern of sexual relationships among adolescents is the well-known serial monogamy. They remain faithful to their partner until the relationship is over and then move to another relationship.

Adolescents have sexual intercourse sporadically and less frequently than older single people. The frequency of sexual intercourse among adolescents is related to the proportion of actual sexually active youth; 35 percent of sexually experienced girls and 39 percent of sexually experienced boys did not have any sexual relationship in the last three months. Whereas 26 percent of girls and 35 percent of boys had sporadic sexual intercourse, only 27 percent of girls and 14 percent boys have had sexual intercourse regularly, every week.

Generally, young women report longer sexual relationships than young men do. Almost half of sexually experienced girls, in contrast to 17 percent of boys, reported that their longest sexual relationship lasted six months and longer; 27 percent of girls, and only 5 percent of boys, had a sexual relationship that lasted more than a year (Štulhofer, Jureša, & Mamula 1999).

C. Adults

Reflecting the current state of Croatian sexology, no nationally representative sexual behavior surveys are available so far. The only empirical evidence regarding adult sexual behavior comes from two studies funded by popular newspapers. Both studies used relatively large samples of over 1,000 respondents and were exclusively urban. Data on sexual behavior, presented in this chapter, were collected in the more recent of the two studies (*Sexual Styles Survey*, 1998-1999; see also: Štulhofer 1999a, b, 2000). It should be emphasized that younger, more educated, and financially better-off respondents are greatly over-represented in the samples used for the following analyses.

Premarital Relations

Premarital sexual relations are a rule in contemporary Croatia. Most people start their sexual life as teenagers; the average age at first intercourse is 18 for women and 17 for men. Premarital sex is generally viewed as perfectly normal and its absence is often considered suspect. In a nationally representative survey on social attitudes and values (Štulhofer, Karajic, Meštrovic 1996), only 16 percent of respondents, mostly older and of rural background, were disapproving of premarital sexual relations.

Sexual Behavior and Relationships

Heterosexual behavior in Croatia seems to be stamped by numerous gender differences. As in most international sex surveys, women have fewer lifetime sexual partners than men. On average, adult women report four sexual partners whereas men report nine partners. The difference is already present in adolescence.

The analysis of sexual pleasure points out another notable difference. Women experience orgasm every second time they have sex, whereas men climax nine times out of ten. This gap is partially responsible for the fact that almost 60 percent of female respondents faked orgasm at least once. However, the correlation between the frequency of orgasms and satisfaction with one's sex life is weak.

In terms of the frequency of sexual intercourse, most respondents have sex two to three times a week (39 percent) or once every week (32 percent). For an equal number of people (15 percent), sex happens either considerably less frequently ("once a month"), or considerably more frequently ("almost daily"). Asked whether they found the frequency of sex in their relationship "too low," "too high," or "just right," 25 percent of women and 40 percent of men answered that it was "too low." On the other hand, there are 23 percent of women and 13 percent of men who found the frequency "too high." Unexpectedly, when analyzing gender differences in accepting a partner's sexual advances for the sake of his or her pleasure, both female and male respondents rejected a traditional perception. Compared to women, men were almost twice as likely to engage in sex just because their partner wanted it (Štulhofer, Karajic, Meštrovic 1996).

Because of the relational model of female sexuality and related social expectations, the ideal of romantic love has traditionally been somewhat more appealing to women. One indicator of this is the differential willingness to engage in fleeting sexual encounters or "one-night stands." More than half of women surveyed (54 percent) and one quarter of men claimed no such experience.

There is a popular belief in Croatia that women are more open and talkative about their sexuality. Men, it is believed, are less likely to discuss their sexual experience, either because of their "machismo" or because they lack the skills necessary to communicate emotionally charged personal matters. Empirical data provide some support for this perception. A significantly larger number of women (63 percent) than men (45 percent) "often" talk about their sex life with friends. Only 2 percent of women never discuss sex with their partners, in comparison to eight times as many men.

There is a notable absence of gender differences in overall sexual satisfaction, whether measured directly or indirectly. When asked directly, 59 percent of women and 51 percent of men consider their sexual lives satisfactory. On an indirect measure, the results are similar: 37 percent of women and 38 percent of men stated that "imagination is better than sexual reality" (Štulhofer, Karajic, Meštrovic 1996).

As previously mentioned, romantic love is the dominant schema of heterosexual relationship in Croatia. The ideals of long-lasting love and erotic passion, open communication and understanding, emotional support, and loyalty are the very core of the contemporary concept of intimate relationship. It is widely recognized that, in reality, one usually has a hard time trying to realize these ideals, but nevertheless, most Croats, especially younger generations, firmly believe that romantic love is the highest intimate accomplishment. Potential partners are evaluated accordingly. When asked to rank the three most important qualities in an ideal partner, women state tenderness, loyalty, and charm. According to men, the top three characteristics are charm, fidelity, and tenderness. Physical beauty, financial success, intellect, and sensuality seem to be of secondary importance.

Marriage and Family

Marriage remains a highly important social image in Croatia. Most people regard it as a *conditio sine qua non* of happiness and fulfillment in life. According to a 1995 nationally representative survey by the Faculty of Political Science in Zagreb, 87 percent of Croatian citizens disagreed with the statement that "marriage is an outdated institution" (World Value Survey Croatia 1995).

In another large-scale social survey (Štulhofer, Karajic, & Meštrovic 1996), 70 percent of respondents described marriage as "extremely important." In comparison, 85 percent stated that children are "extremely important in life," but only 52 percent said the same for sex. The high status of marriage is also reflected in the fact that Croats marry at higher rates than neighboring Slovenes, Hungarians, or nearby Austrians and Italians.

In reality, marriage in Croatia is still far from the ideal picture of gender equality that most people start with nowadays. Because most married women work outside the home, a customary practice from the 1950s on, they are quite often faced with a double workload. Homemaking and raising children are still disproportionately woman's obligations, especially outside the few metropolitan centers. It should be noted, though, that among younger couples, there seem to be a lot more equality and a less-rigid division of spousal roles than was the case before. Another important trend is an increase in the number of single households. In 1991, they comprised 18 percent of all the households in Croatia.

Cohabitation

Cohabitation is rare in Croatia, even in metropolitan settings; recent surveys suggest that only 2 percent of population are living together "as married." The primary reasons for such a situation are the low standard of living and high apartment rents. There is a push factor for marriage, because the resolution of a young couple's housing problem requires, in principle, the pooling of two families' resources. Even when the financial situation is not a restrictive factor, cohabitation is usually perceived, by the couple, their friends, and families, as a prelude to marriage. Only 7 percent of the children in Croatia are born out of wedlock.

Divorce

Divorce rates have been surprisingly stable since the 1960s. In 1966, there were 15 divorce cases per 100 new marriages; in 1998, there were 16. As a consequence, most children grow up in families with both parents present. The situation is somewhat different in the four largest cities (Zagreb, Osijek, Rijeka, and Split), where there are, on average, 31 divorces per every 100 new marriages (*Statisticki Ljetopis* 1999).

Sexual Satisfaction

In comparison to sexually active singles, married individuals are more satisfied with their sex lives. Among the former, 18 percent are dissatisfied and 55 percent are satisfied with their sexual lives; only 9 percent of married respondents are dissatisfied and 60 percent are satisfied. It seems that the declining frequency of marital sex may not be of central importance for sexual (dis)satisfaction, at least for married couples under the age of 50, most of whom have sex about twice a week.

Extramarital Sex

According to the media, there is a rampant sexual infidelity among married couples in Croatia. Thus, it is no wonder that almost 50 percent of urban women and almost 40 percent of urban men are not sure if their partner is faithful. By contrast, our data suggest a much lower incidence of extra-marital sex. One third of men and 16 percent of women admit that they had other sexual partners while in marriage.

Sexuality and the Physically Disabled and Aged

At the moment, there are no studies on the sexual behavior of older people, and none on the sexuality of disabled persons. In addition, these topics are never even touched upon by the media and they remain completely invisible. The only information about the social perception of older people's sexuality can be found in the jokes that circulate in public. All of them, but especially those involving older female characters, reflect extremely youth-centered, prejudicial, and negative attitudes.

Oral and Anal Sex

There are no legal restrictions on any type of sexual contact. Oral sex, both fellatio and cunnilingus, seems to be a widespread practice, almost universal among the younger generations. Among urbanites between 18 and 48 years of age, 10 percent of women and 13 percent of men were never orally stimulated, and 11 percent of women and 9 percent of men have never orally stimulated their partner. Most people surveyed, men and women alike, placed oral sex at the very top of the list of sexual sensations they would like to experience more often. Anal sex is considerably less prevalent: 56 percent of metropolitan women and 61 percent of men have experienced it at least once. The relatively high numbers of respondents who tried anal sex undoubtedly reflect the specific character of the sample and cannot be generalized (Štulhofer, Karajic, & Meštrovic 1996).

The difference between the incidence of oral and anal sex can be explained, at least partially, by pointing out the powerful negative attitudes surrounding the latter sexual outlet. Anal sex is often identified with homosexuality and therefore regarded as deviant. Moreover, traditional body taboos and hygienic restrictions operate against anal eroticism, suppressing experimentation.

6. Homoerotic, Homosexual, and Ambisexual Behaviors

To describe, in short, the position of homosexuals in Croatia, one can use the phrase "absorbed by silence." During the 1970s, in the period when the gay and lesbian movement in the United States and Western Europe was becoming a recognized political factor, Croatia was a part of communist Yugoslavia, a country where homosexuality was invisible and never discussed. It was mentioned only jokingly or used as an insult. The situation changed somewhat in the 1980s. As the AIDS epidemic became a global concern prompting discussion about various aspects of human sexual behavior—and thus rising questions about differences—the Croatian Ministry of Health started an AIDS-prevention media campaign, in which homosexuality, when mentioned, was lumped together with prostitution and drug abuse. Many gays in Croatia remember the 1980s as the beginning of an awakening. The first gay organization appeared at the time, and later, when some bars started to welcome gay audiences, a rudimentary gay scene was created.

During the first half of the 1990s, the war for national independence and a conservative right-wing government fostered the "building of a strong Croatian society" based on Catholic traditions and ethnic identity. At the same time, however, the civil sector started to develop with support from the international community. New non-governmental organizations (NGOs) focused on the protection of human rights, which provided a much-needed counterpoint to the official line. Still, the rights of sexual minorities were never openly discussed or promoted.

Homosexuality is rarely mentioned in the Croatian media. When it is covered, there is often a criminal subtext (homosexuality is presented as a cause or facilitator of crime) or in other "scandalous" contexts which serve to reinforce prejudices. No wonder that gay men are commonly defined as effeminate types unable to resist affectation. Lesbians are usually stigmatized as heterosexual, men-hating women going through a perverse phase, or are considered to be men trapped within a female body.

According to the results of two large national surveys (Štulhofer 1999b; Crpic & Rimac 2000), around 50 percent of respondents are extremely homophobic. In 1995, 53 percent of respondents stated that they would not like to have a homosexual person as a neighbor. Four years later, 46 percent of respondents were of the same opinion. Among women and the younger generations, especially in large urban centers, the social distance from gays and lesbians is less pronounced. Almost two thirds of the students of the University of Zagreb stated that their friend's sexual orientation is irrelevant to them.

It is important to note that there is no positive term for homosexual persons in Croatian. Aside from the neutral *homoseksualac* (homosexual), only demeaning and offensive labels exist, with *peder* (faggot) being used most frequently. Thus, as Croatian translators at the European Parliament have recently discovered, the word *gay* is impossible to translate.

Gay and lesbian issues are occasionally explored in off-theater plays, alternative exhibitions, and translated books. Most of these cultural events escape the public eye and media coverage. It is interesting to note that the first (and still the only) sexological book on homosexuality was published in 1986 by Košicek. Encouraging normalization and social acceptance of homosexuality, it met only marginal attention. Partially because homosexuality is still invisible, and the lack of self-organizing and activism, rare attempts to promote gay and lesbian rights and/or expose discrimination are usually perceived as "tasteless," and the are dismissed with comments such as: "Why do they have to advertise their private affairs?"

A. Children and Adolescents

The first sexual activities among children, often of a same-sex nature, are understood as exploratory play and, therefore, are perceived by most parents as a part of the growing up process. For most gay men, adolescence represents the period, confusing and conflicting, in which the self-defining process and confrontation with social expectations begin. Finding yourself different from others makes it equally hard to be accepted, as well as to accept your own difference. Bisexual feelings and activities are often a part of this self-defining phase. Unlike a couple of decades ago, first same-sex contacts and intimate relationships occur mostly among peers. Contacts between adolescents and adults, it seems, have almost disappeared.

B. Adults

Sexual Outlets, Relationships, and Lifestyles

If we analyze personal ads in newspapers and on Web pages, we notice two distinct types of partner-seeking. The first is focused on sexual encounters with a more-or-less specific outlet. The second type emphasizes meeting and befriending a man, which may or may not include sex. What seems to be most interesting is the fact that both types of partner-seeking include the similar set of criteria for "Mr. Right." He has to be discrete, masculine, an outsider to the gay scene, and sexually inexperienced. He is someone whom you could introduce to your non-gay friends and parents as "my best pal" without arousing suspicion. The gay male who should be avoided at any cost is the *tetka* (aunt). He is too much of a "she," i.e., effeminate and passive, well known to the homosexual community, and indiscriminate in his choice of sex partners. As one of the most frequent remarks regarding gays who are "too sensitive" goes: "They embarrass us. Just look at them—no wonder that society doesn't like our kind."

Beyond placing a newspaper personal advertisement, the possibilities for finding Mr. Right involve cruising areas such as parks, public toilets, and, in the summer, the beaches along the coastline. Every larger city has at least one nonofficial gay place, a coffee shop or a discotheque. In 1999, the first openly gay nightclub (Bad Boy) was opened in Zagreb. For men living in smaller communities, weekend visits to the closest urban center have been a typical aspect of gay life. For many of them, these visits are the only chance to express their sexual identity. During the second half of the 1990s, the Internet has had a major role, both in finding partners and in strengthening homosexual identity. The first Croatian gay Web site was started in 1996. Today, there are several sites offering information on gay culture and lifestyles. They provide chat services, a virtual meeting space, and forums for discussing gay issues.

For most gay men, meeting in public is not easy. Because they are still closeted or have only partially come out, the choice of place is a difficult one. "I should avoid being seen in gay company," and "Do I want to be spotted in a bar that is considered to be a part of the scene?" are frequent dilemmas. An additional problem for coming out in Croatia is that, because of the economic situation, a large number of men in their late 20s still live with their parents. Economic independence is quite rare. Unlike others, gay men who manage to live with their partners have usually come out fully.

There is no specific type of relationship between gay men in Croatia. Some are open, others are monogamous. Sexual exclusivity is, usually, a matter of mutual agreement. Some couples adopt the heterosexual model of gender roles.

In regard to the lesbian population, long-term lesbian relationships are rather rare. Increased sustainability of such relationships is noticeable between more-experienced lesbians (women over 30). The economic situation, the high unemployment rate, and the pressure of Catholic and patriarchal morality all work against long-term relationships. Women who have moved to larger cities feel the need to gain experience and expand their circle of acquaintances, thus becoming the most visible lesbians on the scene. Women who are in serious relationships avoid the scene and larger gatherings in order to protect their exclusive relationships. The presence of a *butch*-and-*femme* dichotomy varies according to social class and the level of lesbian awareness. Copying the *macho* patterns of Croatian society, most Croatian lesbians tend to feel more *butch*. This should be partly understood as an attempt to reject the stereotype of the "real" woman. However, the *butch*-and-*femme* dichotomy is less present among younger lesbian women.

The lesbian community operates in small closed groups. They are highly stratified and do not allow for mixing of different social classes, professions, or social ranks in general. Within the current scene, most lesbian women have no interest in feminism or lesbian human rights. Political activism is not what the average young woman in the lesbian community has on her mind. Being interested primarily in sexual activity, they often absorb the sexism and machismo of the wider society.

Lesbian women living in provincial towns usually migrate to the capital. Some continue their migration and move permanently to Western countries, mostly the Netherlands, Finland, Sweden, the USA, and Germany.

Thus far, 1999 was the most fruitful year for lesbian activities. Kontra, the lesbian network, organized numerous workshops, and the Center for Women's Studies offered lectures in lesbian theory. Nevertheless, lesbian women are still inert when it comes to activism, so the basic need for a safe, women-only, gathering place has still not been met. Many lesbians are trying to find a substitute in cyberspace using the Croatian Lesbian Web Site.

Legal Aspects and Social Status

There is no legal prohibition of different sexual practices as long as they involve consenting adults. Homosexual, both gay and lesbian, couples are not allowed to register their partnership, nor are they allowed to marry. Furthermore, they cannot seek assisted procreation nor adopt a child. During recent discussions regarding the latest changes in family legislation, some NGO activists were trying to push for a more tolerant view on same-sex unions, but without success.

The Catholic Church is very influential in Croatia. Its status has been strengthened during war times because it represented ethnonational identity and tradition. Interestingly, the Church has been extremely silent in regards to homosexuality issues. Only recently has the Catholic press begun to echo Vatican statements on the World Gay Pride parade in Rome in late 2000 and the question of same-sex marriage.

The press has also recently explored homosexuality in the army. Unfortunately, the coverage was exclusively focused on a case of alleged same-sex abuse. It remains to be seen if homosexuality in the armed forces will become an issue to be publicly discussed. So far, there have been no such indications.

C. Activism, Problems, and Perspectives

By the end of the 1980s, the development of civic initiatives in the former Yugoslavia had some impact on gay issues. The beginning of the war put an end to further organizing and the promotion of gay and lesbian rights. The initiative was renewed in 1999, prompted by the opening of the first gay nightclub. An NGO was founded and registered, but to this day, it has not had its public debut. At the end of 2000, a fragmentary discussion of same-sex marriage began, which included several lawyers and politicians. However, it received almost no publicity.

If one can judge by mailing-list discussions on gay Web pages and personal communications, there is a palpable dissatisfaction with the state of human rights among the Croatian gay population, especially in regards to marriage and child adoption. However, gay men still seem to be reluctant to voice their interests in the real social arena.

Feminist NGOs were the starting point for lesbian organization in Croatia, and they have remained the main support. Within the women's organizations, there were a couple of lesbian women whose efforts made a lesbian network possible. In the second half of the 1990s, Kontra was founded to motivate lesbian women from all over the country to establish a communication network. It was envisioned as a community that would join the strivings and activities of lesbian women from small towns, as well as the capital, and link them to similar international organizations. Kontra's main activity is a lesbian SOS hotline—"for women who love women." It was launched on November 24, 1997. In addition, Kontra activists organize gatherings, lesbian film evenings, and lesbian exhibitions, workshops, and lectures. Parallel with the founding of Kontra, a lesbian publishing project was launched. Because Press is oriented toward the improvement of lesbian culture and literature. In 1998, the first collection of Croatian lesbian poetry (Sagasta 1998) was published, as well as a lesbian fanzine, *Just a Girl*, serving as a discussion forum by lesbians for lesbians and a source of information for lesbian women in Croatia.

D. Bisexuality

Croatian society treats bisexuality almost the same way as it treats homosexuality. Both bisexual and homosexual men and women are "invisible." The only difference is that whereas homosexuality occasionally finds its way into the press, this never happens with bisexuality. At the moment, there is no specific bisexual activity; bisexual men usually gravitate toward the gay community.

The relationship between the gay and bisexual populations is intriguing. Among gay men, one can often hear that bisexuals are in fact gay men who are unable or unwilling to accept their homosexuality. Although there are no reliable data on the number of bisexual men, most gay men are convinced that it must be high. One often encounters men in committed heterosexual relationships who seek male sexual partners. Some of them readily admit that "It is much easier to live a double life, than to be exposed." As mentioned before, many gay men recall their bisexual attempts as a phase in life.

7. Gender Conflicted Persons

It is very difficult to get insight into the prevalence of gender-conflicted persons in Croatia. No public data exist, but almost 100 hospital admissions a year have been attributed to diagnoses that can be related to transgender or transsexual health problems.

Transvestites, transgenderists, and transsexuals can be regarded as a phenomenon with marginal public concern. The country's development after the disintegration of the former Yugoslavia has turned the public interest to other more-immediate concerns of daily life, such as overall well-being, unemployment, and related problems, socioeconomic differentiation, and other pressing matters. However, gender-conflicted persons have been recognized, and the phenomenon has been presented in the media. In contrast to a decreasing ethnic tolerance in the last decade, public opinion regarding gender-conflicted persons has shown positive development. One could say that there is a public "silent approval" and acceptance of gender-conflicted persons. Their specific needs have been approved and their specific ways of living have been accepted.

On the other side, one could say there is a "silent disapproval" of transgender intervention among the medical professions. In spite of the absence of legislative obstacles to sex-change operations—since 1993, a person can request the change of sex in the state register—the procedure is very complicated because of the resistance of medical professionals to become involved in such procedures. Psychiatrists tend to demand extended psychological testing, counseling, and prolonged psychotherapy before approving sex-reversal surgery. Surgical procedures and hormonal treatments are difficult to fit within the health-insurance scheme, causing economical obstacles to sex change. There is neither a special institution nor doctors educated for transgender patients. A few sex-assignment-surgery procedures have been performed each year, but it is reasonable to believe that the hidden demand for transgender interventions might be much higher.

Legal issues related to sex changes are also complicated, but the law defines the problem, and the new gender status can be legally recognized. Gender-conflicted persons have not yet been organized either in formal organizations or in informal support groups. At the moment, it seems that the Internet is the most significant source of information and (international) support for transgender people in Croatia.

8. Significant Unconventional Sexual Behaviors

A. Coercive Sex

Child Sexual Abuse, Incest, and Pedophilia

The child sexual abuse issue is relatively new in Croatia. It has been highlighted in the past few years because of an increase in media coverage and the efforts of professionals working in the field. This, in turn, has led to an increased public awareness that cases of sexual abuse do occur in Croatia. Greater awareness from both professionals and the public has had an effect on the process of reporting cases of child abuse. The data from the Ministry of Internal Affairs show a substantial threefold increase in the number of reported cases of sexual offenses against children (under the age of 14) during the past five years: 1995, 63 cases; 1996, 89 cases; 1997, 72 cases; 1998, 140 cases; and 1999, 207 cases.

Along with the increased awareness, there have been few other factors contributing to this change. One has been the formation of a special department within the police force. The Department Against Juvenile Delinquency now employs specially educated and trained professionals dealing with the issue of child sexual abuse. Furthermore, in October 1997, a hot line for abused and neglected children, Brave Telephone, was established. In the last three years of its existence, the number of calls has tripled. More than 20 calls are received each week during a six-hour daily shift.

Unfortunately, there is still a serious lack of educated professionals and dedicated institutions. The problems of identification and prosecution of child sex abuse cases (in 1999, five persons were convicted of child rape), treatment of victims and families, and possible interventions remain. It is often the case that some professionals fail to report a case because of their ignorance, lack of information or courage, or simply because they resent legal obligations (court testimony, etc.). Another problem of vital importance is the slow implementation of the existing laws that protect children in cases of sexual abuse, both in court and during the investigation. There is no multidisciplinary approach during interviews, legislative process goes on for a long period of time, and the predominant attitude is to dismiss the child's statement because of the lack of the court-admissible evidence. Recently, there have been some new developments in the court procedure that allow for the child's testimony to be taken in front of a camera. Because it is a skilled professional who is conducting this filmed interview, which has the legal power of testimony, this situation is not nearly as stressful as the one in which the child has to confront the alleged perpetrator and be cross-examined (Šuperina & Garacic 2000).

Sexual Harassment

Sexual harassment became a public topic only recently. Media coverage is sporadic and unsystematic, which reflects the lack of a commonly shared definition. Thus, raising awareness about the problem is still in its infancy. Like all other forms of sexual coercion, sexual harassment is, above all, gender related. Far more women than men are its victims, whereas the perpetrators are in most cases men.

There is no integrated approach to the problem. If anything, it is usually sexual harassment at the workplace that is discussed. So far, there have been a couple of television shows on the subject, as well as a booklet published by a non-governmental agency. Other forms of sexual harassment—obscene phone calls, sexual suggestions whispered or yelled in the street, sexist jokes in schools and academia, etc.—are only rarely mentioned. Not surprisingly, most forms of sexual harassment remain unrecognized, i.e., they are not perceived as problematic. Women's complaints are often dismissed as hysterical, humorless, or simply malicious. It is not rare that a harassed woman refrains from voicing her protest, fearing that she will be perceived as overreacting.

Sexual harassment is not punishable by criminal law, but it can be part of an offense against an employee's duties. At the moment, there is only one big company in Croatia that has incorporated sexual-harassment prevention and sanctioning. Furthermore, its workers have participated in gender-equality training provided by a women's organization.

Rape

Sexual violence, especially rape, is still a taboo, a topic rarely discussed. In spite of the efforts of women's organizations to sensitize public opinion, the general perception is that rape is an extremely rare crime. In addition, rape myths are occasionally evoked, resulting in a trivial framing of sexual violence. Even people who encounter victims of rape in their line of duty, such as health care workers, the police, and court officers sometimes express similar views. This directly influences the number of filing charges and the prosecuting of such cases. On the other hand, women's experiences and data collected by women's groups and non-governmental organizations suggest that sexual violence in Croatia is much more frequent than presented by the police, criminal courts, or media. According to the records of the State Bureau for Statistics, there were 100 cases of rape reported to the police in 1999. The prosecution was started in only 66 cases; 55 persons were convicted for rape and 13 for attempted rape (Šuperina & Garacic 2000).

However, if we take into account the records of women's organizations, the real numbers seem to be significantly higher. According to a preliminary analysis of data collected from five women's counseling centers (called Stop the Violence Against Women), for each reported rape, there may be up to 19 unreported rapes. In a study carried out on a sample of urban women between 18 and 48 years of age, only 3 percent of all cases of sexual victimization were reported to the police (Stulhofer 1999b). The reasons given for not reporting rape are numerous. Usually the perpetrator is an acquaintance, friend, or lover of the woman, which makes reporting socially more complicated, not to mention the additional difficulties such relationships create in the legal case. Furthermore, women often face an embarrassing and frequently humiliating court procedure, disbelief, and even ridicule. Police and court officers do not receive any training in dealing with victims of sexual violence. Finally, many sexually assaulted women, especially those living in rural areas, are unwilling to disclose what happened to them because of shame and/or fear of stigmatization, both within and outside their families.

According to the 1997 Criminal Code, rape is defined as coercive coitus or a coital equivalent (anal or oral penetration), and penalties range from 1 to 10 years of prison. It is important to note that in present legislation, since 1997, rape is considered as a criminal offense both inside and outside of marriage. The law proscribes that if an offender and a victim live in a marital union, the offender will be prosecuted only by the victim's private lawsuit. Because the recognition of marital rape is a relatively recent legal innovation in Croatia, and also a rarely discussed one, a large number, or even the majority, of women may be unaware of it (Šuperina & Garacic 2000).

B. Prostitution

The available data concerning the scope of prostitution are very partial and more often based on estimates than on real documentation. So far, there has been only two social science studies on prostitution in Croatia, both of very limited scope. The actual number of prostitutes in Croatia, therefore, remains unknown. Here, as well as in most other countries, police reports represent the only source of information regarding the scope of prostitution. In 1999, there were 365 registered prostitutes in Zagreb only. (Some recent journalistic estimates go as high as 500.) If we talk about trends, there is a clear increase in the number of prostitutes registered by the police (120 registered in 1996 versus 365 in 1999), but it has to be taken into account that the forms, or types of prostitution, are changing too (Šuperina & Garacic 2000).

Croatian law defines prostitution and sexual solicitation as a punishable offense against public order and morality. Convicted persons are fined or sentenced with up to 60 days of prison time. On the other hand, organizing prostitution (pimping) is a criminal act. The police generally focus on prostitutes who are lower in the hierarchy, that is, those who solicit on the streets, while prostitutes from hotels, massage parlors, and the like, are usually "protected," often because of their clients' social status. Because of the legislative regulations, sex workers are not only stigmatized and marginalized, but also deprived of any kind of healthcare. There are no state or NGO-sponsored programs offering medical, legal, or educational assistance to sex workers. Recently, the STD and HIV/AIDS concerns were stated as the main reason behind a low-key initiative for decriminalization of prostitution in Croatia.

The post-communist turmoil (transition) and related social costs, the war and the arrival of international military forces, the development of a market economy and booming entrepreneurship, as well as the opening of state borders have led to the increase in prostitution and the development of different forms of prostitution, previously unknown in Croatia. This mostly applies to massage parlors, escort services, call girls, and nightclubs. Contemporary prostitution in Croatia generally exists in three forms: street prostitution, the so-called cell-phone prostitution, and the elite prostitution.

The majority of women who solicit on the streets are Croatian (70 percent), but there is also a significant number of women from Bosnia and Herzegovina. The majority of elite prostitutes, working in nightclubs, hotels, or escort agencies, come from Eastern Europe, mainly from the Ukraine (52 percent). Only 10 percent of the high-class prostitutes or call girls are local women. A comparison of the age of street and elite prostitutes reveals that street prostitutes are significantly older, generally 39 to 43 years old, than elite prostitutes (24 to 28 years of age). Another significant difference between street and elite prostitutes is their education. Whereas most street prostitutes have only an elementary-school education—none of them has any college or university education—those of higher rank have, on average, completed secondary-school education. In addition, every fifth elite prostitute has a college or university degree (Šuperina & Garacic 2000).

As has already been stated, the war, the arrival of international forces, and the social costs of transition have, both independently and combined, prompted the growth of prostitution in Croatia. There seems to be a growing number of trafficked women from Eastern Europe feeding this growth. According to police reports, most of them came illegally to Croatia in the hope of finding good paid work in nightclubs, massage parlors, and the like. Of those arrested and then deported, 47 percent have been working and living in nightclubs.

C. Pornography and Erotica

Croatian law does not prohibit the production and distribution of pornography, unless it is child pornography. However, legal sanctions penalize the broadcasting of pornography on radio and television. Although there is no explicit legal definition of "pornography," public exposure and the sale of publications with explicit sexual materials are prohibited, unless wrapped in non-transparent covers, everywhere, except in sex shops. In reality, explicit magazines are sold on every newsstand.

There are a dozen sexually explicit magazines currently sold in Croatia. Soft-core magazines include Croatian editions of *Playboy* (circulation about 45,000) and *Penthouse*. Sex shops can be found in all larger cities. Explicit videotapes are available in all video-rental stores. (According to a recent study carried out on a metropolitan sample, 26 percent of women and 41 percent of men find sexually explicit movies "considerably arousing.") The video revolution has driven all but one X-rated movie house, located in the Croatian capital, out of business. As elsewhere, the fast-growing popularity of the Internet offers wide new possibilities of pornography consumption. Although their popularity is in decline, it is interesting to note that peep-show theaters are registered as providing "cultural entertainment."

9. Contraception, Abortion, and Population Planning

A. Contraception

How common is unprotected sex among Croatian youth? Recent surveys found that 53 percent of adolescents used condoms during their first intercourse; at the most recent intercourse, 48 percent of girls and 57 percent of boys used condoms. Ten years ago, the figures were 10 percent and 24 percent, respectively. The surveys confirmed that younger generations are more likely than older generations to practice safer sex at first intercourse. Still, 22 percent of sexually active adolescents use no means or methods of contraception, and 21 percent use unreliable methods such as coitus interruptus or natural methods. Only 6 percent of surveyed adolescents use hormone pills. Forty percent of adolescent girls and 43 percent of boys believe that the pill jeopardizes the health and looks of young women.

Although condom use has increased substantially, contraceptive use is far from consistent. Less than half (43 percent) of urban adolescents in Croatia use some form of protection regularly. We can only speculate about the rates of contraceptive use in rural areas, but they are most probably significantly lower. Because Croatia lacks any systematic sex education, inconsistent contraceptive use should not be surprising. According to Hiršl-Hecej, Šikanic-Dugic, and Dobravc-Poljak (1998), 67 percent of the surveyed secondary-school students received basic information about family planning and contraceptives in schools. Only 46 percent of them have talked with their parents about those issues.

In Croatia, teenage women can obtain hormonal pills from a gynecologist, but the low dose pills appropriate for this age are not covered by medical insurance. Their high price makes them unaffordable for a large number of young women. The majority of contraceptives are not included in the national health-insurance system. Reproductive health and contraception counseling centers for teenagers are extremely rare, and there is a pronounced deficit of youth-friendly reproductive health services, birth control counseling, and distribution of contraceptives in Croatia.

Sexual behavior and reproductive health are still sensitive issues for youth, issues fraught with social taboos and personal inhibitions. The major source of information about protection from pregnancy and sexually transmissible diseases (STDs) are teen magazines and television. Knowledge about STDs is fragmentary, except for HIV/AIDS. Less than a quarter of adolescents have ever heard of chlamydia trachomatis (16 percent) and human papilloma viruses (23 percent). However, the knowledge and awareness of HIV/AIDS has significantly contributed to the increased use of condoms. Although the share of adolescents not using contraception has decreased and the number of adolescents using condoms has increased, there is still a high percent of sexually active adolescents who use no protection. This reflects the lack of sexual and health education, accessibility and availability of counseling services, and affordability of contraceptives.

Because no representative sex-behavior study has ever been carried out, data on adult contraceptive use are fragmentary and illustrative at best. In a sample of metropolitan residents between 18 and 48 years of age (Štulhofer 2000), 30 percent stated that they always use some form of protection. On the other hand, almost every fifth respondent (19 percent) never uses contraception. Most urbanites use condoms (43 percent) and hormonal contraception (25 percent). Of other methods, 14 percent use the IUD, 6 percent use "natural methods," and 10 percent practice coitus interruptus (withdrawal). Among those who have one-night stands, more than a third (35 percent) never use condoms. A slightly lower percentage of respondents (32 percent) use condoms every time they have a brief sexual experience. When asked if the responsibility for contraceptive use should be placed more on women than men, 27 percent of respondents agreed and 49 percent of respondents disagreed with the statement. Among the latter, women and younger respondents were over-represented.

B. Teenage (Unmarried) Pregnancies

Only 5.2 percent of all live births in 1998 were to mothers 15 to 19 years old; slightly more than one quarter of these (25.7 percent) were unmarried. There has been an overall decline in adolescent birthrates in the last decade. The percentage of total live births to mothers under age 20 was 8.4 percent in 1989, which decreased to 5.2 percent in 1998. In 1991, the adolescent birthrate, live births to women under 20 years of age per 1,000 women aged 15 to 19, was almost 30; in 1998, it decreased by almost half (16.5). It is unclear whether and how much the decrease in teenage pregnancies was caused by changes in female education and living conditions during the transition period.

Aside from the decline in adolescent birthrates during the last decade, another important change has occurred. Marriage rates have declined even more quickly, and more births than before are occurring among *unmarried* teen mothers. The share of non-marital births to mothers under the age of 20 was 17.1 percent in 1989, which increased to 25.7 percent in 1998.

C. Abortion

Since 1978, abortion can be induced on the request of a pregnant woman until the tenth week after conception. After ten weeks, an abortion has to be approved by a professional committee, taking into account medical reasons or the fact that the conception is a consequence of a sexual crime. A 16-year-old woman can seek an induced abortion by a simple request. For younger persons, the consent of the parents or another legal representative is required. In spite of legal obligations, some hospitals refused to perform abortions during the 1990s, following the neo-conservative, pro-life ideals of the right-wing government. This refusal to perform abortions was based on an organized and coordinated conscientious objection of gynecologists "following their religious and moral feelings." As of late 2000, abortion was not included in the health-insurance system. The costs, exceeding US$200, are roughly two thirds of an average monthly salary.

In 1999, a little over 8,000 notifications of legally induced abortion were received, a continued decline in comparison to previous years. Most women who requested an abortion were between 30 and 39 years of age and already had two children. According to official statistics, the incidence of abortion remained stable for the fifteen years prior to 1990, with about 40,000 to 50,000 abortions per year, or 70 to 80 abortions per 100 live births. In the last ten years, the number of legally induced abortions has declined sharply: 1990, 38,644; 1992, 26,223; 1994, 19,673; 1996, 12,339; and 1999, 8,064). However, these statistics do not include abortions carried out in private clinics, a practice that is illegal. The abortion rate, the number of legally induced abortions per 1,000 women age 15 to 49, was 34 in 1990 and 7 in 1999! The abortion rate among women under age 20 was 8 in 1991, which decreased to less than 4 in 1998. The abortion ratio, abortions per 100 live births, was 84 in 1990, which decreased to 19 in 1998.

D. Population Programs

In the past three decades, the number of births in Croatia has decreased by more than a third, from 69,229 in 1979 to 45,179 in 1999. The falling child delivery trend in younger age groups (below age 20) and the rising child delivery trend (above the age of 35 years), characteristic of the developed countries, have also been found in Croatia. The decline in number of births that has lasted for years was accelerated by the war-related events. As a result, Croatia entered a depopulation trend (negative population growth) in 1991. The war was only one of the factors triggering negative population growth. Among others were and still are the rising unemployment rate, decreasing social and economic well-being, and other transition-related factors. During the 1990s, the government made some efforts to promote population growth. Aside from occasional nationalistic and patriarchic declarations emphasizing motherhood as the prime female contribution to the new Croatian State, there was hardly any clear and systematic policy. A limited amount of money was provided as a "child incentive," both as a bonus and tax reduction. Families with three or four children received additional benefits. None of these efforts have produced any effect.

10. Sexually Transmitted Diseases

A. Incidence, Patterns, and Trends

At present, the incidence of the "classical" sexually transmitted diseases (syphilis and gonorrhea) and HIV/AIDS is relatively low. There are no signs of an STD epidemic developing as a consequence of war-related and/or transitional conditions. The incidence of gonorrhea and syphilis steadily decreased during the 1980s and the 1990s, as shown in Table 1.

Table 1

The Incidence of Syphilis and Gonorrhea

Incidence of Syphilis		Incidence Rate of New Cases
1985	129 cases	
1989	80 cases	1.71 per 100,000 inhabitants
1995	50 cases	
1998	14 cases	0.31 per 100,000 inhabitants
Incidence of Gonorrhea		Incidence Rate of New Cases
1985	1,597 cases	
1989	446 cases	9.52 per 100,000 inhabitants
1995	52 cases	
1998	48 cases	1.07 per 100,000 inhabitants

Interestingly, the opposite trend is present in the adolescent population. The incidence rate of newly registered cases of syphilis and gonorrhea among individuals under the age of 20 was 8.6 in 1989, which increased to 12.9 in 1998.

Our clinical experience and STD research reveal a notable increase in the incidence and prevalence of all other sexually transmitted diseases, including chlamydia trachomatis, HPV infections, genital herpes, nonspecific urethritis, hepatitis B, pelvic inflammatory disease (PID), and dysplasiae (CIN), particularly among adolescents. Within various samples of sexually active adolescent women in Croatia, the prevalence of chlamydia was 10 to 27 percent, HPV infections 9 to 2 percent, candida infections 28 percent, and abnormal cervical cytological findings of PAP smears (CIN I, CIN II, CIN III) 22 percent.

It should be noted that the accurate number of sexually transmitted diseases is currently unknown because the health statistics are notoriously incomplete. Presumably, the incidence of the so-called "new" sexually transmitted diseases equals the rates in Western European countries. The incidence of the "classical" STDs seems to be much lower than reported in Eastern Europe.

B. Availability of Treatment and Prevention Efforts

The law requires that all new cases of the "classical" STDs must be reported to the central epidemiological service and the National Institute of Public Health. Infected persons are required to disclose information about sexual partners to health professionals. Diagnosis and treatment are easily available in all larger cities.

11. HIV/AIDS

A. Incidence, Patterns, and Trends

Croatia is among the countries least affected by the HIV/AIDS epidemics. The incidence rate of AIDS in Croatia is less then 4 per 1,000,000 inhabitants. HIV transmission occurs through sexual activity and needle sharing. Because of the social stigmatization of homosexuality and the complete absence of relevant behavioral research, there is no systematic information about male-to-male HIV-infection routes.

The first case of AIDS in Croatia was reported in 1986. In the next 13 years, there were 151 other cases, 84 percent of them involving male patients. As of the end of 1999, almost two thirds of those patients had died. The number of new cases remained stable during the 1990s, with 11 cases (1989), 14 cases (1993), 15 cases (1995), 16 cases (1997), 12 cases (1998), and 15 cases (1999). The structure of all AIDS cases between 1986 and 1999 is shown in Table 2.

Table 2

Populations Affected by AIDS

Population	Percentage of Total
Homosexual/Bisexual Individuals	46.7 percent
Heterosexual Individuals	25.0 percent
Partners of HIV-Positive Individuals	10.5 percent
IV-Drug Users	9.2 percent
Hemophiliacs	5.3 percent
Children of HIV-Positive Mothers	1.3 percent

Regarding young people, one case has been reported in the 15-to-19 age group and six in the 20-to-24 age group.

In recent years, the proportion HIV/AIDS-infected persons who are homosexual or bisexual has decreased. At the moment, the prime risk group seems to be composed of heterosexual men whose profession requires spending long periods of time abroad, such as sailors. There are no new HIV/AIDS cases among hemophiliacs, confirming that blood products are controlled and safe; HIV testing is compulsory for blood donations.

The low incidence of HIV infection in Croatia is well-demonstrated by the results of preventive and anonymous screening for HIV. In the anonymous testing of 179,919 persons in 1999, only 45 were found to be HIV-positive, a very low percentage of 0.025 percent. The incidence is even lower among blood donors (0.001 percent). Keeping in mind that a rapid assessment study of heroin use in five Croatian cities in 1998 pointed out a widespread needle-sharing practice, there is still a surprisingly low percentage of HIV-positive persons (0.6 percent) among drug addicts (Ajdukovic, Ajdukovic, & Prišlin 1991).

B. Availability of Treatment and Prevention Programs

Triple anti-retroviral HIV/AIDS therapy, consisting of a protease inhibitor plus two nucleoside analogue reverse transcriptase inhibitors, is currently available in Croatia. Since 1999, the therapy is covered by the national health-insurance system. (The national insurance also includes the treatment following the accidental professional exposure of health workers.) Consequently, the proportion of HIV-positive individuals who developed AIDS-related symptoms has decreased substantially. The new prognostic techniques using viral-load tests have been available in Croatia since 1998.

Serological examination regarding HIV status was inaugurated in Croatia in 1986. Voluntary testing for HIV antibodies is encouraged, and counseling for HIV-positive persons is provided. According to a special instruction, health professionals are obliged to protect the anonymity of HIV-positive persons and AIDS patients.

An HIV/AIDS-prevention and control program prepared by the National Commission for HIV/AIDS Prevention in 1990 includes the implementation of a broad range of preventive measures. These include strict control of human blood products, relevant public education, staff training, and the development of diagnostic facilities. Several NGOs joined in organizing needle-exchange programs and educational campaigns that were usually focused on adolescents. In the second half of the 1990s, the Ministry of Health started a large and expensive campaign aiming at HIV/AIDS prevention among the general population. Brochures, fliers, television advertisements, and billboards promoting responsible sexual conduct were all over the country for more than six months. The main characteristic of the campaign was the way it specified the notion of sexual responsibility. It stressed the importance of sexual monogamy and alluded to condom use, although condoms were never mentioned by name nor graphically presented. The huge campaign completely refrained from providing the central piece of information regarding condoms in HIV/AIDS prevention. No evaluation study was ever carried out.

For the majority of the Croatians, the main source of information about HIV/AIDS is the mass media. Adolescents have more and more accurate information about AIDS than the rest of the population. As could be expected, attitudes toward HIV-positive individuals and AIDS patients are more negative among older generations. In the recent European Values Survey (Crpic & Rimac 2000), 46 percent of respondents in a nationally representative sample said that they do not want AIDS patients as neighbors.

12. Sexual Dysfunctions, Counseling, and Therapies

In contrast to the broad public and medical attention to contraception and STDs, sexual dysfunction has never been an issue of great interest for Croatian medical professionals. There is no comprehensive approach to sexual dysfunctions that makes a rather strict distinction between different types of dysfunction. At least three different types have been recognized, and each is diagnosed and treated by a different medical specialist.

Sexual dysfunctions related to an underlying chronic disease causing the dysfunction, for instance, impotence in male diabetic patients or painful intercourse in postmenopausal women with vaginal atrophy, are considered as a complication of the chronic disabling disease, and accordingly, are diagnosed and treated by an internist, a vascular surgeon, or a gynecologist. Various medicament treatment possibilities are available for these medical problems, and most of them are covered by health insurance. However, surgical procedures, such as penile prosthesis implantation, are not available and patients in need have to be surgically treated out of the country.

Sexual dysfunctions related to psychological causes are considered a psychological medical problem. Impotence or sexual aversion caused by a psychological dysfunction is usually referred to a psychiatrist or a psychologist both to confirm the diagnosis and for treatment. The treatment includes psychotropic drugs or psychotherapy, both mainly available within the health-insurance scheme.

Finally, sexual dysfunctions related to partner-relation problems are considered a relationship problem. Mostly, these conditions are confirmed by family doctors and treated by various experts: family physicians, psychologists, marital counselors, and others. If generated in the premarital relations of youngsters, these dysfunctional problems are regarded as the problems of adolescence. Treatments are based on different psychological approaches not always covered by health/social insurance.

This division in diagnostics and treatment of sexual dysfunction problems are the result of a lack of any specific education in sexual dysfunction. There are no specialists in scxology, and sexology courses in medical training are rare and insufficient. For that reason, there is no comprehensive approach to the treatment of sexual dysfunction. Moreover, because there is no medical data collection specifically on sexual health issues, it is impossible to get an insight into the incidence and prevalence of sexual dysfunction. As previously explained, these problems can be registered as complications of chronic diseases, psychological problems, or marital problems. In these circumstances, family physicians are regarded as the medical professionals who have more experience with patient complaints related to sexual dysfunction than any other specialty. However, there is no evidence to support that estimate, nor is there any evidence about how well the family physicians respond to patients' complaints.

13. Research and Advanced Education

A. Graduate Programs and Sexological Research

At the moment, sex research in Croatia is an exception, a strange enterprise within the social and medical sciences. There are no sexological institutes, research units, or programs educating future sexologists. Also, there is no sexological association or any related civic initiative at the moment. The reasons behind this sorry state of affairs are several. The main one seems to be the lack of any sexological tradition in Croatia before the 1970s. In addition, sex research is considered to be of marginal scientific importance, both within social and medical science circles. Consequently, very few scholars and/or practitioners have incentives to specialize in sexology, which, as mentioned, requires studying abroad. Finally, there is a funding problem. So far, sex research in Croatia has been financially supported either by international health organizations or by local popular journals.

A brief history of sex research in Croatia begins in the 1970s, when the first surveys exploring the sexual behavior and attitudes of primary and high school students were carried out by a group of gynecologists and social medicine specialists. Similar studies, mostly small-scale, continued in the next decade. Because almost all of them were marked by a lack of theoretical concept and methodological and statistical naiveté, they have resulted in very limited advancement in scholarly understanding of the observed phenomena.

Recognition of the HIV/AIDS problem at the end of the 1980s prompted a new phase in sex research in Croatia, marked by the entry of the social sciences. As a result, the first (and still the only) large-scale sex study was carried out on a national sample of young people (Ajdukovic, Ajdukovic, & Prišlin 1991). Theoretically and methodologically well-grounded, it measured shared information on HIV/AIDS, related-risk assessment, and risk-taking behaviors. Unfortunately, societal concerns with HIV/AIDS were too brief and failed to produce more studies or engage more than a half-a-dozen psychologists. The third phase started in the mid-1990s, with a rising affinity for sexology among the younger generation of sociologists and psychologists. Stirred by a new undergraduate course, Sociology of Sexuality, which was offered at the University of Zagreb as the first course dealing exclusively with human sexuality in the history of Croatian higher education, this interest resulted in thematic issues on human sexuality in two leading Croatian social science journals. At the moment, it seems that sex research is gaining popularity among social scientists, but losing popularity within the medical sciences.

In recent years, only two semi-training programs have been offered. Both were designed and organized by medical experts. The first, Sexology for Family Medicine Practitioners, focused on providing general information on human sexuality to family-medicine practitioners. The second and more extensive program, Knowledge, Love, and Happy Family, offered comparable content to high-school teachers and school psychologists. Occasionally, there are one-day seminars on child sexual abuse and STD and HIV/AIDS prevention. In the last couple of years, various non-governmental organizations and women's groups began organizing seminars focused mainly on sexual harassment and sexual violence. A summer school in Family Planning, held once a year at the Inter University Centre (in Dubrovnik), is an interdisciplinary seminar discussing links between reproductive health issues, reproductive rights, sexuality, and sex education.

B. Programs for Advanced Study

There are no graduate programs in human sexuality. Because there are just a few sex researchers in Croatia with various scholarly backgrounds, future programs will necessarily have to be of interdisciplinary character. Considering the traditionally rigid divisions between disciplines, this seems to be an additional problem for the development of sexology.

There are no sexological journals in Croatia. However, in recent years there has been a marked increase in the number of scholarly papers on human sexuality submitted to social science journals. It is promising that most of the authors are young scholars beginning their careers.

In 2001, an international conference on sexuality in post-communist countries (Sexualities in Transition held in Dubrovnik) brought together sex researchers from central, east, and southeast Europe, and the West. Focused on the impact of a macro social change (the transitional decade: 1989-1999) on various aspects of sexuality, this event boosted Croatia's emerging leadership in Eastern European post-communist sexological studies.

References and Suggested Readings

Ajdukovic, D., Ajdukovic, M., & Prišlin, R. 1991. *AIDS i mladi* [*AIDS and youth*]. Zagreb: Medicinska Naklada.

Crpic, G., & Rimac, I. 2000. Pregled postotaka i aritmetickih sredina: Europsko istraživanje vrednota—EVS 1999 [Basic descriptive analysis of European values survey—Croatia 1999]. *Bogoslovska Smotra, 52*(2):191-232.

Grujic-Koracin, J., Dzepina, M., & Beluhan, A. 1993. Spolno ponašanje hrvatske mladezi i njen odnos prema kontracepciji [Sexual behavior of Croatian youth and their relation toward contraception]. *Gynecol. Perinatol., 3*:147-150.

Hiršl-Hecej, V., Šikanic-Dugic, N., & Dobravc-Poljak, J. 1998. *Survey on knowledge, attitudes and sexual behavior of adolescents—Students of secondary schools in Zagreb*. Zagreb: Children's Hospital Zagreb.

Košicek, M. 1962. *Seksološki leksikon* [*Sexological lexicon*]. Zagreb: Privreda.

Košicek, M. 1965. *Seksualni odgoj* [*Sex education*]. Zagreb: Epoha.

Košicek, M. 1986. *U okviru vlastitog spola* [*In the realm of one's own sex*]. Zagreb: Mladost.

Sagasta, S. 1998. *Igre ljubavi i ponosa* [*Games of love and pride*]. Zagreb: Because.

Štampar, D., & Beluhan, A. 1991. Spolnost adolescenata u Hrvatskoj [Sexuality of Croatian adolescents], *Arhiv ZMD, 35*:189-205.

Statisticki ljetopis [*Statistical yearbook*]. 1999. Zagreb: Central Bureau of Statistics.

Stein Erlich, V. 1966. *Jugoslavenska porodica u transformaciji*. Zagreb: Liber. (English edition, 1971: *Family in transition: A story of 300 Yugoslav villages.* Princeton, NJ: Princeton University Press.)

Štulhofer, A. 1999a. Hypnerotomachia Poliae: Seksualni stilovi urbanih zena u Hrvatskoj [Female sexual styles in urban Croatia]. *Revija za Sociologiju, 30*(1-2):1-17.

Štulhofer, A. 1999b (August 6). Seksualno stanje nacije 1999 [Sexual state of the nation 1999]. *Globus, 452*:58-63.

Štulhofer, A. 2000. Govoriti jedno, ciniti drugo? Spol, stavovi o spolnosti i heteroseksu-alno ponašanje u urbanoj Hrvatskoj [Gender, sexual attitudes, and heterosexual behavior in urban Croatia]. *Revija za Sociologiju, 31*(1-2):63-79.

Štulhofer, A., Jurcša, V., & Mamula, M. 1999. *Longitudinalno pracenje znanja o spolnosti, spolnog ponašanja i relevantnih stavova adolescenata* [*A report on adolescent sexual knowl-edge, attitudes, and behavior*]. Zagreb: State Office for the Protection of Family, Motherhood, and Youth.

Štulhofer, A., Karajic, N., & Meštrovic, M. 1996. *Sociokulturni kapital Hrvatske—Istrazivacki izvještaj* [*Social capital in Croatia — Research report*]. Zagreb: Ekonomski Institut.

Šuperina, M., & Garacic, A. 2000. Ucestalost kaznenih djela protiv spolne slobode i spolnog cudoreda u Republici Hrvatskoj [Frequency of criminal offenses against sexual freedom and sexual morality in the Republic of Croatia]. *Hrvatski Ljetopis za Kazneno Pravo i Praksu, 7*:399-456.

Trenc, P., & Beluhan, A. 1973. Ispitivanje stavova i aktivnosti u seksualnom zivotu srednjoškolske omladine [Experience and attitudes of secondary school students concerning sexual life]. *Arhiv ZMD, 17*(6):269-320.

World Value Survey Croatia. 1995. *Research report.* Zagreb: Erasmus Guild.

Cyprus
(*Kypriaki Dimokratia*) (Greek)
(*Kibris Çumhuriyeti*) (Turkish)
(The Republic of Cyprus)

George J. Georgiou, Ph.D.*
with Alecos Modinos, B.Arch., A.R.I.B.A.,
Nathaniel Papageorgiou, Laura Papantoniou, M.Sc., M.D.,
and Nicos Peristianis, Ph.D. (hon.)**

Contents

*Communications: George J. Georgiou, Ph.D., P.O. Box 2008, Larnaca, Cyprus; drgeorge@avacom.net.

**Note. The authors welcomed the opportunity to prepare this chapter on Cyprus because very little has been published on Cypriot sexuality in the international literature. This has been because of the lack of adequate funding and professionals to conduct methodologically sound research on the island, a lack of a coordinating body, the difficulties involved in collecting data given a conservative and sexually inhibited society, the suppressive influence of the Orthodox Church on human sexuality, and other factors. We have collected, analyzed, and integrated whatever information we could find, including statistical data, the results of professional experience and clinical work, and anecdotal reflections from professionals in fields related to sexology.

Demographics and a Historical Perspective

A. Demographics

Cyprus, the third largest island in the Mediterranean Sea, lies off the eastern shore of the Greek Islands, the southern coast of Turkey, and the western shore of Syria, with Lebanon, Syria, and Israel to the southeast. Measuring 141 miles by 60 miles wide, the island's total land area is 4,867 square miles or 12,606 square kilometers, about the size of the state of Connecticut. The island is divided between Greek and Turkish regions, with 3,572 square miles (9,251 square kilometers) comprising the Republic of Cyprus and 1,295 square miles (3,355 square kilometers) in the Turkish Republic of Northern Cyprus. Two mountain ranges cross the island from east to west, separated by a wide, fertile plain.

According to the 1998 estimate, 78 percent of the 754,064 Cypriots are Greek with a Greek Orthodox religious affiliation, and approximately 18 percent are Turkish Muslims. About 70 percent of Cypriots live in the cities. All but about 0.5 percent (about 500) of Greek Cypriots live in the southern Republic; 1.3 percent of Turkish Cypriots also live in the south. The majority of Turkish Cypriots, 98.7 percent, live in the northern Turkish Republic. Cyprus also is home to 4,500 (0.6 percent) Maronites, 2,500 (0.3 percent) Armenians, 700 (0.1 percent) Latinos, and 23,000 (3.1 percent) other nationals, mainly British, Greek, European, Lebanese, and Arab.

One quarter of Cypriots are under the age of 15, 64 percent between the ages of 15 and 65, and 11 percent over age 65. Cypriots have a total fertility rate (TFR) of 2.3, slightly above replacement level, which ranks the nation 146 out of 227 nations. The 1995 estimated life expectancy was 74 years for males and 79 years for females. The birthrate in the Turkish Republic is 18 per 1,000 inhabitants; the Greek birthrate is 15 per 1,000. The Turkish infant mortality rate is 12 per 1,000; the Greek infant mortality rate is 8.2 per 1,000. The overall annual natural increase for Cypriots is 0.9 percent, with a 0.746 percent increase on the Greek side and 1.14 percent increase among the Turks. The 1992 literacy rate was 94 percent, with nine years of compulsory schooling. The island has one hospital bed for every 162 inhabitants and one physician for every 677 persons. The 1995 estimated per capita income was $13,000 per person in the Greek area and $3,900 per person in the Turkish area.

B. A Brief Historical Perspective

Recent excavations on the island of Cyprus have yielded evidence of human society at least 10,000 years old. The Mycenean (Greek) culture flourished in the second millennium B.C.E. After Phoenicians colonized the island in the tenth century B.C.E., Cyprus remained a major *entre-pôt* for trade in the eastern Mediterranean. Annexed by Rome in 58 B.C.E., Cyprus later became part of the Byzantine Empire until the English King Richard I (Lion-Heart) established a crusader state there in 1191 C.E. The Lusignan dynasty ruled until 1489, when Venice annexed the island. In 1571, Cyprus became part of the Ottoman Empire.

In 1878, the Congress of Berlin placed Cyprus under British administration. After annexing the island in 1914, Great Britain made it a British colony in 1925. Between 1945 and 1948 the British used the island as a detention area for "illegal" Jewish immigrants trying to reach Palestine.

After 1947, the Greek Cypriot community expanded its long-standing agitation for union (*enosis*) with Greece, a policy strongly opposed by the Turkish Cypriot community. After violence in 1954 and 1955, Cyprus gained full independence under a 1960 agreement that forbade either *enosis* or partition and included guarantees of the rights of both Greeks and Turks. Efforts by the president, Archbishop Makarios, to alter the Constitution in favor of the Greek majority led to more violence in 1964.

A Greek-Junta-inspired military coup against Makarios in 1974 led to Turkey's invasion of Cyprus and the *de facto* partition of the island and declaration of the northern 40 percent of the island as the Turkish Federated State of Cyprus. Some 200,000 Greek Cypriots were expelled from the Turkish area to the Republic, while many Turks fled the Republic for safety in the north. The Republic has experienced a return of political stability and economic prosperity, with agriculture, light manufacturing, and tourism leading the way. The economy in the Turkish sector has been generally stagnant, as the international community refused to recognize the 1983 declaration of independence by the Turkish Republic of Northern Cyprus. Tensions have eased since the United Nations-sponsored Greek-Turkish talks on Cypriot unity, even though little progress has been achieved thus far.

1. Basic Sexological Premises, and
2. Religious and Ethnic Factors Affecting Sexuality
NICOS PERISTIANIS*

A. Character of Gender Roles

Ethnographic and anthropological accounts of Cyprus (Peristiany 1974, Markides et al. 1978) stress the importance of the nuclear family as the paramount institution of Cypriot society, so much so that "an individual exists only as a member of a family," and the self cannot be conceived independently from its familial roles. This is in marked contrast to Western "solitary" conceptions of the self (Mavratsas 1992). The family has acquired such significance because it was, and still is to a large degree, the primary social, economic, and moral unit of Cypriot society.

---

*Note: This combined section on gender roles, marriage, family, and ethnic and religious factors was written by Nicos Peristianis, president of the Association of Cypriot Sociologists, based upon his research and that of his colleagues.

The Traditional Cypriot Family and Gender Roles

The economy of Cyprus maintained its predominantly agrarian character well into the twentieth century (Christodoulou 1992). The perennially heavy financial demands of conquerors and the especially hostile ecological factors—the strategic resources of water and land were always in limited supply and diseases frequently destroyed crops—led to competition being a keystone aspect of life and reliance on the family group being vital for survival. Economic activities were conducted by the entire household for the improvement of their common position, thus enhancing family solidarity and the strong distinctions between "insiders" and "outsiders."

In his survey of rural life in the late 1920s, Surridge, a British colonial officer, noted an internal division of labor within the family, with men being responsible for heavy agricultural work and women (aided by the older children) for the lighter work in the fields, as well as housework. Usually one of the girls would stay behind to look after younger children and help with some housework (Surridge 1930). At the same time, much as in Greece and elsewhere in the Mediterranean, there was a "moral division of labor inside the family," revolving around the cultural codes, or values, of "honor and shame" (Campbell 1983, Schneider 1971).

Honor (*timi*) refers to the value or worth of an individual—but since the individual exists as a "member of a family," whatever worth one earns for oneself automatically "spills over" to the family. Correspondingly, shame (*ntropi*) refers to a loss of honor, esteem, or worth, which brings humiliation, "staining" the individual and family.

It is important to appreciate the salience of these codes on the lives of individuals in traditional Cypriot society. Peter Berger has argued convincingly that contrary to modern societies' emphasis on "dignity," which implies a notion of the self devoid of institutional attachments and roles, more traditional societies put an emphasis on "honor," which "implies that identity is essentially, or at least importantly, linked to an individual's institutional roles." In fact, an individual in a "world of honor" "discovers his true identity in his roles. "To turn away from the roles is to turn away from himself" (Berger et al. 1973). What, then, were the roles through which individual Cypriot men and women discovered their true identities or selves?

The traditional role of the man in Cyprus was that of representing the family to the outside world. As head of the family, he engaged in all tasks necessary to protect and sustain the family. He was the main income earner who made decisions regarding production by obtaining knowledge about environmental conditions, resources, and markets. After work, he would spend time in the coffeehouse (*kafeneion*), where information was exchanged and contacts made, as well as views shared on political and village affairs. The highest value for man was "love of honor" (*philotimo*), that is, self-respect and self-assertive courage, which amounted to assertive masculinity, in all areas of social life, to protect the honor of the family.

The traditional role of the woman was to be responsible for the family inside the home. Her tasks revolved around three sets of duties: first, the duty of being a good mother, hence the tasks of nurturing and caring for the children; second, the duty of being a good housekeeper, responsible for cleaning the house, cooking, shopping, and looking after domestic animals; and finally, the duty of being a good wife, by being obedient, respectful, and submissive to her husband.

The separation of the sexes in traditional society, especially rural areas, was quite strict, even though it has lessened with modernization. A woman would keep away from public areas, which were the domain of men. Women would never enter coffeehouses or athletic clubs; similarly, they would rarely be seen passing through the central square of the village, where most male-dominated coffeehouses were concentrated. In churches, women would occupy the rear and upstairs sections, the front part being reserved for men only. Women could attain more freedom to circulate among men only when they were not considered sexually risk-bearing, i.e., young girls before puberty and elderly no longer sexually attractive women (well past menopause). In these cases, women could walk in the streets more freely, pass through the central square, and converse with men. But in no case could women enter and contaminate in church the holy of holies where the altar is housed.

Women's avoidance of public spaces related to their need to avoid sexual shame. In fact shame-avoidance was the principal value governing all female behavior in traditional society. In his classic study of a Cypriot highland village in the 1950s, Peristiany (1965) noted that "woman's foremost duty to self and family is to safeguard herself against all critical allusions to her sexual modesty. In dress, looks, attitudes and speech, a woman in the presence of men should be virginal as a maiden and matronly as a wife." A woman who behaves in conformity to the "code" regulating the behavior of her sex (femininity/passive modesty), is said to be an honorable woman (*timia gynaika*), whereas the one who doesn't is without honor (*atime*), or, what amounts to the same thing, without shame—shameless (*adiantrope*). Again, honor and shame, respectively, are not restricted to the woman, but "spill over" to her family. Thus, for instance, in case of an unmarried woman, shame taints directly the father and brothers, "who did not protect or avenge her honor." After marriage, these responsibilities pass to the woman's husband.

Whether father, brother, or husband, men bear the responsibility of caring for the women of the family. Indeed, this will be their conformity hallmark that regulates the behavior of their sex ("manliness and assertion of masculinity"). In both cases of non-conformity to the code of honor ("an unmanly man," "an immodest woman") the perpetrators are guilty not of breaking an externally given rule, but of betraying their very nature, their *physis*—because it is considered in the nature of men/women to act in this particular way (Peristiany 1974).

Gender roles are taught throughout the socialization process. A study of the lowland village of Lysi in the early 1970s, provides an account of the different patterns of socialization for the two sexes (Markides et al. 1978). From a very early age, in their games, boys try to imitate their father's behavior and girls their mother's. Until the age of 6, children are free to play in the streets and visit neighbors' and relatives' homes. But after this age, girls begin to spend most of their time at home, playing with their sisters or other friends, but also learning how to clean, cook, sew, etc. As they grow older, they may be allowed to visit relatives or friends, once they have secured their mother's consent. No such limitations apply for the boys, who continue to be free to wander around and play in the streets, and to visit the *kafeneion* or other clubs and public places. Boys are encouraged to develop their masculinity as expressed through "physical courage, tough-ness, competitiveness, aggressiveness, and defending one's honor," whereas girls are taught to cultivate their femininity as expressed through "gentle-ness, expressiveness, responsiveness, tenderness and modesty" (Balswick 1973). The most important virtues that girls must learn are, again, those related to modesty and shame-avoidance. A girl must demonstrate that she is a virgin not only in the flesh, but also in spirit. She should avoid not only physical but also social contact with men, because this could be associated with sexual desire. This entails accepting a number of social prohibitions, such as never to talk to a man in the street, unless he is a close relative; not to fraternize with men, and "when a man looks at her she should avert her eyes and blush; she should not laugh in front of men and if she does so, she must bring her hand in front of her mouth" (Markides et al. 1978).

If this behavior is maintained, her good name and family honor are preserved, which adds to her value as a future bride. Throughout sociali-zation in the family and community, a girl learns to set marriage as the paramount goal of her life, since it allows her to become a wife and a mother. A woman who remains unmarried is destined to remain at the social and cultural periphery of the village, for she is not offered any role to play within the mainstream of society. Her destiny will in fact be to care for the elderly parents and the children of married sisters/brothers, and to engage in church-related activities.

Marriage and the creation of a family is also very important for young men, for it is only through them that they will be considered full and mature members of society with equal rights and responsibilities. A man reaches manhood only when he marries. Until then, he is still a *kopellin*, a "lad," which means he cannot hold any responsible position within the power hierarchy of the village.

Social Change, Modernization, and Gender Roles

The roots of Cyprus's modernization can be traced back to the beginnings of British colonialism. Prior to British control, Cyprus had been subject to

Ottoman rule for approximately three hundred years, during which time the land was owned by the State; the peasants had the right to use the land in exchange for the appropriate taxes. British colonialism introduced a connection between individual production and the right to private property. Peasants could now own the land they cultivated; but they could also lose it! Indeed for various reasons, such as bad agricultural years and overspending on their children's dowry, many peasants found themselves in heavy debt to insurers, to whom they had resorted for borrowing money, and to whom many eventually lost their land because they could not repay their mortgage.

Such destitute peasants sought employment in other sectors of the economy, namely the mines and small industries that started developing in the urban centers early on in the twentieth century. After Wold War II, when Britain was forced to abandon her bases in the Middle East and to grant independence to India, Cyprus acquired enhanced strategic value. In response, the British constructed two large military bases on the island, at Episkopi and Dhekelia, with the resulting construction industry providing new employment opportunities. Furthermore, the increased needs of the British military and administrative personnel provided further jobs and new commercial possibilities.

During the 1950s, the final decade of British rule in Cyprus, the average annual rate of growth of the economy reached 12 percent, an indicator of the progress that was being achieved. Urbanization had also grown dramatically: whereas at the beginning of British rule the urban population was only 17 percent, by the time they left, it amounted to 36 percent. As Attalides (1981) showed in his study of social change and urbanization in Cyprus, the majority of the people who migrated to the towns were those who had no land of their own and no work, mostly unmarried men and women. Another major reason for migration was the decision to attend high school. This was due to the recognition that education provided a way out of the villages and hard toil in the fields, into "a better life" in the towns and employment possibilities in the newly created white-collar jobs.

Gradually the urban centers became the foci of the economy as well as of social and cultural life. This, along with the emergence of a sizable urban middle class, led to a restructuring of power relations—a shift of power from the village to the city. As a result of these modernizing processes, the family underwent considerable change. Functions earlier performed by the family were gradually taken over by other institutions, even though not to the extent and with the consequences this had in the West. Thus, even though in many cases the family stopped being a production unit (as in the case of destitute peasants joining the working force in the mines or industry), in many other cases money earned from work in the towns found its way back to the villages to help the family pay off debts and maintain its land and unity. In yet other cases, family businesses were set up in towns, so the family kept its production role in a new context (Argyrou 1996).

It is also interesting to note that, whereas in many other developing societies urbanization led to a break-up of extended family systems into the nuclear system, in Cyprus there was somewhat of a reversal in the process. We have noted how rural Cypriot society was characterized by a nuclear family system; urbanization, in its early stages at least, had an expanding effect, since kin members were added to the nuclear core (usually younger relatives looking for a job in town). Thus, it does not seem that modernization and urbanization negatively affected family cohesiveness and strength (Attalides 1981).

There were, however, gradual changes in gender roles within the family. Two of the most important factors leading to these changes have been education and employment. Education became an important mechanism of social mobility, advancing both the status of peasants to that of white-collar workers and improving the status of women (Persianis 1998). The first primary schools were established by the Orthodox Church toward the end of Ottoman rule. Very few girls attended these schools because women's destiny was to marry and have a family at an early age. Besides, because there were only male teachers at the time, parents were unwilling to allow their daughters to stay in school beyond the age of 8 or 9. For the same reasons, this absence was even more pronounced in the case of the few secondary schools, which were concentrated in the towns. The first girls to attend schools came from the wealthier (bourgeois) class, which valued the cultural benefits of education, expecting their girls to be taught how to be "refined ladies," but also to remain "modest and quiet." It is from the 1920s onwards, the period in which we start having increasing rates of urbanization and industrialization, that we have sizable increases in student numbers, including girls. Most of these new students were children of the wealthier rural and, primarily, urban classes. The motives henceforth became mainly economic because education was now considered instrumental in securing a job in the towns, in commercial shops, trading firms, banks, and similar work. Such motives were further strengthened in subsequent periods, when the economy grew at a faster pace, providing more and more opportunities for work. This was true after World War II, but especially after independence in 1960, when the service sector opened up. Cypriots thought service jobs to be more appropriate for women, since they more closely resembled their traditional roles.

The 1974, Turkish invasion brought destruction of biblical proportions to the Greek Cypriots. Almost 40 percent of the land came under Turkish control; a full third of the population became refugees and had to flee to the south for survival. Most of these ended up in refugee camps at the outskirts of the larger towns, creating a large new wave of "forced" urbanization. Women from such refugee families, especially of rural and working-class background, provided cheap labor for light manufacturing industries, mostly in shoes and clothing, which found unexpected opportunities for growth during this period. Furthermore, the expanded welfare and other state services, which tried to cater to the new needs, provided new opportunities for middle-class women, both refugee and non-refugee alike. The final pull was provided with the economic recovery and unprecedented boost, the "economic miracle," in the early 1980s, which created numerous new jobs in tourism and the wider service sector.

Throughout this period, women's employment increased by leaps and bounds, as did schooling for girls. By 1995, women's employment was 38.6 percent of the total, as compared to 35.17 percent in 1985. In both primary and secondary education, the ratio of girls was equal to that of boys, with some marginal differences at the tertiary level, where more boys than girls study outside Cyprus, whereas more girls than boys study at tertiary institutions in Cyprus.

All these changes have obviously transformed the Cypriot family and gender roles within it, although continuity with past patterns remains strong. Mothers, especially of the younger generations, are not only "allowed," but "expected" to work. Recent research by Papapetrou and Pendedeka in 1998 shows that family members believe the mother to be sensitive, permissive, and flexible toward children's demands. She is over-protective and worries a lot about her children, spending time in discussion with them, certainly more so than the father, which may explain why she demonstrates more empathy and understanding toward the children. This is seen to be related to the fact that she carries the care of the household and family, spends many hours at home, and thus has more opportunities to see each family member separately. This, it is speculated, may also provide her with the opportunity to "administer" or "rule," to know "what" and "when" something must take place. Such powers, however, are not tantamount to the role of "leader," which is reserved for the father. She is expected to work, but she is also expected to ungrudgingly interrupt her career to raise children. After all, woman's working role is seen as a secondary one, important for supplementing the family's income and not as the main breadwinner.

The father is the one considered to be really responsible for the economic well-being of the family. He is still considered to be the leader of the team and his opinions are "determinative" when it comes to "serious" matters, or matters which have an impact upon the whole family. He does very little in the house, his activity being mostly limited to heavy jobs (construction, repair-work) upon mother's requests. Usually he does not spend much time at home, but prefers the coffee shop, a hobby, or a second job; when he stays at home, he usually watches television, especially news reports. He is thus seen as austere, strongly opinionated, and distant. Often he is "unexpressive," since man's socialization into masculinity (competitiveness, toughness, aggressiveness, physical courage, and defending one's honor) teaches him that expressiveness toward his wife and children is a "feminine" characteristic.

Sociolegal Status of Males and Females, Children and Adults

The traditional social and moral order has been sanctioned by the Cypriot Orthodox Church. The family is considered to be a divine institution, relations between its members being comparable to the relations between

God, Mary, and the Christ Child. Icons were traditionally kept in a specific holder (*ikonostasi*) of every home, with an oil-lamp constantly burning, symbolizing the divine protection of the institutions of marriage and family.

During the marital ceremony, considered to be one of the seven "Divine Mysteries" or Sacraments through which God's grace is bestowed to humans, St. Paul's Epistle to the Ephesians is read to the newlyweds, reminding them that in their relationship, the wife must fear her husband and be submissive to him at all times, whereas the husband must love the woman, as Christ loved the Church. Obedience, respect, and submission to husband are moral imperatives that highlight the patriarchal nature of traditional Cypriot society.

Modernization of all spheres of Cypriot life and secularization of the religious sphere have certainly brought about important changes. The 1960 Constitution of the Republic of Cyprus enshrines modern democratic ideals, including equality of men and women before the law. It also specifically prohibits any "direct or indirect discrimination against any person on the ground of his [sic] community, race, religion, language, sex, political or other convictions, national or social descent, birth, color, wealth, social class or any ground whatsoever . . ." (Article 28).

Nevertheless, as has been pointed out by Stavrou (1998), the patriarchal "logic" lurks behind some of the provisions of the supreme legal document of the country. For instance, in determining the ethnic community to which a citizen should "belong," after marrying someone from the opposite community (i.e., a Greek Cypriot marrying a Turkish Cypriot or vice-versa), the Constitution clarifies that: "A married woman shall belong to the community to which her husband belongs." Similarly, in the case of children under the age of 21 who are not married, a child "shall belong to the community to which his or her father belongs . . ." (Article 2: Par. 7).

This patriarchal logic pervades other sociolegal institutions and respective provisions or regulations. Thus, if an alien man marries a Cypriot woman, he does not automatically acquire Cypriot citizenship, unless he fulfills almost all the conditions that any other alien must fulfil in order to acquire citizenship. If, however, an alien woman is married to a Cypriot man, she thereby acquires his residence as well as his domicile.

While there are often no specific laws determining discriminatory social practices, traditional norms and values may produce such outcomes. For instance, there is no legal provision that regulates the name the parties in a marriage should assume. "The practice, however, as has been customary throughout much of the European Christian world, is that upon marriage a woman takes her husband's family name. Also, the children take their father's family name except in the case of illegitimate children, who take the name of the father of their mother" (Stavrou 1998).

In many other instances, the laws may provide for equality and prohibit discrimination, but traditional institutions and practices may still prevail. A most glaring case is that of divorce, traditionally governed by Church law, which entails different divorce provisions for husband and wife. Two reasons that may be invoked only by the husband as against his wife are: First, that the wife was found not to be a virgin on the night of the wedding, which has to be reported to the local Bishop the next day; second, that the wife spent the night with persons unrelated to her (unless she could not find a relative's house to stay for the night, after being ousted from the home by her husband).

The Constitution perpetuated these unequal provisions, by declaring marriage and divorce matters as the domain of the Church. It was much later, when Civil Marriage Law 95/89 amended the relevant article of the Constitution, to allow free choice of civil weddings for Greek Cypriots, and to place matters such as divorce, judicial separation, and family relations, under the governance of special family courts. The Church of Cyprus reacted strongly against these legal changes and exerts all kinds of pressure in order to retain control of the institution of marriage. Until today, the Church insists that civil weddings are illegitimate and refuses to offer perpetrators the services of baptism and other holy sacraments. These pressures by the Church, but also (and perhaps most importantly), the weight of long-adhered-to traditions explain why the vast majority of Cypriots (more than 70 percent) still choose religious, instead of civil weddings. Indeed, civil marriages between Cypriots account for only 3.6 percent of total marriages.

A similar situation prevails with divorce. The procedures for securing divorce through the Church are not only long and laborious, but they are also much more exacting and discriminatory against women. Nevertheless, because of the Church's pressures and the special weight of adhered-to traditions, most Greek Cypriots prefer to put up with the difficulties of Church divorce instead of resorting to civil divorce. They are afraid of getting themselves entangled into a web of socially difficult or embarrassing situations. For instance, should one wish to re-marry in church after a civil divorce, one may find oneself accused of attempting bigamy!

Interestingly, on the issue of abortion, women's span of control or available choices seems to be much greater than in many other countries, even of the developed West. This seems to have to do as much with historical circumstance as with current social realities. Up to the early 1970s, the Criminal Code completely prohibited the practice and provided severe penalties for perpetrators. Developments related to the 1974 Turkish invasion drastically changed the situation when many Greek Cypriot women became pregnant after being raped by Turkish soldiers during the hostilities. Obviously, Greek Cypriot society was not ready to accept the offspring of the "barbarians" into its midst. Many Greek Cypriot men found it difficult enough to accept the raped women themselves, who were violated or "shamed" publicly. Even though the women resisted this violation of their bodies, the public consequences of the rape indirectly brought shame on their families, and especially on their men. As a consequence, the relevant law was radically amended to allow medical intervention for the termination of unwanted pregnancy in such cases. In addition, a provision was made for pregnancy to be terminated if two doctors advised that the life of an expectant mother would be in danger should pregnancy be allowed to continue, or in cases in which a newborn baby would face the risk of serious physical or mental disability.

These loopholes in the law effectively opened wide the doors for abortions under almost any pretext. Although hard data are not available, there are many indications that a large number of abortions are carried out in modern-day Cyprus. This may appear strange for a society that is still quite conservative on a number of other counts. Even stranger is the fact that there hardly appears to be much anti-abortion talk from any quarters, let alone an anti-abortion movement. Finally, the Church, though in theory opposed to all forms of abortion, seems in practice to be only paying lip service to a cause it does not really care to fight for. One suspects that the main reason for this is that the Church cares mostly to control not the private decisions but the public behavior and choices of Greek Cypriots, since it is the latter which serves as an index of its power.

Obviously the historical circumstances, outlined earlier on, explain to some extent why abortions were initially "legalized" and why, consequently, once the legal prohibition was removed, the door was opened for abortions for all kinds of reasons. But why did the phenomenon grow to much larger proportions? It seems that social change and new realities in contemporary Cyprus account for the remaining part of the answer. Indeed, in recent decades there have been fast-pace and drastic socioeconomic changes, which seem to have eroded traditional values and norms, without allowing the time for new norms to develop—the phenomenon of "cultural lag." This is evident in the area of sexual relationships. Many young people are experimenting with sex in their relationships, something that contemporary "open" or "liberated" Cypriot society seems to "allow." Yet the relationships of these young people with their parents (and teachers) do not seem to be so liberated as to allow for straight talk about sex and contraception—thus the many unwanted pregnancies and the use of abortion as an alternative to contraception!

Besides the young, many older people have problems with their marriage; hence the increasing rates of divorce. Both young and older couples also seem to be resorting to relationships outside marriage, which may again lead to unwanted pregnancies and abortions.

To the above must be added the fact that Cypriot males, and sometimes their women partners, seem to think that male contraceptives will somehow render lovemaking "less natural" and enjoyable. Thus contraception ends up being the sole responsibility of women. And if she has not taken the necessary precautions, they end up with unwanted pregnancies and abortions.

The ease of abortions may be an important explanatory factor for the fact that children born out of wedlock are rarely found in Cyprus. To this, of course, we must add the prevailing conservative traditional values, which view unmarried mothers as immoral, since they are seen to be flagrantly violating the sexual code and carrying the "shame of dishonor." Because stigma is a certain outcome for childbearing outside wedlock, and because abortions are so easy to arrange, it is no wonder that illegitimate births are almost non-existent.

Cyprus has, in fact, introduced legislation (Law 243/90) to bring itself in line with the provisions of the relevant European Convention. An interesting example, which highlights all the above issues, concerned a case in the mid 1990s of an unmarried woman working in the Church-run broadcasting station (Logos). When she decided to go against convention and not hide the fact that she was pregnant, she was soon fired, as she was seen to be a case of embarrassment for her employer and a bad moral example for all. The fired woman sued the station and managed to win the case and be awarded compensation (*Fileleftheros*, 9 May 1995).

Another recent law, which aims to protect women from the abuse of traditional norms, relates to the Prevention of Violence in the Family and the Protection of Victims of Violence (47(I)/94). Such a law was of absolute necessity in Cyprus, where many men consider it their legitimate right to uphold their power as husbands and/or fathers in the family through any means possible, including violence, whether it be physical or psychological violence against wife and children, or sexual violence against the wife.

The Sociolegal Status of Men and Women in Work/Employment

For many years, women in the labor force suffered various forms of discrimination as regards inequality in pay for similar work done, conditions of work, type of employment, and opportunities of advancement. Gradually, as a result of a number of factors, such as pressures from women's organizations and the trade unions, and political pressures emanating from the signing by the Cypriot government of various international treaties, the situation has substantially improved, at least as far as legal provisions are concerned. This has not, however, substantially improved the situation for all women, nor has such legal improvements dramatically improved the life of women.

A good example is that of social insurance legislation, enacted since independence, which provides for a marriage grant payable to working women when they marry, as well as a maternity grant and allowance, the former paid to a woman giving birth, the latter paid during a maternity leave of up to twelve weeks. Unfortunately, the plan does not cover self-employed women or unpaid family workers in agriculture who comprise approximately a third of the total number of economically active women. Furthermore, it does not cover thousands of women involved with unpaid housework, as this is not considered "proper" work. This means that a great number of Cypriot women, particularly older women, have to remain in a state of complete dependence on their husbands. Social insurance legislation has been modified appropriately, after ratification of the International Labor Organization Convention 100, and the Equal Remuneration Law (158/89), to provide for equal pay for men and women for work of equal value. This has decreased the gap between male and female wages, although it has certainly not closed it, since equal remuneration is practiced only by the government and a few large corporations, mainly banks, but certainly not by the private sector at large. Among the laws that seek to improve the legal position of women in employment is the "termination of employment" law (24/87), under which sex, pregnancy, or maternity can never constitute reasons for the termination of employment. Again, however, evidence shows that many employers tend to ignore the law, and that in such cases few women proceed to take legal measures against the perpetrators (Varnavidon & Roussou 1995).

Another interesting example, which illustrates how small an effect changes in laws can have on actual social practices, is the abolition of the pre-independence law (180), which prohibited the employment of women during the night. For many years following abolition of this law, social resistance to the idea of women working outside their homes during the night has been such that few women still dare to do so. The result has been an intense shortage of women working in jobs for which night duties are essential, such as nursing and paramedical occupations. For this reason, private clinics have been given permission to employ women from foreign countries. Also, Cypriot women employed in the Cypriot Police Force and the National Guard, as well as those working in the thriving tourist industry, are exempt from night duties.

Lastly, we should underline the fact that in 1985 the Cyprus government ratified the United Nations Convention (34/180) on the Elimination of All Forms of Discrimination Against Women (Law 78/85). This symbolized Cyprus's commitment to eliminate all forms of discrimination against women in all spheres of life, be it education, politics, employment, family, or public life.

In summary, two major comments could be made about legislative change and its impact on Cypriot society. To begin with, most ratifications of international conventions and relevant laws were passed in the recent decades, after independence in 1960, but mostly after 1974. This suggests that, until recent times, concerns about equality and the protection of the rights of various underprivileged groups in society, including women and children, were not a primary issue, because traditional Cypriot society was based on conservative norms, values, and morals. Cypriot life revolves around the central social institution of the patriarchal family with the father enjoying controlling power over the behavior of the other members of the family, especially women, as the preordained "order of things," legitimated by religion.

Modernization and socioeconomic change have contributed to an "opening-up" of society and the gradual espousal of more liberal values and norms. Thus, the introduction of the various laws outlined above. Yet, it seems that Cyprus is going through a period of transition, in which new values co-exist with traditional ones. This, as well as the efforts of traditional male and clerical power holders to cling on to their powers, seems to explain the persistence of inequality between the sexes and generations.

Women themselves have been slow to organize and push for their rights. Traditionally, the main domain of women's participation in public life has been that of voluntary institutions, especially charitable organizations. This is true especially for upper- and middle-class women, the roots of the phenomenon dating back to the formative stages of the bourgeois class in Cyprus and its ideals of keeping women away from the world of production, as "queens" in the private realm of the family, into which men would retreat after work. Women's involvement with charitable institutions was accepted and encouraged, because, in dealing with these, they could expend similar "feminine" services as the ones expended within the families themselves, namely care, love, and affection (Peristianis 1998). Voluntary organizations, and especially charitable ones, seem to have increased in numbers after the Turkish invasion of 1974, with the appearance of new social groups in need of support (Antoniou 1992). Interestingly enough, the leadership of most of these organizations is composed of men, with the exception of a handful of organizations, such as the Cyprus Red Cross and the Association for the Prevention of Violence in the Family.

Women from the working classes had a more prominent role in the trade unions, which started organizing early on in the twentieth century. The oldest such union, PEO (Pancyprian Federation of Labor), is controlled by AKEL, the communist party of Cyprus. SEK (Federation of Cypriot Workers) is controlled by DISI, the right-wing party, and DEOK (Democratic Workers Federation of Cyprus), is controlled by the socialist party EDEK. There are also strong autonomous unions representing government employees (PASIDI) and bank employees (ETIK).

In the labor history of Cyprus, women have fought alongside men for basic labor rights such as social insurance, improvements in wages, and shorter working hours (Pyrgou 1993). However, trade unions do not appear to have actively pursued women's rights for equality in the labor market. In fact, trade unions have accepted pay discrimination against women in labor agreements with respective employers (House 1987). It is interesting that the first law (in 1961), which provided for equal pay for women in the public sector, was enacted, not after trade union pressure, but as a result of a private prosecution by a woman employee who sued the Republic of Cyprus for not upholding the Constitutional Law's provision for equal treatment of the sexes.

Cypriot women have never gone on strike in pursuit of their specific rights as women. One possible reason for this may be the fact that, whereas all unions have departments dealing with women's matters, policymaking of these departments is directed by men (Antoniou 1992). Overall, although women constitute more than a third of the total trade union membership, they seem to exert little influence of their own.

A contributing factor is obviously the control of all general unions by the political parties, who are, once again, male-dominated, and whose primary objectives have to do with furthering their political ambitions. Even more surprising is the fact that women's organizations themselves seem to be controlled or strongly affiliated with political parties. Thus POGO (Pancyprian Organization of Women) is controlled by the communist party; Equal Rights and Equal Responsibilities is controlled by the right-wing party. The Socialist Feminist Movement and the Women's Organization of the Democratic Party are even more forthright in declaring their affiliation in their own names.

For decades now, the primary focus of concern for the political parties has been the ethnic conflict between Greek and Turkish Cypriots, "the Cyprus Problem." This has overshadowed all other issues, including those concerning women, equality of the sexes, and gender relations. Even though the higher officers of these women's organizations have the opportunity to participate in the decision-making processes of the political parties, their voices are seldom strong enough to make a real impact, as the leading teams are always male-dominated. This becomes even more obvious in times of elections, as women candidates seldom if ever make it on parties' lists. Because of prejudices and stereotypes, hardly any women who do make it onto ballots manage to attract enough votes to enter the House. In 1999, there were only three women members out of a total of 53 members. Women seem to do somewhat better in local government, where they appear to be increasing their numbers yearly. Of course, these posts hold negligible political power, so women's gains in this area do not amount to a serious improvement in their status or impact.

General Concepts and Constructs of Sexuality and Love

In traditional Cypriot society, marriages were arranged by parents and had nothing or little to do with the personal preferences of the young people involved. Often a young man coming of wedding age would suggest to his parents a particular girl of his fancy (usually a girl he found attractive in external appearance, but had little knowledge of—since girls were expected to practice "male-avoidance," in order to protect their reputation and honor). If the parents approved of their son's choice, they would proceed to sound out the parents of the girl, usually through the services of a mediator/matchmaker. If the parents disapproved of the choice, their objections usually prevailed, as they were supposed to "know best" because they were "older and more experienced." Obviously the girl's opinion was rarely asked for and her freedom of choice was much more restricted than the young man's.

The paramount criteria for parents' preferences had to do with considerations of their family's best social and economic interests—thus, they had to be satisfied with the economic well-being of the girl's family, the status of her family in the social hierarchy of the village, as well as the moral reputation/standing of the girl and her family in the village. Obviously, a good choice for marriage would enhance both the material resources as well as the status of their family in the village community. Parents would give a "dowry" to the young couple as a material aid to help the newlyweds make a good start in their married life. The bride's family would usually contribute the house plus furniture, kitchen utensils, household linen, and similar items. The bridegroom's side would provide some land and animals. Attalides (1981) notes that marriage settlements imply a bargaining process of matching the assets brought to the new household by the respective partners. Moreover, the practice of giving equal inheritance to all children means that parents must be aware so that what they give to one child at the time of marriage does not jeopardize the share of any remaining children. "In this situation it is understandable that control of pre-marital sexuality should be extremely strict for girls." Thus, if a girl acquires a "bad reputation," the bargaining power of a potential husband is enormously increased, allowing him the chance to make "virtually extortionate demands for a property settlement, thus incapacitating the domestic group from provision for further children" (Attalides 1981). Of course, property considerations were only one set of reasons for the adherence to a strict moral code of behavior for women, but they were surely an important set.

The above constitutes one more set of reasons why families had to always be vigilant of the reputation of their women. Young women had to maintain their chastity until their wedding day. If a woman's sexual purity was questioned, she risked her chance of ever marrying. Virginity was a necessary condition of a woman's moral integrity and the principal prerequisite for marriage. It should be remembered that virginity did not entail only the "physical purity of a girl," i.e., an "intact hymen," but implied that "the girl should avoid any social contact with men that is automatically associated with sexual desire" (Markides et al. 1978).

So important was the value of female purity that during wedding celebrations the visual display of the bloodstained sheets, proving the bride's virginity, had central importance. It has been noted (Argyrou 1996) that the virginity rite "expressed female subjugation but also the wider subjugation of younger people of both sexes to their elders and in particular their parents," for the rite symbolized in a "tangible and indisputable way" that the parents had been managing and controlling the family well. Argyrou (1996) demonstrates how changes to the rite, leading to its disappearance, reflect changes in the power relations between the older and younger generations, as well as between the sexes. The first set of changes became visible in the 1940s, when new employment opportunities were created, giving young men the opportunity to move to the towns for jobs. The sons of wealthier parents moved to towns in order to obtain secondary education. Eventually, with mass education, this became true for all classes and for both sexes. Youngsters were now exposed to new ideas and values through books, magazines, and newspapers. Overall, opportunities for economic independence and education decreased the dependence of the young on their parents and eroded the latter's authority and powers of control, as children could be more knowledgeable or competent than their parents in some areas.

Other developments also contributed to the changing nature of power relationships between generations. For instance, a young man moving to a town often found it practical to stay with his in-laws, so that his fiancée and mother-in-law could look after him and he could also save money to contribute to the costs of building a house. This practicality made vigilant observation of the engaged youngsters difficult for the parents. It also meant that parents themselves chose to avoid the embarrassment of asking for evidence of a bride's virginity, whereas the couple itself increasingly considered the matter their private affair rather than a public spectacle. By the late 1960s and 1970s, "the practice of having fiancees move in with their in-laws became generalized" and "engaged youngsters were sleeping together with the parents knowledge and implicit consent." Loizos (1975) notes that, in fact, by the 1960s, "youngsters had acquired power to veto their parents' choice of marriage partner." Balswick (1973) points out that by this time young people considered "romantic love" to be of primary importance, and this development was responsible for the challenging of parentally arranged marriages. The concept of romantic love was related to changing sexual standards. For if love was felt to be a prerequisite for marriage, then only the young people themselves could determine the existence of love, and this entailed a certain amount of familiarity with members of the opposite sex. Thus "dating" started becoming common.

Such developments cannot be taken to imply that youngsters have now been liberated from traditional values and that virginity and female chastity are no longer important to men. In fact, as Argyrou (1996) reminds us, what has changed has mostly to do with the "timing of sexual access to the bride." Furthermore, the traditional "double standards," requiring a woman to be a virgin till she marries but not so the man, are still prevalent in Cypriot society. Similarly, although some expected that modernization and romantic love would lead to the demise of the dowry system (Balswick 1973), the practice seems to be going strong with some minor changes. Nowadays, the bride's parents are still the ones who contribute to the house and most other items needed for setting up the new household. The groom's parents are expected to have invested considerably in their son's education, which will have led, or hopefully will lead in the future, to very good employment.

After 1974, with the displacement and impoverization of a third of the population who lost all their wealth and became refugees so they could not give any dowry to their children, the tradition suffered a setback. However, traditional values and expectations were so strong that the state was pushed to donate land or money to all unmarried daughters of refugee families as a form of dowry for establishing their own households in the free south. Besides, the economic recovery and boom after the 1980s has enabled Cypriots to continue with the practice (Stavrou 1992). Some analysts point out that the willingness of Cypriot parents "for deferred gratification" in order to invest in their children's dowry, may actually itself be one of the main reasons for the continued success of Cyprus's economy (Balswick 1973, Mavratsas 1992). The above realities may account for an interesting paradox, revealed by social surveys. On the one hand, young Cypriots claim that love is what is important in marriage and that the giving of a dowry is an outdated practice that they do not believe in. On the other hand, they say that parents should "help" with a house and in other ways so the young couple can make a start in life(Intercollege, 1996). This seems to vindicate Argyrou's (1996) position that we are looking at developments in sexual mores and related practices, which are the result of "a struggle in which children won a dominated freedom and parents retained partial control through compromise."

B. Religious Beliefs Affecting Sexuality

In Cypriot society, the religious attitudes and beliefs of the Greek Orthodox Church exercise a strong influence on the sexual attitudes and behavior of the people. Some insight into this factor can be gained from the responses of Greek Orthodox priests to a semi-structured questionnaire regarding seven sexual topics: a) adultery, b) premarital sex, c) masturbation, d) abortion, e) contraception, f) homosexuality, and g) coital abstention. There were 130 (23.2 percent) responses from the total of 560 questionnaires distributed to all priests on the island, followed up with face-to-face interviews of 27 of the priests (Georgiou, 1990).

On the issue of premarital sex, the priests were asked for their pastoral response to the following "situation":

> A young, engaged Christian couple who has been cohabiting for three years is very much in love, but they cannot marry immediately as they have a number of difficulties. As they do not want to have sexual intercourse before the marriage ceremony, but are involved in heavy petting, they approach a priest for advice. (Georgiou, 1990)

For their pastoral advice, the priests chose the following:

- to separate immediately (0.8%)
- to stop all caring gestures (5.3%)
- to stop all passionate caressing that lead to sexual excitement (22.3%)
- to continue as they are now until they get married (21.5%)
- not to the cohabit together, and (8.5%)
- something else (32.3%)

A thematic analysis was performed using subjective responses based on 14 mutually exclusive general categories. The responses were: The couple:

- should get married immediately, no matter what (32.6%)
- should refrain from sexual intercourse until they get married as soon as possible (19.7%)
- should refrain from heavy petting (19.7%)

- should live in separate houses or sleep in separate beds (18.2%)
- should be reminded that sex outside marriage is considered a sin of fornication (15.9%)
- should continue as they are until they get married (14.4%)
- should get married after a very brief engagement, otherwise problems are inevitable (6.1%)
- should use the engagement as a time to know each other, allowing their relationship to mature until marriage, before having sexual intercourse (5.3%)
- could proceed with their committed relationship and have sexual intercourse (2.3%)
- should read religious literature to help them overcome their passions (1.5%)
- should not consider their sexual relationship sinful since their goal is to get married (0.8%)
- should realise that there is a danger that they will have an abortion if they have sexual intercourse (0.8%)
- should separate immediately
- it is not the job of a priest to advise how an engaged couple should behave sexually (0.8%)

Face-to-face interviews with the 27 priests revealed what appeared to be a confused attitude toward premarital sex. They offered a variety of legalistic definitions of premarital sex, which dichotomized sexual acts into "acceptable" or "not acceptable." Some, for example, drew the line of "acceptability" at light kissing between a couple engaged to be married. Others drew the line at a light caress, rejecting all other sexual expressions as either unacceptable or sinful, and so on and so forth. There was also no consensus as to why premarital sex was a sin. The majority said that it was a sin because the Orthodox Church said so. None of the priests, however, could refer to any specific writings of the Orthodox Church to validate their claim. (See other responses from this survey of priests on homosexuality in Section 6B, on contraception in Section 9A, and on abortion in Section 9B.)

3. Sexual Knowledge and Education

A. Government Policies and Programs

There are no specific government policies and programs for sex education. There are no formal sex education programs taught in schools beyond the biology lessons, which cover subjects such as the anatomy and physiology of the reproductive organs, fertilization, twins and genetics, sexually transmitted diseases, changes during puberty, and birthing. These lessons are normally taught by biology teachers, and it is left to their discretion to answer specific questions that may be raised in class. These lessons are taught from the age of 15 upwards.

B. Informal Sources of Sexual Knowledge

There is an element of informal sex education from organizations such as the Family Planning Organization, but this only covers specific groups of people, such as married women seeking gynecological or family planning assistance, soldiers doing their National Guard service, and other minority groups. There is also some teaching in hospitals and schools, but limited staff does not allow for further expansion.

When the main author arrived on Cyprus from the United Kingdom in 1983, there were no explicit sexual articles published in the Cypriot media for fear of reprisals. I wrote my first article on Cypriot male sexuality during this period, but found it impossible to find an editor willing to publish it in their newspaper, as it contained words such as "penis" and "vagina." There seemed to be an inherent fear of publishing sexual articles of any nature, as the editors believed that there would be a volcanic eruption from the Church and the conservative people of Cyprus. They could not have been further from the truth! When a brave editor of a relatively small, radical right-wing newspaper decided to publish the article, there was applause from many sectors of society; one of the long-lasting but super-fluous taboos had been broken! Cypriots were thirsting to learn more about sexuality. After the newspaper editor's initial enthusiasm, I proposed a weekly column, which would allow people to write in their problems anonymously and receive replies in the newspaper. He agreed, and the first sexual column in the history of Cyprus was launched in 1984 in the newspaper *Alitheia* (*The Truth*). The sales of this particular small newspaper increased dramatically in just over a year!

The degree of sexual ignorance from the questions being received was apparent: "Can I get pregnant by swallowing sperm?" "What is the clitoris?" and many, many other questions touching on topics such as anal sex, transvestitism, telephone sex, and sexual problems. At least a dozen letters were received every day. The columns gave people from all age groups and all walks of life an opportunity to write their questions or problems about sexuality, and get a response published in the media for all to read. The weekly column in the popular magazine *To Periodiko*, which ran from 1984 to 1994, reached a peak audience in excess of 30,000 people weekly. More than 1,000 articles covering all aspects of sexuality were published during this period. This, along with a weekly radio program titled *Human Sexuality*, broadcast live every Saturday at lunch time by the author, covered a wide variety of sexual topics and provided a large part of the informal sex education of the population. After a few years, other newspapers began to publish articles, usually translated from foreign magazines. Beginning in September 1999, this editor completed a series of six television programs on human sexuality for EF-EM, a local TV station in Larnaca. (See Section 10, Sexually Transmitted Diseases, for survey data on the knowledge of adolescents regarding STDs.)

In the Knowledge, Attitudes, Beliefs, and Practices (KABP) Survey on AIDS (Georgiou & Veresies, 1990, 1991; see also Sections 5B, Interpersonal Heterosexual Behaviors, Adolescents, 6A, Homoerotic, Homosexual, and Ambisexual Behaviors, Children and Adolescents, and 11C, HIV/AIDS, Availability of Treatment, Prevention Programs, Government Policies, below), 3,176 15- to 18-year-old school children gave us additional insights into their sources of sexuality information. The respondents reported receiving their first sexual information from five main sources: books and periodicals (24.1 percent), newspapers and magazines (15.4 percent), friends (12.0 percent), videos (12.3 percent), and television (12.2 percent). It is not clear from the questionnaire, however, who is actually providing this information in the sources mentioned. Sex differences showed that the boys were more likely to obtain their information from videos (9 percent v. 3.3 percent), probably commercial pornography, while the girls were more likely to obtain their information from books and periodicals (14.7 percent v. 9.4 percent) and mother (4.4 percent v. 0.6 percent). It appears that newspapers and magazines are read equally by both. Subsequent sources of additional sexual information included: television (13.2 percent), school teachers (12.3 percent), and medical personnel (11.7 percent). The same sex difference as those noted above emerged, with the exception of books and periodicals, which are again read equally by both sexes.

When asked, "Where would you prefer to get information about human sexual behavior? (Circle only your first choice)," the great majority of respondents preferred to obtain their information from books and periodicals (24.1 percent), followed by newspapers and magazines (15.4 percent), friends (12.6 percent), videos (12.3 percent), and television (12.2 percent). All the other responses were below the 5 percent level.

It should be noted here that there are no known sex education videos circulating in Cyprus, apart from the commercial pornographic videos that are freely available for rental in most video shops, certainly before the clamp-down on piracy came about. It therefore appears that 12.3 percent of the respondents are obtaining their information from pornographic videos. When asked to name their second preferred source of sexual information, students listed books and periodicals (16.1 percent), newspapers and magazines (14.2 percent), television (13.7 percent), videos (12.7 percent), and friends (11.4 percent). The remaining responses were below the 5 percent level. Sex differences showed that more males than females would prefer the radio as an important second source of sexual information (108 males v. 46 females), newspapers and magazines (105 males v. 70 females), television (224 males v. 194 females), and videos (111 males v. 38 females). More females than males would prefer sources such as books and journals (153 females v. 137 males), mother (191 females v. 56 males), and doctors and nurses (226 females v. 143 males).

The survey gave no information regarding the specific books, videos, and magazines that students used, or how accurate the sex information was. Moreover, it is not clear how the students interpreted the question, "From where do you get information about human sexuality?" in a country where human sexuality courses have never been taught formally at school. Under the circumstances, the concept of "human sexuality" may be a difficult one for teenagers to interpret.

4. Autoerotic Behaviors and Patterns

A. Children and Adolescents

The only data available on child and adolescent autoerotic behavior comes from retrospective histories taken with a clinical sample of 840 patients whom the main author saw in clinical practice between 1993 and 1996. While male masturbation in this sample is far more prevalent than female masturbation (85 percent v. 15 percent), approximately 50 percent of masturbating females felt guilty about this behavior compared with 48 percent of males.

It appears that parents also have fears of the female losing her virginity if she is allowed to "play about down there!" Virginity is related to the "honor" (*timi*) of the family, and this is very carefully guarded. Males, on the other hand, are often encouraged and "cajoled" to continue, if they are caught fondling their genitals in infancy, as this is seen as a normal part of growing up. Given that the females get rather negative messages when caught masturbating, and indeed may be chastised for this behavior, then it is perhaps not a surprise to find that only 15 percent of the females in this sample masturbated.

Still, it may be a little surprising that such a large number of Cypriot girls begin masturbating at such a young age, before age 10. One of the factors is certainly the early growth spurt that females have in relation to boys, but there are probably other explanations also. Most males learn how to masturbate from their friends (77 percent) compared to only 26.5 percent of females. The majority of girls, however, learn to masturbate by themselves, through experimentation or accident (54 percent), compared to fewer boys (21 percent) that learn in this way. Again, more girls (19 percent) learn to masturbate from the media, books, magazines, and the like compared to about 2 percent of boys. It appears that girls tend not to talk as openly as boys do with their peers about masturbating, and therefore this is not the source of their information. Girls, it appears, prefer to find their sexual information from books and magazines, and self-experiment in the privacy of their own home.

The main author's clinical experience has shown that there is a widely reported incidence of childhood masturbation from infancy to nursery school age. These cases are often reported by parents and are accepted by parents and caretakers if the child is male, and it is often joked about: "He's as potent as his father. Look, he's started young." If the child is female, such behavior is often frowned upon, with punishment as a consequence if it continues. Over the last decade, I have had a number of parents coming to the clinic to discuss the "normality" of their young infant daughter's masturbatory behavior, sometimes in horror that their little "innocent" should be capable of such "disgusting" actions! I have yet to see a parent come to discuss their son's masturbatory behavior!

B. Adults

There are no data available for adult masturbation, but from anecdotal evidence in clinical practice I would say that adult masturbation in a stable relationship is quite rare for both sexes. There are the few occasions when masturbation is reported by a married man who has problems approaching his wife sexually because of marital discord, but this occurred in less than 1 percent of the clinical population. I believe that the Cypriot male views masturbation more as a "child's thing," and not the sort of thing that a "man" does, unless compelled to do so by circumstances.

Women, on the other hand, will often refuse to masturbate even when the husband is in therapy, believing that coitus is the "proper thing." They prefer not to become part of the therapy until it reaches a stage where coitus is allowed. It follows from this that the treatment of anorgasmia using the traditional European or American treatment protocols is doomed to failure in Cyprus, as masturbating to orgasm is the essence of this therapy. (In Cyprus, one has to be a very creative sex therapist to succeed!)

5. Interpersonal Heterosexual Behaviors

A. Children

No data have been gathered to date regarding children's sexuality or sexual rehearsal play in Cyprus.

B. Adolescents

The only systematic survey that has been conducted to date in Cyprus regarding adolescent sexuality involves a sample of 3,176 (1,528 male and 1,643 female) Cypriot lyceum students conducted by Georgiou and Veresies in 1990 and 1991. The Knowledge, Attitudes, Beliefs, and Practices (KABP) Survey was organized and completed along the lines of work carried out by the World Health Organization (WHO), the Global Programme on AIDS, the Social and Behavioral Research Unit (SBR), the Cyprus National AIDS Committee, the Ministry of Health, and the Ministry of Education in Cyprus. The whole project was headed by the main author of this chapter as the WHO Principle Investigator.

Even though the premise of the research was to look at the knowledge, attitudes, beliefs, and practices of Cypriot adolescents toward HIV infection and AIDS, many of the 177 questions in the survey touched on other aspects of human sexuality. There were two questionnaires, one for high school adolescents and another for head teachers. A multistage random cluster sampling strategy was used to obtain data for the survey, using 27 schools—20 (79.2 percent of the sample) in urban areas and 7 (20.8 percent) in rural ones. The 177-question survey was answered anonymously, and covered the following areas: sociodemographics, sources of information on AIDS, knowledge of AIDS, attitudes and beliefs about AIDS, attitudes toward people with AIDS, knowledge of sexually transmitted diseases (STDs), leisure-time activities, perceived norms in certain health-related behavior, drinking and drug abuse, attitudes about condom use, and sexual behavior.

Adolescent Attitudes and Behavior

Previous Heterosexual Experiences. Students were asked to respond to a series of questions about individual behaviors ranging from hugging to anal sex. Even though hugging, deep kissing, and petting are not considered sexual activities through which HIV is transmitted, they are often enough preliminary steps toward sexual intercourse. Therefore the percentage of young people engaging in them indicates when these steps toward more advanced sexual activity are first taken (see Table 1).

Table 1

Sexual Behaviors with the Other Sex for 14 to 18+ Year Olds

	Never	1-2 times	3-6 times	7 or more
Hugging	23.3	26.7	13.2	36.2
Deep (open mouth) kissing	47.5	20.4	8.9	22.7
Petting above the waist	54.5	19.0	8.2	17.2
Petting below the waist	63.1	12.8	6.3	16.9
Sleeping together (without sexual intercourse)	71.9	13.3	5.0	9.1
Sexual intercourse	78.5	7.2	3.9	7.5
Oral sex	75.2	8.2	4.2	8.5
Anal (rectal) sex	84.4	8.0	2.3	4.4

Three quarters of the adolescents (76.7 percent) surveyed have experienced hugging at least once. Of these, the majority were boys (1,340 boys v. 1,075 girls). One in six (15 percent) of the boys and one third (32 percent) of the girls were "sexually inexperienced," not having engaged even in petting. About half of the students have experienced deep open mouth kissing and some sort of petting above the waist. Again the majority of these were boys (963 boys v. 439 girls). About one third have petted below the waist (850 boys v. 289 girls) and a further one third have slept together without sexual intercourse (628 boys v. 242 girls). Sexual intercourse was attempted by approximately one quarter (18.6 percent) of the students (550 boys v. 97 girls), which means that about 94 percent of the girls and two thirds (66 percent) of the boys were technically still virgins, even though they may have had other sexual experiences.

Judging from the figures for sex differences, it appears that the boys are not having sexual intercourse with the indigenous females. This raises the question of who their sexual partners are. Is it mostly with prostitutes, either local girls or imported "artists," or is it with tourist girls? This data does not answer these questions, but they are definitely worth further investigation because of the implications for HIV transmission.

A further 25 percent of the respondents reported experiencing oral sex at least once (563 boys v. 103 girls).

There is no doubt that the most dangerous sexual activity in terms of contracting HIV is receptive anal sexual intercourse. Masters, Johnson, and Kolodny (1988) point out that the risk from a single episode of anal intercourse with an infected partner is considerably higher than with other sexual activities—probably on the order of one in 50 to 100. Just over 15 percent of the respondents reported experiencing anal or rectal sex. Of these the majority were boys (424 boys v. 41 girls). It would certainly be worth investigating further whether the boys had homosexual or hetero-sexual anal intercourse, whether they had used a condom, and whether they were the receptors or the perpetrators. It is also not clear why there should be so many boys participating in anal intercourse. If the large majority of girls were involved, this would be understandable given the patriarchal attitudes that prevail in Cyprus regarding the preservation of a girl's ("technical") virginity. Perhaps the males are using anal sex as a means of birth control.

Among the 19.4 percent of respondents reporting having had vaginal intercourse, 11.7 percent (296 males and 75 females) reported having had one or two sexual partners, 4 percent (123 boys and 5 girls) between three and six partners, and 3.7 percent (115 boys and 4 girls) admitted to seven or more partners.

Of those who reported vaginal intercourse, the most frequent age of first intercourse was 14 to 16 years old, 14.4 percent (see Table 2). Girls showed a marked increase in sexual intercourse starting at age 15, whereas

Table 2

Age at First Sexual Intercourse Experience

Age	Percentage	Number of males versus females		
Under age 11	4.2%	123 boys	v.	11 girls
Age 12	1.3	37 boys	v.	4 girls
Age 13	2.1	63 boys	v.	3 girls
Age 14	4.7	145 girls	v.	3 girls
Age 15	5.5	154 boys	v.	22 girls
Age 16	4.2	96 boys	v.	38 girls
Age 17	0.7	8 boys	v.	15 girls
Age 18-19	0.6	14 boys	v.	4 girls

for boys a marked increase was noted after age 13. The figures for the 11- and 12-year-olds appear to be rather high on first impression and need to be examined further (see also Table 6.)

Table 3 shows the most common reasons given for having a first coital experience. Eleven males and only two females reported being raped; from anecdotal clinical evidence, male adolescent rape is uncommon in Cyprus.

Table 3

Reasons Cited for First Sexual Intercourse

	Number Citing	Boys	Girls	Percentage
I have not yet had intercourse	2,275			71.6%
Love for the person	232	160	72	7.3%
Physical attraction	162	152	10	5.1
Curiosity	106	100	6	3.3
To maintain a relationship	99	88	11	3.1
Got carried away by passion	72	64	8	2.3
It was expected by friends	23	0.7		
I was physically forced	13	11	2	0.4
Under the influence of alcohol or drugs	9	0.3		
Loneliness	4	0.1		
Other	99	55	26	3.1

Contraceptive and Prophylactic Condom Use. Knowledge and use of condoms is another important area of adolescent sexual behavior, with 2,298 (72.4 percent; 1,378 boys v. 915 girls) admitting they had seen a condom, and 65.6 percent (1,312 boys v.771 girls) saying they knew how to use them. Of the roughly one-in-four teens who had had sex, 6.7 percent (168 boys and 45 girls) had never used a condom, 7.0 percent (193 boys and 7 girls) had used a condom sometimes, 3.6 percent (108 boys and 7 girls) most times, and 3.9 percent (110 and 15 girls) always.

These findings have dire implications for HIV and other STD transmission. Only one in five students who had had sexual intercourse at least once had always used condoms. Three out of four were unprotected sometimes or all of the time. Moreover, it is not clear from the question whether the condom was used correctly or not, whether it was placed on the penis before any type of intromission, or whether it was placed on the penis just before ejaculation for purely contraceptive purposes. It is also not clear whether the condom was used for other sexual practices such as anal and oral sex, which are also high-risk behaviors. These issues can be incorporated into any safe-sex and health education program.

Kinds and Duration of Relationships. The disparity between a much higher incidence of sexual intercourse for Cypriot males and a much lower incidence for females raises the question about who the females are that these young men are having sex with. Questions were asked regarding the age of the sexual partner, the duration of the relationship, and the demographic identity of sexual partners. Given the very high influx of tourists every year—for the past six or seven years tourists have outnumbered the indigenous Cypriots—questions were asked that differentiated between the kinds of sexual partners Cypriot men and women have. Table 4 analyses the responses to these questions.

Table 4

Frequencies of Coitus with Different Partners

	Freq.	Percent
Cypriot your age whom you have recently met	146	4.6%
Tourist your age whom you have recently met	249	7.8
Cypriot your age whom you have known a long time	434	13.7
Tourist your age whom you have known a long time	195	6.1
Cypriot you had recently met who was much older than you	111	3.5
Tourist you had recently met who was much older than you	132	4.2
Cypriot you had known a long time who was much older than you	118	3.7
Tourist you had known a long time who was much older than you	92	2.9
Cypriot prostitute, man or woman, who has sex in return for money	216	6.8
Foreign prostitute, man or woman, who has sex in return for money	140	4.4

It appears that there are a large number of long-standing relationships with indigenous Cypriots. A total of 434 students (13.7 percent) said that they had a long-standing relationship with someone their own age. Of these, there were many more boys than girls (346 boys v. 88 girls). A further 146 (4.6 percent) admitted to having sexual intercourse with a Cypriot partner their own age whom they had recently met. Again, the majority of these were males (126 males v. 20 females).

Another category of partner preference that has implications for HIV transmission are the large number of students who had sexual intercourse with tourists their own age whom they had recently met. The overwhelming majority of these were boys (236 boys v. 13 girls). Another equally potentially high-risk behavior was with tourists their own age whom they had known a while, even though it is not clear how long a term is indicated by "a while." Of these, again the majority were males (181 males v. 14 females). To the list of potentially high-risk partners could be added the students who had coitus with older tourists whom they had just met (120 males v. 12 females), and the older tourists whom they had known for some time (77 males v. 15 females). Further potentially high-risk partners would include Cypriot prostitutes (212 males v. 4 females) and foreign prostitutes (133 males v. 7 females). It is not clear why there are a small number of females in the prostitute categories, as it is unlikely that they frequented a male prostitute. Perhaps they misinterpreted the question to mean that they themselves were paid for having sexual intercourse—there have been such known cases in Cyprus among the student population.

Cohabitation. In response to the question, "Have you ever lived with a man or a woman as a regular sexual partner without being married?" 148 (4.7 percent; 134 boys and 14 girls) said that they had cohabited with a sexual partner before marriage.

Teen Pregnancy. A total of 73 boys said that they had made their partners pregnant, and a further 11 girls admitted to being made pregnant by their boyfriends.

Age of Marriage. Table 5 summarizes the results of the question, "At what age would you like to marry?"

Table 5

Ideal Age for Marriage

	Number	Percent
Already married or engaged	51 (26 males and 25 females)	1.6%
Do not intend to marry	52 (36 males and 16 females)	1.6
At age 18	190	6.0
Between ages 19 and 20	797	25.1
Between 22 and 25	1,455	45.8
Between 26 and 30	360	11.3
Between 31 and 35	43	1.4
Age 36 or older	18	0.6

C. Adults

The following data were obtained from a clinical population of 840 clients of varying ages and educational backgrounds (see Section 12, Sexual Dysfunctions, Counseling, and Therapies, for details on sample and methodology).

Virginity

It is clear that far fewer males (9.4 percent) than females (69 percent) are virgins when they become engaged or marry. "Family honor" is at stake because of the prevailing belief that a non-virgin or "soiled" bride should be considered a second-rate citizen in no way equal in social and ethical standing to a virgin bride. Indeed, many brides-to-be have been accused of not being a virgin by their fiancés on the first night. This often results in both families getting involved, taking the female by force to be examined by a gynecologist, and deciding whether the couple should stay together based upon the doctor's diagnosis. Needless to say, such affairs are extremely degrading for the female involved. Even if the couple decides to stay together, there is no guarantee their relationship will stabilize and survive. In my clinical practice, I have encountered many cases of males who believe that virgin females should bleed like a chicken with it's head chopped off!

The males expect to see much blood on the sheets, and if this does not happen—which inevitably it does not—then the accusations will begin, and the horrid saga begins. (See also comments on premarital sex under Sociolegal Status of Males and Females, Children and Adults, in Section 1A.)

Non-virgins before marriage who have slept with a partner before making a firm commitment to marriage will often visit a gynecologist and ask for a hymenorrhaphy or hymen-repair operation. This is one way of "fooling" the potential husband and avoid being ridiculed and belittled by the "expert" spouse who thinks that he has the ability to differentiate between a virgin and non-virgin with his penis on the first night. My national live radio program at Radio Proto (1991 to 1992) and my advice column in the best-selling national magazine *To Periodiko* received many questions about hymen-repair operations. Gynecologists I spoke with admitted performing at least two or three such operations a week, for a total of thousands annually on the island.

Tables 6, 7, and 8 summarize some responses from the author's clinical population of 840 adults. There appears to be quite a range in the frequency

Tables 6

Age of First Sexual Intercourse

Age	Male	Female
Up to 16 years	26.3%	11.7%
17-19 years	52.7	35.1
20-25 years	18.3	44.1
26+	2.6	9

Table 7

First Sexual Partner

	Male	Female
Prostitute	66.6%	0%
Tourist*	11.4	5.5
Cypriot	13.3	17.4
Spouse/Fiancé(e)	8.6	77.1

*Tourism is a unique phenomenon in Cyprus, with an annual flow of about 1.5 million tourists to 600,000 of the indigenous population.

Table 8

Frequency of Sexual Intercourse

Times per month	Male	Female
1-2	16.7%	18.6%
3-4	16.6	18.6
5-8	24.7	19.9
9-12	26	25.5
13 or more times	15.8	17.3

of sex, with a fairly even spread between the sexes (Table 8). About two thirds of the sample have sex more than twice weekly, with the remaining third less than once weekly. Remember that this is a clinical sample that has come for sex therapy for some sexual dysfunction or other, which inevitably adversely affects the frequency of lovemaking. This picture may not be so representative of the general Cypriot population. My guess is that, given our Mediterranean temperament, we Cypriots are generally more hot-blooded than this!

There is a clearly significant difference between the sexes regarding the number of sexual partners in their lifetime (Table 9). Two thirds of the

Table 9

Number of Sexual Partners in One's Lifetime

Number	Male	Female
1	6.8%	66.3%
2-3	18.6	25.9
4-10	41.8	6.3
11 or more	31.9	1.3

women tended to stick with only one partner mostly, compared to about 7 percent of males, while very few women have more than two to three partners compared to males (8 percent of females v. 73 percent of males). Whether this reflects the difference between the sexes or the inhibitions and taboos that exist in the Cypriot culture is not clear; the editor's guess is that the taboo placed upon female "promiscuity" by family and society is certainly a hindrance to moving from one partner to the other. Certainly, females that are likely to have multiple partners that are known in society will be labeled with very nasty names, such as "used," "prostitute," "ethically free," and others. These females tend to have difficulties finding a marriage partner, particularly if their behavior is well known. Usually when a marriage is about to take place, both sets of parents will begin conducting an informal "character" assessment by asking various individuals in the close community of the prenuptials for a character reference. If the girl has a "bad name" in this community, then this will be reported to the potential bridegroom's parents who will strongly advise their son not to proceed, and will continue to stand as an obstacle until their son "sees sense"! These societal norms and taboos are enough for young girls not to consciously want to repeat one mistake twice or more.

About one third of males and one fifth of females had never experienced giving or receiving cunnilingus (Table 10). A very small percentage of males tend to dislike giving cunnilingus (7 percent), whereas a much larger number of females dislike the act (21 percent), which could be for a variety of reasons. The most common reason cited by women in this sample was the partner's inexperience, his ignorance about the clitoris, and his or her belief that the vagina is the most stimulating and sensitive of areas. Also

Table 10

Do You Enjoy Giving/Receiving Cunnilingus?

Reaction	Male	Female
Definitely not enjoyed	1.9%	6.8%
Not enjoyed	5.3	14.2
Moderately enjoyed	11.9	16.8
Enjoyed	36.3	25.4
Very much enjoyed	7.1	18.1
Never experienced	37.2	18.5

cited were the inhibitions of females who feel that they are dirty "down there," or that coitus is the only "acceptable" form of sex.

Not surprisingly, very few males do not enjoy being fellated—these being in the older age groups, which tend to be a lot more conservative in their sexual behaviors. About a fifth of the women in this clinical sample did not like giving fellatio to their partners, again probably related to taboos and inhibitions rife within the Cypriot community. Over a third of the men and a quarter of the women had never experienced this sexual behavior, but again these tend to be in the older age groups above 50 years old in the lower working social classes. Certainly one third of the women thoroughly enjoyed it, as did well over half of the men (Table 11).

Table 11

Do You Enjoy Giving/Receiving Fellatio?

Reaction	Male	Female
Definitely not enjoyed	1.2%	5.6%
Not enjoyed	2.8	14.7
Moderately enjoyed	5.1	19.1
Enjoyed	45.8	30
Very much enjoyed	7.8	3
Never experienced	37.1	27.3

A majority of the men and women who reported experimenting with anal sex appear divided about equally between those who tried it once or twice and those who were a bit more persistent, trying it three to six times before deciding not to continue with this sexual outlet (Table 12). A third of the women and 44 percent of the men who tried anal sex appear to have incorporated this outlet into their sex lifestyle on a perhaps more regular basis, despite the disapproval of this behavior by the Greek Orthodox Church and despite it generally being considered a "no-no" by most couples. Perhaps one of the reasons for its fairly widespread occurrence among both sexes is the availability and popularity of pornography. Additional questioning of this clinical population revealed that it is mostly the male who will "subtly coerce" his partner into trying it, mostly for the sake of experimen-

Table 12

Have You Ever Engaged in Anal Sex? If So, How Often?

Given/Received	Male	Female
Never	57.6%	64.8%
Yes	42.2	35.1
Frequency for Males and Females Who Have Engaged in Anal Sex		
1-2 times	25 %	31.1%
3-6 times	29.3	35
7-8 times	1.2	0
9 or more times	44.3	33.7

tation, after viewing anal sex on a pornographic video. In many cases, the reaction of the wife will determine the frequency of anal sex thereafter.

Unfortunately, there has been no epidemiological study of the sexual behavior of Cypriots. This small clinical sample is the only data available at present and it is limited by focusing on details of sexual functioning among a group of people who at some point in their lives developed a sexual dysfunction. In my opinion, this does not necessarily mean that the sexual histories and behaviors of these particular people differ from those without sexual dysfunctions, as this sample of people were also likely "normal"—without dysfunction—at some point before they decided to seek sex therapy. Their dysfunctions did not exist all their lives. The ideal, of course, is to have a methodologically sound, longitudinal epidemiological study with a substantial random sample of subjects. The lack of funds at present has made this very difficult to impossible.

Divorce, Extramarital Sex, Single Mothers, and Domestic Violence

See comments under Sociolegal Status of Males and Females, Children and Adults, in Section 1A.

6. Homoerotic, Homosexual, and Ambisexual Behaviors

A. Children and Adolescents

Previous Homoerotic or Homosexual Experiences

Many adolescents have some kind of sexual interaction with same-sex peers. This fairly common behavior, particularly among young adolescent males, might best be referred to as "homoerotic" rather than "homosexual." Sorenson (1973) found that about 9 percent of young people in the United States had one or more sexuoerotic experiences with someone of their own sex between the ages of 13 to 19. The likelihood of homoerotic activities in adolescence is significantly greater among those who have had same-sex experiences prior to adolescence. Indeed, most adolescents have their first homoerotic experience with another adolescent.

In the Knowledge, Attitudes, Beliefs, and Practices (KABP) Survey (Georgiou & Veresies, 1990, 1991), about 34 percent of the respondents reported having hugged someone of the same sex at least once. Of these students, the majority were girls (722 girls v. 354 boys). A further 7.9 percent had kissed passionately and a further 5.3 percent had petted above the waist—of these the majority were males. Table 13 summarizes the frequency of various sexual activities with a same-sex partner.

Table 13

Frequency of Sexual Activity with a Same-Sex Partner

Behavior	Never	1-2 times	3-6 times	7 or more times
Hugging	62.4%	14.0%	4.5%	15.5%
Deep (open mouth) kissing	88.9	3.7	1.3	2.9
Petting above the waist	90.9	2.3	1.2	1.8
Petting below the waist*	89.8	2.4	1.5	2.8
Sleeping together (without sexual/anal intercourse)	85.0	4.6	1.8	4.8
Sexual intercourse	91.5	1.5	1.3	2.5
Oral intercourse**	91.6	1.5	0.6	1.9
Anal (rectal) sex***	91.6	1.9	0.6	2.3

*Of the approximately 7 percent who reported petting below the waist with a same-sex partner, 192 were males and 31 females.

**A further 4 percent of the respondents reported experiencing same-sex oral intercourse, with the majority of these being males (114 males v. 13 females). It is not known whether the respondents were giving or receiving oral sex. This is an important factor regarding HIV transmission, as the probability of contracting the virus is far higher for the person giving oral sex, particularly if semen is released into the mouth.

***The latter numbers probably indicate that there are between 2 and 3 percent homosexuals on Kinsey's scale 5 and 6 of his heterosexual-homosexual continuum. This is a little lower than what one would expect, compared with other research. Kinsey and associates (1948) reported that during early adolescence, about 28 percent of the early-adolescent boys were involved in same-sex activities. Sorenson (1973) in his study of adolescent sexuality reported that 11 percent of the boys and 6 percent of the girls in his sample had at least one active same-sex experience.

The majority of students who reported experiencing same-sex anal intercourse were males (141 males v. 9 females). It is not clear, however, how these 9 females could be involved in homosexual anal intercourse, unless it was taken to mean anal penetration by a homosexual boy or with a dildo, but the likelihood of this is probably very small. These results are probably because of a misunderstanding of the question, or ignorance regarding anal sex.

When asked, "With how many people of the same sex have you had oral or anal sex?" 88.7 percent reported never experiencing oral or anal sex with a same-sex partner. An additional 4.3 percent had attempted homosexual oral or anal sex with between one to two partners (119 males v. 18 females), and 1.2 percent had with three to six partners.

It appears that the majority had their first homosexual experiences when they were between the ages of 13 to 16 (see Table 14). During these ages, 5.5 percent of the respondents reported having their first homosexual experience. There may be a latent period for homosexual experiences at the age of 12, but this cannot be confirmed by the data. It has been shown by Kinsey and his co-researchers that the age of puberty is related to the age of the initial sexual experiences, including homosexual ones. It is not clear from the data, however, when Cypriot boys reach puberty, even though it might be presumed that it is younger than 11 years old for some boys.

Table 14

Age of First Experience with Oral or Anal Sex with a Person of the Same Sex

Age	Percent			
Never experienced oral or anal sex with a same-sex person	91.6%			
Age 11 or younger	2.0%	61 boys	v.	8 girls
Age 12	0.7	18 boys	v.	3 girls
Age 13	1.0	29 boys	v.	2 girls
Age 14	1.6	49 boys	v.	2 girls
Age 15	1.9	47 boys	v.	12 girls
Age 16	1.0	21 boys	v.	10 girls
Age 17	0.3	6 boys	v.	3 girls
Age 18 or older	0.5	12 boys	v.	4 girls

B. Adults

A Few Statistics

The author's clinical sample of 840 patients cited earlier gives us some idea of homosexual and bisexual behavioral practices in a group of men and women seeking help with some sexual problem or dysfunction. A second bias in this data is the gender balance, with 597 males to 243 females.

The respondents were asked during history taking if they had ever been approached sexually by another person of the same sex. This opening question was chosen as much less threatening than asking whether the client had actual same-sex experiences. If the response was "yes," then they were asked simply, "What happened?" Of the total number of responses, 12.4 percent of the sample admitted to some type of sexual contact to orgasm with a same-sex partner; 11.6 percent were male and 0.8 percent female.

In order to avoid polarizing the population into "homosexual versus heterosexual," the following clinical data were collected using the seven-point rating scale of heterosexual-homosexual attraction/behavior devised by Alfred Kinsey (1953).

Kinsey scale:	0	1	2	3	4	5	6
Male	82%	9 %	4%	0.9%	2 %	1 %	0.3%
Female	95	0.1	0	0.9	0.9	0.4	0

It seems clear from the data that the majority of people who admitted to some type of homosexual contact or experience were Kinsey 1 or 2 (13.1 percent), with very few, 1.7 percent, in Kinsey 5 and 6. This indicates the transitory experiences of these people with a same-sex partner. Indeed, all of the male experiences, with the exception of eighteen cases discussed below, were age 18 to 20, the age when all Cypriot males are required to do their National Guard training as a soldier in an army camp for twenty-six months. It was during this period in the National Guard that most of these experiences occurred. Most of these young soldiers would be "picked up" by homosexuals "cruising" the scene and taken to their army camp. The deal would be struck in the car, and most of the time they were offered a small sum of money ranging from ten to fifteen dollars (US) in exchange for "services," which meant the homosexual fellating the soldier, or the soldier penetrating the homosexual anally, but not the reverse. With most soldiers, this activity was a one-time experience; with a few, it was repeated two or three times.

The five exceptions that had not had these types of army experiences had encountered homosexuals while studying abroad, and they behaved in a similar fashion to what has been mentioned above. The other 18 males had a specifically homosexual orientation, and their homosexual experiences were more varied and more frequent. These homosexuals had voluntarily entered same-gender relationships, and their interest in opposite-sex partners was very limited. The women were mostly patients who had come to specifically discuss their sexual orientation, and they were involved with a single partner with whom they had fallen in love. All were married at the time.

Homosexual Life in Cyprus   ALECOS MODINOS*

For centuries, this island, which is now an independent country only a hundred miles from the coast of Lebanon, was a model of social and familial conservatism. Family ties were close, the patriarchal concept was entrenched, and strict social mores were enforced by both Church and tradition. The pattern of life, while not unduly exciting, was extremely stable nevertheless.

Abruptly, in just a few short weeks twenty-five years ago, the pattern of centuries was destroyed when Turkey invaded and occupied almost 40 percent of the country. A great percentage of the population lost their homes and jobs, and fled to the southern half of the country before the

Note: The following perspective on homosexuality in Cyprus was provided by Alecos Modinos, B.Arch., A.R.I.B.A., president of the Gay Liberation Movement of Cyprus, and a chartered architect.

advancing armies. Thousands were killed or injured and another 200,000 became refugees.

In those short weeks, the entire social fabric of Cyprus was destabilized. Family ties were abruptly loosened or disappeared altogether in the chaos that followed, and even now, 25 years later, there are still over 1,600 missing persons as a result of the invasion. In a small island-state of less than 700,000 people, the effects of the invasion and continuing occupation were profound.

In May 1989, the following headline appeared on the front cover of a popular national magazine and in daily newspapers: "Homosexual Accuses Cyprus to the Council of Europe for Violation of His Human Rights." The article clearly demonstrated how many journalists were not only prejudiced, but knew very little about the subject. Cyprus is one of the few member countries of the Council of Europe that until very recently had not abolished its anti-homosexual laws. The existing criminal law, CAP 154, articles 171-174, considers homosexual acts a criminal offense punishable by five to fourteen years' imprisonment. This law was influenced by the British Colonial occupation of the island between 1878 and 1960, and was incorporated in our legislation in 1929 in accordance with the British "Criminal Law Amended Act of 1885," a good reflection of the Victorian period! In Britain, the 1885 anti-gay law was abolished with the "Sexual Offenses Acts of 1967," but this had no effect in Cyprus, which by then was an independent state. Cyprus thus was left with an outdated colonial law that Britain had abolished 32 years ago. Homosexuality between women is not a criminal offense, but is completely ignored by the law as if it does not exist at all.

The first discussion on homosexuality was organized by the Pancyprian Mental Health Association in the fall of 1979. In the spring of 1982, a two-day seminar was organized by the same association on the same subject. About 500 persons attended; the great majority were women, and the absence of men was obvious! As a result of the second seminar, five gay men began working together. Five years later, after many difficult and laborious efforts, 16 gay men and a lesbian founded the Gay Liberation Movement of Cyprus on December 10, 1987. As of January 2000, less than half-a-dozen persons have come out of their closet, while the remaining hundreds of gay men and women members of the Gay Liberation Movement still remain in the closet for fear of reprisals.

From 1989 onwards, with great caution, two radio stations arranged live interviews with a gay man who answered questions from listeners calling in. Between 1991 and 1992, in a regular weekly radio program titled *Human Sexuality* presented by the main author of this chapter, homosexuality was included as a topic on three separate occasions. After this initial exposure on live radio, homosexuality was more openly discussed on a few other private radio and television stations.

On the December 6, 1990, the European Commission decided unanimously, with 15 Commissioners, in the case *Modinos v. Cyprus* that Cyprus was violating the human rights of homosexual people. The case went to the European Court, as the Government was reluctant to reform the law. Following a hearing on October 26, 1992, the European Court decided eight to one on April 23, 1993, that Cyprus was violating the human rights of homosexual persons, and ruled that the antiquated anti-homosexual law of 1885 must be abolished. The sole dissenting vote was cast by the judge from Cyprus.

The Greek Orthodox Church bitterly opposed this law reform and was supported by the majority of the members of Parliament. However, after a lot of pressure from the European Council of Ministers, over a period of five years, a week before the third ultimatum given to the Government was to expire, the Cypriot Parliament very reluctantly reformed the law in May 1998.

The new law, made to the satisfaction of the Church and the majority of the opposing Members of Parliament, was found unacceptable by Amnesty International, the human rights organizations of the island, practically all the Pancyprian scientific organizations including the Family Planning Organization, the Gay Liberation Movement and, on September 17, 1998, by the European Commission. The amended law, which the Cypriot government submitted in early 1999 to the European Council of Ministers, was rejected because it was full of discriminations. The Cypriot government planned to rewrite the law and submit it again in 2000.

The Cyprus government was obliged to revise the 1999 law in May 2000 because of the discimations that were not accepted by the European Council of Ministers. During the voting procedure in Cyprus, 27 of the 40 Cypriot Members of Parliament walked out, and as the Cypriot media wrote, "it was not for purposes of micturation [urination]!" Of the remaining 13, two were against the law with the remaining 11 passing the amended law.

The main points in the amended law included:

- The title "Licentiousness Against the Order of Nature" has now become "Coitus Between Men."
- The age of consent for homosexuals has been made 18, whereas for heterosexuals it is 16. Cyprus is not the only country with this discrimination.
- Before, it was against the law for more than two homosexuals in the privacy of their homes to engage in sexual acts. This has now been amended to include more than two consenting adults.
- Article 174a stipulates that it is a criminal offence if homosexual males under the age of consent engage in homosexual acts.

Homosexuality is still a subject very few Cypriots talk about, despite the great publicity through the media since 1989. Cypriots in general are sympathetic and sensitive people who oppose any violations to human rights. There is, therefore, no organized movement against homosexual persons at present. General attitudes toward gays are slowly changing in a positive way because of the European Court's decision and the great publicity given by the media to the gay law reform. However, parents are very unhappy and bitterly disappointed if they have a lesbian daughter or a gay son. Given the slow progress toward liberalization, there still exists a lot of prejudice and discrimination from all walks of life against lesbians and gay men, and this is why the vast majority still remain in the closet.

Besides the clinical data gathered by the main author, there are some anecdotal data regarding homosexual behavior gathered from members who attended the weekly meetings of the Gay Liberation Movement, but this is not in a presentable format that would make any scientific sense. There is clearly a need for further research on this important topic of human sexuality, but the lack of funding makes this difficult.

The difficulties that homosexual and lesbian Cypriots encounter stem from the great social stigma associated with the limits on open homosexuality in the small Cypriot society, the legal system, which still considers gays criminals, and the powerful Orthodox Church, which considers homosexual relationships "the gravest of sins."

Most Cypriot homosexuals conceal their identity behind the curtain of wedlock; it is estimated that about 80 percent of homosexual males are married with families. Marriage makes them feel accepted and secure in a patriarchal, very family-oriented society. Homosexual activities outside marriage are usually conducted with other married homosexuals, or indeed, married "heterosexuals" who are willing to "service" the gay partner with anal penetration without this being reciprocated. Other willing partners include tourists who frequent the island; there is a huge choice, given that Cyprus welcomes about 1.5 million tourists annually!

Because Cyprus did not have its own university until recently, a record number of young Cypriots study abroad. Away from home, they are free to join gay groups, become gay activists, take part in gay parades, and thoroughly enjoy a very active gay life, including one-night stands—a way of life forbidden to them at home. Some even develop long-term relationships. After finishing their studies, many settle down abroad. Those who return home have the same predicament that practically all gay people have in Cyprus. Very few of them remain free at home and travel abroad for holidays and business trips; the great majority will get married, have children, and lead a double life.

There are no organized gay bars or clubs on the island. However, there are a couple of bars/pubs in the main towns, usually owned by gay persons, that are known meeting places with a mixed clientele. Beaches, parks, and "cottages" in the main towns are listed in all European gay guides, but are best avoided because many people frequenting these places, especially during the summer months, land in trouble with plainclothes young policemen acting as "provocateurs." Cyprus's many exercise gymnasiums are another popular meeting place. Good cinemas and theatrical productions, recitals and concerts, as well as ballet performances from visiting companies, attract a number of gay men. Often they socialize with other gay friends over coffee, sometimes for dinner, and most of the time with mixed groups of friends without anybody knowing, perhaps not even suspecting, they are gay.

The great majority of adult gay men and women who remain single and tire of one-night stands want to eventually settle down in a permanent relationship. Such relationships are much easier to achieve between women than men and are, thus, more numerous. The majority of adult lesbians have a lasting relationship. Cypriot men grow up to be strong and to conceal their emotions, and they find it very difficult to be tender and loving toward another man. The Gay Liberation Movement and specialists trained abroad, enlightened with the latest scientific discoveries concerning human sexuality, have assisted many gay persons who seek counseling, with the result that we now have over 30 male couples who have been living together for six to ten years in the main towns. Very few of these couples have talked this over with their family. For the great majority, there is unspoken understanding and silent acceptance, a practice terribly common between all who have a gay son or a lesbian in their families.

Lesbians are discriminated against both as women and as lesbians. Practically all get married and have children; very few of them will dare or manage to have a special friendship with another woman. In the past, they were active members of feminist organizations or women's groups, without letting anybody know of their homosexual inclinations. Unavoidably, special friendships were formed and, as a result, suspicion and prejudice made all such women's groups slowly disappear. Some lesbian couples in the main towns live together, but most live with their families or in separate flats, even though they have been together for several years. This provides them with good cover for family, friends, and colleagues alike.

The younger generation of lesbians today are somewhat more rebellious and daring. They refuse to get married, even to socialize with other young men as a cover-up, especially if they are economically independent. They usually live on their own, not with their families. They socialize with small groups of five or six other lesbians of the same age on the look-out for a partner. They usually form relationships lasting only a few months. Sometimes, they may meet the right person and settle down to a more permanent relationship, but many of these will have relationships on the side for quite a while before making a final commitment to one person.

Single lesbians, especially those who have given up hope of finding a permanent friend, avoid the company of straight men and often meet and socialize with gay young men who share the same interests. The necessity to socialize with the opposite sex brought many homosexual men and women together, thanks to the Gay Liberation Movement, which helped to disperse the myths and stop the prejudices that existed between them.

Recently, although they still dare not come out in the open, the women of very wealthy families who have studied abroad live their lives and form friendships with other women. They ignore the drawing-room gossip about them, much as that hurts and makes them and their families miserable. They often put up a fight with their own families, who may accept their sexual orientation, but they are concerned about what the other people say.

Practically all Cypriot gay men take holidays abroad, even those who can hardly afford it. They travel alone or with friends. They are out to enjoy themselves and have as many sexual relationships as possible, trying to make up for that which is forbidden for them at home. Greece is a very popular, with the gay bars of Athens, the saunas, and the gay beaches of Myconos and other Aegean islands coming first. Amsterdam, Paris, London, and other European cities are always resorts for those who can afford them.

Homosexual men are not accepted or retained in the army if their homosexuality is discovered. Except for half a dozen or so cases, all members of the Gay Liberation Movement have served their national service and have excelled in the posts they were assigned by their officers.

Apart from occasional parties at Christmas and special occasions, where about 50 gay men and some lesbians are invited, there are few gay private parties. The first one was in December 1990 to celebrate the unanimous decision of the European Committee, when the 15 Commissioners condemned Cyprus for violating the human rights of homosexual people. The second took place in April 1993 to celebrate the European Court's decision against the Government for the same reason, and since then, two more to raise money for people with AIDS. About 350 gays attended these huge parties that were considered a great success by all who attended.

Cyprus is a divided country, proud to be a member of the Council of Europe and trying hard to become a member of the European Union. To achieve this, a first necessary step is the equality of all citizens in the eyes of the law. But this is a minimum demand. What must be achieved is true equality in the minds of all people in everyday life. To achieve this, we still have a long way to go!

In the main author's 1990 survey of Greek Orthodox priests (mentioned in Section 1/2B, Religious Beliefs Affecting Sexuality), the priests were asked for their pastoral response to a second situation involving an 18-year-old boy who is having a sexual relationship with another boy, and finding it rewarding and fulfilling. He has heard from someone that it is wrong, and approaches a priest for guidance and advice. The responses chosen by the 130 priests responding to the questionnaire were:

- to terminate this relationship immediately (38.5%)
- to terminate the sexual relationship, but maintain the friendship (10.8%)
- to continue as they are (0.3%)
- to visit a Christian therapist (21.5%)
- something else (28.9%)

The subjective responses given by the 27 priests interviewed face-to-face were analysed using a thematic analysis consisting of 16 general categories, some of which are included below:

- the two boys should separate immediately (51.5%)
- homosexuality is considered a cardinal sin (40.2%)
- the boys should visit a Christian therapist because they are sick and need help (27.3%)
- God destroyed Sodom and Gomorrah for the sin of homosexuality (17.4%)
- it would be advisable for this boy to find a woman to marry immediately (12.9%)
- they should visit a Spiritual Father for guidance and confess their sins (12.1%)
- this is an abnormal, unnatural act that can only be considered a disease (9.1%)
- they should remain friends and have no sex; if this is too much of a temptation, then they should separate completely (8.3%)
- God did not create only men or only women, he created both sexes so that they could be united in matrimony (5.3%)
- if the boy truly repents, his sins will be forgiven (3.8%)
- homosexuality was responsible for the spread of AIDS, etc. (2.3%)

The face-to-face interviews elicited more attitudes from the Cypriot priests that were similar to the survey responses cited above. There was a belief that all homosexuals are really promiscuous heterosexuals who choose same-sex partners for fun, as their passions have overrun them, and that this was definitely the work of the devil. The focus appears to be on the homosexual act, as opposed to the homosexual person. This was further reinforced by the belief that the homosexual person was seen to be the person who accepts being penetrated. This "true" homosexual was referred to by many of the priests interviewed as the *passive* partner, whereas the active penetrative partner was not seen as being homosexual by many priests. This appears to be congruent with St. Chrysostomos's belief of gender expectations, or men behaving inappropriately like women.

7. Gender Conflicted Persons

There is no information available on this topic. There are certainly a few transsexuals and transvestites living on the island, as they appeared in media interviews seven or eight years ago, but little is really known about their situation. The main author has also seen a couple of transvestites and one transsexual in clinical practice, mostly seeking advice regarding sex-change procedures and relationship problems.

8. Significant Unconventional Sexual Behaviors
NATHANIEL PAPAGEORGIOU*

A. Coercive Sex

Sexual Abuse of Children and Incest

Because Cyprus is a close-knit community, it is difficult to conceal sexual abuse and incest with children. The police statistics cover only a minor portion of what happens within families. For example, there has only been one case of incest reported between 1995 and 1997. In the same period, 15 cases of sexual assault on a minor between ages 13 and 16 years old were reported, with 5 cases of assault on a minor younger than 13 years of age. From a sample of 840 patient interviews (see Section 12, Sexual Dysfunctions, Counseling, and Therapies, for details), 3.6 percent or 29 females and one male reported sexual encounters with relatives. These encounters were with a cousin (1.8 percent), uncle or grandfather (1.3 percent), father (0.4 percent), and brother (0.1 percent). This rather small sample of the general population indicates that the problem of incest is far larger than what is reflected in police statistics. It seems reasonable to assume that most such cases are "hushed-up" by the families and by the authorities to avoid shame for the family and having to face all the consequences thereafter. If such incestuous practices were known, the family would be stigmatized, and the chances of the female victim finding an appropriate partner for life would be severely affected.

Rape and Marital Rape

Of the 25 cases of rape reported to the police between 1995 and 1997, all involved tourist women visiting the island. Some of the rapes were perpetrated by Cypriot males "on-the prowl," while many others have been by foreigners living or visiting the island. Most of the female victims were from Scandinavian countries, with a few from Europe. There is no doubt that there have been more such cases that were not reported for various reasons.

Perhaps the most common sexual assault is that perpetrated by husbands on their wives. The author has encounter many such cases, including sexual coercion and abuse. If these cases are reported to the police, they are usually covered up and do not go to the courts for fear of shaming the family and destroying its honor. Many times the police and family members persuade the wife to keep this within the family and not to press charges. Even cases that are reported are often "struck-off" the record after intervention by family members concerned about the probable effect on family ties and honor. (See comments at the end of Sociolegal Status of Males and Females, Children and Adults, in Section 1A.)

Note. The editor is grateful to Nathaniel Papageorgiou, Chief Superintendent in the Criminal Investigation Department (CID) of the Ministry of Justice and Public Order, for providing parts of this section on sexual crimes.

Sexual Harassment

Sexual harassment is perhaps the most commonly occurring crime in the workplace and by Cypriot men harassing tourist women. Sexual harassment in the workplace has been a frequent topic of discussion by the local media, as this was a way of life here in Cyprus. In the workplace, it involves male supervisors using their position and power against women, or women who want to improve their work status or to obtain a promotion. This type of behavior still occurs, but not on the scale that it was once practiced.

A study involving sexual harassment was conducted in 1997 by the Research and Development Center of Intercollege, a large private college in Cyprus, using 1,500 questionnaires that were distributed anonymously to both men and women. About 85 percent of the sample felt that sexual harassment was a serious social problem in Cyprus. About 40 percent of the sample actually knew first-hand of people who had been victims of sexual harassment; most of these took place in nightclubs (cabarets) with strippers (96 percent), with foreign home workers (73 percent), in hotels (64 percent), in factories (38 percent), in shops and offices (28 percent), and at schools and colleges (17 percent).

B. Prostitution

There has not been any systematic study conducted on the rather large population of prostitutes in Cyprus. Apart from the local indigenous prostitutes, there is a growing group of foreign artists who have been specially imported by cabaret and nightclub owners for "entertainment" in their clubs. These girls, from the Philippines, Russia, Bulgaria, and India, are given work-permits and visas by the Cypriot government to work as dancers in these clubs. It is estimated that there are over a thousand foreign girls working on the island, plus an unknown number of Cypriot women. The latter are probably dwindling because of the growing number of foreign imports who are favored by the Cypriot males who frequent such clubs. These foreign girls are not officially registered to work as prostitutes, but it is often recognized by the authorities that this happens. These girls are monitored for sexually transmitted diseases on a regular basis by the authorities.

In the last few years, there have been cases where the owners of these clubs have been convicted of coercing these women to have sex with customers against their will. These cases are usually reported because of some dispute over pay for services rendered between the women and their boss. Most of these cabarets are frequented by Cypriot businessmen in groups who are out for a laugh and a bit of fun with their friends; most are married.

C. Pornography and Erotica

Pornography and all types of erotica are freely available in Cyprus to those who want it. Before the ban on video piracy which the government implemented about two years ago, there were literally hundreds of video shops where anyone of reasonable age could go and ask for a porno tape "behind-the-counter." These tapes cover the whole gamut of sexual behavior, from straight heterosexual sex, to anal and oral sex, homosexuality, bestiality, sadomasochism, fisting, and all the other sexual behaviors in between. Cypriots can rent their usual thrillers or soap movies on a regular basis, and while in the video shop, pick up a porno movie to watch while the children are in bed. Many of these tapes were subsequently copied and are still circulating in many households in Cyprus, often entertaining the children as well who happen to find their hidden location while the parents are at work.

There were large groups of Cypriots who out of sheer curiosity and fascination were requesting harder and harder varieties of porn that consisted of acrotomophilia, anaclitism, anolingus, bestiality, bondage, coprophilia, fisting, klismaphilia, and much more. This surfaced about twelve years ago when the author had the opportunity to interview one of the main suppliers of pornographic material on the island. He mentioned that the more "perverse" or "deviant" the sex he could obtain on video, the greater his business!

D. Sexual Crimes

Cyprus, being a small and relatively conservative community, is not expected to have a large number of sexual crimes. In fact, until quite recently, the number of sexual crimes committed each year was negligible (see Table 15). Judging from media articles and news coverage for 1999, it appears that these offenses are on the increase, and it will be interesting to see future statistics.

9. Contraception, Abortion, and Population Planning
FAMILY PLANNING ASSOCIATION OF CYPRUS*

A. Contraception

In the main author's clinical sample, 33 percent reported using the condom, and 21 percent used coitus interruptus. The IUD ranked third at 7.3 percent, followed by 6.7 percent for the contraceptive pill. Very few Cypriot women use the diaphragm, cervical cap, or contraceptive foam—only 0.1 percent for each. Cypriot women tend to have concerns about placing objects in their vagina, not necessarily because they may injure themselves, but because there is a repulsion to placing items in the vagina. This seems to be a cultural attitude reported in the sexual histories taken by the author.

*Note: The editor is grateful for information supplied for this section by the staff at the Family Planning Association of Cyprus.

Table 15

Sex Crimes Reported in 1995, 1996, and 1997

Type of Crime	1995	1996	1997
Rape	8	7	10
Kidnapping	2	5	4
Seduction of a female (age 13 to 16)	6	5	4
Solicitation	N.A.	12	17
Indecent assault against a female	24	14	18
Indecent assault against a male	2	3	4
Pimping	3	11	15
Indecent offense	32	20	24
Indecent exposure ("unethical projection")	8	4	2

"Touching" the vulva seems to be out-of-bounds for most Cypriot women, and this is reflected in the relatively low frequency of women who masturbate. The IUD is slightly more acceptable because this is placed by the gynecologist and does not entail self-insertion. One-in-five survey subjects reported using no contraceptive, and 3.8 percent reported sterility. (See Section 5B, Interpersonal Heterosexual Behaviors, Adolescents.)

In the 1990 survey of priests conducted by the main author, the priests were presented with a case for pastoral counseling involving:

> a Christian couple with five children. The husband is 35 years old and the wife 30. Only the husband is working and earning a small income, which provides the essentials for the family. Under the circumstances, the couple has decided to use artificial contraceptives (that do not allow fertilisation to take place), and go to a priest to discuss the matter. (Georgiou, 1990)

The priests responded as follows:

- all contraceptive methods are disallowed (39.2%)
- the couple should sexually abstain (25.4%)
- contraceptives are allowed in exceptional circumstances (8.5%)
- contraceptives are freely allowed (6.2%)
- the couple should make love during the wife's infertile days (1.5%)
- something else (9.2%)

Older (over 65) and less-educated priests (junior school with additional training in the Theological School of the Cypriot Archbishopric) tended to be more against the use of contraception than the younger, more-educated priests ($p = 0.0002$).

The thematic analysis of the subjective responses included seventeen mutually exclusive general categories, some of which are presented below:

- the Orthodox Church considers the use a contraceptive sinful, and therefore does not allow it (37.9%)
- the couple should coitally abstain during the fertile days (25.8%)
- God gave the command to multiply and fill the earth, which means that we should have as many children as possible (18.2%)
- the couple should humbly accept as many children as God sends them (16.7%)
- the idea would be to completely abstain from sexual intercourse, unless one wants to procreate (12.9%)
- there are many large families of eight to ten children who are healthy and content, so why not others? (8.3%)
- contraception is allowed in exceptional circumstances (7.6%)
- we should believe in God's Providence; He will help us raise our families if we have faith (6.8%)
- God cares for all the animals of the earth, so why would he not care for his people (6.1%)
- the state should provide assistance to large families (4.5%)
- procreation should not be the only goal in marriage (4.5%)
- contraception is freely allowed to be used by all (3.0%)
- the couple should avoid intercourse during the second to the eighth day of the menstrual cycle which are the fertile days [In this self-generated response the priests revealed their own misinformation about the menstrual cycle, because days 2-8 are not the fertile days (Georgiou)]. (2.3%)
- it is better to use contraception than to have an abortion (2.3%)

B. Abortion

Perhaps the fact that over half of the main author's sample do not use adequate contraception should lead us to the conclusion that many Cypriots have abortions or have numerous children. The latter is not the case, and epidemiological statistics for abortion are unavailable. Using the same clinical sample of 840 patients (see Section 12, Sexual Dysfunctions, Counseling, and Therapies), 21.5 percent said they had had an abortion. Examining the statistics from the unpublished Cyprus Family Planning Association study (see Section 9A, Contraception), 20 percent of the total sample of 496 women reported having at least one abortion during the years 1995 to 1997, with 19 percent having at least one from 1985 to 1987. Interestingly, in the 1980s, 25 percent of these women were single, 18 percent were engaged, and 19 percent were married, whereas in the 1990s, only 3 percent were single, with more married women (27 percent) having abortions than before. It is certainly difficult to be certain about precise figures, but a figure of approximately 20 percent of the female population during any one year would be a fair estimate of the incidence of abortion. In the same study, about 7 percent of women had two abortions between the years 1995 to 1997, compared to 11 percent of women who had two between 1985 and

1987. (See also Sociolegal Status of Males and Females, Children and Adults, in Section 1.A.)

It is known that there are about 10,000 births per year, and it has been estimated that there are probably 12,000 to 13,000 abortions yearly. It appears that many Cypriots use abortion as a method of contraception after all else fails. The majority of gynecologists on the island will freely give abortion upon demand, due to a loop-hole in the law amended after the 1974 invasion of Cyprus by the Turks, allowing abortions for women who had been raped by Turkish troops or based on medical grounds with the permission of two medical doctors. This law still exists and allows gynecologists to practice abortion upon demand. There are only two gynecologists on the island whom the author knows that do not perform abortions for ethical and religious reasons.

In the main author's 1990 survey, Greek Orthodox priests were presented with the following situation involving abortion:

> A Christian woman is pregnant with her fourth child, even though her doctor warned her not to have another child as she would be endangering her health. Presently three doctors have told her that if she continues the pregnancy there is a chance that she would die. She has been advised, therefore, to have an abortion. As she is a woman who believes in God, she approaches a priest for advice. (Georgiou, 1990)

The responses selected by the priests were as follows:

- she should listen to the doctors and have the abortion (17.7%)
- she should not have the abortion under any circumstances (60.0%)
- something else (19.3%)

An additional 3.1 percent of the total sample of 130 priests avoided the question.

A thematic analysis of the subjective and "something else" responses produced fourteen mutually exclusive general categories, some of which are examined below:

- she should have complete faith in God (43.2%)
- the Orthodox Church believes that abortion is an act of murder and is therefore a cardinal sin (25.0%)
- she should pray and ask for God's help and make up her own mind (16.7%)
- if the diagnosis is certain, then she should have the abortion so she will not leave her children and husband to suffer alone (15.2%)
- I've seen similar cases where the woman and child had both survived (11.4%)
- we must bear in mind that there are many cases where doctors have been proven wrong (10.6%)

- she should have the baby; I am certain that God will help her and the baby survive (9.1%)
- God is the wisest scientist (6.8%)
- the woman should follow the doctors' orders and she will be forgiven (5.3%)
- it is important not to listen to the doctors in cases like this (3.8%)
- if she presents a letter from her doctor to the Spiritual Father with the facts of the case, then he will allow her to proceed with the abortion (2.3%)
- she should die for the love of her child (1.5%)
- she should have the abortion, and she will be given a heavy penance (1.5%)
- the priest cannot take responsibility for any abortion (0.8%)

C. Population Programs

The total population of Cyprus was estimated at 746,100 at the end of 1997, compared with 741,000 in 1996, having increased by 0.7 percent. In 1997, the number of births in the Government-controlled areas (the Greek Cypriot side) declined from 9,638 in 1996 to 9,275 in 1997, giving a crude birthrate of 14.2 per thousand in 1997 compared to 14.9 in 1996. Both the number of births and the crude birthrate have followed a declining trend in recent years. The total fertility rate (TFR), which describes reproductive behavior unaffected by changes in the age of the population, is 2.3, slightly above replacement level but declining.

Cyprus has one of the lowest rates of extramarital births in Europe, and fertility is almost exclusively marital fertility. In 1997, only 146 children were born out of wedlock constituting a mere 1.6 percent of the total number of births. The mean age of women at the birth of their first child was 25.8 years old, while the mean age at birth irrespective of the older child was 28 years old in 1997. Women in rural areas tend to start younger, compared to urban areas: 24.8 years and 26.3 years, respectively.

At the Special Session of the United Nations on Population and Development in New York, June 30 to July 2, 1999, the Cyprus Delegation reported that:

> Cyprus is undergoing demographic changes worth mentioning. Fertility is falling below replacement level and shows no sign of recovery. Concurrently, mortality is on the decline and currently is at 7.9 deaths per 1000 population. Also, infant mortality is 8.0 per 1000 live births, while maternal mortality is practically zero. Moreover, life expectancy is seventy-five years for males and eighty years for females. These are indications that Cyprus is going through a period of nearly stagnant population growth, 1.0 percent per year in the last five years, a phenomenon of population aging. Although, aging does not mean an old

population, still my Government is worried about the problems that come in its way and in particular the social and economic implications.

Indeed, the government certainly wants to increase the declining population of 600,000 Cypriots on the island, and is giving incentives to this effect. All parents who have four or more children, so-called "multi-sibling" families, receive monetary and social incentives. For example, each child is entitled to a child benefit allowance of about $60.00 per child per month, and mothers receive a "mother's allowance." Also, all health expenses are paid by the government, as well as subsidies on school fees, books, entrance to museums, theatres, low-interest loans for building or repair of existing home, reduction in months spent doing National Service, tax incentives, and others. There is even discussion in parliament at present to offer a duty-free car of choice, which is a huge incentive for most families, as car duties can exceed 100 percent of the value of the car.

> In Cyprus, reproductive health is integrated into the primary health care system, and is provided free of charge by public sector institutions and at affordable rates by the private sector. The total expenditure dedicated to health purposes, from all sources, is on the order of 6 percent of GDP, or 16 percent of all public expenditure. This compares very favorably with most developed countries.
>
> In Cyprus family planning issues are entrusted to specialist doctors in the private sector, but more so to an NGO subsidized mainly by Government. The services provided are not confined within the narrow meaning of population control but also include access to information relating to sexual and reproductive rights, sexual education, including health issues, reproductive choice and gender equality; it also provides counseling on sexual relations and more recently on the prevention of HIV/AIDS. (United Nations Cyprus Delegation, June 30–July 2, 1999)

Some information regarding the work of the Cyprus Family Planning Association (CFPA) is provided in a recent unpublished study. The data were obtained retrospectively by examining 495 patient records of visits to the CFPA between 1985 and 1997. Most of the women visiting the CFPA were married between the ages of 21 and 41. The most commonly requested services were for birth control and cytology tests. The four major services that women requested were Pap tests, IUD insertions, breast examinations, and prescriptions for the contraceptive pill.

10. Sexually Transmitted Diseases

There are no systematic surveys that have been conducted regarding sexually transmitted diseases, as most of the population with STDs saw private practitioners who do not need to report these statistics. There are, however, some official statistics, which are based mainly on the monthly returns from the dermatology clinics of the four Government general hospitals. Although rare, certain cases may be reported by gynecologists, urologists, and possibly general practitioners in the private sector. The diseases recorded are those that are considered notifiable and reported to the World Health Organization (see Table 16). The sharp increase in AIDS cases in 1997 is because of the adoption of a new case definition by the United States Centers for Disease Control in 1993. A workshop on epidemic preparedness was held in November 1999, during which the list of notifiable diseases was revised to include other STDs such as chlamydia.

Table 16

Summary Statistics for STDs from 1995 to 1998 and for AIDS from 1994 to June 1999

STDs	1994	1995	1996	1997	1998	1999
Syphilis		23	32	32	33	
Gonococcal urethritis		56	48	61	42	
Non-gonococcal urethritis		220	206	166	114	
Herpes genitalis		137	118	122	118	
Genital warts		140	81	77	97	
AIDS	40	49	57	85	91	97

From the KABP Survey on AIDS of 3,176 schoolchildren examining their knowledge, attitudes, beliefs, and practices related to AIDS, there were a few questions regarding STDs that would be worthy of note (Georgiou & Veresies, 1990, 1991).

Twelve questions were designed to tap respondents' knowledge about syphilis, gonorrhea, chlamydia, and genital herpes:

- Close to half the teenagers surveyed had heard something about syphilis: 1,498 (844 boys and 654 girls, or 47.2 percent)
- Had heard something about herpes: 1,432 (700 boys v, 732 girls, or 45.2 percent)
- Had heard something about gonorrhea: 965 (517 boys v. 448 girls, or 30.4 percent)
- Only 236 (150 boys v. 86 girls, or 7.4 percent) had heard of chlamydia, probably because it is not an STD that is often portrayed through the Cypriot media.

Overall, it appears that the Cypriot school adolescents are relatively ignorant regarding STDs compared to their American, Canadian, and English counterparts. This relative ignorance, probably related to the fact that there is no formal sex or health education in schools, needs to be addressed.

Asked more specific questions regarding STDs, the great majority of students were "uncertain." Overall, it appears that less than 20 to 25 percent of the students have correct knowledge regarding ways of transmission, therapy, prevention, and asymptomatic status of STDs. Perhaps the most striking finding is the fact that only about 25 percent of the students were aware that condoms can protect against gonorrhea. The overwhelming majority (63.1 percent) were uncertain about the prophylactic use of condoms. There was also high uncertainty regarding syphilis transmission from an asymptomatic person (57.8 percent), and whether a person who has caught syphilis once can catch it again (64.3 percent uncertain, with 15 percent incorrect). It is clear that these issues need to be urgently addressed in any program on human sexuality.

11. HIV/AIDS

LAURA PAPANTONIOU*

A. Introduction

In Cyprus, as in most countries, the main mode of transmission of HIV is sexual intercourse, both hetero- and homosexual. Consequently, our efforts are mainly focused on the first principle, i.e., prevention of sexual transmission of HIV. Implementation of the National AIDS Programme (NAP) is included in the areas of activities described below.

Epidemiological Surveillance

The figures below are current to December 1, 2000, with certain figures to the end of December 2000. *N* is the cumulative total of tests since 1986. Sources of cases have been recorded according to the latest guidelines disseminated by the World Health Organization. The *N* is very low for certain categories, Cypriot prostitutes, IV-drug users, non-IV-drug users, and patients with STDs, because many of these persons go untested. Only registered prostitutes can be regularly tested as a group; patients with STDs visit a large variety of centers, such as private dermatologists and gynecologists; and drug abusers, though tested, are not reported regularly to our services. However, individuals in these categories who do test positive will very likely be reported to our services, since the country is small and there

Note. The following data for HIV/AIDS, from the Ministry of Health, National AIDS Programme (NAP), under the auspices of the World Health Organization, covers the period between the first reported AIDS case in 1986 and 31 August 1999. Laura Papantoniou, M.D., National AIDS Programme Manager, prepared this section, after collating the information provided by several contributors working in her specialty.

is only one center, the Ministry of Health, that collects this data. Sooner or later these people will need counseling, treatment, and socioeconomic support, so they will come to us. The only problem is that, once they are reported, it is impossible to relate them to a definite source population and calculate rates. All we can do in this case is to include them in the pool of seropositives and calculate them as part of the percent distribution of the total. The same is true for the homosexual community, where no regular testing is done at all.

It is a fact that the rate of HIV infection in Cyprus is truly very low at present (0.1%, which is about one tenth of the world mean rate), and this has been confirmed by Geneva Headquarters where our available data have been sent and evaluated. The very low rates among National Guard personnel, aged 17 to 19, is not surprising, because the mean age at diagnosis for Cypriots is around 32, which situates the probable mean age of infection at around age 22 to 25. Of course there is no complacency about this, and we are now planning to conduct sentinel surveillance at the time of exit, after the National Guard personnel have spent 26 months in the service. Nor is there complacency about the fact that the rates among the general population are, for the time being, low, because we know that risk factors exist, should be evaluated, and appropriate remedies accordingly taken. In early 2001, we are conducting a behavioral survey among the general population, and hope soon to be able to conduct more surveys among school youth and among specific groups of the population.

The rate among foreign workers and students appears higher that the actual rate, because a large number are tested in the private sector and only positive cases are reported, while the N in this case includes only the total number tested in the government service. We are cooperating with the Aliens Department to obtain the figures of all those who are tested each year, since 1997, when the data were entered in the computer. This will allow us to calculate the true rates.

Monthly epidemiological reporting is based on data collected from the sources shown in Table 17.

Sentinel Surveillance

Unlinked anonymous epidemiological sentinel surveillance for HIV is being done among STD patients of the Dermatology Clinic of Nicosia General Hospital. This group and site were chosen as being an area of high risk. There have been no positive results among the approximately 1,000 samples tested in this group since the surveillance started in 1992. In the event of a positive result, sentinel surveillance will be resumed among the group of people undergoing the premarital testing for thalassemia, considered to be a low-risk group, where sentinel was already conducted in 1992, with no positive results.

Table 17

Sources of HIV Testing in Cyprus

Source	Rate*	N
Contacts of HIV-infected people	2.52	714
Suspected AIDS patients	80.22	91
Routine diagnostic testing of in-patients in the public and the private sector	0.03	91,320
Voluntary testing in the government services	0.16	64,324
Routine testing of pregnant women in the public sector and partly the private sector	0.003	37,536
Foreign workers and foreign students	0.32	20,815
Foreign bar girls	0.06	62,137
Blood recipients**	0.08	13,957
Routine testing of STD patients of Government dermatology clinics—sentinel surveillance	0.0	1,394
Universal screening of blood donors	0.003	458,288
Registered Cypriot prostitutes	0.0	1,078
Child from HIV+ mother***	25.0	
Intravenous drug users	0.0	36
Non-intravenous drug users	0.0	48
Prisoners	0.06	6,309
National Guard (recruits, sentinel surveillance, 1998)	0.0	3,423
Premarital testing group for thalassemia****	0.0	307

*Rate of infection per 100 persons tested.

**Multi-transfused only are recorded. All known cases were infected abroad before 1997.

***Based on 4 known cases of HIV+ pregnant women.

****1992-1993 sentinel surveillance; we are contemplating resuming sentinel surveillance.

A protocol for sentinel surveillance among army recruits aged 17 to 19 has been initiated in cooperation with an external researcher. To date, 1,600 tests have been conducted with no positive results.

B. Incidence, Patterns, and Trends in HIV Infections

Introduction

The number of cases recorded since 1986 until August 1999 has reached 319, consisting of 190 (59.6%) Cypriots and 129 (40.4%) foreigners. These numbers correspond to rates of 0.029 per 100 populations of all ages (190 cases in Cypriots per 663,300 population—1998) and 0.052 per 100-population aged 15 to 50 (174 cases per 334,000 population). It is estimated that the true numbers are greater and that, as in any other country, there exist a number of cases that have not yet been diagnosed. This is due mainly to the long asymptomatic period during which the HIV-positive status may be unknown even to the HIV-infected persons themselves, so that many cases are not reported to the relevant services.

The number of AIDS cases may be a more reliable index. Ninety-seven adult AIDS cases (83 men and 14 women) were reported. There are no AIDS cases in children under age 15. Forty-six people have died from AIDS since 1986.

New Cases by Year

A total of 354 cases of HIV infection were reported by the end of 2000 (213 Cypriots and 141 foreigners). The number of AIDS cases by end of fourth quarter of 2000 (included in the 354 seropositives) is 125. The sex ratio for Cypriots is 6 males to 1 female. On average, 23 cases have been recorded each year between 1986 and 2000, 14 Cypriots and 9 foreigners. The numbers of new cases by year are as follows:

Up to 1986:	11	1991:	22	1996:	28
1987:	17	1992:	24	1997:	27
1988:	16	1993:	24	1998:	19
1989:	24	1994:	39	1999:	23
1990:	16	1995:	35	2000:	29

Age and Sex Distribution

Out of the 190 Cypriot seropositives, 163 (86.0 percent) are men and 27 (14.0 percent) are women. The sex ratio has remained stable at six men for one woman. Almost 90 percent of all cases are between 20 and 40. The mean age at diagnosis is 32.7 years for both men and women. Given the long asymptomatic period, it may be conjectured that infection takes place between 20 and 25 years old, which is slightly advanced by international standards.

Distribution by Transmission Category

Almost 90 percent of all infections are reported to have been acquired through sexual intercourse. Heterosexual transmission accounts for 44 percent of all cases and homo-/bisexual transmission for 45 percent.

All 8 cases of transmission through blood and its products took place before 1987. Almost all cases after 1986 were infected through sexual intercourse, with the exception of one case of perinatal transmission and five through the use of intravenous drugs.

Based on reported cases only, the rate of infection per 100 population of Cypriots living in Cyprus is 0.03, but this differs by district. The Limassol district of Cyprus has the highest rate at 0.04, followed by the Famagusta district with 0.03, the Nicosia and the Larnaca district with 0.02 and the Paphos district with 0.01.

As noted earlier, a drop in the number of new cases was recorded in the years 1995 to 1998. It is noted that today's rates in new cases per year reflect the trends in transmission rates that existed five to ten years ago, given the long asymptomatic period of the HIV infection. For this reason, current cases cannot provide an adequate picture concerning today's trends and need to be complemented by special surveys on knowledge, attitudes, and behaviors among the sexually active population. Anonymous epidemiological surveys are currently being carried out. The results of these surveys will serve for the formulation of our policy for the control of the epidemic.

C. Availability of Treatment, Prevention Programs, and Government Policies

Health Education

Based on the international experience that knowledge does not necessarily lead to behavior change, a new orientation is now being promoted, with the development of peer education projects in schools. Despite the fact that the first attempts were highly encouraging and successful, peer education has not yet been applied on a routine basis in schools because of a shortage of staff and time constraints. Most other health education activities are also focusing on the area of behavior change in youth and other sections of the population. Such activities are information kiosks, special events, lectures, messages and programs using mass media, youth meetings, and others.

It should be noted that health education is facilitated by the fact that sex issues and the subject of condom use may be easily addressed in Cyprus because of the high level of knowledge and sensitization among the population. Opposition from certain society leaders, mainly the Church, is hampering full implementation of effective health education. New material is being constantly developed, such as brochures, booklets, posters, TV spots, videos, and various advertising items (key rings, T-shirts, etc) as a necessary complement to these activities.

Health education focuses mainly on sexual behavior, but all other important issues, i.e., compassion and avoidance of discrimination, safe blood donation, dangers of drugs and other habit-forming substances, and the hazards of perinatal transmission, are addressed as well.

Clinical Care

Before 1992, AIDS cases were treated in medical wards of hospitals. Between 1992 and 1996, clinical care for AIDS patients had been delivered through the AIDS Ward in Nicosia General Hospital. A new ward was created in 1996, in Larnaca General Hospital, to meet added needs, due to the increase in the number of patients followed by our services and to the introduction of new methodologies for the management of HIV infection. Following two decisions of the Council of Ministers, treatment of cancers and opportunistic infections, and triple antiretroviral therapy are offered free of charge to all HIV-infected Cypriots who satisfy the necessary clinical criteria. With the introduction of the new antiretroviral therapy, new criteria have been adopted by the U.S. Centers for Disease Control for the clinical coding of cases.

The cost of HIV/AIDS treatment is as follows: Antiretroviral treatment (delivery statistics) (1 Cypriot pound (£ CYP) is approximately US$2): 1996, £76,097; 1997, £255,483; 1998, £324,591; 1999, £368,376; and 2000 (through October 5): £122,838. The cost of other components of care are:

1. General treatment costs involving nursing, counseling, laboratory diagnosis and monitoring (including CD4 count and viral load), treatment for opportunistic conditions, and hospitalization costs. The costs for this component of care have not yet been evaluated.
2. Assistance from the Social Welfare Department, according to general regulations applying to the general population. Social workers make home visits for social and financial support.
3. Assistance from the AIDS Fund: Christmas bonus, ranging from £400 CYP to £2,000 CYP.
4. Assistance from non-governmental organizations, in close co-operation with the AIDS Program (e.g., employment of a psychologist for AIDS Clinic needs, financial assistance in urgent cases, and insurance for the education needs and tuition fees of children of HIV-infected people).

Financing is provided as follows:

1. The health care expenses are all covered by the Ordinary Budget of the Republic.
2. The expenses for the support of people with HIV and AIDS are covered in part by the AIDS Fund and in part by the Social Welfare Department and through voluntary activities, as mentioned above.
3. The education campaigns and research activities are undertaken in part by the regular personnel of the Ministry of Health and in part in collaboration with non-governmental organizations. Health education material (including the purchase of condoms) and research activities are financed by the AIDS Fund, the Development Budget, and the Publications Program of the Public Health Information Office.

Counseling and Support Services

All individuals undergoing testing for HIV receive pre- and post-test counseling at the counseling service of Archbishop Makarios III Hospital in Nicosia. HIV-infected individuals and their families are under the constant care and guidance of the counseling service, which works in close cooperation with the Welfare Services of the Ministry of Labor. Increasing workload is dictating the need for the expansion and decentralization of these services to all towns in Cyprus.

Intersectoral Collaboration

The National AIDS Committee (NAC), which is composed of relevant government services and non-governmental and other organizations implementing the NAP. The reorganization of the NAC is currently under study, aiming to adapt available services to the new demands of the NAP.

In the general frame of the latest internationally accepted principles, intersectoral collaboration, and in particular the role of NGOs, is receiving increasing consideration, and program activities are being rescheduled to meet these prerequisites. The main projects developed with the NGOs concern peer education and social support. More resources are needed for the full development of this intersectoral cooperation.

Cooperation with Centers Abroad

Cyprus belongs to the East Mediterranean Regional Office of the World Health Organization. The Ministry of Health is also promoting the development of cooperation with other countries in Europe, in particular, in view of our impending entry into the European Union.

Program Evaluation

Program evaluation is an integral part of the NAP, according to WHO guidelines. Prevention indicators and targets included in our program are based on the WHO prevention indicators and targets.

Indicators and targets were evaluated in 1997 in youth through the KABP surveys (Georgiou & Veresies, 1990, 1991), using a self-administered questionnaire in private schools. The evaluation process in public schools has not yet been initiated, despite efforts to overcome resistance from the Church, who consider that such an approach would increase the risk of promiscuity among young people.

New methodologies are currently being considered for the evaluation of the remaining indicators and targets included in the program and of other related issues in target populations other than youth, including the adult male population and the personnel responsible for delivering STD care. In addition, it should be noted that it is very difficult to have access and conduct evaluation surveys (as well as health education) in the homosexual, drug-user, and middle-aged-male-with-risky-behavior target populations. Efforts are being made to overcome these difficulties, through cooperation with the Gay Liberation Movement of Cyprus and with the Centre for Drug Education and Treatment of Drug Addicted Persons (with little or no response from the latter), and by approaching individuals in various contexts, e.g., where routine testing is conducted for other reasons.

Conclusions

In the light of the above epidemiological and general information, it is evident that the HIV/AIDS situation in Cyprus is comparable to that in other

Western countries. Based on current epidemiological evidence, health education activities are focused mainly on prevention of transmission of HIV through sexual intercourse, with the main emphasis on abstinence, delayed sex, mutual faithfulness, and the correct use of condoms. Peer education in schools and in youth NGOs is being promoted, though at present it has only been implemented on a pilot basis. Program evaluation is planned according to WHO guidelines and constitutes an integral part of the NAP, but has not been implemented to a satisfactory degree to date.

12. Sexual Dysfunctions, Counseling, and Therapies

A. The General Situation

There is scant information on sexual dysfunctions and therapies in Cyprus, mainly because of the lack of qualified, professional therapists who can systematically collect such data. As of 1999, the main author was still the only professionally qualified sexologist with doctoral training on the island. There were a few psychologists who attempted sex therapy using psychoanalytic techniques with very poor results. There were also a number of medically qualified dermatologists, STD specialists, and urologists who advertised as "sexologist," but are not qualified in any form of sex therapy and have no specific training in this field. Their treatments included mostly drugs and papaverine and prostaglandin penile injections for both erectile problems and premature ejaculation, regardless of etiology. In 1999, Viagra was granted an import license, and no doubt this will be used widely. The situation is quite sad really, as many patients fall victim to costly medical treatments without seeing any benefit.

Unfortunately, at present, Cypriot law does not regulate the training, certification, or licensing of sex counselors or therapists. Anyone can advertise freely on their signs whatever they wish, on the condition that they do not use the adjective "specialist." So "dermatologist-sexologist" is a legal sign, but "dermatologist-specialist sexologist" would be illegal if the individual does not have qualifications and clinical training in sexology. Few Cypriots are aware of this distinction and its inevitable consequences for the delivery of effective health care in this specialized area.

B. Some Limited Observations

The Population and Its Problems

The following observations have been culled from 840 clinical cases of Cypriots with sexual dysfunctions who sought treatment at the editor's Natural Therapy Centre in Larnaca between 1993 and 1996. Some additional insights came from a survey of sexual knowledge, attitudes, beliefs, and practices of 3,176 schoolchildren aged 14 to 18 years old conducted under the auspices of the World Health Organization (Georgiou et al.,

1990), a study of the sexual attitudes of Greek Orthodox priests (Georgiou, 1990), a 1995 book on the treatment of premature ejaculation by the editor, and *Homosexuality*, a book written in 1982 by the PanCyprian Society of Psychic Health after a seminar on homosexuality.

A quarter of the editor's clinical population were age 18 to 25, 40 percent between ages 26 and 35, 21 percent from age 36 to 45, 9 percent ages 46 to 55, 4 percent between the ages of 56 to 65, and the remaining one percent 66 and older. One percent of the sample had not completed elementary school, 12 percent had attended junior high school but not graduated, 12 percent had attended school to age 15, 40 percent had completed high school, and about 20 percent were university graduates. Two thirds of the subjects were married, 12 percent engaged, 2 percent separated, 1.5 percent divorced, 1 percent widowed, and 18 percent single. Some of the 840 attending were partnered, but individual histories were taken, and are presented here as such. The sample is quite representative of the spread of occupations on the island, and covers professionals (13 percent), technical—plumbers, electricians, etc. (9 percent), business people (20 percent), clerical (12 percent), civil servants (10 percent), housewife (6 percent), agricultural (11 percent), unskilled (9 percent), students (3 percent), unemployed (1.5 percent), waiters and hotel workers (5 percent), and others (4 percent). All clients completed a sexual history questionnaire covering 75 topics or questions modeled on Wardell Pomeroy et al.'s *Taking a Sex History* (1982).

In terms of the whole sample of 840 patients, the most common problem was secondary erectile dysfunction (30 percent), with an additional 2 percent primary erectile dysfunction. Other male dysfunctions included premature ejaculation (24 percent), retarded ejaculation (2 percent), and male sexual desire disorder (5 percent). Secondary inhibited orgasm (7 percent) was the most common female complaint, with an additional 3 percent presenting with primary inhibited orgasm—the total of female inhibited orgasm: 11 percent. Other female dysfunctions included vaginismus/coital phobia (11 percent) and female sexual desire disorder (6.5 percent). One percent presented with problem paraphilias, mostly "flashing."

Premature Ejaculation

Males suffering from premature ejaculation commonly postpone treatment for years, waiting until the stress and anxiety of the chronic situation makes the problem a lot worse and their marriage is threatened. Only 15 percent of premature ejaculators seek help within three years of onset. 37 percent wait four to ten years, 31 percent wait eleven to twenty years, and four percent wait more than twenty years. In comparison, men with erectile dysfunction are much quicker to seek help, probably because their problem directly threatens their male ego. Ninety-two percent of impotent men sought help within three years of onset, 4 percent within four to ten years, and 4 percent in eleven to twenty years. A strong majority of premature ejaculators recall ejaculating quickly from their early masturbatory experiences.

This appears to support Helen Singer Kaplan's (1983) theory of the ejaculatory reflex being conditioned to ejaculate early from the initial sexual experiences. Very few of the males recalled otherwise. Most of the males who came for treatment for premature ejaculation had the problem for many years, on average about ten years, but only decided to seek help when additional stress factors had exacerbated the problems to such a degree that many were ejaculating before intromission. Certainly the majority where finishing in ten to twenty seconds, to the woman's growing frustration. At this point, additional coercion from the wife resulted the men seeking help.

Erectile Problems

Many cases of erectile problems began with an extramarital partner, and not with the wife or major partner. This may be because of the tremendous performance anxiety that is again related to the huge Mediterranean masculine ego to "conquer" the woman and show her that one is a "man." I have also thought that it may have been because of the anxiety related to the prickling of consciences, but having spoken at length to many of these men, this does not appear to be the case. Indeed, many of them had come to me not so much to improve their relationship with their wives, but to help them "get it up" so that they could "prove" their manhood with their girlfriends. Many actually expressed satisfaction in the wish to "do it just once" with the girlfriend, and that would be enough! The shame, disappointment, anguish, and bruised ego was very apparent in many of these men. The vast majority of them had no sexual or relationship problems with the spouse—their motivation in pursuing an extramarital partner was purely to satisfy their ego, and not much else.

In addition to these psychological problems, I have found causes related to dietary stresses and abuses, smoking, nutritional deficiencies, sub-clinical hormonal imbalances, sub-clinical hypothyroidism, reactive hypoglycemia, toxic metal status, systemic toxemia, and others. These causes I would consider as "organic," but not in the traditional classical medical view of organic. There may not be any obvious pathology that can be measured on blood tests, doppler, or morphological changes, but there is a continuum of health and disease, with a lot of gray areas in between. Many of these men have malfunctioning organs and tissues, which inevitably will affect penile functioning, unless one holds the view that the penis has it's own will and personality and is totally independent of other bodily functions. Cognitive-behavioral sex theory is often quite effective in treating an erectile problem that is strictly psychogenic in etiology, but compound a psychological factor with smoking two packs of cigarettes a day, eating fast foods full of empty calories and fats, working a twelve- to eighteen-hour day, drinking alcohol regularly to "destress," being anxious and insecure about the future, etc., as many Cypriot males do, and it is obvious that something more than traditional cognitive-behavioral sex therapy may be indicated, including nutritional and homeopathic remedies.

Vaginismus

A clinical incidence of 11 percent for vaginal spasms in Cypriot women is much higher that reported in other countries, where the reported incidence ranges between one and four percent. The origin of this difference, I believe, lies in the cultural dynamics, and specifically the sexual messages that both sexes receive while growing up in Cyprus. The male child get messages based around: "You are a male, so it is normal, acceptable, and a sign of your manhood to pursue and conquer females sexually," whereas the woman gets a very different message: "You are a female and must remain a virgin, as this has direct links with your honor, and that of your family—be careful as males are cunning and are only after one thing." Sixty-nine percent of the women in this clinical sample were virgins until they married, compared to only 9 percent of the men. The women had limited premarital experiences, and their sexual knowledge was obtained mainly from friends and media—with all the misconstrued ideas and prejudices that are inevitable from such sources, mixed with a high level of anxiety and neuroticism. A large majority of the vaginismic women reported dwelling on the fear of coitus starting when some friend or cousin shared her initial "painful" sexual experiences, saying that the pain was unbearable, and that they had hemorrhaged. Without exception, these women had high scores on the Spielberger Trait Anxiety Inventory (SPAI), averaging at least one or more standard deviations above the mean for their age group.

Dysorgasmia

There appears to be a problem with the statistics for dysorgasmia, which one would expect to be higher than the 10 percent reported in this limited clinical sample, particularly when 24 percent of the males have a chronic problem with premature ejaculation. Again, the answer may lie in cultural values and conditioning. Cypriot women are very reluctant to discuss their sexual lives with a complete stranger, even when that person is a competent professional in the sex field. Also, Cypriot women have been taught not to consider or make a fuss about the quality of their sexual pleasure, given that their male is performing like an *epividoras* (stud). Cypriot women tend to lament in silence, perhaps until things in the marriage get to such a point where frustrations can no longer be tethered. Other causes may include physical and mental fatigue from coping with home, work, and many children, an insensitive husband who is tender only in bed, limited sexual foreplay because of ignorance and inhibitions, marital discord, and certain "naturopathic" organic causes. Similarly, I believe the incidence of female sexual desire disorder, a scant 6.5 percent in my clinical sample, is not indicative of the actual incidence of female inhibited sexual desire in the general population. Cypriot women are not taught to expect much from their sexual relations, and so they suffer in silence. We simply do not see these people in clinical practice.

Male Coital Phobia

A recent development in this limited clinical sample has been a three- to four-fold increase over the past two or three years (compared with five years ago) in the incidence of males seeking help with unconsummated relationships owing to their own coital fears. I have no explanation for this fascinating phenomenon, which is certainly worthy of being researched.

The main author's clinical experience with over 10,000 patients in the last sixteen years in Cyprus suggests that the treatment of sexual problems in both sexes is getting more and more difficult. Modern Cypriots are more stressed and anxious, more concerned about finances, apprehensive about the future, concerned about personal safety, have less time for relaxation and leisure activities, are more affluent with all the consequences of bad eating and drinking leading to poor health, and more.

13. Research and Advanced Education

Certainly there is much research that needs to be done in the field of human sexuality on the island of Cyprus. Lack of funding for such research has left the island literally virginal territory for sexology.

The tertiary educational establishments on the island, and there are many, do not even have a single course geared to human sexuality. Perhaps the administrators and educators see it as unnecessary, or fear that it would take up additional space on a busy curriculum. Perhaps it is the inhibitions of the governing bodies to include such topics in the curriculum. Whatever the case, these topics do not exist, neither in the private institutions that award undergraduate and postgraduate degrees from external universities, nor in the one and only newly opened University of Cyprus. It goes without saying that there are no sexological journals and periodicals published in Cyprus, or indeed any national and regional sexological organizations. It is difficult to set these up with only one member!

Certainly the talent for research exists on the island. We have the second highest rate of university graduates per population ratio in the world, as well as the technology and infrastructure. We also have keen researchers who would love to participate in ongoing research. If someone will fund, research will progress.

References and Suggested Readings

Alastos, D. 1976. *Cyprus in history: A survey of five thousand years* (2nd ed.). London: Zenou.

Antoniou, C. 1992. *The revolution of Cypriot women in society and their increased participation in civil engineering.* Unpublished Master of Philosophy thesis. London: University of London.

Attalides, M. 1981. *Social changes and urbanization in Cyprus: A study of Nicosia.* Nicosia, Cyprus: Social Research Centre.

Argyrou, V. 1996. *Tradition and modernity in the Mediterranean.* Cambridge, UK: Cambridge University Press.

Balswick, J. 1973. *The Greek Cypriot family in a changing society.* Lanarca, Cyprus: Department of Social Welfare Services, Ministry of Labour and Social Insurance.

Berger, P., Berger, B., & Hansfried, K. 1973. *The homeless mind.* London: Penguin Books.

Campbell, J. K. 1964. *Honor, family and patronage: A study of institutions and moral values in a Greek mountain community.* New York: Oxford University Press.

Christodoulou, D. 1992. *Inside the Cyprus miracle.* Minneapolis, MN: University of Minnesota.

Charalambous, N., & Peristianis, N. 1998. Ethnic groups, space and identity. Unpublished paper presented at the Space Syntax Second International Symposium, Brazilia, Brazil.

Department of Statistics and Research, Ministry of Finance. 1998. *Demographic report 1997.* Lanarca: Printing Office, Republic of Cyprus.

Georgiou, G. J. 1990. *Sexual attitudes of Greek Orthodox priests in Cyprus.* Dissertation for the degree of Doctor of Philosophy in Human Sexuality. San Francisco: The Institute for Advanced Study of Human Sexuality.

Georgiou, G. J. 1992. Sexual attitudes of Greek Orthodox priests in Cyprus. *The Cyprus Review,* 4:2. Nicosia, Cyprus: Intercollege.

Georgiou, G. J. 1995. *Premature ejaculation* (in Greek). Athens: Hellenic Letters.

Georgiou, G. J., & Veresies, K. 1990. *AIDS knowledge, attitudes, beliefs, and practices (KABP) pilot study undertaken in Cyprus: Preliminary report.* Geneva: World Health Organization (WHO).

Georgiou, G. J., & Veresies, K. 1991. *AIDS knowledge, attitudes, beliefs, and practices (KABP) study of Cypriot schoolchildren in Cyprus.* Geneva: World Health Organization (WHO).

House, W. J. 1987. *Population and labour force growth and development.* Nicosia, Cyprus: Department of Statistics and Research, Ministry of Finance.

Intercollege, Research and Development Centre. 1996. *Youth and leisure time in Cyprus.* Nicosia, Cyprus: Intercollege.

Intercollege, Research and Development Centre. 1997. *Sexual harassment in the workplace in Cyprus.* Nicosia, Cyprus: Intercollege.

Kaplan, H. S. 1983. *The evaluation of sexual disorders.* New York: Brunner/Mazel.

Kinsey, A. C., et al. 1953. *Sexual behavior in the human female.* Philadelphia: Saunders.

Kolodny, R. C., Masters, W. H., & Johnson, V. E. 1979. *Textbook of sexual medicine.* Boston: Little, Brown and Company.

Loizos, P. 1975. Changes in property transfer among Greek Cypriot villages. *Man* [U.S.], *10:*503-523.

Mavrastas, C. 1992. The Greek-Cypriot economic ethos: A socio-cultural analysis. *The Cyprus Review,* 4:2. Nicosia, Cyprus: Intercollege.

Mavros, E. 1989. A critical review of economic development in Cyprus: 1960-1974. *The Cyprus Review,* 1:1. Nicosia, Cyprus: Intercollege.

Markides, K. E., Nikita, N., & Rangou, E. 1978. *Lysi: Social change in a Cypriot village.* Nicosia, Cyprus: Social Research Centre.

Mylona, L., et al. 1981. *I Kipria ghineka [Cypriot woman].* Nicosia, Cyprus: Author.

Pancyprian Association of Psychic Health. 1982. *Homosexuality.* Nicosia, Cyprus: Author.

Papapetrou, S., & Pendedeka, M. 1998. *The Cypriot family: The evolution of the institution through time: Trends of change.* Unpublished paper presented at the Annual Conference of the Cyprus Sociological Association.

Peristiany, J. G. 1965. Honour and shame in a Cypriot highland village. In: J. G. Peristiany, ed., *Honour and shame: The values of Mediterranean society.* London: Weidenfeld and Nicolson.

Persianis, P. 1998. *Istoria tis ekpedefsis koritsion stin Kipro* [*History of the education of girls in Cyprus*]. Nicosia, Cyprus: Author.

Pomeroy, W. B., Flax, C. C., & Wheeler, C. C. 1982. *Taking a sex history: Interviewing and recording.* New York: Free Press/Macmillan Publishing.

Pyrgos, M. 1995. *The Cypriot woman at a glance.* Nicosia, Cyprus: Author.

Schneider, J. 1971. Of vigilance and virgins: Honor, shame and access to resources in Mediterranean societies. *Ethnology, 1*:1-24.

Stavrou, S. 1992. Social changes and the position of women in Cyprus. *The Cyprus Review, 4*:2. Nicosia, Cyprus: Intercollege.

Stavrou, S. 1997. Cypriot women at work. *The Cyprus Review, 9*:2. Nicosia, Cyprus: Intercollege.

Surridge, B. J. 1930. *A survey of rural life in Cyprus.* Nicosia, Cyprus: Printing Office of the Government of Cyprus.

Vassiliadou, M. 1997. Herstory: The missing woman of Cyprus. *The Cyprus Review, 9*:1. Nicosia, Cyprus: Intercollege.

Yeshilada, B. 1989. Social progress and political development in the 'Turkish Republic of Northern Cyprus.' *The Cyprus Review, 1*:2. Nicosia, Cyprus: Intercollege.

Egypt
(*Jumhuriyah Misr al-Arabiyah*)
(The Arab Republic of Egypt)

Contents

Demographics and a Historical Perspective

A. Demographics

Egypt is located in the northeastern corner of Africa and the Sinai, a small Asian peninsula between the Middle East and northern Africa. Egypt's borders include a coastline of 1,523 miles (2,450 kilometers) facing the Mediterranean Sea on the north and the Red Sea on the east. Israel is on the northeast border of Egypt's Sinai Peninsula, between the Mediterranean and Red Seas. On the south is Sudan and on the west Libya. Egypt's 386,660 square miles (1,001,450 square kilometers) make it about one and a half times the size of the state of Texas. Almost all of Egypt is arid, desolate,

Communications: Bahira Sherif, Ph.D., Department of Individual and Family Studies, University of Delaware, Newark, DE 19716-3301 USA; Bahira.Sherif@mvs.udel.edu.

and barren, with hills and mountains in the east and along the Nile River. The Nile River and its fertile valley, where most Egyptians live, stretches 550 miles from the eastern Mediterranean Sea south into the Sudan. Three percent of the land is arable and two percent is devoted to permanent crops. Two percent of the land is irrigated.

Egypt's estimated population in 1999 was 66 million, with 36.1 percent of the population under age 15 years, 60 percent between ages 15 and 65, and 3.7 over age 65. Forty-five percent of Egyptians live in the cities, many in poverty and slums. Cairo has a population of 9.7 million and Alexandria (El-Iskandriyah) 3.6 million. Ethnically, 99 percent of Egyptians are of Eastern Hamitic stock or Bedouin (Berber). Ninety-four percent of Egyptians are Muslim, mostly Sunni, with the remaining six percent Coptic Christian and other religions. Arabic is the official language, although French and English are widely understood by the educated classes.

Average life expectancy (1999 estimate) was 60.1 for males and 64.1 for females. The birth rate in 1999 was 27 per 1,000 population, the death rate 8 per 1,000, and the infant mortality rate 69 per 1,000, for an annual natural increase of 1.89 percent. The 1995 Total Fertility Rate (TFR) was 3.4 children per fertile woman, giving Egypt a rank of 89 out of 227 nations. Five years of education are compulsory between ages 6 and 13. Literacy in 1995 was 50 percent. In 1994, Egypt had one hospital bed per 515 persons and, in 1996, one physician per 472 persons. The per capita gross domestic product in 1995 was $2,760 US.

B. A Brief Historical Perspective

Civilization and urban life was born around 5000 B.C.E. in the fertile valleys of the Nile, Indus, and Tigres/Euphrates Rivers. About 3200 B.C.E., King Menes established the first of many dynasties of pharaohs who gradually unified the country from the Nile Delta to Upper Egypt. The pharaohs produced a distinctive ancient civilization of great wealth and cultural brilliance, built on an economic base of serfdom, fertile soil, and annual flooding of the Nile Valley. The decline of ancient imperial power facilitated the conquest of Egypt by Asian invaders, the Hyksos and Assyrians. The last pharonic dynasty was overthrown by the Persians in 341 B.C.E. Alexandrian and Ptolemaic Greek dynasties then replaced the Persians, who were in turn replaced by the Roman Empire. Egypt was part of the Byzantine Empire from the third to the seventh centuries of the Common Era, when it was conquered by Arab invaders who introduced the Muslim religion and Arabic language. (The ancient Egyptian language is still used in the Christian Coptic liturgy.) Around 1250, the Mameluke dynasty, a military caste of Caucasian origin, replaced Arab control. In 1517, the Turks defeated the Mamelukes and Egypt became part of the Ottoman Empire.

In 1798, Napoleon's armies invaded Egypt and occupied Cairo. His effort to block British trade routes to India and establish a Francophone society was ultimately unsuccessful. Nevertheless, Napoleon's invasion had profound repercussions for the Arab and Muslim world, which continue to affect the region's political and social development. This was the first European conquest of a major Arab country in the history of Islam and it signaled the rapid decline of Islam as a world political power. Some analysts even trace contemporary Muslim fundamentalism to this initial shattering defeat.

The French occupation, defeat, and withdrawal destabilized Egypt and left it vulnerable to an internal political struggle that was won by Mohammed Ali, an Albanian lieutenant in the Ottoman army who set about modernizing the economic and educational structure of Egypt. However, the expansion ultimately put Egypt heavily into debt and, at the end of the American Civil War with the resumption of American cotton production, initiated a major recession in Egypt's cotton industry. As a result of the economic crisis, the British began to assume greater control over the country.

The Suez Canal, built by a French corporation from 1859 to 1869, was taken over by the British in 1975. After the British Empire expanded into East Africa and the Sudan, the British established their *de facto* rule in 1882, although Egypt remained a nominal part of the Ottoman Empire until 1914. Egypt became a British protectorate in 1914, and a League of Nations Mandate in 1922. The autonomy of the Egyptian monarchy was strengthened in the Anglo-Egyptian treaty in 1936, although Great Britain continued its military presence in Egypt and its control of the Sudan.

After the heavy fighting of World War II, a growing nationalist movement led Egypt to abrogate the 1936 treaty in 1951. A military uprising the following year forced King Farouk to abdicate. Farouk was succeeded by Gamal Abdel Nassar when Egypt declared itself a republic. British troops were withdrawn from the Suez Canal Zone in June 1956 and the following month Egypt nationalized the Canal. At the end of October, Israel invaded the Sinai Peninsula, and French and British forces came to Israel's aid. United Nations intervention maintained the peace between 1957 and 1967. Egyptian incursions into the Gaza Strip in June 1967 led to a full-scale war with Israel that continued through 1970, when Nassar died and was succeeded by Anwar Sadat. In October 1973, Egyptian forces crossed the Suez Canal and attacked Israeli positions. Eighteen days later, the Yom Kippur War ended in a cease-fire. Meanwhile, Soviet influence had risen with Russian contributions to the Aswan High Dam, and then waned. In 1974, Sadat's government became increasingly friendly to Western and American investment and relationships between Egypt and Israel improved.

Sadat's economic "Open Door Policy" encouraged, in particular, the private sector to increase the productive capacity of the economy. However, as the government withdrew its commitment to guaranteed employment for all college graduates, unemployment increased. Women, in particular, were affected by this policy. While there had been an increasing expectation in the 1960s that women would increasingly enter the labor force, the Open Door Policy surprisingly worked against this expectation. The national dialogue about women's work started to shift and the definition of women as primarily playing a role in the domestic arena gained ground. Justifying ideologies based on sexual division of roles began to appear, supported by the newly emerging Islamic fundamentalist groups, which advocated that a woman's place was in the home (el-Baz 1997:149). Further, a provision was added to Article Eleven of the 1971 Constitution, which declared the state's commitment to help reconciling women's family obligations and their equality to men in the public sphere, "provided that this did not infringe on the rules of the Islamic *shari'a* [the "Way" of Islam, including the law and governance]" The new Constitution represented an important divergence from the secular discourse of the 1960s and created opportunities for Islamic groups to oppose women's rights on the grounds that they were in opposition to Islamic principles (Hatem 1992:241).

Throughout the 1980s, the Open Door Policy became increasingly institutionalized, eventually leading to the current economic Reform Policy. While this policy has been relatively successful on a macro level, it has had negative consequences for the more vulnerable sectors of society, namely the poor, and specifically poor women and their children (el-Baz 1997:149). As key resources, such as health care and education, have become scarcer, it has been lower class women and children who have become least likely to have access to them. Also, affected by the economic restructuring have been individuals who would previously have been classified as middle class, namely civil servants and unemployed graduates.

While the pressures and tensions of a rapidly changing world in the last half of the twentieth century have affected all the nations and peoples of the world, these tensions have been more obvious in the Islamic nations of the Middle East and southeast Asia. In particular, the growing Islamic fundamentalist movement symbolizes the tensions and conflicts between Western and indigenous traditions and beliefs. Further, in Egypt, this movement has centered much of its rhetoric around the "appropriate" roles for women in society. Gender issues, thus, constitute a principal mechanism for understanding issues of marriage and sexuality.

1. Basic Sexological Premises

According to Egyptian societal norms, sexuality and the ensuing children are part of marriage and creating a family, and do not, therefore, belong in any other sphere of life. With this ideology in mind, contemporary fundamentalists often point to the West and the "loose morality between the sexes" in order to legitimize their arguments about sexuality and gender roles. The essence of their arguments is that women should not work outside of the home and should instead take care of their husbands and children. The family structure emerges as all-important for maintaining a well-ordered society, practical morality, and channeling sexuality. As will be seen, gender roles, and in particular woman's role at the center of the family, thus, acquire social importance and political relevance.

2. Religious and Ethnic Factors Affecting Sexuality

A. The Issue of Gender

Egyptian society is organized on the principle that men and women simply have different natures, talents, and inherent tendencies. This becomes most apparent in the realm of the family, where each gender has a different role to play. Men are created for going out in the world and are responsible for providing financially for the family. Women are suited for remaining within family boundaries, caring for the home, the children, and the husband. Further, women's inherent sexuality is believed to be constantly endangering the social harmony of society (specifically, men) and is, therefore, best controlled through women's modesty and women remaining as much as possible within the private sphere of family. This belief is reinforced through cultural and religious norms that increasingly advocate that family roles of both women and men are fundamental in maintaining societal structure. The dominant gender constructions therefore support keeping women in the home and oppose women working and abandoning their primary roles (Macleod 1991:85). Nonetheless, contemporary images of women as economic assets and providers are rapidly coming into conflict with what are perceived as divinely inspired roles.

Gender roles in Egypt derive much of their legitimacy from the Qur'an. In particular, women are often the focus of quotes that supposedly refer to the appropriate roles and behaviors of women. References to the role of women are widely scattered throughout the Qur'an. Some passages focus on women's unique nature, some on women's place in society, and some on women's role within the general congregation of believers. As Fernea and Bezirgan (1977:13) emphasize, even though the Qur'an is the central source of Islamic belief, there is considerable controversy about the meaning of each of these passages and their implications for the status of women. Consider the verse:

> O mankind! Be careful of your duty to your Lord Who created you from a single soul and from it created its mate and from them twain hath spread abroad a multitude of men and women. Be careful of your duty toward Allah in Whom ye claim (your rights) of one another. (Qur'an 4:1)

This verse is used by some interpreters as evidence that women are considered equal within Islamic doctrine. Others, however, point to the following verse:

> Men are in charge of women, because Allah hath made the one of them to excel the other, and because they spend of their property (to support women). So good women are the obedient. (Qur'an 4:3 4)

They cite this as evidence that women can never achieve equality within Islam (Fernea & Bezirgan 1977:18). Selectively choosing Qur'anic verses can either undermine or support dialogues concerning the proper role of women.

Verses from the Qur'an, the *hadith* (traditions about Mohammed, second only to the Qur'an in authority), and theological arguments about their relevance, are often used as empirical data for sociological explanations of a gender hierarchy in which women are subordinate to men (Mernissi 1987; Marcus 1992). Notwithstanding the powerful assertion that Muslim men and women utilize these sources as part of their hegemonic beliefs, contemporary scholarship has shown that, rather than determining attitudes about women, parts of the Qur'an are only used at certain times or occasions in order to legitimate particular acts or sets of conditions that concern women. The Qur'an is part of the way in which the gender hierarchy and sexuality are negotiated and enforced. It does not provide an explanation of gender roles; instead, it is part of a constant process of gender role negotiation. While central to Islam, the Qur'an is neither the only nor the most important part of the beliefs and practices that influence the daily life of Muslim women and men. Differences between men and women are readily apparent in several aspects of Islamic law, which accords certain rights and capacities to both men and women. A Muslim's legal capacity (*ahliyyat*) begins at birth and ends with death. Legal responsibilities are assumed under one's legal capacity and are distinguished as a "capacity of execution" and a "capacity of obligations." A free Muslim man who is sane and considered an adult has the highest degree of legal capacity. A Muslim woman, even though she has certain rights, generally has half the legal capacity of a man. This difference only becomes apparent when men and women reach adulthood.

According to the Islamic legal point of view, an adult is a

> legally and morally responsible person, one who has reached physical maturity, is of sound mind, may enter into contracts, dispose of property, and be subject to criminal law. Above all, he is responsible for the religious commands and obligations of Islam. (Lapidus 1976:93)

When a Muslim man reaches maturity, his legal capacity becomes complete; neither his age nor marital status influences his legal rights, responsibilities, or capacity of execution.

A Muslim woman's legal identity also begins at birth, but in contrast to men, her legal capacity and status undergo various changes throughout her life cycle. For a woman, her legal coming of age and her achievement of physical maturity do not necessarily coincide. She is a ward of her father or guardian as a child and, as an adult, is restricted in legal decision-making. Her legal persona and social status depend on the state of her sexuality whether she is a virgin, married, divorced, or widowed. There is, of course, variation in different Islamic societies as to the perception of the different stages of femaleness. At different times in a woman's life she is treated differently both by the law and by the society. Societally and legally, the young woman (*shabba*) is the focus of a great deal of protection, and her freedom of movement is limited. In contrast, an old woman (*aguza*) is able to move with much greater ease, and may also move in places and participate in situations where the young woman is forbidden even to enter. It is therefore very important to emphasize the fundamental difference between the stability of mature men's status under the law versus the changing nature of women's status. This legal difference pervades and shapes the lives of women all over the Islamic world.

Existing side by side and sometimes in contradiction to the reality of women's daily struggles in Egypt, is the cultural religious ideal of complementarity between the sexes. Within this concept, women are not devalued as persons, or somehow considered to be inherently lesser in value than men, or thought to be lacking in abilities. Instead, Egyptian women tend to emphasize that everyone—man, woman, or child—is thought to be part of an interrelated community, and that gender complementarity is part of the message of the Qur'an and *hadith*. Even though men overwhelmingly act as the public spokespeople for Islam, as *ulama* (teachers and scholars of Islam), or as *sheikhs* (spiritual leaders), women tend to categorically emphasize that they are just as capable of spreading the word of Islam as men.

While women are clearly not always as much in the spotlight as men, they perform their duties in other ways. Women are valued as the first teachers of their children in the ways of Islam, both through their instruction and also by their example in daily life, which extends beyond the home. There are also many examples of women in Islamic history, beginning with the wives of the Prophet Muhammad and in folk Islam, who have become spiritual leaders in their communities (Ahmed 1992).

While both Muslim men and women are expected to be observant practitioners of religious rites, the actual practice of Islam among men and women in Egypt varies. According to the male view of Islam, all believers have the same responsibilities to God and the same duties to perform. This is supported by the Qur'an, which states: "And they [women] have rights similar to those [of men] over them in kindness, and men are a degree above them (2:228)." In one sense, the Muslim community is made up of equals, and this is supported by the belief that all are equal before God. This doctrine is supported by reference to the Qur'an, and serves as the foundation for the assertion that Islam is egalitarian. However, while it is stated that all are equal before God, at the same time men are in charge of women. Mernissi (1987:41) considers the Islamic community, *umma*, to be the male Muslim world, while women's world is the other portion, a kind of sub-universe. However, this is only partially accurate. There is an important distinction between the concept of the *umma* as the imagined moral community to which all people naturally belong, and the society of believers on earth. The two spheres of the moral community and the world of daily life are connected, but in a manner that may not be directly apparent.

B. The Dangerous Sexuality of Women

A dominant gender ideology is an actively negotiated aspect of many Egyptians' daily lives. Contemporary constructions of what it is to be male or female are only partially shaped by Islamic beliefs. Western images, indigenous feminism, new Islamic views of women, and the requirements of the institutions of family and state all contribute to the creation of the ever-changing image of "proper" woman and man. Nonetheless, an Islamic framework is becoming ever more popular as the foundation for gender discourse in certain segments of Egyptian society. Fundamentalist discourse lends legitimacy and cultural authenticity to all positions in the argument. Much of this gender discourse is based on the "dangerous" nature of women and the evils of unbridled sexuality in society.

The contemporary sociologist Halim Barakat comments that in the Arab world in general, "the prevailing religious ideology considers women to be a source of evil, anarchy [*fitna*] and trickery or deception [*kaid*]" (Barakat 1985:32). Throughout Egyptian society, one finds the expression of a pervasive gender ideology that perceives women as posing extreme danger for men.

This same ideology prescribes modesty in the form of dress and behavior for women. Contemporary Egyptian beliefs regarding the modesty of women represent a convergence of ideology with customary practice and modern problems. In Egypt, as throughout the Arab world, descent is traced through the male line, and a woman remains a permanent member of her father's family. Even after marriage, a woman keeps her father's name and returns to him, or to another male relative on her father's side, if she is divorced or mistreated. She remains tied to the prestige structure of her father's family, even though she is incorporated into the household of her husband. The honor of the family is closely bound to the modest behavior of women, and honor is associated with the family group, not just with an individual. Thus, one finds that the actions of one family member affect the honor of everyone in that group. This leads to the complex situation that a woman's dishonorable actions before marriage threaten her father's whole family, but such actions after marriage threaten both her father's and her husband's family. As head of the family, a man must insure the integrity of family honor by watching over the behavior of the women of the group at all times.

One way in which these existing attitudes and practices are reinforced is by the recitation of passages from the Qur'an and *hadith* that relate to women's modesty, and by interpreting them in a way that underscores the social values of keeping unrelated men and women separated from each other. For example, "And when ye ask of them [the wives of the Prophet] anything, ask it of them from behind a curtain [*higab*]" (Qur'an 33:53). The word *higab* in some contexts is interpreted variously as a screen or a cloth used as a space divider in a tent, or in a metaphorical sense as modest dress or maintaining a decorous distance between men and women. A key word relating to the modesty of women is *zina*, which is defined as adornment, ornament, or beauty. The Qur'an states:

And tell the believing women to lower their gaze and be modest and
to display of their adornment [*zina*] only that which is apparent, and
to draw their veils over their bosoms, and not to show their adornment
[*zina*] save to their own husband or father or husband's father, or their
sons or . . . And let them not stamp their feet so as to reveal what they
hide of their adornment [*zina*]. (Qur'an 24:31)

This verse has been alternately interpreted as defining *zina* as adornment,
such as makeup or jewelry, or all of a woman, except for her face and hands
or natural beauty (Hoffman-Ladd 1987:29). It has become increasingly
common in Egypt to hear that a woman must cover all of her *zina* in the
name of honor and for the protection of public morals. In a constantly
changing world, women have thus become the locus for many of the debates
that actually deal with wider issues in the society.

Much of contemporary Islamic discourse on women deals with the
underlying preoccupation with what it means to be a Muslim in a changing
world. As technological developments in transportation, communication,
and the media become accessible to a wider segment of the Egyptian
population, some Muslims are turning to the fundamentalist scriptural
versions of Islam, which are unfamiliar to much of the population. In an
attempt to validate their positions, these Muslims cite the works of medieval
jurists as the basis for their views on the appropriate roles of men and
women. These works provide some insight into current developments with
respect to gender roles.

First, one should note that the Qur'an specifically encourages sexual
relations in the following verses addressed to husbands:

And when they [the women] have purified themselves, then go in unto
them as Allah hath enjoined upon you. (Qur'an 2:222)

Your women are a tilth for you to cultivate so go to your tilth as ye will,
and send [good deeds] before you for your souls. (Qur'an 22:23)

Having said this, medieval jurists regarded women as a major site of
disruption, *fitna*. This was based, in part, on the specific notion of the
potential danger of women's sexuality. In their arguments, the presence of
women presented society, i.e., men, with the ever-present threat of *fitna*.
Nonetheless, this presence was relational. Even though the danger of *fitna*
was located in women, it was not their actual being that represented
disorder, but the possibility of their unregulated relationships with men. A
popular *hadith*, frequently cited in contemporary fundamentalist literature,
states: "I have not left any disorder [*fitna*] more damaging to men than
women." Thus, women's disruptive sexuality presented a constant danger
to a harmonious society.

In their socialization of men and women, the medieval societies of the
Islamic world presumed that the sexes needed to coexist. Nevertheless,

men and women needed to interact in prescribed ways. This was based on an ideology that assumed that women were seductresses and men were susceptible to seduction (Bouhdiba 1988:20-29). Based on an assumption of their innate abilities, men were accorded the responsibility to set limits for women, who were considered to be below them. Jurists based this assumption on the Qur'anic verses that state: "men are a degree above women" (2:228). While medieval jurists' emphasis on *fitna* must have affected attitudes toward other concepts relating to women's modesty, these discussions were not by any means original or exclusive to the societies of that time.

The fear of *fitna*, which was posed by the visible presence of women, added an element of vested communal interest to the seclusion of women, an interest, which was religiously sanctioned (al-Misri 1994:512). Not only was women's modesty supposed to be guarded by men, who did so in order to guard the honor of their family, but women themselves were seen to bear a religious obligation to uphold their own modesty (*Ibid.*). Part of a woman's duty was to prevent *fitna*, to prevent men from feeling aroused, for if a man misbehaved as a result of arousal by a woman's physical presence, she, personally, was to blame. Furthermore, this was considered to be a woman's duty, not just toward her own family, but also toward society at large. Thus, Ibn al-Hajj, for example, writing in fourteenth century Cairo, suggests that in order for a woman not to cause havoc in society, she should leave the house three times in her lifetime: "at the time of her wedding; at the funeral of her parents; and at her own funeral" (1973 1:119). Any contact between men and women was deemed as potentially dangerous, as seen in another of his examples, where he warns the water-carrier to lower his gaze upon entering a house, due to the possibility of seeing an unveiled woman (1973, 3:123). A spontaneous glance, in this case totally without forethought, was quite naturally assumed to lead towards seduction. These examples provide some insight into the underlying issues of gender ideology which are undergoing change in modern Egypt and reveal why women and sexuality remain a central focus of contention in contemporary debates about the centrality of marriage and family.

3. Sexual Knowledge and Education

A/B. Formal and Informal Sources

There is no form of sex education in Egypt. While Islamic culture has a certain fascination with all sexual matters as evidenced in the bawdy nature of A Thousand and One Nights, in contemporary Egypt, no sexual issues are discussed, either in schools or in the media. This is also in contrast to Qur'anic teachings, which encourage married couples to have sex both for reproductive as well as pleasurable purposes. This is evidenced by an Islamic law that says that if on the wedding night, the woman discovers that her husband's penis is smaller than the thickness of three fingers, she may divorce him on the grounds of impotence.

While discussions of sexuality are a common component in Egyptian social life, and part of the role of older men and women is to help younger men and women deal with their sexuality, these informal discussions take place within highly regulated spheres of interaction characterized by gender segregation and, among women, the virgin/non-virgin category.

4. Autoerotic Behaviors and Patterns
ROBERT T. FRANCOEUR

For Muslim men, the loss of semen in masturbation and nocturnal emissions is bound up, as is the menstrual flow of women, with the impurity associated with the evacuation of organic wastes, unlawful (*haram*) relations, and specific taboos of the *ihram* (ritual purity and dedication of the pilgrim), violations of which constitute a capital sin against *zina*. The life of an observant Muslim is a succession of states of purity acquired then lost and of impurity lost and then found again in carefully specified purification rituals. Man is never ultimately purified, nor is he condemned to permanent impurity. Major impurity (*janaba*) results from any emission of semen, menstruation, or the forty-day lochia (*nafas*, the liquid discharged from the uterus following childbirth). Minor impurity is contracted as a result of any excretion by the urethra or anus.

Faithful execution of prescribed purification rituals, following emission of semen, urination, defecation, and the menstrual flow enable a good Muslim to face God. Whatever the body eliminates is impure and sullies the body, and that pollution must be cleansed each time. This has nothing to do with sin, because man's very life involves the pollution of elimination and excretion, and nothing else. The serious nature and detailed prescriptions of the various purification rituals following an evacuation of organic wastes are often a surprise to non-Muslims (Bouhdiba 1985:43-57).

> The nature of the purificatory act is of a metaphysical order. It is the act of sublimating the body, of removing pollution and of placing it at the service of the soul and spirit. A material, physical, psychological or moral pollution is never final in Islam and the purpose of the purificatory techniques is to restore man to his original purity. (Bouhdiba 1985:43)

Not surprisingly, in view of Egypt's Islamic culture and Islam's reticence in discussing sexual issues, female masturbation is not discussed, or even mentioned, in standard references on sexuality in Islam or Egypt. A single reference discovered by the editor in *Sexuality in Islam*, by Abdelwahab Bouhdiba (1985:31), notes that, while both male and female homosexuality are equally condemned, female homosexuality (*musahaqa*) incurs the same reprimand as incurred by autoeroticism, bestiality, or necrophilia. Whether Bouhdiba would include female autoeroticism in this unspecified mention of masturbation is open to speculation.

5. Interpersonal Heterosexual Behaviors

A. Children and Adolescents

Gender Segregation of the Young

An Islamic marriage contract entwines men and women in a set of mutual rights and obligations. The first obligation of marriage is faithfulness and chastity. Any involvement in an extramarital relationship constitutes adultery and is grounds for divorce. This stems from two Qur'anic verses:

> And who guard their modesty—save from their wives or the [slaves] that their right hands possess, for then they are not blameworthy. But who so craveth beyond that, such are transgressors. (23:5-7)

> And all married women [are forbidden unto you] save those [captives] whom your right hands possess. It is a decree of Allah for you. Lawful unto you are all beyond those mentioned, so that ye seek them with your wealth in honest wedlock not debauchery. (4:42)

Traditional practices throughout the Islamic world limit interaction between the sexes, based on the idea that contact encourages adulterous relationships to develop. Contact is thus limited between young boys and girls, and complete separation of boys and girls becomes the ideal after the onset of puberty. These ideals have become extremely difficult to uphold with the advent of large numbers of women working outside of the house, and are presently in a state of negotiation between the sexes.

Faithfulness and chastity also account for the extreme emphasis that families and prospective bridegrooms place on the virginity of the bride. Both sexes believe that virginity guarantees the faithfulness of the woman to the man after marriage "She will not desire others if she has not known men before" is a common phrase that is bantered about. While customarily these rules are not applied as stringently to men, men from "better" families will attempt (at least in mixed company) to portray themselves as very "moral" and as abstaining from women until marriage. It is commonly believed that one is able to predict future behavior based on the past.

Infractions of the moral code of faithfulness and fidelity are more common than is usually admitted by most middle-class Egyptians or than is cited in the literature on women and family. For example, Altorki writes, "In all the families studied, the fidelity of the wives was a principle that was strictly observed, and to my knowledge no infractions occurred" (1986:63). While Egyptians also adhere to a similar belief system where the issue of faithfulness and fidelity is concerned, although the reality may at times differ quite substantially.

B. Adults

Egyptian society is characterized by a general sense of patriarchy as well as sexual frustration. Men dominate over women in all matters of sexuality, and children are from their first day brought up with very strict sexual guidelines. Girls are expected to be virgins at marriage and are not allowed to ask about sex before their weddings. For many young women (especially the less educated ones), the actual sex act comes as a complete surprise on their wedding nights and often results in lifelong frigidity due to the shock of the experience. Further, due to cultural constraints, even if a woman comes to enjoy sex, she is not allowed to show this to her husband, who will otherwise become suspicious of her desire and suspect her of having sex with other men. Also, women are not allowed to be the initiators when it comes to sex. Women are expected to initially be completely innocent and then later to "endure" sex in order to be "respectable" in their husband's eyes.

Men have a different set of challenges. While they are expected to have some "experience" before marriage, men also are faced with maintaining their reputations so that they will be eligible to marry a "morally respectable" girl once they are financially set to do so. This entails secret sexual behaviors, since many men do not marry until their thirties. Further, it is difficult to find women to have sex with. Men, therefore, resort to encounters with prostitutes or with willing married women. However, most of this behavior occurs secretly and a man will never tell his bride about his experiences. Given the sexually repressive atmosphere of the society and the lack of sexual access to women, many men suffer from impotence and are extremely preoccupied with all sexual matters.

In addition, it must be pointed out that there are strong differences in degree between rural and urban areas, as well as class differences, in terms of interpersonal behaviors between men and women in the private sphere. Men from the south of Egypt (Saidi'is) are renowned for their jealous behaviors over their wives. Nonetheless, the rules depicted above apply in some degree to all individuals brought up in Egyptian society.

Concepts of Beauty

The traditional idea that in order to be attractive, women should be pleasantly plump (*mirabraba*) is still around, but it is changing in the upper strata of society. For example, it is now possible to find diet Coca Cola and other diet sodas in Egypt. Also, hospitals have started treating obesity. There are no reported cases of bulemia or anorexia. "*Hilwa mirabraba*" or "pretty and plump" is a standard phrase, as if the two words are automatically attached. To call a woman "skinny as a stick" or a "drumstick" (referring to drums, not a chicken's legs) is an insult. Traditional lower-class women use a different insult, "you rusty needle" (*Iya ibra miSaddiyy*), as a standard insult.

As far as ideals of beauty are concerned, women spend a lot of money straightening kinky hair and trying to whiten their skin using various creams such as "Fair and Lovely" or "Fair Lady." There are commercials for these products on television all the time. Also, the male ideal of a woman in traditional sectors is blond, white skin, and blue eyes. Women tend to find men who are somewhat taller, have a full head of hair, and again fair skin, as attractive. However, women do not attach great importance to men's looks if they have other favorable criteria, such as a job, good education, and respectable family background.

Intimacy and Nudity   ROBERT T. FRANCOEUR

While the Imams and mullahs of Islam are very clear in their interpretations of the Qur'an and what is permitted and not permitted by tradition, there is often, as Perper points out in the Introduction to this volume, a real discrepancy between "proper sex" and "formal values," what the authorities say should be done, and "smart sex" and "informal values," what men and women actually do in their private sphere. The comments of Abdelwahab Bouhdiba in *Sexuality in Islam* are a good example of this distinction applied to the issue of nudity. Bouhdiba (1985:37-38) writes about formal values and proper sex according to the Qur'an:

> To be a Muslim is to control one's gaze and to know how to protect one's own intimacy from that of others.
>
> However, the concept of intimacy is far-reaching, for we are confronted here with the concept of *'aura*, which tradition divides into four categories: what a man may see of a woman, what a woman may see of a man, what a man may see of a man, what a woman may see of a woman.
>
> Between men and women, and also between men before their own wives, the part to be concealed from the eyes of others stretches from the navel to the knees exclusively, with a greater or lesser tolerance for the lower part of the thighs, especially in the case of youths. A woman must reveal only her face and hands. Between husband and wife sight is permitted of the whole body except for the partner's sexual organs, which one is advised not to see for "the sight of them makes one blind." However, this is allowed in cases where it is necessary, for juridical or medical purposes, to examine the sexual organs of the *zani* or woman in confinement.
>
> Certain *fugaha* authorize the partners to look at one another's sexual organs during intercourse. Zayla'i, armed with the opinion of Ibn 'Omar and Imam Abu Hanifa, even affirms that it increases one's ability to reach the quintessence of ecstasy.
>
> Total nudity is very strongly advised against, even when one is "alone." This is because absolute solitude does not exist in a world in which we

share existence with the *djinns* [*spirits lower than angels*] and angels. "Never go into water without clothing for water has eyes," Daylami observes.

When the editor asked Bahira Sherif to comment on the above description of "proper sex" offered by Bouhdiba, she offered the following comment:

> Public nudity in all forms is forbidden for both men and women. The most extreme case of this is that some ultra conservative men will cover their wife's feet with a cloth when she climbs in and out of a bus. Men and women *are* allowed to be intimate and to see each other's sexual organs.

Islamic Law and Egyptian Marriage

In order to understand sexuality in Egypt, it is necessary to clarify the role of marriage in Islamic law (which remains in effect in all issues related to family in Egypt.) In all schools of Islamic law, marriage is seen as a contract whose main function is to make sexual relations between a man and a woman licit. The term *'aqd al-nikah* refers to the contract of coitus. A valid and effective marriage contract outlines certain respective legal rights and duties for wife and husband, together with other rights and duties common to both of them. Very superficially, these rights and duties can be summed up as dowry and maintenance for the wife and children, as well as the good treatment of the wife and children by the husband, the mutual right of inheritance between the conjugal couple, and the wife's obedience to her husband in lawful matters. At the time of marriage, other parties can stipulate certain conditions, provided that they are not contrary to the basis of marriage as defined by jurists.

The essential requirements for a valid Muslim marriage in Egypt are:

1. consent of the wife,
2. consent of the legal guardian or *al wali*,
3. two legal witnesses, and
4. payment of dowry or *mahr*.

While each of these elements must be present for a marriage to be considered valid, there are other features inferred from Islamic legal texts, which combine to make a legitimate, socially respectable marriage. Because marriage is a contract, both parties can stipulate certain conditions. For example, one condition may be the wife's right to divorce, but a condition that eliminates the husband's right to divorce would be void. (Verma (1971:97-104) has provided a list of valid and void conditions related to marriage.)

Beyond its legal components, marriage is also regarded as a religious obligation and is invested with many ethical injunctions. This can be attributed primarily to the fact that any sexual contact outside marriage is considered fornication or a violation of *zina*, and is subject to severe punishment. Furthermore, Islam condemns and discourages celibacy. In this manner, marriage acquires a religious dimension; it becomes the way of preserving morals and chastity through the satisfaction of sexual desires within the limits set by God (Maudoodi 1983:6-7). Muslim jurists have gone so far as to elevate marriage to the level of a religious duty. The Qur'an supports this notion in the verse that states, "And marry such of you as are solitary and the pious of your slaves and maid servants" (24:32), which is commonly interpreted as advocating marriage in order to "complete the religion" (Bousquet 1948:63). A common *hadith*, still often quoted, particularly among men, states that "the prayer of a married man is equal to seventy prayers of a single man." Thus, all individuals are encouraged to marry, and societal provisions, such as the importance of family reputation, discourage being single.

Marriage remains at the center of contemporary Egyptian social life. It is the primary focal point in the lives of both men and women, followed only by the birth of a child. From a legal standpoint, the marriage contract establishes a series of rights and obligations between a couple which have a long-lasting effect on many aspects of their lives. An Islamic marriage contract naturally represents more than a mere exchange of money or material goods. It is a form of social exchange and is thus a legal, religious, economic, and symbolic transaction (Mauss 1967:76). The contract is attended to with utmost seriousness and is preceded by a set of lengthy negotiations, almost all of which center around the material protection of the woman and her unborn children once she enters the state of matrimony. Nevertheless, the marriage contract may include conditions that are advantageous for either or both spouses. Conditions specified in the contract may range from the woman's right to dissolve the marriage, to an agreement that neither party may leave the town they agree to live in, and even that the husband may not marry another woman. The contract, as a matter of course, also acts as a medium for bringing the various members of the two families together and provides them with the opportunity to discuss in detail the preliminary workings of the marriage. Most importantly, the marriage contract symbolizes the public acknowledgment of the formation of a lawful sexual partnership that will be sanctioned both religiously and socially, and which marks the beginning of a family and the care and upbringing of children.

Mut'a *or Temporary Marriage*

While *mut'a* or temporary marriage is not recognized as legitimate by any school of Sunni Islam, its acceptance and practice among the Shi'as highlights the contractual nature of Muslim marriages (Haeri 1989). However, Haeri's argument that all Islamic marriage contracts are basically an exchange of money for sexual intercourse, while thoroughly researched and argued, is incomplete. While that is one element of the exchange, Haeri ignores the other elements of protection of the woman and her children. Even temporary marriages require a contract based on the notion that should a child be fathered, even in a short-term union, the man must claim paternity. This can be observed by the fact that after the short-term-marriage contract expires, the woman is still required to observe the *'idda*, the period of waiting. A *mut'a* wife is not entitled to maintenance, but should children be conceived during a legitimate *mut'a* marriage, they are entitled to inherit from both parents.

For a *mut'a* marriage to be valid, the term of cohabitation must be fixed, and it may be a day, a month, a year, or a number of years; and a dower should be specified. However, it is still incorrect to draw conclusions about the nature of all Islamic marriage contracts, based on *mut'a* marriage contracts. *Mut'a* marriages are outlawed among all other schools of law because they do not fulfill the purpose that the jurists argue is the fundamental reason behind marriage in the first place. While lawful sexual intercourse is one aspect of the contract, the legalities bound up with the relationship, I think, indicate the multidimensional nature of an Islamic marriage. The Sunni jurists emphasize that even under Shi'a doctrine, temporary marriage is not a proper marriage, since it establishes no maintenance or inheritance rights for the woman.

Modern Egyptian legislation dealing with marriage and its actual practice provides insight into the contemporary nature of the founding of an Islamic family through matrimony. Here we can only give a general summary of the issues dealing with marriage and divorce. A general examination of the legalistic intricacies of marriage is relevant to all schools of law in Islam and reveals the rights and obligations of both men and women that are established through the marital bond. It is not within the scope of this chapter to expound on the social and cultural customs that vary across the regions that are today primarily Islamic. While these variations are very important, they are not central to our discussion here, because of the prevailing uniformity of the legal issues. Few fundamental conceptual and legal differences exist among the various schools of Islamic law concerning the basic rights of women (e.g., dowry, financial maintenance), inheritance laws being the exception. Since the legal structure for marriage and divorce, which constitutes most of the laws dealing with women, is described in detail in the Qur'an (especially *suras*, chapters of the Qur'an, 2:221-41; 4:3-35; 65:1-7), they are believed to be immutable. Historically, Islamic societies have avoided making changes to the structure of family law because of its derivation from religious text. Thus, it is of contemporary relevance to examine some of the legalistic aspects of marriage with respect to their derivations from the Qur'an.

Sources such as the Qur'an and Islamic law represent norms; they do not describe what is or what was, but what should be. They constitute the mechanism of an ideally functioning Islamic society, the goal being to provide for humankind the path to happiness and paradise. However, this does not mean that these sources have no relation to reality. In fact, they do from two aspects. On the one hand, the solutions that they suggest to human questions and problems are often derived, in particular relation to issues about marriage and family, out of the existing circumstances, even in those instances when they seek to change existing conditions. On the other hand, these guidelines influence the given society, leading to changes in social practice including marriage, family, and gender roles.

Sexuality Within Marriage

Islamic justification of sexual intercourse through the marriage contract can be seen in a variety of provisions (Bousquet 1948:63-74). For example, a Muslim marriage only becomes completely valid when it has been consummated. If a man declares his wife divorced three times, he can only remarry her once she has contracted a marriage with another man and consummated the new marriage—a *hadith* refers to this as "tasting a bit of honey." [As Zeynep Gulçat, author of the chapter on Turkey in this volume, explained when asked about this by a graduate student in the Editor's class, this *hadith* is meant to protect the wife from repeated, impulsive declarations of divorcing a wife for minor irritations and then remarrying her on reflection (Editor)].

Also, once husband and wife live together, the marriage is to be consummated within a certain period of time. The different schools of law vary on the specified time period, but one year seems to be the average (al-Misri 1994:531). A woman may not refuse her husband's sexual advances at any time, even if she is menstruating, unless it will cause her discomfort. She, in turn, has the right, not just to sexual intercourse, but also to sexual satisfaction. It is said that if a woman pleases her husband sexually, she can be assured of paradise, and if she refuses him, she will be penalized both on earth and in heaven. If a man swears an oath that he will not touch his wife any more, then she has the right to divorce him after four months, unless he resumes sexual relations with her again (Qur'an 2:226). All of these prescriptions indicate how important and potent Islam considers sexuality to be. Both men and women are to be satisfied sexually in order to prevent adultery and consequent chaos in the society.

The importance of sexuality in the married life of Egyptian women is very apparent in their conversations, which are often, by Western standards, very explicit. Married women will not speak of their sex lives in front of other men or unmarried young women. Nevertheless, once they find themselves alone with other married women, the conversations will become very detailed about the various strengths or weaknesses of their married lives. Women will advise one another on all aspects of sex and on how to best "deal with one's husband."

A major issue among married women is the issue of frequency of sex. Some women feel that their husbands place undue demands on them, given the fact that they work, have children, and are running a household. Interestingly, some other women have the opposite complaint. According to a couple of my informants, several of their husbands kept them on a strict schedule of sex. Thus, the men initiated sex with their wives regularly but in a limited fashion on, for example, Tuesdays and Thursdays, Thursdays being the most common night for sex before the holy day on Friday. Any attempts on the wife's part to deviate from this schedule were met with great opposition. Thus, women are constantly advising one another on "seductive" techniques to force their husbands to vary the schedule. Men, however, feel that it is necessary to preserve a strict regular sexual schedule in order to keep their wives' sexuality under control. Men tend to fear that, as they age, women may want or expect too much from them, and that once they are not able to perform as well, this could initiate a marital crisis. Furthermore, many men fear that anything beyond basic sexual knowledge could potentially make their wives "promiscuous" and "uncontrollable." A major complaint on the part of women is their ignorance about sex when they married and their husband's lack of interest in educating them in this matter.

While Thursday night is considered "sex night," Friday is traditionally known as bath day. This is the day that ritually men get cleaned up to go to Friday prayer. Because of the traditional association of sex with full ablutions required after a major impurity, water is strongly associated with sex. This can even be seen in the term *Imayya suxna*, hot water, a phrase used by parents for something that the children should not be allowed to hear.

Among many Egyptians, part of the role of older men and women is to help younger men and women deal with some of the fundamental aspects of marriage. While sexuality, within the legitimate institution of marriage, is an active, much discussed component of Egyptian social life, these discussions take place within highly regulated spheres of interaction characterized by gender segregation and, among women, the virgin/non-virgin category.

To an individual brought up in the West, Egyptian women's discussions of sexuality are striking because of the many allusion to the Qur'an. While many women do not actually know what the Qur'an says, they do know that it urges all individuals to marry and that sexuality is encouraged and considered of primary importance for both men and women. "The Qur'an says it [sexuality] is part of our nature," or, conversely, "sex is part of their [men's] nature," are common comments and complaints among women. Especially among older women, jokes and anecdotes about sex and their husbands are afternoon entertainment. Younger women tend to be quite proud of the new power they have over their husbands and again validate these feelings with religious references, such as, "the Qur'an urges us to reproduce—and we are helping them [their husbands] to become good Muslims," or ,"We are helping them to fulfill their religious obligation." Some of the less-happily-married women in my study (in particular the older ones) repeatedly emphasized to me that, even though they were not satisfied with their husbands, "this was God's will," and that they were trying to please their husbands in all aspects, including sex, "because it is part of our religion and we will be rewarded in the afterlife." Religious references are used by both older and younger women to validate their positive and negative marital experiences. Nonetheless, none of the women seemed to have concrete knowledge of the actual *suras* or *hadiths*.

The complete social prohibition of young people's sexual activities outside of marriage naturally leads to the almost nonexistence of illegitimacy among this societal group. Illegitimacy is only spoken of in hushed tones and is associated with unusual occurrences, such as a maid getting pregnant through the advances of one of the men in the household. The Western phenomenon of older, educated, unmarried women having children is unheard of and evoked expressions of extreme surprise among my acquaintances. "That is *haram* (forbidden). Why would a woman do this to herself!" or "A woman bears children for her husband. Children need a father. How can this be?" A unanimously shared Egyptian belief is that reproduction belongs to the realm of the family and is thus, like sexuality, highly regulated by legal, as well as social rules and responsibilities.

Divorce

Until 2000, Egyptian and Islamic law provided the wife with a very limited right to initiate a divorce, one of these being the right of the wife to divorce her husband on the grounds of impotence if she discovered when the marriage was consummated that his penis did not exceed the thickness of three fingers.

A major development occurred in late January 2000 when the 454-member Egyptian Parliament voted to allow women to divorce their husbands without first having to prove to a judge that they had been mistreated. Under the new legislation, which was quickly approved by President Hosni Mubarak, divorce will still be more complicated for a woman than a male.

With the new law, an Egyptian woman now has two choices. She can still use the often-protracted procedure, which requires her to have witnesses to prove to a family court judge that her husband mistreated her badly enough to justify divorce. In the end, the court procedure usually results in a ruling against the wife. Despite these disadvantages, 1.5 million such requests are filed each year, according to government statistics.

The new option, which allows a woman to demand a divorce on the basis of incompatibility, requires a six-month wait for a woman with children, and a three-month wait if there are no children involved. If a judge fails to reconcile the couple in this period and she still wants a divorce, the judge has to grant a divorce. However, the woman has to return all money, property, and gifts she received in the marriage and forego alimony. Prior to the new law of 2000, a Muslim man in Egypt could end his marriage by saying three times, "I divorce you," or by filing with a government registrar a document testifying to his action. Under the new law, a man must file the divorce paper.

The situation of the six percent of Christian Egyptians remains as burdensome as before, because religious courts, which administer family law, rarely grant Christian women a divorce unless she can prove adultery.

Many leading clerics supported the change, including the government-appointed *mufti* (legal advisors on religious matters) and the sheik of Al Azhar University, the oldest Islamic teaching institution in the world. Supporters of the change point out that even the Prophet Muhammad allowed an unhappy woman to divorce her husband over his opposition, provided she first returned her dowry.

In the impassioned debate on the new law, opponents argued that Islam gives only men the right to initiate a divorce. Extending this right to women, whom they described both in Parliament and the media as emotionally capricious and vengeful, would lead to a massive breakdown of family life. "This will only lead to more and more splits within the society," Ayman Nour, a member of Parliament claimed; "This law will instigate women to be corrupt. A woman could just get together with another man and agree to divorce her husband."

Establishment of a woman's right to initiate a divorce is a major advancement for women in Egypt in light of the strong fundamentalist movement.

Polygyny

While polygyny is allowed by the Qur'an, it is virtually nonexistent in Egypt. In contrast to the stereotypical Western image of Muslim men with multiple wives, Egyptian men bemoan the difficulties of supporting one wife in today's economy, and strong social sanctions work against their even considering polygyny as a viable option.

Male and female reactions must be seen in light of a 1979 ruling, also known as "Jihan's law," so named after Sadat's unpopular modernist wife, who introduced a decree outlawing polygyny as an option for men. Considerable debate ensued in the media and among secular and religious elites concerning the Personal Status Laws and their relationship to the *shari'a* (Islamic law). This amendment was eventually partially abrogated on procedural grounds in 1985. However, in June of that year, a similar law (Law No. 100) amending the 1925 and 1929 laws was enacted and is now the law in place (Karam 1998:145). The new law stipulates that in the case of a polygynous union, the first wife retains the right to seek divorce, but it is no longer an automatic right. Instead, she now has to prove that her husband's second marriage is detrimental to her either materially and/or mentally. Further, the first wife now only has the right to sue for divorce in the first year of the new polygynous marriage. It is socially unacceptable among the middle and upper classes for men to engage in polygynous unions and, in fact, is not seen as an option. The revisions in the law are important on a symbolic level in terms of giving men certain legal rights over women in the context of the family.

6. Homoerotic, Homosexual, and Ambisexual Behaviors

While there is no public acknowledgment of homosexuality in Egypt, there is a largely hidden but thriving bisexual and homosexual community (Murray 1997c). Nevertheless, families will never acknowledge that one of their members is potentially homosexual. Men will remain living in their natal family for most of their lives and there will never be any public discussion about their reasons for not marrying. Islam condemns male homosexuality and popular culture further reinforces this message. In reality, homosexuality is widely practiced but is divided into two categories: the active versus the passive partner. The active partner has little stigma attached to him, or at least much less than to the *khawal* or passive partner, who is heavily stigmatized. According to one *hadith*, there are three kinds of male homosexual: "Those who look, those who touch, and those who commit the criminal act" (Bouhdiba 1985:32).

There is also traditional pederasty between older men and younger boys. Long-term domestic relationships between men are unknown, given social norms that force all unmarried individuals to remain in their natal families until they marry. Since there are many situations in which males can interact with other males, opportunities for male homosexual encounters are available. Egyptian culture, for instance, encourages intimate interactions between men and it is common to see men holding hands, embracing, or kissing each other on both cheeks without, again, any sexual overtones.

There are no similar venues for women who are under the constant supervision of their families. Thus, there is no information available on the prevalence of lesbianism in Egyptian society. Also, it is considered quite appropriate for women to interact with other women in very intimate settings (such as helping each other bathe) without there being any sexual overtones to these encounters (Murray 1997b).

After pointing out that the Islamic world rests on the bipolarity of the sexes and their union in marriage, Bouhdiba (1985:30-33) notes that "homosexuality is a challenge to the order of the world as laid down by God and based on the harmony and radical separation of the sexes."

> "God has cursed those who alter the frontiers of the earth." In these terms the prophet condemns any violation of the separation of the sexes. Tradition has it that four categories of person incur the anger of God: "Men who dress themselves as women and women who dress themselves as men, those who sleep with animals and those who sleep with men." Homosexuality [*liwat*] incurs the strongest condemnation. It is identified with *zina* and it is advocated that the most horrible punishment should be applied to those who indulge in it.
>
> In the final analysis, *liwat* even designates all forms of sexual and parasexual perversion. Nevertheless, in Islam, male homosexuality stands for all the perversions and constitutes in a sense the depravity of depravities. Female homosexuality [*musahaqa*], while equally con-

demned, is treated with relative indulgence and those who indulge in it incur the same reprimand as those condemned for auto-eroticism, bestiality or necrophilia. (Bouhdiba 1985:31)

7. *Gender Conflicted Persons*

There is no information available on transvestites or transsexuals because they cannot come out in public. This topic is not considered legitimate for discussion in Egypt.

8. *Significant Unconventional Sexual Behaviors*

A. Female Circumcision

In the West, the most controversial and publicized issue concerning women's health in the Islamic world and Africa is the practice of female circumcision. This practice is extremely widespread in Egypt, especially among the poorer classes and in rural areas. It is considered imperative for girls to be circumcised due to cultural norms that stigmatize uncircumcised girls and prevent them from marrying. Estimates range from 50 to 90 percent of all Egyptian women are circumcised, but precise figures are not known. A recent study conducted by researchers from Ayn Shams University found that 98 percent of all girls in the Egyptian countryside and poor girls in Cairo had been circumcised, both Muslims and Coptic Christians, while the estimate for upper-class girls in Cairo was approximately 30 percent (Botman 1999:106). The 1995 Egypt Demographic and Health Survey (EDHS-95) indicates that female circumcision is still a common practice despite government portrayals to the contrary. Among women with one or more living daughters, 87 percent report that at least one daughter has already been circumcised or that they intend to have the daughter circumcised in the future.

Most circumcisions take place before puberty; the median age at circumcision among both respondents and their daughters was 9.8 years. Traditional practitioners were responsible for more than eight to ten circumcisions among respondents, while trained medical personnel performed more than half of the circumcisions among the daughters of respondents.

The majority of women surveyed (82 percent) think female circumcision should be continued. Seventy-four percent believe that husbands prefer their wives to be circumcised and 72 percent believe that circumcision is an important aspect of religious tradition. Relatively few women recognize the negative consequences of circumcision, such as reduced sexual satisfaction (29 percent), the risk of death (24 percent), and the greater risk of problems in childbirth (5 percent).

This clinic-based study, one of the few of its kind, was carried out at five university hospitals, several rural hospitals, and two urban clinics. It included a total of 1,339 women for whom both questionnaires and physical examinations were completed. All clients coming to the sites for family planning or gynecological examinations were interviewed about their experience with female circumcision. In addition to the interview, pelvic examinations were conducted on all the women in the study. As part of the examinations, specially trained gynecologists determined whether there was physical evidence of circumcision and, in the case of circumcised women, the amount of tissue excised during the circumcision.

The results of the study permit a classification of circumcised women according to the type of circumcision performed. Because the interviews were conducted prior to the physical examinations, it was also possible to compare the woman's own report as to her circumcision status with the results of the physical examination. For 94 percent of the women in this clinic-based study, there was agreement between the reporting of circumcision and the findings of the subsequent physical examination.

While female circumcision is often presented as a requirement of Islam, this is in fact a fallacy. To the great embarrassment of the Egyptian government, the issue was raised at the 1994 International Conference on Population and Development in Cairo. Subsequently, a decree was issued to limit the practice to hospitals. The government refrained from completely outlawing the practice due to pressure by Islamic groups who deem female circumcision as necessary based on a saying by the Prophet Muhammad. Critics, however, point out that the Prophet's own daughters were not circumcised and that circumcision is not practiced in Saudi Arabia, the most conservative Islamic country in the Middle East. In 1997, under pressure from Islamic fundamentalist groups, the government lifted the ban on female circumcision. Despite international efforts to publicize the physical and psychological dangers of circumcision, the practice is gaining legitimacy as Islamists revive the belief that it is religiously mandated. The controversy around female circumcision is indicative of the tension between ingrained cultural values with respect to gender, Islamists' quests for "authenticity," and Western perspectives that advocate universal women's rights with respect to control of their bodies.

B. Coercive Sexual Behavior

Incest

Although all cultures have some kind of incest taboo, the boundaries restricting who is an acceptable sexual and marital partner vary. In Egypt, for instance, sexual relations and marriage between first cousins is not considered incestuous behavior and historically was very common. Even today, it is not uncommon for first cousins to marry. In fact, many families, particularly in the poorer and rural areas consider this form of arranged marriage preferable to marrying outside of the family. The rationale for this includes the idea that one has an insider's knowledge about one's own family and, therefore, knows "what one is getting." Also, first cousin marriages keep the land and wealth within the family.

Rape

Incidents of reported rape are infrequent in Egypt because young girls, especially from middle-class and upper-class families are very protected. They tend to only move in the company of members of their families and they themselves take great care to protect their reputations in order to remain "marriageable." Girls from poor families who work as domestic servants are at a much greater risk of rape because they have little power to protect themselves from the advances of male family members. These cases tend to go unreported and are not of interest to most members of the society. Also, the surge in an underground drug culture has led to a greater risk for women to be sexually exploited.

Unconventional Sexual Outlets

Although there are no recorded cases, some people claim that rural males occasionally use animals, such as sheep, as a sexual outlet. Especially in isolated villages, where sexual outlets for unmarried adolescents are lacking, sexual intercourse with animals is not uncommon.

C. Pornography and Erotica

Pornography as well as prostitution are forbidden by Egyptian law. That said, there are attempts to smuggle in pornography from the West, in particular now through the Internet. A crackdown on this behavior has been advocated by the government to the extent that at Internet cafes, users must sign a form saying that they will not attempt to access or download pornography.

D. Prostitution

Although information about prostitution in the religiously conservative nations of the Middle East is limited, prostitution is known to exist in most Arab countries, including the urban areas of Egypt (Inhotn & Buss 1993). Even though prostitution is outlawed in Egypt, Cairo is widely known as offering males access to many classes and types of prostitutes. With the increasing conservative climate in Egypt, the social phenomenon is increasingly hidden and not easily observed. Prostitution rings catering to traveling Western businessmen are known to operate out of private apartments, while other prostitutes frequent the large hotels with a high percentage of Western guests. It is difficult to regulate this form of prostitution because Egyptian prostitutes do not exhibit the same overt signals as their Western counterparts. There is no published data on prostitution in Egypt.

9. Contraception, Abortion, and Population Planning

Family planning is a problematic area even though Egypt has the longest history of contraceptive initiatives in the Middle East. In 1996, the former Ministry of Population and Family Planning was abolished and a new Ministry of Health and Population was created to underscore the renewed importance the government is giving to issues of population growth. Egypt's population problems are two-fold: rapid rates of population growth related to high fertility and an unbalanced population distribution. The highest fertility level is found in rural Upper Egypt, 5.2 births per woman, compared to a lower fertility level of 2.7 births per woman in urban Lower Egypt (Chelala 1996:1651).

In order to help curb population growth, the government has consistently advocated the use of family-planning methods. However, the quality of family-planning services is often poor, contraceptives are not readily available, and especially poor and rural women are reluctant to use artificial birth control methods which they have heard rumored to be detrimental to women's health. Many unwanted pregnancies end in self-induced abortions because abortion is prohibited in Egypt except in cases where pregnancy threatens the life of the mother. The 1995 Egypt Demographic and Health Survey, a nationally representative survey of 14,779 married women aged 14 to 49 shows a leveling off of the contraceptive prevalence rate at around 48 percent from 1991 to 1995. Although contraceptive use in Egypt doubled between 1980 and 1995, from 24 percent to 48 percent, most of the increase happened in the 1980s with no significant change in the overall rate of contraceptive use between 1991 and 1995. The 1995 survey also revealed significant differences in the level of contraceptive use based on region, with women in Lower Egypt showing the lowest contraceptive use. This high discrepancy can be attributed, at least in part, to lower socioeconomic conditions and traditional practices and beliefs.

A primary issue discussed during the International Conference on Population and Development held in September 1994 in Cairo was the relationship between religion, family planning, and women's rights. Abortion turned out to be the most controversial topic. Muslims vehemently argue against abortion as a means of family planning but believe that abortion should be tied to the family unit. They believe that abortion may be practiced in exceptional cases where the health of either the mother or the fetus is in danger. The government's stance is that women must avoid abortion as a method of family planning, but the government does not provide treatment and counseling for women forced to resort to this measure.

Herbal and folk contraceptives are still popular, particularly in rural areas. Midwives are popular sources for information on preventing pregnancies and inducing abortions. Midwives are also often indirectly involved in the hymen-breaking ceremony of young virgins on their wedding night.

Should a young woman not be a virgin or be worried about the intactness of her hymen, she may go to a midwife who will arrange for her to place a small sack with chicken blood into her vagina, so that when the marriage is consummated on her wedding night she will bleed.

Infertility, even though it is barely acknowledged or studied, is also an important problem that culturally afflicts primarily women in Egypt. In a society where it is imperative for women of all classes to bear children and, thus, attain social status through motherhood, the inability to bear children leads to serious social consequences. Alternatives to motherhood and domesticity are largely absent and adoption is not allowed under Islamic law. Thus, for all women, biological parenthood is imperative, especially since under Islamic law a man has the right to replace an infertile wife through divorce or polygynous marriage. While polygyny is not an option that is exercised by upper- and middle-class men, the threat of divorce hovers over childless marriages. Among all classes and educational levels, women are typically blamed for reproductive failings, and they also bear the burden of overcoming this condition through a therapeutic quest that is often traumatic and unfruitful (Inhorn 1994:5). Further, women face extremes of social judgment, for they are cast as being less than other women, as depriving their husbands and their husband's families of off-spring, and as endangering other people's children through their supposedly uncontrollable envy.

10. Sexually Transmitted Diseases

Information about sexually transmitted diseases in Egypt is scattered and often anecdotal. Nevertheless, evidence suggests that sexually transmitted diseases are widespread in the general population. The only study, which provides some indication of the prevalence of sexually transmitted diseases, is research on reproductive morbidities, including reproductive tract infections, conducted among 502 women in two villages in rural Giza, 1989 to 1990. Sixty-four percent of the women sampled had a reproductive tract infection at the time of the survey, which may be in part because condoms are rarely used in Egypt. While solid data is lacking, the 1995 Demographic and Health Survey reported that only 14 percent of married women used condoms for family planning. It is, therefore, unlikely that condoms are commonly used in Egypt for disease prevention (Lenton 1997:1005).

As in many other countries in sub-Saharan Africa, the migration-prostitution-STD triad is operative in Egypt. Studies indicate that, in particular, male labor migration, which is currently over 2 million, brings with it a variety of social ills, including STDs. Given strict cultural norms regarding women's premarital virginity and marital fidelity, Egyptian women find themselves on the receiving end of a variety of sexually transmitted infections. Their husbands, many of whom migrate for extended periods of time, contract gonorrhea, genital chlamydia, and other sterilizing infections, primarily from foreign prostitutes. Emerging studies from both rural and urban Egypt indicate that rates of various STDs are rising in similar proportions to the West. Often men contract STDs from either female or male prostitutes, and, given cultural norms that discourage this form of behavior, avoid seeing doctors. The infection therefore becomes chronic in men's prostates and they transmit the diseases directly on the first wedding night to their new brides. Women, thus, may start their marital lives with tubal infections that potentially lead to infertility. This has major societal implications because infertile women face their greatest threat from their husbands who have the right under Islamic law to replace an infertile wife through divorce or a polygynous remarriage. Such replacements are often encouraged by the husbands' families who view an infertile wife as, at best, useless, and, at worst, as a threat to the social reproduction of the patrilineage (Inhorn 1996:4).

Another factor that may influence the spread of STDs is the fact that Egypt remains a popular tourist destination, both for visitors to the pyramids and pharaonic treasures and, more recently, for seekers of sand, sea, and sex who visit Red Sea resorts. Despite the growing conservative fundamentalist movement, Egypt is still more liberal than other Arab states.

11. HIV/AIDS

According to United Nations statistics, North Africa and the Middle East account for less than one percent of the total number of people infected worldwide with HIV. In this region, 27,000 people have died from HIV-related illnesses, compared to 170,000 in Europe and 46 million in sub-Saharan Africa. The National AIDS Program in Egypt recently published the number of units of blood that have tested positive for HIV in each of the last seven years. The prevalence of infection is low and there is no real evidence of an upward trend. For example, in 1990, 136,422 blood units were tested and only 4 were positive for HIV; in 1996, a quarter of a million units were tested and only 3 were positive (Lenton 1997:1005). The data from blood donations is particularly interesting because all blood collected in Egypt's public-health facilities is voluntarily donated by family members of patients. There is no evidence of either voluntary or non-voluntary donor referral. Egypt's medical surveillance of blood units is, therefore, a good indicator of the prevalence of HIV in the adult population.

Despite worldwide increases in the AIDS epidemic, AIDS is so far not spreading in any perceptible numbers in Egypt. Nonetheless, factors that contribute to the spread of HIV definitely exist and anecdotal evidence suggests that other sexually transmitted diseases are widespread in the general population. However, while reliable survey data is not available,

Egyptian medical experts claim that the negligible spread of HIV infection and AIDS in the general population is possibly the result of the Islamic moral code which forbids adultery, sex before marriage, and homosexual practices. This indicates that widespread adherence to this code could mean that, while HIV infection occurs in small groups practicing sexual behaviors that increase their chance of infection, only rarely do individuals in the general population come into contact with at-risk individuals. Nonetheless, research into patterns of sexuality is needed in order to explain the low prevalence of AIDS in Egypt. Also, the lack of reliable data makes it difficult to gauge the real situation from the picture presented by official sources.

12. Sexual Dysfunctions, Counseling, and Therapies

While there are no official studies on sexual dysfunction in the Egyptian population, it is widely known that Egyptian men are obsessed with enhancing sexual performance. While the men define enhanced sexual performance as prolonging intercourse, all remedies used suggest underlying occurrences of impotence. In recent years, Viagra has become very well known and popular in Egypt. During Ramadan 1999, better varieties of dates, which are very popular as one of the favorite foods for breaking the fast, were being sold under the names "Viagra" and "Monica" dates. Even melatonin, when it initially became popular on the world market, was seen by Egyptian men as some kind of aphrodisiac, as a means for bringing one's youth back. Other remedies that are thought to be good for men are hashish, tea (but not mint or *karkadeh* or hibiscus tea), and other things which are "relaxing," for example, pigeon, sheep's feet, and also nutmeg. There are other more medicinal remedies available at the traditional pharmacies. In addition, there is *dahaan*, "ointments" of various kinds, local anesthetics also supposed to prolong erection. Many Egyptian men at the time of their wedding will seek advice on sexual aids in order to ensure that everything will "function properly."

Women's medicinal and folk medicinal remedies tend to center around issues of conception, pregnancy, and nursing. While many people are aware that female circumcision may lead to frigidity, as was mentioned above, it is still extremely common. Also worthy of mention is the cosmetic practice of hymen repair. Due to the fact that female virginity plays an enormous role in terms of the honor of a family and the bride involved, some doctors have developed the practice of sewing up ruptured hymens before an upcoming wedding night. This practice is particularly common among upper-middle-class and upper-class families where the girls have been permitted more freedom in terms of their interactions with men before marriage, but where female virginity on the wedding night remains just as important as among the lower classes.

13. Research and Advanced Education

Sexological research is only in the initial stages in Egypt. While issues of family planning, mother and infant mortality, and women's reproductive concerns have been at the forefront of the Egyptian research agenda for quite a long period, other topics concerning sexuality are not. The growing fundamentalist movement further impedes any research that deals with issues of sexuality not directly related to reproductive issues.

There are no sexological organizations or publications in Egypt. The Egyptian Family Planning Association has its offices at: 66 Gazirat El Arab Street, Al Mohandissen, El Giza, Cairo, Egypt. Phone: 20-2-360-7329; fax: +20-2-360-7329.

References and Suggested Readings

Abdel Kader, S. 1992. *The situation analysis of women in Egypt.* Cairo: Central Agency for Population, Mobilization, and Statistics (CAPMAS) & UNICEF.
Abudabbeh, N. 1996. Arab families. In: M. McGoldrick, J. Giordano, & J. K. Pearce, eds., *Ethnicity and family therapy* (2nd ed., pp. 333-346). New York: Guilford Press.
Ahmed, L. 1982. Feminism and feminist movements in the Middle East: A preliminary exploration: Turkey, Egypt, Algeria, People's Democratic Republic of Yemen. *Women's Studies International Forum,* 5(2):153-168.
Al-Ali, N. 1997. Feminism and contemporary debates in Egypt. In: D. Cahtty & A. Rabo, eds., *Organizing women: Formal and informal women's groups in the Middle East.* Oxford: Berg Publishers.
Amin, Q. 1976. *Tahrir al-mara* [*The liberation of women*]. Reprinted in *Muhammad 'Imara, Qasim Amin: Al-amal al-kamila* (vol. 2). Beirut.
Anderson, J. N. D. 1968. The eclipse of the patriarchal family in contemporary Islamic law. In: J. N. D. Anderson, ed., *Family law in Asia and Africa* (pp. 221-234). London: George Allen and Unwin.
Badran, M. 1995. *Feminists, Islam, and nation: Gender and the making of modern Egypt.* Princeton, NJ: Princeton University Press.
Badran, M. 1991. Competing agenda: Feminists, Islam, and the state in nineteenth- and twentieth century Egypt. In: D. Kandiyoti, ed., *Women, Islam and the state* (pp. 201-236). Philadelphia: Temple University Press.
Badran, M., & Cooke, M. 1990. Introduction. In: M. Badran & M. Cooke, eds., *Opening the gates: A century of Arab feminist writing* (pp. xiv-xxxvi). Bloomington, IN: Indiana University Press.
Baron, B. 1994. *The women's awakening: Culture, society and the press.* New Haven, CT: Yale University Press.
Beck, L. G., & Keddie, N., eds. 1978. *Women in the Muslim world.* Cambridge, MA: Harvard University Press.
El-Baz, S. 1997. The impact of social and economic factors on women's group formation in Egypt. In: D. Cahtty & A. Rabo, eds., *Organizing women: Formal and informal women's groups in the Middle East.* Oxford: Berg Publishers.
Beijing National Report. 1995. Cairo: The National Women's Committee, National Council of Childhood and Motherhood.
Botman, S. 1999. *Engendering citizenship in Egypt.* New York: Columbia University Press.
Bouhdiba, A. 1985. *Sexuality in Islam* (A. Sheridan, trans.). London: Routledge and Kegan Paul.

Bousquet, G. H. 1948. La conception du nikah selon les docteurs de la loi musulmane. *Revue Algerienne*, 63-74.

Brooks, G. 1995. *Nine parts of desire: The hidden world of Islamic women.* New York: Anchor Books/Doubleday.

CAPMAS (Central Agency for Population, Mobilization, and Statistics). 1986. *National Census.* Cairo: CAPMAS.

CAPMAS. 1990. *Labour force sample survey* (LFSS), Cairo: CAPMAS.

CAPMAS and UNICEF. 1991. *Women's participation in the labour force.* Cairo: CAPMAS and UNICEF.

Chelala, C. 1996. Egypt faces challenge of population growth. *The Lancet, 348*:9042, 1651.

Fernea, E. W. 1998. Egypt. In: *In search of feminism: One woman's global journey* (pp. 240-288). New York: Doubleday.

Haeri, S. 1989. *Law of desire: Temporary marriage in Iran.* London: I.B. Tauris.

Hatem, A 1992. Economic and political liberalization in Egypt and the demise of state feminism. *International Journal of Middle East Studies*, 24.

Inhom, M. 1994. *Quest for conception: Gender, infertility and Egyptian medical tradition.* Philadelphia: University of Pennsylvania Press.

Karam, A. 1998. *Women, Islamisms and the state: Contemporary feminism in Egypt.* New York: St. Martin's Press.

Lenton, C. 1997. Will Egypt escape the AIDS epidemic? *The Lancet, 349*:9057, 1005.

El-Nashif, H. 1994. *Basic education and female literacy in Egypt.* Cairo: Third World Forum, Middle East Office.

Macleod, A. E. 1991. *Accommodating protest: Working women and the new veiling in Cairo.* New Haven, CT: Yale University Press.

Mernissi, F. 1993. *Islam and democracy: Fear of the modern world.* Reading, MA: Addison-Wesley.

Mernissi, F. 1991. *The veil and the male elite: A feminist interpretation of women's rights in Islam.* Reading, MA: Addison-Wesley

'al-Misri, A. I. al-N. 1994. *'Umdat al-Salik wa-'Uddat al-Nasik. Reliance of the traveller: The classic manual of Islamic sacred law* (In Arabic with facing English text, N. H. M. Keller (trans.), rev. edition). Evanston, IL: Sunna Books.

Murray, S. O. 1997a. Male homosexuality, inheritance rules, and the status of women in medieval Egypt: The case of the Mamluks. In: S. O. Murray & W. Roscoe, eds., *Islamic homosexualities: Culture, history, and literature.* New York/London: New York University Press.

Murray, S. O. 1997b. Woman–woman love in Islamic societies. In: S. O. Murray & W. Roscoe, eds., *Islamic homosexualities: Culture, history, and literature.* New York/London: New York University Press.

Murray, S. O. 1997c. The will not to know: Islamic accommodations of male homosexuality. In: S. O. Murray & W. Roscoe, eds., *Islamic homosexualities: Culture, history, and literature.* New York/London: New York University Press.

Murray, S. O., & Roscoe, W., eds. 1997. *Islamic homosexualities: Culture, history, and literature.* New York/London: New York University Press.

Najmabadi, A. 1991. Hazards of modernity and morality: Women, state and ideology in contemporary Iran. In: D. Kandiyoti, ed., *Women, Islam and the state.* London: Macmillan.

Parrinder, G. 1980. *Sex in the world's great religions.* Don Mills, Ontario, Canada: General Publishing Company.

Talharni, G. 1996. *The mobilization of Muslim women in Egypt.* Gainesville: University of Florida Press.

UNICEF. 1993. *Report on the state of women and children in Egypt.* Cairo: UNICEF.

Verma, B. R. 1971. *Muslim marriage and dissolution.* Allahabad, Egypt: Law Books. Co.

Iceland
(*Lveldi Ísland*)
(The Republic of Iceland)

Sóley S. Bender, R.N., B.S.N., M.S., Coordinator,*
with Sigrún Júliíusdóttir, Ph.D.,** Thorvaldur Kristinsson,
and Gudrún Jónsdóttir, Ph.D.

Contents

Demographics and a Historical Perspective

SÓLEY S. BENDER

A. Demographics

Iceland is an island located just south of the Arctic Circle in the North Atlantic Ocean. Geographically isolated until 870 when the first settlers arrived, Iceland's nearest neighbors are Greenland about 190 miles (300

Communications: Sóley S. Bender, R.N., M.S., Department of Nursing, University of Iceland, Eirberg, Eiriksgotu 34, 101 Reykjavík, Iceland; ssb@rhi.hi.is.

**Sigrún Júliíusdóttir, Ph.D., Department of Social Work, Faculty of Social Sciences, University of Iceland, IS-101 Reykjavík. Iceland; sigjul@rhi.hi.is.

kilometers) to the northwest, Norway about 620 miles (1,000 kilometers) to the east, and the United Kingdom 500 miles (800 kilometers) to the south. Iceland's total land area is just under 40,000 square miles (103,000 square kilometers), with a coastline of 3,100 miles (4,988 kilometers). About 65 percent of the country is mountainous, with glacial rivers coursing through sandy deserts and lava fields. About 11 percent of Iceland is covered with glaciers (Hagstofa Íslands 1998).

There are innumerable hot springs both in the lowlands and in the mountains. Natural hot water is used to heat houses. There are many geysers in Iceland, the most famous being the Great Geyser in Haukadalur, which gives its name to geysers all over the world. The climate is insular and much warmer, because of the Gulf Stream, than the name of the country suggests. Icelanders import grain and vegetables but are self-sufficient in meat and dairy products. Fishing, the main industry, accounts for 71 percent of the country's exports and 20 percent of the nation's gross domestic product. One seventh of Iceland's workforce is employed in the fishing industry (Hagstofa Íslands 1998). In 1998, the nation's estimated per capita gross domestic product was $30,126 (Iceland krona) or US$21,000 (Hagstofa Íslands 1999c). Iceland's unemployment rate in 1998 was 2.7 percent, 3.3 percent for females and 2.3 percent for males (Hagstofa Íslands 1999b). The majority of Icelandic women, 83 percent, participate in the labor force, which is higher than in the other Nordic countries (Nordic Council of Ministers 1999).

Schooling is compulsory from age 6 to 16. The language is Icelandic, which is actually similar to the language spoken by the Vikings who settled in Iceland in the early days. Most education is free. The number of women graduating from universities is rising, with 59 percent of the 1995-1996 graduates being women and 41 percent male, compared with a 93:7 ratio in the early 1950s (Hagstofa Íslands 1997). The literacy rate for adults was 99.0 percent in 1997 (United Nations Development Program 1999).

Ethnically, Icelanders are a homogeneous mixture of descendants of Norwegian and Celtic settlers who arrived over 1,300 years ago. Over 90 percent of the people are Evangelical Lutherans, 3 percent other Protestant and Roman Catholic, and 1 percent have no religious affiliation. In 1999, 61.5 percent of Icelanders lived in the Reykjavik metropolitan area.

Iceland's population on January 1, 2000, was 279,049, with 139,665 men and 139,384 women (Hagstofa Íslands 2000a). The age distribution was:

Age	0-14 years	15-65 years	65 and older
All	23.32%	65.1%	11.58%
Men	23.79	65.8	10.41
Women	22.85	64.4	12.75

(*Source*: Denmarks Statistiks 2000a)

Icelander's average life expectancy at birth in 1999 was 81.43 years for Icelandic women and 77.54 years for men (Hagstofa Íslands 2000a). In

1940, the average life expectancy was 66 for women and 61 for men. The crude birth rate per 1000 live births in 1999 was 14.8 and the crude death rate 6.9 per 1000 (Hagstofa Íslands 2000). The infant mortality rate per 1000 live births in 1999 was 1.9 for boys and 3.4 for girls (Hagstofa Íslands 1999b). Usually the infant mortality rate has been higher for boys than for girls. In 1997, infant mortality was 3.0 for girls and 7.9 for boys; in 1940, it was 2.8 for girls and 4.4 for boys (Nordic Council of Ministers 1999). The annual population increase was 1.25 percent in 1999 (Hagstofa Íslands 1999a). Iceland's population increased by 25,202 people or 9.9 percent between 1990 and 2000, which is about 0.95 percent annually (Hagstofa Íslands 1999a). The total fertility rate in 1999 was 2.048 children per fertile woman (Hagstofa Íslands 1999b). Two years earlier, in 1997, Icelandic women had a lower TFR of 1.8 children, placing Iceland 156 among 227 nations. The mean age of having the first child in 1998 was 25.1 years and the mean age of women in general to have a child was 28.8 (Hagstofa Íslands 1999b).

B. A Brief Historical Perspective

The first settlers of the volcanic island of Iceland were Vikings who arrived from Norway in 874 C.E. accompanied by a number of Scots and Irish. The Icelandic people are therefore mainly Scandinavian, genetically very homogeneous because of their long-standing geographic isolation. In 930, the Vikings established their legislative assembly, the Althing at Thingvellir, the world's oldest parliament. Christianity arrived in Iceland around the year 1000. In the year 1262, Iceland came under Norwegian rule. In 1380, it came under the rule of Denmark when the Danes gained control of all of Scandinavia. In 1918, Iceland became an independent sovereign state in union with Denmark through a common king. In 1944, with the Nazis occupying Denmark, Iceland deposed its king and declared itself a republic. The republic developed a Scandinavian-style welfare state, with comprehensive social benefits, that have produced one of the healthiest and best-educated populations (Olafsson 1989, 1990, 1999). Since 1944, Iceland has been an independent republic with the president chosen by a general election every four years.

1. Basic Sexological Premises
SIGRÚN JÚLIÍUSDÓTTIR

The character of gender roles, the sociolegal status of males and females, and general concepts of sexuality in Iceland are dealt with here as the product of the interaction between macroconditions and cultural values on the macro level, and lifestyle and adjustment on the meso or family level within Icelandic culture. These three basic sexological premises are discussed on the basis of statistics and research as well as clinical experience.

A. Character of Gender Roles

The rather young and small Icelandic society is known for its ancient literature, the *Sagas*, from which some basic cultural values derive. From the thousand-year-old Saga period, we have colorful and influential descriptions of powerful gender characteristics of men and women and their equally esteemed gender roles, as Vikings and Valkyries.

The written sagas and their narratives reflect cultural-ethical values and social norms, which have been transmitted through the generations, in written texts, oral history, and developing myths. They have brought with them strong ideas or even ideals for modern men and women, for good and for bad. Also, some of the old values linked to survival and social adjustment in a tough natural environment under poor socioeconomic conditions in earlier times are still today reflected in men and women's tough attitudes to work, love, and children (Juliusdottir & Asmundsson 1987). Accordingly, the modern woman sees herself as strong and independent, but simultaneously she still assumes almost single-handedly the responsibility for the internal life of the family, reproduction, emotional care, and survival. Modern young men still see themselves as socially and economically responsible for the family's external, reproductive, and economic survival.

A family study on coping strategies in Icelandic families with children includes an analysis of the interaction of old cultural values and modern lifestyle. The results show how the ties to earlier times shape a set of gender-based complementarity of responsibilities enchaining both sexes to old hidden loyalties, which often seem to be a stumbling stone to individual freedom and career goals (Juliusdottir 1993).

Strivings for equality in Iceland started more than a century ago with women's movements and activity in different social organizations. Several factors, such as different formal human rights early in the twentieth century, have contributed to the development of a myth about the strong Icelandic woman. Icelandic women gained eligibility and the right to vote in 1915 and the first woman was elected to the parliament in 1922 (Erlendsdottir 1993; Kristmundsdottir 1997). Other historical events are often referred to as verifying instances of gender equality and the somewhat special position of Icelandic women. These are the strong Redstocking Movement (for sexual equality) around 1970, the celebrated "Day of Women's Strengths and Solidarity" (*Kvennafrídagur*) on October 24, 1975, the Women's Slate Movement and the subsequent Women's Party from 1982 onwards, and the election of Vigdis Finnbogadottir in 1980 as the first woman president of a nation in the world. Also cited are the establishment of the Society for Sheltering Battered Women in 1979, followed by the first study of violence against women (Olafsdottir et al. 1982; Juliusdottir 1982), and the Women's Counselling Service in 1984. All these are evidence of the progress modern Icelandic women have made in their endeavors for solidarity with victims of violence and injustice.

Being strong, however, is not the same as being free and independent, a distinction that may apply to both men and women. In spite of the positive image of the strong Icelandic women, statistics give another picture. Figures on the low wages and occupational status of Icelandic women, and their poor participation and lack of recognition in the public sphere, in politics and the economy, show the opposite, i.e., a much lower status of women than men (Hagstofa Íslands 1999b:67, 184).

The increasing pressures of globalization have reduced the historic isolating effects of Iceland's geographical distance from other countries. Modern electronic and computer/Internet media rapidly import new scientific knowledge and convey the latest ideas from abroad about gender equality and behavior patterns. Ideas about the personal freedom to choose and plan one's educational path, occupational career, children, and family obligations thus often collide with the persistent old values related to the virtue of personal sacrifice, hard work, and social adjustment in Iceland.

The labor force is in short supply and both professionals and qualified and unqualified workers are badly needed. Thus the relatively few inhabitants are not only expected to contribute with long working hours, but also are simultaneously expected to find for themselves effective solutions for family matters such as child care and care for the elderly. A strong informal family network often comes into play when public services and support are lacking for dual-career couples. Another example of how social concerns are dealt with in the private sphere is the expectation that married couples will successfully negotiate their own marital/familial roles and responsibilities (Rafnsdottir 1994; Olafsson 1990).

There is strong social pressure to reach the goal of a first-class housing standard, high educational level, and modern material consumption pattern for all Icelanders. Simultaneously, the old values of still having many children, taking care of one's own parents, and other "old fashioned" family obligations often put young parents in a situation of heavy conflicts in their daily lives.

B. Sociolegal Status of Males and Females

The small, traditionally rural Icelandic society changed rapidly after World War II. The process of urbanization with a civil environment and modern lifestyle did not appear until the 1950s. Iceland is supposed to share the welfare-state ideology of the Nordic countries. The implementation of constitutional and juridical issues is, however, somewhat different (Olafsson 1999; 1989). Iceland's health care expenditure is in line with the other Nordic countries and even higher in some cases. In Iceland, consumers of health services, however, pay a larger part of the medical costs themselves. The high-quality health-service results include the lowest infant mortality rate and the highest life expectancy in the Nordic countries (NOMESCO 1998:67-69, 161, 164).

On the other hand, the government's economic contribution to social and family matters is much lower than it is for the health services. Thus, day-care centers and services for the elderly are insufficient to meet the needs of the people (NOSOSCO 1996). The difference is striking when long working hours, the number of children, and the considerable number of three-generation households are taken into account. In spite of the high divorce rate, approximately 40 percent of the weddings, the strong and still increasing familialism, with its emphasis on building families early and having many children, makes the percentage of intact families (married or cohabiting with their own children) up to 50 percent plus. At the same time, the number of single-parent households is 8.5 percent and 7.3 percent for stepfamilies (Hagstofa Íslands 1999b:33, 60, 65; Juliusdottir et al. 1995:40-41).

Statistics show that on average men between the ages of 25 and 54 have a workweek of 54-plus hours and women 45 hours (Hagstofa Íslands 1999b:88). Ninety-six percent of the men and 85 percent of the women between ages 25 and 54 are actively employed (Hagstofa Íslands 1999b:79). The choice of fields in this labor market is highly segregated by gender. The proportion of women is highest in public services, health care, and education, whereas that of men is highest in administration, special techniques, fishing, and agriculture (Hagstofa Íslands 1999b:86). The wages of women are only 52 percent of those of the men, and that has not changed in recent years (*Heilsufar Kvenna* 2000).

Icelandic women have reached a high level of education. Among the 20-year-olds, 42.3 percent of the women and 28.5 percent of the men pass the matriculation examination. Also proportionally more women than men are admitted to universities, and they graduate more frequently than men, both with undergraduate and graduate-level degrees (Hagstofa Íslands 1999b:269). Women do not seem, however, to realize their potential in a vocational career to the same extent Icelandic men do, as already pointed out above.

After World War II, the work of Icelandic women outside the home increased and their educational level improved considerably. There has, however, been a significant difference between single and married women. The latter continued to give birth to many children and take care of their parents, although the day-care system and services for the elderly did not expand in proportion to the demand. As elsewhere, the social care services have developed as a gender issue, both regarding the employed and the families as consumers (Rauhala et al. 1997).

During the last decade, several improvements of crucial importance for equality have been legislated. One sign of progress for equality of the sexes was new legislation on parental leave of nine months at childbirth, which is to be implemented in steps in the next few years. It allows three months leave for the mother, three months for the father, and three months to be divided as the parents choose.

In 1992, Iceland was late in introducing legislation on joint custody for children of divorced parents. A new study on the experience of this alternative shows that parents who choose joint custody adjust in several ways better and more equally to their new life circumstances. Both parents and children report better health on average, and the frequency of depression and social isolation is less than among parents with divided custody. They use alcohol less often and the contact with families of origin is more frequent, especially for the fathers. The parental responsibilities also came out more equal for both sexes than when custody was divided (Juliusdottir & Sigurdardottir 2000).

A recently established public Family Council, followed by the Year of the Family in 1994, has played a role in preparing an integrated and comprehensive family policy, recommending political initiatives, and facilitating actions in family matters, such as family planning and family life education. The Family Council is also supposed to serve as a consulting organ for the government.

The rapid socioeconomic evolution has caused a cultural lag, where families and couples are struggling with adapting to the new society's demand for consumption and self-realization, but at the same time taking on family obligations in the spirit of the still-alive old values and images.

Sometimes the loyalty to old values is beneficial and sometimes it restricts the changing character of Icelandic gender roles. The influences of the macro- and mesofactors mentioned above often appear strikingly in parental roles and in couples' intimate relationships affecting their emotional and sexual lives. A comparison between two Icelandic and Swedish counseling services shows that the reasons for seeking professional help are different. The Swedish clinical population in marital and family therapy seems more prone to seek help to improve couples' emotional relationships and communication when dealing with personal and interactional conflicts. This may, unlike the case in Iceland, have to do with the fact that Swedish parents are not so busy struggling with practical (e.g., financial, housing, working, and daycare) problems of daily life as Icelandic parents are. Such practical needs and problems related to them are not so prominent in Sweden. They are, to a greater extent, taken care of through effective family policy with sufficient official family support (Juliusdottir 1993).

In modern European societies, where the public is generally well educated and conscious about qualities of life, there is also increasing emphasis on harmonious proportioning of work, private life, leisure, sex, and pleasure. In Iceland, some similar changes in cognitive attitudes are appearing. In a comparative European study, 66 percent of Icelanders agreed with the statement, "The government must offer extensive social services, even if it requires higher expenditures and increased taxes." This percentage of agreement was similar to that in other European countries. On the other hand, 79 percent in the Icelandic sample were strongly against the statement, "Social service is too expensive and must be cut down" (Olafsson 1999; Olafsson et al. 1998).

C. General Concepts of Sexuality and Love

Icelandic constructs of sexuality related to family building, health, work, values, and moral attitudes provide a third domain of basic sexological premises.

The Icelandic population, in general, holds rather permissive attitudes regarding sexual relations and other related social-moral issues. Although the age of majority for males and females is 18 years, young people start working already at an earlier age and consequently identify with adult behavior in many regards. Icelandic adolescents, boys earlier than girls, start petting early in comparison to other countries, often before age 16, and have their first sexual intercourse, on average, at age 15 (Jonsdottir & Haraldsdottir 1998). Approximately 55 percent of 14-year-olds, girls more often than boys, have started smoking. A somewhat higher proportion at this age has started drinking. There is no difference between the sexes until the age of 17, when the proportion is significantly higher for the girls (Adalbjarnardottir et al. 1997). Another Icelandic study confirms these results, but also shows that young Icelandic adolescents in general use alcohol and drugs to a somewhat lesser extent than those in the other European countries (Thorlindsson et al. 1998).

Young people, on average, leave home at the age of 20-plus and start cohabitation or marriage, on average, about the age of 21. It is most common to start "going steady" at about the age of 18 and to have experienced two longer relationships before cohabitation. At least 40 percent start cohabiting in the housing of their parents or parents-in-law (Juliusdottir et al. 1995:52).

The generally liberal attitudes of Icelanders are reflected in the Icelandic part of an international opinion study of a nationwide representative sample (Jonsson & Olafsson 1991). In some moral attitudes and values concerning sexuality and family life, Icelanders do not differ from the average on most items. Approximately 24 percent agree on a requirement of "totally free and unregulated sexual behavior," whereas the other Nordic countries are harder on that issue. Icelanders differ from other Scandinavians on average in holding more positive attitudes towards divorce, abortion, and homosexuality. On the other hand, Icelanders are, on average, more negative than other Scandinavians when it comes to marital infidelity.

In the 1991 family study just cited, approximately 80 percent of responding husbands and wives said that it never occurred in their relationship. The respondents, however, reported that they would discuss it rather than see it as a reason for divorce. Asked about their attitudes to their own sexual life, they commonly reported that they have intercourse six to ten times per month (45 percent of the men; 49 percent of the women). They emphasized caring more than intercourse (45 percent men; 70 percent women), and preferred showing physical closeness and warmth (30 percent men; 21 percent women) (Juliusdottir 1993:186, 190).

In an international study of 60 countries (Gallup 1999) with a representative sample of Icelanders, the respondents evaluated similar factors as the other Nordic countries as most important in life, specifically, good health and happy family life. A recent nationwide Icelandic opinion study on moral values and virtues showed similar results (Proppé 2000). What Icelanders saw as more important to care about and to pursue were family and friendship (50 percent) rather than education and vocational career (11 percent). This was especially true among younger people.

2. Religious and Ethnic Factors Affecting Sexuality

SÓLEY S. BENDER

A/B. Source and Character of Religious/Ethnic Values

In Iceland, about 89 percent of the population are registered members of the state Lutheran Church, 3.6 percent belong to the Lutheran free churches, 3.3 percent belong to other religious organizations, and of those there are 1.4 percent Catholic (Hagstofa Íslands 1999b). There is not a strong religious influence on sexual life. According to the Lutheran religion, people should only have sex within marriage. In the earlier days, marriage was arranged between two clans. Both the bride and the bridegroom had to have enough money to be able to get married (Gudmundsson 1990).

In Thorvardarson's 1978 study, students in the age group 16 to 18 were asked about the importance of teaching about Christian values, especially regarding sexuality and marriage. Only 10 percent considered it very important to teach religious values in sex education. This issue had the lowest value when compared to other topics in sex education, such as sexually transmitted diseases (97 percent), contraceptive methods (92 percent), where to get information (86 percent), and sexual problems (61 percent).

Nowadays, marriage is not a prerequisite for living a sexual life. Cohabitation is common and some people never get married, although they may have several children. Icelanders widely accept single persons having a sexual life.

3. Sexual Knowledge and Education

SÓLEY S. BENDER

A. Government Policies and Programs

In the 1950s, sex education in Iceland's schools was limited. For the most part, it consisted of two pages in the human health book. In many schools, the teachers skipped these two pages. In 1948, *Sexuality* by Fritz Kahn, M.D., was published in Iceland. It was a popular possession of many families at that time. Through the years, several books about sexuality have been translated into Icelandic. Some of these books have been used in teaching sex education. In 1976, *The Man, Birth, Childhood and Adolescence* was written by Icelanders to be used for sex education (Eiriksdottir et al. 1976). It has since been widely used for fifth and sixth graders (10- and 11-year-olds). *Human Reproduction*, published in 1983 (Kjartansson & Brynjolfsson). was another Icelandic addition to textbooks for sex education in the schools. It has been widely used in the schools for 13- to 16-year-old students.

The 1985 diagnosis of the first person in Iceland with AIDS raised the importance of preventive work in the schools. This meant increased emphasis on sexually transmitted diseases and the importance of condom use. Because of AIDS, new Icelandic educational material about sexually transmitted diseases was published in 1988 by the Ministries of Education and Health for use by teachers and others in sex education. In 1989, the Ministry of Education issued a curriculum plan for grades one through nine. In this plan, sex education was emphasized as a part of many subjects in the schools, like Christianity, sociology, and biology. Teachers in the schools and health professionals from the local community health center were encouraged to work together on sex education. In the fall of 1999, a new curriculum plan was released by the Ministry of Education for grades one through ten and beyond. Presently, teachers in every school make their own teaching plan, and the number of hours devoted to sex education can vary considerably. Sex education is therefore in the hands of individual teachers and schools. Some schools have very good sex education whereas others are very limited.

A standard curriculum for sex education was lacking for many years. It was not until 1991 that a holistic curriculum for sex education for the eighth through the tenth grades was introduced in the schools. This program, *Human Sexuality, Values and Choices,* was an American sex education curriculum from Minnesota. It was translated, adapted to Icelandic culture, and pilot-tested in seven schools in 1990 (Axelsdottir et al. 1990). The pilot test was based on an experimental design. It showed that there was a significant increase in knowledge among those in the experimental group compared to those in the control group, but it showed very limited changes of attitudes. This sex education curriculum is based on 15 lessons, with lessons about the biological facts of human sexuality, but also about feelings and intrapersonal relations. It does stress identity, feelings, how to make decisions, and knowing what to do when it comes to making decisions about sexuality. It has a comprehensive handbook for teachers, with objectives and the contents of the lessons, as well as projects for the students. It also has a video of 120 minutes that has short episodes of certain sex education sessions meant to facilitate group discussion. There is an additional handbook for parents.

The teachers are supposed to have three meetings with the parents about the curriculum. Many projects are intended to be completed by the students in cooperation with their parents or other adults. This program is now in use in many schools and it has made a considerable difference for sex education. A 1993 study showed that this curriculum was used by 63.6 percent of the 60 schools participating in that study (grades eight through ten) (Palsdottir & Hardardottir 1993).

No comprehensive curriculum has been developed for students younger than 13 years old or for those older than 16 years old. There is no sex education in the junior colleges except when students arrange it themselves. Representatives from the Icelandic Association for Sexual and Reproductive Health have been asked to go to several schools to give sex education. Also lacking are regular training courses about sex education for teachers and school health nurses. The last time such a training course was offered was in 1992.

A regulation about health promotion in schools from 1958 is probably one of the oldest legal documents that deal with sex education. In addition, sex education is based on 1975 laws about information and counseling regarding sexuality and responsible parenthood, abortion, and sterilization, 1976 laws about gender equality, and 1978 laws about sexually transmitted diseases. A 1975 law stated: "Educational authorities should in cooperation with the chief school health physician give information about sexuality and moral issues regarding sexuality in the compulsory school system. Additionally information should be given in other educational programs."

In Thorvardarson's 1978 study, 6.4 percent of boys and 13.7 percent of girls in the sixth grade said that they received good enough sex education. In the eighth grade, the percentages were 2.9 percent for boys and 3.7 percent for girls. In the same study, 79 percent of the sixth graders and 96 percent of the eighth graders wanted the school to provide sex education. A nationwide study of sex education, based on a sample of 60 teachers in 60 schools, showed that the mean hours of sex education for the ninth grade was 19.7 hours, and for the tenth grade, it was 15.6 hours (Palsdottir & Hardardottir 1993). In this same study, participants were asked how they taught each issue. More teachers reported that they taught the contraceptive methods (condom, pill, diaphragm, IUD, etc.) well, than reported that they taught the STDs (gonorrhea, chlamydia, herpes, etc.) well (91 percent to 84 percent for contraception versus 62 percent to 81 percent for STDs). Eighty-eight percent thought they taught about puberty and human reproduction very well, and 81.8 percent felt they did well teaching respect for the decisions of others (Palsdottir & Hardardottir 1993).

Although the 1993 study showed that there were several issues considered by the teachers to be taught well, the survey results can give us only limited information about the actual sexual education on these topics. The study had a response rate of 60 percent, and it is a question whether the 40 percent who did not answer did not respond because they were not motivated to teach the subject or because of some other reasons. These study results do not agree with the results of three interviews with student focus groups, who frequently stated that they got very limited sex education in grades eight through ten (Johannsdottir 2000).

What needs to be done in the future is to have sex education as a compulsory subject in the school system, to have training courses on a regular basis, and to develop a curriculum for junior college (age groups 16 to 20).

B. Informal Sources of Sexual Knowledge

People have had access to sexual information from books, magazines, films, and the media. There has been a considerable increase in the publication of educational material about sexual and reproductive health from the Director of Public Health, from the Icelandic Association for Sexual and Reproductive Health, and from the Icelandic Incest Center (*Stigamot*). In 1990, Ottar Gudmundsson wrote *Íslenska Kynlífsbókin* (*The Icelandic Sexuality Book*), the first comprehensive Icelandic book about sexuality. Before that time, the books that were available were translated from other languages and cultures. Over the last few years, especially after AIDS got into the picture, sexuality has been discussed more openly on television and on the radio.

4. Autoerotic Behaviors and Patterns
SÓLEY S. BENDER

There are many negative terms in the Icelandic language for masturbation, starting with *self-pollution* (*sjálfsflekkun*). In *Sexuality* by Fritz Kahn, which was translated and published in Iceland in 1948, masturbation was explained in a detailed manner for both genders. It was stressed that masturbation was not bad for the health and that this behavior was not related to diseases. Kahn mentioned that Simon André Tissot, who published a treatise on the vice of "onanism" in 1760, had a considerable negative influence on attitudes toward masturbation. Tissot described the terrible effects of masturbation, ranging from nervousness to insanity.

There is no Icelandic study that provides any information about masturbation. Today, it is stressed that masturbation is a good way to get to know oneself. It is considered important to know one's own body sensations before sharing it with someone else.

5. Interpersonal Heterosexual Behaviors
SÓLEY S. BENDER

A. Children

No Icelandic studies have been done about the sexual explorations of young children.

B. Adolescents

A 1977 study by Sigurgestsson showed that among 14-year-olds, 23.2 percent of the boys and 21.2 percent of the girls said they had had sexual intercourse. This was considerably higher than in countries like Denmark, and the difference between genders was less in Iceland compared to other countries like Norway. A 1990 study showed results similar to those reported by Sigurgestsson: 25.6 percent of 14-year-old boys and 22.5 percent of the girls said they had had sexual intercourse (Axelsdottir et al. 1990).

A study by Jonsdottir (1994) showed that the mean age at first sexual intercourse was higher among the older age group than the younger, suggesting that the age of first sexual intercourse has been going down. For 50- to 60-year-olds, the mean age at first sexual intercourse was 17.6 for males and 18.6 for females. For 16- to 19-year-olds, the mean age at first sexual intercourse was 15.1 for males and 15.4 for females. Among the 50- to 60-year-olds, 4.1 percent had never had sexual intercourse, 48.7 percent were 16 or younger when they had their first sexual intercourse, and 47.2 percent were 17 or older. Among the 16- to 19-year-olds, 25 percent had never had sexual intercourse, 64.3 percent were 16 or younger when they had their first sexual intercourse, and 10.7 percent were 17 or older. This is a considerable difference for the age group 50 to 60, where 3.3 percent had never had sexual intercourse, 32.9 percent had sexual intercourse at age 16 or younger, and 65.8 percent were 17 or older.

A 1996 study showed that the mean age of sexual conduct was 15.4 years for both genders. The main author of this chapter conducted this national study based on a random sample of 1,703 people in the age group 17 to 20 years old (Bender 1999a). Table 1 shows the age distribution for first sexual intercourse.

Table 1

Age at First Sexual Intercourse

Age	Percent	Cumulative Percent
12 or younger	1.2	1.2
13	6.4	7.6
14	17.9	25.5
15	27.2	52.7
16	24.8	77.5
17	15.5	93.0
18	5.7	98.7
19	1.2	99.9
20	0.1	100

(*Source:* Bender 1999b)

C. Adults

Marital Data

Between 1961 and 1965, the rate of marriage per 1000 population was 7.9; in 1995, this was 4.6 (Hagstofa Íslands 1997). In 1998, 34.5 percent were married or cohabiting, 56 percent were not married, and 9.3 percent had been previously married and divorced (Hagstofa Íslands 1999b). The divorce rate has been increasing, doubling from 0.9 in 1961 to 1.8 in 1995 (Hagstofa Íslands 1997). The mean age of people who get married has also been going up. In 1961 to 1965, the mean age was 24.4 for brides and 27.4 for bridegrooms. Thirty years later, it was 29.9 for brides and 32.4 for bridegrooms. The attitudes of people to having a child out of wedlock are quite relaxed. A Gallup study (1997) showed that 95 percent did not think this was wrong.

Heterosexual Behaviors

A study conducted in 1992 by Jonsdottir and Haraldsdottir (1998) about sexual behavior and knowledge of AIDS showed that the average number of sexual partners is nine over the life span. Men have more sexual partners than women (12 versus 6). There is an identical ratio of men compared to women who have had anal sex (16.2 percent and 16.3 percent). The majority of men, 62.7 percent of those between ages 16 and 60, had experience with cunnilingus.

Those who have had two or more sexually transmitted diseases have had much higher numbers of sexual partners (26.4 percent) than those who were infected by one STD (11.9 percent) or none (6.2 percent). Casual sex is most frequent among those who are 16 to 25 years old.

This same study asked if participants had or knew about someone close to them who had had an affair while married or cohabiting. The results showed that 71.8 percent answered yes to this question (Jonsdottir & Haraldsdottir 1998). This may not very reliable or accurate information, but it is the only available information about extramarital affairs.

6. *Homoerotic, Homosexual, and Ambisexual Behaviors*
THORVALDUR KRISTINSSON

As of late 2000, no study provided reliable information about the frequency of homosexuality in Iceland. A study conducted in 1992 came closest to this by asking the participants about the sex of their partners. This national study of sexual behavior and knowledge about HIV had a sample of 971 people 16 to 60 years old. The response rate was 65 percent, with 53 percent of the respondents being women and 47 percent men. The percentage of people who reported having had sex with a person of the same sex ranged from zero to 1.8 percent for different age groups, with an overall average of 0.7 percent. In the age group 16 to 19, 1.8 percent reported a same-sex partner. Among 30- to 34-year-old respondents, only 0.6 percent reported a same-sex partner. Of those who had had homosexual experience, 0.3 percent were married, 2.2 percent single, and 5.6 percent divorced (Jonsdottir 1994; Jonsdottir & Haraldsdottir 1998).

Until the 1970s, lesbians and gay men were practically invisible in Icelandic society, which surrounded them with contempt and a massive silence. Their reaction was either to hide their sexual orientation completely, finding an occasional escape from the oppression while touring abroad, or to move to the metropolitan cities of continental Europe and

North America. Many of those people never returned, being later referred to as sexual political refugees. The silence was first broken in 1975 when the first gay Icelandic man, influenced by the international liberation movement, revealed his sexual identity publicly in the media. Three years later, *Samtokin 78*, the organization of lesbians and gay men in Iceland, was founded by some twenty people. After twenty years, it has become the most powerful force in the gay liberation movement of Iceland with a little less than 400 members. Typical of the prejudice and hostility that met this small group on its way to visibility in its early years, was the case of a discotheque in Reykjavik, which in 1983 advertised in newspapers: "Everyone is welcome—except gays and lesbians." Another example from the same year took place in the Nursing School of Iceland, which forbade its students from meeting with the educational group of *Samtokin 78*, a meeting which the students themselves had organized after a gay student found himself forced to leave the school because of group harassment and hazing.

Nevertheless, the few who had the courage to speak up for homosexuals saw remarkable progress in the 1980s. They rejected, for instance, the commonly used derogatory Icelandic terms such as *kynvilla* (sexual aberration) for homosexuality, a term analogous to the older word *truvilla* (religious aberration) for heresy. For a decade, they fought with the Icelandic State Radio against being labeled in such a derogatory manner, and suggested their own popular words, *lesbia* and *hommi* for themselves, and *samkynhneig*, a compound of same-sex and orientation, for homosexuality. Finally they won.

Since then, gay activism in Iceland has been characterized by educational and legislative work with positive results. Several other gay associations have recently appeared, including an association of gay, lesbian, and bisexual students at the University of Iceland, and an association of gay junior college students (Stonewall), both founded in 1999. In 1983, a new political party, the Socialdemocratic Alliance, was the first one to place gay human rights on its agenda, and two years later, a recommendation was presented in the parliament by four political parties demanding action to abolish discrimination against lesbians and gay men. It never passed, and it was not until 1992 that a similar recommendation passed parliament, after the original recommendation had been reworked by five political parties. As a result of the research work ordered by this recommendation, a law on registered partnerships for same-sex couples passed the parliament in 1996, although it denied same-sex couples any right to adopt children or to seek insemination in an official clinic. With this law, Iceland became the first country in the world to legalize common custody of children brought into a same-sex partnership from previous marriages. At the same time, the Protestant Lutheran state church did not approve of a formal church wedding, causing friction and open fights with the church authorities, which are still unresolved. In the year 2000, the parliament passed a new law on registered partnerships giving same-sex couples the right to adopt stepchildren who are brought into the partnership. An anti-discrimination law passed the parliament in 1996. It is worth noting that the parliamentary opposition in the debate preceding these legislative improvements was minimal, compared to the parliamentary opposition in other Nordic countries. To find an example of organized opposition, one has to go to the very small Christian fundamentalist congregations functioning outside the state church of Iceland.

Opinion polls nowadays show a surprising change of values in the society, and they express, in fact, more respect and tolerance towards gay men and lesbians than in other Western societies. When asked by an international opinion survey in 1990 about to what extent certain acts were justifiable on a one-to-ten scale, Icelanders expressed more tolerance than people in other nations regarding homosexuality, showing an average of 5.5. Other nations placed around 4.7 on the average, with the United States at a low 3.0. An international opinion survey of the same kind from 1984 gave the Icelanders an average rate of 3.3. This positive change is generally confirmed by what lesbians and gay men experience in their everyday life (Olafsson 1991). In a surprisingly short period of time, Icelandic society has left its homophobic attitude of the past and opened up for new visions and ideas.

7. Gender Conflicted Persons

SÓLEY S. BENDER

There is no study that provides information about Icelandic persons with gender conflicts or confusion. Given the clinical experience and incidence figures for gender-conflicted persons in nearby culturally similar countries, it seems reasonable to assume that a few hundred or more of the 280,000 modern Icelanders experience various forms of transsexualism, transvestism, hermaphroditism, pseudohermaphroditism, and intersexualism. Given the presence of support groups for gender-conflicted persons on the Internet and World Wide Web, one can reasonably assume that some gender-conflicted Icelanders may find local counselors and psychologists sensitive to their needs and explore possible medical help on the island and abroad.

8. Significant Unconventional Sexual Behaviors

SÓLEY S. BENDER AND GUDRÚN JÓNSDÓTTIR

A. Coercive Sex

Sexual Harassment

No prevalence studies have been done regarding the frequency of sexual harassment, but the Icelandic Office for Gender Equality has made some small surveys in a limited number of workplaces. They show that between 12 and 16 percent of the female workers have been subjected to sexual harassment in their workplace. In the last few years, employees have been better informed than before about their rights if they are victims of sexual harassment. However, many myths still exist regarding this issue.

Sexual Abuse and Incest

No prevalence studies have been conducted regarding sexual abuse and incest in Iceland. Even so, it was clear to a group of women who had been working as volunteers in different services for women that incest and sexual abuse of women and children is not unknown in Iceland. In 1986, these women formed a group whose purpose was to develop services for survivors of sexual violence. The group was named the Working Group Against Incest. In 1987, when an office was opened half a day, the demand for the service increased steadily. The Stigamot (The Icelandic Incest Center), which opened in 1990, is the product of this movement. Stigamot is an information and counseling center for women and children who have experienced sexual violation. In its first decade, Stigamot helped a total of 2,811 persons, with 213 new individuals seeking help in 1999. The two main reasons women and children have come to Stigamot are incest (about 60 percent) and rape (about 30 percent). Those who use the service are mainly 19 to 49 years old (80.2 percent); the majority have limited education (Jonsdottir & Sigurdardottir 2000).

The Government Agency for Child Protection does coordinate and strengthen child protection in Iceland. In 1997, this agency recommended to the Minister of Social Affairs that a special Children's House (Center for Child Sexual Abuse) should be developed to coordinate the work of child protection authorities, social service, police, the state prosecution, doctors, and others when investigating sexual abuse, to improve the quality of the service for children, and to protect the child from having to go through many traumatic forensic interviews and possibly relive the difficult experience. In November 1998, this Children's House started as a two-year experimental project. In 1998, there were 21 children referred to this center and in 1999, there were 119. In 1999, laws were passed about new procedures for court cases, which gives the responsibility of the forensic interview to the judge (Gudbrandsson 1999). The experience has been that not more than 10 percent of cases go to court. The center also offers treatment services. On average, each child has about fourteen interviews during the treatment process. This center serves the whole country. In late 2000, the future of the center was uncertain.

The criminal law about incest (1940) states that a parent who has sexual intercourse, vaginally or by other means with his child, shall get up to six to ten years in prison. Conviction for other types of sexual harassment by a parent towards a child can bring a prison sentence of up to two years and four years if the child is younger than 16 years old. Whoever has sex with a child younger than 14 years old can get imprisonment up to twelve years. Other types of sexual harassment and assault can lead to imprisonment up to four years.

In 1998, 58 legal charges of sexual abuse were brought in all of Iceland (Ministry of Law and Justice, personal communication, 4 July, 2000). Since 1981, the number of prison sentences stemming from sexual crimes has been rising. Between 1981 and 1985, there were 11 prison sentences and in 1998, there were 28. The mean number between 1985 and 1998 was 19.1 annually (Hagstofa Íslands 1999b).

Rape

In 1984, a group of women formed a group of counselors for survivors of rape. In the City Hospital in Reykjavik, a rape trauma center was established in 1993. As of mid-2000, 640 individuals had been attended to by the service. Seven were mentally retarded. In 1999, 103 individuals, 97 women and 6 men, used the service (Arsskyrsla Sjukrahuss Reykjavikur 2000). The majority of clients are females, but annually three to four men seek help. The clients range in age from 12 to 78 years, with 65 percent to 70 percent 25 years old or younger. The service is free of charge (Jonsdottir 2000). Rape is punishable under a 1940 law with imprisonment of between one and sixteen years.

B. Prostitution

Prostitution has probably been organized in Reykjavik, but valid information is hard to obtain. In recent years, several nightclubs offering nude dancing have opened both in Reykjavik and other cities. The women there have mostly come from abroad, particularly from Eastern European countries, to work as "dancers." This is probably hidden prostitution.

Sexual telephone service has become more and more obvious and is advertised in one of the main newspapers. This service was temporarily advertised with porno pictures. This was recently changed and now there is only text in the advertisements. These advertisements for sexual telephone service are also probably hidden prostitution services.

The 1992 study of sexual behavior and knowledge of AIDS showed that there were 71 individuals who had had sexual experience with a prostitute. Most of them were men and two were women. The majority were in the age group 25 to 39. The greater majority, 91 percent, had this sexual experience abroad (Jonsdottir & Haraldsdottir 1998). A person convicted of making a living by being a prostitute can get a prison sentence of two years. A person who gains a living from organizing the prostitution of others can get four years imprisonment. A person who encourages someone who is younger than 18 years old to work as a prostitute can get up to a four-year sentence in prison.

D. Pornography and Erotica

Pornography and opposition to it have existed in Iceland for centuries (Gudmundsson 1990). In the twentieth century, there has been some control over pornography in books and movies. Today, there seems to be very limited control. Books, magazines, movies, and videos showing pornography are easily available.

According to the 1940 criminal law, it is illegal to make, import, sell, and/or distribute pornographic material. It is also criminal to give pornographic material to a person younger than 18 years old. It is also not allowed to store pornographic material of children. These offenses can lead to a fine and/or up to six months in prison.

9. Contraception, Abortion, and Population Planning
SÓLEY S. BENDER

A. Contraception

Contraception is available through Iceland's community health centers, gynecologists, and some hospitals. Around 1994, the only specialized family planning clinic, which served mostly young people, closed. In 1995, the Icelandic Association for Sexual and Reproductive Health started an information and counseling service for young people on sexuality, STDs, and contraceptives. As with the early clinic, mostly young women have used this service.

Few studies have been conducted about the use of contraceptives of women in their reproductive years. In the 1977 Sigurgestsson study, young people 14 years old gave information about their use of contraceptive methods at their first sexual intercourse. Overall, 40.6 percent of the respondents, 43.7 percent of the boys and 36.7 percent of the girls, said they had used contraception for their first full sexual intercourse. A 1990 study showed that the most frequent reasons for not using contraception were: not having thought about it, 61.7 percent; not daring to go to the community health center, 61.1 percent; being too shy to discuss this with their partner, 51 percent; and believing coitus interruptus was sufficient contraceptive protection, 49.2 percent (Axelsdottir et al. 1990). A 1996 study of 1,703 individuals ages 17 to 20 showed that 59 percent used contraception at first coitus. The methods most used were the contraceptive pill, 7.6 percent; condom, 61.7 percent; diaphragm, 0.58 percent; and other, 1.0 percent. After first coitus, the pill, the condom, and coitus interruptus were in that order the most frequently used methods (Bender 1999). There are no national studies of contraceptive use among the over-age-20 population.

Some data from the Cancer Society have been analyzed. This data shows that the most frequently used contraceptive method for younger women is the contraceptive pill and for older women the intrauterine device. In the 20 to 44 age group, 35 percent of contracepting Icelanders used the IUD and 18 percent the contraceptive pill (Geirsson & Gudmundsson 1988, 1987). In 1997, sterilization was used as a permanent method by 640 (83 percent) of contracepting women and by 130 (17 percent) of contracepting men. In 1983, this gender ratio was 95 percent for contracepting women and 5 percent for men.

A 1988 survey exploring information and counseling about sexual and reproductive health in Icelandic community health centers showed that the more common subjects for counseling and information were: contraceptive methods, 84.4 percent; menopause, 72.8 percent; STDs, 72 percent; pregnancy tests, 67.1 percent; and premenstrual syndrome (PMS), 65 percent. Less frequently provided information dealt with: abortion, 23.4 percent; sexual problems, 29.8 percent; and sexual health, 30.2 percent. Most of these services were provided by family practitioners (Bender 1990).

The present legislation about contraception, abortion, and sterilization took effect in 1975. This twenty-five-year-old law suggests that people should get subsidized contraceptive methods, but this has not been acted on.

B. Teenage (Unmarried) Pregnancies

The incidence of teenage pregnancies is considerably higher in Iceland than it is in other Nordic countries. Table 2 compares the rate of teenage pregnancies in these countries.

Table 2

The Rate of Teenage Pregnancies per 1000 Pregnancies in 1997

Country	Rate per 1,000
Iceland	46.2
Norway	31.7
Sweden	25
Finland	19.2
Denmark	23.5 (1996)

(*Source:* NOMESCO 1999)

Although the birthrate among young women in Iceland has been dropping significantly, from 73.7 per 1,000 in 1970 to 24.9 in 1998, it is still much higher than in the other Nordic countries. Table 3 compares the birthrates in these countries.

Table 3

The Birthrate Among Young Women per 1000 Pregnancies in 1998

Country	Rate per 1,000
Iceland	24.9 (1998)
Norway	12.7 (1997)
Finland	9.0
Denmark	8.4
Sweden	7.2

(*Source:* NOMESCO 1999)

The percentage of live births by mothers under age 20 as a percentage of all live births in Iceland declined from 15.3 percent in 1977 to 6.3 percent in 1998 (Hagstofa Íslands 1999b). Table 4 shows comparable Scandinavian percentages for 1998.

Table 4

Live Births by Mothers Under Age 20 per 1000 Live Births in 1998

Country	Rate per 1,000
Iceland	6.3
Norway	2.7
Finland	2.6
Denmark	1.7
Sweden	1.3

(*Source:* Haagensen 1999)

A recent study showed that the birthrate among young women in Iceland is considerably less in the capital area compared to other places in Iceland, but the abortion rate is also higher (Adalsteinsdottir 2000). At the same time, as the birthrate among teenagers (15 to 19 years old) there has been declining, the abortion rate has been rising (5.8 per 1000 in 1976 and 21.7 in 1997). Now, close to 50 percent of pregnancies end in abortion and 50 percent in childbirth. A descriptive study of the health of teenage mothers (15 to 19 years old) during pregnancy and the health of their newborns, compared to older mothers (25 to 29 years old) and their newborns, based on a sample of 50 mothers in each group and 50 newborns of both groups, showed that the mean numbers of prenatal visits were identical in both groups. Teenage mothers attended 11.0 times and the older mothers 12.0 times. The younger mothers did not start to attend the prenatal visits later than the older mothers did. Health problems, such as pre-eclampsia and anemia, were more common in the older age group. There were fewer medical and surgical interventions during the delivery for the younger mothers. The percentage of low birth weight was identical for both groups (6 percent in each). The younger mothers, on the other hand, smoked more than the older mothers (25.5 percent versus 18 percent) and had higher frequency of delivering before the thirty-seventh week of gestation (6.3 percent versus 2.1 percent). The easy access to and no cost of prenatal service seem to contribute to fewer health risks among young mothers (Lorensdottir et al. 1994).

Young people do encounter some hindrances in obtaining contraceptive methods based on their insecurity, shyness, and the cost of the product. They also consider the health service at the community health centers to be too expensive and difficult to obtain, in contrast with the no-cost and easy availability of prenatal care (Johannsdottir et al. 2000). Young Icelanders want sexual and reproductive health services that are organized according to their needs. They have special needs regarding open hours and are sensitive to the environment and the interactions with the health care providers (Bender 1999a). This was further verified in a recent focus group study. This focus group study was based on three interviews of young people 16 to 19 years old, and showed that their special needs were better service hours in the afternoons or evenings, health care providers who show respect to young people, and a friendly staff attitude and friendly environment. They want to have music channels on the television in the waiting room, but not educational movies about STDs (Johannsdottir et al. 2000).

Most young mothers are probably single. Often they get good support from their families. A study based on two focus group interviews with young mothers showed that it was their mother who mostly helped them. They sensed the great responsibility of being a mother. Their inexperience, however, was demonstrated in being intolerant to breast-feeding and not knowing what to do when caring for the child. In spite of that, they felt good about being alone with the child, but often sensed insecurity when they were with others. Oftentimes, they felt that adults were interfering with their child-rearing practices. They sensed that they had little time for themselves, had less freedom, and often felt isolated from their friends. All of the participants had some future vision. Most of them wanted to go to school or to finish the school they were attending (Sveinsdottir & Gudmundsdottir 2000). These results show the need of young mothers for support and guidance about childrearing practices.

Based on the high teenage pregnancy rate, more preventive efforts need to be made. Sexuality education needs to be improved, and specialized sexual and reproductive health services for young people need to be developed.

C. Abortion

The present law legalizing abortion took effect in 1975. Anyone can apply for an abortion for medical or social reasons or following a rape. Abortions can only be done within a hospital setting. According to the legislation, permission is required for the intervention to be performed. The application form needs to be signed either by a social worker and medical doctor or two medical doctors depending on the reason. Women who apply for an abortion report low use of contraceptives. In 1977 to 1980, about 30 percent of women seeking an abortion had used some type of contraception at the time of conception; in 1981 to 1984, contraceptive use rose to 37 percent (Oskarsson & Geirsson 1987). Because of the rising number of abortions, a contraceptive counseling service has been developed within the National Hospital for women before and after an abortion.

Abortion is free of charge, but there is small outpatient fee for the laboratory tests and physical examination before the operation. The majority of abortions are done for social reasons. The rate of abortions for all age groups has been rising over the last twenty-four years and is now identical to those in other Nordic countries; but their abortion rates have has been going down over the years (Bender 2000). Between 1976 and 1980, 472 abortions were preformed; in 1998 the number was 901. Table 5 shows the abortion rate by age group in 1998. Between 1976 and 1980, the abortion rate for the age group 15 to 19 was 9.4 per 1000. In 1996, the abortion rate among 15- to 19-year-old Icelandic women was the highest among the Nordic countries.

There has been a group opposed to abortion in Iceland, but it has never been very active.

Table 5

Abortions in Iceland in 1998

Age Group	Abortions per 1,000 women
15 to 19 years	24.1
20 to 24	23.2
25 to 29	16.2
30 to 34	11.0
35 to 39	9.1
40 to 44	3.8
45 and older	0.2

D. Population Programs

Iceland is a pronatalistic country, as demonstrated by the positive attitude to having many children. In 1997, a Gallup study showed that about 70 percent of Icelanders wanted to have three or more children. Eighty-five percent of those surveyed considered it necessary to have a child to feel fulfilled. This pronatalism is also evident in the fact that there are no government-run teenage clinics. Teenage pregnancy is high and seems to be generally accepted. There is a trend of population movement from the rural to the urban areas. In some rural areas, there are recent efforts to increase the local population by using some financial incentives for young people to have children.

The discussion about the need for better contraceptive counseling services for people at reproductive age is new. The Icelandic Family Planning Association (The Icelandic Association for Sexual and Repro-ductive Health, or IcASRH) was established in 1992. This Association has been giving information to professionals and the public about these issues. One of these issues has been about emergency contraception. IcASRH published a special pamphlet about emergency contraception in 1996 and this has been widely distributed. The 1996 study about the attitude of young people to sexual and reproductive health services showed that only 35 percent of the 17- to 20-year-old participants knew what emergency contraception was.

In 1991, an infertility program was established at the National Hospital in Reykjavik. Before that time, people had to go abroad to have infertility treatment. The success rate of the Icelandic in-vitro fertilization (IVF) program has been high.

10. Sexually Transmitted Diseases

SÓLEY S. BENDER

A. Incidence and Trends

Iceland's national registration of sexually transmitted diseases does not provide accurate information about the prevalence of those diseases. The most accurate information about the rate of STDs is based on data from the Department of Infectious Diseases at the National Hospital in Reykjavik. Based on their information, there were 9,415 chlamydia cases between 1981 and 1990, about 941 annually. The number of positive tests for chlamydia has been dropping from 26 percent in 1981 to 11 percent in 1990 (Steingrimsson et al. 1991). From 1991 to 1997, the incidence of positive tests was 11 to 13 percent.

Chlamydia trachomatis has been the most frequent sexually transmitted disease in Iceland for several years. The number of gonorrhea cases has been dropping over the years, but herpes and condyloma have increased. The 1992 sexual behavior study showed that there were 9.3 percent who had gotten *pediculus pubis* (pubic lice), 8.4 percent chlamydia, 8.0 percent scabies, 5.6 percent condyloma, 4.5 percent gonorrhea, and 2.5 percent herpes (Jonsdottir 1994). In the same study, 20 percent of the participants said they had had one STD, while 6.8 percent reported two or more infections, with men having a higher frequency at 9.3 percent compared with 4.7 percent for women (see Table 6).

Table 6

Percentage Infected with STD

	All (*n* = 966) percent	Men (*n* = 450) percent	Women (*n* = 516) percent
Never infected	73.1	70.2	75.6
Once infected	20.1	20.4	19.8
Infected by two or more STDs	6.8	9.3	4.7

(*Source:* Jonsdottir & Haraldsdottir 1998)

B. Treatment and Prevention Efforts

There is one STD clinic in Reykjavik offering diagnosis and treatment. People can also visit their family practitioner at community health centers all over Iceland. The diagnosis and treatment is free for the client.

There are many aspects that need to be considered regarding prevention and risk reduction efforts regarding STDs in Iceland. The 1992 study showed that about 8 percent of those surveyed had had casual sex once or more often in the last three months before the study was conducted. Casual sex was most frequent in the age group 16 to 24. About 10 percent of those who had casual sex were always or most often under the influence of alcohol or drugs during sexual intercourse (Jonsdottir & Haraldsdotttir 1998).

In the same study, 9 percent of men 16 to 24 said it was difficult to talk to their partner about the use of condoms; 5 percent of the women in the same age group shared this difficulty. Fifty-two percent of the men and 44 percent of women felt that the condom spoiled sexual pleasure. In the 16- to 19-age group, 23.1 percent of participants who had had casual sex in the last twelve months before the study never used a condom during that time. The average non-use of condoms for all other age groups was 14.9 percent (Jonsdottir & Haraldsdottir 1998).

STD preventive efforts in Iceland have been focused on the importance of increasing knowledge about STDs and influencing attitudes. There are several hindrances that make this preventive work not as effective as it could be. In Icelandic society, as in many other countries, there are not many healthy role models for young people regarding the use of condoms. Most movies show sexual intercourse without anyone mentioning the need for protection against STDs or pregnancy.

11. HIV/AIDS

SÓLEY S. BENDER

A. Incidence and Trends

As of January 2000, Iceland had 140 individuals diagnosed with HIV. The annual number of individuals diagnosed with HIV has ranged from zero to a high of sixteen. Most of those who became infected were homosexuals, but the number of infected heterosexuals is growing. Men have a higher frequency of HIV infection than women, as shown in Table 7. As of the end of 1999, a total of 50 cases of AIDS had been diagnosed and reported to the authorities; 33 Icelanders have died of AIDS.

B. Treatment, Prevention Programs, and Government Policies

In 1988, a national AIDS committee was formed by the Ministry of Health. The role of this committee included creation of guidelines regarding prevention of HIV. This committee decided to conduct a study about the sexual behavior of Icelanders and their knowledge about HIV/AIDS (Jonsdottir 1994; Jonsdottir & Haraldsdottir 1998). This study showed that Icelanders were interested in three ways to promote safer sex behaviors in order to reduce the risk of HIV infection: increasing the use of condoms, having fewer casual sexual partners, and being more careful with the use of alcohol and drugs.

Table 7

Incidence of HIV from 1985 to 1996 per 100,000 Population

	Total	Women	Men
1985	7.5	1.7	13.2
1990	2.0	—	3.9
1991	3.9	1.6	6.2
1992	4.2	0.8	7.6
1993	1.1	0.8	1.5
1994	3.0	1.5	4.5
1995	1.9	1.5	2.2
1996	1.9	1.5	2.2

(*Source:* Hagstofa Íslands 1997)

12. Sexual Dysfunctions, Counseling, and Therapies
SÓLEY S. BENDER

A. Sexual Dysfunctions and Availability of Therapy

Since only very limited studies about sexual dysfunctions have been done in Iceland, very little is known on a national level about the prevalence of these problems. Sexual dysfunctions have been reported postpartum in relation to postpartum depression. Sexual dysfunctions are mostly presented in connection with other problems that people have when they visit their family practitioner. It therefore depends on the sensitivity of the attending physician to discover the oftentimes hidden problem. In general, people seem inhibited about discussing sexuality in general and sexual problems in particular. This reluctance often seems to apply to medical practitioners as well. The 1992 study about sexual behavior showed that 28.2 percent of the respondents had had some discussion with a family practitioner or a nurse at the community health center, and 16.8 percent had discussed sexuality with a health care professional in a hospital (Jonsdottir 1994). From the health care providers' perspective, 29.8 percent said they often and rather often provide information and counseling in the community health centers about sexual problems (Bender 1990). Psychiatrists, psychologists, social workers, urologists, and gynecologists are the practitioners most likely to be consulted or involved in diagnosing sexual problems. Some people turn to the IcASRH for advice about their sexual problems.

There is no one certified as a sexual therapist by the Ministry of Health or a professional association in Iceland, and no sexual treatment center run by the government of Iceland. In 1975, a treatment center was launched and functioned for about ten years. Information and counseling services about sexuality and its relation to diseases are lacking within the hospital setting. There is no therapist practicing in Iceland who has a master's or doctoral degree in sexology.

13. Research and Advanced Education

SÓLEY S. BENDER

A. Graduate Programs and Sexological Research

No undergraduate or graduate sexology programs are offered at the University of Iceland or in other universities in the country.

Very few Icelandic studies have been done about human sexuality. Before the 1975 abortion law took effect, there had been considerable discussion about the issue and members of parliament were stressing the need for preventive work. Following this, Sigurgestsson completed a psychology dissertation in 1977 based on a sample of 1,420 young people and conducted among all 14-year-old students in the Reykjavik area. The response rate was 92 percent. This study was the first of its kind to explore sexuality among this age group. The focus of this study was on puberty, sexual activity, and sex education. A year later, in 1978, Thorvardarson conducted a study of sex education as part of a Bachelor in Education program. This study was based on a sample of young people in the sixth grade ($n = 460$), eighth grade ($n = 480$), and among 16- to 18-year-olds ($n = 345$).

Following the first cases of HIV/AIDS, the first national study about sexual behavior and knowledge of HIV/AIDS was sponsored in 1992 by the Directorate of Public Health (Jonsdottir 1994; Jonsdottir & Haraldsdottir 1998). The purpose of this study was to get information for the direction of preventive strategies regarding HIV and AIDS. This study was a cross-sectional postal survey based on a national sample of 971 individuals in the age group 16 to 59. As noted in Section 6, Homoerotic, Homosexual, and Bisexual Behaviors, the response rate was 65 percent; 47 percent of those responding were males and 53 percent females.

Another national cross-sectional study was done in 1996 based on a stratified random sample of 2,500 young people 17 to 20 years old, 20 percent being teenage boys and 80 percent being teenage girls. The crude response rate was 68 percent. This study explored the attitudes of young people to sexual and reproductive health services, sexuality and the use of contraceptives, and the use of contraceptive services (Bender 1999).

B. Sexological Organization and Publications

The Icelandic Sexology Association was established in 1985 and was active for the first ten years. Its goal was to promote sexology and the cooperation of people working as teachers, therapists, and researchers in the field of sexology. It was a member of the Nordic Association for Clinical Sexology (*Nordisk Forening for Klinisk Sexologi*, NACS).

The Icelandic Family Planning Association (The Icelandic Association for Sexual and Reproductive Health, IcASRH) was established in 1992. The Association has been focusing on teenage sexuality and the special needs of young people. It has published several pamphlets, postcards, and a semi-annual newsletter. It is a member of International Planned Parenthood Federation (IPPF) and belongs to the European Network of IPPF. The address of the Association is: P.O. Box 7226, 127 Reykjavik, Iceland; e-mail: fkb@mmedia.is; home page: www.mmedia.is/fkb.

Stigamot (The Icelandic Incest Center), discussed in Section 8A under Sexual Abuse and Incest, has a home page at www.stigamot.is.

There is no Icelandic sexological journal or periodical published exclusively about sexology. There have been some articles published in the Icelandic medical and nursing journals about sexuality. The Icelandic Sexology Association published a few issues of a newsletter, and the Icelandic Association for Sexual and Reproductive Health currently publishes a newsletter two times a year.

References and Suggested Readings

Adalbjarnardottir, S., Davisdottir, S., & Runarsdottir, E. M. 1997. *Áhættuhegun reykviskra unglinga* [*Risk behavior of adolescents in Reykjavik*]. Reykjavík: Félagsvísindastofnun (The Institute of Social Sciences) Háskóla Íslands.

Adalsteinsdottir, H. 2000. *unganir, fæingar og fóstureyingar meal unglingsstúlkna.* [*Pregnancies, births, and abortions among teenagers*]. Unpublished Bachelor of Science degree thesis. University of Iceland, Department of Nursing.

Almenn hegningalög, nr. 19/1940 me vibótar breytingum [*General criminal law with additional changes*]. 1940.

Arsskyrsla sjukrahuss reykjavikur [*The annual report of the City Hospital*]. 2000. Reykjavík: Sjukrahus Reykjavikur.

Axelsdottir, A., Atladottir, A., Davidsdottir, H. S., Skuladottir, K., Rikhardsdottir, K., Runarsdottir, R., & Hedinsdottir, S. 1990. *Könnun á kynfræsluefninu Lifsgildi og ákvaranir* [*A pilot study of the curriculum, human sexuality, values and choices*]. Unpublished Bachelor of Science degree thesis. University of Iceland, Department of Nursing.

Bardarson, H. R. 1965. *Iceland.* Haarlem: Joh.Enchede en Zonen.

Bender, S. S. 1990. Fjölskylduáætlun í íslensku heilbrigiskerfi [Family planning within the Icelandic health care system]. *Heilbrigisskrslur* (Fylgirit nr. 2). Reykjavík: Landlæknisembætti (The Directorate of Public Health).

Bender, S. S. 1999a. Attitudes of Icelandic young people toward sexual and reproductive health services. *Family Planning Perspectives, 31*(6):294-301.

Bender. S. S. 1999b. *Study of attitudes of young people toward sexual and reproductive health services.* Unpublished report.

Bender, S. S., Bjornsdottir, A. G., Hermannsdottir, G. E., Jonasson, M. R., Bjarnadottir, R. I., & Gudjonsdottir, Th. E. 2000. *Skrsla um fóstureyingar og agengi a getnaarvörnum* [*Report about abortion and access to contraceptive methods*]. Reykjavík: Heilbrigis og Tryggingamálaráuneyti (The Ministry of Health and Social Security).

Broddadottir, I., Eydal, G., Hrafnsdottir, S., & Sigurdardottir, S. H. 1997. The development of local authority social services in Iceland. In: J. Sipilä, ed., *Social care services: The key to the Scandinavian welfare model* (pp. 51-77). Aldershot: Avery.

Denmarks Statistics. 2000. *Statistics across borders.* Denmark: Denmarks Statistics Trykkeri.

Eiriksdottir, E., Haraldsson, H., Kjartansson, H., Gardarsson, P., Bjarnason, R. & Ketilsdottir, Th. 1976. *The man, birth, childhood and puberty.* Reykjavík: Namsgagnastofnun (National Center for Educational Materials).

Gallup. 1999. *The Gallup millennium survey.* Reykjavík: Gallup Iceland.

Gallup Organization Princeton. 1997. Family values differ sharply around the world. Gallup Poll Release. Princeton, NJ: Gallup Organization.

Geirsson, R. T., & Gudmundsson, J. A. 1987. Er pillan betri en af er láti? [Is the contraceptive pill better than what is said?]. *Heilbrigismál, 4,* 12-15.

Geirsson, R. T., & Gudmundsson, J. A. 1988. Lykkjan hefur kosti og galla (The IUD has its pros and cons). *Heilbrigismál, 4,* 28-31.

Gudbrandsson, B. 1999. *A report of activities during 1995-1999.* Unpublished report.

Gudmundsson, O. 1990. *Íslenska kynlífsbókin* [*The Icelandic sexuality book*]. Reykjavík: Almenna Bókafélagi.

Haagensen, K. M. 1999. *Nordic statistical yearbook 1999* (vol. 37). Copenhagen: Nordic Council of Ministers.

Hagstofa Íslands [Statistics Iceland]. 1997. *Konur og karlar* [*Women and men in Iceland*]. Reykjavík: Hagstofa Íslands. (Home page for Iceland Statistics, www.hagstofa.is.)

Hagstofa Íslands [Statistics Iceland]. 1998. *Ísland í tölum* [*Iceland in numbers*]. Reykjavík: Hagstofa Íslands.

Hagstofa Íslands [Statistics Iceland]. 1999a. *Fréttatilkynning nr. 88/1999. Mannfjöldi á Íslandi 1. Desember 1999, Bráabirgatölur.* [*News release nr. 88/1999. Population of Iceland 1. December 1999, Estimations*]. Reykjavík: Hagstofa Íslands.

Hagstofa Íslands [Statistics Iceland]. 1999b. *Landshagir 1999.* [*Statistical yearbook of Iceland 1999*]. Reykjavík: Hagstofa Íslands.

Hagstofa Íslands [Statistics Iceland]. 1999c. *Iceland in figures.* Reykjavík: Hagstofa Íslands.

Hagstofa Íslands [Statistics Iceland]. 2000. *Landshagir 2000* [*Statistical yearbook of Iceland 2000*]. Reykjavík: Hagstofa Íslands.

Heilsufar Kvenna [*Health of women*]. 1998. Reykjavík: Heilbrigis-og Tryggin-gamálaráuneyti (The Ministry of Health and Social Security).

Johannsdottir, B. H., Gudjonsdottir, E. O., & Eyjolfsdottir, H. R. 2000. *Kynheilbrigisjónusta fyrir unglinga* [*Sexual and reproductive health service for teenagers*]. Unpublished Bachelor of Science degree thesis. University of Iceland, Department of Nursing.

Jonsdottir, E. 2000 (July). Hópnaugungum fer fjölgandi [Group rape is increasing]. *Dagblai Vísir,* bls. 4.

Jonsdottir, J. I. (1994). Könnun á kynhegun og ekkingu á alnæmi [A survey on sexual behavior and knowledge about AIDS]. *Heilbrigisskrslur* (Fylgirit nr. 2). Reykjavík: Landlæknisembætti (The Directorate of Public Health).

Jonsdottir, J. I., & Haraldsdóttir, S. 1998. Kynhegun og ekking á alnæmi [Sexual behavior and knowledge about AIDS]. *Heilbrigisskrslur* (Fylgirit nr. 5). Reykjavík: Landlæknis-embætti (The Directorate of Public Health).

Jonsson, F. H., & Olafsson, S. 1991. *Lífskoun í nútímalegum jófélögum* [*Values in modern societies*]. Unpublished manuscript. Reykjavík: Félagsvísindastofnun (The Institute of Social Sciences).

Juliusdottir, S. 1982. Våld i isländska familjer [Violence in Icelandic families]. *Nordisk Socialt Arbeid,* 4(2):3-15.

Juliusdottir, S. 1993. *Den kapabla familjen i det isländska samhället. En studie om lojalitet, äktenskapsdynamik och psykosocial anpassning.* [*The capable family in the Icelandic society*]. Reykjavík: University of Gothenburg/University of Iceland.

Juliusdottir, S., & Asmundsson, G. 1987. The emphasis on work and income in Icelandic families and its effect on family life. In: N. Schönnesson, ed., *Nordic intimate couples: Love, children and work* (pp. 45-65). Copenhagen: Nordisk Ministerråd/JÄMFO.

Juliusdottir, S., Gretarsson, S. J., Jonsson, F. H., & Sigurdardottir, N. K. 1995. *Barnafjöl-skyldur. Samfélag. Lífsgildi. Mótun* [*Childbearing families, society, values, and influences*]. Reykjavík: Félagsmálaráuneyti.

Juliusdottir, S., & Sigurdardottir, N. K. (in press). *Joint custody. A nation-wide comparative study on divorced parents' experience.* Reykjavík: Háskólaútgáfan.

Kahn, F. 1948. *Sexuality.* Reykjavík: Helgafell.

Kjartansson, H., & Brynjolfsson, S. H. 1983. *Human reproduction.* Reykjavík: Namsgag-nastofnun (National Center for Educational Materials).
Kristmundsdottir, S. D. 1990. *Doing and becoming: Women's movements and women's person-hood in Iceland 1870-1990.* New York: University of Rochester.
Lög um jafna stöu og jafnan rétt kvenna og karla, nr. 65/1985 [*Law about equal status and equal rights of women and men*].
Lög um rágjöf og fræslu varandi kynlíf og barneignir og um fóstureyingar og ófrjósemisagerir, nr. 25/1975 [*Law about information and counseling about sexuality and childbearing and about abortion and sterilization*].
Lög um varnir gegn kynsjúkdómum, nr. 16/1978 Me vibótarbreytingum [*Law about STD with additional changes*].
Lorensdottir, A. S., Sigurdardottir, E. O., Matthiasdottir, G., & Valgeirsdottir, G. A. 1994. *Ung og ábyrg fyrir nju lífi* [*Young and responsible for a new life*]. Unpublished Bachelor of Science degree thesis. University of Iceland, Department of Nursing.
NOMESCO. 1998. *Health statistics in the Nordic countries.* Copenhagen: NOMESCO (Nordic Medico Statistical Committee).
NOMESCO. 1999. *Health statistics in the Nordic countries.* Copenhagen: NOMESCO (Nordic Medico Statistical Committee).
Nordic Council of Ministers. 1999. *Women and men in the Nordic countries 1999.* Halmstad, Sweden: Bulls Tryckeri AB.
NOSOSCO. 1996. *Social tryghed i de nordiske lande* [*Social support in the Nordic countries*]. Copenhagen: NOSOSCO (Nordic Social Statistical Committee).
Olafsdottir, H., Juliusdottir, S., & Benediktsdottir, . 1982. *Ofbeldi í íslenskum fjölskyldum* [*Violence in Icelandic families*]. *Gevernd, 17,* 17-32.
Olafsson, S. 1989. *The making of the Icelandic welfare state. A Scandinavian comparison.* Reykjavík: Félagsvísindastofnun (The Institute of Social Sciences). *See also:* Variations within the Scandinavian model. Iceland in a comparative perspective. In: E. J. Hansen, H. Uusitalo, & R. Erikson, eds., *Welfare trends in Scandinavia.* New York: M.A. Sharpe.
Olafsson, S. 1990. *Lífskjör og lífshættir á Norurlöndum. Samanburur á jófélagi Íslendinga, Dana, Finna, Normanna og Svía* [*Living conditions in the Nordic countries. Comparison between Iceland, Denmark, Finland, Norway, and Sweden*]. Reykjavík: Iunn.
Olafsson, S. 1991. *Lífsskoun í nútímajófélögum* [*Values in modern societies*]. Reykjavík: Félagsvísindastofnun (The Institute of Social Sciences).
Olafsson, S. 1999. *Íslenska leiin. Almannatryggingar og velfer í fjöljólegum samanburi.* [*The Icelandic way. Public insurance and welfare in multisocial comparison*]. Reykjavík: Tryggin-gastofnun Ríkisins/Háskólaútgáfan.
Olafsson, S., Kaldalons, I., & Sigurdsson, K. 1998. *Vihorf til velferarríkisins á Íslandi.* [*Attitudes to the welfare state of Iceland*]. Unpublished manuscript. Reykjavík: Félagsvís-indastofnun (The Institute of Social Sciences).
Oskarsson, Th., & Geirsson, R. T. 1987. Fóstureyingar og notkun getnaarvarna [Abor-tion and use of contraceptive methods]. *Læknablai* [*The Icelandic Medical Journal*], 73:321-326.
Palsdottir, J. B., & Hardardottir, Th. 1993. *Könnun á hvernig kynfræslu er hátta í efri bekkjum grunnskóla út frá sjónarhóli kennara* [*Survey of sexuality education according to the teachers' perspective*]. Unpublished Bachelor of Science degree thesis. University of Iceland, Department of Nursing.
Proppé, J. 2000. Dyggirnar og Íslendingar [The virtues of Icelanders]. *Tímarit Máls og Menningar, 61*(2), 6-17.
Rafnsdottir, G. L. 1995. *Women's strategies against suppression. A discussion about female trade unions in Iceland.* Lund: Lund University Press.
Rauhala, P.-L., Anderson, M., Eydal, G., Ketola, O., & Nielsen, W. 1997. Why are social care services a gender issue? In: J. Sipilä, ed., *Social care services: The key to the Scandinavian welfare model* (pp. 131-156). Aldershot: Avebury.

Sigurgestsson, A. (1977). *Ungdom og seksualitet* [*Young people and sexuality*]. Århus: Psychologisk Institute, Århus Universitet.

Steingrimsson, O., Olafsson, J. H., Kristinsson, K. G., Jonsdottir, K. E., & Sigfusdottir, A. 1991. Eru klamydíuskingsar á undanhaldi á Íslandi? [Are chlamydia infections reducing in Iceland?]. *Læknablai* [*The Icelandic Medical Journal*], 77:369-372.

Sveinsdottir, M. Th., & Gudmundsdottir, V. B. 2000. *Unglingsmæur, skynjun á móurhlutverkinu* [*Teenage mothers, their perception of motherhood*]. Unpublished Bachelor of Science degree thesis. University of Iceland, Department of Nursing.

Thorlindsson, Sigfusdottir, I. D., Bernburg, J. G., & Halldorsson, V. 1998. *Vímuefnaneysla ungs fólks. Umhverfi og astæur* [*Drug use of young people: Environment and conditions*]. Reykjavík: Rannsóknarstofnun Uppeldis-og Menntamála.

Thorvardarson, J. 1978. *Um kynferisfræslu* [*About sex education*]. Reykjavík: Kennarahaskóli Islands.

United Nations Development Program (UNDP). 1999. *Human development report 1999.* New York: United Nations Development Program.

Indonesia
(*Republik Indonesia*)

Wimpie I. Pangkahila, M.D., Ph.D. (Part 1)*
Ramsey Elkholy, Ph.D. (cand.) (Part 2)**

Contents

*Communications: Wimpie I. Pangkahila, M.D., Ph.D., The Master Program in Reproductive Medicine, Udayana University Medical School, Jl. Panglima Sudirman, Denpasar, Bali, Indonesia; wim@denpasar.wasantara.net.id.

**Communications: Ramsey Elkholy, Ph.D. (cand.), 105 Fifth Avenue, Apartment #6E, New York, NY, USA 10003; ramseyelkholy@hotmail.com.

PART 1: NATIONAL AND URBAN PERSPECTIVES

WIMPIE I. PANGKAHILA

Demographics and a Historical Perspective

A. Demographics

Located in the archipelago southeast of Asia along the equator, Indonesia comprises some 13,700 to 17,000 islands (depending on who does the counting). While only about 6,000 are inhabited, the island of Java is one of the most densely populated areas of the world (see below). Besides Java, Indonesia includes four other major islands: Sumatra, the largest and most western of the Indonesian islands, Kalimantan (most of Borneo), Sulawesi (formerly Celebes), and the "Paradise Island" of Bali, as well as the western half of the island of New Guinea, formerly known as Irian Jaya.*

The mountains and plateaus on the major islands have a cooler climate than the tropical lowlands. In the eastern island of New Guinea, the mountain peaks may be snow-covered. The Indonesian archipelago lies southeast of the Asian mainland. Straddling the equator, Indonesia's neighbors are Malaysia to the north, Papua New Guinea to the east, Australia to the south of its western islands, and the Indian Ocean to the west. Situated in a part of the "ring of fire," Indonesia has the largest number of active volcanoes in the world. Earthquakes are frequent. The "Wallace line," a zoological demarcation, divides Indonesia, marking the separation of Asian and Australian flora and fauna.

In 1999, Indonesia had an estimated 216 million people with more than 300 ethnic groups, most of which are very small minorities. The major ethnic group is Javanese, comprising 45 percent of the total population. Fourteen percent are Sundanese, 8 percent Madurese, 8 percent Malay, as well as smaller percentages of Minahasans, Balinese, Bataks, Dayaks, Timorese, and Papuans. Some very minor ethnic groups still live in the jungles where they maintain their traditional cultures. As noted, Part 2 of this chapter examines

---

[*Editor's Note: The cultures of the eastern half of the island of New Guinea, the nation of Papua New Guinea, are covered under that nation in this volume by Shirley Oliver-Miller. In Part 1 of this present chapter, Wimpie L. Pangkahila and J. Alex Pangkahila provide insights into the national and urban perspectives of sexuality in Indonesia. In Part 2, Ramsey Elkholy reports on the Indonesian Orang Rimba minority group. Elkholy's report on Indonesian New Guinea and Oliver-Miller's discussion of the many indigenous groups of Papua New Guinea offer some interesting complementary insights. (Robert T. Francoeur)]

the sexual culture of the indigenous hill tribe of the Orang Rimba. There are other ethnic groups, including Indonesian Chinese, Arabs, Indians, and Europeans. Each ethnic group has its own culture and language. Fortunately, there is one Indonesian language as a national language, so that people of the different ethnic groups, with the exception of small geographically isolated peoples, can usually communicate with each other.

Five out of six Indonesians, 87 percent, follow the religion of Islam, 9 percent are Christian, and 2 percent Hindu.

The 1999 age distribution of the population was: 30.4 percent under age 15, 65.5 percent between ages 15 and 65, and 4.1 percent over age 65. The nation's overall population density in 1999 was 292 per square mile, but the island of Java, just east of Sumatra, is one of the most densely populated areas of the world with over 2,100 people per square mile and over 100 million people on the island of only 51,023 square miles.

Life expectancy at birth in 1999 was 60.8 for males and 65.3 for females. The 1995 birthrate was 22.78 per 1,000 and the death rate 8.14 per 1,000, for a natural annual increase of 1.46 percent. The infant mortality rate was 57.3 per 1,000 live births. The Total Fertility Rate (TFR) in 1995 was 2.6 children per fertile woman, ranking Indonesia 120 among 227 nations. Indonesia has one hospital bed per 1,630 persons, and one physician per 6,570 persons. School is compulsory between ages 7 and 16, and 97 percent attend at least primary school. The literacy rate is estimated at 84 percent but the criteria are not clear.

Indonesia is a developing country with major problems in the social, political, and economic areas. Most people still have a low-subsistence standard of living. However, the small middle-and upper-class populations have a very good standard of life. Some Indonesian businessmen even have their companies in some other countries. This means that there is a wide gap between the poor, as the majority, and the rich, as a very small part of the population. It is estimated that the country will join the developed countries in the near future. The 1999 estimated per capita gross domestic product was $4,600.

B. A Brief Historical Perspective

It is generally believed that the earliest inhabitants of the Indonesian archipelago came from India or Burma (Myanmar). Later immigrants, known as Malays, came from southern China and Indochina. This later group is believed to have populated the archipelago gradually over several thousand years. Hindu and Buddhist civilizations reached Indonesia about 2,000 years ago, taking root mainly on the island of Java. In the fifteenth century, Islam was spread by Arab traders along the maritime trade routes and became dominant in the sixteenth century.

In the seventeenth century, the Dutch replaced the Portuguese as the dominant European power in the area. The Dutch gained control over Java by the mid-1700s, but the outer islands were not subdued until the early

1900s, when most of the current territory of Indonesia came under Dutch rule. On the other side, the Dutch and the Portuguese also brought Christianity to the Indonesian people.

After the Japanese occupation of 1942-1945, nationalists fought four years until the Dutch granted Indonesia its independence. Indonesia declared itself a republic in 1945. In 1957, Indonesia invaded Dutch-controlled West Irian (the western half of New Guinea); in 1969, tribal leaders voted to become part of Indonesia, a move sanctioned by the United Nations.

Indonesia also invaded and annexed East Timor in 1975-1976, as Portuguese rule collapsed. However, this annexation brought many internal social, economic, political, and security problems and tensions in Indonesia's international relations. After the fall of President General Soeharto in 1998, the transitional president, B. J. Habibie, proposed East Timorese vote on two options: independence or integration as a part of Indonesia. Through a self-determination vote under United Nations supervision in 1999, the East Timorese decided to be independent from Indonesia. The level of unrest and violence remains high in East Timor.

In the same year, the Indonesian people held the most democratic general election to that time to choose the people's representatives in the Parliament and Assembly. Through the Assembly, Indonesian people now have a legitimate president, K. H. Abdurrahman Wahid, and vice president, Megawati Soekarnoputri, for the period 1999 to 2004. This, however, does not mean that the country has already been freed from its major problems. These economic, political, and security problems are the major problems faced by Indonesians under the new legitimated government.

1. Basic Sexological Premises

A. Character of Gender Roles

In traditional Indonesian society, women clearly occupy a lower social status than men. This is still the dominant value in Indonesian culture. The idea that a female's place is in the kitchen is still easy to find, especially in the villages. The husband–wife relationship is a chief–assistant relationship rather than a partnership.

Nevertheless, the role of women is improving in modern Indonesian society. Many women work outside the home, particularly in restaurants and in garment and cigarette factories, even though their wages are lower than those of males. Many female physicians, notaries, and lawyers are found in modern Indonesian cities. A few women have achieved high political positions as Cabinet and Parliament members. Vice President Megawati Soekarnoputri, elected in 1999 by the people's representatives in the most democratic general election, is a female.

In modern Indonesian society, the husband–wife relationship is also improving, with a gradual shift to a partnership. Husbands increasingly treat their wife as a partner rather than as an assistant. It is no longer strange to see a husband taking care of his baby, while his wife is working outside the home. Unfortunately, this improvement mostly occurs in well-educated couples, which are only a small part of the population. Furthermore, sometimes the change of the husband–wife relationship results in the disharmony of the relationship, mostly because of the negative response of the husband. For example, the husband will feel unhappy if his working wife's salary is more than his, or he will get angry if his working wife does not prepare dinner for him.

B. Sociolegal Status of Males and Females

From the standpoint of national law, males and females enjoy the same rights in schooling and careers. However, in some areas, traditional and cultural laws discriminate against females. Only males, for instance, have a right to receive a legacy from their parents. This contributes to a higher status for males.

Another consequence of traditional values is that parents insist on having a son, even though the government has proclaimed a limit of only two children per family, regardless of sex. Many women come to clinics seeking male-sex preselection, even though there is no method that can give a 100-percent guarantee of having a male child.

In many families, parents give special treatment to the son over the daughter. For example, parents are more likely to support higher education for a son than they would for a daughter. This is based on the stereotype that females will ultimately end up working in the kitchen, while males, as the chief of the family, will work hard to gain money.

Another more serious consequence of the traditional law is that males feel they have a higher social status, and therefore feel more powerful, than females. This effect appears in the relationship between a husband and wife where the husband feels he has power over the wife and acts as a chief in the family. Husbands also feel free to do what they want, including having sexual intercourse with other women.

However, among the Miharg Kabou of West Sumatra, females have a higher status than males. Unlike other regions of Indonesia where the male courts the female, Miharg women court the men.

C. General Concepts of Sexuality and Love

Traditionally, Indonesian women connected sexuality with love and engaged in sexual activities only with the males they loved, specifically their husbands. A woman, it was believed, was not able to have sex with a male unless she loved him. In contrast, the traditional view fully accepted males as having sex with any female they liked. In essence, females were only sexual objects, designed for male pleasure.

This traditional view is changing in modern Indonesia. For many, sex and love are easy to separate and are frequently viewed as two different things. Many females, especially among the young, want to engage in sexual intercourse with anybody they like without the necessity of loving that person or without any interest in marriage. This concept, of course, is not well received by the older generation.

This concept change does not seem to occur only in the large cities, but also increasingly in the villages. Some studies performed of the young of the villages showed that there is no significant difference in sexual behavior between the young in the village and in the city. The difference is only in the physical environment and other circumstances that facilitate or permit sexual intercourse. Whether in the city or in the village, the young have the same perceptions about pregnancy, abortion, and family planning. The sexual knowledge and behavior of the young seem to be a new dimension, which is separated from the settings and culture of traditional social organization, family, and religion. The opinion that the village is a traditional and homogeneous community, which holds strongly the cultural and religious norms and is not easy to change, is no longer a reality.

2. Religious and Ethnic Factors Affecting Sexuality

A. Source and Character of Religious Values

During the first few centuries of the Christian era, most of the islands came under the influence of Hindu priests and traders, who spread their religion and culture. Moslem invasions began in the thirteenth century, and most of the area was Islamicized by the fifteenth century. Today, 88 percent of Indonesians are Moslem, with Hindu, Buddhist, and both Protestant and Catholic Christian minorities. There is a commendable degree of religious tolerance among the people.

Evidence of the Hindu influence can be found in some large ancient temples, like Borobudur, Prambanan, Mendut, and Kali Telon in Middle Java, and Jago temple in East Java. The temple in Borobudur is ranked by many as one of the seven miracles in the world. Many reliefs in the walls of these temples portray erotic themes. In the wall of the Kali Telon temple, for example, there are relief figures of males and females having sexual intercourse. In the Mendut temple, people can see in relief figures a scene of a male and female petting.

Christian Portuguese traders arrived early in the sixteenth century, but were ousted by the Dutch around 1595. In the early 1800s, the British seized the islands but returned them to the Dutch in 1816. After the end of the Japanese occupation and World War II, Indonesia declared its independence from the Dutch.

In the past, conservative religious and cultural values had a strong influence on sexual attitudes and behaviors. For instance, it was taboo for male and female adolescents to walk together in public. A daughter who became pregnant before marriage created disastrous consequences for her whole family.

However, the influence of religious and traditional cultural values has decreased in recent decades, most noticeably since 1980. This decrease can be seen in the fantastic changes in the sexual attitudes and behaviors of the people, especially among the young. The widespread distribution of contraceptives, which the government initiated as a national program in 1970, brought many changes in the sexual attitudes and behaviors of the people.

The incidence of abortion among the young, which is estimated at around one million per year in the whole country, shows that the strength of religious values has decreased in today's Indonesian society. On the other hand, attendance for all the different religious services is very high.

B. Character of Ethnic Values

Each ethnic group has its own culture and sexual values. The Javanese, Sundanese, Minahasans, and Balinese, for instance, are more "modern" than the Dayaks and Papuans. In general, however, sex is considered something private and even secret. Sex is appropriate only between husband and wife. Women are like maids; they are only for their husbands' benefit. Wives are subservient to their husbands in everything, including sexual contact.

In a certain Javanese art community of East Java, known as the Reog Ponorogo, some men engage regularly in homosexual behavior because they believe that they have supernatural powers that will disappear if they have sexual contact with women. These men, known as *waroks*, take care of young males called *gemblaks* who are treated as females. *Waroks* engage in homosexual intercourse with *gemblaks* instead of with females.

In relation to supernatural belief or culture, in a certain community sexual intercourse is practiced as a part of ritual. Many people, hoping to receive a blessing, visit a cemetery on Mount Kemukus in Central Java. However, to receive the blessing the visitors must fulfill one erotic condition. The condition is that the visiting petitioners have to engage in sexual intercourse with each other. They are forbidden to have sex with their own partners during the visit to the sacred cemetery. The other condition is that the sexual intercourse must be done in seven visits with the same partner. It is hard to imagine hundreds of couples having intercourse in the open air under the trees covered with clothes. This cemetery is still visited today by many people from different places, and the free sex among the sacred cemetery visitors continues to the present.

In certain isolated ethnic groups living in remote areas, there is a custom whereby a man may borrow another's wife. This custom is based on the fact that the number of females in the group is very limited and out of balance with the number of adult males. This custom allows a man to enjoy the other man's wife for a few days, but after that he has to bring her back to her husband.

In today's globalization trends, sexual attitudes and behaviors are changing rapidly in all the cultures of Indonesia. Premarital sex, for example, is now common among adolescents. Even premarital pregnancy is easy to find and, for many parents, it no longer has the disastrous consequences it did only a generation or two ago.

There is a homogenous tendency in sexual perception, knowledge, and behavior especially among the young, which crosses the ethnic and religious boundaries.

3. Sexual Knowledge and Education

A. Government Policies and Programs

Sex education is not a priority in the government's program. Until the year 1999, school curricula did not offer students any education on sexual topics or issues. However, the Department of Education and Culture has recommended a book, *About the Sexual Problems in the Family*, by Wimpie Pangkahila, as a source of sexual information for high school students. This 152-page text, published in 1988, discusses many sexual problems that occur in Indonesian families as a result of misinformation, misunderstanding, and myths, such as the belief in the harmful consequences of self-pleasuring or the impossibility of pregnancy if sexual intercourse occurs only once a month.

The Indonesian Health Department and the National Coordinating Board of Family Planning have a program for Reproductive Health Education. This program, designed for young people, provides seminars on topics of reproductive and sexual health.

In recent years, some secondary high schools have introduced a small segment of sex education as part of their extracurricular offerings. Outside experts are invited to talk about sexuality in these seminars. The era of reformation in Indonesia has also changed the policy of the government on sex education. The new government, through the Department of Education and Culture, has legalized sex education for students under the title of "healthy reproductive education." Now sex education is formally a part of school curricula.

B. Informal Sources of Sexual Knowledge

Despite public reticence about sexuality, the Indonesian people are eager for and need more information about the subject—hence, the popularity of public and semi-private seminars on sexual topics. Many social organizations for young people and women sponsor seminars for their members with outside experts invited to speak about sexuality. The seminars are not only held in the big cities, but also in the small cities and suburbs.

Some magazines, newspapers, radio broadcasts, and TV stations also have columns or programs in which sexuality and sexual problems are discussed. Readers, listeners, and viewers write or call in asking about some sexual issue or problem they are facing or they want to know about.

Television viewers can watch advertisements for condoms every day in the context of HIV/AIDS prevention.

With the advent of cyberspace, some Indonesian Web sites now offer popular sites for dialog about sexuality. The popularity of these sites among Indonesians makes it hard to believe the view of some people that sex is still a taboo topic among the Indonesian people.

4. Autoerotic Behaviors and Patterns

A. Children and Adolescents

Autoeroticism is common among children in the phallic stage of their psychosexual development. Although some parents report that they watch their children pleasuring themselves to orgasm, many parents are afraid when they discover their children self-pleasuring because they believe this to be an abnormal act.

Autoeroticism is also common among adolescents as a way of tension release. One unpublished study by Wimpie Pangkahila found that 81 percent of male adolescents and 18 percent of female adolescents aged 15 to 20 years old engaged in self-pleasuring. Most reported using their fingers, sometimes lubricated with a liquid. Some rubbed against a pillow or mattress. Only a few females reported using a vibrator.

However, there is still considerable misinformation and misunderstanding about autoeroticism. Many adolescents still believe that autoeroticism or masturbation may result in various health problems, like decreased memory, erectile dysfunction, infertility, and decreased bone marrow.

On the moral side, many adolescents feel that autoeroticism is sinful. But they continue to practice this sexual activity. Questions about autoeroticism appear very often in many informal sources of information about sexuality, such as seminars, interactive Internet chat groups, newspapers, and radio programs. The questions are usually related to the consequences of autoeroticism for the practitioner's health.

B. Adults

Autoeroticism is very common among adults, especially single adults. The pattern is the same as among adolescents. The use of sexual accessories, like various kinds of vibrators and doll partners, are becoming common even though these materials are still illegal. No legal sex shop can be found anywhere in the country, even in the larger cities. One sex shop did open early in 2000 in Surabaya (East Java), Indonesia's second largest city, but the police quickly closed it on the grounds that the sex shop did not have a license from the government and that such shops are contrary to Indonesian culture and morality. It is really difficult to understand such reasoning, especially when this episode triggered a flood of questions in various media—questions, such as "Why close a sex shop? Why don't the police shut down the prostitution?" However, some drug shops still sell those sex accessories illegally, and people can buy from them.

Masturbation among married men or women is practiced in certain situations, like when they stay apart from their partners, if they cannot reach orgasm by sexual intercourse, or if the partner is not able to engage in sexual intercourse for some legitimate reason. Some wives practice masturbation directly in front of their husbands after they have had sexual intercourse without reaching orgasm. A few of them use vibrators or other sexual accessories, whereas others do not want to do it in front of their husbands. The result is that the husbands often do not know that their wives are not reaching orgasm by intercourse and are relying on masturbation for this.

Even though autoeroticism is very commonly practiced among both adolescents and adults, many people still believe that autoeroticism is morally wrong and will result in harmful physical and mental consequences.

5. Interpersonal Heterosexual Behaviors

A. Children

Sexual exploration and sex rehearsal play are common among children as a natural part of their psychosexual development. However, many parents are afraid of such behaviors, believing that the child is suffering from some sexual abnormality or that this behavior will result later in life in some sexual abnormality. Some parents bring their children to psychologists to find out whether their child has had actual sexual intercourse.

Many adolescents are afraid of not being virgins because they had sex rehearsal play a long time ago during their childhood. Some of them even come to the clinic to make sure that they are still virgins. Others seek answers to their questions about childhood sexual rehearsal play and virginity from the dialog columns on sexuality in the newspapers.

B. Adolescents

Puberty Rituals

Some ethnic groups, especially in the remote areas and among tribal people, have ritual ceremonies for adolescents. These ceremonies differ greatly from one ethnic culture to another.

In certain areas, there is a ritual ceremony for the female on the occasion of her first menstruation. This ceremony is actually a way to inform the community that this young female now has become an adolescent and is ready to marry. In one area in East Nusa Tenggara province, male adolescents have to practice sexual intercourse after they are traditionally circumcised. For practical reasons, these male adolescents tend to practice with sex workers. With the unhealed penile cut, this practice, of course, can result in transmission of STDs. This practice also poses a high risk factor for the transmission of HIV/AIDS. However, these ceremonies are no longer practiced in most modern areas of Indonesian society.

Premarital Sexual Activities and Relationships

Premarital sexual activities are still generally considered taboo. In general, older persons and parents oppose all sexual activities engaged in before marriage. However, during the past decade, there has been a change in sexual attitudes and behaviors among adolescents. Some small studies in a few Indonesian cities reveal a growing trend among adolescents to engage in premarital sexual activities such as necking, petting, and even intercourse.

These sexual activities are also becoming common among adolescents in the villages and suburbs. Today there is no significant difference in sexual perception and behavior between the young in the big cities and the villages.

However, knowing that parents and the older generation oppose premarital sexual activities, young people hide their activities from them. On the other hand, parents frequently give their children more opportunities to be alone with their boy- or girlfriends, and many adolescents take advantage of these opportunities for sexual activities.

In their sexual activities, oral sex is becoming popular among adolescents. There are at least two reasons why adolescents prefer oral sex. First, with oral sex they can avoid the risk of premarital pregnancy. Second, the female feels secure because oral sex leaves her hymen, a mark of her virginity, intact. A few adolescents engage in anal sex for the same reasons.

Unfortunately, the changes in sexual behavior, which tend to be freer today than in the past, are not accompanied by any increase in sexual knowledge. Most adolescents have many questions about their sexual lives and experiences, which, if expressed, bring negative responses from the older generation, who still believe that such questions are not appropriate for adolescents to inquire about. However, it seems that the general public tends to be more permissive of these changes. Of course, the lack of sexual knowledge results in some negative personal consequences for adolescent life: feelings of guilt and anxiety, unwanted pregnancy, abortion, and STD transmission.

C. Adults

Premarital Courtship, Dating, and Relationships

Dating and premarital sexual relations among adults are very common in modern Indonesian society. The culture requires a particular kind of courtship when a couple wants to marry. In this courtship, the parents and family of the male approach the parents of the female to make the arrangements.

In some ethnic groups, a courtship document is signed when presents, such as cows, buffaloes, gold, and jewelry, are given. For many people in these groups, this custom is very expensive, because they need to save enough money to buy the presents for courtship. Presently, this custom is still practiced among certain ethnic groups, particularly those who live in the areas where they have little contact with outsiders. This custom actually implies that the male has bought and now owns the female.

However, traditional courtship customs are no longer practiced by people who live a modern lifestyle, especially those who live in big cities far from their original area. It is much more practical for them to abandon the traditional customs of courtship, which are both expensive and impractical. The simpler courtship custom of modern Indonesians calls for the parents of the young man to visit the parents of the young woman and agree to their children courting, but without expensive presents.

Sexual Behavior and Relationships of Single Adults

Self-pleasuring is a common sexual behavior among single adults, even though it is not allowed by religious and moral values. Sexual relationships among male and female single adults are also taboo. However, some data show that many couples engage in sexual relations before they marry. A 1991 study by Wimpie Pangkahila suggested a rate of 53 percent for urban couples. Another unpublished study of rural, pregnant women found a premarital intercourse incidence of 27 percent.

This incidence is now believed to be much higher because of more liberal relationships, between single adults and adolescents as well. The term "the other man or woman" has become very popular in the last few years. It is no longer a surprise if somebody is said to have a relationship with an extramarital partner.

Many single adult males have sexual contact with prostitutes. Prostitution exists in many places in Indonesia, whether it is legal or illegal. The range of services comes in various classes from low/cheap to high/expensive (see Section 8B, Prostitution, below).

Marriage and Family

Indonesia has had a marital code to regulate marriages since 1974. The law requires that a marriage be performed in a religious ceremony and then be registered in the civil act office for Christians, Buddhists, and Hindus. The marriages of Moslems are registered in the Moslem Religion Affairs Office.

Generally, marriage in Indonesia involves the families of both partners. It is uncommon for a marriage to be conducted without involvement of the families of both spouses. In case the families cannot agree for whatever reason, there are two choices for the couple. Adult couples who insist on marrying can arrange their own marriage. The other choice is to delay or cancel the wedding. Couples who insist on marrying, even though their families do not agree, usually attempt to repair their relationships with their families.

Divorce is prohibited in Christianity. However, Christian couples who want a divorce may apply to a state court for a civil divorce. In Islam, Hinduism, and Buddhism, divorce is allowed for certain reasons, mainly infertility and adultery on the part of the wife.

In some areas, the incidence of divorce is very high because of financial problems, family conflict, and infidelity. For example, in Lombok Island (West Nusa Tenggara Province) there are many young widows with or without children. Of course, this becomes a serious social problem in the society.

Extramarital intercourse is common, especially among males. Many married men seek prostitutes or have sexual relations with single or married women. Extramarital intercourse is also found among married women, but at a lower incidence than among husbands. Although married women do have sexual relations with single and married men, most people consider this as very bad and unacceptable behavior. In a typical, double moral standard, extramarital sex by males is considered something usual, even though it is forbidden by religion, local morality, and law.

Sexuality and the Physically Disabled and Aged

Most Indonesians believe that sex is only for physically normal and young people. Most feel uncomfortable when a disabled or aged person still thinks about or expresses an interest in sexual activities. A disabled young woman wrote her complaint and protest in a newspaper because she was discriminated against by a dating and marriage service. The manager of the organization had refused her membership because she was a disabled person. The male manager mentioned that nobody would be attracted to a disabled female.

Even though there is discrimination against disabled persons, marriages do occur between disabled persons, or between disabled and able-bodied persons. Some disabled and many aged people do come to sexual clinics with their sexual problems for counseling and treatment.

The misinformation that sexual intercourse should not be performed after menopause may lead a male with a postmenopausal wife to seek sex with another woman—prostitutes included. Erectile dysfunction is the most common sexual complaint of older males. On the other hand, pain during sexual intercourse is the most common sexual complaint of older females.

Incidence of Oral and Anal Sex

Generally, Indonesians do not accept fellatio, cunnilingus, and anal sex as foreplay or sexual outlets. Most people consider these behaviors as abnormal or sinful. On the other hand, many people do engage in fellatio and cunnilingus, but not with their own spouses.

Many men seek out prostitutes only for fellatio, because their wives refuse to engage in it. Some women do like to have cunnilingus, but refuse to perform fellatio for their husbands. Still, many couples enjoy both fellatio and cunnilingus as a part of their normal sexual activities.

Fellatio and cunnilingus are becoming popular among the new generation as a sexual alternative to vaginal intercourse, and as foreplay as well. Generally, they decide to practice fellatio and cunnilingus after watching this behavior on pornographic cable television or on videocassettes. Very few couples engage in anal sex.

6. Homoerotic, Homosexual, and Ambisexual Behaviors

A. Children and Adolescents

Homoerotic and homosexual activities are not common among Indonesian children, although some sexual exploration involving exhibiting the genitals is known to occur. Some children who experience homosexual experience with adults may be drawn into long-term homosexual behavior, but no data are available on the various outcomes of child–adult same-sex experiences.

Some adolescents engage in homosexual activities as a sexual outlet, while others engage in this activity for material gain as homosexual male prostitutes. In one Javanese society of traditional artists, known as *Reog Ponorogo*, some adolescents engage in homosexual activities to serve adult males who are believed to have supernatural powers (see Section 2B, Character of Ethnic Values).

B. Adults

In general, Indonesians consider homosexuality and bisexuality as abnormal acts forbidden by morality and religion. Despite this taboo, thousands of adults engage in homosexual and bisexual relationships. An organization called the Functional Group for Gays and Lesbians exists, with branches in some of the larger cities. This organization also publishes a newsletter/bulletin to help homosexual persons keep in touch and build support.

Most gays and lesbians, however, hide their orientation and activities, because they know that most people oppose homosexual behavior. Only very few male homosexuals want to be open and frank about their sexual behavior. Some homosexual males hide their sexual orientation by marrying a woman for social status and conformity. Their wives only learn that their husbands are homosexual after the marriage occurs. Some of these marriages end in divorce, but some others remain intact for social or religious reasons.

Some men gradually discover their homosexual orientation during adolescence or early adulthood. Others may be drawn into a homosexual lifestyle, because they had homosexual experience during their childhood. Some engage in homosexual behavior strictly for profit as male prostitutes, and then discover that they have a homosexual orientation.

Since same-sex marriage is illegal, homosexual persons are limited to living together arrangements and cohabitation without legal sanction. In terms of socializing, some of the larger cities offer places where homosexual persons can gather and meet each other. Sexual outlets among homosexual, lesbian, and bisexual-oriented adults include oral sex, anal sex, and mutual self-pleasuring. Some lesbians use vibrators or other sexual accessories. But unlike male homosexuals, lesbians are much less obvious in this society.

7. Gender Conflicted Persons

There are no precise statistics on the incidence or sexual lives of gender-conflicted persons. It is commonly assumed by professionals in the field that there are thousands of male transsexuals in Indonesia. *Banci*, a slang term, and *waria*, an abbreviated combination of *wanita* (female) and *pria* (male), are popular terms for gender-conflicted persons in Indonesia. In Surabaya, the capital city of East Java, Perkumpulan Waria Kotamadya Surabaya, the Association of Waria in Surabaya, provides members with support, education, and career training as beauticians, artists, or dancers. These skills, they hope, will allow *waria* to support themselves and avoid a life of prostitution. Support groups also provide information about HIV/AIDS prevention.

In modern-day Indonesia, people can see many transsexuals working as beauticians, dancers, or entertainers. However, on the other hand, many of them also work as low-class prostitutes. This gives all transsexuals a negative image in the eyes of the wider Indonesian society.

Only a few male transsexuals, usually well known artists, can afford to have surgery to change their sexual anatomy. The average cost for such surgery is the equivalent of thirty to forty times a lower-class worker's monthly income, about US$2,000 to US$3,000.

8. Significant Unconventional Sexual Behaviors

A. Coercive Sex

Child Sexual Abuse, Incest, and Pedophilia

There is no research on child sexual abuse, incest, or pedophilia in Indonesia. What is known about these issues comes from reports in the newspapers detailing some incidents of coercive sex involving children. Legal penalties exist for persons convicted of child sexual abuse, incest, and pedophilia. The social response to these acts is very negative, and the perpetrators are viewed as criminals.

Many street children, whether female or male, experience child sexual abuse. Many male street children are sexually abused by female lower-class prostitutes, who believe the myth that anyone who has sexual intercourse with children or adolescents will remain young.

Incest usually occurs among poor and uneducated families, although this may be a myth. The housing situation of poor families with a single bedroom facilitates the occurrence of incest. Some cases of incest come to public attention when the victims become pregnant and the perpetrators cannot hide the incident. Neighbors and family normally become angry and physically abuse the perpetrator when they learn of such incest.

In the last few years, as the terms pedophilia and sex tourism have become common in Indonesia, knowledge of the incidence of sex with children is increasing. The victims are children of poor families in the villages, while the perpetrators are foreign tourists from other countries. Parents of the children do not object to the foreign tourists who visit their family and offer to help their children. Frequently, the parents agree when the tourists want to bring the children to the city.

It is reported that the organizers are members of an international syndicate of promoters of pedophilia. A video of pedophilia involving Indonesian children is reported to be widely available in many countries.

However, it is necessary to study whether the tragedy inflicted on the children of poverty-stricken families is really the result of paraphilic pedophilia or whether it occurs more because of the belief that sexual intercourse is safer with children who are assumed to be "clean," free from STDs including HIV/AIDS.

Sexual Harassment

Even though there are no significant data about sexual harassment, it is believed that it is a common occurrence in Indonesia. Many women who work in factories or offices, or walk along the street, suffer from a variety of sexual harassments, although few women realize they are victims of sexual harassment. Conviction on a change of sexual harassment may result in three to six months in prison.

Fortunately, in recent years, some women leaders have been trying to educate women, teaching them that sexual harassment is illegal and that women have the right to prosecute those who engage in it.

Rape

As with other forms of sexual coercion, there are no significant data on the incidence of rape in Indonesia. Rape incidents perpetrated by an acquaintance, boyfriend, or stranger, and rapes that end in murder are sometimes reported. However, most rapes reported to the police do not end up in a court trial. One of the reasons for this is to protect the victim from public embarrassment in the mass media. Another reason is that the punishment for rapists is considered to be very light.

Marital rape is not reported in the news media, although some wives in counseling or therapy do report being raped by their husbands when they refuse to have sexual intercourse. However, none of the wives want to report this to the police, because they never realize that it is a rape if done by a husband to his own wife. Some wives, however, resist their husbands and threaten to divorce them when forced to have sex against their will.

Some taxi passengers are raped by the drivers, and have ended up being murdered. According to the confessions of the taxi drivers, at the beginning they only want to rob the passengers, but this in the end resulted in sexual arousal, assault, and murder. Some wives and their daughters become the victims of gang rapes perpetrated by robbers when they are discovered at home during a robbery.

B. Prostitution

Prostitution is widespread and occurs in many locations from small to large cities, even though it is often illegal. In some jurisdictions and cities, where prostitution is illegal, the law may prosecute either the prostitutes or those who manage the business of prostitution.

In a few large cities, prostitution is legal. Many prostitutes ("sex workers") of different ages, from adolescence to middle-aged, can be seen. The sex workers are not only local or Indonesian females. There are also some foreigners working as prostitutes. They are divided into different groups based on their appearance, with low-, middle-, and high-class categories. The price of sexual services offered by the sex workers varies, depending on the class determined by their managers. It varies from only 25,000 Rupia (Rp.) (US$3) to Rp. 3,000,000 (US$400) for a short time and one coitus.

Beside legal and illegal prostitution, there is also a hidden prostitution. This is a form of prostitution concealed in other businesses, such as a massage parlor, beauty parlor, or karaoke place. In terms of STD transmission, this sort of prostitution is worse because the masseuses, the beauticians, or the karaoke escorts do not feel that they are prostitutes; on the other hand, the male customers do not feel that they have had sexual intercourse with sex workers. As a result, many males are unknowingly infected with STDs after they have intercourse with masseuses, beauticians, or karaoke escorts.

Childhood prostitution is often supported by wealthy tourists from the Middle East, Europe, Japan, and other countries, but it is not the extensive problem it is in neighboring nations, like Thailand, Cambodia, Myanmar, and Vietnam. The increase of childhood prostitution is related to the myth that children are "clean" and free from STD infections.

In a few large cities, male sex workers also operate. Their customers are widows, women of middle age or older, and female visitors from foreign countries. Some of them operate quietly as masseurs providing special services for women.

In certain tourist areas, such as Bali, some foreign tourists end up marrying a sex worker whose services they originally sought for pay.

C. Pornography and Erotica

In keeping with our conservative Indonesian tradition, pornography is illegal throughout Indonesia. However, it is not difficult to find "blue" or hard-core video material. Some people sell pornographic books, magazines, and pictures, despite their being illegal. People, including adolescents, can easily rent pornographic videos and videodisks in many rental places for a low price because so many of them are illegal copies.

Police have caught some criminals who illegally produce or import copies of pornographic video material. However, the illegal business never stops, and people can always rent or buy such hard-core video materials. There is no protection for adolescents from pornographic materials, so they can rent or buy it easily. The video renters/sellers do not feel a moral responsibility to protect adolescents from the effects of the hardcore materials they sell.

In the era of cyberspace, it is much more difficult to protect adolescents from pornography, because it is very easy to access pornographic Web sites. In big cities, there are many places where people can gain access to the Internet and no one can control this access to pornographic Web sites on the Internet.

9. Contraception, Abortion, and Population Planning

A. Contraception

Indonesia has a national program promoting contraception to help married couples plan their families. This program addresses only married people, and not adolescents or unmarried adults. Information on contraception is provided through women's social organizations, newspapers, and radio and television broadcasts.

In 1970, the government began providing free contraceptives at public health centers. In 1988, with an improving economic situation and people recognizing the need for family planning, the government gradually began reducing its support, encouraging people who could afford them to obtain contraceptives from physicians in private practice or midwives with reasonable fees. The poor can still obtain free contraceptive services at public health centers where the only charge is for an inexpensive admission ticket.

The most popular contraceptives are the oral hormonal pill, hormonal injections, and IUDs. Women have to be examined by a physician before they can obtain a prescription for oral hormonal pills, but renewal of such prescriptions is not limited. Hormonal injections and IUDs are administered by doctors or by midwives. The other contraceptives are hormonal implants and tubectomy. As for males, acceptance of contraception is very limited. There are at least two reasons for this resistance. First, perceived male social superiority results in males not accepting their responsibility for contraceptive decisions and use. Second, there are only two alternatives in choosing male contraceptives, condoms or vasectomy. Condom users account for only about 5 percent of the total number of contracepting men and women.

Despite the limiting of contraceptive information to married women, some adolescents and unmarried women also use contraceptives. They are available in pharmacies (apothecaries or chemists), and include the condom and vaginal film (tissue). Often the hormonal pill can be obtained without a physician's prescription.

In general, the people do not agree that unmarried people should have access to and use contraceptives. Thus, there is no formal education in the schools about contraceptives for adolescents. Sexually active adolescents and single adults have only informal sources of information about contraceptives: newspapers, television, radio programs, and seminars sponsored by interested social groups. As a result, not many adolescents understand how to prevent unwanted pregnancies. They do not even understand how to estimate their fertile period. However, with the government agreement on sexual education as a part of the curriculum in the schools, adolescents will have access to complete information about sexuality, including contraceptives.

B. Teenage (Unmarried) Pregnancies

Unmarried pregnancies are not uncommon, but data are nonexistent. What little information is available from routine clinical statistics simply documents the number of unmarried pregnancies in different years. Unpublished data from one urban clinic, for instance, reported 473 unmarried pregnant women seeking aid in 1985-1986, a second clinic served 418 pregnant unmarried women in 1983-1986, and a third clinic reported 693 unmarried pregnancies in 1984-1990.

These reports provide only raw data with no perspective, and the frequency and incidence of unmarried pregnancies are much higher than these few studies indicate. Likewise, there are no data that would allow one to compare the incidence of unmarried pregnancies in the cities and rural areas. However, the incidence of abortions performed illegally by medical doctors or traditional healers suggests that unwanted pregnancies are not uncommon, either in the cities or in the rural areas.

Of course, not all unwanted pregnancies result in abortion. Some pregnant adolescents are forced to marry even though they do not want to. The unwanted babies born by unmarried adolescents or young adults that are taken care of in orphanages also indicate that unmarried pregnancies are not uncommon. Some unwanted babies are left by their mothers in the clinic after delivery. Others are simply left in front of somebody's house to be rescued.

Based on an estimated one million teenage abortions a year, and the fact that not all unmarried pregnancies result in abortion, it is believed that the actual number of teenage unmarried pregnancies is well over a million a year.

C. Abortion

Abortion is illegal throughout Indonesia, except in rare medical cases to save a mother's life. It is impossible to obtain any realistic number of abortions performed in Indonesia, simply because it is illegal. However, many abortions are performed. In addition to abortions performed illegally by medical doctors, abortions are also performed by native or traditional healers, who use traditional methods that are often unsafe and result in complications. One such method uses the stem of a coconut tree leaf, which is inserted into the uterus through the vagina and cervix. This method, of course, is very risky because it is not sterile and the healers do not understand the sexual anatomy. Some deaths are reported after abortions by native healers because of uterine rupture, bleeding, or infection.

Some doctors are caught by the police because they perform abortions in their clinics. A few of these cases were reported in the news media when police found many dead fetuses buried in the yard of a clinic or in plastic bags thrown into the garbage bins or dumps.

It is estimated that around 2.5 million abortions are performed each year throughout Indonesia, for both married and unmarried women. Of these, around one million are abortions performed on teenagers.

D. Population Programs

The success of Indonesia's national program of family planning was recognized in 1989 when the United Nations gave its Population Award to the president of Indonesia. Efforts are being made to achieve zero population growth in the near future.

These efforts are particularly important considering that the island of Java is one of the most densely populated areas of the world with 2,100 persons per square mile and over 100 million people on the island of 51,023 square miles. By comparison, the states of New York, North Carolina, and Mississippi are each roughly the same size as Java, but have only 18, 6.6, and 2.5 million people respectively.

One important effort is to increase the participation of males in family planning. Up to now, the participation of males in family planning is very low. The involvement of males in family planning is only 6 percent of the contraceptors because of various factors. The male superiority is one of important factors that inhibit males accepting responsibility in family planning. Most males are not interested to using either condoms or vasectomy.

10. Sexually Transmitted Diseases

Although no survey and reliable clinical reports are available, it is the clinical experience of the authors and their colleagues that sexually transmitted diseases are common among Indonesian adolescents and young adults, indicating that the taboos against premarital sex are not observed. The incidence is highest among those between ages 20 to 24, and lower among the 25- to 29-year-olds and 15- to 19-year olds. As would be expected given the social customs, the incidence among males is higher than it is among females. The most commonly reported STDs are nonspecific ure-thritis, gonorrhea, ulcus molle, and genital herpes. Syphilis is no longer common, although it appears to be increasing in recent years.

Transmission of STDs is caused by unsafe and high-risk sexual behavior, including intercourse with sex workers. The use of condoms is not popular among males who are involved in high-risk sexual behavior.

Treatment for STDs is available at all health clinics throughout the country. Some years ago, the government sponsored a program to reduce the spread of STDs by providing prostitutes with penicillin injections. Unfortunately, the program is no longer available.

Currently, sex workers have taken the initiative in preventing STD transmission. However, their effort is often medically unsound because it is only based on misinformation from friends or other lay people. The most popular method employed by sex workers is consuming an oral antibiotic after sexual activity. The other is irrigating the vagina with antiseptic. These methods, they believe, can prevent STD transmission, including HIV/AIDS. On the other hand, the customers also believe that if the sex workers do not have any visible signs of an STD, they are not at risk of being infected even though they do not use condom.

The prevention efforts by the government and non-governmental or-ganizations (NGOs) focus on providing information in seminars and the mass media, including the newspaper, radio, and television.

Some informal studies of STD prevention have found that most Indo-nesians do not understand well the nature and character of STDs. The obvious question, then, is whether the strategy and/or technique of pre-vention efforts have to be reevaluated, and probably even changed.

11. HIV/AIDS

The first case of AIDS found in 1987 in Denpasar (in Bali) was a Dutch visitor. This incident scared many people, including the hotel staff where he stayed and the hospital staff where he was treated a few days before he died. Fortunately, in revealing that HIV/AIDS was indeed present and active in Indonesia, this incident raised the awareness of many Indonesians, including doctors and government officials.

Until the end of 1987, there were only 6 cases of HIV/AIDS reported in Indonesia. Thereafter, this incidence has increased rapidly as reported by the Indonesian Department of Health (see Table 1). In the first two months of the year 2000, 103 new cases were reported, suggesting the start of an

Table 1

Incidence of AIDS in Indonesia, 1988-1999

Year	Cases	Year	Cases	Year	Cases
1988	7	1992	28	1996	137
1989	7	1993	113	1997	118
1990	9	1994	87	1998	200
1991	18	1995	89	1999	225

exponential increase, with perhaps a tripling of cases to about 600 for 2000. The cumulative number of HIV/AIDS cases until February 2000 was 1,146, consisting of 853 cases of HIV positives and 293 cases of AIDS. However, it is believed that the real number of HIV/AIDS cases is much higher than the reported number. The real number of HIV/AIDS cases is estimated around 100 to 200 times greater than the reported number (Indonesian Department of Health, 2000).

The 1,146 cases of HIV/AIDS reported as of February 2000 are spread throughout Indonesia's 23 provinces. These involve 679 males and 412 females, with the sex of 55 patients unidentified. Most of the HIV/AIDS cases in Indonesia resulted from heterosexual contact. Most of those infected are between 15 and 39 years of age (Indonesian Department of Health).

Sex workers are believed to be one source of infection transmission, but the freer sexual behaviors among today's people has also become a prominent factor. In the early years of HIV/AIDS transmission in Indonesia, it is estimated that some HIV-positive foreign tourists who came to popular tourist centers like Bali introduced the virus through sexual contact with sex workers or local people.

Prevention efforts have been provided for some groups of people, such as sex workers, both female and male, people who work in the tourism industry, university and high school students, long-distance truck and bus drivers, women leaders, and religion leaders. These efforts involve providing information, education, and training on how to reduce the spread of AIDS, and include blood tests for HIV infection. Campaigns to popularize the use of condoms are now conducted through the mass media, including newspaper, radio, and television. However, it is not easy to make people aware and encourage condom use if they engage in high-risk sexual intercourse.

The classical belief that using condoms inhibits the joy of sex is still fixed in the mind of almost all Indonesian males, as well as females. The simple distribution of condoms to sex workers does not solve the problem. Most males seeking sex workers do not want to use condoms because of the classic myth of inhibiting pleasure. Sex workers are in a very weak bargaining position, so they do not have enough power to refuse the customers who do not want to use condoms. If they insist and refuse the customer who does not want to use a condom, they will have to answer to their manager, and this could lead to further difficulties. No one seems to know what policy could best convince those who have sex with sex workers that condoms are a must in today's world. Indonesia very much needs a national policy to encourage men frequenting sex workers to use condoms, or to press sex workers not to do their job if the customer does not want to use a condom. If such a policy is not found and implemented effectively, Indonesia faces the distinct likelihood of an explosion of cases of HIV/AIDS in the near future.

12. Sexual Dysfunctions, Counseling, and Therapies

The diagnostic paradigm used by Indonesian sexologists is basically that of William Masters and Virginia Johnson, with presenting cases of inhibited penile erection (erectile dysfunction), early (premature) ejaculation, inhibited (retarded) ejaculation, male and female dyspareunia, inhibited female orgasm, and vaginal spasms (vaginismus).

However, the development in diagnostic tools has changed both the results of the diagnosis and the strategy of case management. With some diagnostic tools like erectiometer, doppler pen, and Rigiscan, a more accurate diagnosis can be achieved. For example, before the new diagnostic tools were developed, most erectile dysfunction was considered to be psychological in origin. But after the development of new diagnostic tools, it is found that most erectile dysfunctions are organic. This finding, supported by the new medicines like sildenafil, has changed the strategy in the management of erectile dysfunction. Now the treatment of erectile dysfunction is divided into three steps: first-, second-, and third-line therapies. First-line therapy consists of sexual or psychosexual therapy, oral erectogenic agents (primarily Viagra), and a vacuum constriction device. Second-line therapy includes intracavernosal injection and intraurethral application. Third-line therapy is the surgical procedure of penile implant. These advanced treatments are available only to a small minority of Indonesians living in urban centers who can afford them.

A common psychological sequel for males with a sexual dysfunction is a feeling of inferiority with regard to their partner. This feeling is often what brings the male to seek treatment.

Many women, on the other hand, tend to hide their sexual problems and feel shy about seeking treatment. Many married women never have orgasm and never tell their husbands. At the same time, many husbands are unaware or do not even suspect that their wives never have orgasms. Many of them are simply unaware of their wife's sexual dysfunction even after the wife complains to a sexologist.

Out of 4,135 women who came for consultation at the authors' clinics for their own or their husband's sexual problem, 2,302, or 55.7 percent, have never had an orgasm, and 527, or one in six (12.7 percent), have experienced orgasm only rarely. Among those who never reached orgasm, 60 (2.6 percent) experienced dyspareunia, 67 (2.9 percent) experienced hypoactive sexual desire, and 27 (1.2 percent) suffered from vaginismus.

The high incidence of sexual dysfunction among Indonesian females is caused by poor communication between husbands and wives, poor sexual knowledge, and male sexual dysfunction. However, good diagnosis and treatment for sexual dysfunctions are available in only a few urban clinics, and are available only to those who can afford it.

13. Research and Advanced Education

A few Indonesian sexologists have finished their education and training in the United States, Belgium, and Australia. Some informal unpublished clinical studies of sexuality in Indonesia have focused on sildenafil and alprostadil for the treatment of erectile dysfunction, on sexual perception and behavior among the youth in cities and villages, and sexual knowledge, perception, and behavior of STD patients. Some studies are currently in progress, including management of erectile dysfunction using the new medications, and high-risk sexual behavior in relation to HIV/AIDS transmission.

Advanced education on sexuality is available only in the Master Program in Reproductive Medicine at Udayana University in Denpasar, Bali. This program offers sexology lectures and study as a part of the curriculum. As a postgraduate program, it requires a two-year study course in sexology, spermatology, experimental reproductive biology, reproductive endocrinology, embryology, family planning, and infertility management. Instruction in sexology includes perspectives on sexuality, gender and sexual behavior, childhood, adolescence, and adulthood sexuality, sexual fantasy, sexual variation, sexual dysfunction, sexual deviation, and premarital and marital counseling.

The mailing address of this center is: The Master Program in Reproductive Medicine, Udayana University Medical School, Attention: Prof. Wimpie I. Pangkahila, M.D., Ph.D., Jl. Panglima Sudirman, Denpasar, Bali, Indonesia.

References and Suggested Readings

Pangkahila, W. 1981. *Changes in sexual perception and behavior in adolescence.* Presented at the National Congress of Sexology, Denpasar, Indonesia.

Pangkahila, W. 1988. *Sexual problems in the family* [in Indonesian]. Jakarta: PT Gaya Favorit Press.

Pangkahila, W. 1991. *Premarital sex in married couples: A survey* [in Indonesian]. Presented in many public and professional seminars.

PART 2: THE INDIGENOUS ORANG RIMBA FOREST PEOPLE

RAMSEY ELKHOLY

Demographics and a Historical Perspective

[*Editor's Note*: Because there are over 300 distinct indigenous ethnic groups in Indonesia, the authors of Part 1 of this chapter focus mainly on urban and village Indonesians, for whom some data are available. Here, in Part 2, Ramsey Elkholy, a sociocultural anthropologist, expands on this picture of sexuality among modern urban and village Indonesians with insights from his field work with the indigenous Orang Rimba hunter-gatherer forest people of Sumatra, Indonesia. For additional insights into the sexual attitudes and behavior among other indigenous peoples, the reader is referred to the sections on the aboriginal people of Australia and Brazil, Canada's First Nation People, and the indigenous people of French Polynesia in volumes 1 and 2 of this *International Encyclopedia*, and on Papua New Guinea elsewhere in this fourth volume. (Robert T. Francoeur)].

A. Demographics

The Orang Rimba are an indigenous minority population inhabiting the primary and secondary lowland forests of south-central Sumatra, the largest and most western of the Indonesian islands just south of Malasia. *Kubu* is the most commonly used exonym by local villagers and the general Indonesian populace, and it is the most common referent found in the anthropological literature (see Van Dongen 1906; Loeb 1942; LeBar 1972; Sandbukt 1984, 1988a, b; Persoon 1989; Suetomo 1992). However, it is a title they resent being designated by, as it is a pejorative term connoting "savage" or "primitive."

They practice a nomadic or semi-nomadic form of hunting and gathering economy, occasionally supplemented with basic slash and burn (swidden) agriculture. Precise population figures are difficult to obtain, but 2,600 to 3,000 are realistic estimates, with the large majority living in Jambi Province, and nearly one third of the total population concentrated in the Tembesi-Tabir interfluve, where slash and burn agriculture has intensified in recent decades, thus leading to higher birthrates. Significant numbers are also found in South Sumatra Province, while remnant populations and new migrants can also be found in West Sumatra and the Riau Provinces.

Group sizes range from small nuclear domestic units to larger swiddening (slash and burn) camps, which can reach one hundred or more persons (Sandbukt 1988a). In cases where residential groups consist of nuclear family dwellings, it is common for two or more kin-related families to consolidate their efforts by sharing game and other wild foods to compensate for their small group sizes. In recent decades, some groups have adopted a more sedentary life, shifting their economic orientation towards subsistence horticulture and rubber tree cultivation and tapping. This has led to higher birthrates among women, but infant mortality remains high, particularly in areas where deforestation has occurred, where they are coping with the transition to sedentism without proper health care and hygienic education.

B. A Brief Historical Perspective

For centuries, the Orang Rimba have avoided sustained contact with neighboring agricultural peasantries, preferring to trade only with a select few trusted villagers. Various historical accounts report that in certain areas they had practiced a form of "silent trade" whereby forest products were placed on the fringes of the forest to be collected by villagers, who would exchange these products with needed goods, such as salt and metal for spear heads and machetes, by placing them in the same spot—both sides never meeting face to face (Boers 1838; Forbes 1885). This form of barter may have been replaced, in some cases, with face-to-face encounters with a Malay intermediary known as *jenang* or *bapak semang*. He was seen as a guarantor of their autonomy, and the forest products they forfeited to him (e.g., rattan, damar, "dragon's blood," and honey) were often of much greater value than the goods received (e.g., salt, tobacco, metal tools, and clothing), which were to be seen as gifts rather than direct equivalents of the goods offered (Sandbukt 1988b:112-13). This system lasted until recent years and still persists in some areas, but in a less paternalistic and strictly economic form.

Such extreme xenophobia may have been a response to the fears of slave raiding in past times. According to Sandbukt (1988a:111) and Marsden (1811:41), slave raiding on the inter-local level was a real and serious threat to the Orang Rimba until only a few generations ago. Such dangers may have increased with the spread of Islam from the fourteenth century onwards. In the Islamic faith, it is forbidden to enslave other Muslims. The non-Muslim indigenous populations of the interior, such as the Orang Rimba, were, therefore, obvious targets for slave raids and other forms of persecution (cf. Denatan et al. 1997).

Their long history of avoidance of the outside world is deeply rooted in an ideology, passed down from their ancestors, that envisages the bifurcation of humanity into two types: Malays—who live in permanent villages and follow the dictates of Islam; and the Orang Rimba—who live in the forest and follow the traditions and customs of their ancestors (see Sandbukt 1984). This distinction is the inspiration and guiding principle of their lives, and any crossing or confusing of these two domains would be seen as a breach of the sacred mode of life passed down from their ancestors. The Orang Rimba identify all that is sacred with the forest and, concomitantly, view many of the Islamic customs practiced by their sedentary village-dwelling neighbors as somehow impure and, therefore, taboo. Commensality practices perfectly illustrate this, in which two groups can reside in the same area without competing, because they have independent or different values and customs. The foods commonly eaten by Muslim villagers, such as goats, cows, buffaloes, and chickens, are foods that are forbidden to the Orang Rimba, whereas certain forest game, such as wild boar, turtle, and snake, foods quite common to the Orang Rimba, are taboo to the Muslim villagers.

The Orang Rimba integrate and associate religion, the supernatural, notions of well being, subsistence practice, and survival in general with their forest environment. Richly imbued with nurturing and life-giving qualities, their forest world is viewed as a pantheistic totality where a wide variety of deities reside under the auspices of a benevolent and omnipotent Godhead (*Behelo*). Forest deities are contacted regularly by experienced shamans who, while in trance, are endowed with the special ability to see and communicate with these otherwise invisible beings. Such sacred communication insures protection from physical and supernatural dangers and promotes success in hunting and the general well being of the group. It also serves to maintain and regenerate the delicate dialectical balance between themselves and the forest, and the sacred mode of life practiced therein.

Despite their rich and complex system of beliefs, they are, nonetheless, considered pagan savages or "infidels" by their Muslim agriculturist neighbors. Moreover, these encompassing agricultural peasantries, along with a continual influx of transmigrants from Java, continue to clear Orang Rimban forestland for their slash and burn fields. More threatening still to Orang Rimban environments are the large-scale logging operations that continue in both South Sumatra and Jambi Provinces. These days many groups camp on the side of logging roads in order to gain easier access to outer-market goods and services. Exchange contacts have also increased and diversified as a consequence of their broadening knowledge of the outside mercantile economy, and they no longer accept the paternalistic relationships with Malay intermediaries whereby "gifts" are received for their labor and forests products. Although they are enjoying greater access to the wider market economy, which has provided them with unprecedented opportunities to amass personal wealth (usually measured in sheets of cloth, gold, currency, and outer-market goods), there are few, if any, Orang Rimba environments that are not somehow threatened by the forces of encroaching development.

Aside from the destruction of their forests, the Orang Rimba have been under increasing pressures from central and local governments to assimilate. In the 1960s, the Department of Social Affairs (*Depsos*) initiated an assimilation campaign in an attempt to settle the Orang Rimba permanently in Malay-style villages and encourage them to practice subsistence agriculture. In coordination with Indonesia's Department of Religion (*Dinas Agama*), and occasionally through missionaries—sometimes foreign—attempts have been undertaken with varying degrees of success to convert them to Islam, the nation's predominant religion. Christian missionaries have also played an active role in persuading the Orang Rimba to abandon their traditional mode of life in the forest and assimilate to Malay ways, which involves taking up permanent residence in or near one of the nearby villages. Since Indonesia's independence in 1945, most villages have established Government-sponsored primary schools, where Pencasilan national philosophy and modern Indonesian is taught. This has promoted a sense of nationalism and broader regional awareness that is largely absent among the Orang Rimba, who by and large still remain separate geographically and culturally, and continue to see the world from a purely provincial or local perspective.

While the pressures of deforestation and development are causing rapid social changes and challenging the resiliency of their traditional way of life, domestic practices, including gender roles and relations, have remained relatively unaffected, aside from higher incidence of male defection to local villages where intermarriage is sought. No known precedence has been set for villager males marrying into forest-dwelling Orang Rimban camps. As such, these groups remain ideal contexts for studying traditional internal social dynamics. However, the Orang Rimba's well-established history of avoidance behavior had, in the past, undermined many attempts at conducting in-depth anthropological investigation, particularly regarding sensitive matters such as gender and sexuality, which require intimate contact on the domestic level and access to women by researchers. The information reported here is based on a field study of close to two years, when the author lived among the Orang Rimba on the domestic level. The demands of local customs necessarily restricted the author's access to Orang Rimban women.

1. Basic Sexological Premises

A. Character of Gender Roles

The Orang Rimba use kinship categories as the basic societal building blocks of their social organization. Kinship ties determine residential arrangements, distribution of resources, and key social alignments, in effect producing and reproducing their ideational ties and wider social order. Populations who may be separated by hundreds of kilometers will maintain contacts with their near and distant kin, either directly or through intermediaries. Through these "kinship networks," one enduring cultural type—however dispersed—may be said to exist. Gender relations are equally conditioned and affected by kinship relations and, therefore, kinship affiliation plays a fundamental role in shaping Orang Rimban social values and general modes of behavior.

Post-marital residence is uxorilocal. A male will marry-in to his spouse's group and, after an unspecified period of bride-service to his father-in-law, he will remain under his authority and be expected to provide his labor power and moral support indefinitely. He will eventually replace his father in-law's position, either by usurping his power when he is physically unfit or too old to make important decisions (e.g., resolving disputes, representing the group and their needs to outsiders, etc.), or when he finally dies. Marriage is normally a strenuous affair for in-marrying males as well as for both families involved. Most family members, fathers and brothers in particular, will fiercely resist any attempts by an outsider male to marry into the family. The outsider male must first gain the family's trust, and the suitor's bride-service is aimed at achieving this end. Cross-cousin marriage is preferred over unions with non- or distant kin, as trust has already been established through previous consanguinal relations between siblings.

An Orang Rimban man will commonly exhibit "macho"-like characteristics, asserting a "don't fool with me" status to other men. Such a disposition is largely because of the ever-present need to claim one's rights to women, particularly spouses, but also female children of marriageable age who are increasingly coming under the eyes of amorous young bachelors. While a male's masculinity is often exaggerated in manner, he may be openly affectionate and nurturing towards his young children, particularly infants. Men will also display affection openly by embracing and weeping upon uniting with long-separated male relatives. Group weeping (*bubugha-tongpon*) in cases where long-separated parties unite is also common, as well as in the event of death, in which case weeping may continue sporadically for weeks on end. Embracing, however, is restricted to the same sex, and it is more common that a woman will bow her head and sniff the hand of a male relative, which signifies respect during such greetings and farewells.

Traditionally, the role of an Orang Rimban man is that of "the hunter," the provider of meat and the protector of women and children. A woman's role is twofold, that of "the gatherer" of wild food, which includes digging edible tubers, and that of "the nurturer" of the young. While Orang Rimban society appears to be male-dominated in most respects, women often enjoy considerable autonomy and hold considerable political sway over their spouses, particularly when their fathers and male siblings are nearby, where they can voice their complaints and thereby summon their support (see Sandbukt 1988a).

Domestic space is delineated by the male and female domains in their split-level shelters. The upper level is the male domain, where visiting men are welcome to sit, smoke tobacco, and pass the time of day; the lower level is strictly for women and children. The lower level physically marks off a boundary from the rest of the shelter and is strictly off limits to all adult males except for a woman's spouse.

These days, collecting forest product for external exchange is increasing, as the Orang Rimba's ever-growing dependency on outer-market goods, such as cigarettes, coffee, sugar, and rice increases. It is now more common for women to frequent village shops to buy supplies and to sell their forest products. In some areas, however, women are still fiercely protected from the perceived dangers of the outer world and are forbidden to enter the village without male accompaniment. In more rare cases, where traditions still strongly prohibits contact with outsiders, women are forbidden from entering the village altogether.

Labor power is a central concern in Orang Rimban society, and every member, if able, is expected to contribute to the well being of the group. Even child labor is utilized to its fullest extent. As soon as children can walk, they learn, mostly through imitation, the tasks appropriate to their gender. Girls will look after their younger siblings, fetch water, cook, weave sleeping mats, collect firewood, help clear swiddens, and other household chores. Boys will also help clear swiddens and follow older boys and adult males on fishing and hunting excursions.

Young girls will be expected to take care of and nurture younger siblings, and it is not uncommon for a 7-year-old to spend an entire afternoon looking after younger siblings while her mother is out collecting forest products. On other occasions, they may accompany her on short excursions to dig for edible tubers. At this age, a girl will mix freely with boys, but as she approaches menarche her domestic responsibilities will increase along with her increasing awareness of her sexuality. She will already understand and adhere to the social sanctions regarding excessive contact with males. When she reaches her menarche, and for the remainder of her pre-marriage years, the only men she will interact with will be her male siblings and father. It is not uncommon, however, for an adolescent or young-adult girl to eschew intimate contact even with her male family members who, following the same code of conduct, may speak to her only when necessary.

Female children are particularly coveted and prized. Aside from helping with household chores, such as cooking, collecting firewood and water, nurturing younger siblings, and various other domestic tasks, they will someday fetch a bride-price or fine, often paid in sheets of cloth. In more recent times, gold and currency have also been used. Female children are also valued for the subsequent labor-power of an in-marrying male they will bring. More pressure to be self-sufficient is brought to bear on boys, and they will be encouraged to collect forest products or go fishing at the early age of 7 or 8. As they approach their adolescent years, they will accompany men on hunting excursions and increase their proficiency in forest-product collecting. They will commonly give their earnings to their mother for safekeeping or for the group's immediate needs. The logic behind expecting young boys to produce and contribute to the camp's subsistence base lies not only in their inherent abilities, but also in the recognition that they will provide their labor power during their growing years, but eventually will leave the camp to marry-in to another group. Moreover, they will need such survival skills in order to seek a wife and support a family someday.

Obedience to adults, particularly fathers, is an enduring characteristic of Orang Rimban family life. Unlike most of the world's egalitarian hunting and gathering societies, where children enjoy great personal autonomy and are expected to respect but not necessarily obey their parents (Denatan et al. 1997), Orang Rimban children are highly disciplined and are expected to both respect and obey their elders. A child that does not obey a parent is referred to as "evil" (*jahat*) and, in extreme circumstances, may be subject to physical punishment. This is more common among same-sex parent–child relations. For example, a father will not beat his daughter, and a mother will rarely, if ever, beat her son. More commonly, however, children are scolded verbally to invoke a sense of shame that is expecially felt when their behavior is called into question publicly before the scrutiny of the camp.

B. Sociolegal Status of Males and Females

The Adult World

As mentioned above, most of the world's hunting and gathering peoples are egalitarian in their social organization. The Orang Rimba are an exception in this regard, in that competition between men based on unequal access to women creates distinct inequalities between men. As a result, disputes commonly arise between men over their "rights" to women. Out of the need to protect one's claims to women, fathers over daughters and husbands over wives, the Orang Rimba have developed strong notions of law and social order. A male's voice is often oratorical and loud, and their strong sense of law and moral propriety is revealed in the content and character of their speech. In some areas, they have assimilated to an archaic Malay hierarchy, one which the Malays themselves no longer ascribe to, where various ranks preside under the authority of a high-ranking headman (*tumenggung*). These hierarchies most likely served as a mechanism through which they could be governed, however loosely, by the wider rural society, and to extract valuable forest products for external exchange. But they also serve as a legal mechanism through which serious disputes can be resolved. Incumbents are elected to office by their own kinsmen after demonstrating their mastery of formal *adat* customary law, which is exhibited through a public recital of its precepts. In areas where the Orang Rimba have not assimilated to this hierarchy, marked inequalities between men still persist, mainly as a consequence of uxorilocal post-marital residence and the requisite subordination of in-marrying male's to their father-in-laws.

A deep mistrust between distant or non-kin males regarding access to women is a pervasive characteristic of Orang Rimban social relations. Women are fiercely protected from outsiders, and restrictive taboos on interaction with women by non-kin males are strictly adhered to by all but the southernmost groups. Local residential camps, therefore, are usually comprised of only close kin. Groups with distant or no kinship ties, although cooperating occasionally, perhaps by sharing game or storing foodstuffs for one another, will occasionally suspect each other of wrong doings. The nuclear or extended family, therefore, is the core and basic building block of Orang Rimban social life. Constituting their domestic sphere, it is the fulcrum from which all notions of self and collectivity, as well as relations with others, emanate.

Women are normally regarded as legal minors (Sandbukt 1988a, b); but while women are normally subordinate to either their spouse or male relatives, they do often enjoy considerable autonomy within the domestic context, holding considerable influence in private family matters and in the unconditional loyalty they receive from their children. In legal matters, however, in cases of dispute or whenever personal rights are called into question, women are always subordinate either to their male consanguines or affines. Adultery, "wife stealing," and excessive intimacy with an unwed girl (*gadis*) are the most serious breaches of Orang Rimban customary law, and severe punishments may be administered by a headman when such transgressions occur. In cases when a headman is not present, a male litigant, perhaps a father or male spouse, will demand payment of a fine outright, as compensation from the accused male. Such fines are commonly paid in cloth, gold, and cash currency. When disputes cannot be effectively resolved by the two parties concerned, a headman or local villager, perhaps a village headman, will be summoned to mediate. In most cases, the woman involved will not be held accountable. Her actions are more often viewed as a subconscious response to the male offender's sorcery or "love magic." Full responsibility, therefore, is brought to bear on the actions of men, while strict behavioral constraints are adhered to by both sexes in order to temper suspicions and prevent such transgressions from occurring.

The World of Children

The legal status of children is called into question when a parent dies. For example, in instances when a mother has died, her brother, rather than her spouse, will claim legal custody of the children, as is prescribed by traditional *adat* law. This often leads to a dire situation for fathers, who are pressed to either run off with their children or mount a defense against their brother(s)-in-law for custody. Life-long discord between men often results out of such situations, leading to disputes that may never be effectively resolved. "Legally," however, a widowed male will be required to join the group of a brother-in-law and remain subordinate to him. A man who loses a spouse, therefore, also loses a degree of autonomy over his children and himself if he wishes to remain with his children without fleeing the area.

In cases when a father dies, men, particularly those wishing to acquire a second wife, will often assert their claim to the widowed woman. In such instances, a woman can be taken against her will if her male relatives are unable to ward off such men. This happens when the male siblings are too young or simply unable to effectively assert themselves. Having a second wife increases a man's prestige and contributes greatly to the labor force, particularly because child-labor is also utilized. Moreover, female children will one day fetch bride-service and the requisite subordination of any in-marrying male. Orang Rimban life, therefore, is highly political, and power relations between men very much hinge on their ability, or inability, to claim and maintain their "rights" over women and children.

In many cases, women are enjoying greater autonomy these days as contact with neighboring village populations increases. They often travel to village markets to buy supplies unaccompanied by men. This would have been unheard of only a decade ago when women were still fiercely protected against the dangers of the outside world. In some areas, the Orang Rimba still maintain such taboos regarding excessive contact with outsiders. In all cases, however, a woman will not travel to the village unless accompanied by another woman or by children. Unwed and newly wed women are particularly restricted from excessive contact with outsiders, and they often do not leave the general vicinity of the camp unless they are deep in the forest. Boys, however, are free to travel as they desire, shifting their residence as personal whim dictates, often without announcement. Only when a male marries will he be obligated to other persons.

C. General Concepts of Sexuality and Love

There is only one word in the Orang Rimba's lexicon that corresponds to the Western notion of "love" (*sayang*). While translating literally into the English notion of "pity," it more accurately connotes empathy and endearment. Often asexual in its usage, it is most commonly used to describe feelings toward children and long-acquainted spouses, particularly where bonds have grown and strengthened throughout the years. Romantic love is a much less articulated notion, most probably because it commonly occurs among young persons and leads to tensions between the two families involved, who must negotiate a solution, such as marriage or payment of fines to the girl's family in cases where excessive intimacy, which can consist of mere flirting, has occurred. Where marriage is consummated between first cousins, strong bonds may quickly develop through the pre-existing stable relationship between families, particularly in cases where the spouses have been acquainted since childhood.

While the complexion of any relationship is highly contingent on the individual personalities involved, the ability to bear children and perform adequately in household and subsistence-related activities is a necessary prerequisite for both sexes in order to allow a stable union to develop. Both sexes will seek an industrious mate, but in many cases their families will assist, or even determine, their children's spouse, particularly in the case of females. In the female context, bearing and nurturing children, forest-product and tuber collecting, and general domestic efficiency are highly valued attributes. A barren woman is either divorced or relegated to the subordinate status of second wife. In the male context, good hunters and natural leaders who are brave in articulating the groups needs to outsiders, thereby politicking effectively, are sought out, and in some cases, are able to marry more than one wife.

Lust is considered a natural inclination among men, but is downplayed in women. Far from embracing a woman's natural sexual desires, the Orang Rimba see women as innately vulnerable and, therefore, in need of protection against the predation and charms of men. Strict rules prohibiting male–female contact outside of marriage serve to combat or remedy a male's natural proclivity to seek a female. Although sex is accepted as a human urge, its referent, *mengawan*, is rarely spoken in the presence of women. Sometimes a young man's desire for a woman will prompt him to run off with a girl without the consent of her father, particularly in cases where he either does not wish to perform bride-service, does not have the resources to pay a bride-price, or is simply unable to gain the trust and acceptance of the girl's family (see Section 5B, Interpersonal Heterosexual Behaviors, Adults, on Courtship and Marriage). Whatever the method of consummation, strong emotional dependencies will develop through the course of a lifetime, and the losing of a spouse is met with uncontrollable weeping that can last for weeks on end. (Keep in mind the hardships and loss of status experienced by widowed men and women discussed above.)

2. Religious and Ethnic Factors Affecting Sexuality

Among males, loincloths are worn that cover the genitalia while exposing the buttocks. Women wear wraparound skirts known as sarongs and often go bare-breasted, particularly if they are nurturing young children. No sense of embarrassment is felt by such bodily exposure, because domestic units are comprised of only close kin. However, while in the village to trade, Orang Rimba now adhere to village etiquette and wear Western-style trousers, Indonesian sarongs for women, and shirts. Back in their forest camps, however, they revert back to their traditional attire. Men these days, however, are increasingly wearing short pants, even while in their forest camps.

Since their introduction in recent decades, brassieres have been commonly worn by women, often with no shirt. In the past, women wore brassieres outside their shirts as decorative attire, ceasing only when local villagers explained the proper manner in which they are to be worn. Orang Rimban women, nonetheless, continue to wear only brassieres without shirts while in their forest camps to provide easy access for breast-feeding an infant.

Children will remain naked until they reach the age of 3 or 4. During these years, they will mix freely with few, if any, behavioral constraints relating to gender. At this early stage in a child's development, however, a boy's sexuality will be exalted. This is best exemplified by the playful attention a boy's genitalia receive from camp members. The foreskin of the penis is often squeezed and the residual odor on the fingertips is smelled with much fervor and delight by all, who will claim it smells "sweet." A female's genitalia, however, do not receive such attention; on the contrary, they are rarely, if ever, referred to. A male infant will also receive a kind of "erotic" nurturing from his mother, who will adore and kiss him by smelling or sniffing while breastfeeding, or massage his penis and anus with no inhibitions. Female children, however, do not receive such attention from either parent.

As children grow, maternal bonds weaken and they are encouraged to be independent, both economically and emotionally. They will increasingly seek the company of their age-mates, with whom they will play and venture into the forest to search for food and forest products. They will no longer be permitted to sleep with their mothers, not only in order to encourage independence, but also to discourage incestuous desires in the boys. By the time adolescence is reached, both sexes will be well versed in the particular modes of conduct appropriate to their gender. Boys avoid all contact with young unwed females, while the latter eschew contact with all men.

A girl will cover her breasts during her adolescent years, exposing them once again only after marriage, when she will need to nurture her young.

Expressions of female sexuality and displays of femininity are, therefore, systematically discouraged; and whereas only men are held "legally" responsible for their actions, heavy responsibility also rests on women to uphold ideals of purity and chastity, a task which often proves to be increasingly difficult as they come of age and become the temptation for acquisitive young bachelors or older males wishing to acquire a second wife. Should a woman fail in upholding these ideals, a sense of shame and embarrassment will be brought to bear on herself and her family.

3. Sexual Knowledge and Education

A. Government Policies and Programs

The vast majority of Orang Rimba live in geographically isolated areas outside the main network of roads that connect most larger rural villages and towns and, therefore, have little or no access to formal schooling. Only those settled groups that are near roads have access to the primary schools found in nearby villages. Even in these cases, however, attendance is sporadic, as children are often required to help their families with subsistence-related work and/or parents may be unwilling to permit children to attend for fear of enculturation into the "village-world," where Malay customs and Pencasillan national philosophy are taught. (Recall the Orang Rimba's staunch opposition to village ways described in the opening section on Demographics.)

In some cases, however, the Indonesian Department of Health (*Dinas Kesehatan*) has sent health care workers to those Orang Rimban settlements that are accessible by road to hand out hygienic supplies and offer advice on contraception and family planning (see Section 9, Contraception, Abortion, and Population Planning).

B. Informal Sources of Sexual Knowledge

As camp life is normally public and informal in nature, unmediated by walls or strong notions of privacy, children are free to overhear whatever they may take an interest in. Young children may overhear or see the silhouettes of their parents making love in the same shelter should they awaken in the middle of the night. As married men will always be on alert for any undue attention or sexual overture towards their spouses, they will rarely discuss matters that are sexual in nature with other married men so as to avoid attracting such attention to her. However, boys and young men may discuss sex among themselves, outside the company of women. While uttering the word *mengawan* (sex) in the company of females is forbidden, young boys commonly discuss young girls, as well as their own sexuality, among their close age-mates. Masturbation and female anatomy may also be discussed, often playfully, by young males. Girls may have similar discussions, albeit in a less explicit manner.

Almost all sexual knowledge, therefore, is gained in the informal context of the camp, either through overhearing adults or through rehearsal with their same-sex age mates. Such rehearsal or "play" may occasionally lead to homosexual behavior among boys (see Section 6, Homoerotic, Homosexual, and Ambisexual Behaviors). While girls may overhear the discussions of older women and are well aware of the process of conception, they are generally less experienced in terms of pre-marital sexual exploration, because of the considerable pressures they are under to uphold ideals of chastity. It is therefore most probably the case that women learn the techniques of sexual intercourse only after marriage, following the lead of their spouse. This may simply involve assuming the bottom position, as the act of coitus is always performed in the "missionary" position.

4. Autoerotic Behaviors and Patterns

As mentioned above, the genitalia of male infants and children are the object of much playful affection. As male children reach adolescence, and often in their pre-pubescent stage, they will begin to explore their own bodies and perhaps even the bodies of their male age-mates. Young boys who have developed intimate relations with one another are extremely uninhibited with their bodies in each other's presence, and it is not uncommon for young boys to touch and comment on the dimensions, size, and general qualities of an age-mate's penis. At the site where this author collected data for this report, pre-adolescent and adolescent boys were well aware of which boys could and could not ejaculate through masturbation. And while this was most commonly performed in private, they did not feel any sense of shame or embarrassment when detected by the author of this chapter or their peers.

Among adults, masturbation is looked upon as something natural to the male gender. Women, on the other hand, are expected to live up to the ideals of purity and loyalty to men, and are thus discouraged from showing any expression of sexual enjoyment outside of marriage. It is therefore unlikely that masturbation would occur with anything near the same frequency as found among males because of the behavioral restraints imposed upon them.

5. Interpersonal Heterosexual Behaviors

A. Children and Adolescents

Puberty Rituals, and Premarital Sexual Activities and Relationships

Orang Rimba do not practice any formal puberty rituals or rites of passage. However, when both genders have demonstrated a degree of self-reliance, which for boys includes proficiency in hunting and forest-product collecting—the former a skill required to perform adequate bride-service and eventually feed a family, and the latter as a means of cash income—they will be accorded relative degrees of respect by their elders. An indication that a child or adolescent has reached a level of self-sufficiency may be when she or he has a personal debt recorded in a villager's debit book. This implies that debts will be paid for products credited (e.g., rice, cigarettes, sugar, coffee, flashlight batteries, etc.) without the help of the young person's parents. In some rare cases, parents will wait until the child reaches this degree of sufficiency before giving a name.

Other indications that a child has "come of age" might be smoking cigarettes bought with their own earnings with other males, and for girls, covering the breasts with a sarong. This may occur well before menarche is reached, as the girls become increasingly aware of their sexuality and the appropriate modes of conduct incumbent on them. Marriage, however, is the decisive indication of adulthood, perhaps more so for men than women. A woman achieves the full respect accorded to womanhood when her first child is born.

As noted earlier, adolescents and pre-adults are required to adhere to strict taboos on touching or flirting with the opposite gender, and any act perceived as constituting excessive intimacy is grounds for adults to convene in order to discuss the matter and administer a fine to the accused. Because of such fear of punishment, pre-marital affairs of any sort are uncommon and always secretive. In almost all cases, the male will be blamed for "corrupting" the girl and he will be required to pay a fine (*dendo*), most commonly in cloth, currency, and occasionally gold. In cases where sex has occurred between the couple, they will be required to marry, but only after the male endures a frenzied beating by the girl's younger siblings for the shame he has caused her family.

Any sort of premarital sexual activity, therefore, is very rare, as it is considered among the most serious of crimes in Orang Rimban society, and is punished accordingly. In most cases, men also have no sexual experience with a woman prior to marriage. These days, however, pre-adult males are in increasing contact with local villagers and, in one case that was reported to the author, young Orang Rimba men were beginning to seek the services of prostitutes for "unattached" sexual enjoyment.

B. Adults

Courtship and Marriage

Marriage is rarely consummated as a result of a woman's personal preference. She may, however, be able to refuse a male suitor, depending on the nature of her relationship with her family and their own position on the matter. In most cases, however, daughters will acquiesce to the wishes of parents, their fathers in particular, as after many years of segregation from males outside the immediate family, they have developed no other ties with men, romantic or otherwise, and, therefore, may see marriage as an opportunity to progress to the next stage in their development. They would rather enjoy the accorded prestige and status of marriage, rather than remain a subordinate member in their cognatic family. In other cases, however, girls may be afraid and apprehensive of leaving the security of their parents' guardianship to enter into a new and unfamiliar living arrangement with a man. This may be particularly true when girls are betrothed at an early age to a male that they are relatively unfamiliar with or do not have feelings for.

In many cases, marital unions will occur between first or second cousins, most preferably where their parents are siblings of opposite gender. It is considered a mild form of incest (*sumbang*) when persons descending from same-sex siblings marry. In such cases, the male suitor must pay a fine to the family of his bride. In cases where a woman's family approves of the union, the father will fix a bride price, which will be paid to the father and, in some cases, be distributed to the bride's male siblings as well.

Loyalty is the most important quality sought in a son in-law, and the latter's bride service is aimed at gaining the trust of the bride's family. During this period, which can last months or years, the male suitor is scrupulously tested for his honesty and generosity, which he demonstrates by sharing the spoils of his hunting and whatever other resources he acquires, such as coffee, cigarettes, and other products bought with his earnings from forest-product sales. He is also expected not to be "proud" (*banga*), which might be revealed through not showing proper respect to the bride-to-be's family or "saying one thing and doing another." If he is unable to demonstrate proficiency in subsistence-related skills, including collecting forest products, the male suitor will be thought to be either insincere in his intentions of marriage or simply incompetent in his ability to support a family and, consequently, he will be deemed an unworthy candidate for marriage into the girl's family.

In many cases, after being refused marriage by a woman's father, and finding no other welcoming host families, a suitor is pressed to either run off with the girl or express his intentions of marriage to her in private, in an attempt to circumvent the authority of her disapproving family. In such cases, the union may take place, but only after he pays a fine and possibly endures a beating by the bride's female family members and younger siblings for his unduly intimacy with the girl (Sandbukt 1988b:114-15). The bride may also be severely beaten by her mother for her defiance and the consequent shame she has brought upon her family.

Payment of a fine is preferred by the host family, as it does not carry implications of bride ownership as does the outright payment of a bride-price. This type of union, *kawin lari* (literally, "marrying on the run"), often brings a sense of embarrassment and shame to the family of the groom, but nonetheless occurs with at least the same frequency as arranged marriages. Elopement of this sort may also occur between first cousins where the bride's family does not approve of the union. In one recorded case, a young man threatened to defect to a nearby village and "enter Islam" if his male cousin, whose father was deceased, thereby entrusting him by default with the authority to betroth his sister, refused to give her in marriage. This young man was competing with another cousin and with his own father, who wanted to take the girl as a second wife.

In extremely rare cases where marriage occurs between male villagers and Orang Rimban women, the couple will always take up residence in the village. As such, this sort of marital arrangement is deeply resented by the Orang Rimba, in terms of the loss of a female family member, the lost labor power of an in-marrying male, and perhaps most significantly, in the act of making the prohibited cultural crossing of forest and village domains. Consequently, the family will often break ties with the female defector.

In cases where a woman's father is deceased and her siblings are either too young or unable to assert themselves with an older, more dominant male, the latter may bring enough pressure to bear on the situation that the girl will be taken by coercion and he may simply pay a compensatory fine to her male siblings. Having no father-in-law to provide bride-service for or be subordinate to in an uxorilocal residential arrangement, he may simply adopt the new wife to live in his own group. As such, this sort of marital arrangement is highly undesirable to the family of the bride and, concomitantly, is much sought after by Orang Rimban men, as it provides them with a high degree of personal autonomy that would not otherwise be achieved until the death of a father in-law.

In another instance, an adult male of approximately 24 years of age (Orang Rimba do not keep track of age or birth dates) violated the above courting and marriage customs on two separate occasions by expressing his intentions of marriage directly to the girl and, later, by approaching another girl's father and not adequately performing the incumbent bride-service duties or producing the specified bride-price at a later date. In the former case, he was fined five grams of gold, whereas in the latter, he was required to pay sixty sheets of cloth to the offended father. This young adult male, having exhausted all internal options for marriage, eventually defected to a nearby village and adopted Islam, albeit superficially, in order to increase his mating selectivity in a new social environment. In such cases of defection to local villages, Orang Rimba are considered only marginal members of the wider rural society and are treated accordingly. During the time of this writing, the aforementioned male had yet to find a spouse, because of what local villagers claimed was the typical Muslim man's unwillingness to betroth a daughter to an Orang Rimban male for fear of causing shame to the family, or producing "stupid" offspring. This reasoning is based on the assumption that intelligence, or lack thereof, is hereditary, and the Orang Rimba are inherently inferior with limited intellectual capacities.

Among some groups, particularly in the southern areas, newlyweds will leave the group to camp alone for several days. In some cases, a week of prohibition on sexual intercourse is observed (*pantangan*), during which time parents of the bride will bring food to the couple, who are also not permitted to leave their shelter to engage in subsistence-related activities. In all cases, newlyweds will construct a shelter in which they will cohabit, signifying the commencement of their new marital arrangement. Consisting of tree stalks for scaffolding and tied with vine with logs sometimes overlain with bark for flooring, these temporary shelters are not built with walls and are customarily constructed by women. The birth of the first child symbolizes a stable union, while inability to produce a child is commonly seen as infecundity on the part of the woman and may be grounds for divorce.

A married male will be required to remain subordinate to his in-laws, continually sharing resources and providing moral support while residing in the same camp. Occasionally, the couple will reside in another camp should resource distributions necessitate, but are nonetheless always required to share any captured game and other resources. They are expected to return eventually to the camp of the bride's family. This ensures the bride will have sufficient moral support while her family will reap the benefits of her spouse's labor.

In time, a wife's loyalty will grow toward her husband, but she will also be expected to devote her loyalties to her blood relatives. Occasionally, tensions arise when nuptial and consanguiness obligations conflict, such as in cases where a woman complains to her father or brothers of maltreatment or insufficient food provided by her husband. In such cases, a husband will feel betrayed and may threaten to kill his wife. It should be noted, however, that homicide among the Orang Rimba is virtually unheard of, and such displays of anger more commonly serve as mere outlets for one's frustration and/or a strategy for dissuading a wife from further pursuing the matter.

Polygamy is a common conjugal arrangement and second wives are most commonly divorcees, orphans, or lack a father and/or other male consanguines. In the latter cases, a woman's matrimonial value is decreased and she is also rendered a more vulnerable target because male support is lacking—a situation that males will capitalize on without exception. An upper limit of seven wives has been reported, while at one field site in this author's study, a man was cohabiting with five wives, the fifth wife being an adopted daughter. In most cases, however, monogamy is the most common arrangement.

When a second wife is taken, she must first endure a ritual beating by the first wife for the shame that has been caused to her that her husband would seek another spouse, and to assert her seniority in their new residential arrangement. The new wife is not permitted to strike back or retaliate at any time and she is expected to remain subordinate to the former indefinitely. Their shelters may stand as little as three feet from one another, and the husband normally alternates residence with no fixed pattern; his original wife, however, may be given preference. Should a first wife discover her spouse in the act of coitus or other intimate activity with a second wife, the latter may once again undergo a severe beating for arousing jealousies and her perceived insolence in displaying her affection.

Divorce is not uncommon but becomes increasingly rare after the first child is born. Divorce may be initiated by the family of the bride, often when a husband does not adequately provide for his wife and children, or does not share with or show the proper respect to his spouse's consanguines, particularly her father, but also her mother and brothers.

If a woman wishes to remarry, she will be expected to wait at least two to three years in order to avoid being perceived as overly eager in her desire to form a union with another man. If she has been proven guilty of adultery in the past, she may be forever stigmatized and forbidden to remarry, in theory at least. If a woman remarries shortly following her divorce, she will be fined five hundred sheets of cloth by her ex-husband and may lose custody of her children. A man is expected to abstain from marriage for at east six months, and a lesser fine, perhaps twenty sheets of cloth, must be paid to the family of his first spouse in the event that he remarries too soon.

Wife stealing is a reported occurrence, and in such cases the woman in question may not be held liable (see Section 1B, Sociolegal Status of Males and Females). The "stolen" wife's family and spouse may prefer rather to accuse the male culprit of enticing or alluring the woman with sorcery or "love magic." In one instance, a male was known to have "stolen" four wives, all on separate occasions. The putative punishment would have been severe fines or death by the spear of the woman's male siblings or husband. In this case, purportedly, no male siblings or husbands were courageous enough to seek retribution, and the fearless offender, aside from being banished from the area, was said to only have endured a physical thrashing by the women's younger siblings. However, if it were perceived that the woman fled intentionally and was willingly cohabiting with another male, she would also be the subject of death threats made by her male siblings, father, and/or husband for her immoral conduct.

Sexual Behavior

Immediately after marriage, a couple will take up residence in the same shelter, but in many cases, sexual activity will not commence until a much later date, when the girl overcomes her initial fear of sex with her new spouse and gradually adjusts to her new residential arrangement. Such a disposition is created by years of avoidance of males, which in many cases has instilled a deeply inculcated sense of embarrassment towards men as well as her own sexuality. This may be particularly true in cases where girls marry at an early age. A newly wed wife, therefore, may require up to two to three years before she is comfortable with engaging in sexual intercourse.

Occasionally, couples will reside a short distance apart from the rest of the group for the sole purpose of conception. This is particularly so in polygamous marital arrangements, in order to remain out of the purview of other spouses so as not to arouse jealousies. In most cases, because their simple temporary shelters do not contain walls, the couple will engage in sexual activity discretely during the night while others are sleeping or camped a safe distance away. Once children are born, the couple must engage in sexual activity only when children are sleeping, or during their infancy years when they are too young to be aware of their parents' behavior. Recall the rule prohibiting children, once they reach the age of 5 or 6 from sleeping with their mothers. This also insures that a couple will have sufficient privacy to engage in sexual intercourse in the confines of the small family shelter.

In most cases, the male initiates sexual activity. His spouse will normally not refuse him, particularly in polygamous arrangements where time may be divided between wives. In cases where a male has been effectively subordinated to his in-laws, a woman may exercise her power to refuse him or voice her opinion regarding the matter. Also, where couples are first cousins, a considerable rapport may develop, thus creating an arrangement through which mutual compliance dictates their course of action regarding such matters.

Acts of fellatio and cunnilingus are unheard of within traditional modes of sexual intercourse. Coitus is always performed with the man on top and woman on bottom in the "missionary" position. As is the custom in most areas of the Indonesian archipelago, kissing is not performed with the lips but, rather, involves the smelling or sniffing of the nose and facial area. Incidentally, mothers and fathers also practice this behavior in their nurturing of infants and young children.

6. Homoerotic, Homosexual, and Ambisexual Behaviors

Male homosexual behavior has been reported in rare instances among adolescent boys and young adult males, whereas it is practically unheard of among married men. The actual form and nature such relationships take is unclear, and in most cases may amount to mere sex rehearsal or exploration. One case, however, has been reported first hand to the author by two married men of their engagement in anal intercourse during their adolescent years. After being detected by an adult, they were each fined twenty sheets of cloth and stigmatized for a brief period. As married adults with children, both men recounted the episode with humor and expressed no shame or embarrassment. While no cases are known of married men engaging in homosexual activity, informants claim that this may have occurred in previous generations. They could not recall actual incidents, but claimed that the men involved must have been punished severely, perhaps even killed by the male members of the wives' families. (Recall that homicide is more commonly threatened and rarely actually occurs.)

Despite the lack of information regarding incidence of female homosexuality, the sense of shame and ideals of purity regarding the female body and sexuality that are so deeply inculcated in a girl during her years of development and throughout her entire life may inhibit any actual lesbian activity from occurring, even if such desires should arise. However, while questioning men regarding the issue, they claimed that such conduct would not be seen as a serious offense, most probably because it does not threaten the delicate balance of power relations between men as do other forms of sexual misconduct, such as adultery.

7. Gender Conflicted Persons

In the small Orang Rimbal population of less than 4,000 persons, incidence of gender-conflicted persons is statistically rare. No cases have been reported of transvestite, transgenderist, or transsexual individuals. Even if such tendencies are harbored in individuals, they may never be realized because of the ever-present pressures to assimilate. Cases of specially gendered persons, such as hermaphrodite, hijra, berdache, xanith, or intersexual, are also unreported.

8. Significant Unconventional Sexual Behaviors

A. Coercive Sex

Child Sexual Abuse, Incest, and Pedophilia

Child sex abuse has not been reported, but informants claim that such occurrences may occur between men and adopted daughters, but never between men and their natural-born children. Purportedly, an offender would be speared or liable to pay severe fines if detected. Pedophilia involving two males, although virtually unheard of, is not considered a serious offense, mainly because the male body is not seen as an object of purity to be coveted. Death, however, is the stated punishment if such an occurrence involved a young girl. Again, it should be emphasized that actual cases of homicide are extremely rare, and it is more commonly the case that only death threats are made, but never actualized in violent action.

Incest taboos are strictly adhered to, and there are no known cases of sibling or parent–child unions or sexual relations. Indirect forms may occur, but are subject to varying interpretations as to whether they constitute actual incest. For example, the above-mentioned instance where a male married an adopted daughter was not seen as constituting incest by the former; but his sons, who were raised with the girl and considered her a natural sister in every way, strongly disagreed. Despite their attempts to prevent the union from taking place, which included a report to the chief of a nearby Malay village, their father insisted he was not committing incest, as the girl was not related to him by blood.

Sexual Harassment and Rape

Incidence of sexual harassment and rape is rare and always subject to interpretation by the parties involved. For example, in the above-mentioned cases where men elope with women in an attempt to bypass the authority of the latter's disapproving family, the family of the girl may claim that the she was carried off against her wishes or while under duress. If the daughter agrees that this was the case—which may be in her best interest in instances where she fears punishment—her family may claim abduction, or even rape, if it can be established that sexual intercourse had occurred. In such instances, the male would be required to marry the girl and pay severe fines, as well as endure a beating by the girl's younger siblings.

Other sorts of harassment initiated by men towards women will, almost without exception, be interpreted as sexual in nature. In one case observed by the author, an adolescent male was accused of following a girl in the forest while collecting forest products. During a series of meetings between both fathers, which lasted three days, the accused male claimed to have been coincidentally working in the same area of forest, while his father, knowing well that his son was attracted to the girl and was indeed following her, tried to "settle amicably" by suggesting the two marry. The father of the girl refused vehemently in typical Orang Rimban fashion, and the young male was fined twenty sheets of cloth for a kind of "sexual harassment," even though physical contact, or even verbal communication between the two, did not occur.

9. Contraception, Abortion, and Population Planning

Plant contraceptives and abortifacients are not used and infanticide is unheard of. A postpartum taboo on sexual intercourse is adhered to for several years after a child is born, in order to allow for a sufficient weaning period. During a swiddening cycle, taboos are more lax; hence, when groups revert back to nomadic foraging, a woman may have more children to feed than she can comfortably manage. "Blood money" (*bangun*) is paid to a woman's parents if a child is thought to have died of milk deprivation caused by closely spaced pregnancies, which are thought to disrupt an infant's weaning cycle (Sandbukt 1988a, b).

Most groups are inaccessible to the Indonesian Department of Health's regional and local offices, which deal primarily with neighboring rural village populations. Groups of Orang Rimba living in government-sponsored settlements, or who have settled on their own accord, may be visited by Department of Health nurses, workers, and, occasionally, government bureaucrats. Advice on infant care and family planning is given, and most recently, contraceptive injections have been offered, but widely refused, mainly because of mistrust and disapproval on the part of their spouses, who would prefer that the government not get involved in private family matters. Their visits are seen as mere formalities with distracted objectives. Such meetings involve little or no evaluation and are sporadic with no routine follow-up visits. During these "courtesy calls," soap, combs, and other toiletries are handed out, which the Orang Rimba find insulting, along with biscuits and cigarettes! For this reason, the Orang Rimba, males in particular, may resent the efforts of representatives of the Department of Health, which they perceive as being insensitive to their true needs.

10. Sexually Transmitted Diseases

Not much is known about the incidence and types off sexually transmitted diseases among the Orang Rimba. Male informants can name at least three different classes of sickness attributed to sexual contact:

- *Koreng*, literally "scabies": symptoms include itching and skin irritation in or near the genitalia. Instances are said to occasionally lead to divorce in cases where symptoms have not dissipated.
- *Sakit bini/sakit laki or sakit koncing*, literally "wife/husband sickness" or "urinating sickness": symptoms include urinary tract infection characterized by a burning sensation during urination.
- *Buntal*, or "swelling," which is said to feel like biting crabs. Buntal can infect the urinary tract and eventually lead to erosion, with death in rare cases. A tale was recounted (whether symbolic or literal is unknown) of a man's father spearing to death his daughter-in-law for allegedly afflicting and eventually killing his son with this disease.

The Orang Rimba employ a limited range of plant remedies, mainly derived from bark, leaf, and root extracts. For venereal disease, however, only bamboo water is used. Normally for the treatment of *koreng*, pulp water is drunk directly from the fillings of a species of bamboo shoot (*aee kurung bamboo*).

11. HIV/AIDS

Intermarriage with local village populations is rare, and in cases where intermarriages do occur, Orang Rimba will marry into the village rather than vice-versa. Their forest-dwelling populations, therefore, are somewhat pristine, from a genetic point of view. This, coupled with the very low incidence of sex outside of marriage, has rendered their populations relatively safe from the wide range of sexually transmittable diseases that may occur among the surrounding Indonesian populace. There are no reported cases of HIV or AIDS among forest- or village-dwelling Orang Rimba.

12. Sexual Dysfunctions, Counseling, and Therapies

Male impotency is a sexual dysfunction that is rarely reported; but inability to conceive when males do not suffer from impotence may also be considered a form of sexual dysfunction, for which a female spouse will most commonly be blamed. In cases where the woman is known to be fertile, as in second marriages where she has produced offspring during her first marriage, she may seek a divorce on the grounds of her spouse's infertility. In cases of male impotency, an aphrodisiac is used to induce penis erection.

This remedy is a root extract from a species of plant locally referred to as *penyega*, and can be boiled and drunk with water, or eaten directly.

References and Suggested Readings

Boers, J. 1838. De Koeboes. *Tijdschrift voor Nederlandsch-Indie, 1*(2):286-295.
Collier, J. F. 1988. *Marriage and inequality in classless societies.* Stanford, CA: Stanford University Press.
Collier, J. F., & Rosaldo, M. Z. 1981. Politics and gender in simple societies. In: S. B. Ortner & H. Whitehead, eds., *Sexual meanings: The cultural construction of gender and sexuality.* Cambridge, UK: Cambridge University Press.
Dahlberg, F., ed. 1981. *Woman the gatherer.* New Haven, CT: Yale University Press.
Denatan, R. K., Endicott, K., Gomes, A. G., & Hooker, M. B. 1997. *Malaysia and the original people: A case study of the impact of development on indigenous peoples.* Boston/London: Allyn and Bacon.
Dongen, G. J. van. 1906. Bijdrage tot de Kennis van de Ridan-Koeboes. *Tijdschrift voor het Binnenlandsch Bestuur, 30*:225-263.
Endicott, K. 1981. The conditions of egalitarian male–female relationships in foraging societies. *Canberra Anthropology, 4*:1-10.
Endicott, K. 1999. Gender relations in hunter–gatherer societies. In: R. Lee & R. Daly, eds., *The Cambridge encyclopedia of hunters and gatherers.* Cambridge, UK: Cambridge University Press.
Forbes, H. O. 1989/1885. *A naturalist's wanderings in the Eastern Archipelago: A narrative of travel and exploration from 1878-1883.* London: Oxford University Press (original publisher unknown).
Klein, L. F., & Ackerman, L. A., eds. 1995. *Women and power in Native North America.* Norman, OK: University of Oklahoma Press.
LaBar, F. M. 1972. Kubu. In: *Ethnic groups of insular South East Asia.* New Haven, CT: Human Relations Area Files Press.
Lee, R. 1982. Politics, sexual and non-sexual, in an egalitarian society. In: R. Lee & E. Leacock, eds., *Politics and history in band societies.* Cambridge, UK: Cambridge University Press.
Loeb, E. M. 1942. *Sumatra: Its history and people.* Vienna: Institute fur Volkerkunde der Universitat Wein.
Marsden, W. 1966/1811. *The history of Sumatra.* Kuala Lumpur/New York: Oxford University Press.
Murphy, Y., & Robert, F. 1985. *Women of the forest.* New York: Columbia University Press.
Persoon, G. 1989. The Kubu and the outside world: The modification of hunting and gathering. *Anthropos, 84*:507-519.
Sandbukt, O. 1984. Kubu conceptions of reality. *Asian Folklore Studies, 42*:85-98.
Sandbukt, O. 1988a. Resource constraints and relations of appropriation among tropical forests foragers: The case of the Sumatran Kubu. *Research in Economic Anthropology, 10*:117-156.
Sandbukt, O. 1988b. Tributary tradition and relations of affinity and gender among the Sumatran Kubu. In: T. Ingold, D. Riches, & J. Woodburn, eds., *Hunters and gatherers I: History, evolution and social change.* Oxford, UK: Berg.
Shostak, M. 1981. *Nisa: The life and words of a !Kung woman.* Cambridge, MA: Harvard University Press.
Strange, M. Z. 1997. *Woman the hunter.* Boston: Beacon Press.
Suetomo, M. 1992. *Orang Rimbo: A structural functional study.* Doctoral dissertation. Bandung, Indonesia: Universitas Pajajaran.
Turnbull, C. 1982. The ritualization of potential conflict between the sexes among the Mbuti. In: R. Lee & E. Leacock, eds., *Politics and history in band societies.* Cambridge, UK: Cambridge University Press.

Italy
(*Repubblica Italiana*)
(The Italian Republic)

Bruno P. F. Wanrooij, Ph.D.*

Contents

Demographics and a Historical Perspective

A. Demographics

Italy is a large peninsula extending into the central Mediterranean Sea. It borders with France on the northwest, with Switzerland and Austria on the north, and with Slovenia on the northeast. The peninsula also contains the two small independent states of San Marino and Vatican City. Italy has a total of 116,334 square miles (301,230 square kilometers), including the islands of Sicily with 9,926 square miles and Sardinia with 9,301 square miles. The alluvial Po Valley drains most of the northern portion of the

---

Communications: Professor Bruno Wanrooij, Syracuse University in Italy Program, Humanities and Social Sciences Department, Piazza Savonarola, 15 50132 Firenze, Italy; bpwanroo@syr.fi.it; wanrooij@dada.it.

country. The rest of the country is rugged and mountainous, except for intermittent coastal plains like Campania, south of Rome. The Apennine Mountains run down the center of the peninsula. The island of Sicily, at the southwestern tip of the Italian peninsula, is 180 miles by 120 miles with a 1992 population of 5 million. A second major island, Sardinia is about 115 miles west of Rome and Naples, south of Corsica, which is a part of France. Sardinia had a 1992 population of over 1.6 million.

On January 1, 1999, Italy's resident population was 57.6 million, with 27.9 million men and 29.7 million women. Regionally, the north has 44.5 percent of the population, central Italy 19.2 percent, and the south 36.3 percent. The age distribution in 1999 was 15 percent under age 15, 68 percent between 15 and 64, and 17 percent age 65 and over. Life expectancy at birth in 1999 was 76 for males and 81 for females. In 1996, the birthrate was 9.2 per 1,000 population; the death rate 9.5 per 1,000. Italy's Total Fertility Rate (TFR) in 1998 was 1.2 children per fertile woman, giving Italy a rank of 221 among the 227 nations of the world. The infant mortality rate in the first year was 6.1 per 1,000 live births. The natural growth rate of a negative 0.8 percent per 1,000 population is offset by a positive immigration rate. The total number of immigrants legally present in Italy on January 1, 1999, was 1.1 million, about 2 percent of the total population. In recent years, family reunifications, mixed marriages, and the increase in the number of children born of foreign parents have led to a decline in the overrepresentation of young, single males among the immigrant population.

The major ethnic group is that of Italians, but small clusters of German-, French-, and Slovene-Italians exist in the north, and of Albanian-Italians and Greek-Italians in the south. The national language is Italian; German is predominant in parts of Trentino-Alto Adige, and there is a French-speaking minority in the Valle d'Aosta region and a Slovene-speaking minority in the area of Trieste-Gorizia. Immigrants come from many different countries. The most important groups come from Morocco, the former Yugoslavia, Albania, and the Philippines. Ninety-seven percent of the total Italian population age 15 and over can read and write.

Seventy-eight percent of Italians define themselves as Roman Catholics, and fourteen percent more generally as Christians; seven percent do not profess any religion and one percent belongs to "other" religions. The number of those adhering to other religions is increasing, partly as a result of immigration. Identification with a religion does not coincide with active participation: 8.7 percent of Italians never attend religious services; 39.6 percent do so only rarely.

Since World War II, Italy has changed from a rural society to an industrial or post-industrial society. Agriculture now contributes only 2.9 percent to the Gross Domestic Product, against 32.1 percent for industry and 65 percent for the service sector. The service sector employs 60.1 percent of the labor force against 32.5 percent for industry and a scant 7.4 percent for agriculture. The per capita income in 1996 was $21,190, with clear differences on income, higher in the north and lower in the south.

B. A Brief Historical Perspective

The earliest human settlements within the territory of present-day Italy date almost certainly to some 500,000 years ago and correspond to the Lower Paleolithic period. From the beginning of the first millennium BCE, there were increasing contacts with Phoenician and Greek colonists, and Italy entered the historical period. While the Greeks settled on the southern coasts of the peninsula, Etruscan civilization developed in central Italy. During the fourth and third centuries BCE, the Roman state expanded its territory to the entire peninsula. Expansion continued, and by the end of the second century BCE, Rome had become the major military power in the Mediterranean. Territorial expansion was accompanied by the growing importance of commercial activities in addition to agriculture and pastoralism. The following centuries saw a gradual decline of Italy's preeminence in comparison with other provinces of the Roman Empire. With the end of the Western Roman Empire in the fourth century of the Common Era, the Catholic Church sought to take over the authority and prestige of Rome, assuming the government in the territories under its control. In the eleventh and twelfth centuries CE, agriculture, crafts, and commerce prospered, the latter two in particular becoming the foundations of an urban economy that was to produce the city states of central-northern Italy. Tuscan and Lombard bankers played an ever more important role in financing the military undertakings of European sovereigns and the papacy, thus increasing their own prestige and political influence. Arts and humanistic studies flourished, and during the Renaissance of the thirteenth and fourteenth centuries, Italy became one of the major cultural centers of Europe.

The lack of political stability and the frequent wars among the various Italian states, however, allowed the great European powers to intervene, and by the second half of the sixteenth century, Spain had established its predominance over Italy. What followed was a slow decline of the political role of Italy in Europe, and of its contribution to cultural and scientific developments. Spanish predominance in Italy, extending over some two centuries, had rather negative consequences for the country, in terms of economic decline and of a growing imbalance between part of the southern regions and other areas of the country.

The period of French rule, which followed the conquest of Italy by Napoleon Bonaparte, saw the reemergence of a sense of national unity among the intellectual and middle-classes. In 1861, after a number of wars of independence against Austria, the Risorgimento resulted in the creation of a United Kingdom of Italy governed by the House of Savoy. Rome was conquered only in 1870. The problems, which the new kingdom had to face, regarded the Catholic Church's refusal to recognize the new state, and, more generally, the integration of the older states, and the gap between the political elite and the lower classes of the population, especially in the rural areas.

After World War I, social tensions and the growth of New Socialist and Catholic Mass parties convinced the ruling groups to help the Fascist movement, lead by Benito Mussolini, to take over power. The Fascist regime pursued a policy of repression of the working-class movement while favoring at the same time colonial expansion. Family policies were inspired by the desire to increase the fertility rate and to reinforce the position of the male head of the family. This policy received full support from the Catholic Church after the Lateran Treaty of 1929, which made Roman Catholicism the state religion until 1984 when a new agreement was signed between the Catholic Church and the Italian government which cancelled most of the priviliges enjoyed by the Church.

Fascist family legislation remained valid in Italy even after World War II, and the national government, dominated by the Catholic party, Democrazia Cristiana, opposed changes in family and gender relations. However, developments in the late 1950s and 1960s, including growing industrialization, migration from the rural south to the industrialized north, secularization, and higher standards of education, brought the traditional structures under attack. The youth movement, the feminist movement, and the gay movement also played an important role in promoting profound changes, but maybe even more important was the diffusion of consumer culture.

While Italy in the 1990s has much in common with other European countries, some of the peculiarities of Italian society—the importance of the family, the strong regional differences, and the role of Roman Catholicism, among others—can only be understood in their historical context. For example, in the past in northwest and central Italy, the incidence of patrilocal residence and multiple family households was high. In these regions today, about one third of the population lives for some time in an extended family or in a multiple family household, and contacts with the husband's family tend to be stronger (Barbagli & Saraceno 1997).

1. Basic Sexological Premises

A. Character of Gender Roles

Sexuality, as we understand it today, is not merely a biological and "natural" fact, but above all a historical construction, resulting from the pressure by manifold forces, and, as such, it is the outcome of complex historical transformations. Gender roles, in particular, are not only based on physical or biological premises, but are primarily the result of the conditions of life of males and females in a given social class, time period, and geographical location.

During the last decades of the nineteenth century, emancipationist movements in Italy started to question the traditional gender roles, which were based on the identification of males with production and public affairs, and of women with reproduction and private affairs. The prescribed female gender role contrasted sharply with a reality, which—especially in the northern and central regions—saw an active participation of women in the production process. The need to maintain industrial production led to a further increase of the female employment rate in industry during World War I.

The Fascist regime, which came to power after World War I, tried to reinforce the role of the male breadwinner by introducing legislation favoring male employment and by introducing discriminatory measures against female workers. Women received lower salaries and had no access to certain positions in state administration. A quota system was introduced to limit the number of women working for private companies. The government measures failed to reduce significantly female employment, but public appreciation for the female role in the family contributed to strengthen already existing familist tendencies. The desire to conform to the traditional female role of mother and housewife explains the drop in the female employment rate coinciding with the economic boom of the 1960s.

Since this period, new ideals of independence and autonomy have created a trend of growing participation of women in the labor market. Nevertheless, in the 1990s, the female activity rate is still much lower than that of men, while, partly because of protectionist measures, female unemployment is higher. In addition, women are over-represented on the "black" labor market, where wages are lower, working conditions worse, and social benefits and job security non-existent.

In 1995, Italy ranked tenth on the United Nations world list of male–female equality. Since the 1960s, the level of education of women has rapidly improved, and today more women than men obtain a university degree. Also in private business and in public administration, women in Italy have made important progress in the last few years, even though there is still a long way to go for real equality.

The participation of Italian men in household chores is relatively low. While the majority of men—especially in the northern regions—take an active part in the education of children, and a growing percentage is willing to cook, to set the table, and do shopping, very few men participate in activities like cleaning, doing the laundry, or ironing. On the contrary, almost all married women, both housewives and women with full-time employment, participate in domestic work.

B. Sociolegal Status of Males and Females

Women received the right to vote in 1945, and in 1947, the Italian Constitution was approved with Article 3 recognizing equal rights for men and women. According to Article 29 of the Constitution, however, the need to guarantee the unity of the family justified limits to the legal and moral equality of husband and wife. It took several decades to adjust the existing legislation to the principle of equal rights and to change traditional views about the role and position of women. Until 1968, adultery was considered a crime for women, whereas men could be punished for adultery only in special circumstances. Other discriminatory conditions deriving from the male position as head of the family survived until the general revision of family legislation in 1975. The new law, based on the principle of male–female equality and on the recognition of the rights of children, abolished the position of the head of the family, and attributes equal rights and duties to husband and wife in terms of residence, work, education of the children, etc. Married women in Italy keep their own family name, and can add their husband's name if they wish to do so. Proposals are in discussion to give couples the choice to transmit to their children either the name of the father or that of the mother.

Legislation regarding crimes of honor—recognizing special mitigating circumstances for those who, enraged by an offense to their personal and family honor, killed their wife, daughter, or sister, or the person with whom their female relatives had an illicit sexual relationship—was canceled in 1981, but had become obsolete in most parts of Italy long before.

Discrimination against women existed also with regard to labor: women were excluded from many positions and were paid less. This discrimination has been gradually abolished. In 1960, for instance, the Constitutional Court eliminated a law dating back to 1919, which excluded women from many higher-rank positions in the public sector. In 1977, a law was approved which guarantees equal rights for males and females in issues like recruitment and hiring, career, and the like.

C. General Concepts of Sexuality and Love

In Italy, the prevailing ideology links love and sexuality. Love is presented as a necessary precondition for sexual relations, while happy sexual relations are generally considered necessary for the success of a love relationship. Yet, 60 percent of women and 74 percent of men admit sexual desires regarding persons for whom they feel no love (Sabatini 1988). In this case, the fact that the statistics were based on a questionnaire distributed among the readers of *Duepiu*, a progressive magazine with a clear pro-sex attitude, may have influenced the results. Later surveys, however, confirmed that, especially among young men, sexual relations without love were rather common.

Faithfulness is considered an important value for couples, but a recent survey among young people (Buzzi 1998) shows that about one third of young men and one sixth of young women had sexual relations with persons other than their partner. Adhesion to the values of romantic love and faithfulness thus often is more formal than real.

2. Religious and Ethnic Factors Affecting Sexuality

A. Source and Character of Religious Values

In Italy, the values of consumer society seem to have replaced religious values in many issues, especially among many young people who refuse to accept the moral guidance of the Catholic Church. In 1996, religious marriages made up 79.6 percent of the total number, compared to 20.4

percent of civil marriages. According to a recent survey, the religiosity rate—calculated on the basis of the importance of religion in personal life, and on participation in the activities of the religious community—is close to zero or low for 28.5 percent of Italians, and high only for 12.3 percent (Cesareo 1995).

Notwithstanding the on-going process of secularization, the Catholic religion is still the main source of values affecting sexuality, and the public pronouncements of the Pope are widely discussed in the mass media. Due to the Catholic Church's opposition to a separation between procreation and sexuality, it has been impossible to introduce clear legislation regarding artificial insemination and other forms of medically assisted procreation. An administrative rule dating back to 1985, which applies only to hospitals and clinics falling under the public health system, admits medical assistance for procreation in case of married couples, but excludes the use of donors. Therefore, medically assisted procreation with the use of gametes from donors takes place only in private clinics, with possible health risks because of insufficient public control. Due to Catholic opposition, a new bill regarding medically assisted procreation, which was approved by the Commission for Social Affairs of the Chamber of Deputies in January 1998, still had not become law by the end of 1999.

B. Character of Ethnic Values

Immigration to Italy is a relatively recent phenomenon, and as yet the values cherished by immigrants have not had much influence outside the various ethnic groups. In this sense, Italy is not yet a multicultural society. In a medium- or long-term perspective, there is no doubt that the presence of large ethnic groups, which do not share many of the views about family values, gender relations, and extramarital sexuality commonly held by Italians, will be a challenge. Contrasting views may lead to greater appreciation of diversity, but may also become a source of growing social tensions and conflict.

3. Sexual Knowledge and Education

A. Government Policies and Programs

The introduction of sexual education as part of the regular program of primary and secondary school has met with opposition from Catholics who question both the responsibility of schools in this area and the content of education. Catholics have changed their long-standing view that sexual education could lead to the premature arousal of sexuality in young people, but still insist that sexual education is above all the responsibility of parents. Moreover, they deny the value of an education that focuses on the physical aspects of sexuality if it does not place these aspects in a more general context, and if it ignores moral issues.

For these reasons, and notwithstanding the fact that a majority of Italians favor sex education in school at an early age (Durex 1998), until early 1999, sexual education occurred in schools only on the initiative of individual teachers. Only recently has the Ministry of Education decided to sustain these initiatives formally.

B. Informal Sources of Sexual Knowledge

Peer group conversation and the mass media are the primary sources of sexual knowledge. Parents, above all the mother, rank third as a source of information. Magazines and both public and private television offer instructive articles and programs dealing with sexual issues. Moreover, publishers have responded to market demands, and have supplied sexual information both in printed form, in videocassettes, and on compact disks (CDs).

In contrast with the past, sexual education today is less focused on procreation and on genital activity, and tries to explore the relations between gender identity and sexual identity. Moreover, sexual education no longer wants to prescribe sexual behavior on the basis of ideological or religious principles, but rather aims at providing the cultural instruments for self-realization (Cipolla 1998).

Today, young Italians are generally well informed. It should be noted, however, that a high level of information does not automatically translate into sound practices. Knowledge of the risks of sexually transmitted diseases, for instance, does not always lead to the use of condoms.

4. Autoerotic Behaviors and Patterns

According to the most recent survey among young people, nine out of ten men, and four out of ten women, admit to masturbating (Buzzi 1998). However, earlier surveys give higher numbers for female masturbation, even though the number of women who never masturbate remains five times higher—20 percent against 4 percent—than that of men (Sabatini 1988). Men start masturbating earlier than women: 16.3 percent before age 12, 33.3 percent between age 12 and 13. In any event, the vast majority—both men and women—consider masturbation part of the sexuality of every normal human being. This idea is the outcome of radical changes in the consideration of masturbation.

In the nineteenth century, masturbation was the object of severe repression, and was said to be the cause of numerous physical problems. Moreover, masturbation, especially if performed in the presence of other people of the same sex as might occur in boarding schools, was believed to lead to homosexuality. In the twentieth century, opposition against masturbation was based above all on the idea that masturbation undermined the individual's capacity to use sexuality as a form of communication. Alternatively, masturbation was considered a substitute for "real sex," an act which could be performed by young people without stable partners, but which denoted a lack of sexual maturity in the case of adults. Still, in the 1978 sex survey by Giampaolo Fabris and Rowena Davis, 31 percent of males and 28 percent of females expressed the opinion that masturbation was unhealthy, while 26 percent of males and 36 percent of females expressed their moral condemnation of this activity. Today, even though taboos have not disappeared altogether, masturbation generally is rated more positively as a source of pleasure and as an experience allowing the increase of self-awareness and knowledge of the self (Rifelli 1998).

5. Interpersonal Heterosexual Behaviors

A. Children

In the beginning of the twentieth century, expressions of infantile sexuality were considered a form of perversion, and were severely repressed. Today, on the contrary, most Italian parents acknowledge the sexual curiosity of children, but at the same time fear that games with a sexual overtone may lead to over-sexualization. Moreover, Italian parents are afraid of the sexual abuse of children by adults, which is the object of general severe condemnation and repression.

From a legal point of view, sexual relations with minors under age 14 are considered statutory rape. The age limit is higher, 16, in the case when the adult person cohabiting with the minor is a relative, guardian, or other person with educational responsibilities over the minor. A minor who has sexual relations with another minor is not guilty of any crime, on the conditions that the younger partner is at least age 13, and the age difference between the partners is not more than three years.

B. Adolescents

Puberty Rituals

In Italy, no specific rituals exist marking the passage from childhood to adolescence or adult age.

Premarital Sexual Activities and Relationships

Only a limited number of general surveys about the sexual life of the Italians exist, and most of them were based on the responses of a sample of a preselected population, such as the clients of public family advisory agencies. Most of the information about the sexual life of young people presented here comes from a survey of 1,250 persons aged 18 to 30 by the IARD Institute (Buzzi 1998).

According to this survey, males in contemporary Italy have their first complete sexual relations with penetration when they are 17 to 18 years old; the age of their first sex was not much different from that of their fathers. The average age for females is 18 to 19. The 1998 Durex global sex survey (Durex 1998) does not make a distinction between males and females, and indicates an average age for first sex at 17. The tendency to start sex at an earlier age began with the generation of women born in the 1950s and 1960s.

It is more common for young women aged 18 to 21 from central and northern Italy to have complete sexual relations than it is for males of the same age group (females 71 percent vs. males 66.3 percent). The opposite is true for females from the south: Only 51.8 percent of females aged 18 to 21 had complete relations compared with 64.8 percent of males from the south. For the age group 26 to 30, the percentages are 84.7 for females and 88.2 for males. Moral values determine why young females do not engage in sexual relations; for males the main reasons are the lack of opportunity or the refusal of the partner (Buzzi 1998).

The first sexual partner for both males and females in almost half of the cases is a person of the same age; the partner of 41.8 percent of females is somewhat older (21.6 percent for males), and is somewhat younger for 25.9 percent of males (4.7 percent of females). Major age differences are rare. Especially for males, it is very rare that the partner of their first complete sexual relations is their wife (0.8 percent); it is more common for females to have this experience with their husband (10 percent).

The "first time" is appreciated positively by 48.7 percent of males and by 38.6 percent of females, for whom embarrassment, fear of pregnancy, and pain play a greater role. Young women are also more prone to admit sexual passivity (10.7 percent), absence of sexual desire (8.8 percent), and major psychological difficulties (15.3 percent). Without making a distinction between the sexes, the Durex (1998) survey reports that first sexual intercourse was disappointing for 32 percent of Italians, and better than expected for 29 percent.

First time intercourse is often at risk for pregnancy and sexually transmitted diseases: condoms are used on this occasion by about 40 percent of Italians. Coitus interruptus is used as a method of birth control by 24 percent. The low incidence of teenage pregnancy in Italy is therefore not a consequence of better contraception, but of the fact that young Italian females start to have sexual relations at a later age than in other countries. Statistical data relating to premarital conception, extramarital pregnancy, and induced abortion showed a radical change in the ten years between 1969 and 1978, when the incidence of these events increased rapidly. The increase affected unmarried females of all age groups. In the following years, however, the growth in the number of extramarital pregnancies stopped, while the increase in premarital conceptions slowed down.

Stable relationships become more common with the increase of age, but a relatively high percentage of young people aged 26 to 30 have no stable partner (38.5 percent of males and 21.2 percent of females). Love, physical attraction, and trust are the elements that determine the creation and the duration of a relationship.

C. Adults

Premarital Courtship, Dating, and Relationships

Although there is no strong social condemnation of the cohabitation of
unmarried couples, cohabitation is relatively rare, and marriage is considered the natural conclusion of a stable heterosexual relationship. In 1991,
cohabiting couples made up 1.6 percent of Italian couples. The rate of
cohabitation is significantly higher in the northern regions than in the
south, for example, 4.1 percent in the region of Val d'Aosta against 0.5
percent in the Basilicata.

Notwithstanding a generally positive view of marriage, there is a tendency
to delay the time of marriage, and, partly as a result of this, the nuptiality
rate in Italy is low: In 1997, it was 4.7 per 1,000 population. The average age
at a first marriage in 1994 was 29.3 for males and 26.5 for females; in 1984,
it was 27.4 for males and 24.3 for females. Italians in the south are distinguished by a higher nuptiality rate: In 1994, it was 5.6 per 1,000 population
against 4.8 in the regions of the north and the center, and at an earlier age
at marriage, 25.6 for females and 28.7 for males (Barbagli & Saraceno 1997).

Most Italians leave the parental home only when they get married, and
this holds true even for the older age groups: 68 percent of Italian males
aged 35 and over and 63.3 percent of females who never married live with
their parents. Divorce or separation often results in a return to the parental
home: About 20 percent of divorced or separated Italians (25.2 percent of
males and 17.1 percent of females) cohabit with their parents (ISTAT 1996)

"Long families" are the combined effect of the low cohabitation rate and
a relatively late age of marriage: The majority of unmarried young people
aged 18 to 34 continue to live with their parents (58.8 percent in 1998). It
is more common for young men to stay with their family (66.5 percent)
than for young women (50.9 percent). The percentage of young people
living with their family is increasing, especially among young women: In
1983, only 40.4 percent of them were living with their family.

Economic circumstances, high unemployment among young people,
and the difficulty of finding housing also contribute to the incidence of
"long families," but do not offer a sufficient explanation for the fact that
young people in Italy do not "strike out" on their own. "Long families" are
in fact as common in the northeastern region, where unemployment is less
a problem, but where 59.5 percent of young people aged 18 to 34 live with
their parents, compared with the south, where economic problems are
much more serious, and 59.8 percent of young people live with their
parents. An alternative and more positive explanation of the growing
incidence of "long families" is the democratic character of the modern
Italian family, where young adults have the possibility to re-negotiate their
position. In this way, young adults are able to have a satisfactory level of
autonomy and independence, while at the same time enjoying the "fringe
benefits" of family life in terms of financial advantages and services (Barbagli & Saraceno 1997). For a high percentage of young people (57 percent

in the northeast, 34.2 percent in the south), the reason for staying is that they are happy to stay and enjoy a fair amount of freedom. Satisfaction increases with age as the reasons for tension decrease (ISTAT 1999b).

The high level of interaction between married adults and their parents is further proof of the importance of the family network in Italy: 3.8 percent of married Italians under age 64 whose mother is alive live with their mother. Of those who are not cohabiting, 77.8 percent see their parents at least once a week and one third of them every day. One partial explanation of the high interaction with parents is the low level of geographical mobility: 28 percent of married Italians live at a distance of less than one kilometer from their parents (ISTAT 1996).

Marriage and Family

According to the 1975 family law, the legal age of marriage is 18 for both partners. Legal courts can give exemption from this requirement, provided that the partners are at least 16 years of age. Generally, the courts do not consider pregnancy a valid motive to grant permission for the marriage of minors. The same 1975 legislation abolished the possibility of reparatory marriage, which in the past had been used by persons accused of crimes like rape and forceful abduction, who could avoid punishment by marrying their victim.

The average frequency for sexual intercourse was 92 times per year (Durex 1998). According to an earlier survey, on average, men and women had sexual intercourse about eight times per month, but there were important differences according to age, with the highest levels of sexual activity in the age group 18 to 25 for women and 35 to 44 for men. The fact that females under 25 showed a higher frequency of sexual intercourse than males of the same age can be explained as a result of their earlier participation in stable relationships and marriage. A similar explanation is proposed for the fact that young women have more sexual partners than men, while the situation is inverted in the higher age groups. In this case also, the higher tolerance of male pre- and extramarital sexual relations may play a role (Fabris & Davis 1978). The more recent survey published by Carlo Buzzi (1998) confirms the higher sexual activity rate of young women, 33.8 percent of whom have sexual intercourse two to three times a week (against 27.4 percent for males). Also the percentage of young women who had no sexual intercourse during the previous three months turned out to be almost half that of men (12.4 percent against 23.5 percent).

According to the 1978 survey, women, more often then men, had sexual intercourse not because they desired to have it, but to please their partner. While 49 percent of males would like to increase the frequency of sexual intercourse, this was true for only 25 percent of females, most of whom were satisfied with the frequency (56 percent against 43 percent for males). Thirteen percent of females—mostly in the higher age groups—desired to reduce the frequency of sexual intercourse as compared with 3 percent of males. These gender differences may be explained as the result of a greater pressure on males for sexual performance, but also by the fact that more women found sex less enjoyable. Many of them in fact complained that before, during, and after sexual intercourse, men paid insufficient attention to their desires.

The brief duration of foreplay and sexual intercourse, limited almost exclusively to penetration, is more common among the uneducated, among more religious couples, and among the higher age groups. The average duration of foreplay was about 13 minutes, that of coitus about 9 minutes (Fabris & Davis 1978). A more recent survey indicates the duration of sexual intercourse, excluding foreplay, is 14.2 minutes (Durex 1998).

It should be noted that the statistical data regarding the frequency and duration of sexual intercourse, as well as other aspects of sexual life, should be treated with caution. Not only do the averages ignore important differences in individual reactions, but it is also possible that the responses are influenced by the desire of those interviewed to satisfy the presumed expectations of the interviewer, or—more generally—by the desire to make a positive impression. For these reasons, it is wrong to use these data as a measure of "normality."

Seventy-six percent of male partners and 72 percent of female partners in stable couples rated their sexual life "good" or "very good." More negative judgments were expressed by 3 percent of males and by 7 percent of females. The degree of satisfaction with their sexual lives increased during the first ten years of the relationship, and remained the same or decreased thereafter (Fabris & Davis 1978).

According to the 1978 survey, 69 percent of males and 26 percent of females always experienced orgasm during sexual intercourse. About one fifth of women never or rarely experienced orgasm. Young, educated, and non-religious women had a higher orgasm rate. Of the women who experienced orgasm, 29 percent experienced orgasm as a result of the oral or manual stimulation of the genitals, and 27 percent experienced it during penetration, whereas for 44 percent of these women, both activities resulted in orgasm.

At least 41 percent of Italian males and 14 percent of females have had extramarital sexual relations. Especially for women, the adultery rate increases with the level of education; it was 20 percent for women with a university degree. The adultery rate and the number of partners are lower for women, but the extramarital relationship is also characterized by a higher emotional investment (Fabris & Davis 1978). More recent figures indicate that 38 percent of Italians admit to having been involved in more than one sexual relationship at a time (Durex 1998).

Divorce and Remarriage

Divorce became legal in Italy in 1970, and a 1974 referendum confirmed the existing legislation with a 59.1 percent majority. Between 1985 and 1996, the number of divorces increased from 15,650 to 32,717. In the same period, separations increased from 35,163 to 57,538. The numbers were highest in the region of Lazio, followed by the more industrial northwestern regions. The divorce rate was much lower in the south. Even though there is a clear tendency toward an increase in the divorce rate, the stability of marriage is higher in Italy than in any other European country. This impression remains true, even when taking into account both separations and divorces: In 1994 in Italy, 16 out of 100 marriages were dissolved as a result of legal separation, 8 out of 100 because of divorce. In the same year, the divorce rate was 44 percent in the United Kingdom and Sweden and 29 percent in the Netherlands. In 1996, the divorce rate in Italy was 0.6 per 1,000 population against a European Union average of 1.8 (ISTAT 1999).

The main reason for the relatively low divorce rate is probably religion. Added to this factor is the importance of the family, not only as a source of emotional support and the context for the development of profound personal relations, but also for many other aspects of social life, from financial support to finding a job. Divorce is seen primarily as evidence of personal failure, and the end of the relationship is considered, above all, the beginning of a difficult period in personal life, rather than as a possible new start and an occasion to regain freedom and independence.

Incidence of Oral and Anal Sex

Oral sex, which in the past was condemned as "unnatural," is practiced more or less often by 55.2 percent of young Italians, and only rarely by 26.8 percent. Earlier surveys indicated that 47 percent of females and 58 percent of males experienced oral sex (Fabris & Davis 1978). Oral sex is a common element in the sexual fantasies of Italian males, especially during masturbation; this is less true for women. Both men and women prefer their partner to perform oral stimulation of their genitals, fellatio and cunnilingus, rather than performing these sexual acts themselves on their partners.

While anal intercourse is not part of the fantasies of the majority of women, it is part of the fantasies of 75 to 80 percent of men. However, the incidence of this practice is relatively low. According to the 1978 survey, 35 percent of males and 23 percent of females had experienced anal sex. A more recent survey among young people indicates that 78.6 percent of females and 62 percent of males never experience anal sex (Buzzi 1998).

6. Homoerotic, Homosexual, and Ambisexual Behaviors

A. History

With the noteworthy exceptions of the Kingdom of Sardinia and the regions under Austrian rule, the Italian states in the first part of the eighteenth century had no legislation against homosexual acts. After Unification, the repressive legislation of the Kingdom of Sardinia was extended to the other regions of Italy, excluding the territory of the ancient kingdom of Naples. With the introduction of a new penal code in 1889, regional differences in the treatment of homosexual acts were eliminated and homosexuality was decriminalized. Legal persecution of homosexuals continued, however, based on accusations regarding indecent acts, etc. Especially in southern Italy, however, the general attitude regarding homosexuality was rather tolerant, and by the end of the nineteenth century, male homosexual communities existed on the island of Capri and in towns such as Taormina. In this same period, Italy attracted a fair amount of sex tourism from countries like the United Kingdom and Germany where existing legislation against homosexuals was applied more severely.

Homophobic attitudes were prominent in the nationalistic propaganda during World War I, which often made references to sexual scandals in the German imperial court, and used accusations of homosexuality against all those who opposed the Italian war effort, including neutralists and pacifists.

The attitude of repressive tolerance that characterized public reactions to homosexuality, continued during the Fascist period, when attempts to introduce more specific legislation were blocked to safeguard the virile reputation of Italian men. Homosexual communities were thus allowed to survive, but at the same time, police measures were used against homosexuals who dared to "come out." Especially after 1938, when racist legislation was introduced in Italy, many homosexuals were condemned to legal confinement.

While at the level of legislation, the situation remained unchanged after the fall of Fascism in 1945, during the 1950s, some isolated publications voiced the need to improve the social status of male and female homosexuals. These attempts, however, met with the opposition of medical doctors, and especially the Italian specialists of the new discipline of sexology, who insisted on considering homosexuality a perversion or disease, and advocated anything from sports and sexual encounters with prostitutes to electroshock therapy to cure homosexuals. During the 1960s, members of Parliament tried to introduce legislation against homosexuality, which would punish not only homosexual acts between consenting adults, but also any public discourse in favor of homosexuality. These attempts failed because of the prevailing attitude of repressive tolerance.

Within the context of the sexual liberation movement of the late 1960s, which in the first phase was not sympathetic to the problems of homosexuals, the first Italian group of organized homosexuals emerged. In April 1972, the Unitary Front of Revolutionary Italian Homosexuals (FUORI; the acronym also means "out") contested the power of medical science at a congress of sexologists. The lack of support from the traditional leftist parties and the radical opposition from the right-wing parties and from the Catholic party, Christian Democracy, convinced the leaders of FUORI in 1975 to establish institutional links with the Radical Party, which had a tradition of civil rights actions. However, the decision led to a split between the reformers and those who considered themselves part of a revolutionary movement; new groups with links to the extreme left-wing parties were then created. In 1982, FUORI was dissolved.

The first nucleus of a new organization of homosexuals, Arcigay, was created in Palermo in December 1980 as a reaction to the tragedy of a double suicide of two gay lovers who had become the victims of public ostracism in the small town of Giarre, when their story became public. The first national congress designed to unite the local groups, created with the support of a dissident Catholic priest, Don Marco Bisceglia, took place in Palermo in 1982. It saw the participation of the most important leaders of Arci, a leisure-time and cultural organization traditionally close to the parties of the left (the communist and socialist parties). The connection between the homosexual movement and the traditional parties of the left, created through Arcigay, was the result of the innovative political strategy of attention for new social groups, feminists and homosexuals, inaugurated by the Communist Party in 1977. This initial connection was followed by a debate on the conditions of homosexuals in the party press (Giovannini 1980). Finally, in 1985, Arcigay was given a more structured national organization, with the election at the second national congress, of Franco Grillini as national secretary and Beppe Ramina as president.

The relations between lesbian women and gay men have not been easy, due, among other reasons, to the separatist tendencies of the most radical lesbian groups. In 1990, however, a group of lesbians created Arcigay Donna, and for the first time a woman, Graziella Bertozzo, was elected national secretary. In 1992, the association itself was rebaptized Arcigay Arcilesbica. In 1996, the association was once more restructured and became a federation of different groups; Arcilesbica chose to become autonomous. The most recent strategy aims at the construction of a gay and lesbian community offering services, institutional support, and the solidarity necessary to allow lesbian and gay persons to express their sexual identity just like non-homosexual persons.

B. Legal Status

Article 3 of the Constitution of the Italian Republic, approved in 1947, recognizes the equality of all citizens, and condemns discrimination based on sex, race, language, religion, political opinion, and personal and social conditions. The Republic has the obligation to remove social and economic obstacles, which de facto limit the full development of the human personality. While this can be interpreted as including the protection of the right of each individual not to be discriminated against on the grounds of his or her sexual orientation, there is no explicit mention of this in the Italian legislation. A campaign to introduce sexual orientation among the conditions mentioned in Article 3 of the Constitution started in 1998.

The creation of Arcigay has given more visibility to the problems of homosexuals in Italian society, and has made it possible to recognize and fight stereotypes, prejudices, and homophobic attitudes. The recognition of the role played by Arcigay in the defense of the interests of homosexuals became clear in 1987, when a group of members of Parliament attended the Third National Congress of the movement. Together with the fight against all forms of discrimination of homosexuals in Italian society, Arcigay has dedicated much energy to the issue of the recognition of the rights of homosexual couples. In 1997, a proposal was presented to Parliament in favor of the public recognition of relations not based on marriage. The proposal defines these so-called "civil unions" as relations between two consenting adult persons of any sex who have led for at least one year a common spiritual and material life. Legal recognition of these unions would entail the possibility of formal registration, and the extension to the partners of these unions of all rights commonly recognized to the partners of traditional couples, including unemployment benefits, compensation for injuries to the partner, priority access to public housing projects, the recognition of the right to reside in Italy for foreign partners, etc.

A recent survey among Italian Catholics (Inchiesta 1998) indicated a 72.2 percent majority in favor of giving "de facto unions" the same rights as legal families. In this case, an insufficient understanding of the term "de facto unions" probably invalidates the results. However, according to a recent survey (Buzzi 1998), 47.1 percent of young people agree with the idea that "homosexual couples should have the same rights as heterosexual couples," while only 30 percent disapproved. The ideas that homosexuality is a disease or a form of sexual perversion that should be illegal obtained, respectively, the support of 17.4 percent and 8.3 percent of the respondents.

Notwithstanding this public support, the proposal for the recognition of "civil unions" has made no progress in Parliament, because of numerous groups voicing their objections and the opposition of the Catholic Church and its allies.

According to a 1988 survey, homophobic attitudes are strong, especially among the lower social classes and among the elderly. But 35.3 percent of all Italians declared that they would simply acknowledge the discovery of a homosexual relative, while 23 percent would try to help homosexual relatives to express their sexual orientation without anxiety (Fiore 1991). This relatively open-minded attitude at the individual level contrasts with the social rejection of homosexuality. Still, 11.2 percent of Italians proposed legal measures against homosexuality and, while 48.8 percent are in favor of the recognition of the equal rights and dignity of homosexuals, 45.3 percent of Italians see the diffusion of homosexuality as a social peril.

C. Behaviors

Most males discover their homosexual desires during puberty, between the ages of 11 and 15 (42.6 percent), or adolescence, age 16 to 20 (20.9 percent). Females become aware of their desires at a later age. They also start having sexual relations at a later age (22.3 percent before age 15, against 42.1 percent in the case of males). Whereas homosexual contacts precede the acquisition of a homosexual identity in the case of males, in the case of females, the first homosexual experiences usually take place after the acquisition of a sexual identity. The main reaction in the case of females is happiness (64.5 percent against 47.2 percent in the case of males). However, fear and a sense of guilt continue to play a role. The high number of partners of male homosexuals—12.9 percent declared sexual contacts with over 400 partners—is in contrast with the declared preference for monogamous same-sex couples.

The limited information available (Fiore 1991) indicates that the most common sexual practices among homosexual couples are: mutual masturbation (practiced in all sexual contacts by 25 percent of males and 41.9 percent of females), followed by oral-genital contacts and penetration. Sadomasochistic practices are much less frequent. Generally speaking, sexual practices among homosexuals are polymorphous and depend on the partner, the place, and other specific conditions.

7. Gender Conflicted Persons

During the late 1970s, a group of transsexuals created the Movimento Transessuali Italiani (MTI) (Movement of Italian Transsexuals or MIT). With the support of the Radical Party, this movement succeeded in 1982 in convincing Parliament to change the existing legislation. The original proposal would have made it possible to change one's sex simply by requesting a change in the sex indicators on official documents. The final approved compromise introduced a two-step procedure for changing one's sex. First, a court has to give permission for the surgical adaptation of genitals on the basis of medical and psychological evidence. Certification of the surgical intervention is then needed to change the indication of sex in the documents.

The law is based on the assumption that only two sexes exist, male and female, and, while acknowledging the right of transsexuals to recreate the unity of body and mind, the law offers no solution for transsexuals who intend to change their sex status without undergoing surgical interventions.

8. Significant Unconventional Sexual Behaviors

A. Coercive Sex

Child Sexual Abuse and Incest

A number of serious crimes committed in Italy and abroad has brought the problem of sexual abuse of children to public attention. The activities of the telephone help service for children, Telefono Azzurro ("Blue Telephone"), have also contributed to making the problem better known to the general public.

Reacting to the increase in the number of cases of sexual abuse of children that have reached public attention, the Italian Parliament introduced in 1998 new legislation against the sexual exploitation of minors in prostitution, pornography, and sex tourism. The clients of prostitutes aged 14 to 16 risk a term of prison from six months to three years, or of four months to two years if the client is under age 18. Similar punishment is attached to the acquisition of pornography involving minors. The main innovations of the law regard more severe punishment for those who produce, sell, or transmit pornography depicting minors, and for those responsible for supporting the prostitution of minors. Those responsible for traffic in minors for prostitution risk a punishment of six to twenty years. The law can also be applied if the crimes are committed abroad, so that travel agencies have the obligation to warn their clients about the risks of sex tourism.

In order to combat sex tourism and the distribution of pornography involving minors, police forces are allowed to work undercover, participate in organized travel abroad, and create Internet sites and discussion groups.

The recent legislation has been criticized for confirming existing stereotypes and for calling for new crusades or "witch hunts." The main criticism centers on the fact that the law tends to focus on persons who are unknown to the child, whereas, in reality, in the majority of cases, those responsible for child abuse are family members or members of the community.

Indictment for incest involving two adults takes place only on complaint and in case of public scandal. Generally, police and judiciary authorities do not take action unless a formal complaint has been filed.

Sexual Harassment

The majority of Italian women aged 14 to 59 have been the victim of at least one of the following forms of sexual harassment: obscene telephone calls, acts of exhibitionism, physical harassment, and/or sexual intimidation on the job. The persons responsible for acts of sexual harassment are generally outsiders not known to the victims.

Proposals to clarify the legal status of some forms of behavior with a sexual connotation that are clearly offensive came up for open discussion, but early public opinion has resisted all attempts to introduce a more extensive notion of sexual harassment. In many cases, these attempts are considered part of a moral crusade imported from the United States.

Rape

The Fascist penal code defined rape as a crime that offended public morality and not as a crime against the person. Like many other parts of Fascist legislation, the articles regarding sexual violence remained valid during the first decades of the Italian Republic. Rape was considered a crime against morality, and no mandatory prosecution existed. The victim had to file a complaint, and often would be as much on trial as the perpetrator, because the defense would insist that the victim had provoked the crime. Evidence of the sexual history of the victim could be presented to the court. Moreover, the fact that the men responsible for this crime could escape punishment if they married their victims, often led to heavy pressure on the victim. In any case, punishment of the crime was relatively mild.

Given this legal situation, and taking into account the psychological problems that still today make it difficult to denounce acts of sexual violence, the statistics have no direct relation with the real incidence of the crime, but are linked with the attitudes prevailing in society, and especially among women. Until the early 1960s, the number of denunciations of rape was highest in the southern regions of Italy, where legal pressure was used to obtain extralegal solutions, like marriage, which could restore the honor of the family (Sabadini 1998).

During the 1970s, changes in sexual mores led to a decline of the number of denunciations in the south. The general increase of denunciations in the 1980s is linked with changes in public opinion, which had grown more aware of the importance of women's rights, while the police forces and judiciary system also changed their attitudes. Women's organizations have played an important role in this change. Already in the 1960s, women's organizations had started to campaign against the existing legislation, underlining the importance of sexual violence against women. The existence of anti-violence centers and of other assistance services organized by women, like the Telefono Rosa ("Pink Telephone"), convinced more women to denounce violence.

Still today, most cases of sexual violence are not denounced, and this is even more true when the person responsible for the crime is someone known by the victim, as is often the case. Only in 21.7 percent of the reported cases of sexual violence was the person responsible totally unknown to the victim; most other cases regarded friends, relatives, employers, etc. Friends, relatives, and (ex-)boyfriends are responsible for 54.3 percent of reported incidents of sexual violence; violence on the job by employers or colleagues accounts for 10.7 percent. Street violence accounts for 22.5 percent.

In February 1996, new legislation was introduced. Sexual violence is now considered a crime against the person, and is punished more severely than in the past. By abolishing the distinction between rape (sexual violence with penetration) and other forms of sexual violence, Law n. 66 has eliminated the need for specific medical checks and for a detailed discussion of the acts. According to the new legislation, sexual violence, meaning sexual relations obtained with the use of physical violence, threats, abuse of authority, abuse of conditions of physical or mental inferiority, or deception, is punished with a term in prison from five to ten years. The punishment is six to twelve years if special conditions occur, as in the case of gang rape. Prosecution is mandatory only in special cases, such as when the victim is under age 14. In all other cases, it is necessary to file a complaint within a period of six months from the time of the crime. It is not possible to retract this complaint.

B. Prostitution

In 1860, the new Italian kingdom followed the French and Belgian example of allowing regulated prostitution in closed houses, where prostitutes were subjected to mandatory medical control and deprived of many civil rights. Notwithstanding the opposition of the abolitionist movement and feminist groups, the system of regulated prostitution remained in vigor, with relatively minor changes, until 1958. The system was justified on the grounds that it gave young men a safe outlet for their sexual desires, and helped to avoid both masturbation and the socially more disruptive problem of the seduction of "honest" girls. Moralistic arguments played an important role as well in the discourse of the abolitionists, who refused to recognize that prostitution could be a choice for poor women for whom the alternatives offered by the labor market often were not much more attractive. Medical science viewed regulated prostitution as a necessary protection against the diffusion of sexually transmitted diseases. Moreover, positivist scientists like Cesare Lombroso (1836-1909), an Italian physician and criminologist, claimed that prostitution was the "biological destiny" of women who shared certain physical and psychological characteristics.

In 1948, Lina Merlin, a socialist member of Parliament, proposed a bill for the abolition of closed houses of prostitution. The proposal, which was not approved until 1958, met with the open opposition of brothel keepers who financed a campaign in the newspapers against the "Salvation Army mentality" of Lina Merlin, and accused her of disregarding male privileges. Protests were expressed also by the national association of venereologists, who warned that the abolition of mandatory medical checks on prostitutes would lead to a rapid increase of syphilis and other venereal diseases. The group of abolitionists was internally divided because some saw the abolition of organized prostitution primarily as a way to reconstruct the moral bases of male superiority, or as part of a more complex effort of moralization, including measures against premarital sex, adultery, and contraception. The main cause of the delay, however, was the silent opposition of the male members of Parliament who simply refused to put the issue on the agenda.

The new legislation, which was finally approved in 1958, did not make prostitution, as such, a crime, but punished only persons involved in procuring and in the exploitation of prostitution. Therefore, those who organized prostitution now ran most of the legal risks, while the prostitutes themselves had little to fear. The result has been that most prostitutes turned to streetwalking; only those prostitutes who could guarantee a high income, and who did not represent special risks of being minors or drug addicts, were employed in illegal brothels.

In the 1980s, prostitutes, or sex workers, started to organize themselves, and the year 1983 saw the first meeting of the Comitato per i Diritti Civili delle Prostitute (Committee for the Civil Rights of Prostitutes), created on the initiative of Carla Corso and Pia Covre. The main aim of this organization was to limit the extensive interpretation of the existing law against the exploitation of prostitution, which was often applied against the husbands and partners of prostitutes. An attempt was also made to reeducate the male clients, and to convince them of the necessity to use condoms.

The presence among prostitutes of drug addicts willing to accept lower prices and not requiring the use of condoms limited the successes of the organizations of prostitutes. In the early 1990s, the arrival of women from

Eastern Europe and Africa created further problems. According to a report published by the Ministry of Internal Affairs in September 1997, the total number of women working as prostitutes in Italy is about 50,000. Thirty-five thousand of these women have migrated to Italy from abroad, with the major group coming from Albania. In 1996, 4,387 persons were denounced for the exploitation of prostitution.

Prostitutes can be divided into three categories, depending on differences between the level of personal autonomy, the prices paid for their services, the level of integration in society, and age. At the top level are the call girls who are autonomous in the organization of their activities; they attract their clients through advertising in newspapers and in specialized magazines. Unlike the call girls, the second group of women, who work officially as actors, dancers, hostesses, strippers etc., cannot refuse clients who are procured by agencies or by the owners of night clubs.

The working conditions of streetwalkers, many of them illegal immigrants, are worse, because their legal situation makes them easily exploited. Moreover, many of these prostitutes, especially those coming from Albania, are minors, and are forced to work on the streets. These young women are often exploited by criminal gangs, who force them to hand over all the money they earn. Moreover, they are the frequent victims of the violent actions of the procurers, especially when they stand up against their exploiters, and refuse to work as prostitutes. Streetwalkers also run more risks in their contacts with clients. Police actions against these forms of violence have been notably inefficient.

The rapid increase in the number of prostitutes and their growing visibility has led to a recent debate about the possible reintroduction of some regulation of prostitution. Proposals have been forwarded to force prostitutes to exercise their profession only in certain locations, and/or to allow them to organize themselves in cooperatives, without being accused of "favoring" the prostitution of their fellow sex workers. In 1998, many city councils introduced repressive legislation, using the existing rules regarding traffic and public order, to force prostitutes and their clients to change locations. At the national level, proposals were discussed to coordinate police actions against the exploitation of women and to create public facilities for prostitutes who want to abandon the streets. Moreover, illegal immigrants are offered the right to reside in Italy in exchange for their help in dismantling the criminal organizations responsible for the "traffic in women."

Transsexuals and transvestites also participate in prostitution, where the two categories are often lumped together under the name *viados*. Male homosexual prostitution, which created Italy's reputation for sex tourism early in the twentieth century, is concentrated in the major cities, and takes, above all, the form of streetwalking. As in the case of heterosexual prostitution, some of the prostitutes offering their services to homosexual clients are minors, and a relatively high percentage is recruited among (illegal) immigrants. Male heterosexual prostitution is less common, but according to journalistic sources, there is an increase in the phenomenon. Unfortunately, little research has been done on this. In recent years, the larger Italian cities have attracted Brazilian and other Latino transvestites, who can earn a much better living as prostitutes than they can in South America.

Not much information is available about the clients of prostitutes. Until 1960, about a quarter of Italian young men had their first complete heterosexual experience with prostitutes. Visits to brothels were considered part of the process of coming of age for young, unmarried men, even though in reality middle-aged married men made up a large part of the clientele.

Today, there is a growing demand for sexual services, which seems to be linked with the more general phenomenon of the commoditization of human relations. About 16 percent of sexually active Italian males have sexual intercourse with prostitutes, with a higher percentage in southern Italy (Cutrufelli 1996). The increase in the demand, however, has not kept up with the increase on the supply side. As a result, it has become ever more difficult for prostitutes to refuse certain clients or particular sexual acts. Also, the safety risk is higher, as the request to use condoms is often disregarded by clients.

A recent public opinion survey (Buzzi 1998) shows that most young Italians have a more severe judgment about the clients than about the prostitutes. Prostitution, however, is seen above all as a problem of public order, and 64.7 percent of young people agree with the idea of reestablishing brothels. Moreover, the majority of young men do not exclude the possibility of going with prostitutes.

C. Pornography and Erotica

While it is difficult to find precise data about the production and commerce of pornography in Italy, there are no doubts about its diffusion. The gradual blurring of the distinction between pornography and other forms of erotica has led to a high level of social acceptance of pornography and opened new markets. In public debate, the anti-pornography position is weak, and pornography is often presented as a form of sexual liberation. Even some Catholic moralists have recognized that pornography can help couples to improve their sexual life as long as it does not replace "natural" sexuality.

The pornography market can satisfy most requests in genres from heterosexual and homosexual to transsexual, and from sadomasochism to sexual acts involving animals, and products including magazines, videocassettes, telephone services, and sex toys. A great diversification exists in the distribution system, which includes normal newsstands, video shops, porno shops, and mail-order services. From the economic point of view, the most important sector of the porno market is the sale of videocassettes, the success of which has been made possible by the wide distribution of videocassette players. With the increase in the sale of videocassettes, the importance of the so-called "red light" cinemas, with their almost exclusively male public, has decreased rapidly, from 122 in 1987 to 85 in 1992. Soft-core magazines, as well, have entered a period of crisis: The October

1991 issue of *Playboy* sold 51,000 copies, whereas during the late 1970s, the average sale had been about 120,000 copies. Hardcore magazines did not suffer the same decline, thanks to the greater diversification of their content. The total yearly sale of porno magazines is about 30 million copies.

Compared to porno cinemas, videocassettes offer the possibility of greater privacy, and cater to the needs of a more mixed public, including women and couples. Pornographic videocassettes are distributed primarily through video shops, where they can also be rented, and at the typical newsstand. The newsstands have fewer legal problems in selling the hard-core cassettes, which are formally attached to magazines, because, according to a law issued in 1975, the owner of the newsstand is not responsible for the content of the publications that he or she sells. This legal situation has made the newsstands the primary channel for the sale of pornographic cassettes, and has thus determined a high level of visibility for pornography. Video shops, however, offer the advantage of greater anonymity, especially, in the case of automatic dispensers, and the technical quality of the cassettes is usually higher. Estimates of the economic value of pornographic cassettes vary from 250 to 1,000 billion Italian lire per year.

The star system is a characteristic of hardcore pornographic movies produced in Italy, and actresses like Ilona Staller, Moana Pozzi, Jessica Rizzo, and Eva Henger have achieved some popularity also outside the world of pornography, thanks to their presence as guest stars in non-porno television shows. The best-known pornography stars have tried to exploit their popularity also, through the creation of pay sites on the World Wide Web. Not much is known about the consumption of pornography though Internet services, but the growing number of sites in Italian seems to indicate an expanding demand.

Surveys regarding the consumers of pornography (Eurispes 1993) indicate that about fifty percent of both males and females are sexuality excited by erotic films. However, whereas females prefer erotic films where sexual acts are embedded in a narrative context, males are more easily excited by viewing mere nudity and sexual organs. Earlier surveys (Sabatini 1988) defined the interest for pornography as predominantly male, and suggested that female curiosity increased with age. Moreover, female consumption of pornography seems to take place in the context of the couple, whereas for men it is more linked with solitary sex. The gender differences in the consumption of pornography are probably related to its male focus. Notwithstanding this, generally speaking, there are indications of an increase of the consumption of pornography by couples.

9. Contraception, Abortion, and Population Planning

A. Contraception

According to a 1997 survey (De Sandre 1997), the most common method of contraception in Italy is withdrawal, which is used by 29.2 percent of women of fertile age with a stable relationship. The incidence of this method is highest among women in the age group 20 to 24 (38.0 percent), where the contraceptive pill ranks second with 32.9 percent, and in the age group 45 to 49 (39.6 percent). Condoms are the most popular method of birth control for women aged 35 to 39 (28.1 percent); the contraceptive pill prevails in the age group 30 to 34 (30.8 percent). Nine percent of women with a stable relationship do not use any method of contraception.

The situation is completely different among women without a stable relationship: 48.7 percent use the contraceptive pill, and 30.8 percent use condoms. Differences between the age groups are less important for this category, with the exception of women belonging to the age group 45 to 49, whose use of the contraceptive pill is equaled by the use of other modern methods of contraception (both 22.9 percent). Condoms are used by 7.6 percent of the 45 to 49 age group, whereas 38.9 percent of this group does not use any method of contraception. Differences between the age groups are less pronounced among women without a stable relationship. Only the women aged 45 to 49 distinguish themselves: The use of the contraceptive pill is lower for this group (22.9 percent), and the difference is even more striking for the use of condoms (7.6 percent). Thirty-nine percent of women without a stable relationship aged 45 to 49 do not use any form of contraception.

Condoms and other means of contraception were not easily available in Italy until World War I. However, the existing methods of birth control, sexual abstention and withdrawal, were not popular among men from the higher classes, who often preferred the sexual exploitation of domestic servants and peasant women. The ideals of neo-Malthusianism gained more popularity in the first decades of the twentieth century when rubber condoms became available. In 1913, Luigi Berta and Secondo Giorni founded the neo-Malthusian League. The success of this movement was hampered by the advent of World War I, which seemed to show the need of population growth, and gave birth control an anti-patriotic image.

Eager to win the "demographic battle" in favor of population growth, the Fascist leaders introduced in 1930 legislation prohibiting publications and any other form of propaganda in favor of birth control. The production of condoms, as such, was not affected, because they were deemed necessary as a protection against venereal diseases. Subsidies and tax reductions for large families, jobs and better career chances for prolific fathers, higher taxation for bachelors, and health care for mothers and children were introduced in this period, but did not convince men, and above all women, to have more children. The main result of the prohibition of contraception was, therefore, an increase in the number of abortions. In addition, there was an increase in the number of illegitimate children, because economic hardship made it difficult to set up new households.

In the years after World War II, there was growing opposition against the Fascist legislation regarding contraception, which had remained valid in Italy even after the fall of Benito Mussolini. In 1956, the Italian Association for Demographic Education (AIED) was founded with the aim of defending the idea and the practice of a voluntary and conscious limitation of the number of children, and of combating the existing legislation against birth control. AIED had the support of the secular lay forces in Italy, of the socialists and of the communists, but its proposals were strongly opposed by the Catholics, who upheld the existing legislation. Still, in 1965, the Constitutional Court declared that detailed information about contraceptives should remain illegal because it offended public morality. In 1971, the legislation forbidding "propaganda in favor of birth control" was declared unconstitutional.

Since the legalization of contraception, the fertility rate has accelerated its decline. Notwithstanding the opposition of the Catholic Church, which has repeatedly reaffirmed its condemnation of contraception in the 1969 Encyclical *Humanae Vitae* of Pope Paul VI, the use of the contraceptive pill has increased, and almost tripled in the ten years between 1985 and 1996.

Some taboos survive however. In 1997, the installation of condom dispensers in a public high school caused a major outcry in the conservative press. The official newspaper of the Vatican, *L'Osservatore Romano*, spoke about an act of arrogance committed by a minority, even though according to public opinion polls, 79 percent of the Italians were in favor of the initiative. Earlier, in 1993, an anti-AIDS campaign in high schools was blocked because it endorsed the use of condoms. Furthermore, a recent agreement among private and public television networks excludes publicity for condoms during prime time.

Especially among young people, who seem to be aware of the risks of unprotected sexual relations in terms of STDs and pregnancy, the use of condoms is limited, because it is assumed that they make sex less enjoyable, because it is embarrassing to buy them, and also because the risk of not using condoms in contacts with occasional partners is judged acceptable. The low incidence of extramarital pregnancies is nevertheless an indication of the widespread use of contraception. The majority of unmarried women above age 20, in fact, have complete sexual relations, but only a few of them cohabit or have children. This is even more significant taking into account the distance between the age of first sex and marriage.

B. Abortion

Although induced abortion was not allowed during the Fascist period, legal measures against contraception, and the high incidence of premarital sex in certain regions, made abortion a common method of birth control. The first exception in the general prohibition of abortion was made in 1975, when the Constitutional Court ruled that induced abortion should be possible in the case of serious health risks for the woman. After a campaign by pro-choice feminist groups, abortion was legalized in 1978, and women were granted the right to terminate a pregnancy upon request during the first trimester. However, the law contained a number of restrictions: Legal abortion is confined to women whose physical and psychological health are at risk or for whom social conditions, economic conditions, or the family situation make it extremely difficult to educate children. Further limitations regard the obligation to consult a medical doctor, and the mandatory waiting period of seven days between the medically certified decision and the actual intervention. Minors need to obtain permission of a parent or guardian. The male partner of the woman is involved in the decision process only if the woman wishes so.

After the first three-month period, induced abortion is legal only in case pregnancy or childbirth creates serious health risks for the woman, or when the fetus presents pathologies that entail serious risks for the physical and mental health of the woman. All induced abortions have to take place in public hospitals, where the medical staff has no obligation to cooperate if abortion is in conflict with their moral and religious convictions. Partly as a result of the limitations to the freedom of choice, illegally induced abortion has not disappeared in Italy. For obvious reasons, no exact data are available, but the Ministry of Health estimated that 50,000 clandestine abortions were carried out in 1993, 70 percent of which were in the south.

Attempts to change the existing legislation failed in 1981, when two different referenda, one aimed at eliminating the restrictions, the other designed to severely reduce access to abortion, were voted down by majorities of, respectively, 88.4 and 68 percent. Abortion remains controversial in Italy, however, and is severely condemned by the Catholic Church. The condemnation was reiterated in a recent Papal Encyclical on ethical questions, *Evangelium Vitae*. The Italian pro-life movement tries actively, but without much success, to convince the political leadership of the need to change the existing legislation. Most of its resources, however, are spent in providing alternative solutions and facilities for single mothers.

After the introduction of Law no. 194, abortion rates rose modestly, increasing from 13.7 abortions per 1,000 women aged 15 to 44 in 1979 to 16.9 per 1,000 in 1982. Since 1984, there has been a steady decline, reaching 9.8 per 1,000 by 1993. A similar pattern was displayed by abortion ratios (the number of abortions per 1,000 live births), which reached 213 in 1996 after having reached a peak of 389.5 in 1984. While the abortion ratios are relatively high because of Italy's low fertility rate, the general trends are similar to other western European countries. (Salvini Bettarini 1996). Abortion rates and ratios vary considerably according to regions. Since legalization, abortion rates have dropped most in the northern regions, where family planning services are more extensive, but both abortion ratios and rates remain higher in the northern and central regions than in the south.

As far as age patterns are concerned, the abortion rate is relatively low for young women (7.6 per 1,000 women at ages 15 to 19 in 1981, and 4.6 in 1991). This may be due, in part, to legislative restrictions, but it is also linked to the fact that Italian women start to have sexual relations at a relatively late age. Generally speaking, the trend in the distribution of age-specific abortion rates is shifting upward. In 1981, the abortion rate was highest among women aged 25 to 29 (25.3 per 1,000 women), whereas in 1991, the abortion rate was highest among women aged 30 to 34 (16.9 per 1,000 women), with women aged 26 to 29 coming second (15.7 per 1,000 women).

The most recent data (ISTAT 2000) show that the total number of voluntary abortions has stabilized at between 138,000 and 140,000 per year, after a slight increase in 1997 when the number of abortions was 9.5 per 1,000 women of fertile age. Thus, in the years 1980 to 1997, the average number of abortions per woman has diminished by 40.7 percent against a diminution by 29 percent of the fertility rate in the same time period. The decline in the abortion rate and in the fertility rate indicate a more frequent, or more efficient, use of techniques of birth control. The decline in the abortion rate is highest among married women in the most fertile age groups, 25 to 28, and 30 to 34. An opposite tendency can be noted among very young women, aged 15 to 19, among whom the abortion rate has increased since the early 1990s, reaching 6.6 per 1,000 in 1998. A more consistent increase regards the abortion rate of immigrant women, which reached the number of 32.5 abortions per 1,000 women in 1998.

C. Population Programs

Under Fascism, public authorities shared the Catholic Church's positive view about large families, and after the fall of Mussolini, they were slow to change their position. Not until 1971, did the Constitutional Court declare that ideas about population growth dating back to the Fascist period were not sufficient to justify the existence of legislation against contraception. To advance information about contraception and to promote responsible parenthood are part of the duties of the public family advisory agencies created in 1975.

In the postwar period, population planning concentrated on various maternity benefits. The first important legal measure was taken in 1950 when employers were prohibited by law from dismissing pregnant women or mothers of small children. The same law prohibited employing pregnant women in activities that would endanger their health or the health of the unborn baby. Finally, a new law introduced a paid maternity leave of three months before childbirth and two months after childbirth. Mothers have the right to six more months of unpaid maternity leave, during which they retain their position. In the attempt to invalidate the attempt of employers to dismiss women as soon as the possibility of pregnancy increased significantly, a 1963 law specified that marriage was not a valid reason for dismissal. The rules regarding mandatory leave of absence for maternity were reaffirmed and elaborated on in Law n. 1204 of 1971.

Today, Italy's birthrate, expressed in Total Fertility Rate (TFR) is, with that of Spain, the lowest of 227 nations: 1.19 children per fertile woman. A TFR of 0.8 in the northern industrial city of Bologna underscores the social challenges Italy faces. The actions of the Italian governments in the field of population planning are strongly influenced by the fear that this low fertility rate and a relative decline of the active population will make it impossible to finance pensions for the retired and other welfare projects. Most measures aim at improving the conditions of working mothers, and try at the same time to eliminate gender-specific discrimination, by extending rights, such as leaves of absence for the care of children to men. According to recent proposals, financial compensation for maternity, until now limited to employed women, will be extended to non-employed and self-employed women. Further measures focus on the creation and funding of childcare facilities, and, more generally, aim at reducing the financial burden of families with children.

10. Sexually Transmitted Diseases

Historically, sexually transmissible diseases (STDs) were seen primarily as a consequence of sexual contacts with prostitutes, and the legal interventions regarding prostitution and STDs were closely connected. The need to control the diffusion of STDs was one of the main arguments for the introduction, in 1860, of regulated prostitution. In 1870, the obligation to notify health authorities of infectious diseases was introduced, together with more specific laws regarding STDs. In 1888, the clinics for the mandatory treatment of infected prostitutes were reorganized and transformed into specialized clinics for the free treatment of contagious venereal diseases. New legislation, approved in 1901, defined syphilis, gonorrhea, and chancroid (*Hemophilus ducreyi*) as "venereal diseases." According to legislation approved in 1923, venereal clinics had to be created in all major cities. While reaffirming the principle of free treatment, Law 837 of 1956 and successive laws updated existing legislation and established a list of four diseases (syphilis, blennorrhagia (a profuse gonorrheal discharge), chancroid, and lymphogranuloma venereum (*Chlamydia trachomatis*) for which there is an obligation to report. This law is still in effect. Moreover, the terminology used in official documents still refers to "venereal diseases," and has not yet adopted the broader term of sexually transmissible diseases (STD).

While venereologists denounced a rapid increase of venereal diseases after 1958, when the abolition of regulated prostitution made mandatory medical checks on prostitutes impossible, in reality the statistical data could be interpreted in various ways.

In 1972, responsibility for the diagnosis and treatment of STDs was transferred to regional governments. The result has been a growing differentiation in the treatment and operational conditions of various STD centers, with important differences, both between regions and within the same region. In the past, venereology was associated above all with dermatology, but recent developments have shown the need for a more interdisciplinary approach.

The precise incidence of STDs is unknown, not only because there is a legal obligation to report only a few diseases, but also because medical specialists tend to disregard this obligation. The Higher Institute for Health (Istituto Superiore della Sanita, ISS) has estimated that the number of unreported cases is at least 100 to 150 percent higher than reported cases. In September 1991, a national STD surveillance agency was created to collect and analyze data coming from some 48 STD clinics. The aim is not to register the total number of cases, but rather to monitor developments and to gather the data necessary for a better description of STDs (Giuliani & Suligoi 1994).

The results of the first year of the survey confirmed the existence of important regional variations in the registration and/or recourse to STD centers for treatment: 67.4 percent of the 9,527 STD cases were registered in northern Italy, 19.3 percent in central Italy, and 33.6 percent in the south. In order to assist the large number of foreigners involved (10.4 percent), in 1992, a special project was created for the prevention and treatment of STDs among this group. Heterosexual contacts were responsible for 92 percent of the cases, and homosexual or bisexual contacts accounted for 8 percent. The most frequent pathologies were *condyloma acuta* or venereal warts, 28 percent; nongonococcal urethritis, 11.2 percent; nongonococcal vaginitis, 18.6 percent; and quiescent seropositive syphilis, 10.4 percent.

11. HIV/AIDS

The first case of AIDS in Italy was discovered in 1982, and until 1995, there was an annual increase in the number of persons diagnosed as being infected with HIV (see Table 1). HIV infection is unevenly distributed over the national territory, with the highest numbers in the regions of Lombardia, Lazio, Liguria, and Emilia Romagna. Between October 1997 and September 1998, the AIDS rate per 100,000 population was 6.5 in Liguria, 9.1 in Lombardia, 6.0 in Emilia Romagna, and 8.1 in Lazio, against 0.6 in the region of Molise and 1.2 in the Basilicata. In 1997, women constituted 23.2 percent of the cases.

Among the men diagnosed as being infected with AIDS, drug addicts are the major category (63.6 percent), followed by men with homosexual experiences (19.7 percent). Heterosexual experiences are held responsible for 15.2 percent of the cases of AIDS, but heterosexual contact is the second most important cause (34.2 percent) for HIV infection in women after the abuse of drugs (59.9 percent). The average age at which AIDS is diagnosed is increasing: In 1985, it was 29 for men and 24 for women, compared to 37 for men and 34 for women in 1997.

While at first gay organizations interpreted the alarm about AIDS as an attempt of the medical professions to regain control and use the discourse about health risks to moralize "disorderly sexual conduct," the real dimensions of the problem soon became clear. In May 1985, Arcigay, together

Table 1

Annual Distribution of New Cases of AIDS and Mortality Rate

Year of Diagnosis	New Cases	Mortality Rate
1982	1	0.0%
1983	8	87.5%
1984	37	100.0%
1985	198	93.9%
1986	457	93.4%
1987	1,029	93.0%
1988	1,773	90.4%
1989	2,480	90.8%
1990	3,135	89.1%
1991	3,826	88.7%
1992	4,261	85.6%
1993	4,818	77.6%
1994	5,521	72.7%
1995	5,654	56.9%
1996	4,993	36.7%
1997	3,728	20.7%
1998 (to 30 September 1998)	1,430	13.6%
Total	42,899	67.5%

(Istituto Superiore di Sanità, Notiziario, XI, 11 November 1998)

with the Abele group from Turin, promoted the publication of the first Italian book about AIDS, written by Giovanni Dall'Orto (1985). Since then, Arcigay has promoted many public debates and information campaigns about safe sex. Other initiatives included the free distribution of condoms and the creation of homosexual health centers managed by the association itself with the support of the Ministry of Public Health. The success of these actions is shown by the fact that homosexuals in Italy make up a much lower percentage of the victims of AIDS than in most other countries.

12. *Sexual Dysfunctions, Counseling, and Therapies*

A. Sexual Dysfunctions

The notion of sexual dysfunction itself is subject to change, and definitions of sexual dysfunctions often mirror changing attitudes toward male and female sexuality. Thus, inhibited female orgasm (anorgasmia) was not considered a problem in a context where female sexuality was linked almost exclusively with procreation. Premature ejaculation became more of a problem with the emergence of the myth of simultaneous orgasm, and also the idea of (heterosexual) sex as pleasure-created pressures and tensions. Finally, the growing resistance to a compulsory idea of sexuality as necessarily linked with orgasm might eliminate the tendency to treat alternative expressions of eroticism as sexual dysfunctions.

About 11 percent of Italian males have erectile dysfunctions. More widespread are problems regarding orgasm: About one third of Italian males have had at least some experience with problems of early (premature) ejaculation. The most serious problem, however, is a decreased libido. The incidence of physical problems and, above all, psychological factors, like the identification of virility with sexual potency, and the desire to please the female partner, have created a market for new pharmaceutical products. Among women, the sexual dysfunctions with the highest incidence are painful intercourse (dyspareunia), vaginal spasms (vaginismus), and inhibited orgasm (anorgasmia). Also, among women the loss of sexual desire is common.

Recent research among young people aged 18 to 30 indicates that, among males, 10.2 percent presented erectile dysfunctions, and 30.1 percent presented problems of premature ejaculation. Inhibited orgasm was mentioned by 13.2 percent of young females, while painful intercourse was reported by 50.7 percent. Difficulties in experiencing orgasm were reported by 11.5 percent of males and 39.8 percent of females, while 14.1 percent of males and 28.4 percent of females complained about the lack of sexual desire (Buzzi 1998).

Other male problems involve fertility. A comparison of the results of sperm analyses of 4,518 men without fertility problems, carried out by the Centro di Andrologia based in Pisa between 1975 and 1994, has confirmed the thesis of a general decline of the number and of the motility of spermatozoa. In this twenty-year period, sperm counts went down from 71 million to 65 million spermatozoa per millimeter. The decline of the motility was even more serious, as the number of spermatozoa with progressive motility decreased from 50 percent to 32 percent. Oxidation caused by environmental pollution is the main cause of this phenomenon.

B. Counseling and Therapies

In 1948, the first Italian family advisory agency was opened in Milan by Don Paolo Liggeri. La Casa and its sister organizations functioned as a social movement, where volunteers tried to transmit values and ideals, not as a service agency where paid professionals offered their services to clients. For this reason, the use of American manuals for marriage counseling, with their pragmatic attitude, often created problems. Nevertheless, these Catholic marriage advisory agencies were often innovative, because they underlined the positive role of sexuality in marriage and favored a more active role of fathers in the education of their children. However, as far as the female gender role was concerned, they subscribed to more traditional ideas about the female biological destiny of motherhood, and women's generally more passive attitude in sexuality.

Law n. 405 of 1975 created a network of public family agencies, which were to offer psychological and social assistance to couples and families, and to assist couples in choices regarding procreation and responsible parenthood through information and the distribution of contraceptives. The same law allowed for the public funding of private family agencies. Both Catholic and feminist-oriented advisory agencies thus received funding. The prerequisite of client-oriented, non-directive counseling was satisfied, not by the single agencies, which maintained their ideological premises, but by the system as a whole.

Among the therapies often used in combination to combat sexual dysfunctions, it is possible to distinguish these: psychotherapies focused on improving the understanding of sexual problems, and thus modifying reactions and behaviors; behavioral therapy using special assignments to modify and improve the perception of pleasure and the idea of sexual pleasure itself; and autogenous training and pharmacological therapies.

13. Research and Advanced Education

In 1921, the *Società italiana per lo studio delle questioni sessuali* was founded by Aldo Mieli, with the aim to improve the level of information about human sexuality. The journal published by the Society, *Rassegna di Studi Sessuali*, introduced in Italy the themes and ideas developed by progressive German sexologists, and greatly contributed to a more open discussion. The rise to power of the Fascists in 1922, however, reduced the possibilities for reformist action. This was one of the reasons why, in 1928, Mieli submitted his resignation as editor-in-chief of the journal and left Italy for France. By 1931, when Corrado Gini took over control, the journal had become an instrument of the Fascist population policy.

Sexology had to start again in the postwar period. In 1959, a group of medical doctors, headed by Professor Giacomo Santori, created the Centro Italiano di Sessuologia (Italian Center of Sexology, CIS), which is active, above all, in the sector of training and information. The CIS (Via O. Regnoli, 74, 40138 Bologna) promotes an interdisciplinary approach that draws on the results of medical science, psychology, and anthropology, and favors an interpretation of human sexuality that takes into account the biological and medical aspect, as well as the social and relational aspects, without excluding moral aspects. The CIS is a founding member of the World Association of Sexology (WAS), and a member of the European Federation of Sexology.

Aspects of sexology are part of medical training, and specialized schools are attached to some universities. Among these, the Center of Andrology of the University of Pisa, founded by Professor Menchini Fabris in 1975, deserves special mention. Numerous other institutes and associations do research and offer training in sexology, among them:

- Istituto Internazionale di Sessuologia, Via della Scala, 85, Firenze, Italy (founded in 1981);
- Instituto di Sessuologia Clinica, Via Fibreno 4, 00199 Roma, Italy;

- Società Italiana di Sessuologia Scientifica, Istituto di Sessuologia Clinica, Via Fibreno 4, 00199 Roma, Italy; publication: *Rivista di Sessuologia Clinica*;
- Società Italiana di Sessuologia ed Educazione Sessuale, c/o Prof. Gabriele Traverso, Via Circonvallazione 28, 10015 Ivrea, TO, Italy;
- Centro Italiano di Sessuologia (CIS), Via della Lungarina, 65, Rome, 00153, Italy; phone: +39-6-51-245-785;
- Instituto di Sessuologia di Savona, 17026 Noli, Via la Malfa, 5, Savona, Italy; phone: 39-19-748-5687; fax: +39-19-748-5687; Associazione per la Ricerca in Sessuologia (ARS), Via Angelo Cappi 1/8, 16126 Genova, Italy.
- The Centro Italiano di Sessuologia (CIS) is the publisher of the *Rivista di Sessuologia* (CLUEB, Via Marsala 24, 40126 Bologna, Italy; www.clueb.com).
- Other publications in the field of sexology are *Rivista di Scienze Sessuologiche* (Edizioni del Cerro, Via delle Orchidee 17, 56018 Tirrenia, Pisa, Italy) and *Rivista di Sessuologia Clinica* (Franco Angeli, Viale Monze 106, 20127 Milano, Italy; www.francoangeli.it; frang@tin.it).

The results of sexological studies often receive great attention in the mass media, and some sexologists—Willy Pasini, to name but one—have gained national popularity as guests on television talk shows and through their articles in the popular press.

References and Suggested Readings

Barbagli, M., & Saraceno, C., eds. 1997. *Lo stato delle famiglie*. Bologna: Il Mulino.
Buzzi, C. 1998. *Giovani, affettività, sessualità. L'amore tra i giovani in una indagine IARD*. Bologna: Il Mulino. (IARD Foundation, Via Soncino 1, 20123 Milano, Italy).
Cesareo, V. 1995. *La religiosità in Italia*. Milano: Mondadori.
Cipolla, C., ed. 1996. *Sul letto di Procuste. Introduzione alla sociologia della sessualita*. Milano: Franco Angeli.
Cutrufelli, M. R. 1996. *Il denaro in corpo. Uomini e donne. La domanda di sesso commerciale*. Milano: Marco Tropea.
Dall'Orto, G., with R. Ferracini. 1985. *AIDS*. Torino, Italy: Gruppo Abele.
De Rose, A. 1992. Socio-economic factors and family size as determinants of marital dissolution in Italy. *European Sociological Review*, 8(1).
De Sandre, P., et al. 1997. *Matrimonio e figli: Tra rinvio e rinuncia*. Bologna: Il Mulino.
Durex. 1998. *Global sex survey. 1998.* [Available at www.durex.com].
Eurispes. 1997. *Terzo rapporto sulla pornografia 1992*. Eurispes, *L'Italia sotto la lente 1982-1997. Quindici anni di lavoro di ricerca sulla società italiana* [CD-Rom]. Roma: MGE Communications.
Fabris, G., & Davis, R. 1978. *Il mito del sesso. Rapporto sul comportamento sessuale degli italiani*. Milano: Mondadori.
Fiore, C. 1991. *Il sorriso di Afrodite. Rapporto sulla condizione omosessuale in Italia*. Firenze: Vallecchi.
Giovannini, F. 1980. *Comunisti e diversi. Il PCI e la questione omosessuale*. Bari: Dedalo.

Giuliani, M., & Suligoi, B. 1994. La sorveglianza in Italia delle malattie sessualmente trasmesse. In: M. Dolivo et al., eds., *Malattie sessualmente trasmesse* (pp. 245-255). Milano, Parigi, Barcellona: Masson.

Inchiesta. 1998. 'I diritti della famiglia e le 'unioni di fatto.' In: *Famiglia Cristiana*. Vol. LXVIII, n. 31.

ISTAT (Istituto Nazionale di Statistica). 1996. *Famiglia, abitazioni, servizi di pubblica utilità. Indagini multiscopo sulle famiglie. Anni 1993-1994*. Roma: ISTAT.

ISTAT. 1998. *Annuario statistico italiano 1998*. Roma: ISTAT.

ISTAT. 1999a. *Annuario statistico italiano 1999*. Roma: ISTAT.

ISTAT. 1999b. *Rapporto annuale. La situazione del paese nel 1998*. Roma: ISTAT.

ISTAT. 2000. *L'Interruzione volontaria di gravidanza in Italia. Evoluzione e tendenze recenti*. Roma: ISTAT.

Rifelli, G., & Moro, P., eds. 1989-1995. *Sessuologia clinica. Vol. 1, Sessuologia generale; Vol. 2, Impotenza Sessuale maschile. femminile e di coppia; Vol. 3, Consulenza e terapia delle disfunzioni sessuali*. Bologna: CLUEB.

Rifelli, G. 1998. *Psicologia e psicopatologia della sessualità*. Bologna: Il Mulino.

Sabadini, L. L. 1998. *Molestie e violenze sessuali*. Roma: ISTAT. [Available at www.istat.it].

Sabatini, R. 1988. *L'eros in Italia. Il comportamento sessuale degli Italiani*. Milano: Mursia.

Salvini Bettarini, S., & D'Andrea, S. S. 1996. Induced abortion in Italy: Levels, trends and characteristics. *Family Planning Perspectives, 28*(6):267-271.

Sgritta, G. B. 1988. The Italian family. *Journal of Family Issues, 40*(3):372-396.

Stella, R. 1991. *L'osceno di massa. Sociologia della communicazione pornografica*. Milano: Angeli.

Tatafiore, R. 1994. *Sesso al Lavoro. Da prostitute a sex-worker. Miti e realtà dell'eros commerciale*. Milano: Il Saggiatore.

Wanrooij, B. P. F. 1990. *Storia del pudore. La questione sessuale in Italia 1860-1940*. Venezia: Marsilio.

Morocco
(*Le Moroc*) (French)
(*al-Mamlaka al-Maghrebia*) (Arabic)
(The Kingdom of Morocco)

Nadia Kadiri, M.D.*, and Abderrazak Moussaïd, M.D.,** ***
with Abdelkrim Tirraf, M.D., and Abdallah Jadid, M.D.
Translated by Raymond J. Noonan, Ph.D., and Sandra Almeida

Contents

Demographics and a Historical Perspective

A. Demographics

Morocco is situated on the northwestern coast of Africa. It shares its borders with Algeria to the east and south, and with Mauritania to the southwest.

Communications: Nadia Kadiri, M.D., Professor of Psychiatry, Centre Psychiatrique Universitaire, Rue Tarik Ib Ziad, Casablanca Morocco; nadiakadiri@hotmail.com or n.kadri@casanet.net.ma or nadiakadiri@yahoo.com.

**Abderrazak Moussaïd, M.D., 38, Boulevard Rahal El Meskini, 20 000 Casablanca, Morocco.

It is bordered on the west by the Atlantic Ocean and on the north by the Mediterranean Sea, the two expanses of water being separated by the Strait of Gibraltar, which is situated to the north of Morocco. The area of Morocco is 172,400 square miles or 710,850 square kilometers, slightly larger than the state of California. About 20 percent of the land of Morocco is arable. Fertile plains extend the length of the Atlantic coastline: in the regions from the center-north, the plain of Fès-Saiss; to the south, the plain of Souss-Massa; and to the south-southwest, the Tadla. To the east of these plains, the Atlas Mountains, which peak at 4,165 meters (Toubkal), extend from the southwest of Morocco to the confines of the Algerian borders in the northeast. To the north, the Rif Mountains connect the northwest coast of Morocco to West Algeria (l'Ouest Algérien). Among the great wealth of Morocco, along with farming and its human resources, is the mining of phosphate, which is found in great abundance in the central regions of Morocco, the city of Khouribga, and in the Moroccan Sahara. Until 1976, the Moroccan Sahara represented one of the last vestiges of French colonialism in Morocco.

In 1997, the population of Morocco was estimated at 30,391,423; in 2000, more than half of this population, 53 percent, lived in the cities. The regional distribution of the urban population remains marked by the concentration of 56 percent of this population in two areas: the center and the northwest. The axis of the cities of Casablanca-Rabat-Kenitra clusters 35 percent of the urban population of Morocco. Ethnically, Morocco is very homogeneous, with 99 percent of the population Arab-Berber.

The great majority of Moroccans are Muslim (98.7 percent); 1.1 percent are Christian and 0.2 percent are Jewish. Sunni Malikite Islam is the state religion. The 1998 age distribution of the population reveals that about 80 percent of the population were less than 40 years old, the active population, 15 to 60 years old, comprised 56 percent, and those over 60 years represented only 7 percent of Moroccans. The life expectancy from birth in 2000 was 66.85 years for men and 71 years for women. The birthrate in 2000 was 25.78 per 1,000 population, the infant mortality rate was 50.96 per 1,000 live births, and the death rate was 6.12 per 1,000, for an annual natural growth of 1.96 percent. In 1998, the average Moroccan woman of fertile age was expected to bear 3.1 children (the Total Fertility Rate, TFR), placing the country 90 among 227 nations of the world. In 2000, the literacy rate in the rural areas was about 25 percent, with two thirds of the urban population being literate. With school attendance compulsory from age 7 to 13, the estimated overall literacy rate is just 50 percent and 25 percent for women (Fernea 1998:110). In 1994, Morocco had one hospital bed for 978 persons and one physician for 2,923 people. The 1997 estimated per capita Gross Domestic Product was $3,500.

***Note*: The editor, Robert T. Francoeur, has added additional comments, indicated by [. . . (Editor)]

B. A Brief Historical Perspective

Morocco is rich in Paleolithic remains, particularly in parts of North Africa and the Sahara, which were populated until the Neolithic era. The people who settled in the region soon after that were probably natives of Europe and Asia. They became the ancestors of today's Berbers. In the seventh century BCE, the Phoenicians laid the foundations of commerce on the Mediterranean coast of North Africa at sites having Berber names that became the great ports of Tingi (Tangier), Melilia (Russadir), and Casablanca. The conquest of Carthage by the Roman Empire in the first century BCE assured Roman domination of the entire African Mediterranean coastline to the Straits of Gibraltar. From 25 to 23 BCE, Juba II, a Berber sovereign, administered the Berber kingdom of Mauritania (Algeria, Morocco, and a part of Mauritania). Around 42 CE, the emperor Claudius I annexed the whole empire of Mauritania to the Roman Empire. In 429, Morocco underwent the invasion of the Vandals. The Byzantine general Bélisaire regained the region in 533. After the conversion of the emperor Constantine I the Great in the fourth century, Christianity expanded in the Roman regions.

It appears that Islamic troops reached the Atlantic Ocean in 681 under the command of Oqba Ibn Nafii. The real conquest started later on, between 705 and 707, under the direction of Moussa Ibn Nousair. The Muslim establishment was in the meantime long and difficult. Many Muslim dynasties, claiming Arabic origins for religious reasons or prestige, ruled in various areas of the country. In 788, Idriss I, descendant of Ali, son-in-law of the Prophet, founded the dynasty of the Idrissides. It is from this age that dates the founding of the city of Fès, which became an important religious and cultural center of the Islamic world under Idriss II. The rigorist Almoravide warriors of Islam went on to dominate the region beginning in 1062, the date at which they founded Marrakech as the crossroads of commercial routes between the Arab world and the Sahara. A new reform movement, the Almohades (the Unities), launched by Ibn Toumart in the first half of the twelfth century, put an end to the Almoravide empire in 1147, marking the triumph of the seated Berbers of the anti-Atlas under the aegis of Abd Al-Moumen (1130-1163). The Almohades exercised their authority over what is currently Algeria, Tunisia, Libya, and part of Portugal and Spain.

In 1269, the Mérinides, of the Arabic Berbers, took over the throne, but they could not maintain the unity of the North African empire of the Almohades. During the reconquest of Spain, which exiled the Arabs and the Jews, the great majority of Spanish Muslims found refuge in Morocco they took over. In 1415, Ceuta (Sebta) was occupied by the Portuguese. In 1497, Melilia fell to the Spanish. The intrusions of the Europeans provoked the rise of the Beni Saâd (or Saâdiens), who became master of the country in 1554. Moroccan Saâdiens, aided by Moorish and Jewish refugees from Spain, created a prosperous and unified country. In this period, Moroccan architecture and arts flourished. In 1664, Maulay Rachid founded the Alaouite dynasty, which still reigns to this day in Morocco. The Alaouite dynasty knew its apogee under the sultan Moulay Ismail (1672-1727), the builder of the city of Meknès. His reign was followed by a long period of family rivalries. At the end of the eighteenth century, only the northern third of Morocco remained under the administration of the sultan.

On March 30, 1912, the sultan recognized the French protectorate. Spain, for its part, assumed control of the north of Morocco, from the enclave of Ifni (southwest) and from the Moroccan Sahara (west). The occupation of the country was not total until 1934. After World War II, the Moroccan nationalist resistance forced independence in 1956, opening the era of the constitutional monarchy in Morocco. The last vestiges of European colonialism persisted until the recent past. The enclave of Ifni was not returned to Morocco until 1964, and the Moroccan Sahara was not recovered until 1976 at the end of a popular nationalist march called the "Green March." Two other enclaves, small ports situated on the Mediterranean coast west of Tangier, Ceuta and Melilia, are still occupied by Spain.

1. Basic Sexological Premises

A. Character of Gender Roles

The traditional family structure remains very faithfully attached to the archaic patriarchal scheme. The father is, in general, a patriarch who inspires respect and to whom one owes obedience and acknowledgment. The mother is the housekeeper "wife-mother" who does everything. She is the one who makes the decisions in the social sphere. But she prepares her own strategy for managing her ecosystem by imposing a strong personality in the household. She reveals herself to be more conservative than the man. When a woman becomes a mother, she is always considered a potential danger, because she is perceived as having a devastating effect on the man. However, our Islamic religion adopts an ambivalent attitude toward women. On one side, she is considered as being more wily than *Iblis* (Satan) whom she incarnates in our collective unconscious; on the other side, the *Hadith* (*Words of the Prophet*) considers woman as a simple being of spirit, whose faith is incomplete. This notion is largely predominant in the rural population, whereas city women have begun to rebel against this state of things (Moussaid 1992; Naamane 1990). [In terms of Moroccan cultural change, there are continuing tensions between the people of the *magzken* in the urban organized government and the people of the rural and tribal *bled.* These tensions often focus on the differences between modern Western sexual and marital values and those espoused by the tribal and rural cultures (Fernea 1998:63). (Editor)]

B. Sociolegal Status of Males and Females

In the legal sphere, the rights of the individual man or woman are governed by the penal code, the code of commerce, and the code of family law (*mudawana*). Morocco's penal and commercial codes are identical in scope, with men and women sharing the same rights and obligations. On the contrary, the code of family law, which regulates man–woman relations in the domains of marriage, repudiation, filiation, custody of the children, guardianship, and inheritance, is far from being equitable (*Statut du Code*, 1996).

[A first step in reform of the *mudawana* came in the early 1980s, when the Union de l'Action Feminin and other groups gathered over a million signatures in support of a petition urging the King to reform the family law regulating marriage, divorce, inheritance, child custody, and polygamy. There is still no central office to deal with alimony or child support. The new code is known as the *Statut du Code Personnel "Mudawana"* (1996) (Fernea 1998:106, 113, 120). (Editor)]

If the penal and commercial codes are inspired by French law, the Moroccan code of family law is inspired by the *Chariâ* (*Islamic Law*), especially that of the Malékite rite. Although the *Chariâ* accepts polygamy with up to four legitimate wives, Moroccan law adopts some restrictions with the view of limiting the practice of polygamy, and poses conditions of equality in the treatment of the co-spouses. Polygamy is to be avoided when a disparity is to be feared (Article 30.1).

On the other hand, Moroccan women still have not been able to reach a real emancipation and autonomy vis-à-vis men, despite the important changes observed in our modern society. The Moroccan woman still commonly estimates the man to be superior to her, tolerates work of a temporary nature, judges having children, especially boys, as all important for inheritance, thinks that virginity is of major importance, and accords a great place to the ceremony of marriage. The woman in our society is a woman in evolution, but she remains linked to the group (Amir 1988; Kacha 1996; Moussaid 1992). This woman is opposed to the total transformation of those who might lead us toward an insecure situation. This opposition is because of internal resistance that is linked to the educational and external schemas in the measure where the social milieu brakes this desire for change (Amir 1988; Kacha 1996).

On March 12, 2000, two rival demonstrations by several hundred thousand Moroccans bore testimony to the transitional tensions and evolution evident in our country. The issue of both demonstrations was a government plan for a variety of social and human rights reforms proposed by the new King, Mohammed VI, who came to the throne after the death of his father, King Hassan II, in July 1999. Among other reforms, the government plan would fully replace with a court divorce the practice of repudiation, in which the husband can divorce his wife by a triple verbal declaration. The reform would also provide for equal division of money and property in a divorce, and support a literacy program for rural Moroccan women, over 80 percent of whom are illiterate. In the capital, Rabat, 200,000 to 300,000 members and representatives of women's groups, human rights movements, and political parties ended their march supporting the reform with a concert. In Casablanca, at least 200,000 men and women marching in separate columns—some claimed twice that number—denounced the reform (Associated Press 2000).

[In terms of judiciary power, Morocco is far ahead of Egypt, with 20 percent of its judges being women, compared with no Egyptian female judges. On the other hand, whereas Egyptian President Sadat appointed 35 women to his country's Parliament in 1981, Moroccan women had to wait 37 years following independence to have two women elected to the Moroccan Parliament (Fernea 1998:117). (Editor)]

C. General Concepts of Sexuality and Love

In Islam, the love of God occupies a big place in the heart of the believer with regard to carnal love. This has not prevented sexuality from flourishing with the advance of Arab-Islamic civilization, across the different dynasties, in passing through the great sociocultural cities of Damas, Baghdad, and Cairo (Malek 1995). Since those early times, the arts, knowledge, amorous poetry, and sexual culture have not ceased to deteriorate. This degradation puts in relief the contradictions that exist between the religious law and the traditions that are a part of what is prescribed by Islam concerning sexuality and what is forbidden within the family, in the extended community, and in the whole society. While the Muslim religion is more permissive, in contrast to Christianity, it gives primacy to carnal pleasure within the framework of marriage as a means of union with the other and with God. This glorification of sexual pleasure is a necessary ornament to the existence of the believer. Sexual abstention is, consequently, advised against, almost forbidden: "Rahbaniatan: The monasticism that they [Christians] have created has not ever been recommended or enjoined by us," the Koran tells us. The *nikah* (marriage), the religious and judicial framework in which sexuality exerts itself, organizes the sexual connections, their breaks, their changes, and the practical consequences that they entail.

2. Religious and Ethnic Factors Affecting Sexuality

[To understand Moroccan culture, one needs to have some sense of the Spanish, French, Portuguese, Berber, and Arabic influences that have been blended together to create modern Moroccan linguistic heritage and customs. In Moroccan civil law, we are dealing with Islamic law, local customary law, and the resonance of tribal law, Spanish and Portuguese customs, and the French penal code. Attitudes toward women, for instance, come not only from Islam, but also earlier presences, such as the Tuareg nomads in the south and the mountains. When Herodatus spoke of the "blue men of the desert," he commented on how socially strong the Tuareg women were, and called them Amazons. When the Tuaregs became Muslims, they kept their tribal laws (Fernea 1998:63-64). (Editor)]

A. Cultural Factors

The sexual behavior of humans is largely influenced by their sociocultural context. In our societies, to bring up the subject of sexuality is *hchouma*. This word is delicate to translate: On the one hand, it means "disgrace," on the other hand, it means "modesty." It is a code to which one conforms without reflecting on it and which legislates all the situations of existence. *Hchouma* presents itself thus like a thick veil that separates two worlds in total opposition: The one is governed by local customs and excludes every possibility for a being to affirm oneself as an individual, except for the social model. The other universe is done in silence and in secret. It is the world of the person beyond the conventions (Naamane 1999).

In the Arab world, sexuality remains a taboo, the oppression of women keeps their appearance more archaic; however, many voices are being raised against this state of things. Thus, many voices are being raised to denounce the situation of women in the Arab world and especially the sexist discrimination: polygamy, the wearing of the veil, and their non-participation in public life (Attahir; Cherni 1993; Kacem 1970).

In Morocco, the role of the woman and her status varies as a function of her ethnic origin, of her rural or urban setting, and of her socioeconomic and intellectual level, among others. Thus, according to the last census (1997), only a quarter of the urban women are illiterate, compared with 89 percent of rural women. Likewise, with the practice of polygamy, which varies according to the regions. The Berbers and the Fassis are less polygamous than the inhabitants of the Chaouia (region of the center). Women of the Moroccan Rif and of certain regions of the north work in the fields, assuming the rougher tasks, while men are generally passive. However, these women benefit from more experience, the right to education, and the right to work. But despite the recent changes in women's personal status [*mudawana*], more limits are emphasized in the persistence of polygamy, no right to divorce (the husband's prerogative), and no equality for inheritance, where a daughter inherits half of what a son receives.

However, misogyny remains common currency in Morocco; the woman holds a social status of second rank. She often remains less desired at birth than the boy. She frequently has less access to education. If she works, she has to do double work: professional activities and household activities. And she owes obedience to her husband.

B. Source and Character of Religious Values

Knowing that 99 percent of Moroccans are Sunni Muslims, a remark must be made immediately: Islam is far from being the religion most repressive of feminine sexuality as it is current to believe; well to the contrary, Islam's view of sexuality takes more of the sense of a sacred duty, where erotic practices are encouraged, pleasure is pursued, and the satisfaction of the woman is indicated. Islam distinguishes itself in this way from the Judeo-Christian culture, where sexuality is a "regrettable necessity," a moment of victory of the body over the soul according to classical duality (body/soul, good/bad).

In considering woman as an erotic and seductive being, but also deceptive, Islam creates fears of the ominous role she can play in destabilizing society. Thus the prophet said: "I will not let this point be the cause of worse discord for men than for women."

Mernissi (1983) writes in this framework: For Islam, the woman is an invincible seductress, the undoing of the man is inevitable if he does not have recourse to God. The prophet orders his disciples: "Do not visit the women alone, Satan will seize you" (Berrada et al.). In order to avoid the ominous consequences of that sensual and seductive tyranny over the social equilibrium, the Koran has foreseen the following measures:

- *Prohibition of Coeducation.* However, in Morocco, coeducation in the primary and secondary schools and universities is a current practice. Women have the right to enter any profession or job. Just recently can one find women employed as traffic police.
- *Wearing of the Veil.* In Morocco, one finds great freedom regarding the wearing of the veil. Despite the extremist events that have occurred over the years, Morocco has witnessed a rise of integration and accommodation. Although the number of women who wear the veil has increased greatly, the wearing of the veil is a trivial act, neither rejected nor required.
- *Sexist Discrimination and Oppression of Women.* Islam has attributed to women the status of minors. During all periods of life, it is the man (father, husband, or son), who manages her life. She owes him obedience and submission. She can be beaten in the case of disobedience (*Les Femmes IV*: Sourat 38).
- *Polygyny.* Islam gives to man the right to have four wives at the same time (*Les Femmes IV*: Sourat 3). In defense of this right, the Imam Ghazali explains: "There are some men whose sexual desire is so ebullient, that a single woman does not satisfy them and does not protect them against the risk of becoming adulterous. It is desirable in this case that they marry several women (from one to four) (Al Ghazali 1992). Thus, on the one hand, for Islam, it is the woman who is a seductress and nymphomaniac. On the other hand, it is the man who needs four women to appease his needs! Mernissi (1983) poses the question whether it is not the dreaded polyandry that is at the base of the conclusions regarding the erotic nature of women. The sexual satisfaction of women is taken into account by such laws that made sexual satisfaction of the woman a conjugal right in the case of polygamy and that authorized divorce in the case of the impotence or abstinence of the husband. Thus, the sexually satisfied woman will not try to look for sexual pleasure in illicit extramarital relationships.
- *Control of Women's Sexual Practices.* Islam constrains the woman to make love with her husband every time that he wants. In the case of refusal,

she exposes herself to the curse of God. The prophet, reported by Boukhari, said: "The woman who refuses to satisfy the needs of her husband is cursed until she accepts."

Islam gives the woman the right to accept sexual pleasure. Thus, "the preliminary games [loveplay] (*mulaaba*) are warmly recommended by the prophet," "caress your women until they are tender." These preliminaries are destined for the satisfaction of the woman, just as the sexual act is not a bothersome duty, but the happiest gift from heaven (Boudhdiba 1986).

The frequency of marital contact has also been regulated. Thus, the Imam Al Ghazali (1992) recommends that Muslims make love with their wives as frequently as possible. He proposes for the polygamous at least one contact every four days.

Sodomy is prohibited. "Cursed are those who take the woman by the anus," said the prophet (Al Ghazali 1992). Sexual contact during menstruation is forbidden by the Koran (*The Génisse II*: Sourat 22). Masturbation, even though not forbidden, is not recommended. It is permitted only in the case of the risk of adultery or in the event marriage is not possible. Sexual contacts outside of marriage are prohibited.

3. Sexual Knowledge and Education

A. Government Policies and Programs

Sexual education, such as is seen in European and North American countries as part of the programs of academic study, does not exist in either primary or secondary academic programs. What is taught is provided in the form of scientific knowledge of the anatomy of the sexual organs and of the biology of fertilization. This sexual education is centered on procreation and prevention of sexually transmitted diseases.

B. Informal Sources of Sexual Knowledge

The expression "sexual education" is part of the multiple taboos that characterize our society. The subject frightens and worries Moroccans, because there has always been confusion between sexual education and sexual freedom. Discussing sexuality with parents remains a strong taboo in Morocco. A certain difference exists between the two sexes. For all young children, boys are encouraged to display their genital organs, whereas girls are supposed to hide their intimacy. At the time of preadolescence, the girl has discussions with her mother who believes her role is to inculcate in her daughter the obligation to preserve her virginity and to avoid all sexual contact before the bonds of marriage. During these discussions, she prepares her daughter for puberty. The principal role of the mother is to obligate her to preserve her virginity with a talk full of modesty and *hchouma*. On the other hand, the preadolescent boy is left to his own devices, and has no one with whom to talk about his bodily transformations other than his friends and companions. A study in 1992 (Naamane 1999) showed that in 360 Moroccan men, divided equitably between the urban and rural areas, no man had ever gotten information from his father. In one case, the father made an allusion to the puberty of his son to ask him to begin to fast. Thus, in these situations where the young lack total communication about anything sexual with their parents and elders, it remains only to the young of their age, the media, and popular speech.

4. Autoerotic Behaviors and Patterns

Autoeroticism, in its broadest sense, is not condemned by the *Fikh* (religious law). Moreover, no Koranic verse mentions masturbation as a prohibited practice, so it is both a quite common and well known sexual outlet. The point of contention concerns the obligation of ablutions after involuntary touching of the genitals (Rissala in Malek, 1995, p. 29). In the rural areas, masturbation, as much as zoophilia, remains the instrument most used in a male youth's apprenticeship in sexuality. Adolescents masturbate themselves, often in a group, making from this event a competition that consecrates the one that ejaculates quickly and most strongly. If masturbation among adolescents is hushed, ignored, but not tolerated, that of adults is almost a sacrilege. It is a *hchouma*, more than a disgrace, without being truly illicit. In the popular mind, the fingers of the hand can symbolize the spelling of the word *Allah*: The little finger indicates the letter *A*, the ring and middle finger represents *LL*, and the closed index finger and thumb represents *H*, so the hand symbolizes *Allah* and must not be used as a sexual instrument.

5. Interpersonal Heterosexual Behaviors

A. Children

Infantile sexuality absolutely is said not to exist in our context. Instead, from early childhood, one inculcates an implicit sexual education totally antagonistic to the consideration of the two sexes. The sexuality of a boy is praised and valued. He must forge his virility from his young age; he must be the stallion who must get hard in the presence of a woman (Malek 1995). The sexual education of girls is done traditionally by the women of the family, by mothers, aunts, and older sisters. The older women tell the young girl what is forbidden and what is recommended in terms of repressing their sexuality.

B. Adolescents

Female adolescence is dominated by the repression of sexuality with the objective of preserving an intact hymen, the symbol of chastity, until the wedding day. The education of the senses of the body is negative and tends to block the personality of the girl on both the physical and psychic planes. The adolescent girl carries the mark [*prégnante*] of *hchouma* (disgrace) and honor, which crystallizes itself in the obsession with virginity (Naamane 1990). This education is perpetuated by the mothers, who make each step of the evolution of the girl a shock lived in anxiety. However, a study in the urban areas observed that "in three decades, the proportion of women initiated in the elementary principles of their sexuality changed from 38 percent to 55 percent." This initiation touches on two essential questions, menstruation and the gaining of knowledge of sexual contact (intercourse) (Naamane 1990). Paradoxically, in the large cities like Casablanca, girls have access to sexual information at a precocious age.

C. Adults

The sexuality of adults is only conceived of within the framework of marriage. The couple is then an inescapable notion and an obligation that brings one to social conformity. However, the stakes of control in this institution are varied. Contrary to the apparent patriarchy, there are many households that are managed by women with strong personalities. This reality is reinforced by the number of children: The more children a woman has, the greater is her power. And it is not by chance that polygyny is predominant in certain regions more than others.

[In the northern coastal region of the Rif, patterns of authority in the traditional Moroccan family are changing because of a major economic reality. Local unemployment has drawn 60 percent of the fathers and sons in the Rif to Europe in search of employment, leaving many households headed by women. At the same time, Morocco is witnessing an increase in the number of young and middle-aged women choosing to remain single. Almost invariably, these singles by choice are economically self-sufficient and well-educated (Fernea 1998:104, 116)

[The preliminaries to a traditional Islamic marriage negotiation are concerned with class, family histories (blood), and the dowry. Marriage in Morocco today involves new concerns about common goals, joint religious faith, educational background and career potential, and love and romance. In the High Atlas Mountains, the Ait Haddidou tribe follows a very different set of marriage customs. During the annual *moussem* or festival season in Imilchil, men and women arrive looking for mates. The divorced, single, young, and middle-aged come in hopes of finding true love or at least a suitable partner. The village notary publics register the couples, so there is some record, but it is commonly understood that the couple can split up after a day or a month or a year, with no cost, no hard feelings, and no religious stigma (Fernea 1998:64, 88-89, 104). (Editor)]

As for extramarital relations, they are illicit. But socially, the "treachery" of the woman is much more condemnable than that of the man. In reality, after 30 or more years of marriage, the woman often becomes much more demanding with regard to her husband and does not hesitate to get involved with extramarital relations. In urban areas, despite the traditional norms and ideals, marriage is more and more inaccessible because of material constraints, particularly, the high cost of living and high unemployment which make marriage impractical for many young men. The "detribalized" urban space creates intense sexual needs, but offers very few possibilities to satisfy them (Dialamy 1995).

In 1971, the average size of households was over 5.6 persons; this rose to 5.9 persons in 1982. In the same year, 1982, the rate of occupation was 2.3 persons per room. Many couples do not have a private bedroom. Thus, the beginning of a couple is hypothetical because of the absence of this exclusive and independent space that permits the spouses to isolate themselves during their sexual play, the condition imposed by the *Chariâ* and tradition.

Divorce by "repudiation" is an absolute weapon available only to the man, who can use it when he desires, even though the last modifications of the code of family law (1993) tend to humanize it more. The custody of children remains the full right of the mother, who to receive it should remain single until the boy is 12 years old and the girl is 14, the age at which a child has the right to choose the parent with whom he or she wants to live. When the mother remarries, the custody of the children returns automatically to the father (*Statut du Code* 1996).

Access to sexual pleasure is an inalienable right, prescribed by our religion, for both spouses to the same degree. Consequently, pleasure opens the path to all sexual practices. Only sodomy is prohibited by all the theological traditions. Instead, according to irrational popular ideas, the missionary position alone is well accepted. The other positions are seen as being generators of disorders and diseases.

6. Homoerotic, Homosexual, and Ambisexual Behaviors

A. Homosexuality

Homosexuality (*liwat*) derives from the name of Lot, whose person and tribe is mentioned on numerous occasions by the sacred books (Malek 1995). In Morocco, male homosexuality is considered a punishable offense by both the *Chariâ* and the civil penal code. This attitude pushes homosexual practice into a clandestine realm, with all the obvious consequences associated with such social denial. Conformity to all important social rules requires a male, regardless of his sexual orientation, to get married and have children. Within this façade of social conformity, homosexual males create well-closed spaces, cafés, cinemas, nightclubs, etc., where they can meet other like-minded males without endangering their façade. They are completely sealed to all who come to these places for encounters.

Female homosexuality or *sihaq* is not mentioned in the Koran. It is prevalent in certain regions of Morocco, particularly the north, but remains hidden, unmentioned, and unstudied.

B. Homoerotism

Westerners consider certain behaviors of Arabs in general as signs of latent homosexuality. It is a matter of certain completely acceptable male behaviors, like holding hands, putting an arm around another man's shoulder, embracing the face, bathing together (Moorish bath), and masturbating in a group during adolescence in rural areas. From our point of view, these behaviors have nothing to do with being sexual. They are part of our everyday culture.

7. Gender Conflicted Persons

No scientific work has been performed in the transgendered field. The real transsexual subject is rarely seen as anything other than an isolated entity. They are generally confused with homosexual persons or persons with other deviant behavior. Casablanca has been known for a long time as a city where transsexuals came from all over the world for sex change surgery. Although available, these operations were always practiced in a clandestine way.

However, cases do arise in the course of psychological consultations, in which the young behave in school or during everyday life in a manner opposite their sexual identity. In the course of follow up, some of these persons experience depression syndromes because of this conflict between their sexual identity and their social identity. Management of such cases is difficult in Morocco, where there is a complete legal void concerning this clinical entity.

8. Significant Unconventional Sexual Behaviors

Sexology in our context must take account of sexually deviant or perverse behaviors. The particularity comes from the fact that what is perverse for us in the East may not be considered so in the West and vice versa. In this framework, it is the conformity to the prevailing social rules that sets the criteria for normality. All behavior that does not obey the said social criteria, is considered in our society as an offense. The question that is posed then is: Why are we seeing many transsexuals and transvestites in the West and very few in our Islamic countries, and then only in very specific and close circles? In our point of view, the answer lies in the close relationship between behavior and the system (society and power) in which we are living. If the social system is too liberal, too permissive, it will favor easy access and freer expression of more sophisticated "perversities." At the same time, a too rigid and repressive system will favor the appearance of a meager, weak, and repressed sexuality (Moussaid 1997). See also the discussion of transvestism in Section 8D, Paraphilias, below.

A. Sexual Abuse of Children

The sexual abuse of children seems to be frequent, but is usually hidden by the families. In the legal field, these abuses are very seriously punished whether that abuse involves a male or a female child.

B. Prostitution

Prostitution or *zina* has always existed in our Arab-Muslim landscape, as it has in all historical civilizations. In the recent past, at the time of the French protectorate, prostitution was regulated and supervised in brothels. Today, it is repressed and constitutes an offense, which leads to other negative effects and risks. In effect, there is a "sexualization" of different social factors, which are becoming more obvious in our country. This "sexualization," evident in the prostitution relationship (giver-receiver), is generated by the material concerns and the crushing weight of the entire social system, which neglects the woman to the point where she is reduced to her body and to her sexual appeal, and is forced to rely on prostitution to survive. Prostitution may sometimes be ignored, because it is occasional, but even then, it does raise some problems. This appearance of sexual freedom is in fact a kind of slavery of the young girl who has affairs with many men, some old, some rich, some strangers, some unfaithful spouses, and some dissatisfied husbands (Moussaid 1997; Naamane 1990).

C. Pornography and Erotica

The pornographic industry, *khalâa*, as it exists in the West, is not present in Morocco. Instead, consumer spending has become more and more widespread, even while it is limited to certain social classes that are in contact with the Western world. The intrusion of the media, particularly satellite television and videocassettes, in our audiovisual field, has changed the previous situation by giving all levels and social classes access to pornographic images and materials. Meanwhile, the possession of pornographic documents, films, magazines, etc., constitutes a criminal offense. On the other hand, Morocco was unique in the Arab world, being the only Arab country where the ancient works of Arab erotology of the fourteen century, *The Perfumed Garden*, etc., were available. These books, which deal with sexual behavior and erotic pleasures, are now perceived as true pornographic documents, especially by young adolescents.

D. Paraphilias

Frotteurism

Frotteurism is a very prevalent behavior in our country, generated by the great frustration of the citizens. This frustration is a consequence of the years of repression, which censures all sexual relations outside the bonds of the marriage. The favorite place for this practice is the crowded public transportation system.

Zoophilia

In the rural world, zoophilia is still very widespread and not blameworthy. With masturbation, it constitutes an obligatory passage in the adolescent male's apprenticeship of sexuality. Although this practice has never been mentioned in the Koran, it is prohibited without question by the *Chariâ*: "He who has copulated with a beast, kill him and kill the animal."

Transvestism

Takhanout is more or less tolerated, insofar as in the past, women were absent from the artistic scene, and cross-dressing men played the role of women. This practice has always existed and exists still in certain domains where women have not yet gained access. These transvestites are in general homosexuals who practice without any impunity, as long as there is no public act.

9. Contraception, Abortion, and Population Planning

A. Pregnancy Outside of Marriage

Pregnancy outside of marriage is prohibited and remains punishable by law and religion. It appears that such pregnancies are more frequent in the urban than the rural areas, but no statistical study has touched this problem. However, there exist a not insignificant number of abandoned infants born out of wedlock, of which the state takes temporary charge in anticipation of their being adopted by welcoming families.

B. Abortion

Only therapeutic abortions are authorized and practiced in a hospital setting. Non-therapeutic abortions are practiced secretly by physicians in private practice following standard medical methods. There are no accurate official statistics. Moreover, considering that contraceptive methods are not taught to young girls who get involved with illicit sexual relationships, their pregnancies are candidates for the voluntary interruption of pregnancy (IVG, *interruptions volontaires de grossesses*). These IVGs are also frequent among married women who utilize IVG in case of undesired pregnancies.

C. Family Planning

Family planning is a program integrated within the healthcare system. It is based on the spacing of births and not on their limitation. It has contributed to reducing considerably the risks of morbidity and maternal and infant mortality. It is also an essential component of the strategy of the socioeconomic development of the country. The principal actors are the state in the public sector, the private sector, and the ONGs (*organisations nongouvernementals* or nongovernmental organizations, NGOs), in particular the Moroccan Association of Family Planning. The latest study documents the results of their efforts: 99 percent of married women have heard of at least one contraceptive method, and 92 percent know where to obtain information or services for at least one method.

By decreasing order, the best-known family planning methods are the pill, the intrauterine device, tubal ligation, condoms, the injectables, and the vaginal methods. The pill remains the contraceptive method the most used, with 64 percent in 1995 compared to 68 percent in 1992. The rate of contraceptive use has increased significantly since 1980. In effect, in 1995, 50 percent of married women utilized some contraceptive method compared to 41.5 percent in 1992, 35.9 percent in 1987, and 19.4 percent in 1980 (all methods combined).

The principal objectives of Morocco's family planning program are:

- To respond to the expressed and potential needs of the population concerning family planning and contraception;
- To attain a contraceptive prevalence in favor of the long-term methods;
- To modify contraceptive use in favor of the long-term methods;
- To involve the societal agents of the different agencies in our society— youth, sports, social affairs, agriculture, etc.—to participate in the promotion of the concept and methods of family planning; and
- To augment participation of the private sectors in the supplying of contraceptives to attain a balance between both private and public sectors, a kind of social marketing project. At the present time, the private sector accommodates 38 percent of the demand for contraceptive products.

10. Sexually Transmitted Diseases

The sexually transmitted diseases (*maladies sexuellement transmissibles, MST*) and AIDS (*SIDA*) are illnesses known all over the world, and Morocco and the Arab Muslim countries are not exceptions.

At the present time, there is the Program to Fight Against STD and AIDS under the direction of the Epidemiology and the Fight Against Illness Division of the Ministry of Health, which organizes those activities in coordination with elected leaders, the local authorities, and the ONGs (NGOs). Table 1 lists the incidence of several STDs since 1991.

The incidence of STDs is progressively increasing; it increased from 50,567 cases in 1991 to 189,021 cases at the end of 1997 and 100,827 cases in the first half of 1998, despite the underreporting of cases in the public sector and its almost complete absence in the private sector.

Table 1

Statistics on STDs in Morocco, 1991-June 1998

Disease	1991	1992	1993	1994	1995	1996	1997	1998 (June)
Yeast / Fungal	26,646	68,176	69,119	102,214	106,621	108,621	133,716	72,886
Urethritis	14,402	23,207	19,948	27,012	28,260	32,397	35,603	17,916
Syphilis	4,952	5,506	5,635	5,226	5,015	5,084	5,226	2,507
Chancre	2,161	2,981	3,153	3,720	4,742	4,289	5,807	3,081
Condyloma	761	775	429	451	804	1,138	662	285
Hepatitis	792	1,594	1,195	1,367	948	1,138	2,008	1,024
Genital Herpes	598	651	477	502	458	574	561	220
Other STDs	225	544	1,108	2,013	3,793	2,722	5,438	2,902
Total	50,567	103,434	101,065	142,505	150,541	156,722	189,021	100,821

(*Note Ministérielle No. 491* 1996)

The incidence of vaginal discharges (leukorrheas) is much higher than that of urethral discharges. In the early 1990s, syphilis outranked chancres (*Hemophilus ducreyi*), but this has been reversed in recent years. Eighty percent of the cases reported occur among 15- to 44-year-olds, with females accounting for 71 percent of the cases.

A variety of factors have contributed to the increase in STDs in Morocco, including:

- More than half the population is young;
- Tourism jobs in the country;
- The proximity of Europe and the important number of Moroccan nationals returning from abroad;
- The low socioeconomic level;
- The delay in the average age of marriage, which now approaches 30 years old;
- Self-medication by carriers of STDs;
- The anarchistic, unregulated prescription of antibiotics; and
- The poor use of condoms among those with extramarital relationships.

In 1999, the Ministry of Health launched a new public policy and strategy for taking charge of the STDs. This strategy adopts the syndrome approach, based on treating the patient at para-clinics without waiting for the results of biological tests. This approach, which seeks to intervene immediately to break the chain of transmission of these diseases, is based on epidemiological public health considerations, following the USAID project strategy, with the contribution of AIDSCAP and the University of Washington. In coping with the STDs in Morocco, one should not ignore the fact that half of the carriers of STDs self-medicate with antibiotics. This poorly advised and unregulated use of antibiotics is the cause of atypical and asymptomatic, highly contagious forms of STDs (*Note Ministérielle No. 26* 1997).

11. HIV/AIDS

The first case of AIDS was diagnosed in Morocco in 1986. Its appearance was one of the elements that has allowed the very wide development of programs for the prevention of STDs using all the latest approaches. Tables 2 and 3 summarize the AIDS statistics in Morocco.

Table 2

The Epidemiology of AIDS in Morocco, as of June 30, 1998

Cumulative number of cases of AIDS disease	510 cases
Number of declared cases in 1997	92 cases
Number of declared cases (June 1998)	46 cases
Number of adults affected (15-40 years)	351 cases
Number of children affected (age < 15 years)	21 cases
Cumulative number of deaths from AIDS	139 cases

Table 3

The Incidence of AIDS over Time

Year	New Cases	Accumulated Cases	Year	New Cases	Accumulated Cases
1986	1	1	1993	44	172
1987	9	10	1994	77	249*
1988	14	24	1995	57	306
1989	20	44	1996	66	372
1990	26	70	1997	92	464
1991	28	98	1998 (June)	46	510
1992	30	128			

*19 of the 77 new cases reported in 1994 had been previously counted as ARC (AIDS-Related Complex)

The age group predominantly affected is from 15 to 40 years old (69 percent). Ninety percent of the HIV-positive children are infected perinatally. Males account for 70 percent of the cases. The other particulars of AIDS in Morocco are: 42 percent are bachelors; 35 percent are married women; 85 percent were infected while living in Morocco; and 15 percent are recent immigrants.

Transmission modes include: heterosexual, 61 percent; homosexual, 10 percent; intravenous drug use, 9 percent; multi-risk, 8 percent; transfusion, 4 percent; perinatal, 4 percent; and unknown, 4 percent. Before the 1990s, the main modes of transmission were homosexual contact and IV-drug use; at present, the dominant mode of transmission is heterosexual intercourse.

In 1995, males with AIDS outnumbered females by three to one. The age distribution of AIDS cases was: 15 to 29, 24 percent; 30 to 39, 43 percent;

and 40 to 49, 12 percent. STD patients, tuberculosis patients, and pregnant women showed an approximate seroprevalence of AIDS of 1 per thousand. Eighty-three percent of the cases were urban, with the most cases reported in Oujda, Rabat, and Tangier. The transmission by blood products has noticeably diminished thanks to the screening by the Centers of Transfusion of the Kingdom, from 11.4 percent to 4 percent in 1998. However, the prevalence rate of HIV among blood donors, which was 1.3 per 10,000 in 1996 and 2 per 10,000 in 1997, had changed to 8 per 10,000 at the end of June 1998.

The actual prevalence rate of AIDS disease is 0.02 percent, which places Morocco among countries less touched, at the same level as the countries of the Maghreb in the western extremity of the Islamic world (northern Africa) and the Middle East.

In April 1998, the Ministry of Health adopted a national strategy to take charge of the HIV/AIDS challenge (*Circulaire Ministérielle No. 7* 1998). This strategy defines the modalities of the diagnosis of HIV, the prescription and utilization of the antiretrovirus (ARV) medications, the biological follow up, and the reporting of cases. The program is financed in its majority by the Ministry of Health, as well as by certain ONGs (NGOs).

The new program is based on two major, well-equipped facilities, the Hospital Ibn Sina in the capital city of Rabat, which serves the north of the country, and the Hospital Ibn Rochd in Casablanca, which covers the southern part of the country. These two centers work in close collaboration with referring centers at the regional level. Reporting cases of HIV/AIDS is obligatory in accordance with the 1995 decree of the Ministry of Public Health. In Morocco, because the country has endemic tuberculosis, the early pursuit of the *Koch bacillus* bacterium is systematic among seropositive patients.

Another aspect of the campaign against HIV/AIDS are sensitization and education programs, especially those for women, which are reinforced every year on December 1, on the occasion of the worldwide day of the fight against AIDS. Sensitization programs have also been implemented for health care professionals. HIV-detection equipment at all centers for blood transfusions has clearly improved the quality of donated blood. At the same time, a considerable effort was made to educate all professionals traditionally at high risk, such as barbers and dentists. More basic in the prevention of STDs and AIDS is the improvement of the socioeconomic level of the country.

12. Sexual Dysfunctions, Counseling, and Therapies

A. Female Sexual Dysfunctions

Although female sexual dysfunctions are frequent in our society, they are usually concealed by society. Vaginismus represents the most frequent motive for a sexological consultation, because it puts the life of the couple's relationship in danger. Women who suffer from vaginismus do not consult a professional counselor or therapist until they are driven to do so by the partner and/or the family. In Morocco, the causes of vaginismus are, most often, a restrictive religious education, negative beliefs relative to the anatomy of the hymen, misconceptions about the mechanism of penetration, and sexual assault traumas (rapes and attempted rapes), which, unlike in the West, are rarely reported.

Anorgasmia, or inhibited female orgasm, is also frequent, but rarely constitutes a motive for a sexological consultation. Here, as with vaginimus, the causes are restrictive education, negative beliefs relative to female sexuality in general, the awkward behavior of the man, a lack of the development of fantasies [*agénésie fantasmatique*], and the prohibition of childhood and adolescent masturbation.

B. Male Sexual Dysfunctions

Erectile dysfunctions (ED) are very frequent among men and affect all ages and all social classes. An epidemiological study in the general population with a representative sample ($N-651$) showed that globally, 54 percent of the men presented some erectile dysfunctions, distributed as mild in 38.8 percent of men, moderately troubling in 15.1 percent, and severely troubling in 1.1 percent (Berrada et al.). But only a small minority of males who admitted to ED were willing to take responsibility and seek treatment. That is because of their socioeconomic conditions and certainly because of the feeling of disgrace and devaluation that the patient experiences when he sees in the therapist a rival who will judge him. Also keeping the patient from seeking help for ED are the irrational folk ideas that accompany sexual impotence, which suggest that it is because of *tqaf*, a form of sorcery, which is treatable by a faith healer (*marabout*). Apart from the well-known organic causes of diabetes, high blood pressure, cardiopathies, cholesterol, iatrogenicity, smoking, etc., the psychogenic causes are more frequent for men over 40 years old. These may include conjugal monotony associated with the lack of fantasizing, and may be aggravated by performance anxiety. In effect, the process of fantasizing, in our society, is associated with adultery, and accordingly, are prohibited and inhibited for the majority of men. Among young adults, the relationship of circular causality, where various psychogenic factors—for the most part, religious and educational— interact, is a common cause of erectile dysfunction (Bonierbale 1991).

Premature ejaculation is beginning to become a very frequent symptom and a motive for consultation, more than before, when it was considered an indication of virility that one learns in the course of the collective masturbation during adolescence. At the present time, men are becoming more and more conscious of the frustration of their wives, and are thus beginning to take responsibility for it. A very frequent symptom in our cultural context is an association of premature ejaculation with the feeling of having a small penis. Constrained to conceal his assumed handicap, the subject will ejaculate quickly in a hurried sexual encounter.

C. Therapies

The therapeutic modalities available for male and female sexopathies are varied. Therapy is available from general practitioners, urologists, psychiatrists, endocrinologists, gynecologists, etc., as well as by sexologists and andrologists, who are a small minority in the health care community. However, almost all of the patients will consult first, if not in an exclusive way, with the traditional faith healers (*marabouts*). The therapeutic arsenal from which medical personnel can draw is rather rich. The most recent products, intracevernous injections (IIC), Viagra, and aphrodisiacs, were available in Morocco before the majority of European countries made them available in the market.

13. Research and Advanced Education

The domain of teaching and of sexological research is still timid in our country. The Moroccan Association of Sexology (L'Association Marocaine de Sexologie, AMS) began an ambitious program in this domain after 1994. This program rests on the organization of an annual congress, with the participation of numerous experts in the sexological world, and of round-tables on a particular theme. Meetings and congresses of the AMS are organized in a different city and under the aegis of a different university each year. Among the objectives of the AMS is the installation of a program of teaching or a course of sexology within a university framework, and the organization of fundamental research oriented especially toward anthropological, psychological, psychoanalytic, sociological, neurological, biological, judicial, medicolegal, physiological, pathological, experimental, and therapeutic aspects of sexual behavior. This research should result in a conceptualization of sexology that is adapted to our Moroccan context. Given that the actual sociopolitical climate is not favorable, the AMS has decided to limit this discipline to the medical domain (sexual pathology). This adoption of sexology by the medical sciences may be only beneficial in the short run. The focusing on sexual behavior, in the long term, needs a reaffirmation and an acceptance of this science by society and by the medical community. Because sexology carries at the present time a pejorative connotation, research on sexual behavior is marginalized (Moussaid 1997).

Three professional organizations deal with sexological issues in Morocco:

The Moroccan Association of Family Planning (Association Marocaine de Planification Familiale, AMPF), 6, Rue Ibn El Kadi Casablanca, Morocco.

The Moroccan Association of Sexology (L'Association Marocaine de Sexologie, AMS), Abderrazak Moussaid, M.D., 38, Boulevard Rahal El Meskini, 20 000 Casablanca, Morocco; +212-2-298-381 or +212-2-298-331; fax +212-2-221-114; psych@casanet.net.ma.

Les Orangers, E.Abdel Krim Hakam, Executive Director, Rabat RP, Morocco (or BP 1217, Rabat RP, Morocco); +212-7-721-224; fax: +212-7-720-362; cable: FAMPLAN RABAT.

References and Suggested Readings

Al Boukhari. *Al jamii assahi.h.* Egypt. Imprimerie Principale: Livre 67, Bab 85.

Al Ghazali. 1992. *Attib annabaoui* (in Arabic). Beyrouth: Dar AL Fikr.

Amir, A. 1988. Conditions sur la situation psychosociologique actuelle de la femme algérienne. *Présence Femme*, pp. 133-136.

Associated Press. 2000 (March 12). Moroccans and women: Two rallies. *The New York Times*, (March 13), p. 8.

Attahir, H. *Notre femme dans la législation "Charia" et la société* (in Arabic). Tunis: Société Tunisienne d'Édition.

Badran, M. 1995. *Feminists, Islam, and nation: Gender and the making of modern Egypt.* Princeton, NJ: Princeton University Press.

Beck, L. G., & Keddie, N., eds. 1978. *Women in the Muslim world.* Cambridge, MA: Harvard University Press.

Berrada, S., Kadirin, N., & Tahiri, S. (1999. Unpublished). *Dysfonctions érectiles, étude épidémiologique au Maroc* (*N* = 651).

Bonierbale, M. 1991. L'homme impuissant. Le premier entretien. *Sexologies*, *1*(1).

Bouhdiba, A. 1996/1986. *Sexuality in Islam* (trans., A. Sheridan). London: Routledge & Kegan Paul. *La sexualité en Islam.* Paris: PUF.

Brooks, G. 1995. *Nine parts of desire: The hidden world of Islamic women.* New York: Anchor Books/Doubleday.

Circulaire Ministérielle No. 7. 1998 (February 4).

Cherni, Z. 1993. Les dérapages de l'histoire chez T. Haddad. *Les travailleurs, Dieu et la femme* (pp. 137-147). Tunis: Édition Ben Abdallah.

Dialmy, A. 1995. *Logement, sexualité et Islam.* Casablanca: Edition Eddif.

Fernea, E. W. 1975. *A street in Marrakesh: A personal view of urban women in Morocco.* Prospect Heights, IL: Waveland Press.

Fernea, E. W. 1998. Morocco. In: E. W. Fernea. *In search of feminism: One woman's global journey* (pp. 62-143). New York: Doubleday.

Giami, A. 1991 (December). De Kinsey an SIDA. *Sciences Sociales et Santé, 9*(4):23-55.

Kacem, A. 1970. Libération de la femme (in Arabic). *Le Caire: Dar maarif Egypte*, p. 87.

Kacha, N. 1986. L'algérienne et le changement. *Présence Femme*, pp. 137-140.

Malek, C. 1995. *Encyclopédie de l'amour en Islam.* France: Payot.

Mernissi, F. 1983. *Sexe, idéologie et Islam.* Paris: Tierce.

Mernissi, F. 1991. *The veil and the male elite: A feminist interpretation of women's rights in Islam.* Reading, MA: Addison-Wesley.

Mernissi, F. 1993. *Islam and democracy: Fear of the modern world.* Reading, MA: Addison-Wesley.

Moussaid, A. 1992. Les motivations de la polygamie: Mémoire de le fin d'études de sexologie, University of Paris XIII (unpublished lecture), Casablanca, Morocco.

Moussaid, A. 1997 (September). La sexologie un concept à redéfinir: Communication au 1er Congrès de l'Association de Sexologie (unpublished lecture), Casablanca, Morocco.

Murray, S. O. 1997. Woman–woman love in Islamic societies. In: S. O. Murray & W. Roscoe, eds., *Islamic homosexualities: Culture, history, and literature.* New York/London: New York University Press.

Murray, S. O. 1997. The will not to know: Islamic accommodations of male homosexuality. In: S. O. Murray & W. Roscoe eds., *Islamic homosexualities: Culture, history, and literature.* New York/London: New York University Press.

Murray, S. O., & Roscoe, W. 1997. *Islamic homosexualities: Culture, history, and literature.* New York/London: New York University Press.

Naamane Guessous, S. 1990. *Au-delà de toute pudeur.* Casablanca: Eddif Maroc.

Naamane Guessous, S. 1999. *Enquête sur la puberté, la ménopause et l'andropause.* In press.

Naipaul, V. S. 1998. *Beyond belief: Islamic excursions among the converted peoples.* New York: Random House.

Note Ministérielle No. 26 du 23/06/1997. DELM/35.

Note Ministérielle No. 491 du 18/03/1996. DELM/35.

Note Ministérielle No. 1491 du 02/09/1996. DELM/35.

Note Ministérielle No. 1957 du 12/12/1998. DELM/35.

Parrinder, G. 1980. *Sex in the world's great religions.* Don Mills, Ontario, Canada: General Publishing Company.

Recensement général de la population et de l'habitat au Maroc de 1994. Caractéristiques socio-économiques et démographiques. 1996 (January). Rabat: Direction de la Statistique.

Statut du code personnel "mudawana." 1996. Casablanca: Edition Dar Attaqafa.

Nigeria
(The Federal Republic of Nigeria)

Uwem Edimo Esiet, M.B., B.S., M.P.H., M.I.I..D.,*
chapter coordinator, with
Christine Olunfinke Adebajo, Ph.D., R.N., H.D.H.A.,
Mairo Victoria Bello, Rakiya Booth, M.B.B.S., F.W.A.C.P.,
Imo I. Esiet, B.Sc, LL.B., B.L., Nike Esiet, B.Sc., M.H.P.
(Harvard), Foyin Oyebola, B.Sc., M.A.,
and Bilkisu Yusuf, B.Sc., M.A., M.N.I.

Contents

[*Editor's Note*: This chapter presented an unusual editorial challenge, in that on most issues, two or more contributors chose to provide complementary insights and information. This is particularly valuable because the contributors approached the topic from different gender, professional, religious, and ethnic (tribal) backgrounds that clearly enrich the views and

Communications: Dr. Uwem Edimo Esiet, Action Health, Inc., P.O. Box 803, Yaba Post Office, Lagos, Nigeria; ahi@linkserve.com.ng.

interpretations presented. In Section 8A, Significant Unconventional Sexual Behaviors, Coercive Sex, Christine Olufunke Adebajo, Deputy General Secretary of the National Association of Nigerian Nurses and Midwives, and Imo I. Esiet, a member of the Nigerian Bar Association, present not only their own respective views as a Nigerian woman and man, but also the two complementary views of two women's rights advocates, one a health care professional and the other a lawyer. To identify the contributors of these varied views, their name or names are given at the beginning of a section or in brackets [name] at the end of individual paragraphs.

[This rich diversity of perspectives on one of Africa's major nations is also apparent in the unusual comparisons of tribal and regional differences on sexuality education, menstruation, sexual intercourse, conception and pregnancy, menopause, homosexuality, and male and female circumcision presented in this chapter. The information in these comparisons is based on the responses of local health care professionals who met in Lagos, in January 1999 under the aegis of Action Health, Inc, headed by the main author of this chapter, Uwem Edimo Esiet, with Nigerian government leaders, nongovernmental organizations (NGOs), and international United Nations agencies. The comments are from many health care professionals and social workers based on their field observations and experiences with clients in their own regions (Francoeur, Esiet, & Esiet 2000). (Robert T. Francoeur)]

Demographics and a Historical Perspective

A. Demographics

Nigeria is located on the southern coast of the horn of northwest Africa. Its 356,667 square miles makes it about twice the size of the state of California. Benin lies to Nigeria's west, Niger to the north, Chad and Cameron to the east, and the Gulf of Guinea to the south. Geographically, the country is divided into four east-to-west regions: In the south is a coastal mangrove swamp ten to sixty miles wide; in the north is a semi-desert. In between are a tropical rain forest fifty to a hundred miles wide and a plateau of savanna and open woodland. Nigeria is currently made up of thirty states plus the Federal Capital Territory of Abuja; sixteen of the thirty states are situated in the northern Muslim-dominated part of the country and the other fourteen in the predominantly Christian south.

Like all African nations, Nigeria's boundaries are the capricious result of European colonial conquests and power struggles that ignored ancient tribal and ethnic distributions. To understand sexual attitudes, customs, and behavior in Nigeria, one must be aware of the diversity of tribal, ethnic, and religious traditions among its 118 million people. Nigeria has over 250 distinct tribal groups. Slightly over 20 percent of Nigerians are ethnic Hausa, 20 percent are Yoruba, 17 percent Ibo, 9 percent Fulani, while the remaining one third belong to other ethnic minorities. Half of the population are Muslim and live mainly in the north; 40 percent are Christian mainly concentrated in the south. Ten percent of Nigerians practice one of the indigenous religions.

Nigeria's 1999 estimated population of 118 million was predominantly rural, with 40 percent living in the urban centers. By the year 2001, half of Nigeria's youth were expected to live in cities, searching for better living and job opportunities. The population of Nigeria is expected to double by the year 2025, from its current 118 million to 238.5 million. The people are decidedly on the young side, with 45 percent under age 15 and 57 percent under age 24. Slightly over half of all Nigerians are between ages 15 and 65, and only 3 percent are over age 65. In 1997, metropolitan Lagos and Ibadan, the two largest cities, had an estimated 10.5 and 1.5 million inhabitants, respectively.

In 1999, the average life expectancy at birth was 52 for males and 54 for females. The crude birthrate was estimated at 41.8 per 1,000 population, the infant mortality rate at 69.5 per 1,000 live births, and the crude death rate at 13 per 1,000, giving a natural annual population increase of 2.9 percent. In 1998, the number of births an average Nigerian woman was predicted to have—the Total Fertility Rate (TFR)—was six births per woman, placing Nigeria 26 among 227 nations. In 1994, Nigeria had one hospital bed per 1,070 persons and one physician per 4,496 persons.

Education is free and compulsory between ages 6 and 15, with about 42 percent of the youth attending elementary school. In 1998, over half of the population was literate. The per capita Gross Domestic Product in 1996 was $1,380.

English is the official language, but Hausa, Yoruba, and Ibo are also widely spoken. Because communications have become a major factor in changing sexual attitudes and behavior, it is worth noting that Nigeria has one television set for every 21 persons, a radio for every nine persons, and a telephone for every 118 persons.

B. A Brief Historical Perspective

Between 500 and 200 B.C.E., the Nok culture, in what is today's Nigeria, was one of the richest and most advanced ancient civilizations in west Africa.

Around 1000 C.E., the Muslim Kanem civilization expanded into northern Nigeria. By the fourteenth century, the amalgamated kingdom of Kanem-Bornu took northern Nigeria as its political center, dominating the Sahel and developing trade routes that stretched throughout northern Africa and as far as Europe and the Middle East. During the fifteenth and sixteenth centuries, the Hausa Songhai empire rose to power. The Hausa Songhai were overthrown by the Fulani Muslim leader Uthman Dan Fodio, who created the Sokoto caliphate.

At the same time that the Muslim Kanem civilization expanded into northern Nigeria, around 1000 C.E., southern Nigeria was dominated by the Yoruba, whose Oyo kingdom was centered at Ife. The Oyo kingdom gave rise to the Benin civilization, which flourished from the fifteenth to the eighteenth centuries. The Benin culture is famous for its brass, bronze, and ivory sculpture.

The Portuguese established trading stations on the Benin coast in the fifteenth century. Initially, the contact and trade relations were cordial, and Benin became well known in Europe as a powerful and advanced kingdom. However, with the rise of the slave trade, which began with the cooperation of the Benin kings who brought slaves from the interior, relations became hostile, and Benin declined under European pressure. The Dutch, British, and other Europeans competed strenuously with Portugal for control of the slave trade. Britain seized the port of Lagos in 1861 during a campaign against the slave trade, and gradually extended its control inland with the exploration of the Niger River until about 1900. By the end of the nineteenth century, because Britain had suppressed the slave trade, they transported the slaves they captured aboard European ships to Freetown in Sierra Leone.

In 1861, Nigeria became a British colony. Despite native resistance, the colony was expanded in 1906 to include territory east of the Niger River, which was called the Protectorate of Southern Nigeria. The two areas were administratively joined in 1914.

During the 1920s, Britain began to respond to Nigerian demands for local self-rule. In 1946, the colony was divided into three regions, each with an advisory assembly. In 1954, the colony was reorganized as the Nigerian Federation, and the regional assembles were given more authority. Nigeria became independent on October 1, 1960, and a republic on October 1, 1963. Attempts to partition the country along tribal lines for administrative purposes provoked controversy, and charges of corruption and fraud in elections held in 1964 and 1965 led to violence and rioting. In January 1966, civil war broke out when Ibo army officers overthrew the central government and several of the regional governments. Prime Minister Balewa was killed, along with many other political leaders in the northern and western parts of the country, and the Ibo forces took control of the government

The new government abolished the country's federal structure and set up a strong central government dominated by the Ibo. Anti-Ibo riots broke out in the north, and many Ibos were massacred. In July 1966, the Ibo leader was assassinated by a group of northern Yoroban army officers, who formed a new military government. The people in the eastern region refused to acknowledge the new government. In 1967, they seceded, proclaiming the eastern region as the Republic of Biafra. This plunged the country into a devastating civil war that left over a million dead, including many Biafrans (Ibos), who died of starvation despite international relief efforts. The war ended in 1970, and within a few years, the Ibos were reintegrated into national life.

A civilian government returned to power in 1979 after thirteen years of military rule. Four years later, a military coup ousted the democratically elected government, and has remained in power ever since under various leaders. Revenues from the export of crude oil have made possible a massive economic development program, but agriculture has lagged.

1. Basic Sexological Premises

A/B. Gender Roles and the Sociolegal Status of Nigerian Females with Implications for the Male

IMO I. ESIET

Issues of Nigerian Constitutional Law

The social and legal status of women has, over the ages, been a cause for grave concern in every culture and clime. In some areas, this concern has passed the stage of sympathy and has entered an era of aggressive feminism (Oputa 1989:1). In Nigeria, as in other countries, the time has come to recognize that denial of rights solely because one is a woman is a human rights violation. Practices that expose women to degradation, indignity, and oppression on account of their sex need to be independently identified, condemned, compensated, and, preferably, prevented (Cook 1994:228).

A wide range of evidence can be cited for a constructive trend in modern legislation on women's rights that are relevant to Africa and to Nigeria. Examples of this trend include the Convention on the Elimination of All Forms of Discrimination Against Women, the International Covenant on Economic, Social, and Cultural Rights, the 1981 African Charter on Human and Peoples' Rights (which endorsed the United Nations Declaration on Human Rights and the Human Rights Covenant), and the 1979 Constitution of the Federal Republic of Nigeria. Although the clear trend is to establish women's equality with men before the law, the battle against sex-based discrimination and for equality of opportunity, equal pay for work, equal privileges, and equal access to political, social, and religious power is still raging with unabated fury in Nigeria (Oputa 1989:4).

According to Rebecca J. Cook, the term

> discrimination against women shall mean any distinction, exclusion or restriction made on the basis of sex which has the effect or purpose of impairing or nullifying the recognition, enjoyment or exercise by women, irrespective of their marital status, on a basis of equality of men and women, of human rights and fundamental freedom in the political, economic, social, cultural, civil or any other field. (Cook 1994:235)

The constitutions of most African countries today affirm the right to non-discrimination on the basis of sex. Other rules of law and legislation may, however, discriminate against women in certain instances. Even where provisions of law are not overtly discriminatory, their application to women may yield discriminatory results because of women's economic and social positions in society (Ilumoka 1994:341). In this section, we examine the constitutional provisions for and cultural rights of Nigerian women. (Legal provisions related to marriage, sexual coercion, and prostitution in Nigeria are dealt with in Sections 5C, Interpersonal Heterosexual Behaviors, Adults, and 8A and B, Significant Unconventional Sexual Behaviors, Coercive Sex and Prostitution.)

The Constitution of the Federal Republic of Nigeria (1999) succinctly highlights the fundamental human rights to which all persons are entitled. These are the usual civil and political rights contained in most modern constitutions (Ilumoka 1994:314). Chapter 4, section 39, of the Nigerian Constitution provides that:

1. A citizen of Nigeria of a particular community, ethnic group, place of origin, sex, religion, or political opinion shall not, by reason only that he is such a person
   a. be subjected either expressly by, or in the practical application of any law in force in Nigeria or any executive or administrative action of the government to disabilities or restrictions to which citizens of Nigeria of other communities, ethnic groups, places of origin, sex, religions or political opinions are not made subject; or
   b. be accorded either expressly by, or in the application of, any law in force in Nigeria or any such executive or administrative action, any privilege or advantage that is not accorded to citizens of Nigeria of other communities, ethnic groups, places of origin, sex, religions or political opinions.
2. No citizen of Nigeria shall be subjected to any disability or deprivation merely by reason of the circumstance of his birth.
3. Nothing in subsection (1) of this section shall invalidate any law by reason only that the law imposes restrictions with respect to the appointment of any person to any office under the state or as a member of the armed forces of the Federation or a member of the Nigeria Police or to an office in the service of a body corporate established directly by any law in force in Nigeria.

Section 39 renders all laws, including customary and religious laws, subsidiary legislation, regulations, and official government practices that permit discrimination against women unconstitutional, null, and void. The only exception, stipulated in subsection 3, relates to appointments in the public service, the armed forces, and the police force. In effect, Nigerian women, therefore, have all the human rights stipulated in the Constitution, including the right to non-discrimination on the basis of sex. However, they enjoy no positive rights specifically addressed to their particular needs or vulnerabilities, nor is there any statutory recognition of the need for such rights (Ilumoka 1994:316).

Chapter 2 of the Nigerian Constitution, "Fundamental Objectives and Directive Principles of State Policy," contains principles of economic, social, and cultural rights relating to equal access to resources, provisions of basic needs, an adequate means of livelihood, provision of adequate health facilities for all, and free education. The State has a duty to conform to, observe, and apply these principles and provisions, but cases of alleged non-observance cannot be tried in court (Ilumoka 1994:314). The distinction made between the internationally accepted economic, social, and cultural rights guaranteed by the "Fundamental Objectives and Directive Principles of State Policy" and the fundamental human rights in the Nigerian Constitution clearly indicates that there was no intention to enforce them. Accordingly, Jadesola Akande asserts that:

> The Nigerian Constitution has entrenched fundamental rights and made them justiciable* but economic and social rights have been reduced to a mere declaration of pious hopes because it is believed that they can only be achieved progressively according to available resources of the Nation and the policies pursued by the Government. (Akande 1989:123)

In addition to the various constitutional provisions guaranteeing fundamental human rights, Nigeria subscribes to various international declarations and charters, which aim at eliminating discrimination against women (Oyajobi 1986:16). Article 18(3) of the African Charter on Human and People's Rights became national legislation with Nigeria's Ratification and Enforcement Act of 1983. This Act provides that "the State shall ensure the elimination of every discrimination against women and also ensure the protection of the rights of the woman and the child as stipulated in international declarations and conventions." To be able to ascertain how much real emancipation women have received in Nigeria, we need to examine the treatment of women in Nigeria by the laws of the land (see also Sections 5C, Interpersonal Heterosexual Behaviors, Adults, and 8A and B, Significant Unconventional Sexual Behaviors, Coercive Sex and Prostitution).

Specific Issues of Sex Discrimination

Women's Property Rights. The unmarried woman has the same right to hold property as any Nigerian male under both customary and statutory law. Also, since the passage of the Married Woman's Property Act of 1982 (Otaluka, 1989) as amended in 1993, a married woman has the right to contract as a *femme sole* [single woman] to the extent of her separate property. However, it has been a long-standing custom that women in some areas of Iboland cannot acquire immovable property like land. Iboland women are devoid of such contractual capacity (Otaluka 1989). This issue does not arise in Yoruba custom where both married and unmarried women have the full capacity to contract, acquire, and dispose of all forms of property, including land.

Women's Rights in Sureties. Although there are no legal provisions that distinguish along sexual lines between the rights and/or capacity of any citizen to stand as surety for another in an application for bail, Nigerian

---

*Any breach of such entrenched fundamental rights can be referred to the court for necessary redress.

police regularly deny women this right. This obviously contradicts every legal provision regulating bail practices; it also violates section 39(1)(b) of the Nigerian Constitution, which prohibits any executive or administrative practice that discriminates along sexual lines. The arguments for exempting women from the category of "fit and proper persons" are usually not based on any objective criteria.

Women and Income Tax Law. The Nigerian law on personal income tax discriminates largely against women. The tax system does not treat individuals within the marriage structure as persons in their own right. For instance, it is often generally assumed that the children of the marriage belong to the husband, and so it is to him that tax relief is granted. Married women who wish to claim tax relief for expenses related to rearing children are required to show documentary evidence of those expenses and evidence that the father of the children is not responsible for their upkeep. Men are not required to produce such documents. Although the Joint Tax Board justifies this practice by saying that these measures are designed to discourage duplication of claims, the present assumption in favor of the man is discriminatory and groundless.

Women's Inheritance Rights. Under the Yoruba customary law of intestacy, the succession rights of a male who dies without a will devolve not only on his children but also on his brothers and sisters. The Ibo and Bini Customary Laws are governed by the primogeniture principle, so that on the death of a male without a will (intestate), the eldest son succeeds to his estate. The widow, however, has no customary right to inherit her intestate spouse's property. Although death does not necessarily terminate a common (customary) law marriage, the rights of a wife to retain membership in her husband's family, and possibly maintenance, remain only insofar as she remains in her matrimonial home. This holds whether or not she chooses to marry her husband's kin, except where the latter is not raised as an option, but is made mandatory.

   Islamic law discriminates in the amount of entitlement granted the deceased intestate's children along sexual lines. The male children acquire in equal shares, whereas the daughters receive only a half share each. In a case where the deceased is survived by a single daughter, she would be entitled to only half the net estate, whereas an only son would take the whole estate. The widow is allowed a quarter of her husband's estate, whereas a widower takes half the net estate of the deceased wife (Lewis v. Bankole 1909; Adedoyin v. Simeon 1928).

Women and Passports. When a married woman applies for a passport, she is as a matter of practice required to submit a letter of consent from her husband. Similarly, a woman cannot apply to include the name(s) of her child(ren) on her passport without a letter of consent from her husband. There is, however, no such requirement for male applicants.

Conclusion

It cannot be argued more that there is an urgent need for a reappraisal of the status of women in Nigeria. The need to make all the constitutional rights of women a practical reality that would continually guarantee that they have their fair share of power, education, financial resources, positions, and so forth in our society cannot be overemphasized.

C. General Concepts of Sexuality and Love   UWEM EDIMO ESIET

Whereas sexuality is not openly discussed in Nigerian life, it is an underlying activity that is commonly displayed at publicly celebrated festivals. In most tribal cultures, dance dramas convey sexual values and attitudes as well as other more general messages. Similarly, folk tales and drama are used to depict specific tribal sexual values and expectations. This is particularly true of the tradition of early marriage, whether consented or forced, which is the most accepted means of containing adolescent sexuality. Issues of love of children, especially of males who will perpetuate the family name and heritage, also run deep within the family and society in most cultural settings.

In times past, the virginity of the female at her marriage called for a family celebration with appropriate gifts and visits from the in-laws. In some cultures, especially among the Yorubas, where "hawking" (street vending) and "night marketing" is common, young girls are learning to receive "passes" from men and acquire skills in dealing with these. Since the introduction of Western values and education in Nigeria, women have continued to acquire skills in dealing with males in a culture in transition. This has led to an increased tendency to delay marriage and an increased incidence of premarital sexual relationships. In some tribal cultures, in fact, it is more common today to demand pregnancy rather than virginity as a prerequisite for marriage. This is especially true among the educated young.

Also, most of the popular music and advertisements glamorize sexuality, even though there is still a strong disapproval of open discussion of sexuality.

2. Religious and Ethnic Factors Affecting Sexuality
BILKISU YUSUF AND RAKIYA BOOTH

A. An Overview and a Christian Perspective in Southern Nigeria
RAKIYA BOOTH

Religion and culture in Africa are closely interrelated. While religion has at times been used to oppress and exploit people, it has also been appropriated to enhance political liberation.

Maduro (1989) defines religion

> as a structure of discourse and practices common to a social group
> referring to certain forces (personified or not, multiple or singular)
> that believers consider as anterior and superior to their natural and

social surroundings in whose regard they express their sense of a certain dependency (through creation, control, protection, threat, or the like) and before which they consider themselves obligated to a particular pattern of conduct in society.

Every religion is situated in a specific human context in a concrete, determined geographical space, historical moment, and social milieu. Members of a religion share certain collective dimensions—social, economic, political, cultural, educational, military, etc. Religion is therefore closely linked and interrelated with all the dimensions of the life of a community. Because religion is part of a society, it follows that anything that affects people's lives will affect their religion. Hence, religion affects sexuality.

Nigerian society is dominated by two religions: Islam and Christianity. They are the main source of our Nigerian religious value systems, which affect sexual attitude and behavior. Christianity, for instance, expects men and women to hold in high esteem the religious value of sexual purity. Girls are expected to be virgins at the time of marriage. Islam allows female children to be given in marriage before the age of puberty. These practices ensure that the female child is a virgin at marriage. Similarly, Christianity and Islam emphasize that adultery is unacceptable. However, our culture expects men to do what women are not to do. Our culture allows and even encourages a man to contract polygynous marriages. While extramarital sex is publicly frowned on, a man who engages in extramarital sex is privately hailed for his behavior. The same culture deals severely and ruthlessly with married women caught in adultery. In both the Islamic and Christian religions, a man can ask for and be granted a divorce if his wife is confirmed to have committed adultery. This is not, however, the case if a wife discovers her husband's illicit affairs with other women.

Generally, Nigerian men believe that because woman was created out of a man, a woman must be subservient to man in all spheres of life at all times. Women are described as having a small brain in comparison to men's, being deficient in logic, analytical abilities, and critical thinking. In fact, this is the guiding principle that governs the behavior of Christian women who are the most submissive. While women constitute a larger portion of the church membership, women are not allowed to preach or take leadership positions in Nigerian Christian churches. As a result, women have been consistently kept passive and denied equal status with men in decision-making, both in the family and at the national level. Men believe that the only things women control are fertility and the sex of the child. Thus quarrels and even divorce arise where a marriage does not produce a child or where only female children are born.

Similarly, it is a taboo in the Islamic religion for a woman to lead prayers or pray jointly with men. Besides, local interpretations of both the Islamic and Christian faiths forbid men to accept sexual advances from their women. That is to say that sexual advances should be made by men, and not women.

B. The Muslim Hausa of Northern Nigeria

BILKISU YUSUF

The Hausa people constitute one of the most numerous and influential ethnic groups in West Africa. The majority of Hausa live in northern Nigeria, and in Nigeria's three neighbors, the Niger and Benin Republics and the Cameron. There is also a large population of Hausa living as immigrants in the Sudan Republic. Their language, Hausa, is widely spoken by about fifty million people in West Africa (Coles & Mack 1999:4).

Hausan history dates back to the eighth century when city-states and empires flourished in Western Africa (Crowther 1972). Tradition traces the establishment of the seven Hausa city-states to Abu Yazidu (Bayajidda), a prince from Arabia, who fled his homeland after a succession struggle. On reaching Daura, he killed the snake that had troubled the inhabitants of the city, and Daurama, the Queen of Daura, impressed by Abu Yazida's bravery, married him. They had seven sons who established the seven Hausa states (*Hausa bakwai*), Daura, Kano, Biram, Zazzau, Gobir, Katsina, and Rano.

The single most important factor that influenced the development of Hausa culture was their interaction with the peoples of North Africa through the Trans-Sahara trade. After Islam was introduced to the land of the Hausa by Arab traders, it gradually became the religion of the ruling class, and later the religion of the majority of Hausans. However, pockets of non-Muslim Hausa (*maguzawa*) still survive today and have retained their traditional religion. Although other ethnic groups, such as the Fulani and Kanuri, have mixed with the Hausa for centuries, the Hausa culture has retained some of its original features.

Hausa culture today is predominantly Islamic, making it difficult to distinguish tribal Hausa cultural norms from Islamic injunctions. Although Hausa culture has remnants of non-Islamic and distinctly indigenous practices that are part of their rites of passage, a marriage of convenience has evolved between Islamic injunctions and aspects of Hausa cultural norms that do not conflict with the religion.

Islam is a way of life for its adherents, with rules and regulations guiding all aspects of life. Its strong moral code emphasizes chastity, and prohibits loitering, soliciting, and unnecessary intermingling of the sexes. Islam permits women to go out of their houses only to pursue lawful needs such as the acquisition of knowledge or to work and contribute to societal development. Marriage before age 18 was the norm among Muslim Hausa girls before the colonial era and the introduction of secular education. Most parents in those days preferred to marry off their daughters at age 12.

The Qur'an, the basic source of Islamic law, allows the marriage of girls who have not started menstruation (*Qur'an Suratul Talaq*, verse 4). It is common among the Hausa to marry off preadolescent girls and delay the consummation of the marriage. Although the marriage of minors is lawful, the various schools of Islamic jurisprudence have guidelines about how such a marriage must be performed for it to be valid. Hammudahah Abd al'Ati (1982:70-84) clearly outlines the arguments for and against it. According to jurists and the schools of law, a minor cannot give herself away in marriage.

Her marriage must be arranged by her father and her consent sought. Others argue that the father may give his daughter away in marriage with or without her consent if she is underage, i.e., 9 years or younger, a virgin, and is given in marriage to a suitable and socially equal husband. The father in such a case is also her guardian (*wakil*), and Islamic law stipulates that the *wakil* must be legally and religiously qualified. As a legal guardian, he has authority to do only what is beneficial to his daughter or ward.

Arranged marriages were and are still common among the Hausa. In the past, some were actually arranged through pledges made by the parents while their children were toddlers. It is also quite common for the educated elite and royalty to arrange their children's marriages. Cousin marriages are also widely practiced among both Flausa and Fulani commoners and royalty, particularly so among the latter.

Marriage age in Hausa society is now gradually changing, shifting away from child marriages contracted at 7, 8, or 9 years of age, which were quite common in royal households in the past, and away from teenage marriages contracted at 12 years of age among the other classes. With the increase in the number of females attending school, the average marriage age is now 16 or 17 for secondary school graduates and 13 for those who drop out of school. However, the marriage age may be lower in rural areas, where fewer females attend school. It is a common practice for the formal Islamic marriage (*dauphi aure*) to be performed early, after which the girl continues her schooling for several years and completes it before the Hausa cultural ceremony (*hiki*) takes place and the marriage is consummated.

C. Character of Ethnic Values

Ethnicity develops and is expressed in multiethnic situations where a sense of "us" and "them" leads an individual or group to behave in exclusionary ways. This presupposes the existence of more than one ethnic group, an ethnic group being a group of people set apart from others by language, culture, political organization, territory, and myth of common descent. These shared group values constitute the basis for conscious identity and behavior by members when they relate with people from another group. However, it is important to point out that ethnic groups, such as those in Nigeria, are not necessarily homogeneous entities. Quite often, an ethnic group that contains several subgroups, languages, dialects, and cultural variations is classified as a homogeneous entity by bigots who emphasize selected specific traits as representing the whole group.

As with the Islamic, Christian, and indigenous religious traditions, the culture and norms of every ethnic group in Nigeria affects not only the sexual attitudes and behavior of its members, but all spheres of life. All ethnic groups in Nigeria believe strongly in sexual purity. Girls who are virgins at marriage are praised and showered with gifts. Married women are expected to avoid adultery. Although the same is expected of men, cultural norms give room for men to do otherwise. In a study of concubinage conducted among the Ngwa Igbo in southern Nigeria such norms are viewed as cultural discrimination, especially in a polygynous society that deprives women of sufficient sexual satisfaction and emotional security.

However, the idea of eliminating this discrimination would definitely be considered offensive by decision-makers, both at the family and legislative levels. Such a move, if ever contemplated by a woman, would end the marriage in divorce. Cultural values clearly demand that, because they are family-oriented, women must be honest with their husband and endeavor to prevent family disruption.

Studies have shown that women are more worried than men are by post-divorce problems. Furthermore, the wife's inability to initiate a divorce, the stigma of divorce, and a divorced woman's alienation from her natal descent group, along with early child betrothal and the payment of bride wealth, only increase women's subordination and resignation into acceptance of men's decision-making role in the family.

The subordination of women is most manifest in the family. It is in the family that one finds attitudes and behavior that give priority to education of males over females. Our culture believes that men have stronger sexual drives, need more sex than women do, and have greater control over sexuality. It is tradition and culture that socializes women to be sexually submissive to men. Moreover, it is the family and cultural attitudes that define the attributes of a good wife and, through sanctions, force females to fit into these qualities. To a girl, marriage is the ultimate goal. Hence, following cultural and family dictates, she has to appear less intelligent than men and behave with a certain amount of diffidence in dealing with men if she is to achieve that aspiration.

Economically, Nigerian women are expected to be dependent on men in line with their traditionally assigned roles of wives, mothers, and homemakers. Whereas men are trained for remunerative employment outside the home, the process of socialization prevents, limits, or demobilizes women in their march to economic emancipation. Men are regarded as the breadwinners of the family. Because "he that pays the piper dictates the tune," men make all major decisions in the family. For instance, development efforts that provide men access to factors of production simultaneously deny women access to production inputs, such as credit, ownership of land, and skill training. As the family breadwinner, the husband's domain includes all major decisions, such as number of children the spouse should have, the spacing of births, the couple's sleeping arrangement, use of contraception, and even the type of contraceptive used. Although this is a general cultural value, it does vary with the couple's level of education.

Generally speaking, Nigerian women are sexually submissive to men because of the culturally determined masculine roles performed by men. Men pay the house rent and children's school fees, provide kerosene or firewood for cooking, and fulfill other chores that steer men towards leadership responsibilities and give them the legitimacy of decision-making in the family and in the larger society. Still, the internalization and perpetuation of sex roles are achieved through socialization processes. Although Nigerian role stratification is unequivocally male-oriented, as principal actors in child socialization, women unfortunately are used as instruments for its propagation, enforcement, and perpetuation. There is a thriving attitude in Nigeria that a male child should, among other things, exhibit decision-making skills, whereas a female child is expected to be passive, submissive, and portray the "nice girl" image, an image which attempts to control women socially through value construction.

The Ibo culture gives women more freedom of assertion than either the Yoruba or Hausa cultures. Ibo and other cultural groups agree that household activities, such as the pounding of yam (*fufus*), sweeping, and similar domestic chores, should be jointly done by male and female children. The Yoruba, on the other hand, see such tasks as female responsibilities, thus creating gender gaps in the division of labor in the family. The Ibo allow some women to seek divorce, whereas the Yoruba encourage them to engage in extramarital sex. In both ways, ethnic values affect the sexual attitudes and behavior of people.

Both religious and ethnic values are thus intimately interwoven and most profoundly affect the sexual attitudes and behavior of Nigerians in all spheres of our social existence.

3. Sexual Knowledge and Education

A. Sexuality Education   UWEM EDIMO ESIET AND FOYIN OYEBOLA

Because of the culture of silence on sexuality, there has been little or no structured way of teaching Nigerians about sexuality. In the late 1950s and early 1960s, family planning education was introduced in some areas of Nigeria. However, this met with considerable opposition from cultural traditions and religious institutions. At the time, the only way a wife could have access to family planning services was with the prior consent of her spouse. This situation has changed in recent years and married women can now obtain family planning information and services without the husband's consent.

The government has been working to get POP/FLE (population and family life education) into the schools' curricula, and this effort is ongoing. However, adolescents continue to be denied access to sexual information and services on a national scale. There have been some efforts by non-governmental organizations (NGOs) to assure that marginalized groups have access to sexuality education. This effort is increasing as data from studies continue to show that five out of ten girls and seven out of ten boys have had sexual intercourse at least once by the time they leave secondary school.

In 1996, this effort culminated in the production of *Guidelines for Comprehensive Sexuality Education in Nigeria*. This effort by about 20 government and non-governmental organizations was publicly released by the then-Minister of State for Education chief, Mrs. Iyabo Anisulowo. Despite this laudable effort, the government still did not take the bold step of ensuring access to this education of our youth out of deference to the interests of religious leaders. However, in March 1999, at the Forty-Sixth Session of the National Council on Education, a resolution to integrate comprehensive sexuality education into Nigeria's school curricula sponsored by the Federal Ministry of Education, was unanimously ratified. As a result, the federal Ministry of Education made a historic commitment to implementing sexuality education throughout Nigerian schools. (National Guidelines Task Force 1996; SIECUS 2000). [U. Esiet]

The majority of Nigerians have the misconception that sexuality is equivalent to coitus. This has been a major obstacle to the integration of sexuality education into school curricula and other youth-related activities. Because of this equation of sexuality education with intercourse, the focus tends to be on the biological components. [Oyebola]

Sexual Education and Discussion: A Regional/Ethnic Comparison

The following summaries of the attitudes and practices regarding sexuality education and the discussion of sex of several ethnic groups in eight geographical regions of Nigeria were compiled by the authors during a meeting with health care professionals in January 1999 (Francoeur, Esiet, & Esiet 2000) (see Editor's Note on page 351).

1. Regions: Ipoti-Ekiti, Oyo, and Yorubaland. Ethnic Group: Yoruba
   Sexual knowledge is acquired through storytelling myths, from peers, schools, apprenticeship centers, television, films, romantic novels, magazines, and over-heard adult conversations. There is no positive attitude regarding sexuality education. Educated adults see nothing bad in sexual education, but the uneducated say it is an abomination and such things should not be heard of. Sex is freely discussed in the beer parlor, at home when husband and wife are quarreling, or during marriage preparation in the church or mosque. Otherwise, sexuality issues are never discussed and people are repulsed by sexual talk. When compelled to discuss sexuality issues, the uneducated are very shy and hardly give any correct information of participation. More-educated persons discuss sex mostly among peers and with persons of the same gender.
2. Regions: Kano, Katsina, and Kaduna. Ethic Group: Muslim Hausa
   Most children in these states learn about sexuality through their peer groups, media, and films. Parents do not discuss sex with their children. Parents are very negative about sexuality education in the schools because of the misconception that it will negatively affect the children. People will discuss sexual topics freely among friends and peers.
3. Region: Borno
   Sexual information is acquired from peers as well as parents. The general attitude towards sexuality education in schools is negative. Talking openly about sexuality is clearly taboo.

4. Region: Benue. Ethnic Groups: Tiv, Idoma, and Isala

Children learn about sex from their peers, and through storytelling and the cultural practices of gender roles. Sexual intercourse is learned by experimentation. Mothers tell their daughters about the consequences of sexual intercourse when they start menstruating. They usually provide no knowledge on hygiene. People are generally not comfortable with sexuality education. Spouses rarely communicate about sexuality. They are, however, beginning to discuss family planning. Talking about sex is considered "wayward."

5. Regions: Akwa-Ibom and the Cross River: Ethnic Groups: Efik and Ibibio

Children acquire sexual knowledge by listening to stories told by their elders, by eaves-dropping on adult talk, and from older sisters, cousins, house helpers, school peers, and electronic and print media. Young people also learn about sex during moonlight activities with their peers. In these activities, known as *Edibe Ekok* (hide and seek), children make a ring with a broomstick with a sand heap in the middle, around which they sit, mostly naked. They try to locate a ring in the sand heap. When found, they are joyous and exchange pleasant times, which sometimes results in sexual activity. Knowledge about sexuality is considered inappropriate for children but acceptable for the married. Sexuality education is seen as a way of corrupting the children. People do not discuss sexual topics, but this can be done in private and secretly.

6. Region: Delta State. Ethnic Groups: Uhobod, Ibos, Ijaws, Isaw, and Itsekirus

Children learn about sexuality from their peers and from the media in urban areas. Most people view sexuality education negatively because they believe it initiates the young ones to sexual relationships. Discussion of sexual topics is taboo. Males do, however, discuss sexuality—especially when they want to tell their peers how many girlfriends they have had intercourse with.

7. Region: Edo

Children in Edo learn about sex through their parents but mostly through peers. The general attitude toward sexuality education is negative. Discussion of sexual topics is avoided because it is believed that discussing the subject will result in promiscuity and exposure of adolescents to bad influences. People do not easily discuss sexuality topics because it is considered a taboo.

8. Regions: Imo, Enugu, and Anambra States. Ethnic Group: Ibo

Knowledge about sexuality is picked up accidentally—mostly from peers. There is no formal sexuality education. Parents teach their children through their own attitudes and behavior. Knowledge comes mainly from peers. The Ibo believe talk about sexual matters is vulgar, sexual education should not exist, and sexuality should never be discussed.

B. Sexuality Education Among the Hausa

MAIRO V. BELLO, RAKIYA BOOTH, AND BILKISU YUSUF

Sexuality education among the Hausa is imparted by parents and by the Qur'anic schools (*Islamiyyah*). Parents teach the rudiments emphasizing the gender roles expected of men and women, while the details of sexuality are left to the Qur'anic school teachers who instruct the children in *fiqh*, the law of Islamic jurisprudence. The *fiqh* curriculum for children and adults of both sexes include lessons on the onset of puberty, menstruation (a sign of maturity for girls, when fasting becomes obligatory), and ritual purifications after menstruation, sexual intercourse, and childbirth. For the boys, instruction includes the discussion of wet dreams and voice changes as marks of the onset of puberty, when fasting becomes obligatory. Boys are also instructed in the requirement of a purification bath after sexual intercourse and wet dreams. All Muslim Hausa children routinely attend *fiqh* lessons, which prepare them for the prayers and fasting, the two fundamental requirements for Muslim men and women. *Fiqh* lessons also focus on what constitutes sexual intercourse, the virtue of abstinence for unmarried people, and what the law stipulates about fornication and adultery. [Yusuf]

Although adolescents in the predominantly Muslim Hausas are expected to learn about sexuality in *fiqh*, many Hausa boys, and most of the Hausa girls, are withdrawn from school, both Qur'anic and public, before they get to the stage of learning about *fiqh*. Those girls and boys who stay in school to the stage when *fiqh* deals with sexuality, often find that the instruction does not include much, if anything, beyond the rituals, purification baths, marriage, and divorce, because of shyness that is part of the societal culture and the culture of silence that surrounds sexuality issues in the Hausa society. [Bello]

Fiqh teaches that married couples are entitled to sexual satisfaction from their partners, and the absence of sexual satisfaction is a valid reason for divorce. Likewise, *fiqh* enjoins Muslims to maintain their chastity and avoid high-risk sexual behaviors. Affliction with a communicable disease, such as leprosy, and perhaps by extension one could add HIV/AIDS, is also a valid reason for divorce. [Yusuf]

Among Hausa parents, sexuality education is constrained by the cultural practice of *kunya* or modesty, whereby parents are too embarrassed or shy to impart sexuality education to their children. The observance of *kunya* varies from parents who do not show affection in the presence of their children and do not talk to their first child, to those who only refrain from calling the child's name and/or feel too shy to discuss sexual and reproductive topics with their children. In the extreme cases, *kunya* ensures that the child grows up without knowing who his mother is, with the father, stepmother, or grandparents filling the communication and affection vacuum created by the *kunya*-observing mother. The practice of *kunya* is being gradually eroded by the interaction of the Hausa with other ethnic groups, and young Hausa mothers these days refrain from observing *kunya*, calling their first children by their names and openly showing them affection. [Yusuf]

However, an aspect of sexuality education solely entrusted to parents in Hausa society is the expression of sexuality during courtship and marriage. Both Islamic and Hausa culture do not permit dating, but the suitor is allowed to visit the girl in her parents' house, discuss with her gifts (*zance*), and give her token money or presents (*toshi*). During such visits, the young couple is not allowed to stay alone in a secluded place. Although Hausa sexuality education and socialization is replete with measures designed to prevent premarital sexual intercourse, such attempts are being steadily undermined by the prevalent Hausa practice of sending children and young girls to hawk (*talla*). These hawkers (street venders) run the risk of early exposure to sexual overtures, sexual abuse, and harassment from unscrupulous men posing as buyers of their wares. [Yusuf]

C. Sexuality Education Among Christian Nigerians   FOYIN OYEBOLA

In Nigeria, the Catholic Church provides some limited sexuality education, emphasizing abstinence education for unmarried persons and the Natural Family Planning method for married couples and condemning other forms of contraception. Other Christian groups, especially the indigenous Christian churches, emphasize menstrual hygiene and the separation of women during menstruation as described in the Old Testament. These churches tend to be more liberal on premarital sex and polygyny. The modern-day Pentecostal churches tend to be more receptive to contraceptive use within marriage, while emphasizing premarital abstinence. Overall, the Christian churches have yet to pay sexuality education its deserved attention. [U. Esiet]

It would be incorrect to say that sexuality education is not being provided in Nigeria. However, what is taught is not as comprehensive as it should be. Whatever is provided can be called moral education. Most adults are not comfortable with the concept of "sexuality education," because of the ambiguity of the term *sex*, and because of the low level of knowledge about sexuality among adults. [Oyebola]

However, in recent years, challenges to societal values and serious public health issues and problems have made sexuality education increasingly acceptable everywhere, including the Christian communities and informal sources. The Christian churches have been recognized as an agent of socialization for young persons in Nigeria. Consequently, most of the churches, especially in the urban centers, have been sensitized by the relevant NGOs through seminars and workshops, while some of the key religious leaders have been trained as counselors and educators. [Oyebola]

The integration of increasingly comprehensive sexuality education into church activities is a slow process for now, but it is expected to pick up with time. Most of the churches plan various activities and invite experts to make presentations on such topics as "Adolescent Sexuality: Making Responsible Decisions," "Bridging the Parent–Child Communication Gap on Sexuality Issues," "Teenage Pregnancy and Abortion: Consequences and Prevention," "Sexually Transmissible Infections," and "Developing Positive Self-Esteem with Others." [Oyebola]

D. Informal Sources of Sexual Knowledge
UWEM EDIMO ESIET AND FOYIN OYEBOLA

There is a definite increase in the informal sources of sexual knowledge in Nigeria. Young people have access to a lot of information, including both foreign and local magazines, television shows (more foreign than native), books (mainly foreign), and peers. There is also what we refer to as "environmentally available sources of sexual knowledge" that accompany and are associated with the prevalence of poverty and unemployment, the increase in commercial sex work, and the international trafficking in commercial sex workers. Sexual knowledge is also picked up in the course of everyday living at neighborhood gatherings, affiliations, and at home as a consequence of the lack of privacy in many housing patterns. In general, the underground information network on sexuality has acquired greater prominence in the lives of Nigerians.

4. Autoerotic Behaviors and Patterns
UWEM EDIMO ESIET AND FOYIN OYEBOLA

A. Children and Adolescents

It is not unusual for the growing child to engage in thumb sucking and some self-body massage. Both behaviors are commonly frowned on by adults, and parents try to discourage both "bad" behaviors. Pacifiers are encouraged as a substitute for thumb sucking, but parents tend to punish masturbation. [U. Esiet]

Masturbation is a common sexual behavior in Nigeria among adolescents and adults alike. However, it is more common in adolescents, who rely on masturbation to satisfy their sexual urges. This they do by fondling the clitoris, breast, nipple, or penis. Masturbation is common in girls-only schools where same-sex relations occur. [Oyebola]

B. Adults

While adults may engage in masturbation, they do not openly admit to this practice, because the whole topic of sex is a taboo. However, some counselors and health care providers are beginning to encourage an open discussion of masturbation and recommending it as an alternative to risky sexual behavior. [U. Esiet]

5. Interpersonal Heterosexual Behaviors

A/B. Children and Adolescents MAIRO V. BELLO, NIKE ESIET, FOYIN OYEBOLA, UWEM EDIMO ESIET, BILKISU YUSUF, AND RAKIYA BOOTH

Puberty, Menstruation, First Sexual Intercourse, and Marriage

The northern area of Nigeria has the lowest age for first marriage. Local studies conducted among Hausa communities in Kano State, in Zaria (Kaduna State), and in Dutse (Jigawa State) have confirmed the prevalence of early marriage. Clara Ejembi, a staff member at Ahmadu Bello University, Zaria, found that 83.4 percent of girls in the Zaria Local Government Area were married before 14 years of age and 98.5 per cent before age 20. A study by Adolescent Health and Information Project (AHIP) in Kano and Jigawa States confirmed that 75.5 percent of girls who do not have formal education got married before the age of 13 years of age, while 99.5 percent were married before 16. Most Hausa adolescent girls are married before or as soon as they enter puberty, which occurs between ages 12 and 15 (Goddard 1995). [Bello]

In an AHIP study of adolescent socialization, most of respondents confirmed that they had their first menstrual period in their husband's house, suggesting that they were taught nothing about puberty before their first experience with menstruation. Research by the International Reproductive Rights Research Action Group (IRRRAG) found that the few young women who learned anything about menstruation before their first experience got their information from friends, books, or school teachers. [Bello]

Recently, however, the increased rate of Western-style education, a downward turn in the country's economy that has made marriage very expensive, and the terrible rate of inflation are affecting the age of marriage for young people. Many girls now get to finish their secondary school, and learn a little about puberty, their bodies, and life in general from school, friends, and the media before they marry. The boys now think that they cannot take wives because they do not have jobs, and families no longer live in communal settings, where feeding is centrally handled. Young Hausans are fast adopting the nuclear-type family setting because they think it is more convenient for them. [Bello]

According to the 1990 Nigerian Demographic and Health Survey, the median age at first intercourse for girls is just over 16 years. By age 18, 63 percent of women have experienced intercourse; by age 20, approximately 80 percent have experienced intercourse. Thirty-four percent of 15- to 19-year-old females are married and 27 percent of adolescent married women are in a polygynous union, with rural and northern women more likely to be in such a union. A 1992 study by Makinwa-Adelzusoye also showed that among urban youth aged 12 to 24, over 20 percent of the females are married compared to 3 percent of the males. [Yusuf]

A common though not recent pattern of marriage among the Hausa is for girls to have many suitors (*samari*) from whom she selects her mate.

Yet, it is not unusual to find forced marriages (*auren dole*) made out of monetary or other considerations in contemporary Hausa society. Victims of forced marriages may accept the union. However, there are instances when such brides leave the husband and return to their parents' home (*yaji*) or go to court to get a divorce. Forced marriages are now on the decline and are usually limited to girls who have not attained the age of puberty or do not attend school. Some girls are also withdrawn from school by their parents and given out in marriage. The prevailing economic hardship has made education too expensive for poor parents, who view marriage as a means of reducing the burden of maintaining their daughters in school (Goddard 1995; see also Section 2A, Religious and Ethnic Factors Affecting Sexuality, An Overview and a Christian Perspective in Southern Nigeria, for information about childhood and arranged marriages among the Hausa). [Yusuf]

Menstruation: A Regional/Ethnic Comparison

The following summaries of the attitudes and practices regarding menstruation of several ethnic groups in eight geographical regions of Nigeria were compiled by the authors during a meeting with health care professionals in January 1999 (Francoeur, Esiet, & Esiet 2000) (see Editor's Note on page 351).

1. Regions: Ipoti-Ekiti, Oyo, and Yorubaland. Ethnic Group: Yoruba
   In Yorubaland, menarche is seen as coming of age, and a young girl is then advised not to be close to a man because she may get pregnant. There are quite a number of taboos associated with menstruation. Powerful people, such as warriors and traditional leaders, are not supposed to copulate with their wives during this period because it neutralizes the efficacy of any charms they are using. Albinos are believed to be the result of conception occurring during the menstrual period. In Ipoto-Ekiti, a menstruating woman is considered dirty and people will not associate with her during this time.
2. Regions: Kano, Katsina, and Kaduna. Ethic Group: Muslim Hausa
   The social and cultural beliefs of the Muslim Hausa treat menstruation with silence. It is simply not discussed. If a single girl starts menstruating in her father's house, she is quickly given off in marriage to any available man. This is referred to as *Sadaka*. Menstruation prior to marriage is considered a bad omen. When a young girl begins menstruating in her father's house, her mother-in-law is faced with the task of teaching her all she needs to know about menstruation. During menstruation, women do not sleep with their husbands, do not say their five daily prayers, and are also not allowed to fast.
3. Region: Borno
   There are no special taboos or rites relating to menstruation in the Borno State.

4. Regions: Tiv-Benue. Ethnic Groups: Tiv, Idoma, and Isala

There are no rites or taboos related to menstruation in the Tiv-Benue State, except that a family must give a daughter in marriage when she begins menstruating. This early-marriage tradition, however, is weakening.

5. Regions: Akwa-Ibom and the Cross River: Ethnic Groups: Efik and Ibibio

Some people in this region see menstruation as an unclean process. They consider a woman dirty during her period. Hence, she should not cook or serve food at this time. Some churches and cults refuse to let women attend services during their period. Young menstruating women must hygienically and properly dispose of used sanitary napkins; otherwise, the enemy may use them to charm the individual. Sexual intercourse during menstruation is taboo. Menstrual cramps are relieved by using hot water to massage the waist and lower abdomen, by drinking illicit gin, and by taking a hot pepperish sauce to flush out the bad blood.

6. Region: The Delta State. Ethnic Groups: Uhobod, Ibos, Ijaws, Isaw, and Itsekirus

For people in these tribal groups, menstruation is a welcome development and a sign of attaining womanhood. In some parts of the Delta State, no special attention is paid to menarche, apart from the mother telling her daughter that she has become a woman and should not "go near men." In other regions, a girl who is already betrothed is visited by her prospective husband as a sign of homage to her family. In some areas, a menstruating woman is not restricted to any area within the compound; in other regions, she cannot stay in the main house with her husband and others. Instead, a mat is used to construct a hut for her, where she stays for about seven days. Some fathers may exempt their daughters from such restrictions. But if they do, the father must perform a ritual cleansing when the daughter's menses end.

7. Region: Edo

During menstruation, women are forbidden to prepare meals for their husbands. In fact, they must refrain from doing anything for their husbands during this period. A menstruating woman must not sleep in her husband's room, or even in their main house. People believe the husband may die if she doesn't comply.

8. Regions: Imo, Enugu, and Anambra. Ethnic Group: Ibo

In the past, a menstruating woman could not cook for her husband. This is no longer taboo. She cannot, however, have sexual intercourse during her period.

Courtship

When courtship reaches an advanced stage, the Hausa suitor indicates his intention to marry the girl by sending money. He also sends cosmetics and items of clothing (*kayan zance*) and money to her parents (*Gaisuwan uwa da uba*). Before the bride is conveyed to her husband's house, the groom's family sends *kayan sa lalle,* a combination of food and cosmetic items such as henna (*lalle*), sweets, perfumes, sugar, millet, and head ties. The millet and sugar are used to prepare *tukudi* for the bride. *Tukudi* is a porridge prepared from dates, millet flour, yogurt, cheese, spices, and herbs that contain aphrodisiac substances given to the bride a few days before she is conveyed to her husband's house. Because a lot of emphasis is placed on chastity, retaining one's virginity is a virtue. Hausa culture makes it desirable, if not compulsory, for the groom to send a gift to the bride's parents after the consummation of the marriage (*kama hannu*) in appreciation of the fact that she remained a virgin until her wedding night. The Islamisation of Hausa culture is steadily eroding the practice of the forceful consummation of marriage and the publicity given to a private marital affair between a couple. *Fiqh* teaches that the couple's sexual experiences are confidential matters to be disclosed only to a marriage counselor for counseling purposes. In contemporary times, especially among city dwellers, nobody asks questions about the wedding night and the status of the bride. [Yusuf]

Premarital Sexual Activities and Relationships
MAIRO BELLO, BILKISU YUSUF, AND FOYIN OYEBOLA

In urban Nigeria, premarital sexual intercourse can be defined as sexual relations prior to the time a woman is socially recognized to be married. Premarital sexual relations with the man a woman eventually marries, as well as with other men, are included in this definition, as long as the sexual activity takes place before the time societal norms confer on the woman the right to have a sexual relationship. Premarital relationships in the Nigerian setting are guided by normative principles and beliefs, whose baseline is premarital chastity. [Oyebola]

Anecdotes drawn from living Yoruba heritage and sexual networking in Ekiti District showed how the traditional Yoruba society attaches a high degree of importance to female virginity. Every new Yoruba bride is expected to be a virgin at the time of consummation of her marriage, that is, during the first night when the woman and the husband sleep together. A virgin bride has been a source of real pride to the family. [Oyebola]

In the Ibo tradition and the attitude towards virginity in urban Nigeria, it is said that "A woman never forsakes the man who breaks her virginity." Other informal studies of the Ekiti in Ondo State confirmed that virginity was so important that two women waited outside the couple's room on the wedding night to take the good news to her parents that the bride had been intact. In traditional Fulani and Yoruba societies, a white cloth was spread on the bed on the night of marriage consummation; in the morning, the cloth was examined for blood marks. The husband sent a gift of money and kola nuts to the bride's parents if the new bride was found to be a virgin. However, in order to forestall any departure from this norm, some girls were betrothed in childhood. [Oyebola]

With the advance of Western values, however, the situation has changed. Previous informal studies have indicated a gradual erosion of the traditional premarital sexual norms. This change in the norms may be a consequence of the transformation taking place in the institution of marriage itself and, in particular, the transition from family-arranged to individual-choice marriages. [Oyebola]

Informal networking among sexuality workers in the Ekiti District of Nigeria revealed that sexual activity begins at about 17 years of age for both males and females and that, while 33 percent of rural females were virgins at marriage, only 25 percent of the urban females were virgins at marriage. [Oyebola]

Other possible reasons identified for the erosion of the traditional premarital sexual norms are the education of young adults, the rural-to-urban drift, and, most recently, the poor socioeconomic situation in Nigeria, which has thrown many female young adults into prostitution or commercial sex work. [Oyebola]

With the breakdown in the traditional value system, the value placed on virginity is gradually decreasing. Among the Yorubas, the practice of spreading a white bed sheet on the couple's bed on the night of betrothal has almost stopped, especially in the urban centers. In the case of the Hausa-Fulani society, it has been reported anecdotally that the new bridegroom now sends money and nuts to the bride's parents whether or not the new bride is found to be a virgin. This observation suggests that attitudes towards premarital sexual relations are becoming more positive. [Oyebola]

Also, the longer period of schooling, the increasing divorce rate, and the fact that there is no longer insistence on the traditional virginity test indicate that the Ibo may not take a bride's virginity seriously anymore. Westernization has therefore shifted the emphasis on virginity from a reality to an ideal. [Oyebola]

This picture of an increase in premarital relations is confirmed by the 1990 Nigerian Demographic and Health Survey, which revealed that by age 18, 63 percent of Nigerian women had had intercourse while only 56 percent had married [Oyebola]. The 1988 Ondo State Demographic and Health Survey revealed greater exposure of young urban people to sexual activity. This was related partly to the influence of the mass media, as well as the availability of effective modern contraceptive methods that greatly reduce the rick of pregnancy in premarital relations. Other reasons why young people engage in premarital sex include:

- Ignorance about sexuality—it is still a taboo to educate young people about sexuality;
- The urge to experiment during adolescence without considering the consequences;
- For the fun of it and for sexual enjoyment;
- Peer pressure—doing it because others did it;
- Girls giving in to boys to show their love in the hope of marriage; and

- The influence of alcohol and drugs at parties, clubs, or drinking places. [Oyebola]

Traditionally, there were strict codes of sexual behavior and strict penalties were prescribed for transgressors. Indeed, the traditional custodians of society's values went to great lengths to ensure parallel but separate development of teenagers. Boys and girls were usually educated in separate institutions supervised by teachers of their own sex. In recent years, however, more and more schools are becoming coeducational. In addition, according to a 1992 study by Professor Makinwa-Adelzusoye, Nigerian youth today are maturing at younger ages and are doing so in an urban milieu that permits them a great degree of freedom from adult supervision. Add to this new environmental mix longer time in school, later marriage, urban mobility and independence, and financial hard times, and it is clear why premarital sexual intercourse is increasing among teenagers. As a result, today's young Nigerians are exposed to a lot of dangers, especially from unsafe sex, sexually transmitted diseases (STDs), HIV/AIDS, unwanted pregnancies, and unsafe abortions. [Bello]

In addition, Hausan youth appear to possess little knowledge of and considerable misinformation about contraceptives and their use. Less than 30 percent of Hausan youths used a contraceptive for their first intercourse. This proportion only increased to about 40 percent for currently young, unmarried, sexually active Hausans. These percentages are, however, higher than national rates as revealed by the Nigeria Fertility Survey (1981/1982). [Bello]

Many older Nigerians and religious leaders express anxiety about the moral decline reflected in premarital sex among adolescents and the increasing number of teenage pregnancies among students. Islam enjoins Muslims to remain chaste. To satisfy their sexual needs, Muslims are enjoined to marry. Although marriage is not compulsory, it is highly recommended as a very strong *sunnah or custom* in the tradition of Mohammed, the prophet of Islam. Muslims who have reached marriageable age and can afford it are enjoined to marry. Indeed, child and teenage marriage is often urged as a precaution against premarital sex and teenage pregnancies. [Yusuf]

Forced Marriages

In its proposal for a new social order for Kano State, the 1987 Committee for Women's Affairs identified forced marriages (*auren dole*), which are often contracted before puberty, as one of the causes of high divorce rates and prostitution. Young girls forced into marriage not infrequently flee their marital homes and seek refuge in brothels (*gidan karuwai*) in urban centers. When this happens, these girls are believed to have "disappeared" into the world (*shiga duniya*) or to have become their own mistresses (*mata masu zaman kansu*). There have been cases of young girls threatening to *shiga duniya* (disappear) if and when they are forced to marry husbands they do not love. [Yusuf]

Early fertility and early childbearing are linked to teenage and child marriage in Hausa society. According to Makinwa-Adelzusoye and Feyiset (1994:99), the fertility rate for women ages 15 to 19 is much higher in the largely rural north than it is in the south: 196 births per 1000 in the northwest, 212 per 1000 in the northeast, and 71 per 1000 in the southeast. The Nigerian Demographic and Health Survey of 1990 showed that one half of all women became mothers before age 20. Ten to 12 percent gave birth before age 15, and 21 to 28 percent gave birth between ages 15 and 17. [Yusuf]

C. Adults   MARIO BELLO, IMO I. ESIET, UWEM EDIMO ESIET,
                                 FOYIN OYEBOLA, AND BILKISU USUF

Premarital Relations, Courtship, and Dating   FOYIN OYEBOLA

Nigerian youths start dating at about age 16. Most of them date without knowing what dating entails, hence they do not know how to comport themselves during dates. There is a general belief that sexual intercourse must take place during dating. Most young people do not see dating as a first stage of courtship. Courtship in the real sense starts when young persons are in the tertiary institutions preparatory to marriage. Generally, the duration of most courtships is relatively short, and the courtship is kept secret from the parents so there is no parental guidance. (See Section 5A/B, Interpersonal Heterosexual Behaviors, Children and Adolescents, above for additional details on dating, courtship, and engagement.)

Conception, Pregnancy, and Sexual Intercourse: A Regional/Ethnic Comparison

The following summaries of the attitudes and practices regarding conception, pregnancy, and sexual intercourse of several ethnic groups in eight geographical regions of Nigeria were compiled by the authors during a meeting with health care professionals in January 1999 (Francoeur, Esiet, & Esiet 2000) (see Editor's Note on page 351).

1. Regions: Ipoti-Ekiti, Oyo, and Yorubaland. Ethnic Groups: Oyo, Yoruba, and Ipoti-Ekiti

   The Oyo do not allow premarital sexual relationships. They also view "modern" (non-male above) techniques of coitus as abnormal and unmentionable. They think sexual intercourse is solely for procreation; pleasure comes second. They prefer male offspring because they will carry on the family name. The Yoruba culture also prefers male offspring. In fact, a Yoruba man will seek a new wife if his current wife produces only girls. Sexual relations are male-dominated, with the male initiating it and dictating the pace. Female response or satisfaction is not considered important. Coitus takes place at night and in the dark. Among the Ipoti-Ekiti, premarital sex is a taboo. The male-above position is standard, and coitus is for procreation and not really for pleasure. Male children are preferred.

2. Regions: Kano, Katsina, and Kaduna. Ethic Group: Muslim Hausa

These cultures frown on premarital sexual relations. Sexual foreplay before coitus is also frowned on; sexual intercourse usually occurs in the dark or semi-dark. The man indicates his readiness to penetrate by clearing his voice. This tells the wife to position herself. The woman always remains clothed or at least semi-nude. At the end of sexual intercourse, both partners have a ritual bath called *Ghusul Janabat*. Male children are preferred because they continue the family name, help with the farming, and assure inheritance.

3. Region: Borno

Premarital sex is a taboo. Contraception is not acceptable. Female children are appreciated more than males.

4. Region: Benue. Ethnic Groups: Tiv, Idoma, and Isala

Premarital sex is not encouraged. A divorced woman, however, is free to have sexual relations with any man. Sexual relations are for procreation; hence polygamy is acceptable. Women abstain from sexual relations while breastfeeding. There is no foreplay before coitus and techniques for coitus are not even discussed. A wife must allow her husband to have a girlfriend, a "sister," from his own clan. The wife relinquishes the bed for the "the sister" and must treat her nicely. A man is always unhappy when his wife has a female child. The wife is believed to be responsible for determining the sex of the child. Fathers are responsible when children are well-behaved and mothers are responsible when a child misbehaves. Aleku is a traditional god of the Idomas. When a man marries, his wife takes an oath to Aleku, who oversees women and checks on their fidelity. During the Aleku festival, the men are allowed to have sex with any girl or woman who has not taken an oath to Aleku.

5. Regions: Akwa-Ibom and the Cross River. Ethnic Groups: Efik and Ibibio

Premarital sexual relations are considered an abomination. The male-superior position is conventional and foreplay is highly valued. However, because intercourse is for the man's satisfaction and for procreation, a childless wife has no place in her own home. Because women are believed to determine the child's sex, a woman who has only daughters is often thrown out of the home. A badly behaved child is usually blamed on its mother. Among the Efiks and Ibibios, during the "fattening period" before marriage, an engaged girl is taught how to manage and keep a clean home, take care of her husband, help him to reach orgasm, treat in-laws respectfully, care for babies and children, cook delicious meals, maintain personal hygiene, and do a full body massage. In this culture, there is no preference for male or female offspring; inheritance is by seniority and is hereditary.

In the river communities, a female is preferred for the first child, whereas the inland communities prefer the first child be a male. This has to do with the fishing and farming activities of the men. Wives visit their husbands in the fishing ports, like Bakasi, where the husbands also keep mistresses.

6. Region: the Delta State. Ethnic Groups: Uhobod, Ibos, Ijaws, Isaw, and Itsekirus

In some regions of the Delta State, sexual intercourse is sacred; in others, it is not a big deal. Premarital sex is taboo and shameful in areas where virginity at marriage is cherished, but it is allowed in other areas. A girl is expected to become pregnant soon after marriage. There is a preference for male children, and a woman who has only daughters is in trouble. More often than not, her husband and his family will hate her. Such husbands may take another wife.

7. Region: Edo

Wives must respond to their husbands' sexual demands. Male children are preferred. Premarital sexual relationships are accepted depending on the girl's age. It is discouraged in the teen years. The male-above position is preferred and intercourse is for procreation and to feel good. Pregnancy should occur in the first year of marriage, and the first child should be male. Female children are not warmly welcomed, although children are considered God-given and many children are a blessing.

8. Regions: Imo, Enugu, and Anambra. Ethnic Group: Ibo

Even though premarital sexual relations were previously prohibited, in some areas of Anambra it is no longer a crime. Pregnant teenage girls are quickly married because it shows they are fertile. The male-above position is preferred. Intercourse is for procreation. Conception is a thing of joy, but male offspring are preferred. Any odd behavior is inherited from the mother; the father only passes on good traits. Pregnant women are forbidden to eat certain foods, like snails and grass-cutter meats (herbivores), because they are believed to cause excessive salivation and prolonged labor.

Women and Marriage in Nigerian Law   IMO I. ESIET

Nigerian marital laws have helped to consolidate sex-role discrimination in the family. Traditional customs, known as the "customary law," is still accorded recognition in the area of family law, and in fact plays a very dynamic role in determining related issues.

Women and Parental Consent in the Bride Price and Marriage. According to Nwogugu, "For a girl, parental consent is mandatory under customary law even where she has attained majority, . . . on the other hand, an adult male may contract a valid marriage without the consent of his parent" (Nwogugu 1974:20). The reason given for this inequality is that the bride price, which is an essential characteristic of customary marriage law, cannot be properly paid, nor can the formal giving away of the bride be properly effected without parental consent. The bride price has been described variously as a gift in kind or monetary payment to the parent/guardian of a female person on account of marriage to that female person (Nwogugu 1974:50). Although bride price is supposed to be a token of appreciation for the worth of the female chosen as a bride, the amount of the modern bride price is less a token of appreciation than evidence that a daughter is regarded as an investment property whose total market value and capital outlay should be realized at the time of disposition. This situation has led to the intervention of the law in some jurisdictions, although the laws are hardly enforced. In 1956, for instance, the Eastern Region enacted a Limitation of Dowry law to regulate the amount that can be demanded as the bride price. The reality of this transaction having an economic and investment nature is evident in the entitlement of the husband to a refund of the bride price upon dissolution of the marriage.

Women and the Right to Consortium. By virtue of marriage, spouses acquire a right to associate in matrimonial circumstances (known as *consortium*) and enjoy certain incidental rights that flow from that marital/spousal relationship. Any interference with this right is actionable against a third party.

1. *Enticement and Harboring.* A spouse may bring an action against a third party for enticing, procuring, or inducing the other spouse to violate the duty to provide consortium to him/her. Whereas a husband can file a tort against another man for "harboring" his wife, a wife cannot make an actionable claim against another woman for "harboring" her husband (Adv v. Gillison 1962:390).
2. *Loss Due to Tort of a Third Party.* Whereas a husband can recover damages from a third party for loss of consortium and accompanying benefits or services of his wife as a result of that third party's action, a Nigerian woman does not have this same right and may not recover for the actual loss of consortium. She may, however, receive damages awarded for matters, which are somewhat incidental to the loss of consortium (Nwogugu 1974:66).
3. *Adultery.* Under statutory law, the right of claims in cases of adultery is mutually enforceable, because it is tied up with divorce grants based on adultery and there can be no separate civil action for adultery. However, in most parts of Nigeria, customary law recognizes only the husband's right to file claim against a third party who commits adultery with his wife. Hence, the husband can claim damages from the third party whether or not he uses the adultery to file for divorce from his wife. According to customary law, a wife can only apply for divorce if she claims adultery as the grounds for the breakdown of her marriage (Nwogugu 1974, chapter 7). In reality, Nigerian customary laws derive from the traditionally prevalent view that the wife is owned by her husband, whereas the husband is owned by no one but himself.

Hence, adultery with the wife offends against the husband's proprietary interest, and payment of some kind must be made to compensate. On the other hand, adultery by the husband does not offend the wife because he belongs to himself (Oyajobi 1986:30).

Women and Maintenance Under Customary Law. Although customary law recognizes the duty of the husband to maintain his wife, it does not provide any judicial machinery for enforcing this duty, except for the rules of the Maliki School of Islamic Law, which allows an Alkali court to issue an order to the husband. However, when a husband fails comply with this duty, even when ordered to comply, the Alkali Court, which is a customary Court, can do no more than grant dissolution of the marriage. The High Court, on the other hand, can enforce compliance to such duty.

Mothers and Child Custody. In the past, customary law gave the father absolute right to the custody of his legitimate children. This position, however, has been altered by recent statutes, particularly the Infants Law 1978 (Oyo State, Section 12:1). Also, the Matrimonial Causes Act (Section 71) places the parents of a child on equal footing, and the decision of the court is to give paramount regard to the interests of the child.

However, the customary legal systems on custody still discriminate against the woman. The right to custody of children is vested in the father, although the child's welfare is considered when the child is of tender years. In this particular case, although the mother may be given physical custody (when the parents are separated), Nwogugu notes that "the father's right is merely in abeyance" (Nwogugu 1974:260).

Women and the Matrimonial Home. Property disputes, especially regarding the matrimonial home, may arise between a couple anytime during the life of a marriage. Oftentimes, there are complaints from women that although they contributed to the acquisition of matrimonial property, their husbands disregarded their interest at later dates and disposed of the property without their consent. The property is usually purchased in the husband's name only. Efforts have been made in other countries to remedy this position; for instance, in 1967, England passed the Matrimonial Homes Act recognizing the rights of a spouse to occupy a matrimonial home whether or not that spouse is entitled by any legal right devolving on contract, by enactment, or estate (Section 1(1)). This was designed to protect a spouse who is not a legal owner against the power of the other spouse to dispose of the property and also against a third party purchaser. The spouse's right of occupation ceases on the termination of the marriage, except if an application is made to the court while the marriage subsists to direct otherwise by an order. Given the years of British colonial rule in Nigeria, legislation such as this protecting women's rights in England is used by women's rights advocates in their efforts of improve the legal status and protection of Nigerian women.

Since the right of occupation terminates with a divorce, the matter becomes one of property adjustment, and the court can be called upon by virtue of section 7(1) of the Matrimonial Causes Act to resolve distribution of the property in a way it considers just and equitable. Because of the special and domestic nature of the marriage relationship, transactions between couples are not evidenced in the same way as commercial transactions. But the position of the courts in Nigeria, as held in Nwanya v. Nwanya (NWLR 1987:3, 697), is that a claimant for settlement must show evidence of her contributions.

Marriage and Family   UWEM EDIMO ESIET

Individual married couples stipulate their sexual norms and values, protected by the male decision-making role and the custom of total silence regarding sexuality. Menopause may bring a major change, but the extent and nature of this effect has not been researched. Within the family incest is not accepted.

Menopause: A Regional/Ethnic Comparison

The following summaries of the attitudes and practices regarding menopause of several ethnic groups in eight geographical regions of Nigeria were compiled by the authors during a meeting with health care professionals in January 1999 (Francoeur, Esiet, & Esiet 2000) (see Editor's Note on page 351).

1. Regions: Ipoti-Ekiti, Oyo, and Yorubaland. Ethnic Group: Yoruba
   Menopause means a woman has finished her sexual activity. She can neither give birth nor give sexual pleasure to her husband. It is the end of her womanhood and her husband hardly gives her any emotional attention. A menopausal woman "is old and should be preparing for the grave." Women don't talk about menopause because there are no issues attached to it and it is not celebrated. Menopause often results in the man taking another, younger wife. Menopausal women are looked at as old people and are recognized as mothers, but not as wives.
2. Regions: Kano, Katsina, and Kaduna. Ethic Group: Muslim Hausa
   Special considerations regarding menopause are unknown.
3. Region: Borno
   "Menopause is like having a sleepy pregnancy." [There is no indication of whether this is good or bad.]
4. Region: Benue. Ethnic Groups: Tiv, Idoma, and Isala
   Menopause is rarely recognized, as life goes on normally. It simply means that a woman is getting close to retirement.
5. Regions: Akwa-Ibom and the Cross River. Ethnic Groups: Efik and Ibibio
   This culture does not accept or see menopause as a natural aging process. It is attributed to the attacks of witchcraft. When this happens,

the man starts looking for a younger wife, while the woman starts seeking a traditional treatment or cure. During menopause, women become psychologically unstable, suspicious, erratic, irritable, and talkative. Menopause means the woman has outlived her reproductive role and her usefulness in the home. A menopausal woman is not expected to continue sexual relations with her husband, so she arranges for a younger girl to live with her husband.

6. Region: the Delta. Ethnic Groups: Uhobod, Ibos, Ijaws, Isaw, and Itsekirus

    Menopause is seen as the end of a woman's reproductive and sexual life. Her husband may take another wife to satisfy his sexual urges. Menopausal women often become depressed when they feel they are no longer useful and therefore not cherished by their husbands.

7. Region: Edo

    Men do not find a menopausal woman useful or productive. People feel that the "bad blood" lost during menstruation now collects in the body, causing problems.

8. Regions: Imo, Enugu, and Anambra. Ethnic Group: Ibo

    Menopausal women gain more respect because they are now considered men. There are usually no acceptance problems for menopausal women. As for the men, they like running away from their menopausal wives, although our society frowns on this.

Cohabitation, Monogamy, and Polygyny   UWEM EDIMO ESIET

In the past two decades, an increase in the incidence of cohabitation has been observed. However, this is far from being the norm as it has become in Euro-American countries. Because this is a new phenomenon in Nigerian culture, the partners are left to work out their own terms and conditions as appropriate, without benefit of or guidance from the legal structure.

Monogamy has been the hallmark of Christian marriages, even though a few indigenous Christian churches allow or endorse alternatives. Polygyny has been a traditionally accepted marriage pattern in Nigeria and it continues to have some support among Islamic adherents and members of some indigenous Christian churches.

Divorce, Remarriage, and Extramarital Sex   UWEM EDIMO ESIET

"'Til death do us part" has long been the Christian marital ethic. However, this is increasingly being flouted, as spouses are now insisting on their personal rights within marriage, including the right to love and be loved, and have mutual respect and care for each other. Despite the Christian ethic, there is an increased incidence of divorce in contemporary Nigeria. Remarriage after divorce is also becoming more acceptable, especially within traditional tribal norms and Islamic practices and tenets.

Extramarital sex is permissible for the man but not for the woman. However, with the downturn in the economy and women being more assertive, such occurrences are becoming more realistic even for women.

Sexuality and the Physically Disabled and Aged   UWEM EDIMO ESIET

The physically disabled have not been overtly discriminated against, as most children and families wish that their disabled family members could have children as a compensation for their efforts in contributing to the family.

   The elderly enjoy their sexuality within their sociocultural norms and values, and like all Nigerians, are left to deal with their sexual desires and needs within the code of silence regarding all sexual matters.

Attitudes on and Incidence of Oral and Anal Sex   UWEM EDIMO ESIET

Anal penetrative sex is frowned on even now, particularly in view of the HIV/AIDS risk. Although oral sex is practiced, it is not glamorized as it is in other countries, primarily because of the general culture of silence on sexual topics.

Aphrodisiacs   BILKISU YUSUF

Traditional aphrodisiacs are quite common in Hausa culture. They vary from those used as food to special chemical preparations. There are different types used by men and women to increase libido and vaginal lubrication, and to ensure that married couples derive maximum sexual satisfaction from their partners.

   While a variety of male aphrodisiacs exists, the most widely used among Hausa men is *Gaggai*, a root which is either boiled, powdered, and mixed with spices and eaten with meat, or soaked with spices to make a drink. For women, *tukudi* is routinely prepared for brides; its content depends on the local aphrodisiac herbs available in a particular area. *Hakin maye*, very common among Hausa in the Sokoto and Kebbi States, is a combination of herbs used as food additives mixed with chicken broth, sprinkled on yogurt, or mixed with honey.

   The herb *Gyadan mata*, which grows in the wild and looks like a nut, is chewed by women. Two groups of aphrodisiacs, known as *Ko gida* and *Ko mota*, are popularly hawked by women: One is taken orally, whereas the other, used as a topical application, is used to tighten the vaginal muscles. *Maganin mata* (women's medicine) is a more general term used in a variety of female aphrodisiacs that include local herbs, a white sweet substance imported from Arab countries, and a dark substance called *laximi* imported from the Indian subcontinent.

   It is quite common to see local female herbalists (*'yar mai ganye*) hawking these aphrodisiac herbs in the markets. Those who prepare aphrodisiacs for brides and other users buy their herbs from the local female herbalist or her male counterpart. After they prepare their special variety of ingredients, they sell their mixes wholesale to retail hawkers, *dillalai,* and it is not unusual to see these aphrodisiac hawkers making brisk business at social gatherings and sharing in hushed voice with friends their experiences on the efficacy of their own brand of tried and tested aphrodisiacs. There is no existing research on these traditional Hausa aphrodisiacs, but their usage is widespread. Dealers in Sokoto, Nigeria, and in Maradil in neighboring Niger Republic are known for their virtual monopoly on some of the most popular brands.

6. Homoerotic, Homosexual, and Ambisexual Behaviors
UWEM EDIMO ESIET

A. Children and Adolescents

From what little is known, the incidence of same-sex sexual behavior among children and adolescents is very low. Incidents have been reported within same-sex institutions.

B. Adults

More adult homosexual behavior is being recorded. One reason cited for this behavior is the myth that homosexual relationships enhance one's personal wealth acquisition. Persons who engage in homosexual behavior tend to be bisexual because exclusive homosexuality is greatly frowned on.

Homosexuality: A Regional/Ethnic Comparison

The following summaries of the attitudes and practices regarding homosexuality of several ethnic groups in eight geographical regions of Nigeria were compiled by the authors during a meeting with health care professionals in January 1999 (Francoeur, Esiet, & Esiet 2000) (see Editor's Note on page 351).

1. Regions: Ipoti-Ekiti, Oyo, and Yorubaland. Ethnic Group: Yoruba
    The people believe that homosexuality does not exist, only heterosexuals. People who engage in same-sex acts are seen as outcasts.
2. Regions: Kano, Katsina, and Kaduna. Ethic Group: Muslim Hausa
    Homosexuals exist. They are not accepted and keep their sexual activities hidden.
3. Region: Borno
    Both homosexuals and bisexuals exist, but such behavior is taboo.
4. Region: Benue. Ethnic Groups: Tiv, Idoma, and Isala
    The people may hear about homosexuality and bisexuality, and it may occur, but no one has ever seen it.

5. Regions: Akwa-Ibom and the Cross River: Ethnic Groups: Efik and Ibibio

There are no forms of homosexuality or bisexuality in this culture: These acts are forbidden. Anyone known to be engaging in this activity is stigmatized and regarded as outcast.

6. Region: the Delta. Ethnic Groups: Uhobod, Ibos, Ijaws, Isaw, and Itsekirus

Special considerations regarding homosexuality are unknown.

7. Region: Edo

There are no forms of homosexuality or bisexuality allowed in this culture.

8. Regions: Imo, Enugu, and Anambra States. Ethnic Group: Ibo

People say they know nothing about homosexuality in this culture.

7. Gender Conflicted Persons

Gender-conflicted persons are not recognized in our culture, which maintains a strict either/or belief regarding male and female gender. Transvestitism is neither acknowledged nor encouraged.

8. Significant Unconventional Sexual Behaviors

A. Coercive Sex   CHRISTINE OLUFUNKE ADEBAJO AND IMO I. ESIET

Coercive Sex and Nigerian Law: An Overview of the Current Status
CHRISTINE ADEBAJO

Sexual abuse, assaults, and harassment all involve violence against women or men. Any of these forms of coercive sex can occur in the home, workplace, or in public. And each, as an issue, remains complex, ambiguous, interwoven, and extremely dangerous in the traditional Nigerian society. They all entail subjugation of the victim and the stripping of her (or his) autonomy and self-esteem. The occurrences against women are more pronounced because such acts are encouraged by the societal perception of a woman's low status. In Nigeria, as described above, women are subject to several dehumanizing and oppressive traditional values, which ultimately dictate how women are regarded, treated, and acknowledged.

As a traditional, tribal-based society, Nigeria has mechanisms that legitimize, cloud, and deny sexual abuse, assaults, and harassment as forms of violence against women in particular. In many instances, even when a particular act of violence is deplored, some conventional institutions, such as the family structure, as well as religious and traditional rulers, protect the status quo, making it more difficult to challenge. For example, most Nigerian communities, if not all, believe in male supremacy; hence, any of these acts is perceived as an acceptable exercise of the male's prerogative over women's sexuality.

Within the context of women's almost helpless social position, ridiculous scenarios and rhetorical questions are widely used in casual conversations to make light of the reality of oppression and subjugation that these acts inflict on women. For example, men and women alike ask, "Why should a man not chastise his wife for an offense?" Note that such "chastisement" can include physical assaults of varying degree. Another question usually asked involves female genital mutilation (female circumcision): "Why should a woman choose to be uncircumcised, or make her daughter an 'outcast' by not allowing her to be circumcised?" This act is not considered sexual abuse, when in reality it is indeed just that. In fact, one would like to ask who and what makes an uncircumcised woman an outcast? Obviously, it is the society. In this perspective, it could be concluded that sexual abuse, assaults, and harassment affecting women are in most cases not accidental; instead, they serve the sociopolitical function of keeping women subordinate. They are most often expressions of power that connote an unequal relationship between male and female sexuality.

The occurrences of sexual abuse, assaults, and harassment against men in Nigeria are very negligible. When such incidences do occur at all, they occur among children and adolescent males. Ironically, when any act of this nature is directed against a male, it is viewed with great seriousness. In some communities, the same powerful institutions that downplayed these acts perpetrated on women view them as an abomination when directed at a male.

Socially, sexual abuse, assaults, and harassment against women are subtly tied to sexism and women's oppressed status, particularly their sexuality. The law is seemingly insensitive to these acts, whether it is dealing with marital rape (see below) or with other more clear and documented cases. A typical case in which the courts evaded and ignored the need for redress is the outcome in the case of Jos N. A. Police vs. Allah Nagari, Nigeria, in which a 7-year-old girl gave evidence against the man she claimed raped her. Her bloodstained clothes were produced as evidence while a medical report confirmed injury to her genitalia. Despite this evidence, the man was not convicted because a clause in the law stipulates that any child less than 8 years of age needs her case corroborated, before the court can rule in her favor. Unfortunately, cases like this abound, even though requiring a witness to the rape makes a mockery of the law's professed lack of bias between the sexes.

Even though economic deprivation in Nigeria affects all groups, ages, and sexes, the worst hit are women and children. Women in particular suffer from unequal and inequitable access to vital development resources such as education, employment, housing, etc. Yet, women are mainly responsible for raising the children. This dependency exposes mothers and children to prostitution and other forms of sexual abuse. They are also prone to assaults and harassment from frustrated husbands and fathers.

With the father's situation highly precarious because of the prevalence of unemployment, male frustration is common in the Nigerian home. Nigerian wives can easily be sexually exploited by their husbands for the benefit of their family. Also, fathers at times encourage their daughters to prostitute themselves, either directly or while hawking goods in the marketplace, in order to help the family's economic stress.

Ethnic Variations   CHRISTINE ADEBAJO

Although sexual abuse, assaults, and harassment occur among people of all ethnic, cultural, religious, and social classes, their pattern and causes can only be understood and remedied in specific social and cultural contexts. However, in all ethnic regions of Nigeria, almost all reported cases of sexual abuse, assaults, and harassment are perpetrated by men. For example, in a study conducted by Francisca Isi Omorodium between 1982 and 1988 in Benin City, Edo State, all cases of battering reported to the Social Welfare Department were perpetrated by men. The same study showed that the men who battered their wives were between the ages of 20 and 45 years while their wives were between the reproductive ages of 18 and 36 years.

The study went further to ascertain that battering was not limited to level of education or class. It showed that 50 percent of the men and 30 percent of the women involved had attained at least a primary school certificate. More frustrating was the finding that 40 percent of the men and 30 percent of the women involved had an educational level ranging from secondary school to college. The findings portrayed a further worrisome fact that most of the cases reported to the Social Welfare Department were from the lower strata while most of the upper-class cases went unreported and were kept secret by the victims.

Certain acts that qualify as sexual abuse, assault, and harassment are seen in some Nigerian communities as normal and hidden under the umbrella of traditional practice, culture, and beliefs. Examples include female genital mutilation, nutritional taboos in pregnancy and children, body scarification, seclusion in labor, hot baths during the six weeks after birth, and a host of others. Some of these acts are perpetrated as a societal norm. In the case of child battering, some communities believe that parents or guardians have a prerogative over their children and thus can scold and beat them to any degree without interference from a third party. In such a circumstance, a child can be ill-treated and badly injured without it being seen as battering. In certain communities where the wife is viewed as the man's property to be used as he desires or sees fit, beating one's wife is therefore nobody else's business. Worse still, in the same communities, a wife who expresses a need or seeks a favor from her husband can be seen as purposely aggravating the husband to beat her. This is because it is believed that such a domestic scuffle would be settled by the husband offering a gift.

Current Data   CHRISTINE ADEBAJO

Statistical information on the extent of sexual abuse, assaults, and harassment in Nigeria is very scanty, as most data has been compiled in small studies. This data therefore provides only a small insight into the incidence, and the data cannot be used as concrete indicators on the extent of these acts in Nigeria as a whole. However, some of the available studies portray serious health, emotional, and physical consequences that cannot be ignored.

For example, after a 1985-1986 study of the national prevalence of female genital mutilation (FGM), Christine Adebajo reported that female genital mutilation was actively promoted and advocated in twenty-one out of the thirty states in Nigeria. The prevalence within the newly adjusted state boundaries and newly created states indicated that 35 percent to 90 percent of the women in eighteen states are mutilated, while in nine other states the percentage of mutilated women was 90 percent or higher.

Other documented cases of sexual assaults, abuse, and harassment include the following:

- In 1987, 12-year-old Hauwa Abubakar from northern Nigeria died after having both legs amputated by her husband after the girl made several attempts to run away from her forced marriage.
- A case of rape of a 10-year-old girl by a police officer was reported in Benin City. The police officer grabbed the girl who was returning from an errand, locked the door, and threw her to the floor, tearing her underclothes. Before her cries could attract a passerby, she had been raped. The only redress was a fine of 2,500 Naira (roughly $2,500 U.S.) which was never paid by the offender.
- In June 1995, some neighbors brought a 37-year old married woman to my husband's private hospital with a fractured collarbone. She had just been mercilessly beaten by her husband, because he suspected that their son told her about his infidelity. Despite the fact that she did not react, the husband's guilt could not hold him back from challenging his wife for knowing of his infidelity. The husband was, of course, reported to the police by the hospital, but the case was eventually thrown out of court as a mere family squabble that should be settled out of court.

These few cases typify the outcome of many reported cases of assault, sexual abuse, and harassment in Nigeria. Unfortunately, the majority of abuse/assault cases are not reported and do not get public notice. A culture of silence seems to be responsible for the inadequacy of documentation and population-based data. In addition, the sociocultural and legal barriers on the issue of violence, particularly relating to sexuality, make it almost impossible to acquire accurate data on any of the acts. Nevertheless, the few available data and several deafening whispers of daily occurrence of violence are sufficient to justify increased attention to this issue.

Sexual Abuse, Assault, and Harassment   CHRISTINE ADEBAJO

In this discussion, we have tried to discuss the various forms of sexual abuse, assault, and harassment, respecting the ways in which these are perceived and categorized in Nigeria. However, sexual abuse, assault, and harassment are so interwoven that one can hardly talk of one without overlapping into the other. Clear operational definitions are difficult to come by, because the distinctions are often subtle and varied according to the interpretations of the victim, varying cultural perspectives, and differences in the way males and females view individual occurrences. The application of definitions, even when such are clearly delineated, is often difficult or impossible, because particular cases frequently involve a combination of various actions which cannot be separated out. Whatever form these actions take, they usually share a common motivation: to gain and sustain dominance and control over the victim. Sexual harassment, abuse, and assault in Nigeria constitute a major component of violence against women, since it is often associated with male dominance, although a variety of assaults are common among adolescents, peer groups, and adults of either gender.

Sexual Abuse. [Christine Adebajo] Sexual abuse is here defined as someone forcing another to engage in sexual activity, or interfering with someone's sexuality, against his or her will and without his or her consent. Such abuse, which may involve a male and a female or persons of the same gender, may result in, or is likely to result in, physical, sexual, or psychological harm or suffering to the victim. Abuse, in private or in a public place, can range from being kissed without one's consent to touching the sex organs to forced sexual intercourse. Sometimes, sexual abuse can occur between an adult and a child or teenager. Most commonly, however, sexual abuse occurs among people with a personal relationship or where they have had such a relationship in the past. While terms such as sexual assault, sexual coercion, and sexual aggression are sometimes used as synonyms for sexual abuse, in Nigeria sexual abuse includes the following acts: verbal aggression/assault, unwanted physical touch, rape, incest, child prostitution, female genital mutilation (FGM), and *Yankan Gishir* (salt cut)—these variations are discussed below individually.

Unwanted Physical Touching. [Christine Adebajo] It is not uncommon in public places such as work and school, especially colleges, for women to experience physical touch with a sexual connotation. This can involve patting the buttocks (bum-patting), open display of sexist images, rubbing of the body, and more overt molestation. In Nigeria, it is difficult to take these particular types of abuse too far, because they are not viewed with any legal seriousness. Perhaps one of the reasons for this is the fact that Nigerians are known to be warm and close people, where touching is generally seen as an act of kindness and friendship. However, where it involves an adult male touching the genitalia of a child, particularly of the opposite sex, it is viewed with more seriousness.

Verbal Assault. [Christine Adebajo] Verbal assault or aggression occurs when words are used to control, dominate, and intimidate the victim by yelling, insulting, speaking unkindly, and name calling. Other forms of verbal assault involve judging and criticizing; discounting what the other says, feels, or thinks, and in repeatedly disagreeing with the victim. Verbal assaults can be very psychologically damaging, making the victim feel dehumanized and belittled. This can lead to serious emotional health problems. Verbal abuse also very often leads to physical assaults. Unlike other forms of violence, verbal assaults are not primarily limited to males against women; they are perpetrated by both sexes and in all age groups.

Indecent Assaults. [Imo I. Esiet] Section 360 of the Criminal Code provides that: "any person who unlawfully and indecently assaults a woman or girl is guilty of a misdemeanor, and is liable to imprisonment for two years." However, according to section 353 of the same Code, this felony is punishable with three years imprisonment when the victim is a male, rather than two years as in a case of female victims. A fundamental principle of criminal law is that all persons should be equally protected from harm of like degree. It is hard to see any justification for creating different offenses with different penalties to cover the same conduct for persons of different sexes.

Sexual Harassment. [Christine Adebajo] In Nigeria, harassment can be categorized under two headings as direct or indirect. Direct sexual harassment, including verbal assault and unwanted touches, such as bum-patting, sexist remarks, open display of sexist images, and more overt molestation, is a major gender issue, particularly in the work setting and in colleges where it can manifest in the form of victimization and/or molestation. Indirect sexual harassment/abuse occurs as a result of traditional practices or beliefs referred to as harmful traditional practices (HTP); see: Section 8.D. Female Genital Mutilation and Other Harmful Practices.

In Nigeria, as elsewhere around the world, sexual harassment is commonly perpetrated by men against women. However, a few cases have been reported of Nigerian female executives harassing their subordinates. Also on record are a few cases of sexual harassment by female college students against their male lecturers. Even though it is common knowledge that sexual harassment of females by males occurs in public spaces, such as the workplace, school, market, and street, it is often very difficult to prove such in a traditional society such as Nigeria, where the behavior correlates with the society's gender power differentials.

In the workplace, sexual harassment has been manifested in limiting the female to designated sex roles through blackmail or other means. For example, in labor unions, an assertive woman unionist is looked on as defiant. This also occurs when women try to move into professional jobs that are believed to be the exclusive preserve of men. In a research work very applicable to the Nigerian situation, Dr. Madeline Heilman of New

York University showed that there is a general consensus that pretty career women have problems on the job. Heilman found that when an attractive woman is looking for lower-level jobs, her looks could earn her a plus. However, when she is in a managerial position, competing with a good-looking man puts her at a disadvantage. A good-looking man is seen as competent, tough, decisive, and hard-nosed, whereas an attractive woman with the same qualifications, background, experience, and recommendation is dismissed as gentle, soft, and indecisive.

Because of the nature of Nigerian social codes and values that stress male dominance of women, sexual harassment often goes unnoticed. This societal posture makes the victim unwilling to report cases of sexual harassment. It has also been observed that victims are not sure of what constitutes sexual harassment.

Domestic Violence and Spousal Abuse. [Christine Adebajo] These are aggressive acts, such as pushing, kicking, slapping, hitting, punching, grabbing, biting, throwing objects, burning, wounding, or in the extreme, killing. Even though physical assaults are perpetrated by both genders, the worst recorded cases are those perpetrated by males against females, particularly those associated with domestic violence. Domestic violence usually leads to severe injury and, in a few cases, to death. Unfortunately, this problem is not receiving adequate recognition from the society, which does not consider it a problem worth addressing. Physical assaults within the family are central to the violence in Nigerian culture at large. It is embedded within the traditional values that place men above women and the concept that domestic violence is a private matter between husband and wife or man and woman. There is a quiet willingness to accept it.

Case studies of wife battering in some parts of Nigeria have documented that the injuries sustained by battered wives include: facial bruises, blackened eyes, cuts on the mouth, loss of teeth, fractures, and severing of hand(s). Another study, conducted by the Akwa-Ibom state branch of Women in Nigeria (WIN), listed the following major causes of violence in home in terms of descending importance:

- arguments over money;
- jealousy and fear of the partner's infidelity;
- a partner's attempt to intervene in the punishment of children;
- arguments over drinking habits;
- being overburdened with family chores;
- in-law interference;
- a partner being blamed for the children's behavior;
- a spouse's desire to go for further studies or to advance her career;
- ignoring a spouse;
- frequent demands for sexual relations; and
- disputes over the number of children wanted.

The same survey went further to elucidate steps taken by spouses to protect themselves. Among the coping mechanisms used were:

- reporting the assault or abuse to parents, in-laws, the police, social welfare agencies, or a religious leader;
- doing nothing;
- leaving the home with the children;
- praying to God to change him; and
- keeping quiet until it is over.

The majority of the respondents considered domestic violence as natural and not to be questioned or challenged. Victims were optimistic that their partners who had shown a violent tendency would change with time, although all of them confirmed that their health was affected when violence occurred. The majority, who sees acts of domestic violence as wrong, still feels that they should stick to their marriage, because:

- divorce and separation are considered shameful;
- there is no place to keep the children; and
- they do not want the children to have different fathers.

Thus, it appears that many marriages have seriously deteriorated, although things are patched up on the surface. Even when physical injury is not inflicted, many women live in perpetual emotional turmoil, obviously with impaired health.

Domestic Violence and Spousal Abuse. [Imo I. Esiet] Although much of spousal assault involves wife battering and is exploitative and abusive of the marriage relationship, keeping in mind the fact of female subordinance in Nigerian society helps one understand the peculiar social setting that exposes the married woman to such an attack on her physical person.

One of the reasons often given to justify wife battering is the right of the husband to chastise his wife and an erring wife's need of discipline. This defense and claim to moral justification is based on the view that by consenting to marriage, a woman consents to revert to the status of a minor. The provisions of law which allow a defense to assault on grounds of reasonable chastisement gives the right only to parents or those who stand *in loco parentis*. In essence, then, this defense places the wife in the same position as her children in relation to the husband's supreme authority. In most cases, we may safely assume that the wife would have attained civil majority. So the question becomes one of whether an adult woman loses her maturity and capacity to be responsible simply because she has married, and her husband decides to discipline her like a child when she errs.

Rape. [Imo I. Esiet] Section 357 of the Nigerian Criminal Code defines rape as "unlawful carnal knowledge of a woman or girl, with or without her consent, or if the consent is obtained by force or by means of threats, intimidation of any kind, or by fear of harm or by means of false and fraudulent misrepresentation as to the nature of the act or in the case of a married woman, by impersonating her husband." The offense is punishable with life imprisonment with or without whipping. This definition in section 357, however, needs to be read with section 6, which excludes forced sexual intercourse between spouses. Marital rape is not recognized in Nigerian law. The customary law reasoning for this exclusion was succinctly stated by Hale (in Smith and Hogan 1983), when he said, "The husband cannot be guilty of a rape committed by himself upon his lawful wife, for by their mutual matrimonial consent and contract the wife has given up herself in this kind unto her husband which she cannot retract."

It would appear from the above definition of rape that rape is deemed to differ qualitatively from the act of mutual and reciprocal lovemaking only on the issue of consent. According to Nigerian law, in consenting to contract marriage, a married woman gives up any right to refuse sexual intercourse with her husband, even when he forcibly imposes his will on her (Oyajobi 1986:18). This legal position has prompted one commentator to ask: "If the law recognizes the need to protect the wife from other physical assaults from her husband, why should she not be entitled to protection simply because the assault this time is of a sexual nature" (Oyajobi 1986:18; Criminal Code sections 335, 338, 351, 352, 362).

There are, however, some situations in which it has been ruled that a husband should be held liable for raping his wife (Oyajobi 1986:19). These situations are where:

- a divorce decree has been given, even though the marriage is still in existence;
- the spouses are living apart under a court separation order;
- one spouse has filed papers to commence divorce proceedings;
- a husband has been given a court order not to return to his wife;
- there has been a separation by agreement; or
- there is a court order prohibiting molestation of wife.

It is important to note that legally the sexual history of the victim is inextricably tied to the issue of whether or not the party gave consent to the alleged forced intercourse. Section 210 of the Evidence Act allows evidence of previous sexual dealings of the accuser with other persons as well as the accused. But the fact that the plaintiff gave consent to having sex with the accused on a previous occasion may not be conclusive evidence that consent was given on the alleged occasion.

Corroboration of evidence regarding the plaintiff's alleged previous behavior is not an express requirement of the law of rape in Nigeria. However, following the customary law trend, our courts have evolved the rule of practice of warning juries about the danger of convicting based on uncorroborated evidence. The difficulties inherent in providing corroboration in rape cases are obvious. This is not unconnected with the fact that these offenses take place in private, and it is unlikely that there will be any human witnesses apart from the parties themselves.

Another View of Rape. [Christine Adebajo] In addition to marital rape and stranger rape, Nigerian women have been subjected to brutal rape as part of war and violence against refugees. This experience was documented during the Nigerian Civil War with Biafra (1966-1970).

The Nigerian Criminal Code section 221 stipulates that it is a criminal offense if a man has sexual intercourse with a woman

1. without her consent;
2. with her consent given under fear of pain or death threat; or
3. if the female is under 14 years of age or of unsound mind, whether with or without her consent.

Ironically, the age of consent for sexual intercourse varies from one part of the country to another. Specifically, the Nigerian Criminal Code puts the age of consent for boys at 14 and for girls at 16 (unless she is married). It will be seen that the law itself can be open to a lot of abuses. Law enforcement agencies are usually not sensitive to sexual rights violations, often making it difficult to establish a case of rape. The record shows that very few cases of rape offenders have been prosecuted. On the other hand, a child victim is often labeled as being sexually aggressive, even by the courts of law.

This unfavorable societal outlook on the issue of rape has not helped in the proper documentation of its incidence. Victims are reluctant to report rape cases because they feel ashamed that the society might insinuate that they made themselves a target of attack. They are also afraid of repeated occurrences by the perpetrator, because the victim is not sure of adequate redress by law enforcement agents. In some cases, victims have been driven to commit suicide because of the stigma and possible dishonor, particularly in cases of illegitimate pregnancy.

A common form of rape in Nigeria occurs with domestic help, usually a teenage girl, when she is molested by her master or by a teenage male child or relation of the master.

Non-governmental organizations (NGOs) and other groups and individuals need to agitate for law reform that will provide adequate redress for victims. Such a law should also facilitate the prosecution of offenders, more so because the present provision under the criminal code makes a case of rape lapse if prosecution does not commence within two months of the offense. The other obstacle is the requirement of providing an eyewitness when the offense itself can hardly be committed in the presence of anyone.

Incest. [Christine Adebajo] It is difficult to provide a clear definition for incest in the Nigerian context, because its meaning varies from community to community. For example, certain ethnic groups permit marriage between cousins. Neither the criminal nor penal codes make provision for incest as a categorical form of crime. Sexual intercourse between father and daughter is illegal and regarded as an infringement on the daughter's sexual rights. Documentation of incest is almost totally lacking. Nevertheless, unreported cases do exist in almost every community. It is known that victims who were abused by their fathers or stepfathers, whose abuse involved genital contact, and whose molestation involved force, are at greater risk of long-lasting effects that can include: nightmares, flashbacks, disassociative responses, emotional numbing, etc. It has also been established that the long-term psychological complications usually manifest as physical complaints, some of which may be linked with chronic pelvic pain, headaches, asthma, and gynecological problems (Koss 1987).

As with rape, a substantial number of cases of incest do occur among cousins, even in communities where cousin marriages are not allowed. The majority of these cases occur among teenagers. Most are never allowed to reach public notice, as the parents collude to "bury" such incidences within the family to avoid "dishonor." Other common cases involve sexual molestation of stepdaughters by their stepfathers, and of stepsisters by their stepbrothers. In recent times, it has been observed that teenage girls are increasingly more likely to initiate incestuous relationships. This development is perhaps linked with two facts: Girls mature biologically at a younger age than boys, and today's society allows girls more freedom, which exposes them to opportunities of early sexual interaction.

B. Prostitution

Adult Prostitution IMO I. ESIET

Adult prostitution is on the increase, especially with the downturn in the economy. The connection between increasing prostitution and increased incidence of HIV/AIDS in this group has created considerable interest among health care providers. Several non-governmental organizations are now working with prostitutes to get them to practice safer sex.

Section 1 of the Criminal Code defines prostitution as "the offering by a female of her body, commonly for acts of lewdness for payment . . .," whereas, by virtue of sections 222A, 223(2) & (4) of the Criminal Code, the male can only be liable for the offense of procuring a female to become a prostitute.

According to Ayo Oyajobi (1986:23), there is hardly any moral justification or logical reasoning for the exemption of males from the definition of who can be a prostitute, while asserting that there is no reason why a man cannot offer his body for acts of lewdness for payment. The truth is that men in fact do so more often than we would like to admit. This assertion is based on the increased obviousness of homosexual activities by males, in which case male prostitution has become more common and evident. But in reality, only less economically fortunate women in Nigerian society find themselves policed and labeled for subsequent discriminatory treatment by the law (Oyajobi 1986:24). Although, economic factors cannot adequately explain prostitution, they must not be treated as marginal considerations. Insofar as our male-dominated society offers relatively limited opportunities for women to earn a good living wage, win promotions, achieve a secure career, and generally attain economic independence from men, women will be only too willing to give their bodies to achieve these ends (Oyajobi 1986:24).

Child Prostitution   CHRISTINE ADEBAJO

Child prostitution, which used to be a taboo, is now a reality in Nigeria. Since the economic downturn that is hitting every family, child prostitution has increased steadily. The practice comes in different forms. In certain situations, parents actually encourage their teenage daughters to prostitute themselves.

In a survey carried out in some cities of Nigeria by a soft-pornography magazine, *Hints,* (March 1996), most children interviewed confirmed that their mothers, the majority of whom are prostitutes themselves, introduced them to prostitution in an attempt to augment the family's earnings. The age range of these girls is from 8 to 13 years. The same survey revealed that secondary-school girls between the ages of 10 and 13 hang around hotels and streets soliciting male patronage. Others who appear physically mature take older men, referred to as "Sugar Daddies," for boyfriends. These men, in return for sexual gratification, assist the girls with their school fees. Another form of child prostitution occurs when young girls aged 8 to 15 are sent by their parents or guardians to hawk goods on the streets. Some of these children are easily seduced by older men and are paid for any contracted sexual act. More worrisome in recent times are a few reported cases of child-prostitute exporters and importers. This is most often perpetrated by foreigners.

In Nigeria, child prostitution and child pornography are illegal. Any such act that reaches the notice of law enforcement agents is handled with seriousness. Although one would have expected constant raids on perpetrators because they usually have specific designated areas, such raids are very sporadic where they exist at all. Child prostitution is a gross sexual abuse because the act is illegal, and most of the time, the act is forced on the prostitutes either by some older person or by circumstances beyond their control.

C. Pornography and Erotica

See Section 3D, Informal Sources of Sexual Knowledge.

D. Female Genital Mutilation and Other Harmful Practices
CHRISTINE ADEBAJO

Female circumcision (FC), or female genital mutilation (FGM) is a traditional practice in Nigeria in which an unskilled person or a health worker cuts off parts or whole organs of the female external genitalia. This practice is tied to culture, religious belief, and myth. Beyond this, it is a gross sexual abuse, which infringes on a woman's rights with abundant negative consequences (Goddard 1995).

The type of FGM performed varies from community to community, mostly based on their beliefs. In a nationwide survey carried out between December 1985 and May 1986 by Christine Adebajo for the National Association of Nigerian Nurses and Midwives (NANNM), the following facts were established:

- In the twenty-one states in Nigeria (out of thirty states) where FGM is carried out, it is believed that an uncircumcised woman is usually promiscuous. In Anambra, Bendel, Imo, Ondo, and Oyo States, more than 90 percent of the women have had some form of female circumcision, compared with only 30 percent in Lagos, the capital.
- In states where type III FGM (infibulation or pharonic circumcision) is practiced, it is done to preserve virginity. Type III FGM involves surgical removal of the whole of the clitoris, the labia minora, and part of labia majora, and the stitching together of the two sides of the vulva, leaving tiny openings for the flow of urine and menstrual products. In parts of Edo State, FGM is carried out on a woman when she is about seven months pregnant. In 1985-1986, over 30 percent of the women in Bendel and Imo States had infibulation.
- Type II FGM (called reduction or excision) involves removal of the prepuce and the glans of the clitoris, together with adjacent parts of the labia minora or the whole of it. People believe that if the head of a newborn baby touches the clitoris, the baby will die. In 1985-1986, Bendel and Imo States had, respectively, a 55-percent and a 60-percent prevalence of excision.
- Among the 1,300 individuals who reported performing female circumcision, only 5 percent were skilled health professionals.
- In some eastern parts of the country, FGM is carried out as part of a pubertal rite. In this case, the extent of mutilation varies, depending on the circumciser's "expertise" and associated beliefs.
- In the western parts of the country, FGM is performed for cosmetic reasons, the belief being that if the female genitalia, particularly the clitoris, is not trimmed, it will grow and elongate like a penis.
- In some areas, Type I FGM (*Sunna*), which involves the removal of the prepuce or foreskin of the clitoris, is performed. In 1985-1986, three quarters of reported female circumcisions were *sunna* circumcisions.

Some of the health consequences of FGM include: injury to surrounding body parts, severe bleeding, shock, fainting during the mutilation, infection, and the inability to pass urine. Other long-term health hazards include: tetanus, blood poisoning, infection to the urinary and reproductive tracts, menstrual disorders, complications during childbirth, scar formation, painful sexual intercourse, and infertility due to fibrosis of the vagina. There is also a wide range of emotional and psychological effects, which may include embarrassment resulting from deformity of the vaginal area, anxiety and irritability, depression, marital problems of varying degrees, sometimes due to painful sexual intercourse, and psychosis as a result of frustration, particularly when one is unable to have intercourse.

Basically, FGM can be traced to a desire of the society to control female sexuality. Behind the various superstitions that perpetuate FGM, what seems to have sustained the practice is that men will not marry uncircumcised women, because they are believed to be unclean and promiscuous.

Male and Female Circumcision: A Regional/Ethnic Comparison

The following summaries of the attitudes and practices regarding male and female circumcision of several ethnic groups in eight geographical regions of Nigeria were compiled by the authors during a meeting with health care professionals in January 1999 (Francoeur, Esiet, & Esiet 2000) (see Editor's Note on page 351).

1. Regions: Ipoti-Ekiti, Oyo, Ile-oluji, and Yorubaland. Ethnic Group: Yoruba

    Both male and female circumcision are traditional practices in Oyo State. Normally, circumcision is done in the first three months after birth. In the old days, one hardly heard of any complications, infections, or other harm to health. Now, because there are many incompetent people handling circumcision, we hear of complications, infections, and harmful effects. Some educated persons in the medical field now discourage female circumcision. In Yorubaland, male circumcision is generally practiced on the eighth day after birth. Male circumcision is accepted traditionally and is encouraged by the dominant religions in this region. In Ipoti-Ekiti, male and female circumcisions are usually carried out on the eighth day after birth. Female circumcision is practiced in some areas and not in others—in Ondo, Ilesha, and Ekiti towns, but not among the Ijebus. Female circumcision reduces a woman's sexual desire and the temptation to promiscuity. It also prevents the death of the child during delivery. It is believed that the child will die if its head touches the clitoris during birth. In Ile-oluji, female circumcision is an initiation into womanhood.

2. Regions: Kano, Katsina, and Kaduna. Ethic Group: Muslim Hausa

    Only male circumcision is practiced in these regions. Males are circumcised at age 6 to 7 years, when they realize that a male must endure pain. An elderly person, a *Wanzami*, carries out this procedure with locally made tools (*Aska*) and medicinal herbs. He begins with some incantations and digs a hole in the ground for the blood to flow into. He then holds the boy's legs apart with two sticks and circumcises him. Afterwards, the cloth the boy sat on, the soap used for washing hands by the *Wanzami*, as well as money and other gift items, are given to the *Wanzami* as presents. The circumcised boy is fed with special food and taken to a home different from his own to recover. The boy is showered with gifts from well-wishers and relatives. These days, the rate of infection from circumcisions has decreased because the *Wanzami* now boil their instruments to disinfect them (although some infections still occur).

3. Region: Borno

    Male circumcision is usually done sometime after age 7 years. Unsterilized instruments are used, leading to infections; excessive bleeding can result in death. Females are not circumcised but may participate in other traditional rituals.

4. Region: Tiv-Benue. Ethnic Groups: Tiv, Idoma, and Isala

    Males are usually circumcised eight days after birth, but some are circumcised at age 4 or 5. Traditional leaders or ordinary people who have gained some skill in male circumcision perform this both in hospitals and in the villages. Males sometimes become infected as a result of poor hygiene.

5. Regions: Akwa-Ibom and the Cross River. Ethnic Groups: Efik and Ibibio

    Among the Efiks and Ibibios, males are circumcised as babies. Female circumcision is done for aesthetic reasons, to avoid promiscuity, and to maintain virginity before marriage. People believe that if females enjoy intercourse, then they are likely to seek it from different men. Females may be circumcised during infancy or childhood, as a pubertal initiation, or just before marriage in "the fattening room," or not at all. Only the clitoral hood is removed. If done with unsterile instruments or by an inexperienced person, female circumcision can be harmful and life-threatening, or not at all. Some believe that female circumcision helps the fetal head descend smoothly during labor. In female circumcision, some practitioners drink illicit gin and spit it on the new wound; some use iodine on it, whereas others use a feather to spread fresh palm oil or engine oil to commence the healing process. Circumcision at birth has no rituals, but at other ages, feasting is usual for those who participate in the ritual as a sign of respect and acceptance or as initiation into the age group. Infections, tetanus, formation of keloids and fibrosis, extensive tears during labor, postpartum hemorrhage, social stigma, psychological trauma, and frigidity, are reported consequences of female circumcision.

6. Region: the Delta. Ethnic Groups: Uhobod, Ibos, Ijaws, Isaw, and Itsekirus

    Males are usually circumcised within a few weeks of birth. Female circumcision is no longer common in some parts of the Delta. In other parts, however, it is still routinely practiced with a lot of importance attached. People see it as a sign of a girl's honor, a sign of maturity, a source of parental pride, and for the prevention of promiscuity.

Usually the girl is between 13 and 21 years of age. In some areas, it occurs when the girl is expecting her first baby. In areas where female circumcision is common, the whole community celebrates and other young girls with their waists beautifully beaded come to stay with the circumcised girl for ten days. She does not do any work and is given tender, loving care by all. If she is engaged to a man, he comes to pay homage to the family, brings gifts, and helps the girl, including grinding her food. Depending on how it is done, both male and female circumcision can result in infection and other conditions that are harmful to health.

7. Region: Edo

Males and females are circumcised seven days after birth to reduce promiscuity. Even though new razor blades are used, males sometimes experience infections, wounds that do not heal, and excessive bleeding. Circumcision of females may interfere with normal sexual desire. In some cases, female circumcision results in injury to the major and minor labia, or a vesico-vaginal fistula (VVF) that can lead to difficult delivery and other complications.

8. Regions: Imo, Enugu, and Anambra. Ethnic Group: Ibo

In Enugu and Anambra, males are circumcised eight days after birth. Previously, in certain areas, like Nsukka, female circumcision was practiced, but generally no longer. When performed for cosmetic purposes or to reduce promiscuity, female circumcision may be done with the low-risk orthodox method or a high-risk crude native method. Complications of the native crude method include infections, vesico-vaginal fistula, and the narrowing of the vaginal opening leading to painful intercourse. In Imo and Anambra States, a male child must be circumcised within eight days after birth. There are no rituals attached to male or female circumcision.

Yankan Gishiri *or Salt Cut*

This traditional "cure," practiced mainly in the northern part of Nigeria by the Hausa in Kaduna, Kano, and parts of Borno, involves a different kind of mutilation of the female genitalia. It is a traditional surgical cut in the vaginal wall of a women who has been diagnosed by a traditional healer or traditional birth attendant (TBA) to be suffering from *gishiri* disease. *Gishiri*, a Hausa term, refers to a wide range of conditions or symptoms, including: pruritis vulvae (itching vulva), amenorrhea (absence of menstruation), infertility, obstructed labor, anemia, malaria, and any condition that presents the symptoms of headache, edema, fainting attacks, or dyspareunia (painful intercourse). Unfortunately, health workers have found it difficult to associate *gishiri* with any clinical condition.

The "salt cut" is usually made on the anterior vaginal wall; repeated cutting over a period of time may extend the incision area to the posterior vaginal wall. The *gishiri* cut is also performed when certain changes occur during pregnancy, such as hypertrophy of the vaginal muscle and vaginal discharge. The cut is performed by a traditional birth attendant (TBA) or healer, few of whom are knowledgeable of the anatomical structure of the area they are cutting. There is no scientific basis for the *gishiri* cut, and despite the fact that it effects no cure, the practice goes on unabated. A *gishiri* cut leaves behind both immediate and long-term health complications, such as hemorrhage, infection, shock, and scar formation. Some of the most debilitating effects include a breakdown in the wound-healing process. This is caused by repeated cuttings, which can be done anytime any of the above-mentioned symptoms surface. Damage can also be done to the bladder, leading to vesico-vaginal fistula (VVF) or damage to the rectum causing recto-vaginal fistula (RVF).

This practice, which has no benefit whatsoever, illustrates the minimal value placed on female sexuality in Nigeria. No Nigerian male would suggest similar pelvic cuts to cure symptoms of *gishiri*, which occur as often in males as in women.

Other Traditional Practices Harmful to Women

There are widespread cultural practices in Nigeria that pose serious health concerns to female victims and can be classified under gender harassment. Some of these include: nutritional taboos associated with pregnancy, childbirth, lactation, and the six weeks following childbirth; forced feeding; rites associated with widowhood; preferences for a male child; inheritance rights; hot bath during the six weeks following childbirth; and discrimination against female infertility, to name a few. In each of these, depending on the ethnic region, women are pressured to go through harmful practices in order to satisfy societal biases.

In the case of nutritional taboos, pregnant women are forbidden to eat specific foods that are rich in vitamins and protein because of the erroneous belief that such foods reduce contraction strength during labor. Other vital foods are prohibited during pueperium for other superstitious beliefs. For example, eating of salt and pepper or palm oil are forbidden for at least seven to nine days after birth depending on the baby's sex. Some communities forbid breastfeeding, whereas others forbid eating of all kinds of nuts for fear of hemorrhoids. As expected, none of all these taboos has any scientific basis.

Forced feeding is a traditional practice whereby an adolescent is made to eat with the intention to fatten her up. This practice occurs during pubertal rites in preparation for marriage. This practice occurs also in areas where it is not acceptable for a man to marry a slim woman. The weight of the woman, not her personality or other characteristics, is the basis of choice. Unfortunately, the women who are subject to this practice live an obese life with all the health risks thereof.

Widows in some parts of Nigeria are forced to go through various dehumanizing rituals that can affect their physical and psychological health. These include sleeping on a concrete floor for upwards of forty days to three months after their husbands' death, drinking the water used to bathe her husband's corpse, and the shaving of her hair, among others. Another form of gender-based cultural belief is the preference for a male child. A male child gets all the family attention, including educational opportunities. The female child, on the other hand, is forced to assist in all domestic chores while the male child is free to play.

The widely documented gender biases and discriminatory harm to Nigerian women resulting from the prevalence of violence and abuse against women, and the fact that few such cases are reported, and fewer still are addressed appropriately in the legal system, clearly indicate that there is a serious need for more research into the factors that favor these acts in order to be able to develop appropriate strategies and programs to combat the resultant problems. Health professionals also need to be exposed to specialized training that will enhance their knowledge when dealing with such cases. There is a need for special counseling units in health institutions where victims can be assisted. More non-governmental organizations (NGOs) in Nigeria need to focus on these unconventional behaviors, with the aim of helping victims to seek redress, as well as combating the problems. The underlying cultural beliefs and social structures that perpetuate these behaviors must be challenged. NGOs should also sponsor laws that criminalize these behaviors in a more direct manner than the present legislation does, which glosses over them.

9. Contraception, Abortion, and Population Planning

A. Contraception

Contraception Among the Hausa   BILKISU YUSUF AND RAKIYA BOOTH

Hausa society frowns on too-frequent and poorly spaced pregnancies (*Kwanika*), and nursing mothers who get pregnant before they wean their babies are sometimes derided. There are many traditional methods of contraception among the Hausa, such as *rubutu*, Qur'anic verses written on a wooden slate (*allo*) with black ink (*tawada*), which is washed off with water that is then administered orally. Others include *guru*, a string of leather, which the woman wears around her waist, and a Qur'anic verse written on a sheet of paper, bound with leather and worn as an amulet. No research has yet been conducted on the efficacy of these contraceptive methods. However, the Hausa practice one of the surest methods of contraception, voluntary abstinence from sexual intercourse. The pregnant Hausa wife leaves her husband's house to live with her parents when her pregnancy reaches an advanced stage, usually seven months; she remains there until she delivers. During this period, known as *goyon ciki*, the young mother is given lessons in pregnancy management, breastfeeding, and childcare. The length of the stay varies from forty days to several months, while some remain in their parents' home until the child is weaned.

Voluntary abstinence from sexual intercourse promotes child spacing. *Goyon ciki* has no basis in Islamic jurisprudence.

Islam recommends contraception, not through voluntary abstinence from sexual intercourse as *goyon ciki* promotes, but by breastfeeding their babies for two years. The *hadith* also recommends *azl* (coitus interruptus) as a method of preventing pregnancy by mutual consent of the couple.

According to scholars of the Federation of Muslim Women's Associations in Nigeria (FOMWAN), family planning, which is permissible in Islam, should be geared towards child spacing to promote the health of the mother, rather than limiting childbirth out of the fear of poverty. Family planning can only be practiced with the full agreement of both spouses who are free to choose any suitable method. FOMWAN specifically prohibits all methods that are harmful to the body, such as oral contraceptives, sterilization, and the injectibles. Condoms are recommended in addition to coitus interruptus (the *azl* recommended by the *Shariah* (Moslem laws and governance).

According to the Nigerian Demographic and Health Survey of 1990, nationwide, 5.9 percent of 15- to 19-year-old females currently use contraception. Two thirds use traditional methods, including rhythm and withdrawal. One percent uses oral contraceptives, less than one percent uses condoms, foaming vaginal tablets, or IUDs.

B. Teenage Pregnancies and Hausan Maternal Health Practices

BILKISU YUSUF AND RAKIYA BOOTH

Teenage marriage poses some health problems for Hausa society. When the husband of a young girl marries a man who is not patient enough to wait before consummating the marriage until she has matured and her body has fully developed, she runs the risk of getting pregnant before she is old enough to take care of the child. These minors, especially in the rural areas, are susceptible to superstitions. Pregnant teenagers living in the rural areas cannot attend pre- and postnatal clinics, and, where poverty and ignorance are rampant and health care facilities either not available or affordable, these young girls are left solely in the hands of untrained, traditional birth attendants (*Ungorzoma*).

There is a sociocultural preference for home delivery among the Hausa, and most husbands are adverse to the idea of male health care personnel attending to their wives. With the onset of labor, these girls are supposed to observe *kunya*, exhibit bravery and silently endure pain. It is considered shameful among the Hausa for women to cry, shout, or express pain during labor (*Nakuda*) and childbirth (*Haituwa*). Yet, protracted labor lasting for days is quite common. The local preventive measure is to give the pregnant woman one of several bitter herbal mixtures that prevent development of *zaki* (amniotic fluid). Literally translated, *zaki* means "sweet." There is a widespread superstition among Hausa that *zaki* obstructs delivery. Hence, pregnant women drink bitter herbs or *tsamiya* (tamarind) soaked in water to reduce the amniotic fluid, and thereby ease labor pains and hasten childbirth. They are also advised to avoid eating sweet foods in order to control *zaki*. This web of cultural practices does not ease the protracted labor nor the trauma most pregnant girls undergo.

Local birth attendants cannot handle other complications of pregnancy, such as eclampsia, which requires monitoring of the blood pressure, and pelvic malformations, which require a cesarean operation. These complications go undetected and often lead to the death of the mother and child; the Nigerian infant mortality rate is 70 to 87 per 1,000 live births. Use of unsterilized instruments by the local birth attendants also leads to life-threatening infections. In some cases, the placenta is not expelled after childbirth, leading to hemorrhaging, infection of the uterus, and death. When a lot of blood is lost, local birth attendants are ill trained and unequipped to provide blood transfusions. Cases of retained placenta and hemorrhage are often referred to hospitals from the rural areas when the patient's situation is critical and hopeless. The 1995 statistics released by the National Council for Population and Environmental Activities (NCPEA) show that Nigeria's maternal mortality rate of 15 per 1,000 births is one of the highest in the world. Teenage girls also account for almost 25 percent of maternal deaths in Nigeria.

Certain Hausan practices also lead to maternal morbidity. During labor, particularly a prolonged one, the local birth attendant performs a local episiotomy to facilitate delivery of the baby. These *gishiri* cuts are incisions made by the local midwife to cut off membranes in the vaginal region during labor, oftentimes using unsterilized instruments. Subsequent infection and the extension of the cut to the anal and urethral areas may damage the muscles that control the passage of the urine, resulting in a vesico-vaginal fistula (VVF). VVF research by Lawanson (1993) has revealed that the Hausa also believe that, in addition to facilitating childbirth, *gishiri* cuts also alleviate amenorrhea, infertility, and painful intercourse. However, these VVF patients often experience involuntary seepage of urine, a defect that requires a costly and complicated operation to correct. (See additional discussion in Section 8D, Significant Unconventional Sexual Behaviors, Female Genital Mutilation and Other Harmful Practices, above.)

Many pregnancy complications go untreated because of inadequate medical facilities and sometimes ignorance on the part of the patients who fail to seek hospital treatment. Those who do seek treatment at a hospital usually compete for treatment, waiting for years for their turn. The seepage of urine makes the VVF patients undesirable, and they are often abandoned in hospitals or treated as outcasts by their families, especially husbands who desert them. These women, most of them in their teens, are thus condemned to living a life of misery. There are currently 200,000 reported cases of VVF in the country, with a heavy concentration in the northern states of Kano, Jigawa, Katsina, Sokoto, and Borno. Several cases have also been reported in the southern Nigerian state of Akwa Ibom.

D/E. Abortion and Population Planning
FOYIN OYEBOLA AND UWEM EDIMO ESIET

Abortion is a criminal offense in Nigeria except when the life of the woman is endangered by the pregnancy. It is not, therefore, an approved method of population planning and family limitation. Nevertheless, the abortion rate is high in Nigeria. Unsafe illegal abortion is one of the leading causes of maternal death in women of reproductive age. Also, abortion affects adolescent women who lack basic information about reproduction and the prevention of pregnancy, as well as the information and resources necessary for obtaining safe abortions. [Oyebola]

The Campaign Against Unwanted Pregnancy (CAUP) conducted a study recently in collaboration with the Alan Guttmacher Institute of the United States of America, focusing on the incidence of induced abortion in Nigeria ("Incidence of Induced Abortion", 1998). In each year studied, Nigerian women obtained approximately 610,000 abortions. Most of these women resorted to abortion as an outcome of an unwanted pregnancy. Sixty percent of the abortion seekers were age 15 to 25 years old, with a third of them being students, and 63 percent never being married. The study recommended better policies to improve access to contraceptive services to reduce unwanted pregnancy and abortion, as well as greater access to safe abortion to help preserve the health and lives of Nigerian women. [Oyebola]

Abortion has continued to generate controversy in Nigeria. Whereas Nigeria has one of the highest maternal mortality rates in the world, over 800 maternal deaths per 100,000 women, consensus as to how the issue of abortion should be addressed has not been agreed on. The 1998 report by the Campaign Against Unwanted Pregnancy mentioned above further corroborated this need. Thus far, the government has not taken appropriate steps to address this scourge, preferring the ostrich approach of burying its head in the sand and wishing the problem were over. There is no doubt that contraceptive usage is low, especially among adolescents, and that sexual ignorance is very high, with about 60 percent of Nigerian youth not knowing that pregnancy is possible at first intercourse. [U. Esiet]

In a 1994 countrywide report submitted by the Federal Ministry of Health and Social Services, Nigerian adolescents accounted for 80 percent of Nigeria's unsafe abortions. The government has responded to Nigeria's high fertility rate of six children in a woman's lifetime by formulating a National Policy on Population for Development, Unity, and Self-Reliance. Unfortunately, this 1988 document is not gender-sensitive. It recommends that each woman should have no more than four children, and that the minimum age for female marriage be 18 years. The document is silent on the age of marriage for men, and takes no notice of the well-known fact that many men have more than one wife and, therefore, father more than four children in their lifetime. Also, the issue of reducing early marriage is not supported by any appropriate legislation, education, or mass mobilization. It is obvious that the gender-interest perspective was not utilized in making this policy—not unexpected in a patrilineal society. Attempts have since been made to link population with Family Life Education in a POP/FLE effort (see Section 3A, Sexuality Knowledge and Education, Sexuality Education). In 1999, this resulted in a paradigm shift on the federal level, with a reproductive health strategy that addresses the people's needs primarily, and then hopes that this will empower the people to address the population issue. All of these strategies are going to be within the framework of a primary health care strategy. It must be acknowledged that government has done much within its new purview, without ignoring the fact that still more needs to, and can be done. Civil societal groups, especially the NGOs, have continued to make family planning services available, accessible, and directed at people's needs. [U. Esiet]

10. Sexually Transmitted Diseases

Data on sexually transmissible diseases (STDs) in Nigeria are limited. The prevalence of syphilis among antenatal clinic attendees in 1993 from sentinel surveillance was 3.8 percent.

STD clinics are underutilized because of stigmatization and the lack of appropriate facilities and specialists in STD management. Manuals for training health workers, and for syndrome management, have been produced with the support of donor agencies and specialists. Several health workers have been trained, and others are being trained to use these manuals. Appropriate drugs and condoms have been made available, and information and education about STDs is being incorporated into Primary Health Care facilities. It is, however, important for Nigeria to have baseline data, so that adequate and appropriate planning and education can be carried out.

Government support has been far below expectations, and it is hoped that NGOs will participate more actively in the near future in Information, Education, and Communication (IEC) activities and training.

Recommendations from various workshops and meetings are that measures aimed at control and prevention should be integrated into other development projects, such as Family Planning and Maternal and Child Health Services. This will ensure that women and children with STDs are treated in the same clinic by the same service provider in one hospital visit. Nigeria needs intensive IEC advocacy and mobilization of specific groups. We also should promote the best practices as a concept and as a tool for effective and expanded responsiveness to STDs (Family Health International 1996; UNAIDS 1994).

11. HIV/AIDS

UWEM EDIMO ESIET

A. The Current Status

Nigeria reported its first case of AIDS in 1986. However, based on the most recent published data by the National AIDS and STD Control Programme, Nigeria can now be identified as a major locus of HIV infection in Sub-Saharan Africa, with a national seroprevalence rate of 4.5 percent. The progression has been 1 percent in 1990, 1.2 percent in 1991-1992, 3.8 percent in 1991-1992, and 3.8 percent in 1993-1994. It has been estimated that one new infection of HIV occurs every minute in Nigeria. Esiet cites data suggesting that 95 percent of all infections are by hetero-sexual intercourse, 4 percent are through blood transfusions, and one percent are through mother-to-child transmission. Nigerian population surveys from both urban and rural areas indicate a seroprevalence rate of 5 to 8 percent in the general population, with a preponderance of HIV infection in females age 15 to 19, whereas for males, the peak age is 20 to 29 years old (WHO 1997; National Symposium 1998; Lagos State Seminar 1999).

Data from population and hospital-based studies indicate that about 80 percent of HIV transmission occurs through heterosexual intercourse while 10 percent occurs through blood transfusions. Vertical transmission (mother-to-child) is also becoming a significant route with the increase of HIV prevalence among women of reproductive age.

Factors responsible for the rapid spread of HIV in Nigeria include:

- low-risk perception, especially among youths;
- cultural and religious attitudes, which make it difficult for women to make decisions about reproductive health issues;
- myths and misconceptions about HIV/AIDS;
- the worsening economic situation;
- low acceptability, availability, and use of condoms;
- lack of appropriate medical care for STDs, opportunistic infections, and AIDS;
- lack of data management for planning and decision making; and
- lack of voluntary testing and counseling services.

All these factors mitigate against the behavioral changes needed for a decrease in the incidence of HIV/AIDS in Nigeria. At the same time, government efforts at all levels to address the epidemic over the past ten years have been grossly inadequate, and certainly not commensurate with the magnitude of the problem (Akinsete et al. 1997, 1999; Akanmu and Akinsete 1999; Federal Ministry of Health 1999).

Many NGOs are involved in the fight against HIV/AIDS, especially in the areas of information, education, and communication, and a few are involved in home-based care for people living with HIV/AIDS. However, their resources are limited although several donor agencies support many of them. Sustainability of programs is a major problem.

The government response has included formulation of a National Policy on HIV/AIDS, the syndrome management of STDs, sentinel surveys, massive mobilization and AIDS awareness, and a national conference on HIV/AIDS, at which programmatically workable solutions were addressed. It must be acknowledged that despite all these efforts HIV/AIDS programs continue to remain underfunded. However, NGOs have also been complementing government efforts in all areas that include IEC and service provision to people with HIV/AIDS. Despite all these efforts, a lot of Nigerians have yet to be reached with the appropriate information and support necessary to bring about altered behavior changes. Condom use is still low, and the abilities of women to negotiate safe sex also low. Even though it has been introduced, the female condom is quite expensive when viewed from the income level of the people.

B. Gaps, Future Challenges, and the Way Forward

Nigeria is still going through a phase characterized by denial, stigmatization, panic, and political instability. The financial and material resources committed by the government fall far below the level required to adequately and effectively deal with the magnitude of the HIV/AIDS epidemic in Nigeria. AIDS cuts across all aspects of life, and therefore the responses must be multisectoral and multidisciplinary (National Conference 1998).

There is a need to intensify advocacy at all levels, private, public, and community, and to prioritize responses. The priorities for action are:

- Promoting rational responses and priority-setting by the government, NGOs, and donor communities based on knowledge and information (accurate data) rather than anecdotes and prejudice. This makes it imperative that accurate assessment of the magnitude of the problem be undertaken for planning and decision making.
- Assembling usable economic data and knowledge to facilitate decisions about where best to spend limited resources.
- Advocating for appropriate budget allocations for HIV/AIDS/STD activities by the government at all levels and by donor agencies.
- Ensuring that there is a fair spread of resources allocated for HIV/AIDS/STD, which includes both prevention, care, and support activities by all stakeholders.
- Promoting the care and support agenda by government, donors, the community, traditional healers, and the public and private health sectors.
- Linking care with prevention at all levels.
- Encouraging private sector sensitization, advocacy, and mobilization in support of intervention programs in the workplace.

- Increasing acceptability, availability, and access to condoms through condom social marketing supported by government and donor agencies.
- Finding funds to support Health Care Systems in dealing with conditions that increase vulnerability to HIV/AIDS, e.g., sexually transmitted diseases (STD), tuberculosis (TB), and malnutrition, through capacity-building for medical personnel. The promotion and support of such services, and their integration into reproductive health services, are necessary.
- Identifying and supporting income-generating activities and credit plans to reduce vulnerability to the poverty that accompanies and abets the epidemic.
- Promoting activities aimed at addressing issues of gender inequality, e.g., developing negotiation skills for women, knowledge of human rights, and income-generating projects for women.
- Providing access and linkages to counseling services and other activities that address the emotional and spiritual needs of both adults and children.
- Supporting and catalyzing groups of people living with HIV and AIDS, and encouraging their involvement in HIV/AIDS programs.
- Supporting activities that advocate legal rights for HIV/AIDS-affected persons, particularly women and children. AIDS intervention must address issues that promote the marginalization of some sectors of the society, thus increasing their vulnerability.
- Recognizing the rights of all individuals to care, as well as legal, economic, and inheritance protection.
- Encouraging accessibility and affordability of drugs for treatment of opportunistic infections and antiretroviral drugs.
- Preventing vertical transmission through breastfeeding.
- Preventing the transmission of HIV through blood transfusions by educating and recruiting voluntary non-remunerated blood donors, screening of blood for HIV, and the training of personnel.
- Promoting programs that are integrated into other routine activities, e.g., schools, cultural and media reporting, agricultural extension programs, etc., because these are more effective in internalizing the epidemic than programs specifically focused on AIDS.

C. Conclusion

As the HIV/AIDS epidemic continues to spread worldwide, we are learning more about how individuals, households, families, communities, organizations, government, and the nation are affected. Strategies to prevent the spread have been focused on the promotion of condoms, the reduction of multiple sexual partners, and the treatment of STDs.

Many of these interventions have failed to address the social, economic, and gender issues, and the care and support of persons living with

HIV/AIDS, adolescent reproductive health, and the disabled. Future interventions need to take into consideration all these factors in all planning. There is a need to be forward-looking, if responses are to keep pace with the speed and impact of this epidemic.

Evidence from different countries, not just industrialized nations, has clearly shown that prevention works. In Nigeria, we need a multisectoral, multidisciplinary approach, as well as political commitment at all levels of our government.

12. Sexual Dysfunctions, Counseling, and Therapies
UWEM EDIMO ESIET

The introduction of Viagra has opened up a public discourse on sexual dysfunction by providing a new, effective therapy for the primary sexual-dysfunction concern of Nigerian males, functional impotence. In Nigeria's traditional societies, many therapies have long been available to most Nigerians for dealing with functional impotence and other sexual dysfunctions. Some of these remedies have already been described by Bilikisu Yusuf in Section 5D, Interpersonal Heterosexual Behaviors, on aphrodisiacs. The efficacy of these traditional remedies has yet to be clinically ascertained. Sexual dysfunctions of women are hardly discussed, because, for the majority of Nigerians, the prime objective of sexual intercourse is not sexual pleasure but procreation. Therefore, the issue of counseling and therapy is not as profound as it should be in our society. Professionals need to educate the Nigerian public about sexual dysfunctions other than male erectile dysfunction, so that both men and women will seek appropriate counseling and therapies. Hopefully, as the study of human sexuality and sexology becomes more developed in Nigeria, challenges such as these will be addressed.

13. Research and Advanced Education

There is no sexological organization or publication in Nigeria. Nor is there any basic research unless it has practical health applications that address the major health issues facing our nation. The contributors to this chapter gained their expertise from training abroad, including The International Women's Health Coalition in New York (USA), and from their extensive fieldwork among the people.

Nigeria has three organizations that deal with sexuality issues. These are:

Action Health Incorporated, Youth Center, Plot 54 Somorin Street, Ifako, Gbagada, Lagos, Nigeria; Phone/fax: 234-1-861-166. E-mail: AHI@linkserve .com.ng.

Association for Reproductive and Family Health (ARFH), 13 Ajayi Osungbekun Street, Ikolaba GRA, Ibadan, Nigeria; Phone: 234-1-820-945.

Planned Parenthood Federation of Nigeria, 224 Ikorodu Road, Palmgrove, Somolu, PMB 12657, Lagos, Nigeria; Phone: 234-1-820-526.

References and Suggested Readings

Abd al' Ati, H. 1982. *The family structure in Islam.* Lagos: Islamic Publications Bureau.

Akanmu, A. S., & Akinsete, I. 1999. *Epidemiology of HIV/AIDS in Nigeria.* (Publisher not known).

Akande, J. O. 1989. A decade of human rights in Nigeria. In: A. Ajomo, ed., *New dimension in Nigeria law* (Law series no. 3, p. 123ff). Lagos: Nigeria Institute of Advanced Legal Studies.

Akinsete, I., Akanmu, A. S., & Okany, C. C. 1999. *Infected adults at the Lagos University Teaching Hospital—A five year experience.* (Publisher not known).

Akinsete, I., Gwarzo, S. N., Koita, N., Nnorom, J., Asiedu, K., Rehle, T., & Williams, E. 1997 (April). AIDSCAP (AIDS control and prevention). *Nigeria Program Review.*

Beck, L. G., & Keddie, N., eds. 1978. *Women in the Muslim world.* Cambridge, MA: Harvard University Press.

Bouhdiba, A. 1985. *Sexuality in Islam* (A. Sheridan, trans.). London: Routledge and Kegan Paul.

Brooks, G. 1995. *Nine parts of desire: The hidden world of Islamic women.* New York: Anchor Books/Doubleday.

Coles, C., & Mack, B., eds. 1991. *Hausa women in the twentieth century.* Madison, WI: University of Wisconsin Press.

Cook, R. J. 1994. State accountability under the convention on the elimination of all forms of discrimination against women. In: R. J. Cook, ed., *Human rights of women: National and international perspectives.* Philadelphia: University of Pennsylvania Press.

Crowther, M. 1972. *The story of Nigeria.* London: Faber and Faber.

Family Health International. 1996 (May). STD prevention: New challenges, new approaches. *The AIDS Control and Prevention (AIDSCAP) Project, Project No. 936-5972, 31-4692046,* 3(1).

Federal Ministry of Health and Human Services. 1992. Focus on AIDS. *Bulletin of Epidemiology,* 2(2):15-16.

Federation of Muslim Women's Associations in Nigeria (FOMWAN). 1986. Communique of the First National Conference on Family and Society, Queen's College, Lagos, July 24-27, 1986. (Conference summary).

Fernea, E. W. 1998. *In search of feminism: One woman's global journey.* New York: Doubleday.

Francoeur, R. T., Esiet, U., & Esiet, N. 2000 (April/May). Ethnic views of sexuality in Nigeria. *SIECUS Report,* 28(4):8-12.

Goddard, C. 1995 (May). Adolescent sexuality in Nigeria. Advocates for Youth (Available from: 1025 Vermont Avenue, NW, Suite 200, Washington, DC 20005).

Ilumoka, A. O. 1994. African women's economic, social and cultural rights. In: R. J. Cook, ed., *Human rights of women: National and international perspectives.* Philadelphia: University of Pennsylvania Press.

The incidence of induced abortion in Nigeria. 1998. *International Family Planning Perspectives,* 24(4):156-164.

Koss, M. P. 1987. Hidden rape: Incidence, prevalence, and descriptive characteristics of sexual aggression and victimization in a national sample of college students. In: A. W. Burgess, ed., *Sexual assault* (vol. 3). New York: Garland Publishing.

Lagos State Seminar/Workshop on HIV/AIDS and Malaria. 1999 (March). Eko Hotel, Lagos.

Lawanson, J. 1993. Vaginal fistulas. *International Journal of Gynaecology and Obstetrics,* 40:14.

Makinwa-Adelzusoye, P. 1992. Sexual behavior, reproductive knowledge, and contraceptive use among young urban Nigerians. *International Family Planning Perspectives,* *18*:67-69.

Makinwa-Adebusoye, P. K., & Feyiset, B. J. 1994. The quantum and tempo of fertility in Nigeria. In: *Fertility trends and determinants in six African countries: DHS regional analysis workshop for anglophone Africa.* Calverton, MO: Macro International Inc.

Mernissi, F. 1991. *The veil and the male elite: A feminist interpretation of women's rights in Islam.* Reading, MA: Addison-Wesley.

Mernissi, F. 1993. *Islam and democracy: Fear of the modern world.* Reading, MA: Addison-Wesley.

Michigan state sexual offences act. 1974. Ann Arbor, MI: The State Legislature.

Murray, S. O., & Roscoe, W., eds. 1997. *Islamic homosexualities: Culture, history, and literature.* New York/London: New York University Press.

Murray, S. O. 1997a. The will not to know: Islamic accommodations of male homosexuality. In: S. O. Murray & W. Roscoe, eds., *Islamic homosexualities: Culture, history, and literature.* New York/London: New York University Press.

Murray, S. O. 1997b. Woman–woman love in Islamic societies. In: S. O. Murray & W. Roscoe, eds., *Islamic homosexualities: Culture, history, and literature.* New York/London: New York University Press.

National Conference on HIV/AIDS in Nigeria. 1998 (December). *Lessons learnt and the way forward.* Lagos, Nigeria.

National Council for Population and Environmental Activities (NCPEA). 1995. *Population and maternal and child health.* In a press kit titled *Nigeria: Family planning and population activities,* released August 22, 1995, Lagos.

National Guidelines Task Force. 1996. *Guidelines for comprehensive sexuality education in Nigeria.* Lagos: Action Health Incorporated.

National Symposium/Workshop on HIV/AIDS in Nigeria. 1998 (June 2-5). Organized by Federal Ministry of Health (NASCP) in collaboration with Roche Nigeria Limited, Lagos, Nigeria.

Nigerian demographic and health survey. 1990. Columbia, MD: Department of Health Services. Cited in *Fact Sheet on "Adolescent Sexuality in Nigeria."* Washington, DC: Advocates for Youth, 1995.

Nwogugu, E. I. 1974. *Family law in Nigeria.* Lagos.

Oputa, C. 1989. Women and children as disempowered groups. In: *Women and children under Nigerian law.* Lagos: Federal Ministry of Justice.

Otaluka, A. O. 1989. Protection of women under the law. In: *Women and children under Nigerian law* (pp. 98ff). Lagos: Federal Ministry of Justice.

Oyajobi, A. 1986. Better protection for women and children under the law. In: *Women and children under Nigerian law.* Lagos: Federal Ministry of Justice.

Parrinder, G. 1980. *Sex in the world's great religions.* Don Mills, Ontario, Canada: General Publishing Company.

SIECUS (Sexuality Information and Education Council of the U.S.). 2000. Approval of 'Guidelines for comprehensive sexuality education in Nigeria' for Nigerian schools. *Making the Connection, 1*(1):1-2.

UNAIDS. 1994. *Management of sexually transmitted diseases. WHO/GPA/TEM/94* (1 Rev. 1). World Health Organization.

Views and comments of the Kano State Government on the report of the Committee for Women Affairs. 1988. Kano, Nigeria: Kano Government Printer.

WHO. 1997 (December). *UNAIDS—WHO computer epimodel estimate for HIV infection* (FSE/6). World Health Organization.

Yusuf, B. 1995 (January 21). *Impact of Islam and culture on marriage age in Hausa society.* Paper presented at the Seminar on Problems of Early Marriage in Nigeria, organized by Women in Nigeria (WIN), Kaduna State Branch, at the British Council Hall. Kaduna, Nigeria.

Outer Space

Raymond J. Noonan, Ph.D.*

Contents

Demographics and a Historical Perspective

A. Demographics

At this point in history, only a few hundred men and women from more than 25 countries have traveled and lived for some period of time in space.** With the advent of the new millennium, the permanent human presence in space is expected to be firmly entrenched with the first inhabitants of the new International Space Station *Alpha*, developed jointly by the United States, Russia, Canada, Japan, and Brazil, and the participating

Communications: Raymond J. Noonan, Ph.D., Health and Physical Education Department, Fashion Institute of Technology of the State University of New York, 27th Street and 7th Avenue, New York, NY 10001 USA; 212-217-7460; rjnoonan@SexQuest.com.

**Citizens from the following countries have flown in space: Afghanistan, Austria, Belgium, Bulgaria, Canada, Cuba, Czechoslovakia, France, Germany, Great Britain, Hungary, India, Israel, Italy, Japan, Mexico, Mongolia, Netherlands, Poland, Romania, Russia, Saudi Arabia, Syria, Ukraine, USA, and Vietnam.

nations of the European Space Agency (ESA): Belgium, Denmark, France, Germany, Italy, Netherlands, Norway, Spain, Sweden, Switzerland, and the United Kingdom (NASA 2001). Because of this virtually unprecedented mixing of cultures in a peacetime endeavor, we must expect that participants' cultural backgrounds will have an impact on gender interactions and any sexual relationships that will inevitably develop in space environments. Certainly, our common biological nature will have a different set of challenges in the sexological realm that will have to be met as well. Evidence for this comes from recent studies by Italian researchers that found that levels of the sex hormone testosterone are temporarily decreased in male astronauts by exposure to space, along with a concurrent decrease in sexual drive or libido (Strollo et al. 1998).

The "territory" of outer space, the study of which broadly comprises the domain of cosmology and astronomy, is open to interpretation. As Fazio (1997) has noted, where space begins depends on the physical properties of the area in question, specifically the problems that need to be resolved to allow humans to travel and live there. For example, extreme cold occurs, and sufficient air to breathe is lost, at considerably lower altitudes rising from Earth than the oxygen needed to power a jet engine. Thus, humans would require physical protection much sooner than they would need a rocket engine, which does not require atmospheric oxygen to fly. In addition, at various points in space, we would be faced with the potential effects of microgravity, several types of radiation, extremes in temperature and pressure, a near-complete vacuum, and the impact of meteorites. Therefore, for men and women to live and work effectively and safely in various space environments, engineers either have or will design vehicles and habitats, including spacesuits, with countermeasures to protect spacefarers from some of these extreme conditions. Others are pervasive, however, like radiation, which could have serious consequences outside of the protection of the Earth's magnetosphere, in which lie the Van Allan radiation belts, and microgravity, which will likely have an impact on sexuality factors.

Perhaps the most critical aspect of space with which we have to contend, however, is a psychosocial environment that is "characterized by isolation (a separation from the normal or daily physical and social environment), confinement (restriction within a highly limited and sharply demarcated physical and social environment), deprivation, and risk" (Connors, Harrison, & Akins 1985:7). In fact, they said that in space, ". . . the physical environment, when not terrifying, is likely to be bland" (p. 9). Pesavento (2000), in a very recent study of the psychological and social effects of isolation in space and during space-simulation analog studies on Earth, said that these may be the ultimate barriers to extended human spaceflight. He noted those factors that have yet to be resolved, including: "depression-like symptoms on orbit [(which Russian space physicians have named "neuresthenia")]; less-than-encouraging social interactions with mixed-gender and mixed-foreign-national groupings; sensory deprivation; as well as the emotional and sexual affects of close confinement on crew members" (p. 1; see also Cabbage 2001).

Yet, many astronauts have also described the profound sense of spiritual and philosophical awareness they gained being in space and viewing the awe-inspiring panoramas, especially looking back at the Earth (White 1987). Some have noted the absence of geographical boundaries, other than land and sea, and the meaning they ascribe to it in terms of the absence of political boundaries and the unity of humanity. Almost certainly, our collective sense of the fragility of Earth's environment has come from some of the widely published photographs taken in space.

For the foreseeable future, however, the laboratory for this grand human experiment will be the International Space Station (ISS), the largest and most complex scientific endeavor ever attempted on an international scale, which began assembly in orbit in late 1998 and had its first real inhabitants in early 2001. When finished, the ISS will have a mass of over 1 million pounds, measuring about 360 feet across and 290 feet long, with almost an acre of solar panels for electrical power. Flying at an altitude of 250 statute miles with an inclination of 51.6 degrees, at which it can be reached by all of the international partners, the ISS will be able to observe 85 percent of the globe, covering 95 percent of the Earth's population. It will be the site of a wide range of scientific endeavors and research (NASA 1999).

B. A Brief Historical Perspective

The realization of the fantasy of space travel is a distinctly twentieth-century phenomenon, having its antecedents in the age-old fantasy of human flight dating at least from the ancient Greek story of Daedalus and Icarus. Combining the human need for exploration and discovery with the political realities of striving for nationalistic prestige and military advantage, and now, with the possibility of vast economic returns, the spaceflight revolution began during World War II with the development of the first V-2 ballistic rockets used by Germany against Great Britain. One of the fascinating stories surrounding the end of the war involves the race, won by the Americans, with the then-Soviet military to capture these rockets after the fall of Nazi Germany, which, in 1946 and 1947, were used by the U.S. to carry its first biological payloads into space (Bushnell 1958). It was the V-2 rocket that made human spaceflight a theoretical possibility, and this, in turn, both stimulated an interest in suborbital test flights and spurred the development of space biology, as well as space medicine, which was first discussed by leaders at the U.S. Air Force School of Aviation Medicine in 1948 (Nicogossian, Pool, & Uri 1994). Thus began the pervasiveness of a military culture, with its similarities yet distinct dissimilarities with the wider culture of which it is a part, which once dominated but still persists in national space programs.

Test flights by the U.S. continued, including two primates in V-2 rockets prior to 1950, various animals in rockets until 1952 and high-altitude balloons from 1950 through 1954, and two men in balloons in the summer of 1957. Similar ballistic rocket flights by the Soviet Union from 1949 through 1957 used dogs as subjects. The Space Age proper is said to have begun with the launching by the Soviet Union in October 1957 of Sputnik-1, the first artificial satellite to orbit the Earth. This was followed a month later by Sputnik-2 carrying a dog named Laika, the first animal in orbit. The U.S. responded with the February 1958 launch of Explorer 1, which detected what would be named the Van Allen radiation belts. Subsequently, both the U.S. and the Soviet Union launched a number of animal flights, using mice, rats, monkeys, dogs, or other small animals, sometimes to test systems that would later contain humans. In April 1961, the Soviet cosmonaut Yuri Gagarin became the first man to orbit the Earth, with Gherman Titov being the second in August 1961. Following two manned suborbital flights by the U.S., John Glenn was the first American to reach orbital flight in Mercury's *Friendship 7* in February 1962. In June 1963, Soviet cosmonaut Valentina Tereshkova became the first woman in space.

It would be almost two decades later, August 1982, before the second woman, cosmonaut Svetlana Savitskaya, would fly; she would later be the first woman to conduct an EVA (extravehicular activity) in July 1984. Although it is widely accepted today that women will always be a part of the American space program, it was over 20 years, almost to the day from Tereshkova's historic flight, before the first American woman, Sally Ride, would fly on the space shuttle in June 1983, and October 1984 for the first EVA by an American woman, Kathryn Sullivan (Cassutt 1993; Nicogossian et al. 1994). Although it is interesting to note that Tereshkova's flight was considered by many at the time to be a Cold War public-relations ploy by the Soviet Union (Santy 1994), the United States had tested women as potential astronauts as early as 1960 (Atkinson & Shafritz 1985; McCullough 1973), although this fact is not widely recalled today. When news of it reached the press, it was treated with skepticism and flippancy. In fact, these women had been systematically barred from the space program, even though it was thought by some in the scientific community that women might be better suited, both physically and psychologically, for the severe requirements of those pioneering spaceflights (Levin 1989). These events illustrate an example of the collision of prejudice (sexism) with scientific knowledge that occurs all too often with sex-related issues (see Noonan 1998a).

Santy (1994) expressed her belief that a contributing factor to women's finally being selected as astronauts, although less obvious, was the fact that the first private toilet had recently been designed for use on the space shuttle:

> The issue of privacy, linked as it was to sexuality and personal hygiene, had been a big factor in NASA's reluctance to include women as astronauts, and the development of the private toilet—probably more than any other reason—encouraged NASA to believe that females could finally (and without embarrassment to the agency) be integrated into Shuttle missions in a way impossible during the earlier missions. In

> *Gemini* and *Apollo* missions, the spacecraft required that crew members
> live side by side without even the most minimal capability of providing
> privacy for personal activities. (p. 51)

In 1978, the first group of astronauts to include women and male minorities was chosen. It was considered a watershed event, signaling a change in the way in which future astronauts would be recruited and selected (Atkinson & Shafritz 1985). In fact, it was probably our first experience with what would later be called the "development of space cultures" (cf. Harris 1996) given that racial and ethnic minorities have distinct cultural attitudes and behaviors, and many regard males and females as having different cultures as well (Francoeur 1997, 1998). Cultural factors later became important in the Space Shuttle Program, which first flew in April 1981, and in the Shuttle–*Mir* Program, including Shannon Lucid's current-American-record 188-day stay on *Mir*, which resulted in unprecedented cooperation and trust between the U.S. and Russian space programs. The Shuttle–*Mir* Program, in which several Americans flew on *Mir* between 1995 and 1998, was designed in part to elicit some of the possible psychological, psychosocial, and human performance aspects of multicultural crews in preparation for the International Space Station (Morphew & MacLaren 1997). All of these experiences led to the present ISS *Alpha*, with its historical antecedents in the early space stations of the U.S. (*Skylab*) and USSR (*Salyut*) in the 1970s.

At the present time, international treaties govern the use of space, including the Outer Space Treaty of 1967, the Liability Convention of 1973, the Moon Agreement of 1979 (which was never signed by the U.S. or Russia), and others, under the auspices of the United Nations Committee on the Peaceful Use of Outer Space. Also, other agreements have been entered into in the telecommunications realm (Harris 1996). In addition, in the United States, Congress and the President determine space policy. Federal agencies also affect space activities, including NASA (the National Aeronautics and Space Administration), the Federal Communications Commission, and the Departments of State, Defense, Transportation, Commerce, and Energy, as well as the military, as noted earlier. Similar national organizations function in other countries. The Space-World Bar Association (Smith 1997) is working further to develop a prototype Lunar Economic Development Authority that would coordinate the planning of more extensive uses of space resources, not the least of which are the mineral resources expected to be mined and the microgravity environment expected to make possible new manufacturing opportunities.

Space tourism, in fact, is expected to be a very important, although initially expensive venue in which ordinary citizens will be able to visit space habitats for their vacations. Just as air travel has become common today with its mass-market availability and the concurrent affordability resulting from it, a few entrepreneurs are already creating private companies to offer the service. One expected attraction is what a former U.S. congressman called widespread public attention to: the honeymoon in space (Gingrich 1995). Such ideas, of course, echoed similar predictions by science fiction writers, such as the space visionary, Arthur C. Clarke (1986), but this was the first time that such an inherently sex-bound human activity was included in a political vision for future Americans (if not for the bulk of humanity).

1. Basic Sexological Premises

A/B. Character of Gender Roles and Sociolegal Status of Males and Females

Early in the space programs of both the United States and Russia, men were virtually the only ones recruited for space missions. Although this has been attributed to the fact that the Eisenhower Administration in the U.S. directed that military test pilots be the first to attempt these early missions because of their skills in testing new aircraft designs, and the inherent danger they entailed, women had been considered as early as 1960 (see Section B, A Brief Historical Perspective, before). At present, women have been an integral part of the various space programs, including commanding the space shuttle, although there is still not a gender-balance in the ranks of astronauts. In addition, some authors have noted that sexist attitudes have been a part of the experience of some women, as well as attitudes that some women still have to prove themselves because they are women (Casper & Moore 1995; Connors et al. 1985). The issue with regard to the development of the toilet, noted above, serves as an example of the constraints surrounding the biological aspects of our differing anatomies, and psychological differences have been cited as well (see Noonan 1998a).

C. General Concepts of Sexuality and Love

Conjecture on the Influence of Spaceflight on Sexological Issues

Levin (1989), a British consultant on reproductive and sexual physiology, has written the most extensive review of the possible effects of space travel on these human systems. In surveying the research literature, he wrote:

> Despite th[e] large number of people who have been exposed to space flight with all its attendant hazards, our knowledge about the effects of space travel on the human reproductive system, and human sexuality, is sparse, bordering on the non-existent. Some of the most elementary questions seem not to have been investigated, indeed in some respects not even to have been asked. For example, it appears that no programme to evaluate the effect of space travel on human spermatozoa was ever initiated despite the obvious hazard of exposure of astronauts to radiation, stress and G forces. Even if asked, answers have not yet appeared in the open literature. (p. 378)

With regard to the lack of research on the behavioral aspects of human sexuality, Levin provided additional insight:

> In some respects this near-complete avoidance of what is a sensitive area of human behaviour represents a significant failure to investigate fully the possible reasons for the known stresses of living in isolated, confined environments. It is remarkable that there is no study as to whether human sexual activity, *or its loss* [italics added], can influence the adverse effects of such environments e.g. boredom, listlessness, sleep disturbances, fatigue, impaired cognition, irritability, hostility, depression and deterioration of personality. (p. 382)

Despite these concerns expressed within the space science literature—and readily available in their headquarters library in Washington, D.C.—little research has been done by the NASA, whose typical response has been that sex is not yet an issue (Date 1992; Vaughan 1992). It is my contention that much of this official response to sexual expression and to sexual research by the U.S. space establishment has been guided by attitudes distorted by a conceptualization of human sexuality as a capacity to be feared, avoided, sensationalized, problematized, or trivialized unless considered within the traditional boundaries of American sexual propriety. Similar negative views of human sexuality have failed to alleviate many of the perceived problems of people on Earth—and, in fact, have created many more problems because of ignorance and irrational fear (see Francoeur & Perper 1997; Weis 1997). Americans, after all, whether educated scientists or the generally scientifically ignorant general public, are Americans first. As such, we have been profoundly influenced by cultural values publicly accepted and promulgated by those who define society's norms, even if those norms have often been privately ignored by significant numbers of people, including, often enough, the very leaders who promote them.

In 1998, the first comprehensive analysis of human sexuality factors in relation to extended spaceflight, *A Philosophical Inquiry into the Role of Sexology in Space Life Sciences Research and Human Factors Considerations for Extended Spaceflight* (Noonan 1998a), was published, in which the author explored the issues and constraints surrounding the study of sex in space and conjectured about the potential impact of our sexual nature on mission success or failure. It suggested new terminology, the *human sexuality complex*, as a useful construct in which to consider the various sexuality factors in which human beings interact in and with their various environments.

The complexity of human sexuality, human sexual relationships, and sexual responses suggests the advantages of adopting a complex systems approach, one that draws on chaos and complexity theories, in future research on sexual phenomena and the interactions of its various components conceived as systems (Noonan 1998a, b). Research on human sexuality in space, it would seem, could definitely benefit from the systems perspective, much as it was essential in developing our space programs. It also seems worthwhile and reasonable to consider the space environment to be a culture in itself, a "microsociety in a miniworld," as Connors et al. (1985:2) described it, although it is also influenced by the outside cultures that sponsor it, much as any organization or workplace develops an indigenous culture, and the cultures of birth and subsequent origin of the individual crewmembers. In time, of course, any group will develop its own culture and norms that may be independent and/or an intricate mix of the others.

On the International Space Station, conflicts will occur when the status of women and men are inherently unequal, or if there is a perception of sexual deprivation among some members of a crew when others are in a sexual relationship there, as has occurred in Antarctica analogs (see Noonan 1998a). An anecdotal story tells of a Muslim passenger on an international spaceflight who had to take directions from a woman. Whenever she addressed him, he ignored her, because his cultural heritage, influenced by his religious beliefs, prohibited such contact between men and women. As a result, directions needed to be given by the woman to a male colleague who then repeated them to the man who then carried them out.

2. Religious and Ethnic Factors Affecting Sexuality

A/B. Source and Character of Religious Values and Character of Ethnic Values

The experiences of U.S. astronauts on *Mir* are well-known examples of some of the problems encountered by international crews of different ethnicities. Pesavento (2000) and Harris (1996) highlight the potential impact that cultural differences have had or might have on future missions. Of particular importance with respect to cultural and religious factors would likely be the compatibility of crewmembers' worldviews, as Francoeur and Perper (1997) have elucidated. The example previously noted of the Muslim crewmember's inability to interact with women as a partial result of his religious beliefs about innate differences between the sexes would also be relevant here. Of equal or greater importance might be the organizational (i.e., NASA's) stance and corporate-cultural beliefs about sexual issues that are transmitted to crewmembers (probably reinforcing similar beliefs in the astronauts), although such beliefs may have the same questionable effectiveness long-term as similar ones do generally in the U.S. and other societies today.

3. Sexual Knowledge and Education

A/B. Government Policies and Programs and Informal Sources of Sexual Knowledge

The impact on extended spaceflight is likely to occur as a result of policies that resist the study of both the potential positive aspects inherent in the human sexuality complex as well as the potential negative ones. There may also be problems in failing to communicate the findings—and their importance—to the space community, Congress, and the American public as a whole, once they have been studied. The sexual myths of individuals at all levels of the scientific, administrative, and other parts of space organizations and their contractors or subcontractors are also likely to have a negative impact, as the myths become the guiding principles that are incorporated in the organizational philosophy. Perhaps another benefit of the space program (the so-called spinoff effect) could be the furthering of sexual knowledge by combining sexuality education and space education. Young people are very interested in both, and each subject could be used to impart knowledge about the other, particularly in the realm of science.

4. Autoerotic Behaviors and Patterns

A/B. Children and Adolescents, and Adults

Today, masturbation is believed to be a generally healthy and normal part of the experiences of human beings throughout their lifecycle. Nevertheless, we are still influenced by some of the beliefs of the nineteenth century, that masturbation (and ejaculation in general) depletes certain personal mental and energy reserves, such as when coaches sometimes suggest that neither be engaged in prior to competing. Money (1985a) has shown that this now-discredited degeneracy theory of masturbation, which some people thought could be counteracted by proper fitness and nutrition, prompted prominent health proponents, such as John Harvey Kellogg and Sylvester Graham, to develop foods they believed would extinguish sexual appetite and masturbation. Today, two of these foods remain associated with their creators, Kellogg's corn flakes and graham crackers, respectively, although their original purpose is long forgotten. Nevertheless, some religious traditions continue to oppose masturbation as moral degeneracy. Both of these traditions—the medical and the religious—are likely to be important in the context of space, because they have and will prevent the study of masturbation as a sexual activity that will likely be practiced in space, in the unlikely event that it has not been already. Among other things, it can help to counteract boredom and stress, and the environment is amenable to it, in that sufficient privacy can be found in which to practice it. Pesavento's (2000) recent study noted that in the early 1970s, a physician suggested that masturbation would be an effective countermeasure to maintain prostate health and avoid urinary tract infections for astronauts on *Skylab*, the longest mission of which lasted 84 days. Children and adolescents will, of course, practice masturbation when they become a part of settlements in space in the distant future, just as they will have hetero- and homosexual experiences, as they do on Earth in various societies today.

5. *Interpersonal Heterosexual Behaviors*

A/B/C. Children, Adolescents, and Adults

Heterosexual behavior encompasses a wide variety of possibilities: in specific activities, such as kissing, oral and anal intercourse, and vaginal-penile intercourse, for example, and in the variety of ways in which they can be done. A device has been patented, the "Belt to Paradise," to enable sexual intercourse in microgravity (McCullough 1992). In addition, there are numerous fantasy behaviors that can be acted out with a partner or imagined alone. Any of these heterosexual activities are very likely to occur in space at some point in the future, if some have not occurred already. Pesavento (2000) has discussed some of the rumored pairings that have occurred, although everyone officially denies that anything happened. However, it seems likely that sexual intercourse and oral sex have already occurred in space. It is likely because, in our culture, sex is pervasive, gender awareness is ubiquitous, and the astronauts are mostly young, healthy people. However, given the current political climate, it is not possible to prove that sexual behavior has occurred. Speculation at this time may be the best approach until the next sex-positive cultural phase, which, if Reiss (1990) is correct in his characterization of sexual revolutions as being cyclical, will probably occur early in this century, that allows and emphasizes healthy sexual experience as the predominant social norm (see also Noonan 1996, 1998b).

Given our experience on Earth, it is also very likely that at least a few astronauts have entertained the notion of being the first to "do it" in space—unknown to the world, but still a shared, cherished, intimate secret. In addition, there is evidence that higher levels of intelligence and overall education—characteristics selected-for in astronauts—increase the likelihood that certain sexual behaviors will be experienced (Hunt 1974). At this point in the space program, the astronauts are a large-enough population so that individuals would likely be able find appropriate partners. Privacy and space in which any sexual activity can occur, albeit scarce, can be made available with appropriate planning. Sexual intercourse can also be done rather quickly, if need be, with very satisfactory results.

Our experience on Earth with some of the heterosexual subcultures, such as multiple sexual partnerships, also would imply that, although they have been sometimes problematic when flaunted in an atmosphere of sexual deprivation for other crewmembers in the analogous Antarctic settings, in the more normal conditions of typical urban, suburban, and sometimes rural settings, extramarital affairs, multiple relationships, and even group sex, have the potential to coexist with the more traditional expressed norms of heterosexual monogamous marriage (Libby & Whitehurst 1977). When these alternative relationship patterns are successful (functional), it is usually because the couple and the subcultural network in which it functions have adopted it, and group norms have evolved that define their expression, often in contrast to how they perceive the outside world's views of their subculture's behavior. In space, because there will be limited populations for the foreseeable future, both with and without a balanced gender mix, the various diverse alternative sexual lifestyle patterns might be an avenue of inquiry to minimize potential problems. Again, given the current political and social climate in the country, it may be necessary to keep it an internal group secret. Nevertheless, a television news magazine reported the possibility that group sex had occurred in space (Anderson 1992).

6. Homoerotic, Homosexual, and Ambisexual Behaviors

A/B. Children and Adolescents, and Adults

Connors et al. (1985) considered the possibility of homosexual relationships in space, although they considered heterosexual relationships to be the more realistic problem. At this time, it appears that homosexual activities in their varied forms are significantly less likely to have occurred in space, even if there are gay astronauts, because the majority of their colleagues are likely to be heterosexual; in addition, the process of coming out (making their homosexuality known to others) would very likely be the end of their career. However, homosexual sex may have occurred, because individuals are often able to find each other by conscious and unconscious subcultural cues. Then, allowing for the accidents of time and scheduling, potential homosexual partners may have been assigned to the same flight, guaranteeing training together for the mission and allowing them to be together in space for sex to occur. I also would not want to prove that homosexual activities have occurred for the same reasons noted above for heterosexuals, but in this instance, I would have to add the potentially greater harm that might come to a gay astronaut if his (or her) sexual orientation were unintentionally made public (although losing one's career would likely hold true for heterosexuals as well).

The number of women who are astronauts would make lesbians even less likely to be represented in the astronaut corps than gay men, and thus would make it less likely that lesbian sexual activity has occurred. Nevertheless, both lesbians and gay men are represented in other aspects of the space program. The likelihood of bisexuals who might be astronauts is more difficult to assess, because many bisexuals typically do not identify themselves as a distinct subculture, but tend to shift between heterosexual or homosexual affiliations. Bisexuals, female and male, who are attracted equally to females and males are less common than those who tend to focus on one sex or the other. With regard to multiple pairings, my comments with reference to heterosexual astronauts would also likely apply, although in the case of gay astronauts, more or less their whole sexual persona would need to be kept secret in the present social climate.

7. Gender Conflicted Persons

At present, this issue probably has no relevance in the space programs.

8. Significant Unconventional Sexual Behaviors

A. Coercive Sex

Sexual Harassment and Rape

Sexual harassment has been cited as a significant problem in the military, and, although it is often used now as a means of extortion or harassment itself, obscuring its real meanings and incidence in general, there is no information as to whether it has been a problem in the training or other professional or social settings involving the astronauts; it could be a problem in a space setting where significant levels of stress might precipitate that or other antisocial behavior. The same might be said for rape, although it is less common than sexual harassment. Clearly, we have not yet found the solutions to these problems in many of Earth's cultures.

Casper and Moore (1995), noting the instances of friction in the analog and space environments that have occurred as a result of the psychosocial stresses covered earlier, at one point highlighted the possible sexual violence that might occur because of these stresses. Apparently rejecting the evidence that shows that mixed-sex groups function more effectively in many ways than single-sex groups (Bishop 1996a, b; Pierce 1991), they wrote:

> These accounts raise compelling questions about the limits of the "complementary sexes" model proposed by NASA as leading to more harmonious and productive work. Psychological disturbances raise the specter of sexual violence, racial violence, and other serious interpersonal conflicts resulting from stress induced by long missions. It is somewhat disturbing to us that sexual behavior in space is assumed to be "total consenting adult free-choice sex." Given contemporary gendered power dynamics, this seems naively idealistic. Yet, an interesting research question is presented by the possible effects of weightlessness on expressions of sexual and other types of violence. For example, how would physical/bodily deterioration affect an individual's capability to overpower, force, and/or injure another astronaut? What does force look like in a 0-gravity context? Despite these concerns, issues of sexual violence are rarely raised with respect to long-term travel, and when we mentioned this possibility to informants they seemed vaguely puzzled. (p. 325)

Coercive sexual behaviors and blatant sexual harassment are not likely to be a problem in space, except in the event of a complete breakdown of the microsociety within the space culture. As Pierce (1991) noted, such microaggressions are usually more verbal and do not result in explosive violence. Rather, Casper and Moore frame outcomes of sexual expression as likely to be negative, reflecting the prevailing antisexualism of our culture, and is a clear example of the victimology concerns noted by Money (1995b).

Nevertheless, Pesavento (2000) noted that an attempted sexual assault did occur in a more-than-six-month-long simulated *Mir* mission module at the Institute for Biomedical Problems in Moscow. Alcohol was involved, as it occurred during a New Year's celebration. Still, it is important to emphasize that possibility does not equal likelihood.

B. Prostitution

Prostitution will likely find its way to space settlements once commercial exchange becomes established there, but it will not likely be an issue in any scenario until some time later in this century. It may well be a part of the expected sex-tourism industry that is expected to occur in the not-too-distant future.

C. Pornography and Erotica

It seems reasonable to expect that there would be a place for pornographic and erotic materials during a long flight. Bluth (1985) has noted that at some Antarctic research stations, "the men liked to watch pornographic films and it's best if a woman is not offended by pornography" (p. 143). This brings up questions of a sexological nature that may have relevance to extended spaceflight. If sexually oriented materials have the ability to relieve stress under extremely trying conditions, then they should be studied to determine if, in fact, they do. They also may serve as a morale booster. In addition, they may have value in places where there is currently a disproportionate ratio of women to men. The issue of sexual harassment would also be a factor when women are also members of the crew, because many courts have adopted the standard that such material sexualizes a workplace because some women (and some men) are offended by it. Although it is unlikely that it in fact does typically sexualize an environment, this position fails to take into account the sexually oriented materials marketed to gay males or lesbians, nor the feminist-produced corpus of literature and films for women. As a result, the ban on such materials as an expression of sexual harassment is typically applied only to materials oriented to heterosexual males.

Recently, Pesavento (2000) revealed that pornographic films were available to cosmonauts on the space station *Mir*, which Russian space psychologists recommended viewing only in the later stages of an individual cosmonaut's flight. He also described the surprise that American astronaut Norman Thagard had when he found that these soft-core French and Italian erotic videos were there. Pesavento also described plans for a movie to be made on *Mir*, in which sexual activity would be filmed, for which the Russian

Space Agency had already been paid millions of dollars for training the actors for their time in space. However, the filmmakers were not able to raise the additional millions needed to save the *Mir* from its planned deorbiting, which occurred at the end of March 2001.

D. Paraphilias

The paraphilias are those behaviors that are dependent on atypical or socially unacceptable things for sexual arousal, such as inanimate objects or parts of the body or events that are linked erotosexually to a person's childhood. They are thought to arise out of a traumatic or similar event that affects psychosexual development at critical periods during a child's life. Nevertheless, one may speculate that a generally sexually repressive environment would, at the same time, facilitate the expression of paraphilias. In relation to spaceflight, therefore, it would be incumbent upon researchers to create and maintain a sexually positive outlook to avoid the problems associated with paraphilic behaviors.

9. Contraception, Abortion, and Population Planning

A/B. Contraception and Abortion

Effective contraception is essential for long-term space travel for heterosexual couples, and efforts need to be undertaken to develop safe and effective contraceptive techniques, both for use on Earth and in space. Pregnancy is currently a contraindication for spaceflight. Abortion would probably be required in the event of failed contraception, because of mixed results found with the development of fertilized eggs of various animals, although the morning-after pill could be available as an alternative of first choice. Because abortion at the earliest stages is relatively simple to perform, the necessary equipment for a menstrual extraction or for a later suction curettage should be available in the medical station, as well as appropriate pregnancy-testing kits.

C. Population Programs

Population planning will become an issue when settlements are needed to be designed for lunar, Martian, or other outposts, and in that case, it is likely to be at the level of engineering the social environment around the professional expertise needed for the various parts of the mission (Harris 1996).

10/11. Sexually Transmitted Diseases and HIV/AIDS

The typical Earth-bound STDs with which we have to contend may present additional problems in space. This is because there is evidence that the immune system is compromised by spaceflight, although Sherr and Sonnenfeld (1997) wrote that some results are difficult to interpret. However, if this is found to be true, they thought it could severely limit long-term human spaceflight. Certainly, additional studies are needed to clarify this possibility, as well as to continue to learn more about our immune systems to be able to meet these challenges. There might also be the possibility that other disease organisms could mutate and become new STDs. The same is true for HIV/AIDS as well. In addition, there is the possibility that studies that gain a better understanding of the human immune system in space may have direct application for dealing with HIV/AIDS. It is also possible, given that drugs are expected to be manufactured in space because crystals form more purely in microgravity, that space science could assist in eradicating AIDS, as well as the STDs.

12. Sexual Dysfunctions, Counseling, and Therapies

Sexual response can be viewed physiologically as essentially a series of cardiovascular and muscular events resulting in a buildup of vasocongestion and myotonia to a psychophysiological peak and release known as climax or orgasm—coupled with a buildup and release of muscular tension. In the human sexual response cycle, as sexual stimulation progresses, blood engorges the vascular tissues of the clitoris, penis, and other parts of the body in the process called vasocongestion, while the buildup of muscle tension (myotonia) occurs. This is usually accompanied by an increase in respiration and metabolic activity. Orgasm releases and is typically considered the climax of this vasocongestion and myotonic buildup of sexual tension, in a paroxysmal, rhythmic, reflexive discharge of energy, typically resulting in a feeling of relaxation throughout much of the body.

Among the most visible physiological effects of spaceflight are the shifts in body fluids, most importantly the blood, which rises from the lower extremities to settle into the chest cavity and head. In time, the cardiovascular system acclimates itself to the new environment. At the same time, with less blood volume and no longer the need to pump blood against gravity, the heart muscles begin to relax somewhat, and the process of deconditioning begins (unless exercise is used to compensate for the loss by forcing the heart to pump harder). A similar condition occurs with overall body muscle tone, especially the large, weight-bearing, anti-gravity muscles that allow us to walk erect and maintain an upright posture. Therefore, we can probably expect a change in our perception of the various physiological phases of the sexual response cycle.

Anecdotal stories confirm that erections can and do take place in space, although a characterization of the quality of these erections has not been done. Information about whether women have experienced clitoral erections and vaginal lubrication has not been forthcoming, although the homologous nature of this aspect of the sexual response cycle would support the conclusion that they have. NASA could be easily monitoring this while the astronauts slept. One may conjecture that both female and male astronauts, when they are not asleep, would perceive a difference in their genital responses from their normal preflight experiences. Using Masters and Johnson's (1966) four-phase model of the human sexual response cycle, each phase might be affected in the following ways. During the excitement or arousal phase, penile erections in men may not feel as physically strong, particularly as the time in space gets longer and the body continues to adapt to weightlessness by deconditioning. The increase in respiration—the heavy breathing or hyperventilation, along with an increase in blood pressure and heart rate experienced during arousal through the plateau phase to orgasm—may also take more effort and feel more tiring as time progresses for the same reason. In women, clitoral erections and vaginal lubrication are likely to be similarly perceived.

Both vaginal lubrication in women and the erection of the clitoris and its homologue in men, the penis, are essentially vasocongestive in character. Vasocongestion forces the lubricating fluids through the pores of the walls of the vagina. This response varies with age, decreasing as women get older. This is likely to have an impact on astronauts who eventually travel to Mars, because older individuals are now thought to be among the prime candidates for such a trip because of the higher exposure risk to radiation in interplanetary flights. The main idea is that because the radiation effects are usually manifested many years later, it would be more likely that the astronauts would approach the natural end of their lives before the radiation effects would become evident. In addition, it is likely that the older astronauts would be well past the stage of starting families than younger ones would, given the impact of the possible and probable effects of radiation on gamete production.

The myotonia, the increase in muscle tension also characteristic of the sexual excitement and plateau phases, is likely to be experienced by the astronauts as being less intense during spaceflight than they normally experience on Earth, particularly in the voluntary muscle groups over which we have conscious control. This effect may increase as the time in space increases because of the progressive deconditioning of the muscles. Sexual activity, thus, might be an ideal part of an exercise program that people would very likely want to do regularly to maintain overall body and sexual fitness.

All of the effects on the human sexual response cycle just described provide possible mechanisms for a breakdown at some point in the cycle. Thus, there is the distinct possibility that any of the sexual dysfunctions experienced by men and women on Earth may increase or be aggravated in the space environment. But, just as Masters and Johnson (1966) indicated with respect to human sexual functioning on Earth, the range of normal functioning in space will need to be clarified before mechanisms and ameliorative actions for sexual dysfunctions can be described. Counseling practices will also need to take into account the unique psychosocial environment and the total space experience to be effective. In addition, countermeasures found to treat space-related sexual dysfunction should have application to the same problems on Earth.

Recently published data support the speculation that there would likely be some effect on sexual functioning, although deconditioning was not the focus of the study. Strollo et al. (1998) measured hormone secretion in four male astronauts pre-, in-, and postflight to test their hypothesis that stress-induced hormone changes might impair gonadal function by reducing testicular androgen (especially testosterone) secretion. In addition to its many roles in the differentiation of the fetus and the development of the secondary sex characteristics at puberty in males, testosterone stimulates the sex drive (libido) in both sexes. Strollo et al. found that "[s]exual drive was reduced inflight and postflight as compared with preflight ($p < 0.05$)" (p. 135), which correlated with a decrease in testosterone levels in the men. In addition, they noted that there were no endocrine signs of acute stress, in that the levels of adrenocorticotropin (ACTH) and cortisol (CS), although high from the preflight anticipation that astronauts typically feel, did not change inflight, although interstitial-cell-stimulating (i.e., luteinizing) hormone (LH) levels unexpectedly increased. LH stimulates the secretion of testosterone in the testes. The researchers also found that testosterone levels recovered dramatically one day following the astronauts' reentry from space. Thus, they noted, "For the first time, space life sciences research has shown reversible primary hypoandrogenism in man during exposure to microgravity" (p. 136). Nevertheless, although testosterone levels recovered quickly (as measured in the saliva), they noted that 15 days after reentry, other measurements suggested that more than two weeks were required for complete recovery at the cellular level. The timeframe for libido recovery, however, was not revealed in the article, or even whether it did recover. The authors stated that further research was needed to clarify whether fluid shifts or altered androgen distribution in the body because of microgravity was responsible for the results.

13. Research and Advanced Education

In the space arena, the time will eventually come when sexological concerns are recognized as legitimate topics for research in support of extended spaceflight missions. Administrators at the top levels of management and those with influence within the space life sciences of national and international space agencies, such as NASA, the Russian Space Agency, and the European Space Agency, need to encourage and support relevant biomedical, psychosocial, and human factors professionals within their organizations to receive advanced sexological training. These professionals should be urged to make contact with colleagues in sexology to find out the advances and concerns within this discipline that might have relevance to their spaceflight responsibilities, as well as to offer their knowledge from the space program that might be relevant to the work of sexologists. The Society for the Scientific Study of Sexuality (SSSS), with its international membership, would be the professional organization of sexologists whose expertise in sex research, counseling and therapy, and education would provide the best interdisciplinary support that would benefit the work of space life scientists. In addition, training programs for space life scientists should incorporate sexological information into their curricula, and sexologists have the expertise necessary to provide knowledgeable input at all levels of the educational spectrum, including advanced medical training for physicians.

Conclusion

It should be clear that the integration of various human and mission components work synergistically to provide the context in which space missions will function and how they might be affected by the human sexuality complex. At the same time, it is not yet as clear that humans on Earth will soon come to terms with their own sexualities, as Perry (1990) has noted, and this should be a cause for concern. Despite this truism and the demonstrated evidence that various space life scientists and others have projected that they are likely to have an impact on future long-term space missions, the intersection between the two scientific specialties whose domains encompass either the space life sciences or sexuality and gender has scarcely begun to be investigated. This should serve as a call to action to prepare adequately for meeting the challenges expressed here. One focus of intervention will need to be directed toward the managers and mission planners; the other focus will need to be on the individual crew-members, as well as their families and intimate partners. My earlier work (Noonan 1998a) might well serve as a rationale and an outline for action for the managers and planners in the space endeavor. Certainly, wherever humanity goes, our sexuality will surely follow.

To me, possibly the most important conclusion to come out of my study was embodied in the new terminology I coined, the human sexuality complex, that conceptualized the various factors of human sexuality to be components of a unified system, one that had characteristics ascribed to chaotic, complex systems. Such a conceptualization, I believe, will allow scientists in both the sexual and space life sciences, as well as policymakers in the public domain, to better understand and address both the potential problems of sex and the role that healthy sexual expression has in society and in space. Once we are effectively able to do that, the consideration of the human sexuality complex in the closed ecological environments of space will appear more justified, and so a space sexology might well be established.

References and Suggested Readings

Anderson, G. 1992 (May 15). Is NASA secretly experimenting with sex in space? *Now it can be told* (Geraldo Rivera television program) [Official transcript]. Livingston, NJ: Burrelle's Information Services.

Atkinson, Jr., J. D., & Shafritz, J. M. 1985. *The real stuff: A history of NASA's astronaut recruitment program.* New York: Praeger Publishers.

Bishop, S. L. 1996a (May). Psychosocial issues in spaceflight. In R. J. Noonan (Chair), *Space Life Sciences Symposium.* Symposium conducted at the 15th International Space Development Conference (ISDC), May 24, 1996, New York, NY.

Bishop, S. L. 1996b (November). Psychosocial issues of mixed-gender crews in space. In R. J. Noonan (Chair), *Women and men in space: Implications for the space and sexual sciences.* Symposium conducted at the 39th annual meeting of the Society for the Scientific Study of Sexuality (SSSS), November 15, 1996, Houston, TX.

Bluth, B. J. 1985. *Space station/Antarctic analogs* (ITT, Antarctic Services Contractor Reports NAG 2-255 and NAGW-659). Reston, VA: Space Station Program Office, NASA.

Bushnell, D. 1958. *History of research in space biology and biodynamics at the Air Force Missile Development Center, Holloman Air Force Base, New Mexico, 1946-1958.* Holloman Air Force Base, NM: U.S. Air Force Missile Development Center.

Cabbage, M. 2001 (March 11). Lust in space: Study tells all. *Orlando Sentinel.* Available: http://www.orlandosentinel.com/news/custom/space/orl spacc031101.story?coll–orl%2Dhome%2Dheadlines

Casper, M. J., & Moore, L. J. 1995. Inscribing bodies, inscribing the future: Gender, sex, and reproduction in outer space. *Sociological Perspectives, 38*(2), 311-333.

Cassutt, M. 1993. *Who's who in space: The International Space Year edition.* New York: Macmillan.

Clarke, A. C. 1986. *Arthur C. Clarke's July 20, 2019: Life in the 21st century.* New York: Macmillan.

Connors, M. M., Harrison, A. A., & Akins, F. R. 1985. *Living aloft: Human requirements for extended spaceflight* (NASA Publication No. SP-483). Washington, DC: U.S. Government Printing Office (Scientific and Technical Information Branch, National Aeronautics and Space Administration).

Date, S. 1992 (June 6). The birds and the bees head into outer space. *The Orlando Sentinel,* pp. A-1, A-6.

Fazio, G. G. 1997. Vacuum, temperature, and microgravity. In S. E. Churchill, ed., *Fundamentals of space life sciences* (pp. 3-9). Malabar, FL: Krieger Publishing Co.

Francoeur, R. T., ed. 1997. *International encyclopedia of sexuality* (Vols. 1-3). New York: Continuum.

Francoeur, R. T., ed. 1998. *Sexuality in America: Understanding our sexual values and behavior.* New York: Continuum.

Francoeur, R. T., & Perper, T. 1997. General character and ramifications of American religious perspectives on sexuality. In: R. T. Francoeur, ed., *International encyclopedia of sexuality* (Vol. 3, pp. 1392-1403). New York: Continuum.

Gingrich, N. 1995. *To renew America.* New York: HarperCollins.

Harris, P. R. 1996. *Living and working in space: Human behavior, culture and organization* (2nd ed.). New York: John Wiley & Sons.

Hunt, M. 1974. *Sexual behavior in the 1970s.* Chicago: Playboy Press.

Levin, R. J. 1989 (August). Effects of space travel on sexuality and the human reproductive system. *Journal of the British Interplanetary Society, 42*(7), 378-382.

Libby, R. W., & Whitehurst, R. N., eds. 1977. *Marriage and alternatives: Exploring intimate relationships.* Glenview, IL: Scott, Foresman and Co.

Masters, W. H., & Johnson, V. E. 1966. *Human sexual response.* Boston: Little, Brown & Co.

McCullough, J. 1973 (September). The 13 who were left behind. *Ms.,* pp. 41-45.

McCullough, N. 1992 (November). Sex in space. *True News,* pp. 24-26.

Money, J. 1985a. *The destroying angel: Sex, fitness & food in the legacy of degeneracy theory, Graham crackers, Kellogg's corn flakes & American health history.* Buffalo, NY: Prometheus Books.

Money, J. 1995b. *Gendermaps: Social constructionism, feminism, and sexosophical history.* New York: Continuum.

Morphew, M. E., & MacLaren, S., eds. 1997 (June). Voyage to discovery: American astronauts aboard Russia's Mir space station [Introduction]. *Human Performance in Extreme Environments,* 2(1), 39-61.

NASA. 1999. *NASA facts: The International Space Station: An Overview* (NASA publication IS-1999-06-ISS022). Houston, TX: Johnson Space Center, NASA.

NASA. 2001. *Human spaceflight.* Available at: http://spaceflight.nasa.gov/station/reference/partners/index.html

Nicogossian, A. E., Pool, S. L., & Uri, J. J. 1994. Historical perspectives. In: A. E. Nicogossian, C. L. Huntoon, & S. L. Pool, eds., *Space physiology and medicine* (3rd ed., pp. 3-49). Philadelphia: Lea & Febiger.

Noonan, R. J. 1996. Survival strategies for lovers in the 1990s. In P. B. Anderson, D. de Mauro, & R. J. Noonan, eds., *Does anyone still remember when sex was fun? Positive sexuality in the age of AIDS* (3rd ed., pp. 1-12/2nd ed., pp. 1-12). Dubuque, IA: Kendall/Hunt Publishing Co. (Original work published 1992)

Noonan, R. J. 1998a. *A philosophical inquiry into the role of sexology in space life sciences research and human factors considerations for extended spaceflight.* Doctoral dissertation, New York University (UMI publication number 9832759). Information at http://www.SexQuest.com/SexualHealth/rjnoonan-diss-abstract.html.

Noonan, R. J. 1998b. The psychology of sex: A mirror from the Internet. In: J. Gackenbach, ed., *Psychology and the Internet: Intrapersonal, interpersonal and transpersonal implications* (pp. 143-168). New York: Academic Press.

Noonan, R. J. 2000 (September 11). The 200 mile high club. *The Position* [online journal of the Museum of Sex]. Available: http://theposition.com/.

Perry, M. E. 1990. Preface. In J. Money & H. Musaph, eds., *Handbook of sexology.* M. E. Perry, ed., *Vol. VII. Childhood and adolescent sexology* (p. v). Amsterdam/New York: Elsevier.

Pesavento, P. 2000. From *Aelita* to the *International Space Station*: The psychological and social effects of isolation on Earth and in space. *Quest: The History of Spaceflight Quarterly* [University of North Dakota], 8:2:4-23.

Pierce, C. M. 1991. Theoretical approaches to adaptation to Antarctica and space. In A. A. Harrison, Y. A. Clearwater, & C. P. McKay, eds., *From Antarctica to outer space: Life in isolation and confinement* (pp. 125-133). New York: Springer-Verlag.

Reiss, I. L. 1990. *An end to shame: Shaping our next sexual revolution.* Buffalo, NY: Prometheus Books.

Santy, P. A. 1994. *Choosing the right stuff: The psychological selection of astronauts and cosmonauts.* Westport, CT: Praeger.

Sherr, D. H., & Sonnenfeld, G. 1997. Response of the immune system to spaceflight. In S. E. Churchill, ed., *Fundamentals of space life sciences* (pp. 121-129). Malabar, FL: Krieger Publishing Co.

Smith, M. L. 1997 (January). The compliance with international space law of the LEDA proposal. *Space Governance: The Journal of United Societies in Space & The World-Space Bar Association,* 4(1), 16-18.

Strollo, F., Riondino, G., Harris, B., Strollo, G., Casarosa, E., Mangrossa, N., Ferretti, C., & Luisi, M. 1998 (February). The effect of microgravity on testicular androgen secretion. *Aviation, Space, and Environmental Medicine,* 69(2), 133-136.

Thagard, N. 1997 (June). Additional comments from Norm Thagard. Sidebar to: Astronaut draws attention to psychology, communication (pp. 42-47). *Human Performance in Extreme Environments,* 2(1), 47.

Vaughan, D. 1992 (December). Sex in space: The final frontier. *Penthouse Forum,* pp. 48-53.

Weis, D. L. (1997). Adolescent sexuality [The United States of America]. In: R. T. Francoeur, ed., *International encyclopedia of sexuality* (Vol. 3, pp. 1479-1498). New York: Continuum.

White, F. 1987. *The overview effect: Space exploration and human evolution.* Boston: Houghton Mifflin Co.

Papua New Guinea

Shirley Oliver-Miller*

Contents

*Demographics and a Historical Perspective***

A. Demographics

Papua New Guinea (PNG) occupies the eastern half of the island of New Guinea, the world's second-largest island, in the southwest Pacific Ocean, north of eastern Australia's Captain Cook Peninsula. The Indonesian province of Irian Jaya occupies the island's western half. To the east are the Melanesian and Solomon Islands and the Coral Sea. North and east of New

*Communications: Shirley Oliver-Miller, The Margaret Sanger International Center, 26 Bleecker Street, 6th Floor, New York, NY, USA 10012; 212-274-7256; fax: 212-274-7299; somatppnyc@aol.com.

**This overview of some attitudes and practices of the people of Papua New Guinea as they relate to sexuality is based on the author's own work experience in PNG over three years, her interviews with Papua New Guineans, studies done in Papua New Guinea, and current anthropological literature.

Guinea are about 600 islands in the Bismarck Archipelago, including Manus, New Britain, New Ireland, Bougainville, and the northern part of the Solomon Islands, which are also part of Papua New Guinea. The total territory of Papua New Guinea is 178,704 square miles or 462,840 square kilometers, making it about a tenth larger than California. Most of the main island, especially the interior, remains isolated from outside contact by rugged mountains, deep gorges, and swamps. The mainland's high plateau climate is temperate, contrasting with the tropical climate of the coastal plains. Two major rivers, the Sepik and the Fly, are navigable to shallow-draft vessels.

In the past, the very rugged topography of Papua New Guinea made communication and movement from one place to the next very difficult. This resulted in extraordinary variations in attitudes, behavior, ethnic groups, culture, traditions, customs, religion, and linguistics throughout the country. There are more than 850 spoken languages in Papua New Guinea. Only one to two percent of the people speak English, the official language, but Tok Pigin English is widely spoken.

Only 15 percent of the 1997 estimated five million Papua New Guineans live in the few cities, about a quarter of a million in the administrative center of Port Moresby. The majority of the people make their living in small-scale agriculture, although only one percent of the land is devoted to permanent crops and a negligible percent of the land is arable. The large majority of Papua New Guineans live in villages with settlements averaging about 800 persons to scattered homesteads with residents numbering no more than five to ten. The average-size village is about 200 to 300 people, located within a half-hour's walk to other neighboring villages. Ethnically, the people are predominantly Melanesian in the northeast, and Papuan mainly in the south and the interior, with some Negrito, Micronesian, and Polynesian.*** A third of the people follow indigenous religions; 22 percent are Roman Catholic, 18 percent Lutheran, and 28 percent other Christian.

Forty percent of Papuan New Guineans are under age 15, 56 percent between ages 15 and 65, and 4 percent over the age of 65. The average life expectancy at birth in 1995 was 56 for males and 58 for females. The 1997 estimated birthrate was 33 per 1,000 persons, the death rate 10 per 1,000 persons, maternal mortality projected as high as 80 per 1,000 deliveries, and the infant mortality rate an underestimated 80 per 1,000 live births, for an estimated average annual natural increase of 2.3 percent. The 1997 total fertility rate (TFR) was 5.4 children per fertile woman, with adolescent pregnancy a major contributing factor. Papua New Guinea's fertility ranks it 64 among 227 nations. The country's health indices remain an abiding

---

***Melanesians, Micronesians, and Polynesians constitute the three main ethnic groups in Oceania, the central and south Pacific. The brown-skinned Polynesians occupy the most-eastern islands of Oceania, from Hawaii to New Zealand, including Tahiti, Samoa, and Hawaii. The Micronesians inhabit the islands north of the equator and east of the Philippines, including the Mariana, Caroline, and Marshall Islands. The dark-skinned, frizzy-haired Melanesians occupy the islands in the south Pacific northeast of Australia.

source of concern. Less well documented quantifiably, but widely acknowledged by health care providers and researchers, is the rapid proliferation
of sexually transmitted infections (STIs) and AIDS, as random sexual
contacts both within and outside marriage increase. Experts project that if
the high rates of fertility persist, the population will double by the year
2020.

The nation has one hospital bed per 234 people, and one physician for
every 12,874 people. The literacy rate is 52 percent, with 65 percent of the
children attending primary school and 13 percent in secondary school.
Illiteracy is disproportionately high among females. For the most part,
women and girls are subjugated and less valued than men. If a choice has
to be made between who goes to school, the boy or the girl, it will be the
boy. Women put the needs of their husbands and children before their
own needs. Consequently, women and girls are often malnourished. The
1995 estimated gross domestic product per capita was $2,400.

Like other developing nations, internal migration from rural communities has resulted in rapidly expanding urban populations. Although 85
percent of Papua New Guinea's population live in isolated rural areas,
urban values exert very strong influences in the village communities. People
seeking a better life in the city find few employment opportunities. Many
have resorted to crime as one way to survive. Today, violence in Papua New
Guinea has become a dominant and critical reality in the country.

B. A Brief Historical Perspective

New Guinea, the world's second-largest island, was settled many thousands
of years ago by waves of Papuans and Melanesian migrants. These many
waves of immigration developed into hundreds of diverse, mutually hostile
tribes of hunters and small cultivators, each with their own language. The
eastern half of the island of New Guinea was first visited by Portuguese and
Spanish explorers in the sixteenth century, but the Europeans did not
become established there until the nineteenth century, when the island
was divided between the Dutch in the west (the current Indonesian Irian
Jaya), and the Germans and the British to the east. In 1884, Germany
declared the northern coast a German protectorate. Britain followed suit
in the south. Both nations then formally annexed their protectorates. In
1901, Britain transferred its territory to the newly independent Australia.
During World War I, Australian troops invaded German New Guinea and
maintained control under a League of Nations mandate that eventually
became a United Nations trusteeship that incorporated a territorial government in the southern region known as Papua.

Australia granted the territory limited home rule in 1951, and autonomy
for internal affairs in 1960. The country attained independence September
16, 1975, when the United Nations' trusteeship under Australia ended. In
February 1990, guerrillas of the Bougainville Revolutionary Army (BRA)
attacked plantations, forcing the evacuation of numerous workers. In May,

the BRA declared Bougainville's independence, triggering a government blockade of the island until a peace treaty was signed in January 1991. However, the independence rebels still threaten and limit foreign investment on Bougainville.

1. Basic Sexological Premises

A. Character of Gender Roles

The societies of Papua New Guinea are male-dominated and the attitudes of men toward women, on the whole, are poor. Women are valued as objects to be owned by men along with pigs and gardens; hence, few women exercise any real sort of power or control over their lives. Men are hunters and warriors; women are laborers, gardeners, and mothers who bring food to the men's house. The penis makes a man incapable of doing onerous gardening and tending the crops of edible sweet potatoes. Cultural tradition makes women subservient and responsive to male needs.

Whereas women's roles are clearly defined, men suffer from the loss of their traditional roles in defending their clan and land. The government of Papua New Guinea has now usurped these powers. Many young men find themselves unemployed and alienated from the society at large. Their capacity to produce income, the single most important prerequisite to securing a lasting relationship, remains the most difficult objective to achieve. These factors combine to make a very negative climate for gender equity both within and outside sexual relationships.

There are many examples of the low status of women in Papua New Guinea, not the least being the extent of violence used against them by males who exert authority and control, batter, and rape them. These social dynamics also contribute to the high risk for STI, including HIV infection, as well as adolescent pregnancy. While babies born out of wedlock are generally absorbed into the extended family without rancor, many girls drop out of school and otherwise foreclose their life options in terms of education and employment. Despite increasing educational opportunities, women continue to take a back seat to men in many aspects of development. Most men view women's development as breaking a long-standing taboo tantamount to entering "a man's house" in a rural culture where men and women, including married couples, often live segregated lives.

Although government officials and community members alike express private concern over adolescent sexual behavior and teen violence in general, a larger programmatic response has yet to be forthcoming.

B. Sociolegal Status of Males and Females

Whereas the vast majority of cultures around the world and in Papua New Guinea adhere to a gender- and sex-dimorphic paradigm in which only males and females are recognized, the Sambians of Papua New Guinea's eastern highlands are among the interesting minority of societies that accept three sex categories: male, female, and a "third sex or hermaphrodite." Classic examples of "third-sex persons" include the *hijra* of India, the *berdache* of American Indian and Eskimo societies, the *acaults* of Myanmar, the *kathoey* of Thailand, the *vehine* of Polynesia, and the *fa'afafine* of Samoa.

The Sambian third-sexed persons, known as *kwolu-aatmwol* ("male thing-transforming-into-female thing") or *turnim man* ("expected to become a man"), are the result of a rare genetic variation known as delta-4-steroid-5-alpha-reductase deficiency, or DHT (dihydrotestosterone) deficiency, first reported in the Dominican Republic as *guevedoces* by Imperato-McGinley (1974) (Francoeur, et al. 1995; Herdt 1981, 1984a, 1987, 1990; Money & Ehrhardt 1972). Individuals with DHT deficiency lack the gene necessary to produce the 5-alpha reductase enzyme that converts testosterone into dihydrotestosterone (DHT), the hormone that causes the undifferentiated external genitals of a fetus in its third month to differentiate as a penis and scrotum. As a result, during pregnancy, the external structures differentiate more or less as a female clitoris and labia. Given this pseudo-female appearance at birth, Sambian parents of such a child may identify and raise the newborn as female or male. However, the pubertal surge of testosterone causes the pseudo-female external genitals to more or less convert to male structures, along with the deepening of the voice, male facial, pubic, and axial body hair, penile enlargement, and labio-scrotal fusion (Gregersen 1996:84).

Unlike the Dominican society, which celebrates the pubertal conversion of a *guevedoces* "daughter" into a son, the patriarchal Sambians are much less comfortable with their third-sexed offspring, even though their ability to function as a male would seem to be considerably more attractive in terms of personal power and prestige. Sambians, however, regard a newborn with ambiguous genitals as a boy with a defect, who is rejected by both parents, teased, and humiliated. After transformation at puberty, the male becomes the fellator (giver) in the sequential bisexual life of a male. When raised as males from birth and later married, they were rejected by their wives as unsatisfying. When raised as girls and married, they were soon rejected by their outraged husbands who found testes and a small penis within the labia when they attempted to have vaginal intercourse (see Section 6, Homoerotic, Homosexual, and Ambisexual Behaviors).

C. General Concepts of Sexuality and Love

In several highland Papuan societies, incest restrictions dictate that wives must be taken from other clans. But, because relationships between different clans are often so hostile as to verge on warfare, men who abduct women from hostile clans trigger armed retaliation and counter-abductions, which result in an endless cycle. "Marriage in these societies, and the sexual relationships within marriage," according to Davenport (1997:126), "are always fraught with fear, hostility and anger."

The Dobo, who live on a small island off the coast of the main island, live in constant fear of sorcery from their wives. Because they believe that they are particularly vulnerable during intercourse, Dobo men have to continually weigh their need for sexual gratification against the possibility of sorcery when they try to satisfy their sexual need (Davenport 1997:126)

2. Religious and Ethnic Factors Affecting Sexuality

A. Source and Character of Religious Values

After a century of Christian missionary influence, most of the indigenous ethnic-based rituals and customs described in the next section no longer exist. Today, Christianity dominates in Papua New Guinea, although a third of the people still practice traditional indigenous religions, especially in the remote mountainous areas.

B. Character of Ethnic Values

Before the 1900s, no Papuan traveled too far from home for fear of being killed or even eaten by more distant neighbors, suggesting that marriage patterns were likely to have been locally endogamous. As most villages are composed of multi-clan hamlets, one might marry a spouse from another hamlet within the same village. The most common marriage pattern was based on the requirement that one must marry outside of one's clan, most of which were patrilineal. For the most part, marriage patterns still show couples come from the same contiguous villages. In the past, unmarried people from neighboring villages gathered together in courting rituals that included dance, song, and pair bonding. Married men looking for a second or third wife also participated in this ritual.

The following examples illustrate the wide range of traditional ethnic factors influencing the sexual attitudes and behavior of the diverse groups in Papua New Guinea. Contact with Western and other outside cultures are altering many of these patterns classic in the anthropology literature of the area, but to what extent in individual tribal cultures is not evident from the anthropological record pieced together over the last century.

- In the Eastern and Central Highlands, elders chaperoned festivities, which allowed young people from neighboring villages to sit opposite each other in pairs and rub-legs, cheeks, or noses while they engaged in singing.
- In the Simbai areas of the Highlands, men adorned with heavy shiny beetle-decorated headdresses came together to dance in a ritual that lasted all night. A woman could take her pick of men during the night and the couple would then disappear into the nearby bushes. In the morning, women carrying men's headdresses were clearly visible. Each

couple then went to the man's house, and word was sent to woman's parents to come to discuss a brideprice. She may have never seen the man before that evening, but, as they were all from nearby villages, the sexual pool was still quite localized.

- In the Trobriand Islands of Papua New Guinea, courting parties were openly explicit sexual events. Boys were called out from villages A and B to have sex with the girls from village C; the host and guest roles were reversed on the next occasion. Public events of sexual mixing among adults were also permissible in some areas. These open sexual events took place only on special occasions, as rituals of reversal, fertility, or renewal, allowing people to have sex with those with whom they ordinarily had no sexual rights, e.g., the spouses of other men and persons within proscribed kinship relationships.

- Plural copulation or group sex was also a traditional pattern in some areas, and took the form of a single woman having sexual intercourse with a series of men in tandem. Among the Ok of the Highlands and the Sepik on the North Coast, this was done as a punitive measure (e.g., Ok, Highlands, and Sepik, North Coast) and in others, it was an honor (e.g., Papuan Coast).

- In the Eastern Highlands, Papuan Plateau, and Papuan Coast, there were also male initiations, which required insemination, either anally or orally, by elder males initiating younger males.

- Every Banaro man has a "ritual brother" as a sort of alter ego with whom he shares mutual access to each other's wives. The Banaro also require that a bride's first intercourse be performed by her husband's father's ritual brother (Davenport 1977:144).

- Among the Fasu of the Southern Highlands, older males had sex with younger males with less ceremony, but still within the context of traditional relationships and ideology.

- The Enga of the Highlands firmly believed that men and women differed in many fundamental ways. Because of these fundamental differences, contact with menstrual discharge could contaminate a man and cause illness, weakness, and even death. But reality told them they could not avoid all contamination, so males and females were highly segregated. The Enga men needed some sexual outlet, for their own release and to produce offspring, so single men almost never engaged in heterosexual intercourse, and married men only reluctantly did so with their wives. Purification rituals were important (Davenport 1997:136).

- The Wógeo added to the Enga menstrual taboo the belief that men in a trance or sacred state were dangerous to women. The sacred state was in fact an imitative menstruation, induced by hacking the penis until it bled freely and was thus purified. This periodic male bleeding rid the body of contaminations received from women. Unlike the Enga, the Wógeo did not avoid heterosexual intercourse to avoid contamination (Davenport 1977:136).

- The Manus treated all aspects of sex as ugly and shameful. Even marital intercourse was sinful, degrading, and to be engaged in only in strict privacy. Women considered intercourse an abomination they endured, however painfully, until they produced a child. The sexuality of men was considered brutish. Sex outside marriage offended the sensibilities of watchful spirits and triggered supernaturally ordained punishments. Sexual talk was not heard, and women were so secretive about their menses that Manus men denied women ever experienced such a thing as a monthly period (Davenport 1977:115, 123-24).

In the exuberance of mid-twentieth-century anthropological research, considerable cultural data, much of it related to sexual beliefs, attitudes, and behavior, were gathered by cultural anthropologists, led by Bronislaw Malinowski (1927) and Margaret Mead (1930, 1935).

One of their favorite subjects was the Melanesian matriarchal Trobriand Islanders, off the eastern end of New Guinea. Trobriand Islanders not only view the expression of sexuality with great favor, they are also quite comfortable with pre- and extramarital affairs, provided these respect certain incest and age taboos. Trobriand Islanders make frequent and open use of love magic to make themselves irresistibly attractive to desired partners. With a few slight alterations in the love magic formulae, they have an equally irresistible aid for their famous overseas exchange system known as *kula* (Davenport 1977:131, 245; Gregersen 1996:268).

Most of these tribal patterns of sexual activity were rationalized as mechanisms to gather the spiritual force residing in sexual fluids, i.e., sexual power, and redirect it to social and material aims, such as improving the growth of boys or strengthening the clan's reproductive powers, both human and agricultural. These belief systems nearly always had within them a strong component of female pollution and associated behavioral taboos. Colonial contacts in the last century and expanded contact with outsiders in recent decades have changed many of the tribal customs so carefully documented by anthropologists. Whatever the extent of enculturation, and regardless of how unchanged these customs remain in the remote and inaccessible regions of Papua New Guinea, their record is important in understanding how sexual diversity plays out within the social fabric of individual functioning societies.

3. Sexual Knowledge and Education

A. Government Policies and Programs

Recently, the Papua New Guinea government implemented a pilot Adolescent Sexuality and Reproductive Health Project, which targets adolescents, church groups, and teachers/lecturers. The program addresses a myriad of issues around sexuality, morality, reproductive health, STIs/AIDS, prevention of rape/child molestation/domestic violence/drug abuse, value clarification, decision-making, and how to talk about sex (traditionally a taboo topic) with others. The project is the first of its kind in Papua New Guinea. Although it is too early to tell what impact the project will have, thus far, students, teachers, parents, and the church community (interdenominational) have welcomed the opportunity to learn more facts about sexuality, reproductive health issues, and the skills to communicate with others about sensitive topics.

B. Informal Sources of Sexual Knowledge

It is important to acknowledge that sexuality education to a greater or lesser degree has always existed in cultures around the world. Culture and traditions are vehicles by which sexuality information and knowledge are transmitted. We tend to forget that there have always been systems that controlled sexual behaviors. The erosion of cultural norms, coupled with today's health concerns about teen pregnancy, maternal and child spacing, sexually transmitted infections, AIDS, rape, child molestation, and domestic violence, have made talking about sex very controversial. It is clear that former systems no longer provide effective approaches to addressing social problems.

Parents make an effort to teach their children what is socially acceptable and what is not in all areas of life, including the sexual. When young people go away to school, it is very difficult for parents to maintain constant input over the years when their children are becoming sexually mature. Instead, their peers have the most influence. Even when children remain at home, peer pressure is often stronger than the influence of parents.

This is true in most societies today. Some parents attempt to strengthen their teachings about proper morality by insisting their children attend church. When parents themselves are sincere followers and doers of the teachings of the church, this has the most effect. But where the church is simply used as another means of control by parents who themselves practice behaviors considered improper by the church, children will not listen. Although sex is a biological drive, all sexual behavior must be learned.

In some communities, young people have few examples of responsible sexual behavior to follow. From childhood, they repeatedly hear tales about who slept with whose wife, who was raped, and who got pregnant out of wedlock. These events are often the subject of public discussions at court hearings and in community gossip. The usual outcome is that someone must pay someone else a fine. Single or married men who make a young girl pregnant are rarely publicly criticized, even though people may talk about them behind their backs.

Knowledge about sexuality and reproductive health is generally low throughout Papua New Guinea at all ages. Younger people have slightly better access to information than did most of their parents. Information levels are higher in cities and towns than in villages. Some parents, especially in the villages, persist in telling their teenagers as little as possible about sex and reproduction. They continue to say that babies come from the garden or from stones, or offer other fanciful explanations. Unfortunately, parents' notions that keeping their children ignorant about sex will keep them from trying sex is completely without foundation. In all areas, the average age at first sexual intercourse is about 15 or 16 for both sexes. This means that many try their first sexual intercourse quite a bit younger than 15, as well as some at ages 17 to 19. [Gregersen suggests that the age of first intercourse is likely earlier than just stated (personal communication, 2000). (Editor)] Few enter a sexual relationship with any knowledge of contraception or STIs.

After a girl has her first menstruation, throughout the country, she is warned to stay away from boys or it will lead to pregnancy. But little else is revealed. Sometimes a grandmother or other relative decides to give a traditional contraceptive spell or herb to a young woman. This is reported to be more common if the girl is in school. Occasionally, a schoolteacher or a kinswoman who is a nurse explains more to a young woman and even helps her obtain modern contraception. But, for the vast majority, the early years of sexual activity are the most dangerous, because the elders have not considered sex one of life's most powerful drives, as a topic to be discussed with young people. With few exceptions, neither the schools nor the churches carry out adequate sex education early enough to be of any value. By the time sexual reproduction is discussed in high school, nearly half of the young people have already begun having sexual intercourse. The health services do not make contraceptives accessible to young people. The result is many unwanted teenage pregnancies and STIs, including HIV. The known age distribution of HIV and AIDS cases up to 1995 in Papua New Guinea, compared to other islands in the Pacific with numerous cases, demonstrates this clearly.

Arguments against sex education, whether in the home or within an institution such as a school or church, focus on the fear that information will increase the desire for sexual experimentation. Evidence from studies conducted in several different countries point in the opposite direction. If young people are given adequate sex education, those who have not yet begun often delay starting, and those who have started do not increase their sexual activities. In either case, both groups are better informed about the pleasures and risks of sex. If sex education is carried out properly, they will then know how to have safer sex.

In *Sexual Networks and Sexual Cultures in Contemporary Papua New Guinea*, Carol Jenkins (1996), principal research fellow with the Papua New Guinea Institute of Medical Research (in Goroka), noted that:

> only a minority of young people reported learning about sex through the school system or from their parents. Most girls and boys first learn from older female or male relatives or friends. Sitting around and telling stories about sex is a favorite pastime of teenagers of both sexes. More than any other factor, this activity spurs the imagination. Many times older young people deliberately try to persuade younger ones to try sex. Cousins, in particular, often help set up the first sexual encoun-

ters for their younger relatives. Sometimes cousins are the first sexual partners. On a world scale, this pattern is not unusual. It is unlikely, however, that older relatives and friends raised under similar conditions represent a good source of information.

Until recently, Papua New Guinea has remained isolated from the rest of the world. Today, Papua New Guinea struggles with all the influences and trappings of modern-day society, including radio, television, drugs, computers, videos, MTV, written literature, pornography, rape, child molestation, domestic violence, commercial sex workers, etc. As more and more people are exposed to modernization, there is an emerging culture whose sexual practices are becoming fairly homogenized.

Agricultural and mining industries require travel to and from rural areas, and this greatly contributes to the diffusion of new ideas. Media, especially video and pornographic magazines, also play a large part in changing sex practices and attitudes. Some copy what they see and learn in urban centers, whereas others condemn what they see. In either case, the eroticism of more complex and commercial societies, both Asian and Western, presents issues of contention in sexuality to Papua New Guinea.

4. Autoerotic Behaviors and Patterns

Although it is seldom discussed, masturbation is widespread and generally considered harmless, but wasteful, particularly for boys. Therefore, the overwhelming pressure, when sexually aroused, is to find a partner of the opposite sex immediately. In some cases, this may lead to rape. Rape is very common in Papua New Guinea and can occur without the aid of pornography, simply because violence against women in Papua New Guinea is widespread and unopposed by strong cultural or legal norms (see Section 8A, Significant Unconventional Sexual Behaviors, Coercive Sex, below).

5. Interpersonal Heterosexual Behaviors

A. Children

Trobrianders, and likely other Papua New Guinea societies, approve of imitative copulation or sex rehearsal play about age 10 or 11 (Davenport 1977:150).

B. Adolescents

First Intercourse and Premarital Sex

The initiation of first sexual intercourse among young people today takes place around the age of 15 for both girls and boys in both urban and rural areas. In general, virginity is not highly valued, but rather society denounces

444 · International Encyclopedia of Sexuality

premenarcheal sexual intercourse for girls and getting pregnant before proper marriage arrangements, i.e., a brideprice, are made. In rural areas where traditional menarcheal seclusion ceremonies are still maintained, young men, often accompanied by their parents, begin to seek a young woman's interests as soon as she is allowed out of seclusion. Unless she is in school, a young woman is considered ready for sex and marriage immediately after menarche. And, as the age of menarche declines, so has the age of first sexual experience. Most rural girls experience their first sexual encounter willingly with young men slightly older than themselves from nearby villages. Others are forced into sex or raped. According to one study, 17 percent in a sample of 116 women said their first sex was with a boy they had just met, while only 8 percent had their first sex with an older man.

Studies conducted by the Papua New Guinea Institute of Medical Research indicate that nearly half of all adolescents in the country are sexually active by the age of 16, and by the age of 20 nearly a third studied reported having had at least one STI. Evidence suggests that sexual activity occurs among girls as young as 14, whose physiological immaturity and poor coping skills place them at particular risk for STIs and HIV.

Following the first experience of sexual intercourse, options for new and different sex partners increase. Young women fantasize that they will be rescued from the labor of rural subsistence farming, and hope for a man with a job, a permanent house, and car in town. Poor rural parents also want their daughters to "marry up," which usually means marrying a man from town. Approximately 25 percent of young women take married men as partners. Half of the women between the ages of 15 and 24 in our recent study of youth stated that they accepted cash, gifts, or both in exchange for sex. In the national study conducted in 1991, 66 percent of the women under 25 ($n = 33$) and 43 percent of those over that age ($n = 37$) had exchanged sex for goods. These young women do not see themselves as sex workers, although they say they earn some of their income through sex (see also Section 8B, Significant Unconventional Sexual Behaviors, Prostitution).

Young men are equally subject to earlier biological maturation, and the adolescent male is no longer subject to the dominating control of elder males as expressed through male initiation rituals. Few societies have maintained these rites of passage, and where they do exist, they are very much altered. Consequently, boys are free to experiment with sex more or less as they choose. Older siblings frequently teach a younger boy about sex in explicit ways, sometimes setting up a woman with whom he can "try his luck," often in a group situation. Two studies suggest some boys first have anal intercourse with each other several years before having intercourse with a female.

Whereas parents are concerned about the health of the mother and infant, they are more concerned about ensuring economic commitment from the purported father of the child.

Young people receive subliminal messages that say, a little sex is all right, but not too much with the same person. Long-term sexual involvement with a single partner implies the likelihood of pregnancy and is definitely to be avoided unless one is ready for commitment. Many people believe that pregnancy cannot take place unless a man has sexual intercourse with woman at least six or more times. Hence, many girls and boys are taught to change partners frequently.

The sexuality of young, unmarried women is placed under fewer constraints than married women. Young women recognize this and seek to enjoy as many partners as possible while they remain unmarried. Whereas most Papua New Guinea societies do not allow a young girl to have sex before the onset of menstruation, Trobriand Islanders allow sex before menarche. First cousins may have temporary premarital affairs but can never marry (Davenport 1977:145). [However, certain kinds of first-cousin marriages may be permitted, such as a marriage with a child of one's mother's brother or one's father's sister (Gregersen, personal communication, 2000). (Editor)]

Courtship

Although Papua New Guineans still have widespread traditional sexual beliefs, practices, and unique customs, which differ by region and language areas, traditional courting customs have often been replaced with disco dances, CDs, cassette players, loud speakers, alcohol, marijuana, and other recreational drugs. Anyone can enter a disco. This marks a major shift from the controlled courting practices in the past.

A Puberty Ritual: Obligatory Universalized Transitional Homosexuality

Gilbert Herdt (1981, 1984a, 1987, 1990) and other anthropologists have reported on a pederastic puberty ritual shared by thirty to fifty Melanesian and New Guinea cultures that may be historically related to similar practices that developed among aboriginal Australians some 10,000 years ago. The focus of intense speculation by anthropologists and fierce opposition from Western governments and missionaries, these ritualized homosexual relationships are a necessary part of the coming-of-age training for boys. Their basis is the belief that boys do not produce their own semen and must get it from older men by "drinking semen," i.e., playing the passive insertee role in oral-genital sex or anal sex before puberty and during adolescence. This is the opposite of the traditional Western view in which the recipient (insertee) of anal or oral sex is robbed of his manhood.

Societies with this ritual practice characteristically maintain:

1. extreme social differences between men and women, with women clearly in an inferior status;
2. the blood of men and women are not ritually differentiated, but their semen and milk are; and
3. marriage often involves men exchanging sisters with no special marriage payment.

Other societies in the same area that do not share these beliefs or ritual pederasty are more likely to view menstrual blood as extremely dangerous and/or require a "bride price" to legitimize a marriage (Gregersen 1996:274-276).

According to the Sambian people of the Eastern Highlands of Papua New Guinea, a young boy must be fed women's milk in order to grow, until he approaches puberty when the men of the village must rescue him from the society of women and feed him men's milk (semen). To trigger puberty and enable a youth to become a mature macho head-hunter, he needs the semen of mature youths and unmarried men provided by young bachelors. After eight to ten years of exclusive homosexual relationships, the 19-year-old youth has completed his defining rite of passage and is ready to marry (McWhirter et al. 1990:42-43) (see Section 6, Homoerotic, Homosexual, and Ambisexual Behaviors).

C. Adults

Marital Relationships and Sexuality

See Sections 1C, Basic Sexological Premises, General Concepts of Sexuality and Love, and 2A, Religious and Ethnic Factors Affecting Sexuality, Source and Character of Religious Values.

Marriage and "Ritual Brothers"

Among the Banaro of Papua New Guinea, every male has a "ritual brother," a kind of alter ego, as a companion and support throughout life. Every "ritual brother" is allowed sexual access to his "brother's" wife. This is not, in our Western sense, "extramarital" sex, because the "ritual brother" is in some ritually real way the other man, the husband, and so is entitled to have sex with his alter ego's wife. The "ritual brother" also plays a role in Banaro marriages. The bride's first intercourse after marriage must be performed by the "ritual brother" of her husband's father, i.e., the father-in-law's "ritual brother"). In the Banaro society, it is the social father, not the procreative or biological father, who is important (Davenport 1977:144).

Coital Positions

Christian missionaries are commonly credited (or blamed) for trying to impose the male-superior coital position on the natives they evangelized, because they considered it "the natural and normal coital position." However, they do not deserve credit for its origins, which historians have traced back to the Stoics of ancient Rome and the early Egyptians [despite some modern assertions to the contrary (Gregersen, personal communication, 2000). (Editor)] Although popular in Western cultures, the male-superior position has not been adopted by the people of Oceania, despite Western advocates. In fact, the people of Oceania commonly view the male-above position as impractical and improper, placing too much weight on the woman, and are uncompromising in recognizing only two natural copulatory positions. The Dobuana and the Wógeo of Papua New Guinea prefer the rear-entry position, with the man standing behind the woman while she bends over and rests her hands on her knees. Also popular is the "Oceanic position," in which the man squats or kneels between the spread legs of his partner who lies on her back. He then pulls her towards himself and completes the intercourse. In a variation of this position, the woman lies on her back and keeps her knees up (Davenport 1977:150).

One benefit of this position is that it can be carried out with minimal body contact, "which encourages young people to have sex with ugly and older partners. On the other hand, as Malinowski has expressed it: '. . . where love exists, the man can bend over the woman or the woman can raise herself to meet him and contact can be as full and intimate as is desired'" (Davenport 1977:148; Gregersen 1996:5, 67). The Tallensi point out another possible advantage (or disadvantage), in that this position enables the woman to push the man over with a kick.

Premarital Pregnancy, Ritual Multiple Intercourse, and Extramarital Sex

A single mother often gives her child to her parents or another relative to rear and she continues with her single lifestyle. When a married man sleeps with a woman other than his wife, it is hardly noticed. If a woman is caught having sex with a man other than her husband, she is beaten. On the whole, sexual infidelity does not cause martial breakups and life continues. In some communities, other sexual issues are more disturbing than sexual infidelity.

Colonial influences have changed the lives of the Marind Anim, a former headhunting people of southern Papua New Guinea, but some of their customs likely continue in remote areas. One tradition involved an unusual ritual of extramarital sex. Traditionally, Marind Anim men and women live in separate housing in their small villages, even after marriage, and always engage in marital sex outside in the bush. Immediately after a wedding ceremony, a few older women take the bride to a place they have prepared outside the village, where the bride has sexual intercourse with the male members of her husband's clan before the groom is allowed to copulate with his wife. These ritual multiple intercourses, *otiv-bombari*, may extend over several nights. Although not particularly satisfying for the wife, this sequential group sex is repeated at various specified occasions, when a woman returns from her seclusion after delivering a baby, when her husband's friends come to visit, or when another man gives the husband a gift of tools or food.

> Apart from this custom, most [Marind Anim] marriages are monogamous and break up rarely. The rule is apparently that affection and love exist between the spouses, and the husband may get violently jealous if his wife should have secret sexual relations with a man without prearrangements and the husband's consent.

Extramarital relations are not supposed to become love affairs. They have the character of a ritual. The birth rate is low. *Otiv-bombari* are supposed to make women fertile. They are also used to collect semen, for semen is considered the essence of life, health and prosperity. Semen discharged from the vagina is ritually prized. After an *otiv bombari* it is collected in a coconut bowl to be used in food or medicine, and for body creams. . . .

Contemporaneously with marriage and heterosexual relations, men have also homosexual relations with young and adolescent boys while the younger ones are passing through an institutionalized phase of homosexuality. Here then one has a society in which the men but not the women are bisexual in experience, with some overlap from the homosexual to the heterosexual phase. (Money & Ehrhardt 1972:132-135)

6. Homoerotic, Homosexual, and Ambisexual Behaviors

A. Children and Adolescents

Same-sex activities, boys with boys or girls with girls, are common in many Papuan societies, but they are generally viewed as play and meaningless, though somehow wrong. However, the ritualized pederasty for Sambian adolescents and their postmarital exclusive heterosexuality (see Section 5B, Interpersonal Heterosexual Behaviors, Adolescents) does raise a major question about the development of sexual orientation, or at least a question about the nature of erotic arousal.

On the one hand, Herdt (1984) suggests that among the Sambia only about 5 percent of the male population become exclusively homosexual—virtually the same percentage Kinsey found for the United States where all homosexual acts are tabu. On the other hand, to discount homosexual arousal altogether in these institutionalized semen transfers seems unrealistic; slavish performance of a ritual does not produce erection and ejaculation unless an erotic component exists as well. (Gregersen 1996:276)

An additional insight, offered by John Money suggests that:

Institutionalized homosexuality, in serial sequence with institutionalized heterosexuality and marriage, as among the Sambia and other tribal peoples, must be taken into account in any theory that proposes to explain homosexuality. The theory will be deficient unless it also takes heterosexuality into account. Culturally institutionalized bisexuality signifies either that bisexuality is a universal potential to which any member of the human species could be acculturated or that bisexuality is a unique potential of those cultures whose members have become selectively inbred for it. There are no data that give conclusive and absolute support to either alternative. However, genetically pure inbred strains are an ideal of animal husbandry, not of human social and sexual interaction. Therefore, it is likely that acculturation to bisexuality is less a concomitant of inbreeding than it is of the bisexual plasticity of all members of the human species. It is possible that bisexual plasticity may vary over the life span. Later in life it may give way to exclusive monosexuality—or it may not. (Money 1990:43)

Another aspect of this complex-orientations picture is the fact that in many South Pacific societies, for example, the Marind Anim of southern Papua New Guinea and the (fictionally named) East Bay Melanesians, pubescent and adolescent boys are free to engage in homosexual relations with their peers and/or older married men. Unlike with the Sambia, these relationships are seldom exclusive or obligatory. In such societies, most men are more or less bisexual, and the women assumedly heterosexual (Beach 1976/1977; Marshall & Suggs 1971; Gregersen 1996:276).

B. Adults

The Trobriand Islanders admitted to Malinowski that homosexuality is contemptible, but also that it was formerly practiced (Gregersen 1996:274). In general, the people of Papua New Guinea view homosexuality in a negative and unacceptable light. They cannot understand how a man might enjoy having sex with another man.

7. Gender Conflicted Persons

See the discussion of Sambian hermaphrodites, 5-alpha-reductase boy-girls, in Section 1B, Basic Sexological Premises, Sociolegal Status of Males and Females.

8. Significant Unconventional Sexual Behaviors

A. Coercive Sex

Rape

To most young women today, a man with money, a car, or even a schoolboy with promise, is a far more attractive prospect than a poor boy with no obvious future. For many young men, having no money with which to buy sex directly, or simply with which to make a girlfriend happy, is a frustrating state of affairs. Some such men state that there is no opportunity for them to have sex at all, unless they rape a woman. Group rape is less likely to lead to trouble than individual rape, although most men who state they rape women do both. Gregersen (1996:149, 358) includes the Trobriand Islanders among the societies that simply prefer to ignore rape altogether.

Rape of any sort is disturbingly common in all areas of the country, rural, town, and city. In addition to commercial sex, there is the issue of "line-ups" or pack rapes. Often associated with "six-to-sixes" (clubs that remain open from 6 p.m. to 6 a.m.) or video showings that run from evening to dawn in both rural and urban areas, a group of men/boys take turns in forcing a woman to have sexual intercourse with them. As they watch each other, the sexual dynamics of rape and homosexuality mix to produce, for some, a highly erotic event. In some communities, line-ups are reported to take place every weekend. Older men, many of whom are married, are also frequently involved. Younger men and even boys of 11 or 12 are able to join with their elders in sexually abusing a woman. One young fellow of 17 years told me about his village:

> In here rape and forced sex exists just like in other parts of the province. It happens especially during disco nights and video shows. When we brought our village girls to the disco or video show, the boys from other places came and took our girls for dance and sometimes take them home to sleep with and have sex with. We thought they slept only with their friends, but somehow the boys arranged it with their village boys and made single file on them [line-up]. When the girls come back they never tell us about it because they are afraid and ashamed. Then we do the same to their sister in return. (Author's field notes)

This type of sexual behavior is extremely dangerous because the men involved are exposed to the semen of many of men, thus raising their risk of acquiring STIs and AIDS, not from the woman, but from the other men involved. The woman is placed at extremely high risk of acquiring STIs and HIV as well.

Many Papua New Guineans do not like to admit that such things are going on, but there is now a great deal of evidence from studies conducted in selected urban areas (i.e., Daru, Port Moresby, Lae, and Goroka) and many rural villages, indicating that such sexual activities are widespread. These sexual activities are highly dangerous from a public health point of view because they spread diseases very quickly, not just among the people who participate in them, but among all those other persons, wives and husbands, new and old boyfriends and girlfriends, with whom these people have sex. These activities are also responsible for many STIs, including HIV, among newborn babies.

B. Prostitution

Across the country, people are complaining that more and more young women are having sex earlier, and often with older, married men. The lure of social status, drinking beer, going to dances or parties, the institution of the "six-to-six" clubs, and, increasingly, payment in cash and/or gifts, are drawing women into commercial sex. Papua New Guinea does not yet have a major brothel-based commercial sex industry, but it does have a large, highly dispersed population of women who are willing to sell sex and men willing to buy it.

Much of the activity among women is driven by poverty, some of which is severe. Single mothers, widows of all ages, urban married women whose husbands do not bring home enough money, and teenage girls everywhere are often poor in cash. There is little shame attached to selling sex in some communities, especially where the woman brings home the cash and food. Brothers, husbands, and other men in the family are often very willing to help a woman find a man who will pay for sex, especially if they can share the rewards. Young women are more saleable, and sometimes very young girls are offered to adult men for sex.

From their earliest contacts, outsiders and missionaries misinterpreted as promiscuity and/or prostitution the "casual" sexual relations and small gifts Trobrianders, and Papuans in general, offer their female partners. This is not the view of the Papua New Guinea people themselves, for whom sexual relations and small gifts do not carry the cultural messages of Western standards and norms. [The contrast here is between the meanings and values insiders attach to some behavior and the way outsiders interpret this behavior from their "objective" perspective. The "objective" views of the outsiders represent what anthropologists label an etic view. In many, perhaps the majority, of customs, the "objective" etic view is quite different from the emic (insider) view of persons within the culture (Gregersen, personal communication, 2000; Reiss, 1997). (Editor)]

C. Pornography and Erotica

In most areas of Papua New Guinea today, pornographic magazines, picture books, and videos are available, despite laws to the contrary. Many adults and young people seem to enjoy looking at pictures of people having sex. They consider it educational, and given the dearth of printed or other media on sex, this is hardly surprising. To some young people, however, the experience is frightening, because they find themselves sexually aroused with little understanding of how to manage their desires.

D. Paraphilias

In spite of fairly extensive reporting of sexual behavior in general, the paraphilia level for Oceania seems to be fairly low. Sexual contacts with animals has been reported in a few cultures, including the Marquesans, but such contacts are denied, condemned, or apparently unknown among the Wógeo and Trobrianders (Gregersen 1996:278).

9. Contraception, Abortion, and Population Planning

A. Contraception

Although male control over women is a significant factor in extramarital pregnancies and teen pregnancies, alcohol use by women and their inability to plan for protected intercourse are also factors. Condoms are readily available, but are deemed inappropriate for women to carry. Other contraceptive methods are unavailable and prohibitively expensive.

B. Abortion

Abortion is illegal in Papua New Guinea and is considered to be morally wrong by the majority of the people. However, illegal abortions are increasing. It is not unusual to hear about young girls and older women inducing abortions. Many of these self-induced abortions result in serious infections and, on occasion, death. The methods of inducing abortions are done by ingesting certain mixtures or herbs, or inserting things into the vagina.

C. Population Programs

Papua New Guinea health indices remain an abiding source of concern, with maternal mortality projected as high as 800 per 100,000 births and infant mortality at an underestimated 80 per 1,000 live births. Within the Action Plan of the 1994 Cairo Conference on Population and Development, adolescent reproductive health is identified as a priority area. Hence, the government of Papua New Guinea, in collaboration with donor organizations, are launching programs to combat the spread of STIs, HIV/AIDS, and unplanned pregnancy, especially among young people.

10/11. Sexually Transmitted Diseases and HIV/AIDS

There is a National AIDS Committee in Papua New Guinea responsible for increasing public awareness and advocating prevention of HIV/AIDS and other sexually transmissible infections. Advocacy is done through media campaigns, advertisement, radio spots, local television, school curricula and classrooms, peer-education programs on university campuses, and community-outreach efforts, including training religious leaders about sexual and reproductive health issues.

Condoms are free but not always available. Efforts are presently underway to break through the walls of silence around issues related to sexuality and reproductive health. Although cultural taboos make this a challenging task, educators and service providers are making inroads by using culturally relevant videos and dramas on STIs and HIV/AIDS, and other related topic areas, to educate people about the facts.

12. Sexual Dysfunctions, Counseling, and Therapies

Over the last few years, the author has conducted several training seminars on sexuality and reproductive health, including issues related to sexual dysfunctions. Common concerns among men were premature ejaculation, small penises, and erectile difficulty. Women complained of vaginal discharges, unpleasant odors, pain during intercourse, and dissatisfaction with their sex lives. Women reported that their husbands or partners use them for their own pleasure.

As in most developing countries, sexual diagnostic counseling is a luxury that most people cannot afford. However, through reproductive health interventions, information is being shared about the various types of sexual dysfunctions and treatment. In many instances, people need basic information about how the body responds sexually. Educators talk about some of the physical and psychosocial factors which can have an impact on sexual performance, including the negative effect that alcohol and other drugs can have on sexual performance. Other important issues that get discussed are gender roles, gender inequities, poor hygiene, and violence.

13. Research and Advanced Education

Despite the obstacles of geographic isolation and linguistic diversity until recent times, anthropologists, like Margaret Mead, Bronislaw Malinowski, Clelland S. Ford, and William Davenport, psychologists, such as Frank A. Beach, and others managed to gather considerable ethnographic data on the peoples of Papua New Guinea. Only recently, as modern transportation and electronic communication have broken down some of the obstacles, the HIV/AIDS and population/family planning crises have brought some limited and focused sex research. Sexological research, however, is just beginning to appear in very limited ways in Papua New Guinea, as it is in most other developing countries.

The main organization promoting sexological research is the Papua New Guinea Institute for Medical Research, P.O. Box 60, Goroka, Papua New Guinea.

Conclusion

Although most societies and cultures around the world are experiencing major social change and tension, few are experiencing the transformation more intensely and radically than the people of Papua New Guinea. However, as Papua New Guinea moves into the new millennium, there is a great deal to be optimistic about. First, people are hungry for information and are open to learning new things about sexuality, as well as other aspects of life. Second, the government is working with agencies to prevent the spread of HIV/AIDS, and to educate the masses about population health issues. Third, the Ministry of Education, the Ministry of Health, and the faith-based communities in Papua New Guinea have developed curricula that address the issues of sexuality and reproductive health. Educators are being trained in sex and sexuality, family life education, reproductive anatomy and physiology, sexual and personal health, family planning and contraception, prevention of STIs and HIV/AIDS, prevention of sexual abuse and violence, and gender equity.

As Papua New Guinea continues to embrace the values and ways of the Western world, there will be many gains and losses. Culturally speaking, Papua New Guinea stands to gain information that will help to save lives. But, Papua New Guinea will no doubt experience all the problems and contradictions associated with Western society. Papua New Guinea's challenge is to maintain its cultural integrity as it struggles to become part of the modern world.

Acknowledgment

We gratefully acknowledge Edgar Gregersen's helpful review and additional comments on this chapter.

References and Suggested Readings

Beach, F. A., ed. 1976/1977. *Human sexuality in four perspectives.* Baltimore, MD: Johns Hopkins University Press.

Davenport, W. H. 1977. Sex in cross-cultural perspective. In: F. A. Beach, ed., *Human sexuality in four perspectives* (pp. 115-163). Baltimore, MD: Johns Hopkins University Press.

Ford, C. S., & F. A. Beach. 1951. *Patterns of sexual behavior.* New York: Harper, Colophon Books.

Francoeur, R. T., Cornog, M., Perper, T., & Scherzer, N. 1995. *The complete dictionary of sexology* (pp. 160-161). New York: Continuum.

Gregersen, E. 1996. Chapter 16. Oceania. *The world of human sexuality: Behaviors, customs, and belief.* New York: Irvington Press. pp. 263-281.

Herdt, G. 1981. *Guardians of the flute: Male initiation in New Guinea.* Berkeley, CA: University of California Press.

Herdt, G. 1984a. *Rituals of manhood: Male initiation in New Guinea.* Berkeley, CA: University of California Press.

Herdt, G. 1984b. Ritualized homosexuality in the male cults of Melanesia. 1962-1982. An Introduction. In: G. Herdt, ed., *Ritualized homosexuality in Melanesia* (pp. 1-81). Berkeley, CA: University of California Press.

Herdt, G. 1987. *Sambia: Ritual and gender in New Guinea.* New York: Holt, Rinehart and Winston.

Herdt, G. 1990. Mistaken gender: 5-alpha reductase hermaphroditism and biological reductionism in sexual identity reconsidered. *American Anthropologist, 92.*2:433-446.

Imperato-McGinley, J., et al. 1974. Steroid 5 alpha-reductase deficiency in man: An ingerited form of male pseudohermaphroditism. *Science.* 191:872.

Imperato-McGinley, J., Peterson, R. E., Gautier, T., & Sturla, E. 1985. The impact of androgens on the evolution of male gender identity. In: Z. DeFries, R. C. Friedman, & R. Corn, eds., *Sexuality: New perspectives*. Westport, CT: Greenwood Press.

Jenkins, C. 1996 (April 14-17). *Sexual networks and sexual cultures in contemporary Papua New Guinea*. An unpublished paper presented at the conference, "Reconceiving Sexuality: International Perspectives on Gender, Sexuality, and Sexual Health," in Rio de Janeiro, Brazil.

Malinowski, B. 1927. *Sex and repression in savage society*. Cleveland, OH: Meridian Books.

Marshall, D. S., & Suggs, R. C., eds. 1971. *Human sexual behavior: The range and diversity of human sexual experience throughout the world as seen in six representative cultures*. New York: Basic Books.

McWhirter, D. P., Sanders, S. A., & Reinisch, J. M., eds., *Homosexualty/heterosexuality*. New York: Oxford University Press.

Mead, M. 1930. *Growing up in New Guinea*. New York: Dell.

Mead, M. 1935. *Sex and temperament in three primitive societies*. New York: Dell.

Money, J. 1990. Agenda and credenda of the Kinsey Scale. In: D. P. McWhirter, S. A. Sanders & J. A. Reinisch, eds., *Homosexualty/heterosexuality* (pp. 41-60). New York: Oxford University Press.

Money, J., & Ehrhardt, A. 1972. *Man & woman, boy & girl: Differentiation and dimorphism of gender identity from conception to maturity*. Baltimore, MD: Johns Hopkins University Press.

Reiss, I. L. 1997. An introduction to the many meanings of sexological knowledge. In: R. T. Francoeur, ed., *The international encyclopedia of sexuality* (vol. 1, pp. 21-30). New York: Continuum.

The Philippines
(*Republika ng Pilipinas*)

Jose Florante J. Leyson, M.D.*

Contents

Demographics and a Historical Perspective

A. Demographics

The Philippines is an archipelago of about 7,107 islands that stretch 1,100 miles north and south in the Pacific Ocean off the southeast coast of Asia. With 3 million square kilometers (115,830 square miles) of total land area, the landmass of the archipelago is about the same size as the state of West Virginia, but slightly smaller than the British Isles. The Philippines is located northeast of Malaysia and Borneo, east of mainland China and Vietnam, south of Taiwan, and a distant west of the Hawaiian Islands in the Pacific Ocean. Ninety-five percent of the 1999 estimated 79.345 million Filipinos

*Communications: Jose Florantes Leyson, M.D., 6 Ranney Road, Long Valley, NJ 07853 USA; Phone: +908-876-5482.

(Pilipinos) live on the eleven largest islands, which are mountainous, except for the heavily indented coastlines and the central plains of Luzon. Slightly over half the nation's population live in the cities, in Manila, the former capital, with a 1990 estimated population of 1.6 million, in Quezon City, the new capital, with 1.7 million, and Cebu City with 612,000. The Philippines is divided into three major regions: Luzon in the north, Visayas in the center, and Mindanao in the south.

The 1999 age distribution of the 79.3 million Filipinos was 37.3 percent under age 15, 59.1 percent between ages 15 and 65, and 3.6 percent 65 or older. Ethnically, the large majority of the people are Malays, with small minorities of Chinese, American, Spanish, and Indian. Twelve percent constitute the ethnic and cultural minorities that include Aetas, Negritos (north), Ifugaos, Igorots, the "hill people" (north central), and the Muslims in the south. Although ten major languages (Cebuano, Bicolano, Ilocano, Pampangino, Spanish, English, etc.) are widely spoken, and there are 80 different dialects, Tagalog (Filipino) became the national official language in 1937. However, English is still widely used today throughout the country and it is the medium of instruction beyond the sixth grade. Eighty-three percent of Filipinos are Roman Catholic, 8 percent Protestant, 5 percent Muslim, and 4 percent other.

Life expectancy at birth in 1999 was 63.8 for males and 69.5 for females. The birthrate in 1999 was 27.88 per 1,000 population; the death rate 6.45 per 1,000, and the infant mortality rate was 33.89 per 1,000 live births, giving an annual natural increase of 2.143 percent. The 1995 Total Fertility Rate (TFR) was 3.6 children per fertile woman, placing the nation eighty-fourth among 227 nations. In 1993, the Philippines had one hospital bed per 860 persons and one physician per 849 persons. In 1995, 95 percent of the people were literate, with 97 percent attending primary (elementary) school and 55 percent attending secondary school. The Philippines also has the distinction of having one of the oldest universities in the modern world, Santo Tomas University, founded in 1645, twenty-five years before Harvard University, the oldest university in the United States.

In 1997, *Time/World News* reported a 7 percent economic growth for the Philippines, with a per capita gross domestic product of $2,600, and considered the Philippines as one of the 10 leading major Asian countries in a business boom. However, in 1999, because of global economic crises, the country is trying to recover and survive in agriculture, aquaculture, and industry.

B. A Brief Historical Perspective

Several waves of Malay peoples arrived in the Philippine archipelago from Southeast Asia long before the arrival of Europeans. These tribal societies and petty principalities coexisted with links to China, the East Indies, and countries in the Indian Ocean. Discovered by Magellan, who was killed there in 1521, the islands were named Las Filipinas (the Philippines) in 1559 by the Spanish explorer Ruy L. de Villalobos in honor of Prince Philip of Asturias, who later became King Philip II of Spain. The first Spanish settlements came in 1564, and a colonial capital, established at Manila in 1571, quickly became the key transit point for trade between Mexico and the Far East. Under Spanish rule, a majority of Filipinos became Catholics, except in the southwest islands where the people remained Muslim. In the shadow of a tepid colonial administration, the Catholic Church grew in power and wealth.

A nationalist movement gained strength in the late nineteenth century, leading to an armed uprising in 1896, the Spanish-American War, and defeat for Spain. In 1898, Spain ceded the Philippines to the United States for $20 million. When the nationalist movement declared the islands an independent republic, the United States refused to accept the declaration. A six-year war followed between 1899 and 1905, in which American troops brutally repressed the guerrilla uprising. In 1916, the Filipinos elected a Senate and House of Representatives, but the President was an American Governor General. In 1935, a Philippine Commonwealth, modeled on the U.S. constitution, was established.

Japan brought the United States into World War II by attacking and then occupying the Philippines in December 1941. On July 4, 1946, the Philippines became the first Asian colony of the United States to gain independence, in accordance with an act passed by the United States Congress in 1934. In the 1970s, Muslim (Moro) secessionists fought repeatedly for their autonomy from the Christian majority on the island of Mindanao. In 1972, President Ferdinand Marcos declared martial law to combat riots by radical youth groups and terrorism by leftist guerrillas and outlaws. Despite some land reform and control of inflation, opposition continued, as a high population growth rate was aggravated by both poverty and unemployment. Opposition to Ferdinand Marcos continued despite his lifting of martial law and his election in 1981 to a second six-year term as president. The 1983 assassination of Benigno Aquino, the prominent opposition leader, sparked demonstrations calling for the resignation of the president. When Marcos declared himself victor in the bitterly contested elections of 1986 despite widespread charges of fraud, Corazon Aquino, the widow of Benigno Aquino, proclaimed herself president and announced a nonviolent "active resistance" to overthrow the Marcos government. The 20-year rule of Marcos ended in February 1986, with the recognition of Aquino as the new president by the United States and other nations. A weak economy, widespread poverty, and communist insurgents kept the political scene unstable between 1987 and 1990. Government forces were able to put down an attempted coup in 1989 with help from the United States military stationed in the Philippines. In 1994, the government signed a cease-fire agreement with Muslim separatist guerrillas, although some rebels have refused to abide by the agreement.

1. Basic Sexological Premises

A/B. Character of Gender Roles and Sociolegal Status of Males and Females

The traditional gender roles in Filopino society are strongly influenced by centuries of Islamic culture, Chinese mores, and 425 years of deep-rooted Spanish Catholic traditions. However, since the 1960s, traditional Filipino gender culture has been transformed by tremendous Western—European and American—influences, except in the Muslim-dominated southern islands, which have been much less influenced by Western contacts. Polygamy, the wife as the husband's chattel, and deferential behavior of women in the presence of men are still strong values in the Muslim-dominated areas. The Muslim ideals of feminine behavior still produce a dependent, inferior, passive, and obedient woman.

In traditional Chinese society, women were to be obedient to the father and elder brothers when young (single), to the husband when married, and to their sons when widowed. For Filipinas of Chinese ethnic origin, marriage was the only means to economic survival. Arranged marriages are still common, with the clear expectation of male offspring who will maintain the "family business" interests and continuity. A wife's position and security within her husband's family remains ambiguous until she produces a male heir. These women have no right to divorce or to remarry if widowed. Those who try to defy these traditions have been ostracized and sometimes driven to depression or even to suicide.

The traditional colonial Filipina was supposed to reach marriage in a virginal state. She was expected to take care of the domestic tasks, go to church, bear and educate children, and support her man in his political, professional, and economic endeavors. The oppressive attitude of colonial Spain toward the Filipinas was first challenged by Mechlora Aquino (Tandang Sora), a non-violent intellectual woman. In the mid-1800s, she was considered as the equal of the French "political" heroine, Joan of Arc, for leading both a political and cultural revolt against the suppression of women's rights. However, the colonial government quickly extinguished the local revolt, and the treatment of Filipinas as second-class citizens remained in force until Spain ceded the Philippines to the United States in 1898.

In the early years of the American occupation, 1900 to 1930, both females and males were provided with free elementary education. However, only the children of the rich had access to a high school and college education. Although women's social standing was improved, it was not until the late 1950s that the majority of women achieved equal rights; but this also happened mainly in the urban areas. For a long time, this double standard of colonial mentality was accepted without open criticism. That has changed since the Philippines gained its independence from the United States, with the democratic government taking steps towards recognizing the social and political rights of women. The Western influences on women have resulted in sociocultural independence from parents, spouses, and/or lovers. Women with a college education and businesswomen have started painstakingly to open spaces in the country's political, economic, legal, and administrative positions. On February 21, 1986, Mrs. Corazon Aquino became the first woman president of the democratic Philippines.

Today, Filipinas occupy key positions in university and medical schools, hospitals, both local and national government, large corporations, research-pharmaceutical companies, journalism, and all fields of the arts. However, discrimination against women and special privileges granted to men continue to exist simply because the males benefit from a deeply rooted and long-standing "male buddy" (*comparé*) network.

C. General Concepts of Sexuality and Love

Virginity is no longer a universally expected prerequisite for the marriage covenant. The 1994 Young Adult Fertility and Sexuality Survey (YAFSS) of 11,000 young people, ages 15 to 24 years, conducted by Dr. Z. C. Zablan, professor of demography at the Population Institute of the University of the Philippines, revealed that 18 percent of Filipino youths approved premarital sex, 80 percent disapproved, and 2 percent were neutral. Today, sexual attitudes are more liberal and accepting of radical changes in sexuality and love because of the influences of the media and global communications. The same YAFSS survey showed that a large number of female college graduates residing in urban areas (35 percent) were exercising their liberal roles, both in their personal and professional lives with flexible sexual attitudes, while 40 percent were more likely to employ contraception. Filipinas in all classes are trying to balance their responsibility as mothers and lovers with some real class distinctions. The mothering role of the middle- and upper-class Filipinas is often supported by housemaids, professional babysitters, and grandmothers. In general, sophisticated, well-educated Filipinas are more comfortable than older women in taking the initiative in foreplay and learning new erotic techniques to introduce a variety of sexual techniques in their sexual lives. Also, these younger middle- and upper-class wives try to increase both the depth and scope in the emotional and intellectual communications within the couple. On the other hand, the 65 percent of Filipinas who live in the rural areas are less educated, more conservative in their sexual lifestyles, less likely to use contraception, and less independent in their personal lives.

The Philippines is a third-world country that enjoys the benefits of a young population, with 37.6 percent under age 15 and 47 percent between the ages of 15 and 49 years. There are also more women than men, with the surplus women finding support as maids or "nannies." The Latino tradition of single women serving as surrogate mothers for infertile wives is morally and legally unacceptable in the Philippines. For some males, especially in the rural areas and in minority groups, it is often difficult to internalize the impact of the women's liberation movement both in their sexual and professional lifestyles. In my observation, most well-educated males, especially urban dwellers, are starting to perceive that they enrich the relationship by participating in the rearing and education of their children, and the sharing of two incomes are beneficial to the family. The sophisticated professional men are also learning to relax during lovemaking, enjoying alternating passive and active roles, and accepting the fact that they can also be seduced and excited.

The majority of the Filipino urban population today is clearly Westernized, but still very conservative in its public and legal sexual values. Because of the dominant and pervasive influence of the Catholic Church, the only sexual behavior considered legal and moral is heterosexual intercourse within a monogamous marriage. Every other imaginable sexual variation is explicitly condemned. Thus, prostitution, pornography (nudity), polygamy (except in some minority groups and the Muslim south), premarital and extramarital sex, cohabitation, homosexuality, and other variant sexual behavior are all illegal. However, quiet homosexuality and heterosexual cohabitation seem to be more socially acceptable today, especially when they involve celebrities and politicians.

2. Religious and Ethnic Factors Affecting Sexuality

A. Source and Character of Religious Values

Although 83 percent of the Philippine population are Roman Catholic, 8 percent are members of the Mormons (Church of the Latter Day Saints of Jesus Christ), Seventh Day Adventists, Four Square Church, Philippine Independent Church (Aglipan), Church of Christ, Jehovah's Witnesses, and Iglesia ni Kristo. Five percent are Muslim, and 4 percent follow Hinduism, Buddhism, Taoism, or the traditional nature worship of the aborigines or hill people. Taoism was introduced to the Filipinos by Chinese merchants during the tenth century. Taoism has both a philosophical and a religious tradition. Before the Spaniards came to the Philippines in the sixteenth century, in 1521, Taoism had some definite ideas about sex. For example, the wife's purpose is to please the husband and conceive more children. If the wife is barren, the husband can have a concubine or mistress to bear children, especially sons, for him. As the traditional Chinese population has aged, Taoist temples are increasingly seen only in few major cities where they serve as tourist attractions, not religious symbols and sites. As octogenarian males are dying and their religion is fading away, modern Chinese males are being Westernized or practice a more popular religious persuasion.

Buddhism was probably first introduced to the Philippines during the eighteenth century from India through the Malaysian peninsula and China. Chinese Buddhism, based on the Mahayana (Great Vehicle, Wide Path) school of India, was handed down from generation to generation by both Chinese traders and immigrants. This form of Buddhism is very similar to

Taoism. More recently, Buddhism has become more of a social ceremonial practice rather than a religion, and its temples have become a tourist curiosity. The "fat-bellied" Buddha statue is a symbol of the family's wealth and fertility that bedecked a Chinese house's foyer or living room.

Nature worship, the traditional indigenous religion of the Philippines, has been practiced from prehistoric times by the aboriginal Aetas, Negritos, Ifugaos, Igorots, and the hill people. Their constant struggle with the forces of nature for their survival has led to a closer relationship with their ancestors and the elements of nature. This form of religion has little if any systematic doctrine. However, there is one basic characteristic: the belief in the spirits of their ancestors who influence the living in every conceivable sphere of life and apply rewards and sanctions where appropriate. These religions also have lesser gods and deities with different powers related to physical health and fertility. The majority of tribal peoples believe that the first woman came from the "split" of the bamboo node, a kind of a tropical, tall, and slender palm with sequenced "nodes" in the trunk. Some tribal customs allow sexual activity as early as puberty, comparing this early exploration with sweet and tender young bamboo shoots. On the other hand, the expectation of virginity—the absence of penile/vaginal intercourse—with the assumed "tight vaginal entrance"—as "tight" like the nodes of an adult bamboo stalk—is favored for marriage.

Islam is practiced by 5 percent of the population, with the majority residing on Mindanao at the southwestern tip of the archipelago. Islam reached the Jolo and Zulu Islands in the Philippines, a century before the Spanish colonialists arrived, through Arab and Persian merchants arriving from the Malayan peninsula. Despite the fact that the Philippine government legally approves only monogamy, local Muslims, known as "Moros," are allowed to have several wives provided they can afford them.

American settlers brought Protestantism to the Philippines after 1898. The sexuality attitudes of both old and new Protestant tenets are based on the basic Judeo-Christian doctrines. However, two off-shoots of the Protestant tradition are homegrown: one established in 1902 by the Aglipay family, the Filipino Independent Church, and the other in 1914 by the Manalo family, Iglesia ni Kristo (Church of Christ). These two Filipino Protestant churches have sexuality restrictions similar to the basic Judeo-Christian principles, but each has added rules imposed by personal preferences from their Filipino religious founders.

The influence of the Roman Catholic Church was and still is hegemonic over ninety percent of the Filipino population. Throughout Filipino history, the political powers have been submissive to the Catholic Church. The Church is determined to maintain its hold on important aspects of civil life, such as education, the availability of contraception and abortion, and even the registration of major events in the lives of the people like births, marriages, child adoptions, and deaths. A very conservative interpretation of Catholic decrees about sexuality and marriage have been inscribed in the minds of the Filipino people, in a way that has proven difficult to alter or delete. Outstanding among these are the Church's views on the social roles of males and females, its insistence that any form of masturbation or premarital intercourse is sinful, and condemnation of homosexuality as unnatural behavior. The Church also places great emphasis on virginity as a prerequisite for matrimony, citing the example of the Virgin Mary, the Blessed Mother of Jesus Christ, who conceived her son without the need of sexual intercourse or a biological father. This sexual innocence and purity is clearly symbolized in the white clothing worn at baptisms, first communions, confirmations, and weddings. Catholicism also offers young men and women a celibate life that is supposedly more spiritual and rewarding in the priesthood and religious life.

B. Character of Ethnic Values

Before the arrival of the Spaniards in 1521, the Philippine islands were inhabited by fierce, indomitable tribes that valued their freedom and had learned to survive by adapting to the climate and resources of the different islands (regions) of the archipelago. It is believed that the chain of islands was a geological product resulting from volcanic eruptions from coastal/mainland China. However, the aborigines came by land and/or ice bridges from the Malayan peninsula. The indigenous people were mostly nomads who fished and hunted wild game. But the "hill people," the Ifugaos, who settled mainly in the north central part of the country about 1,000 years ago, developed and retain to this day unique sexual and marital ethnic values along with advanced engineering land cultivation. For instance, some tribal customs consider breast size and prominence of the hips to be financial assets that equate to the value or size of the dowry; large breasts and wide hips in the prospective bride would make a dowry of a few pigs or chickens unacceptable. The Rice Terraces of the "hill people" are considered one of the wonders of the world still existing today.

When the Portuguese explorer, Ferdinand Magellan, funded by Spain, discovered the Philippines in April 1521, he accidentally landed in the central part of the island country called Limasawa. Literally, "Lima" means five and "asawa" means wife. Limasawa, then, translates into "five wives." Magellan noticed that the natives were practicing polygamy. Most of the men have five or more wives. He did not realize that polygamy was a common marital ethnic norm in most of the indigenous tribes throughout the whole archipelago.

During the tenth century, China was trading regularly with different Philippine tribal clans led by a merchant known as Limajong, who introduced monogamy. The arrival of Chinese traders resulted in about 10 percent of intermarriages with the indigenous peoples. There was also a great variety in the way religious values and sexual customs developed in different ethnic groups and tribal traditions. For example, Islam takes on a slightly different expression among its many followers in the southern part of the country where ethnic plural marriages occur. Most of the ethnic minorities—Negritos, Aetas, Ifugaos, and Igorots of the north—practiced monogamy. The sexual values of these ethnic minorities often allow marriage by the age of puberty, about age 13 or 14 years for girls and age 15 and 16 for boys.

On the other hand, Catholicism introduced to the islands by colonial Spain in 1521, considers males not mature or ready for marriage until age 20 or 21 years, and girls only at age 18 or 19. Masturbation is prohibited by the Church as sinful, "dirty," immature, narcissistic, and unnatural. In the recent years, the traditional awareness of and opportunities for sexual initiation among adolescents have been relaxed, with male sexual exploits provided by an abundance of social opportunities, including birthday and college fraternity parties, community celebrations (fiestas), and public dances, which generally encourage sensual and erotic relationships. ·

The socioreligious education of women in traditional Catholic Filipino society encourages them to play the "cat and mouse" game. Young women are expected to develop social strategies that produce maximum enticement and individual satisfaction. This continual erotic stimulation and the hyper value of masculinity drives young men into the "courting game," leading hopefully to marriages. A young woman's ability to employ her virginity as a "bargaining tool" makes males inevitably impatient. The young male is then caught in an expensive web of socially productive and profitable engagements associated with courtship that resolves itself in betrothal to the young woman and "marrying" her, coupled with the expense of building his masculine image and sexual experience with prostitutes.

3. Sexual Knowledge and Education

A. Early Sex Education Programs

For some 425 years, Spanish colonial rule afforded the Filipinos little political freedom and individual dignity. This began to change in the 1880s, when a multi-talented physician, Dr. Jose P. Rizal, broke through political, racial, and sociocultural barriers by studying medicine in Spain and Germany. Returning to the Philippines, Rizal established architectural and ecological parks, and local health education. He also advocated interracial marriages and later married an Irish woman before his political execution in 1896. At that time, only the most sophisticated elite and rich Filipino students were admitted to the oldest university of the Philippines, the University of Santo Tomas. At the time, only a few colleges offered limited science and social courses, and absolutely no sexuality or health education. All university and college courses placed a heavy emphasis on religious subjects. Between 1600 and 1824, the colonial Catholic Church had a total monopoly over education that kept the people ignorant of the advances in science, technology, and political organization that were taking shape in the Western world.

In 1898, when Americans colonists replaced the Spanish, public education was drastically altered and some individual freedoms were granted. In 1916, the Filipinos elected a Senate and House of Representatives, with its president an American governor general. He was interested in economic growth and political participation. Gradually, in the 1910s and 1920s, free secondary education was introduced in the big cities. In the 1930s, college education was free only in national colleges. With political modernization and the advent of the Philippine Commonwealth of 1935, Filipino society became increasingly Westernized, specifically Americanized. However, there was still no formal sex education or published material on the subject. Sex education was completely limited to information about pregnancy and childcare passed on by word of mouth among the women in families.

When Japan invaded the Philippines on December 8, 1941, at the start of World War II, the political and educational climates changed hands. Between December 1941 to October 1944, the Japanese occupation was characterized by political oppression and indoctrination. The Japanese military government was interested in total sociopolitical suppression, not in education.

The "re-Americanization" of the Philippines began when U.S. Army General Douglas McArthur liberated the islands on October 20, 1944. Two years later, the Philippines was granted its independence on July 4, 1946. Prior to independence, the educational system was reorganized and further modernized. United States soldiers who held educational degrees acted as model teachers and a catalyst for future Filipino teachers. From 1946 to 1968, there was rapid population growth, but still no formal sex education. What was not taught in the classrooms, the students would learn from their families at home and in the streets, although this information was often distorted, incomplete, or outright erroneous.

In 1969, in an effort to reduce the world population, the United Nations, through the World Health Organization in cooperation with the Filipino government, instituted a family planning and birth (conception) control program. In 1970 to 1971, this author was one of the principal instructors and trainers in the family planning program in the suburban and rural areas. The program consisted of teaching basic biology, conception/pregnancy, and the different options for contraception, but mainly the "pill." Although the Catholic Church was overtly opposed to contraception, particularly the "pill," the church covertly supported this education in order to reduce the family's burden of child rearing because of poverty. In 1970, the educational (college) system was rocked by a widespread explosion of "students unrest" demanding more student rights and an expanded curriculum. The author was again one of the medical student leaders who demanded students' rights in a peaceful protest rather than a confrontational or violent demonstration. The college administrations finally settled and included in their curriculum science courses, such as expanded public health, that included information on sexually transmitted diseases and limited information on human sexuality.

During this era, sex education was left to the biology teachers, both in high school and college, who gave very limited information as part of the classes in the biological sciences. In a few cases, when the teacher decided to do so, this instruction was more or less a description of the reproductive organs in plants and animals, with perhaps some references to the role of the ovaries and testes in human reproduction. Explicit mention or pictures of the male and female genitalia were unacceptable and forbidden by custom.

B. The Present Situation

In 1972, President Ferdinand Macros declared martial law and proclaimed a new sociocultural reform, the "New Society," which purported to reduce crime, enhance land reform, and augment economic stability. During this period, the government also approved a program, and directed that formal sex education be taught in all levels of education. Sex education courses were offered, starting at the elementary level in science and biology (human development and population). The high school equivalent to the tenth grade in the American system and college courses included elementary basic-level biological information plus discussion of family planning and separation—divorce being illegal. The information on legal separation (de facto separation) was more in-depth in the public schools because of its high incidence in the lower class as compared to the middle and upper classes (professionals), who sent their children to private schools. In the 1980s, the medical schools supplemented the courses on human sexually with seminars and an international conference in which the author was one of the main speakers. In the 1990s, the government sponsored kindergarten classes. Research on population control, sexually transmitted disease (STD), pre-marital sex, sexual harassment, and AIDS are ongoing. (See Section 5B, Interpersonal Heterosexual Behaviors, Adolescents, for additional insights into sexuality education for adolescents and medical school students.)

Despite the government's crackdown on illegal sex publications, which was supported by Catholic Church authorities, it is obvious to any careful observer that informal sources of sexual information—television talk shows, soap operas, radio-phone-in programs, and different kinds of adult journals and magazines commonly found in metropolitan and other urban areas—are widespread in the Philippines and cannot be controlled by either the government or religious authorities.

4. Autoerotic Behaviors and Patterns

The Catholic Church still maintains its condemnation of self-pleasuring (masturbation), teaching that any sex outside marriage is sinful. At present, a majority of Filipinos still believe that frequent masturbation can cause neuroses, premature ejaculation, and even blindness. In 1969 and 1970, the author conducted an informal sex survey in Central Region colleges and universities, which revealed that only 22 percent of the students, mainly males, engaged in masturbation. Another survey done in 1995, limited to medical school students, showed that 32 percent of the males and 8 percent of the females practiced masturbation (total $N = 280$).

5. Interpersonal Heterosexual Behaviors

A. Children

In Filipino society today, it is not unusual for preteenage boys to engage in exploratory "sex" games with other boys and girls. Such exploratory play allows the child to reassure him/herself of the normality of his or her body. This kind of childhood sexual rehearsal games was more common in the past and in rural areas, when violence and drugs were not as devastating as they are now in the urban areas. In some cases, boys would observe couples kissing and hugging in the park. Occasionally, they sit in the balconies of movie theaters where couples are engaging in heavy petting. In the rural areas and *barrios*, boys commonly compare their bodies with a friend, relative, or schoolmates. Generally speaking, parents and other adults have a mildly negative response when they discover child sexual play, ranging from warnings to spankings.

B. Adolescents

Our knowledge of the sexual attitudes and behaviors of the Filipino youth is limited to a very few anecdotal reports, most of which deal with middle- and upper-class urban teenagers rather than the rural poor and urban street children. In this very limited context, my personal experience was the basis of my premedical school thesis on "First Night Sexual Experience of Young Boys—1968." This study consisted of personal interviews with 80 adolescents in the rural areas of Cebu during social dances and summer festivals. The majority of these teenagers were interested in obtaining information regarding nocturnal emissions, love, sexual intercourse, and, for women, contraception and pregnancy. Most of the males' ideas on sexuality were derived from older boys, brothers, and their uncles. On the other hand, the girls were too timid or shy to answer the sexuality questions.

During the author's return visit to the Philippines in July 1995 as an invited speaker at a college sociocultural conference, he arranged an impromptu meeting with middle and high school students, grades seven through ten. They informed me that most of their teachers believed that they were too young to hear about sex education. The teachers did not allow questions from their students during the lecture on "family educa-tion." Most instructors were too insecure and embarrassed, and so were unable to facilitate any in-depth dialogue. In Catholic Filipino society, the Christian dogma still has a strong influence on the teachers' moral and religious values, so that, despite the presence of a government-mandated educational climate, sexuality remains taboo in public discussion. Unfortunately, these teenagers were afraid to elaborate further, confessing only that it is attitudes like this, repeated in their conservative homes, that make them view society and family cynically.

In Christian colleges and universities, being pregnant out of wedlock can result in expulsion. In most public non-sectarian universities, sex education is still mostly non-existent except for those basic biological courses and family planning programs mandated by the government in 1972. However, in the largest government-run university, the University of the Philippines, sex education courses are more in-depth and liberal, because of the sophistication of the instructors and department heads who are Westernized and comfortable with controversial and sensitive ideas.

Although still limited, some might say elementary, sexuality courses in most urban medical schools are generally open to updating because of the infusion of new ideas from visiting professors and experts in periodic international forums and conferences. The best medical school students can graduate as doctors at the young age of 23, a factor that makes their communications with patients about sexual issues difficult at best.

Pubertal Rites for Boys

The anatomical and physiological changes that herald puberty are universal to the human race. However, in Filipino society, the sociocultural pubertal rites are expressed in a variety of customs and traditions depending on the particular subculture and its religious orientation. In the Christian tradition, the custom is to circumcise all males. Male circumcision is performed either by a medical doctor trained in this surgery or by a traditional medicine man. Filipino boys may be circumcised as newborn infants or somewhere around age 8 to 10 years, when they are in the third or fourth grade. City dwellers and the sophisticated elite have their newborn males circumcised before they are discharged from the hospital. Working class and poor families seldom have their newborns circumcised, but usually wait until the boys are 9 or 10 years of age. The medicine man is not a medical doctor, but a man of ordinary skills who has learned the art of circumcision handed down from his father or grandfather.

Circumcision is done in two ways. In superincision, a dorsal-mesal cut is made along the length of the upper surface of the penis, from the base to the foreskin, or only on the top of the foreskin. In the coronal technique, the excess foreskin is removed with a circular incision, as is the practice in Europe and North America. When a medical doctor performs either of these types of circumcision, the incision is closed by sutures and oral antibiotics are prescribed to avoid post-operative infection. The medicine man, on the other hand, only performs the dorsal slit circumcision, using a specially "cleaned" (not sterilized) sharp knife or a modified slender "machete" as scalpel. The medicine man uses neither antibiotics nor anesthesia.

This pubertal initiation traditionally occurs in the spring or when the schools begin summer recess, somewhere in May or June. The ceremony commences when boys, aged 8 to 12 years old, march in procession, usually in groups of ten to twelve, to the medicine man's house. The medicine man, with the parents' knowledge and consent, will then lead the boys to a secluded place, a clearing in a thicket or on a farm to insure privacy. The boy with pants removed, is seated on the edge of a rock or stump of a tree, while the medicine man sharpens and cleans the knife. Despite this tension-producing build-up, the boy must remain calm and composed to show that he is brave and ready to enter the new realm of adulthood and can handle the rigors of manhood. The medicine man places the knife's sharpest side underneath the tip of the excess prepuce (avoiding the glans penis). He instructs the boy to look up, saying "look for a bird or a plane," diverting his attention. In a split second, a piece of wood or a branch is struck down against the knife, resulting in a midline cut or dorsal slit of the prepuce. Bleeding may be profuse or minimal. The juice of a certain tropical palm plant (*nipa palm*) is squeezed over the wound as a post-surgical anesthetic and caustic agent to stop the bleeding. No wound dressing is applied to cover the fresh and rugged incision. A clamp of cobwebs or a mesh scraped from the underside of a coconut palm branch over the incision serves as a bandage and additional clotting agent (to stop further bleeding). In some parts of the Philippines, the medicine man spits on the wound pre-chewed tobacco or a concoction of guava (a tropical peach-like fruit) leaves to act as a clotting agent. Both the cobwebs and coconut palm scrapings act as mechanical meshes to trap blood platelets in order to stop bleeding. The guava leaves mixed with saliva has papase, a chemical agent that medically can minimize post-operation swelling and sometimes arrest bleeding.

After circumcision, the boys walk home without a sound of complaint or grimace of pain. It is interesting to note that a particular gait can be discerned before and after the circumcision. The boys naturally walk normally on their way to the medicine man's house. When they walk back to their homes, their gait is characterized by a "frog-like" walk, in which the knees are spread away from each other in order to avoid the thighs touching the newly circumcised genitalia. For three to five days, the circumcised boys stay home. Some wear skirts borrowed from their sisters or mothers, not pants, so that clothes do not touch or accidentally hit the sensitive, partially exposed glans (head) penis. Despite daily wound washing in the ocean, a river, or stream, about 90 to 95 percent of these cases of non-sterile circumcision become infected. It takes about six to eight weeks for the wound to heal, usually without ugly scars or deforming penile skin adhesions.

In the 1970s, Muslim boys were not usually circumcised unless their parents were well-educated and health-aware of Westernized attitudes of that time. In the early 1950s, boys of minority families in the north were not circumcised. However, with the arrival of foreign Christian missionaries and their conversion to Christianity, most of the boys are now circumcised either by a medicine man or a physician.

Puberty Rites for Young Females

Christian girls undergo two phases of social transition to womanhood: ritual ear piercing and a *cotillion* or debutantes' ball. Ear piercing is neither a religious nor a pubertal rite. It is just a custom, a traditional "tribal" rite of socially announcing that the person is a girl. The piercing of the ear is usually done between one month after birth and 2 or 3 years of age. In some parts of the country, the girl is much older. Ear piercing is usually done by a hair stylist, a "medicine woman," or medical person. Outpatient procedures by medical personnel use properly sterilized needles. Oftentimes, however, no anesthesia or antibiotic is given when the piercing is done by a hair stylist or a medicine woman. In general, however, infections from ear piercing are not as common as in male circumcisions done by a medicine man with an unsterilized knife. Phase two, the debutante's ball or *cotillion*, is a social introduction of young females ages 16 to 18 years in the form of an elaborate party or dinner dance. The hostess of this social event is an 18-year-old female usually from the rich families. *Cotillion* is an old Spanish tradition, dating back to colonial days, when the daughters of foreign dignitaries or tenured Spanish government officials were introduced to the eligible bachelors of the equally rich in order to secure the daughter's future financial and sociopolitical status as eligible and eminently suitable future wives.

In the Muslim or Moros community, about 10 percent of the Filipino population, the ear-piercing ritual is the same as among Christians. In the early 1950s, the older girls would wear a veil. At present, young females seldom use veils or cover their faces. Some Muslims include the cotillion in their rite of passage, but for others, dancing or any form of partying is absolutely prohibited and considered sacrilegious.

The minorities, Ifugaos, Kalingas, Igorots, and others, account for 3 to 5 percent of the population. These females, like most Filipinas, have their ears pierced at any early age. However, in some tribes, family wealth and status are demonstrated by the number of earrings or the layers of necklaces worn. No form of female circumcision or genital mutilation has been recorded. Anecdotal reports suggest that during the pre-Hispanic colonial days, some tribal females wore multi-appendage rings, nose, and lip rings. These tribal cultures do not observe the cotillion.

Premarital Sexual Activities

Sexual attitudes and behavior differ from one group of Filipino youth to another, depending on their social class, educational level, and place of residence. In metropolitan and large cities, Manila, Quezon, Cebu, Iloilo, Davao, Dumaquete, and Zamboanga, adolescents and young adults are exposed to the cosmopolitan life and consequently receive more information on sex and sexuality. They are also freer to experience numerous options than are less educated youths. Youth in small towns have narrower and more restricted ideas on sexuality, because of the family's and Church's strong control and influence. Furthermore, youngsters in big cities have easy access to adult magazines and entertainment, in which sexuality is openly discussed or shown, even though their parents and the Church try to hide such information from them. The majority of urban youth knows about contraceptives and can acquire these from pharmacies or from friends without problems. Despite the guilt and shame associated with sex, middle- and upper-class urban youth often engage in sexual contacts with girlfriends, household maids, and even prostitutes. For the youths of the poverty belts around the big cities, the situation is compounded by the lack of money and self-control. Even if they would prefer to use a contraceptive, they cannot afford them and there are no places where they can get them free. Oral contraceptives are only given free to married women for family planning purposes by government-run city and municipal health clinics. Although condoms were distributed freely in public high schools in the early 1990s on a mandate from the Secretary of Health as part of an STD and HIV prevention program, this practice was later discontinued because of a public outcry that it was ineffective and because of the Church's persistent objections.

The situation for rural (*barrios*) youth is quite different. They learn and receive information about sex and sexual behavior from observing farm animals, from magazines, from clandestine "boys only" meetings, and from the relations between parents and other family members in homes where there is little privacy. The prevailing Catholic dogma on sexual morality is written deep in the unconsciousness of every boy and girl. Only a few years ago, 98 percent of the youth associated premarital sex with guilt and sin. Only recently has this begun to change. In 1994, the Youth Adult Sexuality Survey (Zablan 1994) revealed that about 18 percent accepted premarital sex, although a majority of 80 percent still believed it was a sin and morally unacceptable.

Only a few general surveys about the sexual life of younger Filipinos exist; most of what is known is based on anecdotal reports. The author's experiences are with interviews of preselected groups of the youth population conducted during periodic sojourns back to the Philippines. The samples mainly consist of middle-class youth, ages 17 to 22, who were encouraged to bring to the meeting problems related to their sexual lives and development. Repeatedly, they expressed regret that these aspects of their lives that engender so much anguish and fears could not be explicitly discussed in the intimacy of their household.

It is becoming increasingly clear that first premarital sexual activities are initiated at an earlier age, especially for those in metropolitan areas, where the basic family structure often disintegrates because of a lack of parental supervision, with both parents working or the father absent and perhaps working overseas. Young males pursuing college and graduate studies in the city are often detached from parental supervision and frequently succumb to the lure of metropolitan temptations, go-go bars, and adult-entertainment houses. Twenty to 25 percent have their first sexual experiences with prostitutes, either out of peer pressure or curiosity. In a few cases, youths in smaller communities who impregnate their girlfriends may be forced to marry them or make an amicable financial arrangement with parental approval. The woman usually keeps the child in her parents' home instead of giving it up for adoption.

In the Muslim communities, premarital sex is absolutely prohibited. But young girls, ages 14 to 16, can be betrothed through the usual (parental) marriage arrangement, mainly to affluent and much older bridegrooms.

Among girls, the memories of being deflowered were somewhat different from those of the boys. Because of guilt and shame, the majority of young females did not bother to get prior information about sexual intercourse and the possible consequences of their first sexual encounters. They perceived their first intercourse as the fulfillment of young love, motivated by peer pressure to keep their boyfriends, and at the same time as a "challenge" to parental authority or a gross transgression of a religious or social taboo. For the well-educated and sophisticated city dwellers, it was a calculated act to get rid of the old-fashioned social taboo (virginity), which they perceived as an obstacle to entering into a more mature and fulfilling sexual life, or plainly to catch the men of their dreams. It is interesting to note that, compared with the United States and other industrialized nations, Filipino teenagers are probably less sexually active; thus teenage pregnancy is less of a problem than elsewhere.

Most of the children born to single mothers are kept in the teenager's mother's home, instead of being given up for adoption. In the 1970s, a pregnant teenager was a social outcast and was subjected to severe parental scorn. However, in the 1990s, because of Western influence and financial difficulties, a pregnant teenager is somewhat more tolerated, and her parents are less condemning and more accepting of any financial help the teenage father might offer.

C. Adults

Courtship, Dating, and Relationships

As mentioned previously, Chinese influence runs deep and the majority of Filipinas adhere to its simple social dictum, "Get married at a marriageable age." Marriage is considered the natural conclusion of a stable heterosexual relationship. Recently, however, Filipinos have started to replace their old-fashioned social concepts with ones that recognize that the right to remain single is as much a personal right as the right to marry. Because of the Western influence on women's liberation, to be a single older woman is no longer considered a social disgrace or the result of any personal inadequacy.

Cohabitation

The colonial view of the sacredness of marriage includes a strong social condemnation of cohabitation for unmarried couples. Thus, cohabitation was relatively rare during the 1940s. The social and legal implications of "common-law marriage" (cohabitation) are not significant in a society of less affluence and resources. Furthermore, the definition of unmarried used in compiling official statistics makes it difficult to estimate the popularity of this behavior in the sense it is understood in the Western Hemisphere. Beginning in the late 1980s, the increased tolerance of non-marital cohabitation in the West began to influence the middle-aged and younger generations. During the author's 1996 visit in the provinces of Cebu, Leyte, and metropolitan Manila, there was an estimated increase of half a percent and an estimated 340,000 couples in unmarried cohabitation. The majority of cohabiting couples in the provinces are separated from their legal spouses because divorce is illegal and they cannot be civilly or religiously married. The rest are college students, youth, artists, and intellectuals who are attracted to this lifestyle.

Courtship is a cherished Filipino tradition with certain specific rules based on religious, sociocultural, and family values. There are five widely shared rules or "commandments" associated with courtship:

1. Say "yes" to the first invitation.
2. It is a prerequisite to have an escort, either a friend or next of kin, on the first date (no escort is necessary for a woman 28 years or older.
3. It is all right to publicly demonstrate decent affection, such as kissing, touching, and caressing.
4. A young Filipina should reserve criticism after the first date, be discreet about her feelings, and the man must cover (pay for) all expenses.
5. If dating leads to marriage, one must remember that marrying entails marrying into the spouse's whole family as a clan.

The majority of young men and women believe that love, physical attraction, similar religious beliefs, and trust are the basic essentials in creating and maintaining a stable relationship.

Adults, Marriage, and the Family

The marriage ceremony is usually preceded by an engagement. For the rich and middle class, betrothal is marked with elaborate parties. On the other hand, the low-income class concludes the occasion with a firm handshake and/or a sip of a local wine or homemade ferment. The engagement and wedding are usually a happy, festive occasion. However, if questions of family honor and shame arise, the outcome may be violent and deadly, as happened at the time of this writing, when a male's family massacred the bride-to-be's family because she slept with another man two days before the wedding. The community accepted the outcome as a proper punishment for the betrayal and unbearable shame caused to the bride-groom's family.

Whereas the legal age for voting is 21 years for both males and females, the legal age for marriage is 21 for males and 18 for females. In the Muslim community, the parents of a girl between ages 14 and 16 may betroth her to an older man. Generally, in the Christian community, the courts do not consider pregnancy a valid motive to grant permission for the marriage of a minor. Legislation has also abolished the possibility of reparatory marriage; in the past a person accused of rape or forceful abduction could avoid punishment by marrying the victim. In the southern end of the archipelago, where the majority of the Muslims live, a dowry is agreed on before a formal marriage arrangement is signed. The dowry, given by the bride's parents to the groom, may be a large sum of money, property, or a sizable wedding present.

Muslim marriages are conducted by a judge or an *imam* (a religious cleric), Christian marriages by a priest or pastor. Civil marriages are recognized and accepted in both the Christian and Muslim communities when conducted by judges and commercial chiefs, such as pilots and ship captains.

Although polygyny had a long history in pre-colonial Filipino civilization and was common in the Muslim community prior to the 1970s, polygynous marriages are the exception today. The majority of sophisticated, highly educated males, whether Muslim or Christian, choose to be monogamous for financial reasons. Middle- and upper-class Filipino families also elect to have fewer children, two on average, as compared to three or more for the less educated and low-income families.

With the advance of information technology, foreigners seeking brides with traditional values can now surf the Internet for a modest fee. Companies also advertise "mail order brides" in different magazines and specialty journals. There are currently about 100 companies competing to lure mail-order bride customers, such as "Cherry Blossoms," "Asian Rose," and "Exotic Girls." The service charge can range from a basic $150 to upwards of $2,500. For $150, the bridegroom-to-be will receive a brief biographical sketch and a photo or video of the woman. He can correspond with her in letters or even phone calls. He can arrange to go to the Philippines and see her at his own expense. For $2,500, the services include airfare, hotel accommodations, and a two- or three-day tour to personally interact with the candidate bride(s). The client is introduced to different women during a party and the couples can interact socially.

A major shortcoming of this venue for finding a mate is that the interested males are not screened properly. These men can be psychopaths, criminals, or worse. In some cases, a syndicate of "Internet bride-merchants" sells young women aged 14 to 18, oftentimes with fake birth certificates, for a mere $3,000. These women are admitted to the United States on a fiancée's visa. Parents with severe income hardship frequently sign the contract believing that their daughters will either be given a job opportunity or be future brides of these unscrupulous foreigners. Recently, a congress-man from the state of New Jersey sponsored a bill in the United States Congress to severely restrict the issuing of these "fiancée's visas" and to stop the practice of "bride-to-be/sex slave" businesses. Newspaper reports and embassy communiqués have documented that many young Filipino mail-order and Internet brides are held captive, raped, divorced, and then pressed into prostitution.

There are no credible published data on marital sexual satisfaction or on the status of Filipino marital life. According to the author's informal survey and radio-talk-show interviews in 1995, 15 to 20 percent of Filipinos are unhappily married. Women, more often than men, reported having sexual intercourse not because they desired it, but to please their spouses. Whereas 35 percent of males would like to increase the frequency of sexual intercourse, especially those in their 20s and 30s, most of the women were satisfied with the frequency of sex; only 5 percent of the females were interested in more frequent sex. These gender differences may be ex-plained as the result of a greater pressure on males for sexual performance to maintain their macho image and maintain total control over women.

A majority of women complained of the brief duration of foreplay and premature ejaculation. Sexual intercourse is limited almost exclusively to penetration, which is more common among the less educated, more de-votedly religious couples, and the older age groups. The average duration of foreplay is about five minutes, that of coitus about five to six minutes. On the other hand, the more educated, sophisticated, younger age group, and the "unchurched" have a longer duration of sexual foreplay and coitus, about twenty-two minutes. Although premature ejaculation is not uncom-mon among males, very few men seek medical help. Husbands generally do not consider premature (early) ejaculation a problem.

In the Christian community, sexual activity is not prohibited during any religious event or celebration. In some cases, Christian women make the personal choice of not having sex during their menstrual period. On the other hand, Muslim custom does not allow any sexual activity during the menstrual period, between sundown Friday and sundown Saturday, and during *Ramadan*, the month-long period of daytime fasting.

It is difficult to gather data on female orgasm because of religious repression and personal shyness. It is believed that Filipinas' sexual satis-faction is based on cultural and religious grounds. The husband's satisfac-tion is primary and the wife's orgasm clearly secondary. Young, educated, and less religious or unchurched women have a higher orgasmic rate as compared to their older, less-educated, (oftentimes) more religious, and shy counterparts. It is believed that for a majority of women who experi-enced orgasms, it was more a result of psychological and religious expec-tation and not so much because of oral or manual genital stimulation. However, the barrage of media and Western influences has increased the proportion of Filipinas who prefer both psychic and physical stimulation. Filipinas are bombarded by the mass media and performing arts with messages about more openness in sexual matters, greater gender equality, information about new techniques for lovemaking, new roles within the couple, and new opportunities for extramarital relationships. These issues are also conversation matter among friends and families, at business meetings, and at almost any social-civic gatherings.

Divorce and Remarriage

The Catholic Church does not allow divorce of any kind, but it will grant annulments, which most Filipinos find socially distasteful. However, generally, we find civil decrees of legal separation, divorce, and annulment are becoming more socially acceptable for Christian and Muslim Filipinos. A civil divorce requires that the ex-husband support the children and provide some assistance to the ex-wife along with household maintenance.

Slightly more acceptable are consensual separations. What is popular today is having a court declare a marriage null and void under the Family Code (Executive order 209, article 36). The Family Code has adopted the grounds of "psychological incompatibility" as a basis for civil annulments. This was the criterion for annulment articulated by the Catholic Church forty years ago after the Vatican II Council, when annulments became much more common. A civil annulment dissolves the marriage and leaves both parties free to remarry. With the incidence of annulments clearly increasing in the mid-1990s, Filipino Senator A. D. (Nikki) Coseteng introduced in the legislature a pro-marriage anti-divorce bill (no. 179), which now legally defines marriage as an inviolable social institution and the foundation of the family.

The incidence of remarriage is not presently known. However, both in the rural and metropolitan areas, cohabitation is on the upswing because of Western influences and financial problems. In major cities, younger, more sophisticated, and affluent women have more chances for remarriage, but priests will not officiate at a second marriage ceremony unless the Catholic Church has annulled the previous marriage. Despite liberalization in the dissolution or annulment of marriages, the main reason why the divorce rate is still relatively low, when compared to the industrialized countries, is most likely the pervasive influence of the Catholic Church and parental moral values. The importance of extended family norms derives, not only as a source of emotional support and the context for the development of profound personal relations, but also for many other aspects of social life, from financial support to finding a job. Legal separation, divorce, and annulment are still frequently perceived as evidence of personal failure and as a "social anomaly." The end of the relationship is not viewed as freedom and independence, but as the beginning of a different period in one's personal life.

Extramarital Sexual Activities

Most of the causes of legal separation involve extramarital affairs. Adultery or extramarital sex is vehemently condemned by the Catholic Church and is socially detested. However, there is an issue of legal terminology and social definition. Under Filipino penal laws, a man does not commit adultery unless he violates the law against concubinage. To be guilty of concubinage, a man must:

1. keep a mistress within the conjugal dwelling;
2. have sexual intercourse with another woman under scandalous circumstances; or
3. cohabit with another woman outside the conjugal dwelling.

Having sexual intercourse with a women who is not one's wife does not in itself violate the law of concubinage. Nor is the ban on concubinage violated if a man fathers a child with a woman who is not his wife. A wife commits adultery simply by having sexual relations with a man who is not her husband, regardless of the circumstances.

The provisions of the Penal Code on female adultery and male concubinage are glaring examples, not only of the inequality between the sexes, but also of the inequity between erring spouses. The law provides a maximum penalty of four years imprisonment for the erring husband. The concubine shall be meted a penalty of *destierro*, wherein she is prohibited from setting foot within the man's residence. A wife found guilty of adultery, on the other hand, may be imprisoned for a maximum period of six years. Some lawmakers have pointed out that it is easier to send a female to jail and that this violates the constitutional provision on equality of the sexes. In simple terms, the law does not criminalize the sexual infidelity of a married man except under certain circumstances. This, some lawmakers point out, seems to imply that the extramarital affairs of men are acceptable as long as they are discreet in handling them—a clear reflection of the double standard mentality of society with regard to sexual infidelity.

A 1996 survey conducted by an advertising and research group revealed that out of 485 married men in metropolitan Manila, 51 percent admitted having had extramarital affairs. The survey results reflect the machismo culture in the Philippines, wherein a man's worth, among other things, is also equated with his ability to lure other women. In an attempt to correct this inequality in 1997, Senator M. Santiago filed a bill simplifying marital infidelity. In her measure, she proposed that the extramarital sex by either the husband or wife be called *adultery*, whether the extramarital partner is of the other or same sex. The House committee made amendments to her bill and put the marital offense under a single crime called "marital infidelity," eliminating the separate provisions on concubinage and adultery, and the consideration of whether the infidelity occurs within the couple's home or elsewhere. Congress proposed a maximum penalty of six years for all parties concerned. Speaking for the Women's Legal Bureau, a non-governmental organization (NGO), E. Ursua claimed that imposing criminal liability on the offenders is not the answer. "We do not think criminalizing is the proper solution. We can't force someone to be faithful."

The new law penalizes the guilty party with imprisonment, regardless of the reasons behind the infidelity. A woman escaping from an abusive or violent relationship, or one who simply falls out of love and finds growth and fulfillment with another person, is treated no differently than a man who keeps several mistresses. In effect, the law also punishes individuals who get out of marriages that are bereft of love, respect, and trust. Some legal organizations propose a modified "divorce" law and/or a new bill to decriminalize sexual infidelity. But Senator Santiago countered that this might send a "subliminal message" to the youth that the state is encouraging "free love."

In the Muslim world, adultery is severely punished, with the perpetrators either made social outcasts or, in rural villages, stoned to death in public. This "fatal justice" is carried out clandestinely as an expression of community justice that government magistrates (*datu*) can do nothing to either prevent or punish. The whole village maintains a "code of silence," because this punishment is written in the Muslim moral marital law. There is no witness to interrogate or testify.

During the Spanish colonial days, 1775 to 1899, rich Filipinos who owned *haciendas* (estates or a large parcel of land) and employed several female domestic helpers could easily have extramarital relations with their female employees, with or without the knowledge of their wives. Today, we still find married men in all walks of life who maintain a long-standing relationship with a second woman, oftentimes with the knowledge and approval of their spouses, and even of their grown children. In some cases, an extramarital affair can end a politician's career; in other cases, an affair, even when its makes headlines, may have no political consequences. Some couples find extramarital affairs a solution that keeps their marriage alive. The man may be freed to satisfy sexual needs he does not dare, because of religious restrictions, reveal to his wife, while the wife is relieved of any pressure to change her sexual behavior. Most wives who adopt this compromise have limited horizons in their lives and a very low sexual appetite. Less common is a marriage in which both the husband and wife have extramarital relationships by mutual knowledge and agreement. In such cases, usually the husband has a job that keeps him abroad for long periods of time, with periodic visits to wife and family. Occasionally, Filipinos who married, found employment abroad, immigrated for a few years, and married a second woman while abroad, bring their second wives back when they return and set up a second household in a different dwelling. Discovery of this bigamous affair can be costly if the courts become involved. Legal penalties for bigamy can bring up to four years in prison and fines for moral and psychological damages between $500 and $1,300 US.

These relationships pose a serious problem in Philippine society because many of these men resist the use of condoms, do not practice safe sex, and pay no attention to the possibility that their regular or occasional partner(s) may be HIV-positive.

Incidence of Oral and Anal Sex

Both the Christian and Islamic sects abhor oral and anal sex acts. The Muslim tradition specifically requires the husband to enter the wife by natural means in penile-vaginal intercourse. Oral sex, which in the past was condemned as "unnatural," is practiced more or less by educated Christians who live in the metropolitan areas. From the 1950s to the 1970s, when there was no constant supply on electricity in many towns and areas of the country, professional couples enhanced their sexual lives by using pornographic and specialty magazines. In the 1970s and 1980s, with electricity more widely available, middle-class and upper-class couples used film projectors, and later videocassette players, to enhance their sexual repertoire and learn about alternatives to penile-vaginal intercourse that could bring renewed vigor to their routine sex lives.

Anecdotal reports suggest that oral sex is practiced by 10 to 15 percent and tried by 20 percent of the professional couples (i.e., doctors, lawyers, and businesspersons who travel a lot). The majority of Filipinos, however, still consider oral sex as dirty and unnatural. For the few who engage in oral sex, cunnilingus is acceptable, but Filipinas will only very rarely engage in fellatio. In general, older and lower-class Filipinos have a more negative view of oral and anal sex.

Modern Filipino youth, however, seem to be taking a new look at Westernized sexual expressions, according to what they said at the author's impromptu meetings. Although no general survey data are available, a segmental study of metropolitan youths revealed two groups of young women based on their responses. One group accepts and practices oral sex as a way of avoiding the risk of pregnancy, maintaining their technical virginity until marriage, and/or as a form of safer sex. For the second group, oral sex was a more intimate form of sexual relationship, somehow more "romantic" than genital intercourse. Youths holding the latter view believed that oral sex should be only engaged in with a stable (engaged to be married) partner and not in the first few exploratory encounters or dates. Some other older girls joined some boys in rejecting this way of expressing love, and thought that only prostitutes could practice fellatio on boys.

Whereas anal intercourse is not part of the fantasies for the majority of devout Christian women, anecdotal reports revealed that 30 to 40 percent of males fantasized about having anal sex with women other than their wives. Prejudices against anal sex are even stronger in less educated youths. Most of the youths I spoke with do not accept anal sex even after marriage, perhaps influenced by the increasing incidence of AIDS in the Orient. Older boys agreed that a woman will never ask for it.

6. Homoerotic, Homosexual, and Ambisexual Behaviors

Early Christian and Muslim colonists brought their religious views of homosexuality as either sinful or at least unnatural and immoral. Today, the Philippines is still, to a large extent, a macho society, and macho men detest gays, whom they see as effeminate and "strange." For a majority of the population, including locally trained physicians, psychologists, and social workers, homosexuality is viewed as a perversion and a disease. Teenagers who feel a strong attraction to persons of their own gender at first experience confusion about their feelings and sexuality. Gradually, as their orientation becomes clearer in their minds, they awake to the unpleasant reality of belonging to a group that Filipino society marginalizes.

Homosexuality in the Philippines, however, is increasingly being tolerated, and a gay movement is gaining strength and demanding their rights. Twenty years ago, this would have been unthinkable. The scorn for gays is stronger among low- and middle-class men than in the upper class. There always were artists, beauticians, fashion designers, writers, and medical and dental professionals whose homosexuality was known among the elite, but which was carefully kept out of scrutiny from the media and the masses. Lesbians are still not too visible in Filipino society, in keeping with the Christian and Victorian tradition, which never wanted to think about sexual activities in a relationship between two females. To be gay or lesbian in a repressive environment whose stereotypes are the macho man and the submissive reproductive woman is not an easy task. Anyone who deviates from strict heterosexual behavior is ridiculed: A gay is not a man and a lesbian is a degenerate woman. The Filipino Armed Forces does not allow gays to join the military and expels them when they are discovered.

To be bisexual, however, is not so annoying, as long as one's same-gender behavior is kept very private. In the early 1970s, it was common for Filipinos to identify or classify two types of gays: those who engage in homosexual sex activities and those who act effeminate but do not engage in homosexual acts. However, in the early 1990s, the former group has been active in promoting gay rights for the whole gay community. Although the "Gay Organization for Liberty and Dignity" is not yet a formal organization, they speak for both the visible and the invisible, helping the latter to openly assume their identities. Part of the emergence of gay and lesbian subcultures are masseurs who advertise their services in the most important papers and magazines and in metropolitan "gay" bars, discos, and hair salons. Some vocal gay groups lobby to influence politicians for future legal status and/or political clout.

Most Filipino gays prefer to mix with the heterosexual mainstream in their own social class and not form exclusively or predominantly homosexual neighborhoods. Those who have a well-defined and highly visible economic or political role are still in the closet. The same is true for members of the Armed Forces and the clergy. To admit their homosexuality would be unthinkable or suicidal. On the other hand, among artists, writers, movie producers, TV personalities-actors, dancers, some doctors and dentists, and university professors, to openly admit they are gay may bring rejection from the most conservative members of society, but they may end up being accepted and sometimes even see their popularity increase. In the medical community, homosexuality is still generally viewed in Freudian terms, as a condition originating in conflicts and childhood sexual conflicts, which can be cured by psychotherapy. Whereas members of the locally trained medical community, with limited experience abroad, view homosexuality as a violation of the laws of nature, the general public continues to believe that homosexuality is a result of growing up effeminate in a family without a masculine image or male role model.

7. Gender Conflicted Persons

Despite the prevailing Spanish machismo mentality, the advent of democracy and Westernized media messages are slowly changing traditional attitudes. Thus, the "eccentric" minorities have had a chance to come out of their closets and express themselves. For the moment, the public reacts with curiosity rather than violence or acceptance. In the world of beauticians, dress makers/designers, and performing artists, there are well-known transvestites. Because these persons are celebrities in Filipino culture, the public, especially the women, accepts them with smiles and gentle jokes. There is an annual summer parade of transvestites in Manila, where some men are indistinguishable from real women in physique and even "beauty." This event is similar to gay, lesbian, and transgender pride parades in San Francisco and New York City's Greenwich Village. In his younger days, this author would cross dress with other young professionals to entertain hometown guests during fiestas and Christmas celebrations. On the superstitious side, folklore in the North Central and Central parts of the archipelago holds that, when someone is confronted by a witch or travels through a haunted region, it is advisable to cross dress so that the witch or the devil does not recognize you. In some rare cases, transvestites have acceptance from their mates, and sometimes from their children, when they live in metropolitan cities, cross dress in the privacy of their homes, and maintain the macho stereotype in their work and social environment.

If life is not easy for non-effeminate gays or non-masculine lesbians, it is more difficult for those who identify themselves as the opposite sex in manners and clothing, and even more so for those who want to see their bodies change towards the features of the other sex. Persons who want to change their physical sex and be socially recognized as being of the other sex have not been seriously considered in the Philippines. The Philippine Medical Association and the Philippine College of Surgeons have not officially reported any case of transsexualism. Transsexuals are provided with psychiatric treatment, not transsexual surgery. The courts have not addressed this situation, and any person who desires to undergo medical (pre-surgical) and transsexual surgery treatments has to seek such services abroad.

8. Significant Unconventional Sexual Behaviors

A. Coercive Sex

Sexual Abuse of Children and Incest

There are no statistics on the incidence of incest in the Philippines. However, it is quietly known that adolescent girls are often raped by older male family members, and fathers often use them as sexual objects after the death of the mother, or when the wife's work takes her outside the home for long periods. Abusive males are usually unemployed people with a past history of family violence, high consumption of alcohol, social inadequacy, and impulsive behavior. Although less frequent, cases of incest are also known in which the male is the head of an upper-class household and respected by his community. Cases of incest in middle- and upper-class families seldom surface while the victim is a minor. The trauma may emerge during private sexual therapy with an older woman, but there is a strong reluctance on the part of most victims to make formal charges. Generally, indictment for incest by judicial authorities does not take effect unless a formal complaint has been filed or in cases of public scandal.

Reacting to the increase in cases of child sexual abuse reported in the media, law enforcement agencies and the courts have started taking this situation seriously. Sexual exploitation of minors is more frequent in the cities, in the form of child prostitution, child pornography, and sex tourism. The clients and supporters of child prostitutes and those who produce, sell, or transmit pornography involving minors risk heavy fines and imprisonment. Crimes of sex tourism are difficult to prosecute because they originate or transpire outside the geographic borders and legal jurisdiction of the Philippines. There is, however, an organization, Hand Extending Love to the Philippines (H.E.L.P.), based in Phoenix, Arizona, USA, whose primary mission is to help sexually abused Filipino children, provide counseling for pedophiliacs, and prevent teenage pregnancy.

Sexual Harassment

The Euro-American concept of sexual harassment has no place in the tradition of Filipina subservience to males that is part of *marianismo*, the symbiotic culture to *machismo*. However, the experience of sexual harassment is emerging in the social consciousness, as Filipinas respond to Western influences and begin to assert their personal and political rights. Women from the barrios and small towns are easily intimidated, but it is the sophisticated and well-educated women who challenge the "old-boy buddy" system and file complaints. Sexual harassment is punished through an administrative indictment that may end with a dismissal from public service. The administrative procedure, however, does not preclude legal action by the alleged perpetrator. The strength of the current law shows that Filipinas are expanding their political presence/clout, and winning the support of men, who know the problem well from inside the system.

Rape and Family Violence

Despite a long colonial period during which wealthy *haciendems* controlled and regularly exploited their indigenous female employees without fear that the victims might find some recourse in the justice system, recent educational reforms and the transition to a democratic government are producing a more humane society. However, there is still considerable violence within Filipino households perpetrated by the male head of the household. Abuse of this kind is seldom reported to police, because women know that the male police usually behave in the same way in their homes.

In the poorest households, girls are conditioned from infancy to accept the violent behavior of their fathers, particularly when they return home intoxicated. The initial physical abuse may lead to sexual intercourse that amounts to marital rape. Faced with a society that until recently did not recognize the possibility of marital rape or a woman's basic rights, abused women capitulate, repress their feelings, retreat into their taciturn dreams, and continue laboring for the survival of their families, especially their offspring. Even then, if she does not manage to hide at least some of her earnings, the husband may spend them with another woman or drinking with friends. Local newspapers occasionally report domestic incidents when a wife inflicts serious genital damage on her husband while resisting his violent carnal advances. Philippine Department of Social Work and Development (DSWD) statistics reported that in the first three quarters of 1998, there were at least 1,152 cases of rape and attempted rape, 656 cases of incest, and 400 cases of lasciviousness.

The seriousness of rape against an individual female was brought to the public eye by the media when a famous actress was "gang raped" in the mid-1960s. The public demanded the severest punishment, the death penalty, and they got it. Execution by hanging, electrocution, or lethal injection as a penalty for rape has been on the books since 1924. The death penalty was abolished in 1987 but reinstated in 1994. There are currently about 900 persons on death row, including a former member of Congress convicted in 1998 and awaiting execution for rape. Even though no actual executions for rape have taken place, the law has been instrumental in helping reduce such incidents.

After nine years of debate, the House of Representatives finally, in 1997, approved the bicameral conference report on a new law that heavily penalizes rape and makes it easier for government prosecutors to prosecute rape cases. This anti-rape law reclassifies rape from "a crime against chastity" to "a crime against a person." Thus, if the victim is a minor and refuses to accuse the perpetrator, only the minor's legal guardian or the court can file a suit. This new law also penalizes marital rape, but opens the door for the spouse to forgive her husband, in which case the charge is voided. The new law also redefines the nature of rape, expanding the traditional definition of forced penile insertion in the vagina to include unwanted insertion of the penis, or any object or instrument, in any bodily orifice of another person. These "other acts" are now part of "sexual assault." The law in the Revised Penal Code also eliminates the gender bias, so that a woman can now be charged with raping a man. Finally, the law makes it possible to present evidence in court, in which presumption is created in favor of a rape victim, so that any overt physical act manifesting resistance in any degree can now be accepted as evidence of rape. Similarly, evidence that the victim was in a situation where she/he was incapable of giving valid consent can now be accepted as evidence of rape.

B. Prostitution

Tribal wars between the aborigines in the Philippine islands turned the vanquished into slaves for labor or cannibalism, but not sexual slaves. When Chinese merchants started trading with the inhabitants of the archipelago in 960 C.E., they intermarried with native women, but did not sexually exploit the women. With the advent of Spanish colonists in the late 1500s, a flourishing slave trade was established between the Philippines, the Caribbean, and Spain. Anecdotal reports revealed that some Filipina slaves were sold as "exotic sex objects" or prostitutes to European brothels. When Pope Gregory XIV abolished slavery in the Philippines in 1591, middle-class Europeans started to immigrate to the archipelago, but the sexual exploitation of Filipinas by the Spanish colonists continued.

During World War 11 (1941-1944), the Japanese Imperial Army forced Philippine women from Manila and surrounding towns to serve as "comfort girls" (military prostitutes) to provide sexual favors to all Japanese soldiers serving in the Philippines and in the Pacific region. In the 1990s, with international (legal) backing, these comfort girls were partially compensated for their humiliation and moral sufferings. When the American troops liberated the Philippines from Japanese imperialism in October 1945, many American soldiers left illegitimate Amerasian children behind. The mothers of these children and their Amerasian children were social outcasts. In order for these mothers to survive, they became part-time prostitutes in the rural areas for single laborers and traveling salesmen and in the cities with all kinds of customers. In 1947, President Roxas signed a military agreement granting twenty-two military bases to the United States. In the following year, the two largest U.S. military bases in the Far East, the Naval Subic Bay and Clark Air Force Base, were established north of Manila. Angeles City, located near Clark Air Force Base, later became the "Mecca of Sex Trade," the military adult-entertainment capital of the Philippines, with every variety of prostitution, exotic bars, pornography, and sex tourism conceivable.

With the advent of information technology and global travel, the old part-time prostitutes have moved to the big cities. Prostitution survives because of poverty, the commercialization of human relations, and the sustained carnal demand. Although for different reasons, all social classes made their contributions to the trade in sexual services. The rich are looking for entertainment and diversity of sexual practices that they would never dare to ask from their wives. These respectable matrons are assigned by society only to bear and raise children, manage households (sometimes businesses), and organize social activities. The out-of-town students, immigrant workers, and wayward youths may be looking for their first sexual experiences and to combat the loneliness of being separated from their family for the first time. The poor frequent the brothels to affirm their masculinity by using many women or to relieve their loneliness.

As in most other countries, there are three types of prostitutes or sex working girls in the Philippines: streetwalkers, entertainment girls (*hostitutes*), and call girls or high-class prostitutes. Streetwalkers are not common, are usually self-employed, and many have pimps. Their safety is at jeopardy on the streets. The majority of the prostitutes fall under the category of entertainment girls. These *hostitutes* include bar girls, nightclub hostesses (waitresses), masseuses, exotic dancers, and those that work in brothels. They are usually business employees and have contact managers (sophisticated pimps). Their safety is secure because they work inside an establishment. However, they cannot refuse clients who are produced by agencies and their managers. They cannot set the prices for their services. Some massage parlors are commercial fronts for prostitutes who offer their services from oral sex to regular intercourse ($25 to $65 US). Call girls comprise approximate about a third of the female sex-worker population. Self-employed or autonomous, they usually do not have managers. They advertise their services in specialized magazines disguised as escort services for sophisticated gentlemen and sometimes ladies. *Hostitutes* and call girls advertise their services through word of mouth, by taxi drivers, bar bouncers, club managers/owners, and hotel bell captains. These agents receive part of the price in exchange for referring clients. In the large sophisticated hotels, the bell captain may have an album with pictures of different prostitutes from which guests may choose. In 1997, a new phenomenon emerged, the *Japosakis*, Filipina *hostitutes* who return home from sex work in Japan and continue serving their Japanese special clientele or sugar daddies on their periodic "business" trips to the archipelago. Recently, there are also reports of an increasing number of *gigallos* or *toy boys* who provide escort services and pleasures for lonely matrons and wealthy widows.

Although prostitution is still illegal, Filipino society believes that some regulation is always needed, based on the premise that prostitution is regulated in order to minimize the damage to society. Local city councils may require filing an application with the city to establish a brothel, indicating the location for legal reasons and/or tax purposes. Local authorities may also restrict brothels to certain areas and regulate any signs that would identify it as a brothel. Prostitutes cannot reside anywhere other than at the brothel itself, which is her official domicile. Brothels also have to have a bedroom for each working woman. The women cannot show themselves at the balconies or in a window, nor can they solicit in the streets. In order to work in a brothel, a woman has to register with the sanitary-health authorities (Bureau of Health). The authorities will check whether she is a victim of deceit or coercion and advise her that help and assistance is available from legal authorities.

Each prostitute is given a "sanitary notebook" with her picture, personal data, registration number (if any), and the main articles of the decree that concern her rights as a provider of a service. Her rights include being free to stay or quit the brothel in which she lives and works, debts cannot be used to compel her to stay in a given brothel, and no one can subject her to any abuse. Each prostitute has to undergo mandatory monthly medical examinations for sexually transmitted diseases (STDs). If an STD is diagnosed, the brothel pays for medical treatment. The sex worker must show her sanitary notebook to any customer that asks to see it. The manager of the brothel cannot accept any "prostitute-candidate" or applicant who has not first registered and passed a medical examination. The manager also has to report immediately to the sanitary authorities whenever a prostitute is ill, be this an STD or non-sexual disease.

It is easy to imagine the rampant corruption that this naive attempt to protect customers and suppliers of contractual sex alike has produced. Police protection is bought, violations are ignored, and politicians and judges are bribed, often on the pretext of protecting the free practice of a fully consensual sex by the client and sex worker. In reality, this law and its application or lack thereof does little to protect the health of the women and their clients. The women have no protection from customers already infected. The prostitutes can request that their clients wear condoms, but cannot demand the performance of safe sex practices. The clients are not subject to compulsory medical "control," and many may be infected but not show any symptoms while others suffer in silence and continue practicing unsafe sex with other prostitutes, lovers, and even wives.

Transvestites also participate in prostitution, especially with unwary foreigners. Male homosexuals and child prostitutes who created Asia's reputation for sex tourism are concentrated in major metropolitan cities.

Sex Tourism

The Philippines has always been known as the "Pearl of the Orient Seas," the Land of the Three Ss—Sun, Sand, and Sea. A fourth "S," Sex, sold in "coolly" wrapped packages, has emerged to the point where it has already warranted the United Nations' attention: sex tourism involving child prostitutes as young as 6 years old.

Angeles City in Pampanga, north of Manila, once home of the mighty Clark U.S. Air Base, is now being developed as an international airport. But the new airport has also become the center of sex tours to the Philippines, openly promoted abroad, arranged by Filipino tour operators and their foreign counterparts, with attractive come-ons for men seeking sexual activities with "virginal" or child prostitutes who they hope are free of STD and HIV infections.

While the government is making major arrests in this trade, and sex establishments are regularly closed down, the front page of major dailies show bikini-clad young girls being led away by operatives, but never the brothel owners, the tour operators, their cohorts, and pimps. The Philippine Congress is still struggling to pass a law making a customer of a child prostitute criminally liable, even if he does not engage the services of a pimp. An increase of the maximum punishment for child labor and exploitation to twenty years was sought. The 1995 law set the punishment for child prostitution at twenty years in prison; the punishment for pornography and pedophilia, however, remained unchanged.

Sex tourism is the third-highest money-making industry in the Philippines. But the current penalties and enforcement policies do nothing to have an impact on the business. As in many other countries, the prostitutes are arrested, but not the clients, managers, and others whose enormous profits make this business so attractive. The punishment for committing prostitution is a US$500 fine or twelve years in jail. While this law, in effect for three decades, applies to women dancing in the nude or in scanty bikini tongs, a major element in the prostitution trade, arrests are seldom made because of corruption and bribery.

In order to reduce the negative moral and economic effects of prostitution, government and some non-government agencies are working together to rehabilitate former prostitutes or entertainment girls who retire or change their "profession." The government's Department of Social Welfare and Development has programs to teach these ex-prostitutes other work alternatives and technical skills as a means to a decent living. A civic action and rehabilitation group, Marriage Encounter, is also training married former prostitutes to help them move back into mainstream society and divert single women from the sex trade by improving their personal skills for future relationships and family life. But funds and enthusiasm for such social programs are too limited.

C. Pornography and Erotica

Under Spanish colonial rule, the Dutch (in 1600), and the British (in 1762), Filipinos were concerned about their personal freedom rather than freedom of the press. In 1820, the Spanish Cortes (government) granted the Filipino freedom of the press, but it was not until 1887, 67 years later, that Dr. Jose P. Rizal, a Philippine national hero, published in Germany the first Filipino novel, *Noli Me Tangere* (*Touch Me Not*). This literary masterpiece exposed the Spanish political, economic, and sexual abuses in the Philippines. However, it was not until the early 1900s that Filipino romantic novelist Francisco Balagtas published *Florente at Laura*, his Filipino variation on the Romeo and Juliet theme.

In 1946, when the Philippines became a republic after 48 years of American colonialism, American and foreign magazines started to pour into the country. Pornographic magazines were illegal, but the rich and some devoted collectors managed to import literary exotic pieces (erotica). By the 1960s, changes were visible in the social attitudes and private interests of Filipinos. Women's magazines are now found everywhere, in homes, hair salons, physician's offices, and in businesses. And in almost every issue, there are articles about sexuality and eroticism. These articles also cover a variety of subjects, such as contraception, the influence of a healthy sexual life on physical and mental well-being, and how to improve a marital relationship.

Although there are no precise data on the production and commerce of pornography in the Philippines, there is no doubt about its widespread distribution and availability. The gradual blurring of the distinction between pornography and other forms of erotica has led to some level of social acceptance of pornography and opened new markets. In public debates, the anti-pornography position is weak, and pornography is often presented as a form of sexual liberation. Even some Catholic moralists have recognized that pornography can help couples to improve their sexual lives, as long as it does not replace the "natural" (romantic) sexuality.

Three types of Filipino magazines deal with sexuality and eroticism:

1. Magazines dealing with sexual issues, but avoiding pornographic images and full nudity, (e.g., *Superstuds, Gossips, Intrigue, Expose, Teen Stars*, and *Soap Opera Stars*). They are moderately to expensively priced, have quality printing, and are directed at informing a public that accepts a scientific (although popular rather than academic) language. *Sex Forum* magazine, published by a lawyer in the mid-1980s, provided sexual information reviewed and approved by the author of this chapter. Among the topics discussed in *Sex Forum* were techniques to enjoy an intense sexuality, to make your bedroom a more erotic place, to renew sexual passion without changing partners, safer sex practices, and ways of taking care of yourself without handicapping your pleasure.
2. Magazines of literary and sexual humor, with pornographic texts, advice columns, letters, and partial or total nudity (e.g., *Tik-Tik, Playboy*, and *Penthouse*).
3. Magazines and packages of playing or picture cards, clearly pornographic and devoid of artistic quality, some with scatological content.

In reality, a wide range of pornography and erotica is readily available, with distribution handled by regular newsstands, video shops, porno shops (major cities only), and mail-order services.

From the economic point of view, the most important sector of the Filipino pornography market is the sale of videocassettes, fueled by the wide distribution of videocassette players-recorders. In the 1960s, before video players, rich couples viewed adult films with an eight- or super-eight-millimeter portable film projector in the privacy of their own homes, or at some occasional college students' "stag parties." Videocassettes offer the possibility of greater privacy, and cater to the needs of middle-class and even poor men, women, and couples. Most of the pornography is produced abroad and imported for rental through video shops and typical newsstands. The legal situation seems to favor the newsstand as the primary channel for the rental/sale of these cassettes. Video shops, however, offer the advantage of greater anonymity and the higher technical quality of the cassettes. The sale and distribution of these pornographic materials are illegal. Although enforcement of the anti-pornography law is weak, sometimes it will produce a dramatic example. In April 1999, a 61-year-old Filipina grandmother was arrested for selling pornographic tapes on the streets of a metropolitan city.

Filipino pornography also comes in the form of "Live Sex Shows" arranged through special parties held in motels or hotels. The movie *UHAW* (*Sexual Hunger*), a soft-core film in the early 1970s, was the first erotica production with the lead female role played by a former national Philippine beauty queen. Hard-core videos, although poor in quality, are also homemade, but lack the better quality of American and foreign imports. The advent of the Internet has brought a wide variety of sexual information and visuals, including local Web sites, like *sex maniacs* (*manyakis*, www.mayakis.com), with a modest monthly access fee.

The author's informal survey of consumers of pornography indicates that about 85 percent of the males and 15 percent of females are sexually excited by such films. Females prefer erotic films where sexual acts are embedded in a narrative context, whereas males are more easily aroused by simply viewing mere nudity and sexual organs. Female consumption of pornography seems to take place in the context of the couple, whereas for men it is more linked with solitary sex. Generally speaking, there are indications of an increasing trend toward increasing consumption of soft-core (clean) pornography by educated, sophisticated, and professional couples.

9. Contraception, Abortion, and Population Planning

A/B. Population Planning and Contraception

Despite the mountainous topography of the Philippines, agriculture is the main source of livelihood. This agrarian living needs workers. In order to provide "cheap" labor, it is advantageous for a Filipino family to sire more children, mainly boys, as workers and helpers in the agribusiness and aquaculture. Despite the deep-rooted influence of Catholicism in favor of large families and its ban on all artificial contraception, family planning has become increasingly popular since World War II. Even though the Filipino population has increased exponentially to 79 million in January 1999 and is projected to reach 105 million in the year 2025, the Total Fertility Rate is 3.6 children per fertile woman. Most of the larger families reside in the villages and barrios, especially among poor families.

The only contraceptive method accepted by the Catholic Church, the rhythm/cervical mucus or Natural Family Planning method, has a very low effectiveness rate because of menstrual irregularity, a reluctance of Filipinas to check their cervical mucus, and limited understanding of the physiology of fertility among those with limited school education. Between 1968 and 1970, the United Nations, through the World Health Organization and Planned Parenthood, initiated a massive population control program distributing contraceptive pills to Filipino families. As one of the trainer/instructors, this author gave public lectures and provided training to all municipal health care personnel. The pills were given free to all married women. Fortunately, there was no strong opposition from the Catholic Church. However, after two years of implementation, because of government mismanagement of funding and pill distribution, there was no significant reduction in the pregnancy rate. With the increasing number of couples living together out of wedlock, the number of illegitimate children will double by the year 2005. Before the government started the "aggressive and formal" family planning in the late 1960s, middle-class couples learned the use of contraception through specialized pamphlets, magazines, and private channels (family doctors and pharmacists).

Nowadays in the large cities, contraceptives of all kinds—pills, condoms, diaphragms, IUDs, and vaginal spermicides—are available to all types of women. These contraceptive aids can be freely bought in pharmacies without prescriptions. Women who can afford to pay can use the services of private physicians to help them acquire the correct kind of diaphragm or to insert an IUD.

The situation is more difficult for women who live in scarcely populated distant rural areas. There, both the birthrate and infant mortality rate are still high when compared to the urban figures. In these less-developed areas, the government has been trying to organize family planning services as part of its program of mother-child care including kindergarten classes. The number of abandoned children in metropolitan cities has increased. The Catholic Relief Services and other non-governmental organizations are trying to house these children and provide contraceptive-control classes, including newspapers and television advertisements regarding practical birth controls for women and families who live in the city's slums and newly arrived urban immigrants. In 1997, faced with declining official development assistance from developed countries, the government requested increased funding for population programs. Former President F. Ramos suggested that developed countries must meet the United Nations target of committing 0.7 percent of their gross national product (GNP) to population control, and that this aid must follow the 20-20 formula on environment and development endorsed by the 1995 Copenhagen World Summit on Social Development.

According to recent studies, the Philippines has nearly 1.5 million street youth. At the same time, 74 percent of all unintended pregnancies in the Philippines occur in women 15 to 24 years old and 18 percent of Filipino youths engage in premarital sex. In late 1999, the Family Planning International Assistance office in Bangkok, Thailand, and the Reach Out Reproductive Health Foundation announced the start of Barkadahan, a new project designed to curb the spread of sexually transmitted diseases and unintended pregnancies among Philippine's street youth, and have launched a program to address their reproductive health needs with sexuality education, treatment for HIV and STDs, and family planning options (World Reporter Asia Intelligence Wire, 11/1/1999).

B. Abortion

From 1581 on, the Spanish colonists suppressed women's rights, including the right to an abortion. Filipinas were considered second-class citizens until 1937, when a plebiscite on women's suffrage gave them the right to vote. For the first time, Filipinas could have some impact on decisions regarding their health. In the 1930s, abortion was controversial and performed in rural areas by quack doctors with improvised instruments and herbal concoctions. These crude gynecological procedures often led to serious complications including death. After World War II, the American influence resulted in most abortions being performed by physicians. However, abortion today is illegal in the Philippines and is severely condemned by the Catholic Church. This condemnation was reiterated in a recent Papal Encyclical on ethical questions, *Evangelium Vitae*. The current criminal code penalizes with prison sentences women who have an abortion and the professional who performs this service. Abortions are allowed in only two situations, when the pregnant woman is mentally deranged and the pregnancy is a result of rape or incest, and when the pregnancy endangers the woman's life. The Catholic antichoice movement tries actively but with limited success to convince the political leadership to tighten the existing legislation and its enforcement. Muslim law supports the national law on abortion.

Abortion is a last resort everybody knows about, but nobody talks about. Instead of fighting against the powerful forces that arrogate to themselves control over women's bodies, Filipino society prefers to tolerate the officially condemned practices with a mischievous twinkle of tacit agreement among professionals and citizens. Criminal prosecution and denunciation of abortion practices are rare, and only occur when a woman dies as a consequence of an abortion performed by a non-professional. Given these conditions, the Ministry of Health has no exact statistics for abortion, but it is believed that its practice is not as widespread as previously thought. In the major cities, women who typically seek medical help for abortion are unmarried, mature women who already have several children or single high school and college students. These women resort to abortion mainly to put a stop to an unwanted pregnancy or to reduce the family size.

Although morally wrong, pregnant teenagers are now being gradually accepted by their parents. They do not resort to abortion, but agree to keep the child in their parents' house despite embarrassment and peer ridicule. Studies on the relationship between abortion and socioeconomic position suggest that middle-class professional women resort to abortion more frequently than high- or lower-class women. Studies in Manila and Cebu City during the 1980s and 1990s revealed that the highest rate of abortion was among women with a college education or college students who temporarily reside in college dormitories on city-owned housing. There are no written records of abortion among the lower classes because they are usually not performed by health care professionals and the women deny having them to avoid problems for themselves and for those who help them in the procedures.

The morbidity rate associated with illegal abortions, especially those performed by non-professionals, could be reduced if the Church and the government would provide appropriate sexual education and promote the proper use of contraceptives, and expand the socioeconomic criteria/indications for legal abortion. In addition, the government and non-governmental organizations should appropriate extra funding to provide better accessibility to well-equipped provincial or regional hospitals to treat the complications of abortion.

10. Sexually Transmitted Diseases

The estimated one million foreign women sold into prostitution in Japan, Singapore, Europe, the Middle East, and Southeast Asian countries and sex tourism are a major source of STD. In metropolitan Filipino cities, the most frequently reported STDs are gonorrhea, genital chlamydia, chancroid, genital herpes, papillomas, and AIDS. There is an alarming increase in the number of cases with the traditional STDs, particularly gonorrhea, herpes, and syphilis. Because of global travel, resistant strains of gonorrhea and trichomoniasis have been reported in some pockets around large Filipino cities with international connections. The lack of appropriate sexual education among mostly the lower social class, an attitude of indifference to prophylactic measures, and a poorly funded medical care system combine to increase the rate at which STDs are growing in the Philippines. The nationalistic policies of the government have meant that doctors are trained and medical services organized to take special care of pregnant women and newborns, not for the prevention of STDs.

Management of STDs is organized on three levels. The first and most advanced environment is provided by private medical practitioners in their offices. In this privileged setting, only prejudice or ignorance can prevent doctors from providing timely prophylactic advice, early diagnosis, and appropriate treatment of STDs. The second environment is industrialized medicine, clinics established by big corporations and specialized businesses. While the quality of care in this setting depends on the training and qualifications of the medical staff, the availability of consulting specialists, dermatologists, urologists, and gynecologists, has helped a large number of workers and their families by educating patients about the risks of STDs and encouraging them to seek early detection and treatment. The third environment is provided by municipal health clinics and provincial and/or regional hospitals. These hospitals are entrusted with two missions: to provide medical services to the poorest sectors of the population and to serve as training grounds for medical students from both private and public medical schools and universities. Initially these services were totally free, but because of escalating labor-management medical costs, these facilities now charge a small fee or donation to defray the recurrent and management costs. This small donation and transportation difficulties may further discourage Filipinos from the shantytowns in the poverty belts around the large cities from seeking early diagnosis and treatment of STDs.

Prostitutes form another subpopulation in the larger cities that requires special focus in terms of being a reservoir of the diseases and implementing measures for prevention. Children and young adults, especially women from the barrios/rural areas, pour into the city and become prey to drug traffickers and pimps. Through shared needles and sexual activities, they are infected with all kinds of STDs, further contributing to the spread in their original milieus and city at large. Because of poor record keeping, there are no precise data or information regarding the incidence of STDs from city health offices. But anecdotal reports from the last ten years revealed that a small percentage of women who came to a medical office or made hospital appointments for gynecological problems, contraception, or family planning are infected with STDs. However, with the increasing population growth and the advent of sexual liberation, young Filipinos are vulnerable to STDs. The government and non-governmental organizations (NGOs), including the Church, must marshal all their informational-educational resources to counteract the spread of STDs. Schools should incorporate STD-prevention information, with intense mandatory sex education starting in the sixth grade or earlier. Information provided by schools, social workers, health clinics, and NGOs should go well beyond this to help the youth develop a positive attitude towards the body, without shame and guilt about one's sexual nature, and to recognize their instinctive drives and develop an ability to establish trade-offs between instinctual urges and the social moral constraints. Poor peasants and sophisticated urbanities can both understand a well-delivered message that these trade-offs do not mean a repression of one's erotic life, but rather its enhancement by seeking to make it free of disease.

11. HIV/AIDS

The current epidemiological explanation of the origins of HIV traces it to a mutant strain of SIV (simian immunovirus) found in "green monkeys" of the sub-Saharan regions of Africa. Two thousand years ago, the ancient Filipinos supplemented their rice and vegetarian diet with meat from a variety of game animals, including native Philippine monkeys. These simian creatures are the main prey of another world-famous carnivore, the Philippine monkey-eating eagle. In spite of their carnivorous appetite, the Filipino aborigines did not contract the HIV virus. Even today, there are

Filipinos who still savor exotic menus of Philippine monkeys. Nevertheless, the HIV virus has reached the Philippines by other routes.

Acquired immune deficiency syndrome (AIDS) was first described in the U.S.A. in 1978. In 1988, an anecdotal report indicates that one infected Filipina prostitute from New York City came home to die in the Philippines. Twenty years after AIDS was diagnosed in California, the first twenty cases of AIDS were diagnosed in the Philippines (1990). Epidemiologists believe a major factor in the spread of HIV is the U.S. military personnel who frequented the sex bars and bordellos in the towns surrounding Clark Air Force Base and the Naval Base in Subic Bay. In 1992, it was estimated that 234 people were infected; by 1994, there were 834 cases. According to L. B. Duchene (1997) of Doctors Without Borders (Médicins Sans Frontières), 1,234 Filipinos were infected with the AIDS virus in 1997. But the World Health Organization (WHO) estimated that the true figures of Filipinos with AIDS in 1998 was approximately 23,350 persons. The dramatic increase in AIDS cases is attributed by MSF to exposure and infection of the virus through prostitution (heterosexual activities), the prohibitive cost of medicines, malnutrition, economic depression, untreated STDs, and limited access to modem medical care. Contrary to the experience in the industrialized nations, mortality is almost 82 percent in the first year of infectivity and 98 percent in two years. WHO and MSF estimate the Philippines will have 30,112 cases by the end of 1999, and about 39,780 cases by the year 2000. That is a 70-percent increase in the incidence of AIDS in just two years in a population of 79 million people.

The Department of Health AIDS Registry showed that 53 percent of the victims are men, 38 percent are women and 9 percent are children. Among persons diagnosed as being infected with AIDS, 55 percent are drug addicts, 40 percent were infected by heterosexual activities (mainly with prostitutes), and 5 percent by homosexual activity. Approximately 1.8 million Filipinos, 50,000 in Cebu City alone, are involved in the illegal drug trade, a US$6.6 billion business. According to Duchene (1997), the drugs and AIDS situation in the Philippines is, for unknown reasons, less serious that it is in India and Cambodia. As of 1999, 90 percent of the world's 33 million HIV/AIDS cases are found in Africa, Latin America, and Asia. Furthermore, the WHO figures estimated that there will be 38 to 40 million people living in the world with the HIV virus by the year 2000. By the year 2001, the Philippines will have an estimated 40 to 42 million cases of HIV and over two million of them will be children.

While the gay community initially interpreted the alarm about AIDS as an attempt by the medical profession to regain control and use the discourse about health risks to moralize against "disorderly sexual conduct," the real purpose of this crusade was to reduce the risks and mortality for gays who are sexually active. Government and NGOs are more actively engaged in the education and prevention of HIV/AIDS.

It is now clear that any plan to decrease the social and economic impact of AIDS in the Philippines, as in any society, requires an emotional engagement that facilitates an important paradigmatic change of beliefs and behavior. This paradigmatic change is essential to practicing abstinence, to increasing the use of condoms, decreasing promiscuity, promoting the use of disposable needles among drug addicts, understanding and respecting those who suffer, and helping individuals everywhere to enjoy sexuality while minimizing the risks for one's self and society.

In addition to emotional engagement, changes in individual attitudes require the active and creative support of social groups to which the individual belongs; namely families, schools, private businesses, and churches. In 1995, a private-civic organization hired Magic Johnson, a famous American basketball superstar, to give talks to Filipino youth about HIV prevention and living a responsible and healthy sex (safe) life.

12. Sexual Dysfunctions, Counseling, and Therapies

A. Concepts of Sexual Dysfunction and Treatment

The Philippines is a conservative society in which definitions of sexual dysfunctions often mirror the changing attitudes towards male and female sexuality. Thus, in the 1970s, inhibited or absent female orgasm (anorgasmia) was not considered a problem in a context where female sexuality was linked almost exclusively with procreation. Premature ejaculation became more of a problem in the 1980s with the emergence of the myth of simultaneous orgasms, promoted by the Western media, and the idea of heterosexual sex as spontaneously pleasant, which taken together created a new set of pressures, expectations, and tensions. Finally, the growing public rejection of the conservative attitude of the Church linking emotionally stable sexuality with orgasm might reduce the tendency to treat alternative expressions of eroticism as sexual dysfunctions.

Prior to the mid-1950s, Filipino physicians had no better knowledge or understanding of human sexuality than the sophisticated Filipino citizen. Both could, but seldom did, read Kinsey's works and Masters and Johnson's book *Human Sexuality*. Even after some sexuality education was introduced into medical training, the information they received was prejudiced and biased. The departments of obstetrics and gynecology in the public health and urology section taught the pathologic aspects of genitourinary (sexual) organs and reproductive mechanisms, but refused to consider with the same vigor or objective the sexual behavior of healthy males and females. In my interviews with medical students and young doctors during my periodic visits to the Philippines in 1984, this author perceived that two years later, the physicians still did not feel comfortable discussing healthy sexuality issues. Some of these doctors even felt personally offended, especially in being asked to deal with the "sexually oppressed" minority social groups, such as the aging, homosexuals, and the mentally and physically disabled (handicapped).

Gynecologists, psychiatrists, urologists, and general practitioners often have limited knowledge when people come for advice on sexual problems, such as frigidity, impotence, ejaculatory dysfunction, painful sex, sex during pregnancy and after delivery, consequences on sex life from drug/alcohol abuse, sex among the aged and physically handicapped, and sexual surgical procedures. Although their scientific information about sexuality is limited and incomplete, they perceive that science and common sense conflict with their ideologies and cultural-religious beliefs. The internal battles between these two opposing patterns of thinking and behavior only add confusion and distress to ignorance.

In 1990, this author initiated the creation of sexuality programs in major Filipino universities and medical schools. *Sexual Rehabilitation of the Spinal Cord Injury Patients* (Leyson 1991), by this author, was introduced, along with other resources, and quickly became popular among medical and paramedical personnel along with judges, lawyers, and teachers who are increasingly more aware of their need for advanced education on sexual topics/issues.

B. Sexual Counseling and Therapies

Prior to the 1960s, the management of sexual dysfunctions was based mostly on folklore and "witchcraft." In the 1970s, management was a mixture of traditional folklore and medical science. In the rural areas, marital dysfunctions (sexual and reproductive) were treated with exotic concoctions and herbal remedies. In the urban areas, impotence was mainly treated with psychotherapy, occasional anti-depressants, and hormones. Premature ejaculation was managed by psychotherapy. In 1998, the most common male sexual problem was impotence, followed by premature ejaculation, decreased libido, and infertility. Premature ejaculation was managed by anti-depressants and psychotherapy, with perhaps some behavioral sex therapy. Impotence was treated with non-specific vasodilators, sex therapy, and, for those who could afford it, penile prostheses. Libido disorder and infertility were treated with psychotherapy and pharmacological remedies. Among women, the most common sexual problems were painful intercourse (dyspareunia), vaginal spasms, and inhibited orgasm (dysorgasmia). Occasionally, older women complained of a decrease of sexual desire. Dyspareunia was treated with psychotherapy and sex therapy. The other sexual dysfunctions were grouped into one disease and managed with sex therapy and pharmacological remedies.

From 1995 to the present, sexual dysfunction management is almost the same as in the United States and Europe for those able to afford it. Most urologists and gynecologists have taken additional training in sex education and therapy. A few American- and European-trained sexologists have opened offices in major cities. With the infusion of new ideas and discoveries in sexology, management of sexual dysfunctions consists of behavioral therapy, sensory amplifications, advanced psychotherapy, and sex therapy. Modern impotence treatment includes erection vacuum devices, oral and intra-urethral medications, intrapenile injection medicines, and solid and inflatable penile prostheses, as well as sexual performance medications like Viagra. However, some herbal remedies for impotence, infertility, and libido disorders have also been revived. The Church and NGOs with social services offer premarital and marital counseling, although the official Catholic position still maintains the traditional female role of motherhood and perpetuates a generally more passive attitude towards sexuality and pleasuring even in marriage.

C. Sexual Counseling for Emigrant Filipinos

Sexual counseling and therapy from Filipinos who immigrate to other countries presents some unique problems. The "Filipino Blend," which represents the majority of Filipinos, is the result of racial diversity and genetic pooling involving over 1,300 years of infusions from China, Indonesia, Malaysia, Indochina, India, Borneo, Java, Spain, and the United States. The profound psychological and cultural result is a Filipino self-concept of being powerless and inferior. This perceived sense of dependency on the benevolence of envied Western masters detracted from the development of a strong national identity and solidarity, perpetuating a subservient mendicant role and passive resistance. A different generation of Filipinos immigrating to the United States and Canada are subjected to a variety of traditional and Westernized cultural and ethnical (values-communication styles) conflicts. This clash of values and behaviors may result in a cultural psychodynamic conflict, a kind of cultural baggage, which may include any or all of the following:

1. The primacy of family and small-group affiliation over the individual, a strongly held value that inhibits free expression of dissent and tends to detract from the creativity and autonomy that are highly prized by Americans.
2. A strict adherence to gender-role stereotypes and patriarchal family structure that goes against the egalitarian norms in the American family.
3. A primacy given to smooth interpersonal relationships that conflicts with the American ideal of openness and frankness.
4. An attitude of "optimistic fatalism" or *bahala na*, that is opposed to American beliefs in future orientation, careful planning, and the drive for excellence and economic development through determined effort.
5. A sensitivity to slight and criticism, which springs from an exaggerated need for self-importance, *amor propio*, and often leads to withdrawal and/or vengeance, in direct opposite to the American style of directness and sportsmanship.
6. A fear of *hiya* (devastating shame) that often inhibits competitiveness. This concern over face-saving is fostered by the use of ridicule and ostracism in child training.

7. The practice of *delicadeza,* or nonconfrontational communication, most evident among females, that is ineffectual in Western societies, where directness is appreciated and competitiveness is encouraged.
8. *Utang nang loob,* or reciprocity of favors, that derives from a sense of gratitude and belongingness, is incongruous in societies that give primacy to individualism and the "bottom line."
9. A strict adherence to Catholic belief on virginity, abortion, contraception, and homosexuality, which can nourish a self-righteous judgmental stance that is out of place in a pluralistic society with emerging alternative lifestyles.

The stress of immigration and acculturation have extracted a heavy toll on Filipinos, which can result in psychological and/or sexual dysfunctions and symptoms of depression, schizophrenia, and paranoia. These adjustment disorders may show up in family and marital conflicts, extramarital affairs, embarrassment from inadequacies in work situations, estrangement from the Filipino family, and even divorce. Unemployment and underemployment weigh heavily on the Filipino male's sense of his own masculinity, and he frequently takes his frustration out on his spouse and children. Filipino women may internalize their frustration against male dominance by developing symptoms of depression and/or arousal or orgasmic dysfunctions.

Santa Rita (1996) emphasized the need of professionals providing sexual and relationship therapy for native and émigré Filipinos to understand the psychodynamics, and cultural and ethnic background of the Filipino personality and their families. The therapist should try to discard the "cultural baggage" of the Filipino colonial mentality by utilizing alternative Filipino cultural norms and practices in the therapeutic role. Such role playing can be used to suggest alternative, more functional ways of interacting as individuals within a family and as a family in a changing Filipino culture or in a different culture. These stage scenarios might include:

1. A scenario for role playing *Lakas ng loob* (assertiveness) may be used to contrast *mahinhin* (self-effacing) and long-suffering, passive behaviors of Filipinos with assertive behavior. Assertiveness is an alternative to playing the martyr, which exacts such a high psychological price in the form of depression and other medical symptoms.
2. *Tinikling* (a bird in a bamboo trap) is the traditional Filipino dance simulating how a bird skips and jumps its way through clashing bamboo poles. This dance can be used to remind the family that like the bird, Filipinos can be resilient and resourceful, and thereby escape whatever traps the colonial masters might concoct. This resourceful dancing-bird image suggests an alternative to maintaining *amor propio* (need for self-importance) and *hiya* (shame) at all cost. These traits are so often exaggerated in both Filipino men and women that failures and disappointments often lead to depression and adjustment disorders, including arousal and erectile dysfunctions.

3. "God helps those who help themselves" is a study theme that can utilize the religious theme of "actively working with God" through one's labor and accomplishments to "glorify" Him. This biblical view suggests an alternative to *Bahala Na* (fatalism) that may result in lack of initiative and impedes economic and social mobility.

4. "In my father's house, there are many mansions" is another basic religious theme common among Filipinos that can be used as an exercise in "hospitality"—welcoming one's fellow human beings. This thesis of "Christian welcome" may help Filipinos become more accepting of other people's beliefs and lifestyles, especially on very emotion-laden issues like contraception, abortion, premarital sex, homosexuality, and bisexuality.

The marital and psychogenic sexual dysfunctions of immigrant Filipinos stem from their sense of vulnerability over their perceived, often acutely subordinate status as a minority in a pluralistic society that reminds them of their colonial history. Culturally sensitive therapeutic approaches are important in order to neutralize the Filipino family's low image of self and provide the family and the individual an opportunity to discover its inner strengths and resources including the gaining of self-respect (Santa Rita 1996).

13. Research and Advanced Education

A. Advanced Education

In August 1887, while on a trip to America, Dr. J. P. Rizal, a foreign-trained eye surgeon and "the Liberator of the Philippines," deplored the American prejudice against Asians and African-Americans and was especially appalled by the laws against interracial marriages in some states. At the time, over a hundred years ago, the Spanish religious teachings were solely limited to family life, and sexual issues were totally suppressed. Despite the declaration of independence from Spain by Filipino nationalists on January 12, 1989, sex education was not formally taught in colleges until the American colonial rule. In the late 1940s, sexuality was introduced to the Filipino educated elite in the form of family planning and topics on reproduction and birth through pamphlets and specialized magazines.

Since the 1980s, despite the proliferation of medical schools, human sexuality courses have been limited to sexuality-related professional degree programs in nursing, psychology, and medicine. In 1996, through the author's encouragement, three medical schools in Manila, Cebu City, and Quezon City established some form of sexuality courses in the gynecology, urology, and public health sections. Today, there is only one so-called accredited post-graduate program in sexuality and humanities, offered by the Population Institute of the University of the Philippines in Quezon City. The Ministry of Health regularly trains nurses and midwives in family planning and contraception through the municipal health clinics. The

Philippine Psychiatric Association and the Philippine Urological Association are updating their diagnostic codes for the diagnosis and management of sexual dysfunctions.

B. Research

Most of the government research dollars and interest have been earmarked for the prevention and treatment of childhood diseases, population control, and combating the spread of HIV/AIDS. The limited research resources from private and civic organizations are directed to traditional medical illnesses, such as heart diseases, hypertension and stroke, and tuberculosis. Some international, foreign medical associations and the Association of Philippines Physicians in America (APPA), and medical alumni associations sponsor research projects that relate to social and practical sexual issues, including:

1. Sexually transmitted diseases and HIV/AIDS;
2. Birth control—the effectiveness of new contraceptives and their side effects;
3. Management of sexual dysfunctions—old treatment and new alternatives; and
4. Sexual attitudes and behavior: child prostitution, sexual violence (rape, incest, and spousal abuse), extramarital sex, homosexuality, and the sexuality of minority groups (blind people and the handicapped).

Conclusion

The peoples of the Philippine archipelago, both indigenous and immigrant, Muslim, Christian, and other, reflect the cultural attitudes and behavior of their mixed Malaysian and Chinese ancestries. There are also wide variations because of the sociocultural and linguistic mix. However, the dominant Catholic Church, the legislative body, and the educational system are essentially an amalgam of the old Hispanic dogma and the modern Western flavor with the present public sexual morality reflecting the values of these enduring institutions.

References and Suggested Readings

Austria, T. 1999. *Sexual customs and attitudes of Filipinos.* New York: Library of the Philippine Consulate.

Avento, G. P. 1982. *Sexuality: A Christian view.* Mystic, CT: Twenty Third Publications.

Bradley, E. 1996 (October 27). R and R in South East Asia. *60 Minutes* [Television news magazine]. New York: CBS Television.

Baxter, J. 1992. Power attitudes and time: The domestic division of laborer. *Journal of Comparative Family Studies, 23*:165-182.

Birk, L. 1970. Shifting years in treating psychogenic sexual dysfunctions, medical treatment, sex therapy, psychotherapy and couple therapy. *Psychiatry Clinics North America, 3*:153-172.

Bonoan, R. J. 1996. Jose Rizal, liberator of the Philippines. *America, 20*:18-21.

Duchene, L de B. 1997 (December 8-14). AIDS cases in the Republic of the Philippines. *The Filipino Express* (Jersey City, NJ).

Evaristo, F. 1995 (August 1). Sex tours: A tourism come on. *Manila Bulletin*, 80.

Fernandez, T. 1995. *Prostitution, sexuality transmitted diseases, AIDS in Cebu.* Cebu City, Philippines: Chief City Health Officer.

Freud, S. 1965. *Standard edition of the complete psychologic works of Sigmund Freud.* London: Hogarth.

Highlights of Philippine history. 1999. *Filipino yellow pages.* New York: The American Kayummanggi Communication, Inc..

Leyson, J. F. 1965. *First night.* Unpublished psychological thesis. Cebu City, Philippines: Cebu Institute Of Technology.

Leyson, J. F. 1982 (June 10-12). *Sexuality for Filipinos update in medicine.* Paper presented at the annual alumni meeting of the Cebu Institute of Medicine, Cebu City, Philippines.

Leyson, J. F. 1987 (May 17-23). *Comparative study between oral and intrapenile vasoactive drugs in the management of impotence.* Paper presented at the annual meeting of the American Urological Association, Anaheim, CA.

Leyson, J. F. 1988 (December 2-3). *Future options in impotence management.* Paper presented at the American College of Surgeons Meeting, Ashbury Park, NJ.

Leyson, J. F. 1991. Controversies and research in male sexuality. In J. Leyson, ed., *Sexual rehabilitation of the spinal cord injury patients* (pp. 483-531). Clifton, NJ: Humana Press.

Leyson, J. F. 1995 (July 6). AIDS and Filipino sexuality. TV Talk Show *Medicine.* CBS, Channel 3, Cebu City, Philippines.

Leyson, J. F. 1996 (June 2 and 3). Sexual dysfunction management for the year 2000. Radio Talk Show *Dyrc and Dyss.* Cebu City, Philippines.

Laurel, S. H. 1999 (January 29-February 4). Malolos Republic glazed first democracy in Asia. *Turning Point Filipino Reporter Newspaper* [Jersey City, NJ].

Loach, L. 1992. Bad girls: Women who use pornography. In: L. Segal & M. McIntosh, eds., *Sex exposed: Sexuality and the pornography debate.* London: Virago.

Moore, S. W., & Rosenthal, D. A. 1991. Condom and coitus, adolescents' attitudes to AIDS and safe sex behavior. *Journal of Adolescence, 14*:211-227.

Morrison, A. 1988 (September 22). HIV may be a 200 year old infection. *Oncology and Biotechnology News*, 2.

Mosher, W. R. 1996 (February 6). *Visionaries.* New Jersey Television Channel, Trenton, NJ.

Paez, M. S. 1999 (March). Department of Social Work seeks NGOs' help to stem rise of child abuse cases. *The Filipino Express* [Jersey City, NJ], p. 10A.

Philippine population—Increased funding population programs sought. 1997 (December 10). *The Filipino Reporter* [Jersey City, NJ], p. 14.

Saludo, A. G., Jr. 1999 (March 22). The first Holy Mass in Limasawa as the embodiment of our faith and reaffirmation of history. Congressional Privilege Speech, House of Representatives Assistant Majority Leader, Philippine Congress, Manila, Philippines.

Santa Rita, E. 1996. Pilipino families. In: M. McGoldrick, J. Giordano, & J. Pearce, eds., *Ethnicity and family therapy* (2nd ed.). New York: Guilford Press.

Sison, J. 1996. Adultery by any other name. *Mr. and Mrs. Magazine* [Manila, Philippines], *19*:14.

World Bank. 1993. *World development report.* New York: Oxford University Press.

Zablan, Z. C. 1994. *Young adult fertility and sexuality survey (YAFSS).* Quezon City, Philippines: Population Institute, University of the Philippines.

Portugal
(*República Portuguesa*)

Nuno Nodin, M.A.,*
with Sara Moreira, and Ana Margarida Ourô, M.A.

Contents

Demographics and a Historical Perspective

A. Demographics

Portugal occupies the western part of the Iberian Peninsula in southwestern Europe. With the Atlantic Ocean on its western border and Spain to the north and east, Portugal has a land area about the size of the state of Indiana, 35,550 square miles or 92,075 square kilometers. It is crossed by many small rivers, and by three large rivers that originate in Spain and flow through Portugal to the Atlantic, dividing the country into three geographic areas. Between the Minho River, which forms part of Portugal's northern border, and the Douro River is a mountainous region with the city of Porto in the

Communications: Nuno Nodin, M.A., Av. Fontes Pereira de Melo, 35, 11-B Edificio Imaviz, 1050-118 Lisbon, Portugal; nunonodin@mail.teleweb.pt.

southwest corner. Between the Douro and the Tejo Rivers, the mountains yield to plains. South of the capital, Lisbon (Lisboa), and the Tejo River are the rolling hills of the drier Alentejo region. Culturally, the northern region is more traditional and religious and the southern region is more secular and less restrictive in gender and sexual matters.

The nine islands of the Azores stretch over 340 miles in the Atlantic, about 900 miles east of Cape da Roca in mainland Portugal. The Azores is a strategic station on the cross-Atlantic air routes. Madeira, Porto Santo, and two groups of uninhabited islands lie in the Atlantic about 535 miles southwest of Lisbon.

Portugal's 1999 estimated population was 10 million. The age distribution was 17.3 percent below 15 years of age, 67.6 percent between ages 15 and 65, and 15.1 percent age 65 and older. The average life expectancy at birth in 1999 was 72.3 years for males and 79.3 years for females. Ethnically, the population is largely homogeneous Mediterranean stock with a small African minority of about 100,000. A third of the population live in the cities, with two thirds in the rural areas. In religious affiliation, 97 percent are Roman Catholic, 1 percent Protestant, and 2 percent other. The 1999 birthrate was 10.49 per thousand population, the death rate 10.25 per thousand population, and the infant mortality rate 6.73 per thousand live births, for an average annual rate of natural increase of 0.024 percent. The Total Fertility Rate (TFR) in 1997 was 1.5 children per fertile woman, giving the country a ranking of 218 among 227 countries. The country has 1 hospital bed per 253 persons and 1 physician per 332 persons. The annual per-capita domestic product in 1996 was $12,400. Education is free and compulsory between ages 6 and 15. The literacy rate is 90 percent.

B. A Brief Historical Perspective

Portugal's roots reach back to the warlike Lusitanian tribes of Roman times. Having gained independence in the twelfth century by the hand of King Afonso Henriques (1128-1185) from a rebellion against his own Castillian mother, Teresa, Portugal was created at the expense of the conquest of territory from the Moors of Morocco who occupied part of the Iberian peninsula until the sixteenth century. The country gained its final form after the conquest of the Algarve (Portugal's southernmost region) in the thirteenth century, and its frontiers have been kept almost untouched up to today. Prince Henry the Navigator (1394-1460) brilliantly coordinated Portugal's expansion that led to a period of great prosperity for the country. In 1488, Bartholomew Diaz reached Africa's Cape of Good Hope. Vasco da Gama followed by reaching India in 1498. By the middle of the sixteenth century, Portugal had colonies in West and East Africa, Brazil, Persia, Indochina, and Malaya.

In 1581, Philip II of Spain invaded Portugal, precipitating sixty years of occupation and a catastrophic decline in Portuguese commerce. By 1640, when the Portuguese dynasty was restored, the Dutch, English, and French had taken the lead in colonizing the world, although Brazil remained under Portuguese rule until 1822 and the African colonies until the 1970s. After years of weak governments, a 1926 revolution brought a strong, but repressive government into power under the rule of Antonio Salazar. The colonial wars of the 1960s placed a terrible strain on Portugal's economy, adding to the country's standing as Western Europe's poorest country. A successful military revolution in 1974 brought a socialist government into power. Fifteen years later, a "democratic economy" was introduced and industries were denationalized. In 1985, Portugal joined the European Community and, between that date and 1992, the per-capita income tripled so that Portugal was no longer the poorest country in Europe.

1. Basic Sexological Premises

A. Character of Gender Roles

In Portugal, there is an influence of traditional Latin perspectives on male and female roles in society, so that social status is still, in part, related to biological sex. Nevertheless, some significant changes have been occurring in recent years. Traditionally, women were expected to have a passive role in society, although generally assuming a leading position at home, taking care of children, and, in many cases, being responsible for the management of the domestic economy. The male was the decision-maker in what concerned major issues at the community level and the main provider of financial maintenance for the household. Women were "naturally" supposed to be good housewives, mothers, and wives.

This situation, a reality for the majority of cases at all socioeconomic levels of society, was maintained and reinforced by the fascist government that ruled in Portugal until 1974. The political and ideological principles of this period, which lasted for 48 years, was strongly influenced by the Catholic Church and also determined social and sexual roles of the male and female. The worship of the Virgin Mary, the *Marianismo,* symbolically reflected the feminine ideal of maternity without sexual involvement to which every women should aspire (Rodrigues 1995).

The Catholic and traditional ideals of the politics and social structure of this era are still a reference for the older generations, but the modernization of Portugal and of the Portuguese society in recent years has brought new values and realities. Women are more and more actively taking part in the social life, and they are also currently the vast majority of the university student population—about 80 percent of all university students are female. The *machismo,* once a value strongly associated with the male, is now considered a fault more than something positive.

Although it has been commonly accepted for several decades that women should also be gainfully employed outside the home to help support the family, gender differences exist here despite Portugal having one of the highest percentages of working women in Europe. The distribution of males and females according to professional categories, as well as to hierarchical levels, is unequal. Females mostly assume unskilled and lower level positions and have the lowest salaries (Amâncio 1994). This fact is quite obvious in the Portuguese Parliament, in which after the 1999 elections only 19 percent of the commissioners are women. However, given the significant increase of college-graduate females, a shift should be expected in the near future.

The professional situation of men and women is not the only area in which gender differences can be found. It is easier for a parent to let a teenage son out at night than it is for a girl to have the same kind of liberty. The so-called sexual double standard also prevails and expresses itself through a more permissive attitude towards men's sexual behavior and a more conservative and repressive posture towards women's sexuality (Machado & Almeida 1996). This way, it is expected and somewhat valued that a male has several sexual partners, whereas the same is disapproved of in a female. However, this double standard has in recent times lessened, with a growing acceptance of female sexuality and the changing in the character of gender roles.

Among a new generation of couples and families, it is possible to find evidence of this change, as young men are more willing to share domestic tasks and are happy to take care of their children. These fathers are proud of their paternity and are assuming the traditional functions of the mother, which is reflected in publicity that uses images of young fathers changing diapers and playing with their infant sons and daughters.

B. Sociolegal Status of Males and Females

According to the Portuguese Constitution, all men and women are equal before the law. Legal majority is achieved at 18 years of age or with marriage after 16. Marriage is allowed at age 16 with parental consent. Nevertheless, as previously mentioned, despite legal gender equality, several differences still exist at various levels of society. To reduce this gap, in 1991, a commission, Comissão para a Igualdade e para os Direitos da Mulher (CIDM, Commission for the Equality and for the Rights of Women) was formed, succeeding a previous organization that had a key role in changing the legal status of women and in achieving gender equality before the law. The main objectives of CIDM are:

- to allow the same opportunities for men and women;
- to reach the same level of responsibility for women and men in what concerns family, professional, social, cultural, economic, and political life; and
- to contribute to the recognition of maternity and paternity as social functions.

Although this commission is mainly concerned with feminine problems and rights, it contemplates the work with men as a way of achieving equality, which is most obvious in the attention given to the questions of paternity.

In October 1999, a new ministry, the Ministério da Igualidade (Ministry of Equality) was created. As in similar ministries in other European countries, the goal is to achieve equality at different levels of society. Gender equality will obviously be one of its main areas of action.

C. General Concepts of Sexuality and Love

As in many other parts of the world, sex and sexuality are uncomfortable topics for most people. Sex and sexuality are mostly discussed between friends, using jokes as a way to lighten the tension involved in these issues. However, in sexual education programs or when asked about sexuality for research purposes, most people will participate and show an interest in the topic. Sex-related issues, such as homosexuality, abortion, and AIDS are also regular subjects of talk shows and programs on television as well as of reports in the press. Nowadays, a wide range of information and services are available and this has, in turn, influenced and reshaped the general Portuguese conceptions of sexuality in recent years. This fact does not necessarily mean that the Portuguese are very open-minded about these issues. A certain resistance exists towards minority forms of sexual expression, which are more likely to be tolerated than truly accepted.

Love and the existence of steady relationships are considered previous conditions for sexual intimacy with a partner, especially for women. Men, as well as individuals from the younger generations regardless of gender, value the hedonistic and pleasurable aspects of sex the most (Pais 1998). One has to assume that there are significant gender and generational differences over what is or is not considered a steady relationship, and also over other general conceptions of love and sex. In any case, the general picture shows us clearly that sexuality is no longer associated with procreation and that relationships are based on affection towards the partner, rather then in formal structures such as engagements and weddings.

The two tendencies in love and sex in the Portuguese mainstream society, i.e., the importance of romantic love and the sexual pleasure ideals, are somewhat in conflict: The first implies monogamous relationships and the second reinforces the search for different and multiple sexual partners. However, it is known that a gap exists between what is said and what is done and, when confronted with a choice, most frequently the romantic ideals lose in favor of a greater sexual freedom.

2. Religious and Ethnic Factors Affecting Sexuality

A. Source and Character of Religious Values

Portuguese society has in the past been greatly influenced by the Catholic Church. In the fifteenth century, the clergy was one of the supporters of the colonial "discoveries" that led to a period of great prosperity for the country. One of the reasons for this support was the opening of new possibilities of evangelism and the spread of the influence of the Church throughout the world. This eventually happened in many parts of the world, in Brazil, India, Macao (China), and Japan, where the Portuguese were the first Westerners to arrive and to introduce the Catholic religion.

The Portuguese Church grew, enriched and hegemonic, especially after the expulsion of the Jews from the country in 1496, which came by royal order, but with a strong Catholic influence. The Holy Inquisition (Tribunal do Santo Ofício), established in the sixteenth century, was for a long time a powerful means of political and ideological repression that was also used to persecute people with sexual behaviors that were considered deviant, like prostitutes and homosexual men. Women who lived their sexuality freely were often considered witches, especially in the interior of the country. Many of the charges of witchcraft against women were, in fact, the consequence of revenge related to cases of adultery.

The Marquis de Pombal (1699-1782), the prime minister during the reign of King Joseph, ruled the country despotically, but introduced many reforms and turned the big earthquake of 1755 that destroyed part of Lisbon into a chance to rebuild the capital according to modern principles. He reduced much of the power and importance of the Church and of the Inquisition that was finally extinguished in 1821. This was also the beginning of the end of much of the religious influence in civil society, which was only again regained during the government of Salazar, in the period called the Estado Novo (1926-1974). The three mottoes of this time were *Pátria, Deus, Família* (Fatherland, God, Family) that, like the Holy Trinity, were the moral references of the Estado Novo. This period left several marks in Portuguese society that still has an influential Catholic community.

Of the majority Catholics, 26 percent go to church regularly and have some degree of religious influence in their lives, whereas 65 percent are non-practitioners (Pires & Antunes 1998). Non-practicing Catholics are believers that do not attend religious rituals, such as the mass, or go to confession very often.

There is an important difference between the practicing and the non-practicing Catholics that can help us understand different positions in Portuguese society, and not just those related to sexuality. In general, practicing Catholics have more conservative positions on such different things as marriage, social intervention, drug addiction, nudism, and tax evasion (Pires & Antunes 1998). Usually in Catholic families, behavioral norms are stricter than in non-Catholic families, and there is a greater concern over the upbringing of children according to religious principles. Most practicing Catholic children go to religious schools that are generally considered among the best private education institutions. The Catholic University is also one of the most prestigious universities in Portugal.

This conservative perspective of the practicing Catholics obviously influences their views on sexuality. In general, they are more repressive over the expression of sexuality, less tolerant towards sexual minorities, and have more traditional ideas on contraception and abortion. Religious practice is also negatively associated with sexual experience and permissiveness among university students, while the simple fact of being or not being a believer is not a condition to explain these kinds of differences (Alferes 1997). What does influence the beliefs about these issues is, again, the assumption of a practicing or non-practicing Catholic position.

Lately, some criticisms have emerged among the Catholic community towards the stagnant position of the Church on different subjects related to sexuality. One such criticism is that the Church still associates several different subjects with sin, this way repelling Catholic couples and individuals who do not find in the Church the answers they are looking for in what concerns their private lives (Ferreira 1993). In 1993, an organization of Catholic students, Movimento Católico de Estudantes (MCE), published a document that considered the ideas of the Church on sexuality inadequate and detached from the scientific speech. It also condemned the use of power in ways that affect the individual experience of one's sexuality in areas such as homosexuality, premarital sexual activity, and masturbation (MCE 1993). Despite these critical movements, the Catholic Church still has considerable influence in Portuguese society, and is economically powerful. This became quite obvious in the recent referendum over the legalization of abortion.

As for other religious beliefs and practices, they also have a strong effect on the permissiveness towards sexual behavior. Little is known about these minorities, but one researcher tells us that people that follow these beliefs have attitudes towards sexuality even stricter than the Catholic majority, especially in what concerns prostitution and adultery (Pais 1998). However, more research is needed in this area in order to study the effect of these attitudes on the behavior of people belonging to these groups.

B. Character of Ethnic Values

Portugal is one of the oldest nations in Europe and its actual frontiers are almost the same since the thirteenth century. There has also been a considerable stability in the constitution of the population in its majority Caucasian character over the centuries. Although having been influenced by several races and cultures throughout history, the Portuguese are essentially a Latin people, with concepts of gender roles and sexuality similar to those existing in other south European Latin countries like Spain and Italy.

After the revolution of 1974 and the independence of the colonies of Guinea-Bissau, Angola, Mozambique, Cape Verde, S. Tomas and Principe, about half a million Portuguese who lived there returned to the mainland (in fact, many had been born and always lived in Africa). This mass return of people with a different experience and kind of living was socially quite problematic, and a certain xenophobic climate appeared against the new-comers who were pejoratively called the *Retornados* (the ones that returned). The *Retornados* must have had an influence on the concepts and practices related to sexuality of the rest of the Portuguese, for in Africa there were not as many restraints as the ones that existed on the more conservative mainland. However, to our knowledge, there are no studies about this topic.

3. Sexual Knowledge and Education

A. Government Policies and Programs

The history of sex education in Portugal begins in the 1960s. Before that, the Catholic Church was responsible for the moral orientation of education, separating boys and girls in public schools, and repressing the study or teaching of sexuality. It was only with the Vatican II Council, which brought new ideas and a different approach to several areas within the Church, that sex education began to be discussed. It was also at this time that new values and attitudes emerged, together with democratic ideals and expectations of liberty.

A new course, "Sexuality, Love, Marriage and Family," started being taught at a seminary in Lisbon, and several articles about sexuality appeared in Christian magazines and newspapers. In public schools, in the existing class "Religion and Morality," mainly taught by priests, the discussion of sexuality was included as a way to guarantee long-lasting and happy marriages for future adults. However, this approach was non-systematic, had no scientific basis, and was frequently inadequate.

In 1967, the Associação para o Planeamento da Família (Portuguese Family Planning Association, or APF) was created, supported by the International Planned Parenthood Federation, which was interested in reaching southern European countries. This organization is not very well accepted by the government, by the Church, or by the most conservative sectors of society, but it has initiated several actions aimed at the training of professionals as well as implementing a service of family planning for the population.

In the early 1970s, the Ministry of National Education created the Commission for the Study of Sexuality and Education. This commission advocated the abolition of separate education of boys and girls and focused on the need for a different approach, integrated and not fragmented, to the human body in schoolbooks (Roque 1999). This commission became extinct one year after its creation.

The revolution of 1974 that ended the dictatorship in Portugal brought a rapid change to society. But although sex education could be and was, in fact, publicly discussed and defended at this time, the disturbed post-revolutionary atmosphere was not favorable to its introduction in the educational system. Other issues, such as abortion and the equality between men and women, were the main concerns over which new legal and practical measures were brought together. The APF became the main organization responsible for sex education in the school context, with actions carried out by professionals. However, these efforts were very limited and could not respond to the real needs of young people. Teachers were trained as a way to enlarge the reach of its intervention, and later, at the beginning of the 1980s, new programs aimed at young people and supported by the United Nations Fund for Population Activities (UNFPA) were put to into action outside the school context. There was an urgent need to legally regulate sex education, and this came with the 3/84 Law, 24 of March 1984. According to this law:

- The state guarantees access to sex education as a basic educational right;
- The state is the responsible entity for the promotion, diffusion, and organization of the juridical and technical means necessary for a responsible maternity and paternity;
- The school curricula should include scientific knowledge about the anatomy, physiology, and genetics of human sexuality, and should also allow the overcoming of the social discrimination based on biological sex and of the traditional division of duties between the male and the female;
- Teachers should be trained in sex education as a way to be able to respond to the needs of young people; and
- Parents should also be supported concerning the sex education of their children.

Although approved and authorized, the means to apply it in the school context were never standardized. Children and adolescents only had access to sex education because of the initiative of some teachers and other organizations. These initiatives were never truly systematic. In the meantime, new activities and classes, like "Personal and Social Development," where created to facilitate the discussion of subjects directly related to the reality and practical needs of young people (Vaz 1996). This allowed a more regular introduction of sex and sexuality in the school system, frequently as a response to the requests of the students themselves. Programs for the prevention of HIV also started, because sex education is considered as a way to fight the growing spread of AIDS. Proposals for including sex education in different branches of education have been made and pilot projects have been introduced in some schools.

In 1998, a commission formed by representatives of several ministries presented a report proposing a plan of action for sex education and family planning, in which practical measures are proposed in several areas. Its goal is to provide students with access to sex education and to insure the availability of family planning services. New laws and initiatives are emerging, but a lot of work still needs to be done concerning the regular and effective availability of sex education for the young and also for the general population.

B. Informal Sources of Sexual Knowledge

Sex and sexuality have become common subjects of television programs and are frequently presented in the media. There is a concerned effort to invite experts to talk about these issues in the media, so that the information that reaches the public is usually of a fairly good quality. A popular and light reading magazine, called *Maria*, is famous for having a section of responses about the sexual problems of the readers. In the past, this was a major source of informal knowledge on sexuality when very little, if any, information was available from other sources.

Several books about sexuality by both national and foreign authors have been published in Portugal and are easily available. Different institutions working in the field frequently publish and distribute brochures and leaflets on subjects such as contraception, special cares during pregnancy, and sexually transmitted diseases. Since the appearance of AIDS, many of these leaflets have also appeared aimed at specific groups of the population, such as women and gay men.

When asked about the sources of sexual information accessed or preferred most young people will refer to the media, with television at the top of the list. Other significant sources mentioned are friends and the partner or consort (Pais 1996). In fact, sexuality is in great part played and learned in a relational context, both with peers in informal situations and with the sexual partner. In adolescence and even in young adulthood, the information obtained from friends is not always the most correct and is frequently filled with popular false beliefs. However, given the known importance of peer influence, some of the most recent health-promotion and HIV-prevention programs developed in Portugal integrate this new approach through the training of young people. It is expected that these programs will produce a positive influence from peers, instead of a negative one.

Intervention in the influence of the sexual partner is more difficult because it occurs in emotional and intimate situations that are hard to change. A person who has information on how to prevent HIV infection or an unwanted pregnancy might, in any case, engage in risky sexual behavior with a partner because of feelings of inadequacy, low self-esteem, or simply because of forgetfulness in the heat of the moment. It should also be mentioned that a high percentage of young people (about 80 percent) think they do not need to be enlightened or to have technical support on sexual issues (Pais 1996). Although this percentage is higher among younger adolescents who are not sexually active and tends to get lower as the age increases, these numbers are still very disturbing. They show a great feeling of self-sufficiency in these youngsters that can be the first step to high-risk behaviors because of a lack of correct knowledge.

A significant percentage of young people get information on sexuality (60.6 percent), contraceptives (49.7 percent), and HIV (30.4 percent) from their parents, with the mother being the most frequently mentioned source of information. A great part also report they would like to have more information from either one of their parents.

In June 1998, a free and confidential telephone helpline, *Sexualidade em Linha* (*Sexuality on Line*), opened to serve the information needs of young people. In its first year, 50,000 phone calls were answered and many more went unanswered because the amount of phone calls far exceeded the service's capability of response. The great majority of callers were between 13 and 18 years of age, and over half were girls (55.9 percent). The questions that led to the calls were varied. In most cases, the objective was to get information about sex (oral and anal sex, masturbation, virginity, etc.), contraceptives, and counseling for relational problems with the partner (GAEP 1999).

4. Autoerotic Behaviors and Patterns

A. Children and Adolescents

Autoerotic behavior is common in children and adolescents, but is usually repressed by parents and society, and condemned by religion. This induces some anxiety, especially for the adolescent who masturbates just the same but often with guilty feelings about it. Adolescents sometimes request counseling over masturbation to know whether it causes illness, impotence, infertility, or pimples, or if it is bad for the health. All these questions reflect popular beliefs about this behavior.

B. Adults

Although also slightly influenced by repressive religious-based ideas about masturbation, Portuguese adults are more and more open to this behavior. A recent survey shows that it is accepted by approximately 40 percent of the population, although another 40 percent feels it should not be accepted (Pais 1998). However, these figures do not coincide with the percentage of individuals who admit masturbating. In a different survey, 69 percent of adults reported having practiced masturbation (Marktest 1995). This percentage was surprisingly steady in all age groups studied, 18 to 45, but significantly different between men and women, the former reporting a much higher practice of masturbation than the latter.

In a study conducted by Valentim Alferes (1997) with college students, 74 percent of the males and 27 percent of the females reported having masturbated in the month previous to the inquiry. It was also possible to determine that men who had had intercourse masturbated just as much as men who had not. As for women, the number of the ones who had not had intercourse and masturbated, more than doubled the ones who had had intercourse and masturbated. Apparently this means that for men, sexual activity is no impediment to masturbation, whereas for women, genital self-stimulation is more frequent in the absence of sexual intercourse, and rarer in its presence.

Men have a more open attitude about masturbation, but individuals of both sexes have a similar level of acceptance over the performance of masturbation by men and women. Differences exist over the acceptance of masturbation according to religious position, age, and social status: the more religious, the higher the age, and the lower the social and economic status, the less accepting will the individual be towards masturbation (Pais 1998).

5. Interpersonal Heterosexual Behaviors

A. Children

Sexual Exploration and Sex Rehearsal Play

Childhood exploration of the body of one's self and others is common, although usually repressed by parents and caregivers. Most Portuguese adults still have some difficulty admitting that children are sexual persons and are thus curious about sex, especially when the adult is not at ease with his or her own sexuality. This is important because sex education directed at children is basically non-existent in the school system and is not done at home. However, from a very early age, children try to get information about sex as they can, usually through their peers.

In some cases, sexual experiences start in childhood or early adolescence. In a survey conducted in an urban sample, 15 percent of the males reported having had their first sexual intercourse before 13 years of age (Marktest 1995). This, however, happens only in the case of the male population, probably caused by early curiosity and partner availability; in most cases the female partner is older.

Among younger adolescents, from age 9 or 10 on, a game called *Bate Pé* (Foot Stomping) is played in small- to medium-sized groups. In this game, each girl and boy alternatively proposes a number to an element of the opposite sex. Each number is related to a given behavior, e.g., number one is a handshake, number two is a kiss on the face, number three is a kiss on the mouth, number four is a French kiss, number five is touching the breasts, and so on. The higher the number, the more daring is the behavior, with sexual intercourse being the upper limit. When the recipient of the proposal refuses, he or she will stomp the foot—hence the name of the game. This game is a common starting ground for the discovery of the opposite sex and of rehearsal without compromise. Needless to say that boys rarely stomp their feet and the numbers rarely pass beyond four or five at age 9 or 10.

B. Adolescents

The fast progress and improvement of life in recent years have affected the lifestyle of Portuguese youth. Major international fashion trends and influences reach Portugal within a few months from the rest of the world. The influence on youth is strongest for music. However, a gap exists between the urban and the rural youth. In the cities, access to leisure and information resources is much easier than in the interior and less-developed rural areas of the country. This makes it difficult to discuss Portuguese youth as a single group because this cohort contains, in fact, a great range of different people. This should alert the reader to the fact that general information, like most of what we present here, can sometimes be misleading in terms of adolescents who live in different contexts. This fact should also be considered when interpreting information about adults and other groups of the Portuguese population.

Dating

Affective relationships in adolescence are frequent, and dating is common, usually starting at 14 or 15 years of age, at least in Lisbon (Silva, Dantas, Mourão, & Ramalho 1996). Dating is not seen as a first step towards marriage, but as a period of experimentation and discovery of the relationship. This pattern is accepted by the majority of young people and is slowly replacing the more traditional ideas about how relationships should be, i.e., a phase leading to marriage. Nevertheless, the large majority of young people (92 percent between 18 and 20 years of age) have marriage in their plans, even if this is an idea that diminishes as age increases (87 percent at 21 to 24, and 81 percent at 25 to 29) (Vasconcelos 1998). This probably happens because of social and economic difficulties perceived as obstacles to marriage or simply because marriage is no longer considered a necessary condition for being with a consort.

First Sexual Intercourse and Premarital Sex

Some decades ago, boys usually had their first sexual experience with prostitutes, whereas, for girls, marriage was a condition for starting their sexual experiences (Miguel 1987). The severe social laws that ruled peer and couple relationships at that time strongly disapproved of sex before marriage, but tolerated the sexual behavior of men who used professionals or "easy women" for their first sexual contacts. These easy women were not necessarily prostitutes, but also girls and women who, without great pressure from men, agreed to have sex without being married. These women were, of course, not seen by men as the traditional "marrying type" and were severely socially reproved.

By the end of the 1980s, sex outside marriage was still seen as reprehensible or even as a dangerous behavior, especially for girls (Figueiredo 1988). Ten years later, only 6 percent of young people considered marriage as a condition for starting their sex life (Pais 1998). Today, affection is the main reason for the sexual initiation of the young, and in fact, most of those who have already had sexual relationships were in love at that time (Alferes 1997). Nevertheless gender differences can still be found in these conceptions, although not as much in behavior. The importance of an emotional involvement with a partner is not considered a prerequisite for sex in the case of boys, as much as it is in the case of girls. This will also influence the psychological situation in which the "first time" takes place. In many cases, there is a strong pressure from the boy to have sex, and the girl will allow it to happen as a proof of her love, even though she might not feel ready for it. For boys, the erotic and hedonistic aspects of love are more important, whereas for girls, romance and love between the partners are the most valuable things.

In any case, sexual foreplay is frequently used as a way to discover sexuality and the body of the partner. There is a sense of inevitability connected with sexual activity in adolescents, for whom their sex life is something that can happen at any time, and often does. However, AIDS is considered one of the main general concerns for these young people, and 96.9 percent are moderately or very concerned with it (Sampaio 1996).

Despite the fact that sexual activity can, in some cases, be found at ages as early as 12, virginity is still considered something precious for many girls, who are sometimes anxious about the possibility of having lost it because of masturbation, sexual rehearsal, or sexual abuse during childhood. Also, the concept of virginity is not always very clear, and the absence of bleeding during the first intercourse can be interpreted as one still being a virgin.

C. Adults

Premarital Relations, Courtship, and Dating

The pattern of love and sexual relations of younger adults is much like the one of teenagers. People usually get together and date with people they like, even if it is against their parents' wishes. There is a growing acceptance of premarital sexual activity, so that the absence of marriage is not considered a reason for not having sex with a loved one. Most people think that sex without love has no meaning, and this reason is often the determinant of sexual activity among young adults (Vasconcelos 1998).

This also explains the fact that the average age for the start of sexual activity has slightly decreased, at least for women. Thirty years ago, the average age for women starting sexual activity was 21.5 years; presently it is 19.8 years. For men, the average age for the start of sexual activity has been quite stable at around 17.5 years (Instituto Nacional de Estatística 1997). However, this gender gap tends to weaken as age advances. By 25 years of age, the great majority of people have already started their sexual activity, and the difference between the males and the females who have had sex is practically non-existent.

As for young adults who still have not started their sexual activity, it is mainly because they have not yet found the right person, because they feel they are too young, or simply because they have not yet had the opportunity (Vasconcelos 1998). The start of sexual activity does not happen until certain conditions are met, foremost being a certain perceived level of self-development and the presence of the "right" situation or person.

Nevertheless, the so-called "one-night stands" do happen, 3.3 times more frequently for males than for females (Alferes 1997). Consistently, men are found to have much more positive attitudes towards casual sex and greater expectations regarding the number of future sexual partners. Real or imagined infidelity is also more common in males.

Marriage and Family: Structures and Patterns

The family is the stage where life and social relations play out, and where the major influences of the society become more acute. This means that the characteristics of gender roles discussed earlier achieve their clearest expression. Traditionally, women are responsible for taking care of the house and children, but their growing participation in the workforce has also granted them an important role in the economic sustenance of the family. Their husbands are increasingly involved in domestic tasks. Relationships between the couple, as well as between parents and children, have become more equilateral and democratic (Vicente 1998).

There is a strong consensus among the Portuguese of different generations on considering the family the most important social organization in everyday life, couple life, procreation, relationships between parents and children, as well as the role of the female inside and outside the house. These findings are counter to the idea, sometimes defended, that there is a crisis in the institution of the family.

Crisis or not, demography shows us that changes are occurring in the Portuguese family. The median number of family members has decreased substantially in great part as the result of a smaller number of children being born, from four in the traditional family to a current average of two (Instituto Nacional de Estatística 1997). Divorce rates have increased to 11 percent in younger generations, and new forms of family are emerging, such as single-parent families, reconstituted families (families formed by partners previously divorced and most times bringing together children from the previous marriages), and cohabitation. The number of families in which the female is the sole adult responsible for the family has grown to about 5 percent, greater than the number of single-parent families headed by a male, currently less than 1 percent.

All of these new realities exist peacefully and are generally unquestioned. The notion of family itself has changed and has integrated these alternative organizations of the household. An example of this is the acceptance of cohabitation as a valid alternative to marriage or, at least, as a first step prior to marriage (Vasconcelos 1998). Actually, cohabitation is more easily accepted than it is practiced.

Family has truly become a place of relational and emotional belonging, and is no longer a rigid and institutional structure that has its own right to existence. This is true mostly for the younger generations, in which there is a rejection of the traditional institution of weddings associated with a clear gender difference, the functional division of the house tasks, and the idea of the irreversibility of the relationship. For many younger Portuguese, the main principles are freedom of association between the couple and the right to end the relationship when it no longer has any meaning for the persons involved.

Arranged marriages were never popular in Portugal, although they sometimes took place in the past, mainly in rural and interior areas. Frequently, however, marriage was a guarantee of economic sustenance, and it was also maintained for the same reason, mostly for women who depended on their husband to survive. Nowadays, the economic importance of the wedding has not disappeared, but it now has a different meaning since women have established their place in the workplace. Most Portuguese men and women consider economic stability a prior condition for getting married. Usually, couples do not get married before having a stable job or economic situation, although some will still rely on the parents for help and financial support.

Nevertheless, love is the main reason why two people get married. Marriage is thus seen as a public institutionalization of an affective relationship between two individuals, but it is sometimes also a way to legalize a situation of cohabitation when children are born (Vasconcelos 1998). One should not forget that the figure of the *bastardo*, a child born out of wedlock that previously was socially stigmatized, only disappeared from the Portuguese law in 1981, and still plays an important role at a more unconscious level, even among more progressive people.

Marriage is considered as a life project planned by both members of the couple, even if some concessions are involved. It is also considered as an engagement for life, which, curiously, is opposite to the idea of the reversibility of the relationship that most individuals defend. While romantic love is the basis for the marital relationship, its loss is also reason for ending a marriage. Separation or divorce is generally accepted and considered a way to reach the happiness that can no longer be obtained in the marriage. This fact might explain the growth of divorce rates in recent years.

Sexuality and the Physically Challenged

In its Rule Number 9 dedicated to the Family Organization and Personal Dignity Dimension, the United Nations calls our attention to the fact that disabled people should not be denied the possibility to enjoy their sexuality, to engage in sexual intercourse, and to have children. It notes that, because of the fact that disabled people may have difficulties in getting married and in having a family, governments should encourage the existence of the appropriate counseling services for this matter. Therefore, disabled people should have access, as other citizens should, to family planning methods and to reliable information regarding the sexual functioning of their body (Secretariado Nacional de Reabilitação 1998). This concern is also present in the lines of the "Rehabilitation Coherent Policy for Disabled People," a European Council Recommendation signed by the Portuguese Council of Ministries in April 1992 (Secretariado Nacional de Reabilitação 1994).

As in other European countries, the United Nations 45/96 Resolution, that establishes the rules regarding Equalization of Opportunities for Disabled People, led to the constitution of Law 9 (of 9 May 1989), called "Prevention, Rehabilitation and Integration for Disabled People," which emphasizes the Basic Principles of the Portuguese Constitution (Secretariado Nacional de Reabilitação 1999). As a result of this law, a permanent national organization included in the Social Security and Solidarity Ministry was created in Portugal. This organization, the National Commission for the Rehabilitation and Integration of Disabled People, is responsible for the planning and general coordination of the National Rehabilitation Policy in cooperation with non-governmental organizations and the sectarian systems of the Portuguese Public Organization.

As an Information Supplier, this commission organized a national Disability Inquiry, and its last results were published in 1996 (Secretariado Nacional de Reabilitação 1996). They included the situations of 142,112 persons and 47,020 families in the Portuguese continental territory. This National Inquiry of the Incapacities, Disabilities, and Disadvantages was very important for understanding the Portuguese reality in this area and made it possible to identify particular priorities and strategies.

Its conclusions, elaborated with the support of the National Statistical Institute and the Instituto Nacional de Servicios Sociales of Spain, showed a national disability rate of 9.16 percent, similar to that of other countries in Europe. It draws attention to the considerable disability rates in children under the age of 9, and also to its major incidence in the periods of the end of the productive life, earlier retirement and retirement (45 to 54 years of age). Also, the disability incidence, especially regarding locomotion, was directly proportional to age.

The Inquiry also stated that, in Portugal, the rehabilitation and integration actions are insufficient and centered in the medical-functional dimension, despite the increased number of organizations dedicated to intervention in disability. Furthermore, there is no structured national program associated with the managing of sexuality in the disabled, in particular for those physically disabled, despite the partial actions associated with the intervention of the organizations dedicated to disability, sexology, and family planning (see Section 13D, Research and Advanced Education, Important National and Regional Sexological Organizations).

Incidence of Anal Sex, Fellatio, and Cunnilingus

There is no legal restriction on the performance of oral or anal sex between consenting adults. Both are practices that can take place between couples, married or not, and apparently their incidence is growing. This might be because of the liberalization of sexual practices and the consequent curiosity over alternative forms of sexual experience.

Most people are pleased with the idea or practice of oral sex, either fellatio or cunnilingus, and over 60 percent report having practiced one or the other (Marktest 1995). Other studies have found values for the practice of oral sex as high as 67 percent, with no significant differences between males and females (Alferes 1997). In research conducted by one of the authors in a sample of young adults, 46.2 percent reported having practiced oral sex at least once with a regular partner, while 11.3 percent had practiced it with an occasional partner and about 1 percent with a prostitute (Nodin 2000).

The practice of simultaneous oral sex, also known as "69," is also documented, with 58.2 percent of respondents expressing enthusiasm or pleasure in anticipation of this activity, and a smaller proportion, 51.5 percent, reporting having practiced it (Marktest 1995). In this case, there is a slight difference between the attitude towards the behavior and the engagement in the behavior, which may happen because the ones who would like to practice it do not have the chance to do it, perhaps for lack of a willing partner.

Opinions are split on anal sex between the male and the female. The proportion of persons who anticipate it with enthusiasm or pleasure, 35.1 percent, is just about the same as the proportion of those who consider it unpleasant or disgusting, 35.0 percent, with 22.8 percent being indifferent about the subject (Marktest 1995). However, 43.3 percent have tried this sexual practice, especially men.

In the same sample of young adults mentioned before (Nodin 2000), 15.8 percent report having practiced anal sex at least once with a regular partner, 5 percent have tried it with a casual partner, and 1.2 percent with a prostitute.

6. Homoerotic, Homosexual, and Ambisexual Behaviors

A. Children and Adolescents

Studies of homosexuality in children and adolescents have not been done, and thus, little is known about its incidence or character.

B. Adults

Incidence and Relational Patterns

There is no consensus regarding the percentage of homosexual individuals in the population. Different studies have arrived at different proportions: 0.7 percent (Nodin 2000), 1 percent (Lucas 1993), and 7.8 percent (Marktest 1995). Others only have specific data related to the incidence of same-sex experience, 2.9 percent in women and 5.2 percent in men (Alferes 1997). The marked differences found in these surveys are probably due more to the methodology used to assess the sexual orientation than to a real oscillation of its occurrence in the population. The highest results are obtained in studies made of urban samples, where it is possible to report that individuals who have had a sexual experience with someone of the same gender are mostly in their 30s, have lower educational backgrounds, and are married, cohabiting with a partner, or are divorced or widowed (Marktest 1995).

The prevailing patterns in relationships between homosexual individuals have not been studied, but it seems that it is very close to the heterosexual one, i.e., based on romantic feelings, affection, and sexual attraction towards the partner. This pattern is probably related to the devastating effects of AIDS in the gay community that led to a slow but obvious change in the relational behaviors of this population.

Bisexuality is admitted as a behavior or tendency by a larger proportion of individuals, although sometimes it is a way to dissimulate a homosexual preference. Many bisexuals marry as a way to have a socially acceptable facade, but maintain a secret double life. The existence of this group was highlighted by the advent of AIDS and its spread to women by sexual contact with boyfriends and husbands previously infected in homosexual contacts. These men usually have problems dealing with their sexual orientation and are thus difficult targets for HIV-prevention programs.

Social Status

For over seventy years, homosexuality in Portugal was considered by the law as a behavior against nature and was considered equivalent to the crime of vagrancy. Individuals accused of this crime were kept, sometimes for years, in the *Mitras*, institutions for prostitutes, homeless, and other excluded persons. Others were blackmailed with the threat of being "outed." Prior to 1974, no form of organization or group consciousness existed for gays and lesbians, although some meeting points existed, like bars, mainly for individuals from the upper social classes. It was only during the national revolutionary process, in 1975, that the first organization of gays and lesbians, called CHOR (Revolutionary Homosexuals Collective), appeared, claiming dignity, freedom, and political rights for this minority (Vitorino & Dinis 1999). This collective had some impact in the community, but also had difficulties in gaining associates within a group that had but a vague consciousness of what the gay identity really was. Two years later, CHOR had disappeared.

The 1980s were a decade in which several things changed in the Portuguese society, among them, the questioning of the restricted sexual morality the country lived with for several decades. Echoes of the gay movements in other countries started to appear and the propagation of gay bars influenced a growing awareness of a national gay community.

A new lifestyle appeared, but unlike in other countries, there were no community organizations to support the minority in its needs and rights. In 1991, a homosexual work group (Grupo de Trabalho Homossexual) appeared inside a small left-wing party (Partido Socialista Revolucionário) that became the face of the gay movement in Portugal. However, because of its political association, it could only work as a group of reflection and public intervention.

It was only with the upcoming of AIDS and its impact in the gay community, together with the non-existence of an active and effective government policy to control this disease, that a slow but growing alert to a need for action appeared. Several non-governmental organizations appeared in the fight against AIDS, many of them integrating gay individuals. It was within these organizations that a group of people, with support from international organizations, created the ILGA–Portugal (International Lesbian and Gay Association), which quickly gathered a considerable amount of members. Its growth was also largely a consequence of the pioneer use of the Internet, which made it possible to reach gay individuals all over the country. ILGA is responsible for the organization of several successful events, such as the Gay Pride Festival and the Gay and Lesbian Lisbon Film Festival, with consistent support from the Mayor of Lisbon. ILGA, which launched an unprecedented awakening of the gay and lesbian community in Portugal, was followed in late 1997 by another institution, Opus Gay.

These institutions have played an active part in trying to change the several existing discriminatory laws against homosexual individuals. Although Portugal has signed international conventions, such as the Amsterdam Treaty, and is a member of organizations that recommend the elimination of legal discrimination based on sexual orientation, it still exists. Most of the time this discrimination in the Portuguese law is not explicit, excluding homosexual people by omission. Marriage, for instance, is not possible between two people of the same gender, which also makes it impossible for a gay or lesbian couple to adopt children, because, according to the Civil Code, only married couples can adopt children. A gay couple who live together is excluded from the recently proposed laws regarding the creation of cohabitation rights similar to those of married couples. Other legal differences can be found, for instance, the consenting age for same-sex sexual relations is 16 years compared with 14 for heterosexual persons. Individuals who admit to being homosexual are considered unable to enter a military career or the police force, and are also not allowed to donate blood (ILGA–Portugal 1999).

Socially, there is also a lot to be done. All forms of sexual behaviors and lifestyles considered different from the mainstream are usually not very well accepted by the common Portuguese. In a recent survey, a large majority of the population (86.1 percent) reported negative feelings towards homosexuality (Marktest 1995), although, in general, women were more open than men about the subject. Almost half the people, 48.5 percent, also think sexual relations should only be allowed between men and women (Pais 1998). Gender identity and sexual orientation are frequently confounded, even among professionals from the social and medical areas, and homosexuality is often associated with effeminate behavior.

Generally, Portuguese people have negative attitudes towards sexual minorities, but demonstrate some degree of acceptance when it comes to people they are familiar with. Perhaps the best word to describe this is not acceptance, but tolerance, which is a general attitude of the Portuguese also in other issues. In this particular case, the tolerance is usually related to the affection that one holds towards the homosexual individual, and that sometimes becomes incongruent with the ideas and positions otherwise held. This, however, is not seen as an internal conflict and is thus not resolved either way. Some degree of tolerance also exists towards public displays of affection between two people of the same sex, even though these are not very common. Gay bashing is almost unheard of in Portugal.

In the specific case of lesbians, they face the double discrimination of being women in a Latin country and of having a homosexual orientation.

The lesbian community has much less visibility than the gay community. It is in any case easier for a couple of women to have a relationship or to live together and go unnoticed.

It is only recently that the lesbian community has started to get organized, with the publication of its first lesbian magazine, *Organa*, in 1990, and three years later of *Lilás* (Vitorino & Dinis 1999). The publication of these magazines, and the debate they launched in the lesbian community, allowed the organization of meetings and of small groups that stood for the rights of lesbian women in Portugal. Today, ILGA includes a group of women that integrates many of the members of those previous organizations and that is actively involved in working towards a greater acceptance and demanding of specific rights for lesbians.

7. Gender Conflicted Persons

A. Sociolegal Status, Behaviors, and Treatment

There are no specific laws in the country regarding transgenderism or transsexualism, only a few court decisions that serve as references about the latter, and these are sometimes contradictory (ILGA-Portugal 1999). According to one of these court decisions, someone that goes through the process of sex change cannot truly become someone of the other gender. The explanations are, in the case of a male-to-female transformation, that the individual cannot get pregnant or maintain sexual intercourse in the same conditions as a woman. Sex change is seen as an error and transsexuals are considered mentally unhealthy people. These ideas are a step back regarding a previous sentence (in 1984) according to which the moral personality of the individual should be respected, the sex change recognized, and the name change accepted by the civil registration.

In fact, name change is possible for any citizen who wishes it and is a relatively accessible procedure, but only when the new name belongs to the same gender category as the previous one or to a gender-neutral name. This last alternative is the one chosen by some transsexuals in order to avoid the complicated procedure to have gender identity recognized. For this, the person has to go through a complicated legal process, and it can only occur with the decision of a court of law.

It is only since 1996 that sex-change operations are possible and occur in Portugal, because the Portuguese Medical Order allowed it to happen. However, no information is available regarding the real number of operations performed in the national territory. The Santa Maria Hospital in Lisbon is the institution that has the major experience with these kinds of operations. Nevertheless, the process to have a sex-change operation is long and implies a severe psychological and psychiatric evaluation to verify whether the candidate is eligible for the process. This difficult process usually takes about two years. Before 1996 and still today, many Portuguese transsexuals went to other countries, like Morocco, or more recently to

England, to have their operations done, sometimes under unsafe conditions.

In a study conducted with a sample of approximately 50 transsexual individuals, some of whom were sex workers and others working in various professional areas, the great majority came from rural parts of the country (72 percent), and many had changed from their birthplace because of their sexual orientation (28 percent) (Bernardo et al. 1998). This gives us important information regarding the problems that these individuals have to face related to their social adjustment. Besides, most of them do not benefit from social security.

Important problems were identified in risk behaviors and situations. Thus, 30 percent of these transsexuals knew they were HIV-positive, although only 61 percent always used a condom. Seventy percent abused alcohol, tranquilizers, or heroin on a regular basis. Fifty-seven percent of this transsexual sample were prostitutes, some having started to work as early as age 11. Eighty-six percent of the transsexual prostitutes were street workers. As this study concluded, "The transgender community in Portugal is an unknown reality, ignored by the public health system. A large majority of its members having a profession that is considered illegal, they do not benefit from any kind of social and medical assistance" (Bernardo et al., 1998).

Besides, transgender persons are not viewed in a positive light by Portuguese society, and so can be ignored, as well as discriminated against. However, as in the case of homosexuality, the traditional Portuguese tolerance is usually prevalent in personal contact with transgendered individuals.

For a couple of years now, several institutions working in the field of HIV prevention and gay rights have organized an annual transvestite gala on the first of December (World AIDS Day) to gather funding for the fight against AIDS. This gala has considerable impact in the media and is also changing the mainstream idea about the transgendered community. Regardless of that, during Portugal's widely celebrated Carnival holiday, it is common to see men dressed as women without that being considered strange.

8. Significant Unconventional Sexual Behaviors

A. Coercive Sex

The present Portuguese Legal Code was designed to protect a recent legal accomplishment: sexual self-determination and freedom. Freedom is understood not only as the free use of sex and of the body for sexual purposes, and the individual sexual freedom of option and action, but also as the right of anyone not to endure actions of a sexual nature against one's will. Coercion and public displays that adversely affect a third person or disrespect a person's sexuality are grounds for charging someone with the crime of violating another person's sexual (rights and) liberties.

The behaviors that qualify by law as sexual crimes are:

- A relevant sexual act specified in the penal code;
- Non-consensual intercourse (coitus);
- Non-consenting artificial procreation;
- White slave traffic;
- Those who profit from adult prostitution
- Child prostitution;
- Exhibitionist actions;
- Pornography (when it involves child corruption); and
- Homosexual actions as specified in the penal code.

Sexual crimes fall under two categories: *Crimes against sexual freedom* and *Crimes against sexual self-determination*. The former involves child sexual abuse (Article 172), adolescent and dependent individual sexual abuse (Article 173), stuprum (Article 174), homosexual actions with minors (Article 175), and prostitution of minors (Article 176). The laws regarding crimes against the sexual self-determination of a child victim distinguish between a minor under age 14 years, a minor between ages 14 and 16 years, and a minor between 16 and 18 years. The penalties for conviction of a crime against self-determination depend of the age of the victim.

Justice statistics show that, during 1995, 306 individuals were convicted for sexual crimes, from a total of 433 victims (62 males and 371 females), of whom 155 were minors under age 14 and 57 between 15 and 19 years of age. However, it is well known that these figures do not correspond entirely to a social reality because of the characteristics of these phenomena: shame, taboo, hidden practices, and the need for medical evidence in order to have a legal process. According to the Legal Medicine Institute, from 1989 to 1993, of the alleged examined victims of sexual abuse, 460 or 76.4 percent were children or adolescents. From the total of the population studied, 380 or 63.1 percent did not present evidence of physical sexual abuse during observation. This absence of physical evidence, in part because of the long period of time that passed before medical observation, does not automatically exclude the possibility of abuse. This absence should be reconciled with cognitive, emotional, and affective signs and symptoms (Costa Santos 1998).

Child Sexual Abuse, Incest, and Pedophilia

No generally accepted definition of what constitutes sexual abuse exists in Portugal. In what concerns pedagogic, therapeutic, penal-juridical, and social intervention, several models of intervention coexist and are applied. However, three criteria are commonly accepted on the base definition of sexual abuse: age differences, power differences, and types of behavior. The different intervention models establish as criteria the maximum age of the victim as 15 or 17 years. Above this age, the action is considered rape or sexual harassment. According to Felix López (1991), child sexual abuse can be singly based in age asymmetry. The age difference implies a biological maturity as well as different expectations and experiences. To João

Seabra Diniz (1999), a Portuguese priest and psychoanalyst, the age asymmetry is in itself a violation. It is conceived that the child has desire, but the pathology lies in the fact that the adult is taking advantage of that desire. Children do not have the physical, mental, or symbolic experience that allows them to understand the adult's sexuality.

In Portugal, the child's complaint is followed by the need for evidence. This is a long and painful process for the child. The bureaucratic machine involves a hard interinstitutional process in the several areas of intervention.

The studies published in this area are recent and use professionals as the main research population. These studies are not theoretical but practical, analyzing the national situation and characterizing the cases of sexual abuse. In the report *Violence Against Children in Portugal* (Nunes de Almeida & al. undated), the number of maltreated children is analyzed according to the family context. From the 755 cases of family violence, 13.5 percent or 102 cases involved sexual practices with female children. The more affected ages are 10 to 14 years, followed by 6 to 9 years and 4 to 5 years.

The General Health Department, in collaboration with the Family and Child Support Project, implemented yet another investigation, according to which, during 1996, each of 384 health professionals from Health Centers identified at least one case of child abuse involving a minor between infancy and age 19). A second questionnaire revealed that close to half of the victims (47 percent) were between 10 and 14 years of age, and 28 percent between ages 5 and 9. When the victim was a female, 48 percent of the cases occurred between 10 and 14 years, and when the victim was a male, the large part of the cases occurred between 5 and 9 years of age. It is important to mention that 17 percent of these cases involved a mentally or physically disabled child. In 68 percent of these situations, there was a family tie between the perpetrator and the victim.

The Justice Ministry Studies and Planning Office (GEPMI) reveals that, during 1996, 137 children under 14 years of age and 65 adolescents between 15 and 19 years of age were sexual crime victims. Of 23 individuals tried for minors' sexual abuse, only 15 were convicted. Of a total of 137 children, 44 were rape victims, 58 coercion, abuse, and sexual fraud victims, 5 were human trade and prostitution victims, 17 were sexual abuse victims, and 13 were victims of other crimes against freedom and sexual self-determination. However, the professionals' experience reveals that many more cases exist besides the ones that were exposed. The fact is that there is a serious increase of cases and a larger visibility of the phenomenon.

In 1990, Portugal signed the Children Rights Convention in New York and approved it to ratification through the Republic's General Assembly Resolution nº 20/90 in June of the same year. Later, in August, the President of the Republic ratified it. According to the 8th article of the Portuguese Constitution, this convention is a part of Portuguese Law and has an imperative character, which means that it can be applied by the courts. However, because of its generality, it is only used as a reference in the interpretation of the Portuguese laws.

In the sexual child abuse area, we draw attention to Article 19º—*Child protection measures are needed against sexual violence in the family performed by those who are close or by the ones that have legal paternal power.* It is also important to reflect on the 34º Article—*The states should take the adequate measures against all forms of sexual exploitation and violence at the national, bilateral and multilateral level, in order to prevent the child from being drawn to perform sexual illicit activities, to be exploited or involved in other illegal sexual practices and exploited in pornography.* In accordance with these international principles, the Portuguese Law establishes in the 69º Article of the Constitution that *children have the right to be protected by the society and by the state, in order to allow their complete development, specially against all forms of abandonment, discrimination, oppression and also against the abusive exercise of authority in the family and other Institutions; The state gives specially attention to orphan children or children that are abandoned or deprived of a typical family environment.* The law establishes that in cases of sexual abuse, the courts can take the necessary and essential measures that are nevertheless unspecified. These measures are often limited to the total or partial inhibition of paternal power, because most cases of sexual abuse take place within the family and are committed by relatives or by people very close to the child.

The Family Court or the Family and Child Court are the entities responsible for putting in action the needed measures in cases of child abuse. Any person with paternal power (meaning a relative) or someone having child custody can request it, as also can the Public Ministry. A special division of this Ministry that works inside the courts, called Minors Curator, defends and promotes child rights, protecting their complete development and rights. The Public Ministry also defends the state's public interest in the protection of people who are vulnerable and incapable of exercising their rights. According to the law, a situation of sexual abuse must be communicated to the Public Ministry, which will take action using the civil-protection structures and penal actions available against the abuser.

Sexual Harassment

Sexual harassment is a recent concept in Portugal. For some, it is the result of the changes in the traditional gender roles and of a growing equality between males and females. The fact that women are leaving the house and trying to get a job can be considered as an invasion of the masculine world. Sometimes, the professional dignity of women is the target of abusive behavior.

In Portugal, sexual harassment is all the manifestations of a sexual nature towards someone without that person's consent. The national newspapers and magazines regularly carry stories in which women in particular are victims of sexual discrimination and abuse. This happens mainly in institutions where males are in control. The level of dependency, the threat of unemployment, and the rightful wish to professional accomplishment reveal the exercise of a male power that often works as a barrier to the established equality of rights and opportunities in the professional world. This problem is spreading in a disturbing way, as revealed by the growing number of complaints filed, even though not always ending in legal incriminations. There are no statistics that detail this phenomenon. However, it is calculated that in Portugal, one in three women has already been a victim of this particular type of violence.

It is also common for women to be harassed on the streets by men who consider it as a sign of masculinity. However, this is becoming a rarer behavior, as new values are replacing those associated with the *machismo* culture.

As in the case of sexual abuse, sexual harassment is also based in asymmetries, not only the hierarchical, social, or economical ones, but also on age asymmetries, with the discrepancy being a particular form of power. This is apparent in cases of sexual harassment happening in Portuguese schools. Sometimes girls allow abusive behaviors from teachers in order to get higher grades or simply because they are afraid of retaliation. However, these situations are usually covered by fear and shame, leading to high levels of secrecy. As the Portuguese say: *hidden pussycat with its tail out.*

Rape

The crime of rape in Portugal is directly related with the exercise of power. Being perpetrated by the consort or by a stranger, it is punished with imprisonment. When it happens within marriage, it can be the cause of divorce or litigious separation. Rape, like sexual abuse, is not a statistically studied situation as it is also involves some secrecy. When it happens inside the family, it is sometimes associated with domestic violence. Fear, embarrassment, and the will to forget, all joined up with self-guilt, keep the victim from filing a complaint. However, the crime does exist, and at a governmental level, there are several projects aimed at the facilitation of the denouncement process, including the training of police officers to deal with rape victims. There is also a concern over the necessity of interinstitutional articulation in the cases of rape and violence among other situations.

New associations, like the Associação Portuguesa de Apoio à Vitima (Portuguese Association of Victim Support, APAV) or the Associação das Mulheres Contra a Violência (Women Against Violence Association) try to act in a coordinated way to provide support and guidance for the victims. This process tries to protect the victim from a double victimization and the consequences of a long process. In 1995, the APAV assisted 1,238 victims; in 1996 this number almost doubled to a total of 2,300. Adding to this number are all the victims who do not search for help. The majority of people who seek help from these associations are women victims of violence and of physical offences. In Lisbon, most of these women are between 25 and 35 years of age; in Porto, the situation occurs mostly with women between 36 and 45 years of age.

528 • *International Encyclopedia of Sexuality*

B. Prostitution

During the nineteenth century, Lisbon was the capital of an intensive bohemian life. The cultural traditions of this city were characterized by deviant behaviors forbidden by the society. The moral and decency imperatives of a society that lived on public virtues and private habits were exposed by an accepted marginality that went along with popular traditions such as *fado vadio* (the national song), bullfighting, and a spread of popular language. During this period, the city nightlife had some preferential spaces, particularly the traditional quarters of the Bairro Alto, Alfama, and Mouraria, which were gathering places for devotees of specific socially deviant behaviors. In these quarters, the participants, prostitutes, *fadistas* (fado singers), *marialvas* (extravagant, indolent people, usually males), bullfighters, vagabonds, and sailors from all social backgrounds, maintained an open get-together, where all the social distinctions, values, and rules were apparently minimized (Pais 1985). The animation of these times and places is well characterized by popular songs such as this one:

> *Correi a ver em cena as putas grulhas, Do Bairro Alto a corja dos pandilhas, Os fadistas pingões e bigorrilhas, Que de noite incomodam as patrulhas* (Run to see the whores, in Bairro Alto, the gangs, the drunken *fadistas*, by night disturbing the patrols).

These Lisbon night places are presently neighborhoods with a significant popular traditional history. Bairro Alto and Alfama are still important local references in the traditional and modern Lisbon night. However, the changes in the entire social process that occurred in Lisbon with the turn of the twentieth century had its effects on bohemian life and prostitution. The places of prostitution and bohemia survived the beginning of the twentieth century, but slowly, everything related to them—words, language, body, and movements—started to have a strong commercial value (Pais 1985).

The Portuguese legal code does not penalize the act of prostitution, but only a third party who profits by it. The prostitute occupies a marginal legal and social status, a sort of no-man's land, which can be more or less accepted. There are no specific data on how many people engage in this practice, but it is a well-known fact that prostitution has increased in recent years. This phenomenon daily involves thousands of individuals—prostitutes (women, men, or children), pimps, and clients. With the spread of services with sexual connotations, such as erotic phone lines and luxury prostitution (also existing in Portugal), we could draw wrong conclusions about this activity. As in the beginning of the twentieth century, prostitution is not viewed as an individual act, but as a commercial enterprise that involves three individuals (the prostitute, the pimp, and the client). In some cases, prostitution occurs in environments involving specific social and economic situations, such as:

- Growing up in large families;
- Child labor;
- Abandonment and emotional privation;
- Parental alcohol-abuse problems;
- Familial disintegration;
- Rape; and
- Unemployment.

Prostitution raises issues of human rights, especially when it involves the sexual abuse of minors. The rising number of children in prostitution—boys and girls in their early teens—is the result of a large demand mostly by married man from all social classes, usually in their late 30s. Frequently, these men are still burdened with some taboos towards sexuality, but they find in prostitution a way to break away from tensions existing in their strict and conservative familial structure. On the other side, the demand for prostitution by young people has been diminishing. Before the 1970s, it was a tradition in Portugal for a young man to initiate his sexual life with a prostitute, sometimes with the father guiding that visit. This process marked the social role of the prostitute. Presently, information and counseling services in sexuality, sex education, and the fear of HIV/AIDS, has brought young people to initiate their sexual life earlier than in the past, but now in the context of an emotional involvement. One exception to this new pattern are young men from the interior of the country who enter compulsory military service and are stationed in the major Portuguese cities like Lisbon and Porto. These two cities are Portugal's main centers of prostitution, as well as a strategic entry passage for women and children from African and Latin America countries who become involved in prostitution.

Although the issue has not been studied, it is a fact that Portugal's strategic location between the rest of Europe and the countries of Latin America and western Africa, along with its tourism industry, make it a key element in the international child-prostitution nets. At present, a large number of prostitutes are also drug addicts who find in this activity a way to make money. Addiction and prostitution thus become a vicious circle of slavery. Although many think prostitution is a highly profitable activity, the fact that it is a marginal activity means that all profits are immediately used to pay bills. There are no credit lines.

Several social solidarity organizations are dealing with this problem, working side by side with prostitutes in their own activity places, providing humane and therapeutic assistance, and working for the social reinsertion of the prostitutes through professional and career training. Others provide medical support, information, and assistance. Drop-in centers exist, as well as mobile units that take professionals to places where prostitutes work. The abolition or legalization of prostitution is a hot topic of discussion. Legalization could be a way to provide effective legal, psychological, and medical support for this work group that otherwise cannot access it.

C. Pornography and Erotica

As in other industrialized countries, pornography has gained an important place in Portugal. One has only to open the advertisement pages of a Portuguese newspaper or magazine to realize the numerous pornographic materials available. Sexuality has become a major, greatly magnified social factor, invading our lives through television, films, and magazines.

Before 1974, any kind of public or private display of pornography was forbidden and severely punished. As a result, the local production of pornographic magazines and videos did not develop in Portugal, so today, Portugal is more an importer than a producer of pornography. In the 1990s, markedly amateur, pornographic films became a commercial venture. At the same time, Portugal was increasingly chosen by many foreign filmmakers and magazine owners as a cheap place to produce pornographic material.

The current visibility of pornography has made it the center of a heated debate in Portugal. Despite the fact that the first sex shops opened only a half-a-dozen years ago in Lisbon, pornographic films and magazines have been available for a long time in different kinds of shops (even in supermarkets) or through mail catalogues. There is even a cable network that broadcasts pornographic films three nights a week. While these broadcasts are popular with a considerable number of Portuguese, including teenagers, the older generations strongly oppose this development.

In general, Portuguese men have a more open attitude towards pornography, which they view as a way to improve their sexual life and as a source of diversion and entertainment. Women tend to consider pornography as immoral, and think it can degenerate in pernicious habits, and should thus be forbidden (Pais 1998). Sexual liberation seems stronger among younger age groups and also among people from higher social classes for which pornography is seen as a diversion that can improve the sexual life.

In a society just starting to develop its sex education programs, and still fighting against all kinds of anti-sexual prejudices—cultural, moral, and religious—pornography is still viewed as pernicious because of its contents.

9. Contraception, Abortion, and Population Planning

A. Contraception

Contraceptives are widely available at pharmacies, hospitals, and health centers. Since 1985, contraceptive pills, IUDs, and condoms have been freely distributed at the various family planning services available. Condoms are also distributed by institutions involved in the prevention of HIV infection. The emergency contraceptive pill, depoprovera, which was not well known until quite recently, became available in late 1999 after some resistance from some public and private sectors of the society. However, unlike the contraceptive pill that can be easily bought in Portugal without a medical prescription, the emergency contraceptive has to be prescribed by a doctor. RU-486 or mifepristone is considered an abortifacient, and is therefore illegal.

The female condom was available in the past, but is not presently, mainly because they were not profitable. Sterilization is also available, and in the Maternidade Dr. Alfredo da Costa, one of the oldest and most important women's hospitals in Portugal, it is performed only after a careful evaluation of the request by a team of a gynecologist and a clinical psychologist.

More recent methods of contraception, like hormonal implants or injections, are available, but used only by a minority. The great majority of Portuguese women use the pill. In the youngest age group, 15 to 19 years of age, studied by the 1997 Inquiry on Fertility and the Family (Instituto Nacional de Estatística 1997), the pill was used by 55 percent of women, while in the following age group, 20 to 39 years, it is the method used by 70 percent of the women. In any case, the pill is followed in popularity by the condom among women, whereas for men, the condom is the most used method from adolescence on. A significant proportion of individuals use the IUD. It is the method chosen by 10 percent of all women, although older women use it more than younger ones.

Among adolescents, where sexual activity is frequently unplanned and occasional, coitus interruptus has been used by as many as 37 percent of all individuals (Pais 1996). In those conditions, most times it is the only method available. Nevertheless, young adults will also use it, as well as the rhythm method, both easily fallible methods used because of the lack of knowledge related to their real efficacy to prevent a pregnancy. The first of these two is reportedly used by 9.5 percent of all individuals, whereas the second, many times not used in a proper way, is reported by 3.2 percent in the same age group (Nodin 2000).

The percentage of individuals who have not used contraceptives in their first sexual contact is very high, 65 percent of women and 73 percent of men. However, it is clear that in the younger generations, the gap between the first sexual intercourse and the first use of contraception is decreasing, when compared with older generations (Instituto Nacional de Estatística 1997).

B. Teenage (Unmarried) Pregnancies

Portugal has a severe problem with teenage pregnancies and it has one of the highest rates of adolescent mothers in Europe. This situation is because of several factors, some of which are external and some of which are internal to the adolescent. Among the external factors, one can point to the non-existence of sex education in schools, the difficulty that many parents have in talking about sexuality, and the lack of resources aimed at youngsters regarding family planning, especially in the rural areas where they are most needed. The internal factors are related to the idea that contraceptives are hard to obtain and to an inhibition related to the discussion of contraceptive use with the sexual partner, among others.

Among today's younger generations, the proportion of women who had their first child before 20 years of age is 3 percent (Instituto Nacional de Estatística 1997). In the past, this figure was significantly higher, but the social context was also significantly different. In fact, people got married younger, and because of this, many teenage pregnancies occurred within wedlock and thus in a more favorable context for the mother and child.

Almeida (1987) conducted a large research study with teenage mothers in a women's hospital. He found that the civil status of the mother had an important influence both socially and emotionally. Unmarried teenage mothers had more problems with the family and a greater intention to have an abortion. Besides that, they also had important medical complications, such as hypertension, pre-eclampsia and eclampsia, premature babies, and small babies for gestational age. However, when the father of the child was positively interested and not absent from the situation, these problems were alleviated.

Teenage pregnancies are generally not well accepted by the Portuguese family, and there are cases of girls being thrown out of their parent's home when their condition is discovered. For these, the solution is to move in with their boyfriend or with his family, or to resort to one of the existing institutions that shelter single pregnant women and mothers who have no place to go. However, in most cases, the family eventually accepts the pregnancy of the girl and tries to find the resources to receive the newcomer. This usually is done with the help of the grandparents or great-grandparents of the baby. Nevertheless, the pregnancy has a significant impact on the life of the girl, often leading to the abandonment of immediate plans of having a proper education.

Among girls who come from lower social backgrounds, in which one of the main life goals is the constitution of a family, pregnancy during adolescence means gaining status. Maternity, in these spheres, is a way to become socially accepted and recognized as a woman (Vilar & Gaspar 1999). Teenage pregnancy might challenge the traditional sexual morality, but it can also be a way for the girl to get closer to her family, to her baby's father, and most of all to her child. The child becomes, for many, a reason to be.

C. Abortion

The Portuguese law on abortion was created in 1984 and changed in 1997. Currently, abortion is allowed at different times of gestation, according to the reason behind the decision to interrupt the pregnancy:

- Before twelve weeks, when a serious and lasting effect to the physical or psychological health of the pregnant women is present;
- Before sixteen weeks, in the cases in which the pregnancy resulted from a rape; and
- Before twenty-four weeks, when there are strong indications of serious disease or malformations of the unborn baby.

Several attempts have been made to change the law to make it more extensive, but without any success. The strongest of these attempts occurred in 1998, when a national referendum, the first in the history of the Portuguese democracy, was conducted over the legalization of abortion after twelve weeks by request of the mother. This referendum launched a large-scale public debate over abortion, and several movements were formed for and against this law. Catholic sectors of the Portuguese society in particular responded very strongly against any kind of liberalization of abortion. However, participation in the referendum was very weak, below 50 percent, and the results showed a clear split in public opinion over this subject, with the number of responses against the liberalization only slightly outnumbering those in favor.

The existence of a restrictive law on abortion doesn't mean that women will not resort to it when confronted with an unwanted pregnancy. In fact, a recent national study showed that, for young adults, abortion was the option of 74.3 percent of women faced with an unwanted pregnancy (Nodin 2000). According to the national statistics, 5 percent of all Portuguese women have used abortion at least once (Instituto Nacional de Estatística 1997). However, in this area, as in others, the actual number is very likely higher than the reported number. Most times, women will not admit to having resorted to abortion as much as they really have. This is still a subject restricted to the privacy of couples and families and not spoken out loud. The legal penalty for abortion, which can be up to three years in jail for the woman, has been applied only a very few times. More often, the abortion provider has been prosecuted and convicted. But even in these cases, a legal charge or complaint is necessary for the process to begin.

While the number of legal abortions performed in hospitals in 1995 and 1996 were less than 300 annually, it is estimated that an average 20,000 to 22,000 occur every year in illegal situations (Rosendo 1998). These illegal abortions are the frequent cause of serious health problems and subsequent hospitalization of the women involved. Some, but not the majority, of the providers of illegal abortions have medical or nursing training. The use of traditional techniques, such as the insertion of objects into the uterus or the ingestion of toxic substances, is not as common as it was in the past, but it still occurs. Many Portuguese women also resort to abortion clinics in Spain, where, curiously, the law is very similar to the Portuguese law, except that there it has had a more liberal application that allowed the opening of abortion clinics. In 1998, 30 percent of all clients in one Spanish abortion clinic close to the border were Portuguese women.

Abortion is more frequent in women after the age of 20, which is also the average age for the start of the sexual life of the Portuguese. The incidence of abortion increases after age 35, and after age 45 about 70 percent of all pregnancies end up interrupted (Instituto Nacional de Estatística 1997). Abortion is also more common in women with a low socioeconomic status and education. However, these are also the ones who have more conservative attitudes towards abortion (Vasconcelos 1998).

D. Population Programs

Unlike other industrialized countries where fertility rates started to decrease at the end of the nineteenth century, in Portugal this tendency is quite recent. It started in the 1960s, but the decrease was quite significant, and in less than twenty years, between 1970 and 1989, the fertility rate that was one of the highest in Europe dropped from 2.8 to 1.5 children per women (Bandeira 1994). One reason for this is the changes in the mating and marrying patterns of the population, formerly restricted by social norms, but recently replaced by individuals and couples taking control over their fertility. Women are delaying the birth of their first child, many times in favor of a professional career.

Another significant demographic phenomenon affecting Portuguese society is the aging of the population. Until 1960, the proportion of people 65 years of age or older was a constant 5 to 6 percent; in 1991, it was 14 percent, and still growing. Nevertheless, there are significant differences between the rural interior and the urban littoral, the former having more older people than the latter. This situation is mostly related to migratory movements that led a considerable proportion of the rural young population towards the cities and towards other countries, like France, Germany, Switzerland, the USA, Canada, and South Africa, in search of better living conditions (Barreto & Preto 1996).

Bandeira (1994) has interpreted the aging Portuguese demographic situation as decaying and entering a potentially irreversible process. According to this author, serious actions need to be taken in order to deal with this situation, but not much has, in fact, been done. He also argues that it is the government that should be responsible for a turnover in politics, facing the reality of the situation and supporting the high costs of having and rearing offspring as well as creating the conditions for the resettling of the population in the interior.

Some of the more recent actions aimed at the promotion of population growth are related to the protection of maternity and paternity. New laws protect women against discrimination at work based on pregnancy, and grant them bigger maternity leaves, to a minimum of six weeks and maximum of a hundred days. The working mother's right to breastfeed her child for at least a year after birth is also now guaranteed. For the first time in Portuguese legal history, the father now has the right to a work leave of up to twenty days subsequent to the birth of a child, and also has the possibility of absence from work to feed the child in case breastfeeding is not possible. Similar rights have been granted to grandparents when they are the baby's caretakers.

10. Sexually Transmitted Diseases

In Portugal, the sexually transmitted disease surveillance and treatment history goes back to the nineteenth century with the March 27, 1879, founding of the Consulta de Moléstias Syphilíticas e Venéreas of the Desterro Hospital in Lisbon, under the direction of the prominent Portuguese physician, Thomaz de Melo Breyner. Later, in the second decade of this century, the Lisbon and the Porto Dispensários Centrais de Higiene Social centralized the surveillance of venereal diseases according to Law 14-803 of December 13, 1927.

Since the 1980s and the demise of the free and confidential Central Dispensaries, monitoring STDs has become the responsibility of the Reference Health Services. Two of these services are the Dermatology service of the Curry Cabral Hospital in Lisbon and the Sexually Transmissible Diseases service in the Lapa Health Center, also in Lisbon. Nowadays, in Portugal, notification is compulsory for gonorrhea, syphilis, and the soft ulcer, all of them bacteriogenic STDs.

In 1993, the results, conclusions, and recommendations of a descriptive, cross-section, longitudinal, and retrospective study regarding sexual behavior in Portugal were published. This report, known as *Portuguese Unprotected Sexuality* (Lucas 1993), focused on the adult population, ages 18 to 49, living in cities with 10,000 or more inhabitants in the continental territory. It was supported by the World Health Organization (Social and Behavioral Investigation Unit of the AIDS Global Program) and by the National Commission Against AIDS. It showed that 12 percent of those surveyed admitted to having had a sexually transmitted disease. The results showed that STDs were more prevalent in the metropolitan areas of Lisbon, Porto, and in the Algarve (in the south of the country), and more common after the age of 25. The incidence of the various STDs was 5 percent for gonorrhea, 4 percent for hepatitis, 2 percent for herpes, and 1 percent for cases of syphilis and urethritis (Santos Lucas 1993). It is important to note that the data were self-reported and so it can underestimate the reality.

At the end of 1997, the Dermatology service in the Curry Cabral Hospital and the Lapa's Health Center noted the stabilized number in cases of syphilis and the lower incidence of gonorrhea and *chlamydia trachomatis*. It is, however, important to note that the 1997 data of the STD service in Intendente, an area of Lisbon traditionally associated with prostitution, draws attention to the fact that only 20 percent of the prostitutes were not infected with an STD, and the percentage of gonorrhea and chlamydia infections was above 30 percent.

Regarding the future of STDs in Portugal, Cardoso (1997) pointed out some difficulties related to the surveillance and treatment of these diseases that are responsible for our intermediate position between developed and less developed countries. These difficulties should be overcome by the reorganization of the STD services in Portugal, with real accessibility and confidentiality of the medical services, with free complementary exams for diagnosis and medication, with the epidemiological evaluation (overcoming sub-notification), and also with counseling.

11. HIV/AIDS

In Portugal, human immunodeficiency virus infections and AIDS have been reported since 1983. The Epidemiological Vigilance Center of the Portuguese Health Institute in Lisbon collects the national data respecting the universal criteria of the Center for Diseases Control in the U.S. The Comissão Nacional de Luta Contra a SIDA (National Commission Against AIDS, or CNLCS.), an organization connected to the Ministry of Health, characterizes the national situation and organizes the national policy, priorities, and strategies in accordance with the United Nations AIDS (UNAIDS) policy.

According to the quarterly and annual information of this Commission, Portugal has had an annual increase of AIDS-related cases since 1983, the first year of notification (Carvalho Teixeira 1993). The official national values do not totally characterize the Portuguese reality, because they do not include untested, undiagnosed, and unreported people.

Since 1985, the year of the first 18 notified cases (and not the time of the primo-infection or first diagnosis), most cases have been related to homosexual and bisexual individuals, the same tendency as in the majority of European countries. This remained the case into the 1990s. #15. Before 1993, the second most affected group were the heterosexuals who were not IV-drug users as was already the trend in the rest of the Europe. After 1993, the heterosexual transmission of the virus in African emigrants from the Portuguese ex-colonies was overtaken by the greater number of reported cases of HIV/AIDS in IV-drug users (Prista Guerra 1998).

At the end of the first three months of 1999, the national percentages of accumulated cases according to the mode of viral transmission were distributed as follows: 45 percent homosexual or bisexual, 27 percent heterosexual, and 12.5 percent IV-drug abuse related. In 1996 and 1997, IV-drug users represented 53.8 percent and 61 percent of the total affected people, respectively (Ministério da Saúde 1997). The most recent rates provided by the Comissão Nacional de Luta Contra a SIDA (1999a, b, c) for the third quarter of 1999 also show a significant increase in the HIV-infection rate in IV-drug users (46.9 percent in September, 46.5 percent in June, and 45.8 percent at the end of March 1999).

In the period between January 1, 1983, and September 30, 1999, 26.1 percent of the total number of AIDS-related reported cases was from heterosexual transmission, 19.2 percent was from homo-/bisexual transmission, and 1 percent was from vertical transmission (mother to child).

Since the beginning of the AIDS-epidemic situation, Portugal had, as of September 30, 1999, a total of 6,263 reported cases, of which 3,928 had already died because of the disease (86.2 percent with opportunistic infections, especially tuberculosis). Of the affected individuals, 85.8 percent were between 20 and 49 years.

Another existing trend in the national data is the increasing incidence of cases in the female population, although affected men still represent the large majority, as in the rest of Europe at the end of the third quarter of 1999, with the proportion 84.2 percent for men and 15.7 percent for women.

Even though the majority of Portuguese cases are HIV-1 infections, there is a great impact of HIV-2 infections and of infections with both viruses. Most European countries do not have specific numbers for HIV2 infections because it is almost non-existent in those countries and the rare cases are simply combined with HIV1 cases. In Portugal, 4.5 percent of cases are HIV-2 and 1.7 percent are infections with both viruses. Most of the notified cases until 1999 were concentrated in the capital, Lisbon, in the second major Portuguese city, Porto, in the north, and in Setúbal, approximately 30 km south of Lisbon.

Because of the epidemiological surveillance, several centers for HIV testing are available, as well as information sources from non-governmental organizations (NGOs) and social solidarity institutions, such as Abraço (The Hug Association), Fundação a Comunidade Contra a SIDA (Foundation to the Community Against AIDS), and the Liga Portuguesa Contra a SIDA (Portuguese League Against AIDS), among others (see list at the end of the chapter). Several therapeutic resources are also available in the central and local health institutions.

Finally, it is important to note the national specificity and intervention priorities in the prevention and treatment areas of the HIV infection. In less than two decades, Portugal ranked highest regarding the dissemination and impact of HIV in Europe, and does not yet follow the stabilization trend of central and northern Europe.

Prevention, the most important weapon against AIDS, will be achieved by the reduction of risk behaviors on an individual level, but mostly by decisive investment in serious improvements in socioeconomic conditions, as well as in the educational and cultural arenas, i.e., in reducing risk situations on a community level.

These objectives imply a global Health Education Policy reaching the individuals who are considered the most vulnerable according to the data, such as homosexual and bisexual men, women, young people, children, drug users, prostitutes, people in jail, and ethnic minorities. Aspects of extreme relevance are condom access and their systematic use, with national information and promotion campaigns, free condom distribution, and initiatives created by drug-abuse prevention programs; real access to anti-HIV antibody testing; a generalized respect for informed consent and confidentiality; and the systematization of multidisciplinary structured responses for the affected persons, and particularly the creation of psychological and socioeconomic structures, such as domestic support. All of these are factors that reduce the personal, social, and financial costs of the AIDS phenomenon (Machado Caetano 1997).

12. Sexual Dysfunctions, Counseling, and Therapies

A. Concepts of Sexual Dysfunction

The diagnosis of sexual dysfunctions is usually done according to the existing specialty international disorders classification systems, such as the DSM and the ICD. However, despite the fact that several sexuality surveys have been conducted in the Portuguese population, questions about dysfunctions are usually left out of them. This reflects the secretive way that the Portuguese deal with these difficulties. Sexuality is a difficult subject to discuss of its own right, and all the problems affecting it are even more. The most frequent strategy used to deal with sexual difficulties is silence. It is only with some difficulty that someone will talk to a physician about a premature ejaculation problem or vaginismus, and when they do, it is usually with a professional that they trust. However, it is estimated that a large number of sexual dysfunctions go unreported.

There is a significant gender difference in the experience of these problems. For men, for whom sex is yet a means to prove their masculinity and virility, sexual problems are a major concern, especially impotence. Men make a great investment in their sexual performance and abilities, and when something goes contrary to expectations, catastrophic scenarios are built and self-esteem is severely affected. As for women, in the past they were supposed to serve their husbands sexually disregarding their own sexual pleasure. This way, many times there was not even the awareness of the existence of a sexual dysfunction when orgasm was not experienced. Today, women are more aware of their own sexuality and are able to seek help when they feel they need it, even though they are not as likely as men to seek help. In the Alferes 1997 survey of sexually experienced individuals, 100 percent of men had experienced orgasm, but only 88.5 percent of women had. In the portion of people who had not had sexual relations, all of the males had experienced orgasm, while only 35.5 percent of women had experienced it.

The sexological tradition in Portugal is strongly connected to a cognitive and behavioral perspective of sexuality. Nevertheless, nowadays the different institutions working in this field have a broader approach to sexuality. The echoes of the International Conference for Population and Development held in Cairo in 1994, in which major emphasis was given to sexual and reproductive health, are having its effects at different levels. A greater concern is being devoted to the special sexual and reproductive needs of individuals in a holistic approach to the problems they face. To accomplish these goals, true efforts are being made especially by non-governmental institutions (NGOs).

B. Availability of Diagnosis and Treatment

Diagnosis and treatment of sexual dysfunctions are available in hospitals in the main urban centers. The cities where specialty sexology services can be found are: Porto, Coimbra, Leiria, Lisbon, Faro, and Ponta Delgada (in the Azores). Many private practitioners, either medical doctors or psychologists, offer their services in other parts of the country. However, not all the people can afford to go to these consultations, nor do they frequently know of their existence. In 1998, the Portuguese Society of Clinical Sexology (Sociedade Portuguesa de Sexologia Clínica, SPSC), together with a pharmacological company, created a telephone helpline called SOS Dificuldades Sexuais (SOS Sexual Difficulties) aimed at an adult public with sexual dysfunctions. The main goal of this helpline is to provide counseling for people with sexual problems, and also to work as a guiding service to indicate which services, both public and private, are available for these kinds of problems.

C. Therapist Training and Certification

Until the 1990s, no specific sexological training was available in Portugal. There was a hospital tradition that provided practical and also theoretical training for psychiatrists, gynecologists, and professionals from other medical specialties that had an interest in sexuality. Others had their training abroad in countries where this kind of training was available. Many of the great names of sexology in Portugal today, like António Pacheco Palha, Francisco Allen Gomes, José Pacheco, Júlio Machado Vaz, or Júlio Silveira Nunes, had their training as part of their specialty training or abroad.

In 1984, following the first Portuguese Congress of Sexology, a commission was formed to create a Society of Sexology, which the following year had a total of 116 members. One of the main and primary goals of this society was to promote and regulate the scientific training in sexology in Portugal. In 1992, the society began seriously exploring the legal, practical, and pedagogical aspects organizing a post-graduate course that would grant a certified title of sexologist.

The first post-graduate course in sexology, was a two-year program started in 1995 with a group of fourteen medical doctors, psychologists, and nurses; a second course started in 1998. This course, organized by the SPSC, is actually the only one that grants a certificate for Sexual Therapist in Portugal. This course is interdisciplinary and aimed at professionals with some experience in the area. It has a duration of two years divided into four semesters: The first semester is solely theoretical, the following two are theoretical and practical with the discussion of clinical material provided by the students and teachers, and the last semester is devoted to the elaboration and execution of a research project.

13. Research and Advanced Education

A. Institutes and Programs for Sexological Research

As in other behavioral areas, there is little sexological research. The tradition of research is incipient and lacks appropriate articulation between universities and companies that would provide financing and practical application of the results of the research. The few research studies that exist within Portuguese sexology occur mainly in universities, usually associated with psychology, medicine, and sociology, and also in the hospitals and centers that offer specialty services in human sexuality.

B. Post-College and Graduate Programs in Sexology

There is no graduate level course on human sexuality. There are some initial efforts in short-duration advanced courses on the subject, but they are infrequent and irregular. There are, however, two post-graduate courses on human sexuality in the country, one of them a master's degree course.

The first post-graduate course in human sexuality ever to occur in Portugal was organized by the SPSC in 1995 (see Section 12C, Therapist Training and Certification, above). In the meanwhile, a private university, Universidade Lusófona, organized a master's degree course in sexology that started in 1998. Many of the teachers of this course are connected to the SPSC and are, thus, the same as the ones in the post-graduate course provided by that society. The master's degree is, however, mostly theoretical and does not grant the title of sexual therapist as the post-graduate course does. The theoretical areas discussed in the master's degree are:

- The historical, social, cultural, and anthropological aspects of sexuality;
- The human sexual response;
- Gender identity and its disturbances;
- AIDS and other sexual transmitted diseases;
- Research methods in sexology;
- Diagnosis and evaluation of the disturbances of the human sexual response;
- Treatment of the disturbances of the human sexual response;
- Minority sexual and erotic preferences;
- Couple therapy;
- Sex education and family planning; and
- Data analysis techniques in sexology.

Although these courses have played an important role in extending the offering of sexological training programs in Portugal, professionals from different areas recognize the need for a more appropriate approach to sexual problems. Many have to deal with these kinds of problems and have no appropriate training to handle them.

C. Main Sexological Journals and Periodicals

Acta Portuguesa de Sexologia, Hospital de São João, 4200-319 Porto, Portugal; Tel:/Fax: +351-225-508-384; email: psiquiatria.fmp@mail.telepac.pt.

Sexualidade e Planeamento Familiar, Rua da Artilharia Um, 38, 2º Dto., 1250-040 Lisboa, Portugal; Tel: +351-213-853-993; Fax: +351-213-887-379; email: apfportugal@mail.telepac.pt.

There are also some periodicals related to AIDS worthy of note:

Abraço, Tr. do Noronha, 5, 3º Direito, 1250-169 Lisboa, Portugal; Tel: +351-213-974-298; Fax: +351-213-957-921.

Informação SIDA, Apartado 1980, 1058-001 Lisboa, Portugal; Tel: +351-213 129 290; Fax: +351-213-129-299.

D. Important National and Regional Sexological Organizations

Sociedade Portuguesa de Sexologia Clínica, Serviço de Psiquiatria, Hospital de São João, 4200-319 Porto, Portugal; Tel:/Fax: +351-225-508-384; email: psiquiatria.fmp@mail.telepac.pt.

Associação para o Planeamento da Família, Rua da Artilharia Um, 38, 2º Direito, 1250-040 Lisboa, Portugal (with branches in Porto, Coimbra, Lisbon, Alentejo, Algarve, and Azores); Tel: +351-213-853-993; Fax: +351-213-887-379; homepage: www.apf.pt; email: apfportugal@mail.telepac.pt.

Telephone Helplines:

Sexualidade em Atendimento (APF), +351-222-001-798.

Sexualidade em Linha, 800-222-002; Ap. 1191, 1054 Lisboa Codex, Portugal; email: sexualidade@ipj.pt.

SOS Dificuldades Sexuais, 808-206-206.

Lesbian, Gay, Transgender, and Bisexual Organizations:

Grupo de Trabalho Homossexual (Partido Socialista Revolucionário), Rua da Palma, 268, 1100 Lisboa, Portugal; Tel:/Fax: +351-218-882-736.

ILGA–Portugal, Rua de São Lázaro, 88, 1150-333 Lisboa, Portugal; Tel: 218-873-918; homepage: www.ilga.portugal.org; email: ilga-portugal@ilga.org.

Opus Gay, R. Ilha Terceira, 34, 2º, 1000 Lisboa, Portugal; Tel: +351-213-151-396; homepage: homepage.esoterica.pt; email: anser@esoterica.pt.

HIV/AIDS Organizations:

Abraço, Travessa do Noronha, 5, 3º Direito, 1250-169 Lisboa, Portugal; Tel: +351-213-974-298; Fax: 213-957-921; homepage: abraco.esoterica.pt; email: abraco@mail.telepac.pt.

Associação dos Direitos e Deveres dos Positivos e Portadores do Vírus da SIDA, Quinta das Lapas, Monte Redondo, 2560 Torres Vedras, Portugal; Tel: +351-261-312-331; Fax: +351-261-312-322.

Centro de Respostas Integradas de Apoio à SIDA, Avenida da Imaculada Conceição, 153, 4700-034 Braga, Portugal; Tel. +351-253-261-500; Fax: +351-253-609-994.

Comissão Nacional de Luta Contra a SIDA, Palácio Bensaúde, Estrada da Luz, 153, 1600-153 Lisboa, Portugal; Tel: +351-217-210-360; Fax: +351-217-220-822; email: CNLCS@cnlcs.min-saude.pt.

Fundação Portuguesa a Comunidade Contra a SIDA, Rua Andrade Corvo, 16, 1º, Esq. , Portugal; Tel: +351-213-540-000; Fax: +351-213-160-000.

Gabinete de Apoio a Doentes com SIDA, Rua João António Gaspar, 40, Bairro Marechal Carmona, 2750-380 Cascais, Portugal; Tel: +351-214-861-429; Fax: +351-214-861-420.

Liga Portuguesa Contra a SIDA, Rua do Crucifixo, 40, 2º, 1100-183 Lisboa, Portugal; Tel: +351-213-225-575; Fax: +351-213-479-376.

Movimento de Apoio à Problemática da SIDA, Avenida Cidade Hayward, Blocos C1 e D2, Caves Vale Carneiros, 8000-073 Faro, Portugal; Tel: +351-289-864-777; Fax: +351-289-846-598.

Projecto STOP SIDA, Centro Laura Ayres, Rua Padre António Vieira, 12, 3000-315 Coimbra, Portugal; Tel: +351-239-828-771.

SOL Associação de Apoio a Crianças Infectadas pelo Vírus da SIDA e Suas Famílias, Rua das Praças, 55, r/c, 1200-766 Lisboa, Portugal; Tel: +351-213-625-771; Fax: +351-213-625-773.

Disability and Rehabilitation Organizations:

Liga Portuguesa dos Deficientes Motores, Rua Sítio Casalinho da Ajuda, 49 Frente, 1300 Lisboa, Portugal; Tel: +351-213-633-314.

Secretariado Nacional de Reabilitação e Integração das Pessoas com Deficiência, Avenida Conde Valbom, 63, 1050 Lisboa, Portugal; Tel: +351-217-929-500.

Sexually Transmitted Diseases Organizations:

Centro de Saúde da Lapa, Consulta de Doenças Sexualmente Transmissíveis, Rua de São Ciro, 36, 1200 Lisboa, Portugal; Tel. +351-213-957-973.

Prostitution Support Organizations:

Associação "O Ninho," R. Actor Taborda, 30, 3º Dto, 1000-008 Lisboa, Portugal; Tel: +351-213-426-946.

Centro "Drop In," Travessa do Maldonado, 3, 1100-329 Lisboa, Portugal; Tel: +351-218-853-249; Fax: +351-218-869-784.

Espaço Pessoa, Travessa das Liceiras, 14/16, 4000 Porto, Portugal; Tel: +351-222-008-377.

Child Sexual Abuse Support Organizations:

Associação Chão dos Meninos, Bairro António Sérgio, Avenida da Liberdade nº 100, 7000 Évora, Portugal; Tel: +351-266-731-079; Fax: +351-266-371-079.

Instituto de Apoio à Criança (IAC), Largo da Memória, 14, Portugal; Tel: +351-213-624-318; Fax: +351-213-624-756.

Domestic Violence Support Organizations:

Associação de Mulheres Contra a Violência, Al. D. Afonso Henriques, 78, 1º esq, 1000 Lisboa, Portugal; Tel:/Fax: +351-218-124-048.

Associação de Apoio à Vítima, Rua do Comércio, 56, 5º esq, 1100 Lisboa, Portugal; Tel: +351-218-884-732, Fax: +351-218-876-351.

Comissão para a Igualdade e Direitos das Mulheres, Avenida da República, 32 1º andar, 1093 Lisboa, Portugal; Tel: +351-217-983-000.

Acknowledgments

For their assistance and valuable help, the authors wish to thank: Ana Paula Manteigas, Delegação Regional de Lisboa da Associação para o Planeamento da Família; Clara de Jesus, Associação para o Planeamento da Família; Francisco Allen Gomes; Jó Bernardo; Mário Lourenço, Sociedade Portuguesa de Sexologia Clínica; Sergio Vitorino, Grupo de Trabalho Homossexual—Partido Socialista Revolucionário; and Sofia Verissimo.

References and Suggested Readings

Alferes, V. 1997. *Encenações e comportamentos sexuais [Sexual stagings and behaviors]*. Lisbon: Edições Afrontamento.
Almeida, J. M. R. 1987. *Adolescência e maternidade [Adolescence and maternity]*. Lisbon: Fundação Calouste Gulbenkian.
Amâncio, L. 1994. *Masculino e feminino: A Construcção social da diferença [Masculine and feminine: The social construction of the difference]*. Porto: Edições Afrontamento.
Associação para o Planeamento da Família. 1998. *1º Seminário Nacional sobre abusos sexuais em crianças e adolescentes [Sexual abuse in children and adolescents: Contributions from the 1st National Seminar]*. Lisbon: Associação para o Planeamento da Família.
Bandeira, M. L. 1994. Envelhecimento demográfico e planeamento familiar: Que relação? [Demographic aging and family planning: What relationship?]. *Sexualidade e Planeamento Familiar* [Lisbon], *3*(2):15-18.
Barreto, A., & Preto, C. V. 1996. *Portugal 1960/1995: Indicadores sociais [Portugal 1960/1995: Social indicators]*. Lisbon: Cadernos do Público.
Bernardo, J., et al. 1998. *The Portuguese transgender community: An unknown reality*. Paper presented at the 12th World AIDS Conference—Bridging the Gap, Geneva.
Cardoso, J. 1997. O futuro das doenças sexualmente transmissíveis em Portugal [The future of sexually transmissible diseases in Portugal]. *Sexualidade e Planeamento Familiar* [Lisbon], *15/16*:17-22.
Carvalho Teixeira, J. C. 1993. *Psicologia da saúde e SIDA [Health psychology and AIDS]*, Lisbon: Instituto Superior de Psicologia Aplicada—CRL.
Comissão Nacional de Luta Contra a SIDA (CNLCS) do Ministério da Saúde. 1999a (March 31). *A situação em Portugal a 31 de Março de 1999 [AIDS: Portugal's situation at*

31 March 1999]. Lisbon: Informação Centro de Vigilância Epidemiológica das Doenças Transmissíveis, Instituto Nacional de Saúde Lisboa.

Comissão Nacional de Luta Contra a SIDA (CNLCS) do Ministério da Saúde. 1999b (June 30). *A situação em Portugal a 30 de Junho de 1999* [*AIDS: Portugal's situation at 30 June 1999*]. Lisbon: Informação Centro de Vigilância Epidemiológica das Doenças Transmissíveis, Instituto Nacional de Saúde Lisboa.

Comissão Nacional de Luta Contra a SIDA (CNLCS) do Ministério da Saúde. 1999c (30 September). *A situação em Portugal a 30 de Setembro de 1999* [*AIDS: Portugal's situation at 30 September 1999*] (Doc 117). Lisbon: Informação Centro de Vigilância Epidemiológica das Doenças Transmissíveis, Instituto Nacional de Saúde Lisboa.

Comissão para a Igualdade e para os Direitos das Mulheres. 1998. *Guia dos direitos das mulheres* [*Guide to women's rights*]. Lisbon: Presidência do Conselho de Ministros, Colecção Informar as Mulheres nº 10.

Costa Santos, J. 1998. Prova médica—Que prova? Reflexões sobre os exames periciais em matéria de abusos sexuais de crianças e adolescents [Medical evidence—What evidence? Reflections on the specialty examinations in cases of sexual abuse of children and adolescents]. In: Associação para o Planeamento da Família, ed., *1º Seminário Nacional sobre abusos sexuais em crianças e adolescentes* [*Sexual abuse in children and adolescents: Contributions from the 1st National Seminar*]. Lisbon: Associação para o Planeamento da Família.

Direcção Geral de Saúde. 1998. *Estudo exploratório de abusos sexuais em crianças e adolescentes* [*Sexual abuse in children and adolescents—An exploratory study*]. Lisbon: Divisão de Saúde Materna e Infantil e dos Adolescentes/Divisão de Promoção e Educação Para a Saúde.

Ferreira, A. C. 1993. Sinais dos tempos [Sign of the times]. *Planeamento Familiar* [Lisbon], *61/62*:16.

Figueiredo, E. 1988. *Portugal nos próximos 20 anos* [*Portugal in the next 20 years*] (vol. II). Lisbon: Fundação Calouste Gulbenkian.

Fundação Portuguesa a Comunidade Contra a SIDA. 1998. *As mulheres e a SIDA* [*Women and AIDS*]. Lisbon: Fundação Portuguesa a Comunidade Contra a SIDA.

GAEP. 1999. *Sexualidade em Linha—Um ano de funcionamento* [*Sexualidade em Linha—One year of functioning*]. Lisbon: Gabinete de Apoio, Estudos e Planeamento da Secretaria de Estado da Juventude.

Gameiro, O. 1999. *Aspectos sociais e políticos da população homo e bissexual em Portugal* [*Social and political aspects of the homosexual and bisexual population in Portugal*] [WWW document]. URL: http://www.ilga-portugal.org/portugues/index.html.

ILGA–Portugal. 1999. *Situação portuguesa* [*The Portuguese situation*] [WWW document]. URL: http://www.ilga-portugal.org/portugues/index.html.

Infante, F. 1998. *Comissões de Protecção de Menores: Síntese dos relatórios de actividade, 1997* [*Minors' Protection Commissions: Resume from the activity reports, 1997*]. Lisbon: Ministério da Justiça Centro de Estudos Judiciários—Jurisdição de Menores e da Família.

Instituto Nacional de Estatística. 1997. *Inquérito à fecundidade e à família* [*Inquiry on fertility and the family*]. Lisbon: Instituto Nacional de Estatística.

López, F. 1995. *Prevención de los abusos sexuales de menores y educación sexual* [*Prevention of the sexual abuse of minors and sex education*]. Salamanca: Amarú Ediciones.

Lucas, J. S. 1993. *A sexualidade desprevenida dos portugueses* [*Portuguese unprotected sexuality*], Lisbon, McGraw-Hill.

Machado Caetano, J. A. 1997. *SIDA em Portugal: Que perspectivas?* [*AIDS in Portugal: What future?*]. Lisbon: Fundação Portuguesa a Comunidade Contra a SIDA.

Madeira, J. & Costa Santos, J. 1998. Prova médica—Que prova? Reflexões sobre os exames periciais em matéria de abusos sexuais de crianças e adolescents [Medical evidence—What evidence? Reflections on the specialty examinations in cases of sexual abuse of children and adolescents]. In: Associação para o Planeamento da Família, ed., *1º Seminário Nacional sobre abusos sexuais em crianças e adolescentes* [*Sexual abuse in children and adolescents: Contributions from the 1st National Seminar*]. Lisbon: Associação para o Planeamento da Família.

Marktest. 1995. *Estudo sobre comportamento sexual dos portugueses* [*Study on the sexual behavior of the Portuguese*]. Lisbon: Marktest—Departamento de Estudos Especiais.

Miguel, N. 1987. A sexualidade na adolescência [Sexuality in adolescence]. In: F. A. Gomes, A. Albuquerque, & J. S. Nunes, eds., *A sexologia em Portugal* [*Sexology in Portugal*] (vol. I). Lisbon: Texto Editora.

Ministério da Saúde Direcção Geral da Saúde. 1997. *A saúde dos portugueses 1997* [*The Portuguese health in 1997*]. Lisbon: Ministério da Saúde Direcção Geral da Saúde.

Movimento Católico de Estudantes (MCE). 1993. *Documento sobre moral sexual* [*Document on sexual morality*]. *Planeamento Familiar* [Lisbon]. *61/62*:17.

Nodin, N. 2000. *A saúde sexual e reprodutiva. Resultados de um estudo nacional sobre factores de riscopara o VIH para gravidez não planeada em jovens adultos* [*Sexual and reproductive health. Results from a national study on the risk of HIV and of unwanted pregnancy in young adults*] [Master's degree thesis in Health Psychology]. Lisbon: Instituto Superior de Psicologia Aplicada.

Nunes de Almeida, A. No date. *Maus tratos às crianças em Portugal* [Violence against children in Portugal]. Lisbon: Instituto Superior de Ciências do Trabalho e da Empresa.

Pais, J. M. 1985. *A prostituição e a Lisboa Boémia do século XIX aos inícios do século XX* [*Prostitution and Bohemian Lisbon from the 19th to the beginning of the 20th century*]. Lisbon: Editorial Querco.

Pais, J. M., coordinator. 1998. *Gerações e valores na sociedade portuguesa contemporânea* [*Generations and values of the contemporary Portuguese society*]. Lisbon: Instituto de Ciências Sociais da Universidade de Lisboa.

Pais, M. 1996. *Sexualidade in jovens de hoje e de aqui.* Caderros Estudos Locais Loures: Dept Socio-Cultural, C. M. Loures.

Pessoa, A. A. 1976. *Os Bons velhos tempos da prostituição em Portugal* [*The good old times of prostitution in Portugal*]. Lisbon: Arcádia.

Pires, L., & Antunes, M. 1998. Vida religiosa [Religious life]. In: J. M. Pais, coordinator, *Gerações e valores na sociedade portuguesa contemporânea* [*Generations and values of the contemporary Portuguese society*]. Lisbon: Instituto de Ciências Sociais da Universidade de Lisboa.

Planeamento familiar e sexualidade [*Family planning and sexuality*] [journal]. 1996. Lisbon: Associação para o Planeamento da Família, *11/12*.

Prista Guerra, M. 1998. *SIDA: Implicações psicológicas* [*AIDS: Psychological implications*]. Lisbon: Editora Fim de Século.

Rodrigues, J. A. 1995. *Continuidade e mudança nos papeis das mulheres portuguesas urbanas. O aparecimento de novas estruturas familiares* [*Continuity and change in the roles of urban Portuguese women. The appearance of new family structures*]. Lisbon: Comissão para a Igualdade e para os Direitos das Mulheres.

Roque, O. 1999. *Educação sexual nas escolas portuguesas: Realidade virtual* [*Sex education in the Portuguese schools: Virtual reality*] (monograph paper). Lisbon: Univeridade Lusófona de Humanidades e Tecnologias.

Rosendo, G. 1998 (June 26). Decisões com consequências [Decisions with consequences] (magazine article). *Revista do Expresso* [Lisbon]. Pp. 56-64.

Sampaio, D., coordinator. 1996. *Escola, família e amigos* [*School, family and friends*]. Lisbon: Programa de Promoção e Educação para a Saúde.

Seabra Diniz, J. 1998. O abuso sexual como rutura do processo de desenvolvimento [Sexual abuse as a rupture of the development process]. In: Associação para o Planeamento da Família, ed., *1º Seminário Nacional sobre abusos sexuais em crianças e adolescentes* [*Sexual abuse in children and adolescents: Contributions from the 1st National Seminar*]. Lisbon: Associação para o Planeamento da Família.

Secretariado Nacional de Reabilitação e Integração das Pessoas com Deficiência 1994. *Uma política coerente para a reabilitação das pessoas com deficiência* [*A coherent policy for the rehabilitation of people with disabilities*] (SNR Nº 1 Conselho da Europa). Lisbon: Cadernos.

Secretariado Nacional de Reabilitação e Integração das Pessoas com Deficiência. 1996. *Inquérito nacional às incapacidades, deficiências e desvantagens. Resultados globais* [*National inquiry regarding incapacities, disabilities and handicaps. Global results*] (SNR Nº 9). Lisbon: Cadernos.

Secretariado Nacional para a Reabilitação e Integração das Pessoas com Deficiência. 1998. *Normas das Nações Unidas sobre igualdade de oportunidades para pessoas com deficiência* [*The Standard United Nations rules on the equality of opportunities for persons with disabilities*] (SNR Nº 3, 2ª Edição). Lisbon: Cadernos.

Secretariado Nacional para a Reabilitação e Integração das Pessoas com Deficiência. 1999. *Lei de bases da prevenção e da reabilitação e integração das pessoas com deficiência* [*Law on the prevention, rehabilitation and integration of people with disabilities*] (SNR Nº 6, 2ª Edição). Lisbon: Folheto.

Silva, M. L., Dantas, A. M., Mourão, V., & Ramalho, H. 1996. *Promoção de saúde dos jovens na optica da prevenção primária do consumo da droga* [*Health promotion of young people regarding the primary prevention of drug addition*]. Lisbon: Fundação Nossa Senhora do Bom Sucesso.

Vasconcelos, P. 1998. *Práticas e discursos da conjugalidade dos jovens portugueses* [Behaviors and opinions of the conjugality of the young Portuguese]. In: M. Cabral, A. Fernandes, J. Nunes, & P. Vasconcelos, eds., *Jovens portugueses de hoj*, Oeiras: Celta.

Vaz, J. M., ed. 1996. *Educação sexual na escola* [*Sex education in school*]. Lisbon: Universidade Aberta.

Vicente, A. 1998. *As mulheres em Portugal na transição do milénio* [*The Portuguese women at the turn of the century*]. Lisbon: Multinova.

Vilar, D., & Gaspar, A. M. 1999. Traços redondos (A gravidez na adolescência) [Round traces (Pregnancy in adolescence)]. In: J. M. Pais, ed. *Traços e Riscos na Adolescência* [*Traces and Risks During Adolescence*]. Porto: Ambar.

Vitorino, S., & Dinis, G. 1999. *Lesbian, gay, bisexual and transgender (LGBT) politics in Portugal: The awakening of a new social movement.* Paper presented at the Euro-Mediterranean Conference of Homosexualities, Marseilles.

South Korea
(*Taehan Min'guk*)

Hyung-Ki Choi, M.D., Ph.D.,* with
Ji-Kan Ryu, M.D., Koon Ho Rha, M.D., and
Woong Hee Lee, M.D.;
redacted with additional information researched by
Huso Yi, Ph.D. (cand.)** ***

Contents

Demographics and a Historical Perspective

A. Demographics HYUNG KI CHOI AND COLLEAGUES (REDACTED BY HUSO YI)

The Republic of South Korea occupies the southern half of the Korean Peninsula in northeast Asia, with North Korea on its northern border, the

---

Communications: Professor Hyung Ki Choi, M.D. Yongdong Severance Hospital, Dept. of Urology 146-92, Dogok-dong, Kangnam-ku, Seoul 135-270, Korea; urol3887@yumc.yonsei.ac.kr.

**Huso Yi: Program in Human Sexuality, Department of Health Studies, School of Education, New York University, New York, NY, 10003, USA; husoyi@sexuality.net.

***Unless otherwise indicated at the beginning of a section or at the end of a paragraph, Hyung-Ki Choi, Ji-Kan Ryu, Koon Ho Rha, and Woong Hee Lee are the authors. In most sections, the material these authors supplied has been redacted by Huso Yi and the editor (Robert T. Francoeur) with additional information. The additional comments are indicated in brackets as [. . . (Huso Yi)] or [. . . (Editor)]. In the areas where the primary authors did not supply information, Huso Yi and the editor have summarized key studies to complete the picture, which are also indicated as above.

Sea of Japan and Japan to the east, the East China Sea and China to the south, and the Yellow Sea and northern China to the west. With a total land mass of 38,023 square miles (99,434 square kilometers), and a coastline of 1,500 miles (2,413 kilometers), South Korea is slighter larger than the state of Indiana. The country is mountainous, with a rugged eastern coast. The western and southern coasts are deeply indented, with many islands and harbors.

The estimated population in 2000 was 47.3 million, with an age distribution of 22.4 percent below age 15, 71.2 percent between ages 15 and 65, and 6.4 percent over age 65. The population is highly homogeneous with only about 4,500 Korean-Chinese and 50,000 foreigners as of 1995. Eighty-three percent of South Koreans are urban, with 11 million living in Seoul, the capital (the 1999 population density in Seoul was 17,000 per square kilometer), 4 million in Pusan, and 2.4 million in Taegu. Life expectancy at birth in 1998 was 70.4 years for males and 78 for females. The 1999 population growth rate was 0.92 percent. The birthrate per 1,000 population was 17, the death rate per 1,000 was 6, and the infant mortality rate was 8 per 1,000 live births, giving a natural annual increase of 1.04 percent. South Korea's total fertility rate (TFR) of 1.7 children per fertile woman placed it 182 among the 227 nations of the world in 1995. [Family Planning has been an important task since the 1960s. Korea's TFR decreased from 6.0 births per fertile woman in 1960 to 4.5 in 1970, 2.7 in 1980, 1.6 in 1990, and 1.5 in 1998. A zero population growth rate is expected by 2021 (National Statistical Office (NSO 1999b). (Huso Yi)]

Forty-nine percent of South Koreans are Christian, 47 percent Buddhist, and 3 percent Confucianist. There is a pervasive coexisting folk-religion influence. Korean is the official language, but English is widely taught in the high schools. Education is free and compulsory from the first to sixth grades. Literacy in 1995 was 98 percent. The 1999 gross domestic product per capita was $8,581, compared with $32,448 in the United States. (For complete demographic information, refer to the Korean Government Homepage, 2000, and the National Statistical Office, 1999b.)

B. A Brief Historical Perspective*

HYUNG KI CHOI AND COLLEAGUES (REDACTED BY HUSO YI)

[According to the National History Compilation of the Republic of Korea (NHCROK 2001), the beginning of Korea dates from 2333 B.C.E. when Tan-gun, a legendary figure born of the son of Heaven, married a woman from the bear-totem tribe and established the first kingdom, Chosun, literally meaning, "Land of the Morning Calm." Korea's early native culture was based on a warrior aristocracy, a shamanistic religion, and a subject class of rice cultivators. The ancient period was followed by the Three Kingdoms from 57 B.C.E. to 676 C.E.; the North–South Unified Shilla

*The strong historical dimensions of this chapter and the recurring references to the historical and contemporary influence of Confucianism and its patriarchal views might seem to be unimportant, because 96 percent of Koreans are either Christian or Buddhist and only 3 percent identify with the Confucian/Neo-Confucian philosophy. However, Confucianism, and particularly Neo-Confucianism, continue to play a major role in Korean sexual culture. (Editor)

period (676 to 935 C.E.); and, starting as a province under the Shilla era, the Koryo dynasty from 913 to 1392 (the Koryo dynasty started as a province in 913 and governed the whole country in 935). (Huso Yi)] In the Yi or Chosun dynasty (1392 to 1910), during which it was known as the Kingdom of Chosun, Korea was a staunch tributary ally of China during its Ming (1368-1644) and Ch'ing (1644-1911) dynasties. The Japanese, who invaded most of Korea in 1592, were finally expelled by combined Korean and Chinese forces in the late seventeenth century. This relationship with China brought a strong adherence to Buddhism and a government system modeled on Chinese bureaucracy. For the next two hundred years, Korea was rigorously isolated from all non-Chinese foreign influence and was known as "the Hermit Kingdom."

Korea's isolation, and its status as a tributary of China, ended in 1874, when Japan imposed the Treaty of Kangwha to guarantee Japanese commercial access to Korea and other interests. The outcome of the Sino-Japanese war (1894-1895) recognized Korea's complete independence, but made the nation a protectorate of Japan. In 1910, Japan forcibly annexed Korea as the colony of Chosun. A harsh colonial policy was established to eradicate all Korean culture and make Korea an integral part of the Japanese empire. All Korean resistance was violently repressed, although resistance movements managed to survive in exile. During World War II, tens of thousands of Koreans were conscripted to work in Japan and in the Japanese-occupied territories. At the same time, thousands of Korean women were forced into "comfort services" for the Japanese military, a reality that was not dealt with publicly until fifty years later in the late 1990s.

Following Japan's surrender in 1945, Korea was arbitrarily divided into zones of Soviet and American occupation. The thirty-eighth parallel split the country geographically, economically, and politically into north and south. Korea's industrial and hydroelectric power was concentrated in the north, where careful Soviet plans established a communist government. In the agricultural south, American attempts to reunify the country under a republican government were inept. By 1948, when it was obvious that the country could not be united, the Republic of Korea was organized in the south, and the United States withdrew its occupation forces in June 1949. In June of 1950, Northern Korean troops invaded the south in an attempt to unify the country under a communist regime. Because it boycotted the United Nations Security Council debate on what response to make to the invasion, the Soviet Union could not veto the United Nations' decision to send troops to repel the invasion. Initially, American forces were successful in driving the communist forces back to the Chinese border. However, when Chinese troops entered the war, the tide reversed and the United Nations troops were driven south. Seoul, the capital, fell to the communists on January 4, 1951. Within two months, the communist forces were driven back to the thirty-eighth parallel, where the battle line stabilized despite intervals of fierce fighting. A truce was finally signed on July 27, 1953, with a demilitarized zone along the thirty-eighth parallel.

Postwar reconstruction of the south followed with major American support. Student demonstrations in 1960 forced the resignation of Korea's first president, Syngman Rhee. In May 1961, a military coup was established. The military government was given some democratic trappings in a 1972 referendum that allowed General Park to run for an unlimited series of six-year presidential terms. Following Park's assassination on October 26, 1979, by the government's chief of intelligence, General Chun Doo Hwan assumed power. Widespread violent political protests followed, although the nation's economy was making great strides, with modernization, industrialization, and a strong urban life. In 1986, South Korea achieved a favorable balance-of-payments ratio in its foreign trade.

Widespread demonstrations in mid-1987 led to new elections and a calmer political situation, although students called for greater efforts for reunification of the north and south, and protests of the large number of American troops continued. North–South talks in 1990 produced an agreement in principle on reunification in the near future. However, South Korea's interest in reunification became more cautious when North Korea faced a major widespread famine. The massive economic burdens West Germany encountered in helping East Germany become a part of a reunited Germany added to South Korea's growing hesitation over reunification. Establishment of diplomatic relations with China in 1992 was a clear signal that Korea will remain a major influence in the region. [In addition, the Korean government began to build up good relationships with North Korea through the so-called "sunshine policy" of President Kim Dae-Jung, who was awarded a Nobel Peace Prize honoring his political efforts for democracy and reunification. (Huso Yi)]

1. Basic Sexological Premises

A. Character of Gender Roles

HYUNG KI CHOI AND COLLEAGUES (REDACTED BY HUSO YI)

[The following examples of typical and popular Korean proverbs concerning women provide an insight into the position of women in Korean culture and the family.

"If you don't beat your woman for three days, she becomes a fox."

"If you listen to a woman's advice, the house comes to ruin; if you don't listen, the house comes to shame."

"If a woman cries, no good luck for three years."

"A woman's mouth is a cheap thing."

"You can know in water 1,000 fathoms deep, but you can't know the mind of a woman."

"When wood fire and a woman are stirred up, the outcome is a great misfortune."

"Get slapped at the government office; come home and hit your woman."

"A bad wife is a grievance for 100 years; bad bean paste is a grievance for one year."

"The good-for-nothing daughter-in-law gets sick on the day of ancestral sacrifice."

"A son-in-law is a guest for 100 years; a daughter-in-law is an eating mouth 'til the day she dies." (Huso Yi)]

Throughout Korean history, Korean women have been treated as second-class citizens regardless of their social and familial positions. In the social system, they have been limited to being bystanders in the main cultural systems, behind bureaucratic male dominance. Korean women have been the subjects of discriminations based on their role in marriage, their fertility, and their lack of a right to end their marriage in divorce, as well as their subordinate role in the public domain.

In the Koryo dynasty, monogamy was encouraged, and divorce and remarriage were widely practiced by both men and women. However, at the end of the Koryo dynasty, polygamy emerged. The Chosun dynasty (1392-1910) proclaimed monogamy and officially frowned on polygyny as a part of a social reformation policy, although powerful men were commonly allowed to have several wives. [The Chosun dynasty reversed the entire previous marriage system by prohibiting women's remarriage, and furthermore, marriage between those of the same surname and family origin (Chung 1998). The law against remarriage was enforced in 1447 and lasted until 1894. The law against same-surname and family-origin marriage still exists in Korea. It will be discussed later. (Huso Yi)] The conflicting system of polygyny and monogamy coexisted without much problem because of the lenient Neo-Confucian morals for males. Those who made the laws were not about to give up their privileged right. Nor were they about to improve the subordinate position of women. Women who openly opposed the practice of multiple wives were maltreated and humiliated. However, in 1899, near the end of Chosun dynasty, a formal protest against polygyny took place, headed by the newly organized woman's association. Their protest ended without any change, but it was a herald of an active organized women's movement in Korea.

Early marriage is another interesting feature of the Korean marriage heritage. Records of early marriage as far back as the Three Kingdom era (57 to 676) document the practice of early marriage, which allowed children about 10 years old to be presented to a family as a bride or groom. The legal age for marriage in Chosun was 15 for boys and 14 for girls, with the exception of 12 years when a child had to assume responsibility for the family. At the time, the average legal age for marriage in other countries was 18 for men and 15 for women. It was generally believed that the risk of inappropriate sexual involvement increased if marriage was delayed, and so the legal age for marriage was lowered. The custom of early marriage continued well into the twentieth century. In the 1991 national tax census, among 1,000 married couples, 10 men and 18 women married before the age of 5, 48 men and 132 women were married between ages 5 and 10, and 159 men and 488 women married between ages 10 and 15. In other words, 217 or one in five of the men and 638 or nearly two thirds of the women were married by age 15 (Chung 1998). These children had no choice in the commitment of marriage and parenthood. With no opportunity to reject or refuse their arranged partners, marriage was simply one's fate. Another surprising fact is that among 100 murderers in prison, 31 of the 47 female prisoners murdered their husbands (Chung 1998).

B. Women of Korea: A Historical Overview

YUNG-CHUNG KIM (SUMMARIZED BY HUSO YI)

Women and Family

As in other agrarian societies, the large patriarchal, extended family was the basic organizational unit in Korea for many centuries, with relatively little change in its basic structure. The rule maintained in husband–wife relations was the rigid distinction drawn in their roles. Whereas the man dominated in public affairs, the woman took full responsibility in the family. The wife was responsible for the education of the children, especially girls up to the age of marriage. There were no educational institutions for girls, and the mother assumed the role of teacher. Her influence was not limited to her daughters' upbringing. She was often honored and rewarded for her model behavior and contribution when her husband or sons were successful in public life.

The woman also took an active part in the family economy. She was expected to be an able and careful manager of family finances. In case the husband was disabled and could not support the family or was neglectful of his duties, the wife had to be able to use her skills to provide for the family. Also, one of the wife's functions in the family system was the performance of rituals in ancestor worship. Filial piety was the prime virtue by which family lineage was preserved, and ancestor worship was its salient feature.

In traditional Korea, it was customary for the ruler and *yangban* (rural ruling-class males) to keep several wives. There was a clear distinction between the primary spouse and the secondary wife/wives or concubines who were at his caprice. In contrast, the woman was subject to strict chastity. When the husband died, ideally the wife must remain chaste the rest of her life; this was the virtuous conduct expected of widows. However, there was less prejudice against remarriage for women in the Koryo period than during either the United Shilla period or the Chosun dynasty. Customs concerning marriage were basic features of the social structure. Because a person's social position was determined by bloodline and family background, a marriage violating or risking such established convention was neither desirable nor acceptable.

The marriage celebration was an expensive one. Such expensive and elaborate feasting and entertainment at weddings (and funerals) were responsible for the ruin of many of the less-affluent *yangban* in the later years of the Chosun dynasty. As the proverb goes: "If a family has three daughters, the pillars of the house will fall." So the marriage expenditures remained a grave social problem throughout the Chosun dynasty, and even today this is true to a great extent.

The position of a woman, on the whole, depended on the status of her father, husband, or son. Women of the ruling class, either by birth or by marriage, could enjoy the same privileges of comfort and honor as men of the same class. Hence, the conduct of women was governed by the rule of three obediences: obedience to the father in childhood, to the husband during marriage, and to the son in old age. The systematic subjugation of women in Korea started during the early reigns of the Chosun dynasty within the aristocratic milieu. The Confucian government started to enact various legal measures harshly discriminatory against women. Remarriage of widowed women was strictly forbidden by law. This prohibition was enforced by disqualifying the sons and grandsons of remarried women from taking the government-service examination.

Social status and rights were transmitted only from fathers to sons. Whereas chastity was thus being forced upon women, men were allowed to expel their wives on any of seven grounds, the so-called seven evils (*ch'ilgo chiak*): disobeying parents-in-law, bearing no son, committing adultery, jealousy, carrying a hereditary disease, talkative to a fault, and larceny. However, even in cases where the wife was guilty of one of these seven evils, the husband could not divorce her if she had served three years mourning for her husband's parents, if the man had gone from poverty to wealth since marrying, or if the wife had no family to depend upon when divorced.

Surprisingly, however, according to the stipulations in the new Confucian code, male and female offspring were both entitled to inherit the father's property. Although there were certain discrepancies between the law and its application, it is important to note that an equal right to property inheritance was recognized by the law, as it was during the Koryo period prior to the Chosun dynasty.

Women "Professionals"

As pointed out earlier, because of firm adherence to the segregation of men and women, few women could engage in any form of activities outside the family compound. There were, however, some exceptions. Three special groups of women wielded considerable influence by performing certain public functions in traditional society. They were shamans, folk healers, and entertainers (*kisaeng*). The women who worked in these special jobs were, almost without exception, from lower-class families.

The mass culture of Korea since ancient times has been shamanistic in its basic character and tone. Records on female shamans first appeared during the early Shilla period. By that time, they had already outnumbered male shamans. The female shamans had three functions: as priests, as exorcists, and as diviners and fortunetellers.

The second group of women, the folk healers, were increasingly in demand during the Chosun dynasty. It was considered improper for a woman to be examined by a man even if he were a physician. When a woman healer was not available, women patients died because they refused to see male healers. It was, therefore, necessary for the government to train women in order for them to take care of female patients. Women healers could also have a law-enforcement role. When authorities needed to arrest a woman of the ruling class for some suspected crime, women healers from the lower class were called upon to act as policewomen.

The women entertainers (*kisaeng*) also belonged to the low social group. Because their occupation was to entertain men, they developed special talents and skills in poetry composition, singing, dancing, calligraphy, and painting. They were the few women who had free access to public events. For this reason, entertaining women most frequently appeared as heroines in ancient tales and novels. To romanticize the lives of the low-born women in these special cases would be wrong; however, compared to the secluded life of the court and *yangban* families, the lives of female shamans, healers, and *kisaeng* permitted them to have broader experiences and development of their talents.

Women in the Modern Era

It is hardly accurate to speak of education for women during the Chosun dynasty. Education had barely developed even for the majority of men beyond the local village schools. Because of the new emphasis on Confucianism, and the government-service examination system, formal education facilities and curricula were expanded during the Yi dynasty. Needless to say, women were excluded from these schools.

Following the signing of treaties with Japan, the United States, and European nations in the 1880s, a modern system of schooling was introduced by government officials and leaders who traveled abroad, and by foreign missionaries who were to play a decisive role in women's education. To be exact, school education for girls began in 1886, when a Methodist missionary founded Ewha Haktang. In spite of persistent resistance by Confucian conservatives to women's education, various women's organizations, individuals, and government leaders founded many schools for women by the government by the turn of the century. During the first decade of the twentieth century, numerous women's societies were organized for various purposes, including modernization and Westernization.

In 1910, following Japan's victory over imperial Russia in the Russo-Japanese war (1904-1905), Japan annexed Korea. Education was the most important method for carrying on the Japanese colonial policy in Korea. Japan hoped to assimilate Korea culturally as well as politically and economically. The discriminatory policy was even more noticeable in women's education, which was perhaps the least concern of the government during this period. No institution of higher education was founded for women by the government. The colonial policy exploited Koreans more than ever through a military draft and forced labor. Women too, were either sent to factories, into forced labor, or as "comfort women" at army camps. Women leaders could not keep their positions unless they pledged loyalty and obedience to Japan.

During the Japanese colonization, on the other hand, women were politically active in the independence movement. In 1913, a teacher at a girl's school in Pyongyang (now located in North Korea) formed an underground organization. Some of the members organized an underground society called the Patriotic Women's League. Some churchwomen were active in support of the independence movement. They collected funds for resistance fighters and succeeded in sending the money to the government-in-exile in Shanghai. Among the various women's organizations that sprang up in the first quarter of the twentieth century, the one that was most outstanding and had the most lasting effect was the Young Women's Christian Association (YWCA). Founded in 1922, this organization has continued, to the present, its activities that have helped promote women's status, social programs, participation, and volunteerism.

A review of the path of women through the centuries of Korean history reveals certain contrasting traits: on the one hand, a state of subjugation, and on the other, a state of self-reliance and full social participation. The differences between the modern era and the past are striking. Women's self-consciousness, buried deep in traditional society, was awakened with the coming of the enlightenment era. By the beginning of the twentieth century, women were participating in the drive for political emancipation, social justice, and equal rights. Korean women were confident in their stride and bold in their ambitions as they stepped into the new age.

C. Sociolegal Status of Males and Females
HYUNG KI CHOI AND COLLEAGUES (REDACTED BY HUSO YI)

In the early twentieth century, a new women's movement started to save Korea from foreign aggression. During the 1920s and 1930s, women's liberation became a key social issue, and some of the intellectuals, artists, and writers actually practiced liberal relationships. The social consensus of the time, however, was not quite ready to accept this phenomenon, and activist women usually ended their lives suffering for their efforts.

After the establishment of the Republic of Korea in 1948, a new Constitution stated the equality of all, including women and children. Other equalities were spelled out in the sectors of politics, economics, general society, and culture, but in actuality such equalities were not well maintained or protected. According to the annual report by the National Statistical Office (1999a), the majority of employed women are limited to part-time work, the opposite of the male employment pattern. The part-time jobs of women are usually low paying and involve blue-color-type work. In 1997, the average wage of women workers was only 59.9 percent of their male counterparts. As for participation in employed labor, the report indicates that in 1985, 72.3 percent of adult males were employed and 41.9 percent of the women. Twelve years later, in 1998, the data were 75.2 percent for men and 47.0 percent for women. [However, when the labor participation is divided by marital status, the report indicates as follows:

1. The percentage of single women working in 1985 was 50.8 percent, which decreased to 46.0 percent in 1998.
2. The percentage of working single men increased from 43.5 percent in 1985 to 48.5 percent in 1998.
3. The percentage of married working women rose from 41.0 percent in 1985 to 47.3 percent in 1998.
4. The percentage of married working men has been relatively stable between 1985 and 1998 (86.8 percent), dropping slightly from a little above 86.8 percent between 1990 and 1997.

Therefore, unmarried women are the only group in which the participation rate has not increased since 1985. (Huso Yi)]

Obviously, the labor participation rate of women has lagged far behind that of their male counterparts. Compared with statistics from developed countries, Korean women between ages 25 and 35 have an especially lower rate of labor participation. This is likely because of women in this age group being forced to choose their marital and childcare responsibilities over involvement in the workplace.

In terms of the educational status of women, as of 1995, women accounted for 34.8 percent of the total enrollment in high school and 13.1 percent of college and post-graduate educational attainment, compared to men, with 41.4 percent for high school and 25.6 percent for college and post-graduate enrollment. In addition, the serious gender imbalance in certain university departments continues to be a problem. The career consciousness of female students tends to be based on the division of societal gender roles. For example, in occupational choice, female students are accustomed to such traditional jobs as teaching and nursing, whereas male students prefer to become scientists and lawyers. [In response to new educational opportunities, the average age of marriage has been pushed later as the number of years women spend in school increases. In 1960, the average age at women's first marriage was 21.6 years old, whereas for men it was 25.4 years old, a difference of 3.8 years. In 1998, this increased to 26.2 years for women and 29.0 years for men, a difference of 2.8 years (National Statistical Office 1999a). (Huso Yi)]

[Meanwhile, after 1980, women began to use legal means to address and remove patriarchal structures and sex discrimination by new legislation, including the enactment of the Equal Employment Opportunity Act in 1987, the Mother–Child Welfare Act (supporting single mothers) in 1989, the Child Care Act (for support of working mothers) in 1991, and the 1993 Act Relating to Punishment of Sexual Violence and Protection of Victims, as well as the prevention of prostitution (for a review of current laws on Korean women, refer to Kim 1996). Another important issue in women's rights is the status and compensation of "comfort women" under Japanese colonialism (1910 to 1945). The Korean Council for Women Drafted into Military Sexual Slavery by Japan (2000), established in 1990, has made concerted efforts to solve the issue of comfort women and Japan's responsibilities for compensation. During World War II, women were sent to all combat areas and territories occupied by Japan. It is estimated that up to 200,000 women were drafted, of which approximately 80 percent were Korean women ranging from age 11 to 32. (Huso Yi)]

[Today, women's issues have become very important in national policy. Since 1994, the Korean Women's Development Institute (2000) has published *Women's Statistical Yearbook* in order to review and analyze the existing social statistics and indicators about the status of women in comprehensive and systemic ways. The women's social indicators system in the book is composed of 36 subareas, 98 detailed concerns, and 435 indicators under eight major categories: population, family/household, education, employment/economic activities, health, social welfare, social activities, and public safety. In February 1998, the Presidential Commission on Women's Affairs (2000), under the direct supervision of the President, was initiated to promote the status of women and expand women's participation in the public domain. (Huso Yi)]

D. Male Preference, Female Infanticide, and the Sex-Ratio Problem
HYUNG KI CHOI AND COLLEAGUES (REDACTED BY HUSO YI)

The influence of Neo-Confucianism has been generally strong since the Chosun era, and it is linked with a male preference in offspring. During this era, the most legitimate method to have children was within a marriage, which was also designed as a joint commitment between two families to produce an heir for the husband's family. Contrary to Confucianism, the traditional Buddhist belief was that all human beings are just transient creatures, prone to be reborn in another life. This resulted in a certain unselfishness and less emphasis on male preference. However, in the Chosun dynasty, the long-term success of the family became the most important goal in marriage. In the eyes of parents, a son will provide economical and emotional supports after his parents' retirement. After their death, he will be in charge of funeral and memorial services. Only a male can head a Korean family. Without a son, a Korean family ceases to be a family, which was an utmost disgrace to parents and ancestors. As the importance of a son increased, his social position became more important. The son had priority in the parents' assets, and in case of the father's early demise, the son oftentimes assumed the role of father in the family.

This pattern of male preference changed social manners and it continues to this day in Korea. However, in 1962, the government introduced a family planning program as part of a powerful economic plan. It encouraged small families with fewer children. With the phenomenal economic growth, the concept of children has changed from a workforce resource to an investment, which requires much time and money. As the average length of education increased dramatically, this burden has also become more prominent. Thus, the small family has become the main pattern.

Widespread abortions have helped to preserve small families in case of unwanted pregnancies. Furthermore, with the advancement of modern reproductive medicine, such as chorionic villi sampling, amniocentesis, and ultrasound scans, the ascertainment of fetal sex has become possible, and small families with an existing male preference have resorted to so-called selective abortion or female infanticide. This has created a sex-ratio imbalance, with 113.4 males born in 1995 for every 100 female babies, much higher than the world average of 106 to 100. This imbalance has been particularly drastic for the third child, where the ratio was 179.4 males for every 100 females. This trend of female infanticide is slowing somewhat, with a ratio of 108.4 to 100 for the first child in 1997 and 134.0 to 100 for the third child (see Table 1).

According to a survey by the Korean Institute for Health and Social Welfare (1991), 71.2 percent of married women between ages 15 and 49 replied that a son is required in the marriage. This trend is more evident in older women with lower education. The reason for this male preference was family succession for 42.2 percent of the women, a sense of security for 34.2 percent, a balanced family for 16.8 percent, and economic security after retirement for 6.8 percent of the women surveyed. In a study of 260 married women in Seoul (Kim 1993), the preferred sex for a second child after a son was 52.8 percent for a daughter and 20.5 percent for another son.

Table 1

Sex Rate at Birth by Birth Order (Males Born per 100 Females) by Year

Birth Order	1971	1981	1985	1991	1993	1995	1997	1998
Total	109.0	107.2	109.5	112.4	115.3	113.2	108.3	110.2
First	108.1	106.3	106.0	105.7	106.5	105.8	105.1	106.0
Second	107.7	106.7	107.8	112.5	114.7	111.7	106.3	108.1
Third	109.7	107.1	129.2	179.5	202.6	177.5	133.6	118.8
Fourth & Over	110.1	112.9	146.8	194.7	237.9	205.4	155.4	155.2

However, after an initial daughter, 83 percent wanted a son, and only 2.2 percent wanted a daughter. In a study of 1,546 married adults, 29.4 percent replied that a son is necessary, whereas 70.6 percent said a son is not a requirement (Chin et al. 1997). These results reveal an improving trend away from male preference compared to the 1991 survey. Still, the deep-seated preference continues for the next child to be a male, especially in families with daughters. Overall, the recent gender imbalance may be attributed to the easy societal acceptance of gender-selective abortion, a male-centered sexual culture in which the responsibility of contraceptive use primarily is attributed to women, and a deep-rooted patriarchal male preference (see Section 9, Contraception, Abortion, and Population Planning). [In their study, as for the question of "why a son is necessary," 43.5 percent claimed that a son is needed for the family succession, 39.3 percent wanted a boy and a girl, 5.8 percent said "daughters will be taken to husband's family," and 5.8 percent "wanted to be respected by the parents of husband." (As noted in Section 1B, Basic Sexological Premises, Women of Korea: A Historical Overview, one of the seven evils for a wife is not bearing a son.) For those who needed a son for family succession, when they were asked, "who most claimed the need of a son," 54.3 percent said the husband himself, 35.5 percent said his parents, and only 6.9 percent said the wife. (Huso Yi)]

[In the traditional idea of the Korean family system, it is said that when a woman gets married, she is no longer considered as a member of her family. This notion is indeed supported by the law of Head of Household. Thus, it should be noted that male preference is closely related to the family law that was initially established in the Chosun dynasty. First, when a woman marries, her name will be eliminated from her family register and transferred to her husband's family register. Not only ideologically, but also legally, married women are not members of their natal families. In addition, according to the law, married women cannot be the primary successor of the family inheritance. For example, when a husband, the first family head, is dead, the headship is inherited by his son or grandson. If a family does not have a male successor, the headship is taken by the family's unmarried daughter, not the wife. The wife is the third order for the headship. Even when a woman gets divorced, the headship still remains on the side of her ex-husband so that it is very difficult for women to head a family. In summary, when a daughter is married, she is "taken" to her husband's family and then has no right for headship and inheritance unless the will specifies her inheritance. If a woman gets divorced, her name can be re-listed in her family register. It is extremely difficult for divorced women to win custody. Another case is the family without a son. After the daughter(s) leave by marriage and her/their father is dead, the headship passes to the mother. But the problem occurs after the mother is dead. Since there is no one to have headship in the family, the family becomes officially extinct (Kim 1992; Chang 1996). Active movements have been organized to correct the law/system of family headship. Critics claim that the law is unconstitutional and violates human rights. A coalition has submitted a petition to the United Nations and, as of mid-2001, was preparing for an appeal to the Supreme Court (Headquarter of the Family Headship Law Abolition 2000; Citizens for Abolition of the Family Headship (*Hoju*) System 2000). (Huso Yi)]

[Such a legal system evokes bearing a son, "to be respected by the parents of husband." It is the most important obligation for married women to have a son. It is said, "A married woman should gift a son to her husband's parents." In that case, it is likely that son is regarded as a "property," as well as the source for family linkage survival. In the Chosun dynasty, if a married woman could not have a son, her husband would adopt a surrogate for a son. These days, it might be happening, but more frequently, women get abortions until they have a son. It is the fidelity and duty of married women to the husband's family. Once women "accomplish" this role, they are "accepted" and "respected" (Huso Yi)]

[Selective abortion is not the only avenue to male preference. In Oriental medicine, there are treatments and pills for son-bearing. In a survey of 203 Oriental medical doctors by *Hankyere* (1996), 34 percent said that they learned in medical school about the treatment for son-bearing, whereas only 6 percent learned about the daughter-bearing treatment in school. Ninety percent of their patients asked for medications for son-bearing and 60 percent of the doctors prescribed it for them. Despite popular prescriptions and treatment, 45 percent of the doctors did not believe in their reliability and effectiveness. No clinical study has been reported about the medications. Another interesting finding was that 51 percent said that sex is determined when fertilization occurs and 49 percent said sex determination is later, around 3 months. It is believed in Oriental medicine that the third month of pregnancy is the time of sex determination, so that sex can be changed by treatment. (Huso Yi)]

E. General Concepts of Sexuality and Love   HUSO YI AND KI-NAM CHIN

Cultural Taboos

Parallel with family succession in Confucian sexual values is "purity of kinship." "Purity of kinship" includes not only the prohibitions of interracial and interclass marriages, but also a third, particularly Korean, prohibition against marriage between persons with the same last names. [In the legal system, this prohibition is quite complicated. For our purposes here, it is sufficient to note the system of Korean kinship. According the Committee of Korean Genealogy (2000), there are 254 surnames from 13 out of 14 Korean alphabets. The official report by the National Statistical Office (NSO 1985) revealed that, among 275 surnames, each of 44 surnames was reported by less than 100 people. As of the 1985 population of 40,410,000 people, 5 surnames were reported by more than one million: 8,780,000 were owned by those who had the last name of Kim, 5,980,000 of Lee (or Yi or Rhee), 3,400,000 of Park, 1,910,000 of Choi (or Choy), and 1,780,000 of Chung (or Jung). (Note: there is no official romanization for Korean as in other languages, hence the alternate spellings.) Thus, 54 percent of the population had one of those five surnames. (The NSO recently finished another investigation in 2000, which will be published in September, 2001). It should be noted that the surname, however, is categorized by three criteria: (1) ancestor, (2) place of family origin, and (3) letter of surname (surname). For instance, although two Korean people have the same surname, they may have a different ancestor and/or place of family origin. Because the ancestor is hard to detect without genealogy, Koreans usually refer to two components, place of family origin and surname. In fact, no official classification for the place of family origin exists. Every genealogical archive shows different numbers. (According to the Committee of Genealogy, one archive reports 499 family origin places for Kim, whereas another notes 600, and others note 623. As for Lee (Yi, Rhee), in the census, only surname and origin is asked because of the incorrectness of the origin of ancestor. (Huso Yi)]

[Korean genealogy started early in the Shilla dynasty, but only people of royal class could have their surnames. In the Koryo dynasty, ordinary people started to have surnames with the place of family origin. At the time, because they made their family origin based on the current living places, it is not unusual to have the same surnames regardless of the origin of the ancestor. Thus, in the early Chosun dynasty, people paid more attention to the place of family origin rather than the letter of surname when married. But, later in the mid-Chosun dynasty, marriage within the same surname and place of family origin was prohibited by the law, which has existed to now (Chung 1998). Today, the law enforces a prohibition of marriage within the same surname and place of family origin in the eighth degree. In a sense, a marriage within the same surname and family origin is constituted as incest, which therefore can violate the purity of kinship. Some family clans even prohibit marriage only within the same surname. The law has been criticized for a long time because of its unrealistic aspects. First, it has nothing to do with the matter of family purity or incest unless it happens within blood relatives. Second, the place of family origin is not always correct, and furthermore, the fact that two have the same family origin does not tell the status of their kinship in all senses. For example, two peoples who have the same name and whose family came originally from the same city do not always indicate whether or not they are close relatives. Third, it is a reality that many who have same name and family origin get married, and, because of this fact, a specific period is granted for such married couples to get a marriage license. (Huso Yi)]

Since the Chosun dynasty, these reproduction-oriented sexual norms have traditionally surrounded sexual acts with a total secrecy. This secrecy remains dominant, within marriage, in the family, and in public. [However, this secrecy is no longer an absolute and universal factor inhibiting communications about any and all sexual issues in Korea today. Modern currents of sexual liberation, and global communications about sexual topics via the Internet and World Wide Web are reducing the traditional secrecy surrounding sexuality in Korean culture. As of the end of December, 2000, the Ministry of Information and Communication reported that the number of Korean Internet users topped 19 million (Korean Government Homepage 2000). Another study by NetValue also reported that Korean Internet users spent 18.1 hours a month online, on average, more than any of the other 12 nations, including Hong Kong (the second at 12.1 hours/month), the U.S. (at 10.8 hours/month), and Singapore (at 9.9 hours/month) (*Korea Herald* 2001). It is not difficult to assume how much the Internet will have an impact upon the lives and sexuality of Koreans. (On the very same day, the Seoul District Prosecutor's Office launched an investigation into adult Internet sites and arrested six Internet adult TV-station operators; the office announced that "we can no longer tolerate the Internet TV's overheated competition by broadcasting lots of lewd programs," and expanded the investigation to all forty Internet adult TV stations (Kim 2001) (Huso Yi)]

Nevertheless, Confucian taboos continue to hinder institutional sexuality education programs, as well as discussions about sexuality within the family. Korean children grow up with a belief that ignorance of sex is good; they are still encouraged not to talk about sexuality. During childhood, they learn negative attitudes about sexuality, which during adolescence, because of their natural curiosity about sex, often turns into irresponsible sexual activities. [In a nation–state study with 2,243 adolescents, 67.2 percent reported sexual violence in the middle/high school, and regarding the question of asking about potential sexual violence, 75.6 percent of the male adolescents and 23.9 percent of the females reported that they felt impulsive and had a terrible desire of experiencing "violent sexual activities" in middle/high school ($p < .001$) (Chung 1990). This negative view of sexuality is also related to the prevalence of verbal and physical sexual domestic violence in Korea (see Section 8, Significant Unconventional Sexual Behaviors) (Huso Yi)]

The Double Standard in Sexual Culture

The most outstanding aspect of sexual culture in male-dominant Confucianism is the different standards of sexual morality for men and women. Such ethical codes are formulated by stressing virginity for women. According to Confucianism, the woman is always placed lower than the man. The husband is compared to the sky and wife is depicted as the ground and, therefore, she is obedient to the husband (see *Woman's Four Book* by King Young-Jo, 1736/1987). [*Woman's Four Book* was originally written by Chinese scholars. King Young-Jo imported and translated the book to correct the morals of women. In his introduction, he began with the metaphor, "Man is the sky and woman is the ground." Besides that dictum, many rules of obedience are described for women. For example, the title of the first chapter is, "The chapter of low and weak status," which implied women. The chapter begins: "The sky is high, the ground is low and *yang* is strong, *yin* is weak. The lowness and weakness is women's destiny. If the woman wants to be strong on her own, it violates the law of justice." (Huso Yi)]

Under the ideology of the gender hierarchy, the moral superiority of the upper class and family purity, and the Chosun dynasty Constitution of 1485, women of the ruling class were prohibited from remarriage after the death of their husband. If a widow was recognized as a moral model, gracious grants were allowed for her entire family. By the end of Chosun era, the control of female virginity and fidelity had been firmly established, widely promoted by books about female domestic education. Contemporary Korean attitudes towards virginity are based on these historical events. To maintain the purity of one's family lineage, female virginity and sexual fidelity were and still are stressed for women, whereas men were and still are generously allowed the varieties of prostitution, polygyny, and other forms of sexual explorations.

The Phallus-Centered Sexual Culture

The male-dominant sexual culture of Korea has been very phallic oriented. Because the male sex is considered sexually superior to the female sex, sexual intercourse is not perceived of as a mutually intimate interpersonal relationship. Rather, it is perceived as a physiological or primitive event, a kind of tension release for the male. In this view, only the phallus is worth consideration. Thus, the entire Korean sexual culture exists for satisfying the male's sexual needs, downplaying the mental and intimate relationship between partners. Women are raised to passively play up to this male-dominant action, and those who are more obedient and passive are encouraged. Men, on the contrary, are portrayed and raised as strong, aggressive, and dominating figures, and this concept is carried into everyday sexual and marital relationships. Because this sexual discrimination is regarded as natural, intimate relationships between men and women are seriously distorted.

[The Korean metaphoric/ideological description of the phallus-centered sexual culture that one finds in Korea has interesting ritual expressions in the traditional phallus-worship ceremonies of Japanese Shintoism and *lingam* and *yoni* worship in Hinduism (Gregersen 1994:232, 355). In Korea, the phallus is literally called "male-root" and the vulva "female-root." Although many phallic stones were destroyed during Japan's colonization and the subsequent modernization, 840 stones and wooden objects have been discovered so far (Kim & Yoon 1997). Those that are made of wood are placed in the temple or hung on the ceiling of a household. (The size and shape of the wooden phalluses are just like modern sex toys). Oh (1997) analyzed 45 historical remains that are preserved for "sexual worship": 26 stones are categorized as being used in prayers for a son, 9 for protecting the village, 5 for preventing a women's promiscuity, 3 for family well-being, and 2 for cultivation. These stones convey a male preference. However, many vulva-shaped stones can be easily found next to phallic stones in a *ying-yang* context or separately. These vulval stones, as well as vulval fountains, are also worshiped, as are phallic stones. Vulval fountains are not only natural ones, but some that are designed on purpose. In order to be pregnant with a son, women not only pray in front of the stone, but also rub their genital areas on it. Many interesting worship ceremonies are still held all over the country. For instance, in a fishing village, fishermen have for hundreds of years carved wooden phalluses and offered them to a legendary virgin of the temple twice a year. It is believed that the virgin died in the ocean longing for sex, so the villagers believe that they should appease the virgin ghost in the ocean with wooden phalluses to avoid any misfortune and accidents. (Huso Yi)]

2. Religious and Ethnic Factors Affecting Sexuality

A. Source and Character of Religious Values
HYUNG KI CHOI AND COLLEAGUES (REDACTED BY HUSO YI)

[As already noted, Korea has developed and adopted several new religions that have molded its sexual values, family structure, concepts of love, and gender roles, both in public and the private space. The ancient shamanistic religion and warrior aristocracy encountered a new religious influence two thousand years ago in Confucianism. Buddhism arrived in Korea around 400 C.E. and was actively persecuted for a hundred years. At the end of the Koryo era around 1400, Neo-Confucianism reversed the previous sex-positive attitudes in Buddhism. In the late 1700s, Catholicism arrived from Europe, followed a century later by Protestantism. Today, 49 percent of South Koreans are Christians and 47 percent are Buddhists. Although only 3 percent of Koreans believe in Confucianism, it remains the basis of criminal law and sexual morals. (Huso Yi)]

Confucianism

Confucianism was first introduced into Korea in the era of the Three Kingdom unification. The Unified Kingdom of Shilla was successful in blending the different lifestyles and cultures from the other two original kingdoms, and also was eager to accept the advanced cultures of mainland China. A new and unique cultural unification took place on the Korean peninsula, and one of the most important advancements was Confucianism. In this new era, the political idea of Confucianism, which stresses loyalty to authorities, was a convenient justification for the totalitarian rule of the kings. In the succeeding Koryo era, Confucianism continued to be the main ideological basis for the kingdom. Its beliefs were accepted as an efficient ideology supportive of the king and the ruling class. This is why, even though its official adherents are few in number in Korea, it has remained a major social influence. This practical social application is also the reason that Confucianism has flourished in the Far East.

Respected scholars were recruited to serve as high-ranking government officers, and all ceremonies and record keeping was modeled on the Confucian system. The government set up a learning center to sponsor further research and discussion of Confucianism. The kings and other nobles tried to practice the Confucian way of life in both their personal and public lives. One important aspect of Confucianism in the Koryo period 600 years ago is that it did not consider Buddhism as a hostile belief to Confucianism. The people of Koryo considered Buddhism as a personal religion for souls, and Confucianism as a bible for everyday human social lives. They respected both beliefs until the end of the Koryo era, when

Buddhism became lavish and selfish. Orthodox followers of Confucianism then rejected Buddhism altogether, banning new recruits and halting financial support to the Buddhist temples. Confucianism was greatly appreciated by the reforming sect of the ruling class, which made it the official belief of the Chosun dynasty. It was the guideline of politics, society, and culture, encompassing all facets of everyday life. This marked the end of a thousand years of Buddhist public influence in Korean culture and the return of Confucianism in a Neo-Confucian form employing negativity against sexuality (Fellows 1979:199-241; Noss & Noss 1990:283-318).

Confucian belief regards the male as a positive being (*yang*) and the female as a negative counterpart (*ying*), based on the concept that the biological differences of the two sexes actually stem from a basic element of nature. Confucianism stresses the harmonious relationship of *yang* and *ying*, but *yang* is always more dominant than *ying* in every aspect. Thus, men are considered omnipotent compared to women, and male dominance and discrimination against women are justified. Furthermore, the Confucian way of life regards sex is an inevitable aspect needed to maintain the family and society, rather than an act of pleasure. Thus, in the Chosun era, sex was first considered as a reproductive process. The Chosun period is also known for its strict caste system, based on the Confucian theory that higher and ruling classes should be morally superior to the subjecting classes. Male preference and a double moral standard in sexual matters are only a few examples of this varied Confucian past (Fellows 1979:199-241; Noss & Noss 1990:283-318). [In addition, it should be noted that these ideologies in Confucianism have been challenged by feminism since 1990, and are having an impact on changing the laws discriminating against the status of women and individuals' lifestyles (Huso Yi)]

Buddhism

Buddhism was first introduced to Korea in the year 372 C.E. during the Three Kingdom period in which it was adopted and encouraged as the new faith by the royal court. Traditional shamanism and conservative nobles opposed Buddhism for 100 years after its initial introduction, but in all three Kingdoms it was accepted by the sponsorship of royal endorsement. In the totalitarian kingdoms, Buddhism was a practical new faith helping to unify the common people. The people considered themselves subjects of both Buddha and the king, and this helped to unify the young kingdoms. The three kings and their royal courts gave generous contributions and slaves to the Buddhist temples to support cultivation of the land. Buddhism in this era was a tool to deepen the philosophical aspects of the people, and the monks were both scholars of learning and teachers (Fellows 1979:129-194; Noss & Noss 1990:157-231).

After the unification of the three kingdoms, Buddhism received more attention internationally by preaching abroad. However, the lavish construction of temples wasted resources, which became one of the reasons of the demise of the unified kingdom of Shilla. In the Koryo era, Buddhism still played a major role as the main religious belief of the kingdom. The monks of the Buddhist temples were exempt from military conscription and service, and even princes became monks in this era. This gave Buddhism a flavor of nobility, but toward the end of the Koryo dynasty, the powers of the Buddhist temples and monks became excessive, and power shifted back to Confucianism. During the Neo-Confucian Chosun period, the monks were subjected to harsh rules, including closure of major temples, seclusion in the mountains, forced labor, and heavy taxes. The social position of Buddhist monks was lowered substantially. Buddhism in this era shifted its base to the poor and unfortunate. Despite this oppression and decline in public image, 47 percent of Korean people still consider Buddhism as their faith. Buddhists in general are instructed to give up all desires, including those related to sex, and sexual activities are prohibited in many sects.

Catholicism and Protestantism

During the mid-Chosun dynasty at the end of the seventeenth century, a Korean scholar introduced a Catholic publication, marking the first recorded evidence of Christianity in Korea. Other books about Christianity followed and naturally became the subject of academic interest. Because Catholic belief differed so from the realistic beliefs of Confucianism, Catholic belief was initially considered similar to Buddhism, and so drew only academic attention and interest.

Towards the end of the eighteenth century, Christianity began to win over increasing numbers of the common people, mostly in the northern provinces near the Chinese border. Catholicism in Korea is unique in the fact that it was not initially introduced by priests, but rather through books imported by scholars and then self-propagated among the common people. Catholicism did not acknowledge the caste system, and thus was considered by the authorities as a threat to the society. Catholic worshipers also neglected the responsibility to conduct memorial services for one's ancestors, which was considered one of the most important elements in Koreans' everyday lives. Soon Catholicism was considered illegal and officially banned. Harsh punishments were given to the worshipers. The Chosun government also prohibited the importing of any Catholic book. Around 1801, some 300 Catholic worshipers, including a priest, were executed. A Korean informer notified the archbishop in Peking and called for a military demonstration by Western powers to stop this repression. This incident only aggravated the religious oppression of Catholics, and by 1839, three Western priests had been executed along with 80 more believers. However, Catholicism gained an underground popularity, so that by 1865, there were more than 23,000 Korean Catholics, with their own Catholic school.

The increasing popularity of Catholicism was in part attributed to the extremely corrupt period of the nineteenth-century Chosun. After the beginning of formal diplomatic relationships with France in 1887, freedom of religion was finally guaranteed in Chosun and an official Catholic Church was established in Seoul. Missionaries quickly set up Catholic parishes and became involved in publishing numerous books.

Protestantism was first introduced into Korea in 1884 by an American Presbyterian missionary named Dr. Horace N. Allen. In the next year, Dr. Horace G. Underwood (Presbyterian) and Rev. Henry G. Appenzeller

(Methodist) arrived in Korea. They started by concentrating on offering practical knowledge on health, medicine, and general education to the poorer segments of the general public. Preaching followed. The Protestant belief of equality and freedom directly confronted traditional Confucianism, and became, as it spread, the foundation of a democratic movement. The Young Men's Christian Association (YMCA) was first established in 1903 in Korea and brought with it initiatives on reforming various aspects of everyday lives, including the prohibition of alcohol, abstinence from smoking, and equal rights. In 1915, the Chosun Christian College was founded, chiefly through the efforts of Dr. H. G. Underwood, the pioneering Protestant missionary who served as the Chosun Christian College's first president. During the Japanese occupation in the early twentieth century, the Protestant churches and schools became a secret stronghold for the independence movement. It is no wonder that many of prominent leaders in this era were Protestants. Both Catholics and Protestants are currently actively involved in medicine, education, and various social movements. (As noted earlier, 49 percent of Koreans are Protestant or Catholic.)

B. Character of Ethnic Values   HUSO YI

Korea is a very homogenous country in terms of ethnicity. Until recently, it was so and it is still rare for many Koreans to have close contact with other ethnic groups. Historically, when the neighboring countries, China and Japan, began to open their borders to Western culture in the late nineteenth century, Korea remained closed to trade with Western countries. Opening to trade with the West might lead to colonization by Japan or by Western nations, as happened with the British in Hong Kong and the Portuguese in Macau. Another reason for this policy of seclusion may be the size of Korea and its geographical location: a small country surrounded by China and Japan. The lack of contact with other cultures naturally restricted the acceptance of various sexual attitudes and behaviors from the outside. In recent years, the influence of globalization and the immigration of foreign laborers have challenged Korea's homogenous character and traditional isolation.

3. Sexual Knowledge and Education

A. Historical Perspective   HYUNG KI CHOI AND COLLEAGUES

Unmarried young men and women in the Chosun dynasty received a very limited form of sexuality education, focused on how to achieve pregnancy and produce better descendants. The most important lesson was instruction on how to select the right time, as well as the best position and behaviors, for achieving pregnancy. When newlyweds started their honeymoon, the bride received a calendar with information about the fertile time. In many instances, husbands were also given this information. In some traditional extended families, married sons were not allowed to sleep in the same room with their wife unless the family patriarch approved, based on the wife's fertile period. Delivering a child was an important, often-sacred event in the Confucian Chosun family. Prenatal care was a mandatory obligation for pregnant couples and was dutifully accepted by all expectant parents. This prenatal care began even before conception and was the focus of sexuality education when taught in the elementary schools.

B. Government Policies and Programs
HYUNG KI CHOI AND COLLEAGUES (REDACTED BY HUSO YI)

The traditional silence of Korean society on sexuality issues and education has left its adolescents almost completely without guidance in dealing with the imported Western sexual cultures. This trend is accelerating with the fast pace of modernization, and the consequences can be observed in the increasing incidence of adolescent pregnancies, sexual abuse, and sexual crimes. The Planned Parenthood Federation of Korea (PPFK) started sexuality education in 1968. Since 1982, counseling centers for sexuality has been provided for adolescents in schools and industrial parks. Besides education and counseling, PPFK has published annual reports on counseling cases and educational projects to help understand adolescent sexuality.

In spite of such efforts and the obvious needs, formal sexuality education in schools has not been well established. What sexuality education exists in schools focuses solely on physical development and gender roles. For female students, the topics of menstruation, pregnancy, and virginity are the main content, whereas male students are taught about sexual transmitted disease and sexual activities. It is assumed that male students are sexually active but female students should not be. Research in the 1990s has noted the limitations and problems of the existing sexuality education in schools. For example, research by Lee (1996) reported that only 5.5 percent of students were satisfied with their school sexuality education program. [In 1996, the Korean Government established the Korea Research Institute for Culture and Sexuality to develop effective sexuality education programs. Government policies, as stated in the Sex Education in the Adolescent Youth Protection Law, state that information and materials on homosexuality are illegal. The policies are based on homosexuals being sexually abstinent and denying themselves any sexual relationships, especially in adolescence. The policies also questioned whether homosexuality should be considered as a part of sexuality education program. (Huso Yi)]

C. Informal Sources of Sexual Knowledge
HYUNG KI CHOI AND COLLEAGUES (REDACTED BY HUSO YI)

In the early 1990s, interest in sexual information increased enormously. Since then, books as well as other materials on sexuality have been produced. To meet academic interest, conferences on sexuality have been held and the mass media has taken up sexuality topics. In 1998, a public sexual education program was offered on television, and the instructor became a celebrity. It is now relatively easy to access information on sexuality.

In two studies by the Korean Research Institute on Sexuality and Culture (Kim et al. 1996, 1997), 37.1 percent of 1,976 male high school students reported that their primary source of sexual knowledge was adult materials and pornography. Fourteen percent of the males learned from their friends, whereas 37 percent of 3,134 female high school students obtained sexual knowledge from their peers, and 25.7 percent learned in school. The percentages were lower for students in the upper grades. These results show an increase in the influence of sexuality education programs in school. The study also tested sexual knowledge. Some examples of the kinds of questions asked include: "The hymen can tear during bicycle or horse riding," "The testis produces blood along with semen," "Kissing can induce fertilization in healthy couples," "Pregnancy stops periodic menstruation," "The sex of a fetus is determined at birth," "Douching immediately after intercourse prevents fertilization," "Condom use lowers risk of contacting STDs," and "Masturbation is not associated with transmission of AIDS." The mean score of the correct answers was 62 for female students and 65 for males. For the questions about STDs, the mean score was 53. The results reflected the current need for more effective sexuality education in Korean adolescents.

4. Autoerotic Behaviors and Patterns

A. Children and Adolescents   HUSO YI

The Korean Research Institute of Sexuality and Culture (Kim et al. 1997) reported that 70 percent of female high school students agreed that "masturbation is natural to release sexual desire." In contrast with their positive attitudes, however, only 15.2 percent of the survey participants had experienced masturbation. For those who had masturbated, the frequency of masturbation was once a month (44.2 percent), two to four times per month (23.1 percent), and five to seven times per month (5 percent). With respect to self-reported feelings after masturbation, 35.6 percent felt guilty, 21.0 percent felt nothing, and 6.3 percent felt good. When asked about their response to a sexual urge, 41.9 percent "just endured," 10.5 percent exercised and/or engaged in favorite habits, 6.2 percent masturbated for relief, and 35.7 percent answered they had no experience of sexual urges. Meanwhile, 49.9 percent of male high school students reported masturbating, whereas 46.3 percent endured the sexual urge. There was a significant gender difference in masturbation.

B. Adults   HUSO YI

Yoo, Oh, and Soh (1990) asked about parents' attitudes toward masturbation to see their relationship to their children's masturbation. In 75.2 percent of the parents showing positive attitudes toward their own masturbation, there was a linear trend by age: 77.8 percent in the parents in their 50s, 75.9 percent in their 40s, and 56.1 percent in their 30s. In terms of religious adherence, Buddhists were least positive about masturbation, 54.5 percent, compared with Protestants, 76.9 percent, and Catholics, 91.7 percent. In terms of negative views toward their own masturbation, more than 60 percent of the male and female respondents said, "It is against moral standards." The second reason showed a significant gender difference: 25.0 percent of the males answered, "It's harmful to sexual activity," whereas 12.5 percent of the females offered a religious reason, saying that "it evokes guilty feeling." Certainly, their attitude on masturbation was related to that of their children's masturbation. Those who feel good about their own masturbation showed positive attitudes toward their children's masturbation as well. Meanwhile, their reasons also revealed a significant gender difference. Half of the parents said children's masturbation is good because it shows "good evidence of physical development." But, in terms of gender difference, masturbation is a "unique method of resolution of sexual tension," answered by 13. 6 percent of the males and 33.3 percent of the females, a "relief of physical tension" by 4.5 percent of the males and 13.3 percent of the females, and a "relief of psychological tension" by 11.4 percent of the males and 2.2 percent of the females.

5. Interpersonal Heterosexual Behaviors

A. Children

Male Circumcision   ROBERT T. FRANCOEUR AND HUSO YI

In 1945, after World War II, very few South Koreans knew there was such a thing as a "naked penis," a penis with no foreskin. Male circumcision was practiced only within the tiny Jewish and Muslim enclaves. Nationwide, fewer than one in a thousand South Korean boys were circumcised, and circumcision was equally unknown in neighboring China and Japan. In Asia, only the Filipinos embraced circumcision, or at least the Spanish version, which involves cutting a slit in the top of the foreskin rather that removing the foreskin altogether. Around the world, 50 years ago, only about 15 percent of boys were circumcised at birth or puberty. Only one "developed nation" stood out as a champion of circumcision and that was the United States, where 90 percent of newborn sons were circumcised. When American soldiers arrived in Korea to implement the United Nations trusteeship (1945-1948) and returned in even greater numbers to South Korea during the Korean War (1950-1953), South Koreans came to believe that practicing circumcision was "advanced and modern."

In the 1960s, South Koreans adopted circumcision with a passion, but also with some differences. Whereas Americans circumcise their sons soon after birth, South Korean physicians decided it was much healthier to circumcise their sons at puberty, when they were 12 years old and could understand the importance of leaving their childhood behind and becoming a man. Unlike most American circumcisers, who until recently used no anesthesia as they operated on the newborn boy, South Korean circumcisers use a local anesthesia. In the 1960s, Korean doctors and advice columnists launched a campaign in newspapers and magazines urging parents to have their adolescent sons circumcised during the long winter break before a boy enters middle school. Infections, the Korean doctors say, are much less likely if circumcision is done in the winter rather than in the summer.

Another reason Korean doctors cite in recommending circumcision is their claim that South Korean men have a gene that causes penile phimosis or "abundant foreskin." In their view, at least 90 percent of Korean men have "too much" foreskin. Strangely, there is no evidence of this alleged genotype for phimosis among South Koreans, where a 1971 study of men aged 19 to 31 entering military service found only 5 percent to be circumcised and fewer than 1 percent of uncircumcised men with phimosis (Jung 1971). The incidence of phimosis is similar to that in the rest of the world. At the same time, Kim, Lee, and Pang (1999) found that most physicians could not define phimosis, yet almost all of South Korean physicians recommend universal circumcision because they believe it eliminates tight foreskins and brings many benefits. Circumcision, they wrongly claim, makes for harder penises, eliminates the bad smell of the penis, reduces susceptibility to various sexually transmitted diseases, cures premature ejaculation, and prevents penile and cervical cancer. Finally, there is the irresistible claim that circumcision produces a definite "cure-all-aphrodisiac effect" in the penis.

Those who were not circumcised believed that they were "naturally circumcised." The common word for "natural circumcision" may be difficult to understand in other countries. But, it is a very popular Korean term, which refers one of the followings: 1. not having phimosis; 2. relatively short prepuce; 3. fully retractable when penis gets erected; and 4. the penis looks more or less the same when erect. Considering the same low rate of phimosis, the uncircumcised men also think circumcision is mandatory, but they feel "naturally circumcised" (Kim et al. 1999). The researchers noted, "nearly all textbooks, encyclopedias, and newspaper articles [in South Korea] essentially advocate universal or near-universal circumcision, and the debate is about when to be circumcised or to circumcise, rather than whether to be circumcised."

For unknown reasons deeply rooted in their ethos, South Korean doctors misinterpret the recent decrease in American parents circumcising their newborn sons—down to 59 percent in 1992—as recommending universal circumcision at about age 12, even though there is absolutely no evidence that American boys are now being circumcised at puberty. The doctors are also puzzled why such "advanced" countries as Japan and Denmark do not recommend universal circumcision. One advice columnist recently wrote that, "If a child feels different because he is not circumcised and his friends boast of having a superior penis because of circumcision, it is good to have him circumcised for psychological reasons." Today, at least 95 percent of South Korean boys entering middle school have had been circumcised. For the other five percent, the question is not whether they should give up their foreskin, but when they should be circumcised. Korean boys simply take circumcision for granted. It is their right of passage to manhood.

B. Adolescents   HYUNG KI CHOI AND COLLEAGUES (REDACTED BY HUSO YI)

Overall, adolescents perceive heterosexual relationships in a positive way. Research with adolescents indicates that 39.3 to 64.1 percent of the participants have had heterosexual relationships.

The main reason adolescents gave for engaging in heterosexual relationships was curiosity about the opposite gender. According to a study among female high school students (Kim et al. 1997), 44.4 percent had had heterosexual relationships. Of those who had not had vaginal intercourse, 47.8 percent reported that they just had not had the opportunity, 18.3 percent did not want to because "we are students," and 15.5 percent were not interested in the opposite gender. These results suggest that, if the opportunity offered itself, heterosexual relationships would be increased. With regard to a question about what sexual intimacies are permissible for unmarried adolescents, 44.7 percent regarded light kissing as permissible, 31.6 percent accepted holding hands, 19.7 percent regarded kissing and petting as acceptable, and only 1.4 percent found sexual intercourse acceptable. The results indicated that female students still wanted to keep their virginity although their attitudes toward sexuality became more open and liberal. In the study, 88.1 percent of the female students reported that virginity should be kept until marriage, whereas 65.7 percent of males favored premarital sexual activity. [In their study, 91.7 percent had no coital experience, and only 7.5 percent had coital experiences. Among those who had coital experiences, 38.7 percent were coerced into having sex, 32.3 percent had sex "because of love," and 11.9 percent were raped. In the study of male students, of the 16.2 percent who had had coital experiences, 74.7 percent had had sex with a girlfriend, 34.1 percent had had intercourse with a woman they "happened to meet," and 16.6 percent had done so with prostitutes (Kim et al. 1996). (Huso Yi)]

Most of adolescents held conservative views of sexual experiences. The study also noted a difference in contraceptive use between males and females; 20.4 percent of female students used contraceptive methods and 52.2 percent of males used them (Kim et al. 1996; Kim et al. 1997). The most frequent contraceptive method was condom use (37.5 percent of the females and 49.1 percent of the males). [The next most frequent "contraceptive" method was withdrawal prior to ejaculation (33.3 percent of the females and 31.1 percent of the males (Huso Yi)] The low percentage of contraceptive usage may come from male partners' ignorance of condom use and/or the lack of opportunity (power) for that. Females have less opportunity to make decisions.

The Korean Sexuality Counseling Center (1997) for adolescents reported that most calls, 86.1 percent, were from boys. One in five boys, 20.6 percent, had questions about masturbation and 16.7 percent asked about sexual impulses. The callers were most curious about physical contacts with the other sex (50.2 percent), followed by pregnancy and delivery (17.4 percent). Boys tended to show self-centered, male-egoistic attitudes about the other sex, whereas girls focused on their responses and passive behaviors. The most frequent concern of high school girls, 31.6 percent, was boyfriends, followed by pregnancy, 12.4 percent, and abortion, 4.9 percent. This reflects passive attitudes about sex on the part of Korean females. The girls usually consulted with their friends, 44.5 percent, or with professional counselors, 33.6 percent. Parents and siblings were less frequently consulted, 12.2 percent and 4.1 percent, respectively. However, only 1.1 percent of girls considered their own schoolteachers as trustworthy consultants. A similar trend was seen with high school boys: 53.5 percent wanted to consult with their friends, but only a few were willing or wanted to share their sexual problems with parents (5.7 percent), siblings (5.1 percent), or teachers (1.5 percent). There is a substantial communication barrier between high school students and their parents and teachers, attributable to strong emotional barriers on both sides, which impede sincere discussion.

[Youn's (1996) study with 849 adolescents revealed similar results that 9.8 percent of the female respondents had coital experiences while 22.9

percent of the males had it. However, the study revealed significant gender difference in sexual experiences. The male respondents reported the maximum number of sex partners, ranging between 25 and 40 partners, whereas the highest number for the females was 6. The average number of coital partners for the males steadily increased by grade, but the number of females' coital partners did not, as Table 2 shows. This may be because of the value of keeping virginity as a treasure to be maintained until marriage and a sort of sexual explosion in the first college year (grade thirteen). With respect to the question of practicing safer sex, 43 percent of the sexually active male adolescents had used contraceptive methods at least once, whereas 28 percent of the females had done so. But, only 7 percent of the respondents used contraceptives consistently. (Huso Yi)]

Table 2

Korean Adolescents Who Experienced Sexual Intercourse by Year in School

Grade	Males			Females			Combined		
	%	n	/ N	%	n	/ N	%	n	/ N
11	14.6	25	/ 171	8.1	7	/ 86	12.5	32	/ 257
12	16.6	38	/ 229	7.8	10	/ 129	13.4	48	/ 358
13	16.5	51	/ 309	10.5	28	/ 267	13.7	79	/ 576
14	21.0	87	/ 415	9.5	37	/ 388	15.4	124	/ 803
15	22.4	99	/ 441	9.3	37	/ 398	16.2	136	/ 839
16	22.9	103	/ 449	9.8	39	/ 440	16.7	142	/ 849

Source: Youn 1996

C. Adults
HUSO YI AND HYUNG KI CHOI AND COLLEAGUES

Premarital Relations, Courtship, and Dating
HUSO YI

In 1991, the Women's Studies Center of Ewha Woman's University surveyed 352 male participants ranging in age from 20 to 40, which indicated that over 80 percent had had heterosexual experiences, and among those, 44.7 percent had their first sexual experiences with a female prostitute, 55.4 percent answered that prostitution should allowed to prevent rape, and 25.6 percent were in favor of the legal regulation of prostitution (Chin et al. 1997).

A study of 1,596 married couples reported that 50.8 percent regarded premarital relations as negative and 36 percent as positive; 75 percent regarded extramarital affairs negatively and 13.2 percent as something positive (Chin et al. 1997). In their study, the responses of male and female participants showed significant differences. Females, and those who were younger, more educated, and had no religious affiliation, held more positive attitudes toward premarital and extramarital relations. An interesting factor was the participants' ambivalence. Around 80 percent were concerned about what they viewed as the current open and uncontrolled sexual culture. On the other hand, 61 percent agreed that Korea's sexual culture is repressed. The usual double moral standard, which is more permissive for males than for females, is more complicated in modern Korea, where premarital sexual experiences and sexual liberation are increasingly accepted, while at the same time, the traditional value of female virginity and sexual passivity is expected in a very patriarchal society. The result, obviously, is psychological stress more for women than for men.

Sexual Behavior and Relationships of Single Adults   HUSO YI

As one might suspect from what has already been discussed, sexual behavior and relationships among Korean single adults are very limited because of negative attitudes toward premarital sexual relationships and the frequency of marriages arranged by parents or according to their socioeconomic status (Kendall 1996). Thus, it is likely that single adults do not feel a need for sexual relationships. Even though sexual liberation has influenced the sexual relationships of single adults, the value of female virginity is hard to be dismissed. In a study of single adult sexual behaviors (Kim et al. 1998), around half of the male and female adults were in heterosexual relationships. But, being in relationships did not mean having sexual relationships: 52.9 percent of the male respondents had positive attitudes to sexual relationships, whereas 37.6 percent were opposed to that. In response to the question of "how one resolves a sexual urge" (multiple answers), 60 percent of males exercised, 52.1 percent masturbated, 38.3 used hobbies as a distraction, 37.0 percent held in their urge, 9.6 percent prayed, 11.7 percent claimed they never had a sexual urge, and 26.2 percent had sex. In the female group, 35.2 percent exercised, 8.1 percent masturbated, 33.8 percent engaged in hobbies, 21.8 percent repressed their urge, 3.7 percent had sex, and (surprisingly) 61.1 percent never had sexual urges. Such female repression of the sexual urge or self-reported asexuality can be related to the most frequent female's sexual dysfunction, inhibited sexual orgasm (see Section 12, Sexual Dysfunctions, Counseling, and Therapies).

Hymen Reconstruction and Plastic Surgery   HUSO YI

Hymen can be translated as "virgin-skin" in Korean. Despite the effort of educating Koreans about the meaning and function of the hymen, the existence of an intact hymen is still highly valued at marriage so that hymen reconstruction and plastic surgery is frequently popular. There was an interesting lawsuit case about the loss of a hymen. In 1994, a 40-year-old woman sued the Korean Medical Research Center because she was extremely psychologically distressed after she lost her hymen during a Pap Smear test. Even though the doctor claimed that the hymen is usually torn during the test (and can even be torn by exercise), the court said, "It is clear that the hymen is still recognized as a symbol of 'virginity' and keeping virginity is valued in society. It is admitted that she was distressed by the lost of her symbol of virginity, therefore the hospital must pay for compensation" (Park 1994). One Korean prenatal genetic clinic offers STD tests with hymen reconstructive surgery, so that women can be free from her "history" of past sexual experiences (http://www.yunlee.co.kr, in Korean). In addition, the vaginal-opening muscle (pubococcygeus muscle) tension surgery (called "beauty surgery") is also commonly provided after delivery or for middle-aged married women. These surgeries are not even approved by the Korean medical association (Seol 2000). Dr. Seol, one of the leading sex therapists, is strongly opposed to such surgeries, based as they are on myths (see Section 12, Sexual Dysfunctions, Counseling, and Therapies).

Marriage and Family: Structures and Patterns
HYUNG KI CHOI AND COLLEAGUES (REDACTED BY HUSO YI)

In 1948, when Korea initiated its own government, the law on monogamous marriage was enforced. According to the census, the crude marriage rate has not changed from 1975 (8.0) to 1997 (8.1). The average age at first marriage in 1987 was 27.3 for males and 24.5 for females, which was delayed to 28.7 and 25.9, respectively, in 1997. However, the crude divorce rate has increased significantly from 0.5 in 1975 to 2.0 in 1997. The number of divorces in 1998 was 124,000, an increase of 30 percent from 1997. It is calculated that 1 out of 3 Korean marriages today end in divorce (see Tables 3 and 4). The annual report also indicated that the most common cause of divorce was the extramarital affairs of husbands. Moon (1993) addressed the factors of dissatisfaction in sexual activities with spouse, husband dominance, lack of respect and affection, male-preferred sexual position, no foreplay, and absence of communication. The sexual activities of married couples were only initiated and led by the husband. It is hardly acceptable for wives to express their sexual interests because of the cultural value of male dominance in sexual relationships.

Table 3
Crude Marriage Rate and Crude Divorce Rate: 1975-1997

Year	Total Marriage	Crude Marriage Rate	Total Divorce	Crude Divorce Rate
1975	282,000	8.0	16,179	0.5
1985	375,253	9.2	38,429	0.9
1995	401,161	8.8	67,858	1.5
1996	389,319	8.5	79,733	1.7
1997	374,429	8.1	83,171	2.0

Source: National Statistical Office 1999b

Table 4
Mean Age at First Marriage: 1987-1997

Year	Male	Female
1987	27.3	24.5
1990	27.9	24.9
1993	28.2	25.1
1996	28.6	25.7
1997	28.7	25.9

Source: National Statistical Office 1999b

According to a survey with 1,200 housewives in 1996, 67.2 percent reported dissatisfaction with their sexual lives and 30.2 percent responded that their sexual lives were satisfactory (Kim 1996). Such a psychological distress of sexual dissatisfaction leads to the increase of extramarital sex and divorce. In recent years, the rate of divorce caused by adultery has been increasing by 15 percent annually.

D. History and Structure of the Korean Family
PILWHA CHANG (SUMMARIZED BY HUSO YI)

Patriarchy

The recently expanding discourses on sexuality and the enlarging diversity of lifestyles in contemporary Korean society might give an impression that the reign of traditional control over sexuality is loosening. However, "legitimate" sexual behavior has been, and still tends to be, limited to marital partners. Patriarchy has a vested interest in defining women's sexuality in a particular way. It has particular sexual scripts, which use sexuality as social control. Women and men's sexuality is treated differently. Women's sexuality has frequently been exploited and degraded and used to sell commodities, even to turn women themselves into commodities. This double standard works against women and in favor of men.

Korean history, from the third century to the end of the nineteenth century, illustrates a gradual systematization of one of the most ideal types of patriarchy in the world. By the end of the sixteenth century, the state completed a patriarchal system by implementing Confucian ideology, with its gender hierarchy and sex segregation, through the gender division of labor and class divisions that upheld the patriarchal family in strict observance of patrilineage (rule of lineage, descent, or continuing family line from father to son), patrinymy (rule of continuing the surname of the father), and patrilocality (residential rule based on patrilineal locality). Women had to prove their worth as mothers, producing sons to continue the family line, and producing food and clothing, to survive in a woman-hostile environment. However strong and capable they might have been, Korean women were systematically denied activities outside the confines of the home, and their education was strictly prohibited.

Only in the national crisis at the end of the nineteenth century, when foreign powers threatened Korea's sovereignty, did some possibilities of cracking this rigidity arise. For about two centuries, some philosophical systems, among them Silhak and Tonghak, began to question the gender relations under new influences. [Very briefly, Silhak can be compared to pragmatism and Tonghak can share its philosophy with a sort of socialism that claims the rights of lower-class people (Huso Yi)] However, it was only in a crisis situation when proper observation of traditional family rituals became difficult or impossible that such thoughts began to be heard and listened to. The national crisis created a space of critical reflection on the traditional ways of life. Within this space, reevaluation of the position of women began. Women's social participation had to accepted, however reluctantly, as essential to national survival. The resulting discourse, however, focused on the national interests, and not on the value of education held for the personal development of women and their fuller participation in society.

In the last hundred years, Koreans have experienced crisis after crisis: the Japanese occupation, two World Wars, the division of the country into

North and South, the Korean War, and the industrial war to join the world capitalist system. These crises prioritized efficiency and expediency, and justified sacrificing individual human rights for the sake of growth and stability. In this context, it was easy to brush aside women's claim for human rights as a luxury, and so the tradition of utilizing women's instrumental values persisted. At the same time, such crises opened some windows of opportunity for women to participate in sociopolitical arenas. Also, it is true that the models of the "developed" world provided a stimulus for women's rights. Consequently, women's suffrage was included in the first modern Constitution in 1947, and primary education became compulsory for girls as well as boys. In the last few decades, Korea has managed to furnish the appearance of "modernity." Despite the appearance and some changes in patriarchal families, the underlying assumptions continue to be patriarchal, with the view that women's identity is only familial, guided by the "three obediences" to father, husband, and son, and without any independent public identity based on her own personal merit.

The marginal position of a daughter in her natal family rests in her future roles as wife and daughter-in-law in another household. Because of this, she was considered only as a temporary member of her natal family, her filial piety being transferred on marriage to her parents-in-law. Her duty of filial piety towards her own parents was not to bring shame and dishonor to her natal family by misbehaving in her new family. With marriage, a daughter had to break her ties with her natal home, "she who left the family and has become a stranger." Her parents told her that she now belonged to her husband's family where she had to persevere, however hard life might have been: "She ought never return to her old home but the ghost of her husband's home." It is another example of how married women are treated. In an old saying, once they are married, they have to finish their lives no matter what happens to them. Once married, a wife who committed any of seven evils could legitimately be divorced, and a divorce brought shame to her natal family. Because a wife could not be protected by her natal family, she had no alternative but to comply with the rules of her husband and his family to survive. In this environment, the sooner a wife made the transition, the easier it was for her in her new role. Physical distance from the natal family helped the process, hence the proverb: "Toilets and the wife's home are best kept at a distance."

Even if the environment of her husband's household was alien and hostile initially, the young wife can gradually establish her own position within the household by producing her own children, particularly sons. Producing the heir secures her status and her acceptance as a full member of her husband's family. Once a wife became the senior lady of the household, mother-in-law to her sons' wives, she had achieved a measure of power. Many women must have softened the hardships by anticipating the day when they would enter the stage of being a mother-in-law. This is another dimension of intrafamily relationships that explains why having a son was, and still is, so much more important to a mother than having a daughter. As filial piety was the supreme principle, a mother's authority was respected, and through her sons she could enjoy a measure of social power.

However, although a mother possessed considerable power and influence within the family, her power did not extend beyond its boundary. A woman's power was based on the private relationship between mother and son, and, however strong an influence she may have on him, it could not extend beyond the scope of the village. As this power was derived from the son, and his power base lay in patriarchy, the mother's power could not and did not challenge the patriarchal system. Rather, the mother actively enforced patriarchal rules in their own interest. This is why, despite the existence of powerful women, the patriarchal system was not undermined or modified to improve the situation of women, nor to institutionalize the private nature of women's power publicly. Under this system, it is far easier for women to perceive other women as a threat to their livelihood and power than as allies to fight against the system.

Problems of Today's Families and Its Direction of Change

There is little dispute that the family has been changing under the process of industrialization. Although this is widely acknowledged by empirical research and a broad range of data sets, the question still remains whether the external trends really confirm the change in the stereotyped ideology of the family, even with the notion that social procedures are now developing for basic functions other than the family. Besides, it is also necessary to notice that not all changes occur at an equal rate, nor do all segments of a society adjust equally to the changes taking place. Then, how much change has occurred in the Korean family and what are the implications of this change?

The decrease in average household size (from 5.2 in 1979 to 3.12 in 1995) may come from the increase in one-person households and non-family households because of the advance of the mean age of first marriage of women (from 21.5 in 1960 to 26.2 in 1998), the great flexibility in adapting to new ways of life, such as marriage, divorce, and remarriage, and more frequent family moving. Despite the changes in the physical organization of the family, traditional Confucian ethics, which stress patrilineage, filial piety, solidarity among brothers, and the importance of domestic harmony, are still pervasive in the Korean family. The unbalanced sex ratio of children, which has emerged as a serious social problem in Korea, shows a good case in point. In other words, the ideal of son preference is still pervasive as a main agent to support the male-centered norms and values of the patriarchal family. The findings from the 1981 Gallup survey of children and mothers (see Table 5) also shows that the traditional Korean concept of the family as a social institution to continue patrilineage is reflected in attitudes toward child rearing.

Despite the gradual changes in recent years, the idea that the role of homemaking belongs exclusively to women is still pervasive throughout Korean society. This has put great pressure on career women and forced them to perform dual roles. Women engaged in full-time homemaking, on the other hand, experience more social alienation and anxiety in the nuclear family life than in the traditional extended family life, which is increasingly more difficult to maintain in modern urban life. Full-time

Table 5

Meaning of Giving Birth and Raising Children

	Mothers Only		Both Parents	
	Korea	US	Korea	US
To transmit my life to my child	34.0	40.8	32.2	30.5
To have a successful child who will further pursue my aspirations	43.2	10.9	32.1	11,4
To continue my family line/name	48.3	23.1	68.2	28.4
To contribute to a generation which will inherit the future society	48.4	52.6	39.6	45.6
To strengthen our family bond	24.8	44.9	25.4	49.5
To have security in my old age	26.8	5.8	37.5	7.8
To mature and enrich myself	13.5	44.2	19.2	53.5
Just to enjoy childbearing	19.3	48.6	18.9	49.8
To be recognized by society	29.3	4.0	10.9	2.2
To obtain additional work power in our family	2.2	2.6	1.8	2.6

Note: Multiple answers may exceed 100 percent. *Source:* Chang 1998

homemakers experience a serious conflict of role expectations and their own identities. Thus, although Korean families appear to be stable, in reality, they are increasingly at a crisis level of psychological dissolution.

Sexuality and the Physically Disabled and Aged   HUSO YI

In a study about sexuality in 65 spinal-cord-injured males (Oh et al. 1990), 24 had problems with erections, 23 had difficulty in maintaining erections, and 24 were unable to ejaculate. During sexual intercourse, 41 had difficulty with erections, but the rest reported suffering from fears of not reaching orgasm, and fears of a passive response and rejection from partners. After the spinal-cord injury, about 80 percent of them said that their sexual and marital satisfaction had decreased. Although they were aware of sexual problems, only 5 had been in sex therapy because of a lack of facilities and accessibility.

The National Rehabilitation Center started a sexual rehabilitation clinic project in 1996. The clinic has provided sex therapy and counseling, couple sex therapy, group therapy, and erectile dysfunction therapy for more than 1,000 physically disabled people and their partners. The clinic also facilitates a place, called that "shelter for love," where physically disabled people and their partners can stay over to enjoy their sexual activities. Since 1998, the clinic staff has organized conferences about sexuality and disability. In 2000, Dr. B. S. Lee, a sexual rehabilitation specialist, published a small handbook, *Sexual Rehabilitation for the Spinal Cord Injured.* The book introduced the importance of sexuality in the physically disabled, cases reports about sex therapy for the foreign and Korean disabled, sexual concerns of the female and male disabled, medical treatment for erectile dysfunction, psychological issues on sexual rehabilitation, and marriage of the physically disabled. (For information: http://www.nrc.go.kr/eng/eindex.htm; contact: nrc1986@chollian.net.)

6. Homoerotic, Homosexual, and Ambisexual Behaviors

A. Historical Perspective   HUSO YI

The earliest Korean record of homosexuality may be from King Hyekong, the thirty-sixth king of the Shilla dynasty in *Samguk-Yusa* (a Three Kingdoms' story) written by Il Yeon in the thirteenth century. King Kyungduk did not have a son, but wanted one very badly because he needed an heir. He kept asking the messenger between God and man to go to God and ask for a son. God insisted that he was not destined to have a son, only daughters, yet the King was persistent. Finally, God let him have a son, but God put a female spirit in the son's body. King Hye-Kong was very feminine and liked only being around men all the time. He became the next king at the age of 8 in 765 C.E. because his father died early. However, he was killed at the age of 22 in April 780 by his subordinates because they could not accept his 'femininity.' Another story in Samguk Yusa is about Myojung, a very young Buddhist monk who lived during the reign of Wonsung (785-798 C.E.), the thirty-eighth king of the Shilla dynasty. It is said that he was loved and sought after by several male Shilla aristocrats, and even by a Chinese Emperor from the Tang dynasty (618-907 C.E.).

One of the best-known homosexual histories is the *Hwarang* or *Flower Boy*, the story of a homoerotic military elite, paralleling the Egyptian mamluks, the Japanese samurai, and the Theban Band of ancient Greece (Murray 2000). Prior to the introduction of Buddhism, ancient Korea maintained a transgendered shamanistic tradition, in which the *hwarang* seem to have been involved. With the transfer of religious legitimization to Buddhism, the code of the *hwarang* began to change from social and religious concerns to political and military programs. In the *Haedong-Kosung-Chon* (*Lives of Eminent Korean Monks*) written by the Buddhist Kakhun in 1215, the first criterion of the *hwarang* seems to have been appearance: "It was handsome youths who powdered their faces, wore ornamented dresses, and were respected as hwarang." After unification of the peninsula, ruled by the Three Kingdoms, in 676, the members of *hwarang* were rewarded with land and slaves.

In the Koryo dynasty, same-sex relationships, mostly between males, were very common among the ruling class. In a historical analysis of *Hallimbuilgok* by Seong, King Chungsun (1275-1325) maintained a long-term relationship with a *wonchung* (male lover), and King Kongmin (1325-1374) appointed at least five youths as "little-brother attendants" (*chajewhi*) as sexual partners. After the fall of the Koryo dynasty in 1392, the Chosun dynasty adopted Confucianism as a governing ideology in order to confirm their dynasty as totally different from the Koryo dynasty. Even though Confucianism had negative attitudes about same-sex relationships, there were still male-to-male relationships among the Buddhists and among the rural ruling class. Lesbian relationships were not treated with the same acceptance, as the palace chronicle from the Chosun dynasty reveals. King Sejong convened a meeting of his cabinet on October 24, 1436, to discuss the rumors that his daughter-in-law had been sleeping with her maidservant. These rumors had been somehow confirmed, so the ministers advised the king to strip his daughter-in-law of her noble status in order to preserve the honor and dignity of the royal family (Chung 1998).

Another historically known homosexual group was the *namsadang* in the Chosun dynasty (Murray 1992), which existed until it was broken up by force to extinguish the national culture under the colonization of Japan in the early 1910s. As a type of indigenous theater, the *namsadang* traveled around the country with various types of entertainment, including band music, song, masked dance, circus, and puppet plays. Reflecting the common peoples' harsh living conditions and their resentment toward the upper class, the *namsadang* was the voice of lower-class people. When boys, called *midong* (beautiful boys), first joined a troupe, they played the penetrated sex role and were probably male prostitutes for the rural ruling class (Leupp 1995). In this era, many members of the rural ruling class maintained boys for sexual purposes. Because same-sex relationships, however, were generally regarded as immoral in the eyes of Neo-Confucianism, the *namsadang* performers were treated as outcasts.

B. Children and Adolescents   HUSO YI

As mentioned below, there is a law against informing adolescents about homosexuality and, in mental health settings, it is easy for lesbian and gay adolescents to be diagnosed as having either sexual maturation disorder, egodystonic orientation, or sexual relationship disorder. In fact, it is likely that mental health professionals will claim homosexual attraction is nothing but a phase of heterosexual development (Yi 2000). In another context, homosexuality may be diagnosed as either pseudo-homosexuality or true-homosexuality (Hong 1996; Lee 1993). Although no research on homosexuality among children and adolescents has been conducted, most research on adolescent sexuality asks questions about homosexual behaviors. Instead of considering homosexual behaviors as normal, these studies by the Korean Research Institute for Culture and Sexuality categorize homosexuality together with "sexual violence" (Lee et al. 1998), or asks females the question, "Have you ever fallen in love with a woman whom you consider as a man?" (Kim et al. 1997). Both studies found that around 13 percent of the female student respondents said they had had sexual relationships with the same gender.

C. Adults

Gender Roles, Courtship, and Relationship Patterns   HUSO YI

Before the emergence of gay identity in the mid-1990s, expressing homosexuality in Korea was somewhat easier than in the West, because the existence of homosexuality was denied at the same time there was a cultural tolerance for homophilic touch. Same-sex friends can hold hands together on the streets just like heterosexual couples. However, it might be inappropriate to see such same-sex friendships as homosexual relationships in the way that Western culture does (Shong & Icard 1996). One of cultural patterns related to homophilia is that when a husband's friend visits, his wife sleeps separately from her husband, who sleeps with his male friend. Also, because same-sex roommates before marriage are common, in fact, more acceptable than sharing with the opposite gender, living as a young "gay" couple is possible, and the neighbors hardly suspect them as lesbians or gay males (Yi 2000). But, because everyone's first role is to continue family linkage, lesbians and gay men are compelled to be married after a certain age. In addition, Christianity is certainly another hindrance for gay courtship, particularly because Korean Christianity is strongly fundamentalist (Martin & Berry 1998). These long-established cultural norms have been challenged by the gay community. Every issue of a gay magazine since 1997 reports the commitment ceremonies of lesbian and gay couples.

Social Status of Lesbians, Gay Men, and Bisexuals

The modern gay community in Korea can be traced from the 1970s. Before that, it is known that places for gays coexisted with other sex places for foreigners. In the 1970s, around 120 lesbians and gay men held a monthly social gathering at a Chinese restaurant. But, the social group did not survive to connect with the current gay community (Lee 1997). Today's gay movement emerged with Sappho, the first Korean lesbian group, organized by an American lesbian soldier. When she came to Korea in November 1991 to serve in the army and found no lesbian bars, she immediately realized that living as a lesbian was very difficult in Korea. Outside of meeting a few lesbians in a gay bar, there was no chance to meet with lesbians. She decided to organize a group for lesbians and placed an advertisement for her lesbian group in English newspapers. Eight foreign lesbians from the United States and Europe gathered together at the first meeting. The membership of Sappho changed often, because most of its members returned to home in the U.S., Canada, Belgium, Sweden, or Australia after two or three years in Korea. Sappho was still holding its small meetings in early 2001.

In the U.S., groups for lesbian and gay Korean-Americans were founded in New York (in December 1990) and in Los Angeles (in August 1993). A few members from these Korean-American groups had been in contact with Sappho and discussed forming Korean gay and lesbian rights groups and providing outreach and support to their various friends. In the meantime, a Korean-American gay man visited Korea and organized the first Korean gay and lesbian co-gendered group in December, 1993. Unlike Sappho, this group was organized by Koreans, and is recognized as the first authentically Korean lesbian and gay men's support group.

Because there is no law protecting lesbians and gay males, Korea has no sodomy laws proscribing oral or anal intercourse, except a military law against homosexual relationships in the army. Meanwhile, in 2000, Korea passed the law of Youth Protection prohibiting distribution of materials that contain incest, animal sex, and homosexuality. In the mental health setting, the Korean Standard Disease Classification (KSDC) states three "Psychological and Behavioral Disorders Associated with Sexual Development and Orientation" (http://www.nso.go.kr/stat/dis/e-diss.htm, in English):

- F 66.0 Sexual Maturation Disorder: The patient is suffering from uncertainty about his gender identity or sexual orientation, causing anxiety or depression. Most commonly this occurs in adolescents who are not certain whether they are homosexual, heterosexual or bisexual in orientation, or older married individuals who after a period of apparently normal heterosexuality, often within marriage, find themselves experiencing homosexual feelings.

- F 66.1 Egodystonic Sexual Orientation: The gender identity or sexual preference (either heterosexual, homosexual, bisexual, prepubertal or uncertain) is not in doubt but the individual wishes it were different because of associated psychological and behavioural disorders, and may seek treatment in order to change it.
- F 66.3 Sexual Relationship Disorder: The gender identity or sexual orientation (either hetero-, homo-, or bisexual) is responsible for difficulties in forming or maintaining a relationship with a sexual partner.

The Classification clearly states that it is adapted from the International Classification of Diseases by the World Health Organization (WHO). However, a crucial difference between the two should be noted.

In the original text in ICD-10, F 66.0, Sexual Maturation Disorder, reads as follows:

> F 66.0 Sexual Maturation Disorder: The patient is suffering from uncertainty about his gender identity or sexual orientation, causing anxiety or depression. Most commonly this occurs in adolescents who are not certain whether they are homosexual, heterosexual or bisexual in orientation, or *individuals who, after a period of apparently stable sexual orientation (often with a longstanding relationship), find that their sexual orientation is changing.* (italics added)

> In the KSDC version, the italicized phrase above has been replaced by: *older married individuals who after a period of apparently normal heterosexuality, often within marriage, find themselves experiencing homosexual feelings.*

In the original ICD-10, the words "normal homosexuality," "marriage," and "experiencing homosexual feelings" do not appear. It seems that Korean mental health professionals regard heterosexuality as normal, but homosexuality as something else.

7. Gender Conflicted Persons

A. Sociolegal Status, Behaviors, and Treatment of Transvestite, Transgendered, and Transsexual Persons

HYUNG KI CHOI AND COLLEAGUES (REDACTED BY HUSO YI)

Until the mid-1980s, the care system for transgendered people was not well established in Korea because of little understanding of transsexualism and the negative attitude and prejudices of medical doctors. In desperation, many transsexual persons turned to non-licensed facilities for sex-reassignment surgery or self-injected hormones for partial physical transition. [Yoo

(1993) has noted that doctors' prejudices and ignorance of transgenderism/transsexualism result in a boundary between them and the patient. As a consequence, it is common that transgendered/transsexual people get more information from resources in Western countries, where the doctors learn about transsexualism from their clients. (Huso Yi)] In 1989, Dr. Koo Sang-Hwan conducted the first sex-reassignment surgery for a male-to-female. As of late 2000, about 50 cases of sex-reassignment surgery have been reported. In 1990, the Korean Urology Association proposed 12 criteria for sex-reassignment surgery (SRS):

1. Accurate psychiatric diagnosis.
2. No success from long-term psychiatric treatment.
3. Establishment of psychosocial adjustment for the desired gender before SRS.
4. No other psychiatric illness or depression.
5. Sufficient period of hormone-replacement treatment with no side effects.
6. Over 21 years old and past puberty.
7. Physical appearance has to fit with the desired gender.
8. Family approval for SRS.
9. Agreement of spouse and/or family regarding infertility.
10. No drug and alcohol history.
11. No criminal record and no possibility for crime.
12. Under good medical supervision.

The transgendered (transsexual) patient has to meet all the above requirements and must get two recommendations from psychiatrists.

Even after the surgery, they cannot change their gender on any legal document. In 1990, the court rejected a male-to-female transsexual's petition stating, "Because the plastic surgery only made anatomical structures that look like those of the female artificially so that it does not change the chromosomal structure, he cannot be accepted as a female from our society's common sense and value. [Added to that, the court ruled that "he cannot legally change his gender because he has no internal parts of the female body which are very important to the woman's role of giving births. Thus, it is not appropriate in our society to change his gender." Since then, all of the cases of gender change have followed this court decision (Cho 1993). It is likely that gender in Korea is constituted by chromosome and familial "role" (Huso Yi)] In the legal system, sex-reassignment surgery is regarded only as a part of plastic surgery and not a gender transition. Also, in a case in which a male-to-female transsexual was raped, the judge said it was not rape, but as a physical attack. [The judge in this case also implied that the rape of a same-sex person cannot be properly constituted as "rape," because such homosexual acts do not fit the sense of "sex." It is the court's stance that sex can only occur between the opposite sexes. (Huso Yi)] Because of these limitations, transsexuals cannot claim any benefits and rights that non-transsexuals have.

8. Significant Unconventional Sexual Behaviors

A. Coercive Sex   HUSO YI

It is very difficult to ascertain the actual frequency of sexual violence in Korea. According to the Korean Institute of Criminology (1998), the report rate for sexual assaults was estimated to be only 6.1 percent of actual incidents, whereas the rate in the advanced countries is around 30 to 40 percent. In 1998, the sexual violence counseling centers under the Ministry of Health and Welfare reported around 25,000 cases of sexual violence, which was as twice the incidence in 1997. Of these cases, 33.5 percent involved rape; 21.9 percent involved physical sexual harassment, and the rest were about verbal sexual abuse. However, only 3.6 percent of the victims reported the incident to the police (Korean Institute for Health and Social Welfare, 1999). The Korean Sexual Violence Relief Center (1999) reported that 95 percent of the victims are women (assaulters are mostly men) and 73 percent of the assaulters are acquaintances of their victims, who range in age from the teens to the seventies. Thirty percent of the victims are children under the age of 13, with 50 percent under the age of 19. Chang (2000) noted that sexual assaulters experienced no guilt for their behavior, believing that sexual violence may occur accidentally as an expression of a natural uncontrollable sexual urge of men. This conception leads men to look at rape as a kind of sexual act, rather than a crime infringing on a woman's body and personality. An interesting legal aspect in sexual violence is that current law does not allow a victim to file a suit against her father, leaving some incest victims with no means to their rights. Frotteurism, the forceful touching and rubbing of the genital area, particularly in the subway, is another sexual assault problem. In 1997, 128 males were arrested by the subway police for rubbing their genitals and half of these sexual offenders were college graduates.

With the effort of the women's rights movements, Korea has achieved several legal enforcements, as noted earlier, to protect victims from sexual harassment. However, research on the public awareness of the anti-sexual violence laws showed that only 2.1 percent were familiar with the laws, 31.6 percent had some familiarity with them, 46.5 percent had heard of them, and 22.2 percent had never heard of them (Kim et al. 2000). Thus, it is necessary to implement an effective educational program to make the public aware of the sexual violence laws.

Sexual Harassment   HUSO YI

Cyber-sexual violence has become a major concern and issue in Korea. In July 2000, for example, a female middle-school student committed suicide after being harassed by Internet postings. In order to prevent sexual harassment on the Internet, the Ministry of Information and Communication established the Report Center of Cyber Sexual Violence in 2000 and has conducted a survey, which found that 58.9 percent of those surveyed had experienced cyber-sexual violence and 14.4 percent had witnessed it. Most cyber-sexual violence occurs in the chat rooms, bulletin boards, and e-mail. The respondents were harassed by verbal abuse, pornographic pictures or movies, private videos (e.g., exposure of the body or sexual scenes), and suggestions of prostitution.

[The issue of sexual harassment emerged when the Korean Women's Hotline opened in 1983. In the first survey of 700 married women, 42 percent reported that they had been hit by their husband at least once. Following up on the issue, the Hotline started to deal with the issues of kidnapping for prostitution and female sex workers. During this time, society began to pay attention to harassment against women. There were two important legal cases about sexual harassment. In 1986, Kwon, In-Sook, a female college student, was interrogated by the police because of her democracy activism. During the interrogation, she was sexually harassed by the police. Later, with the help of an unprecedented 166 lawyers' arguments and human right organizations, she was released. Another case dealt with rape. In 1988, when a woman was raped on her way home, she cut off the offender's tongue. However, she was sentenced to a year in prison. The case stimulated debates on rape and self-defense and the implication of women's self-defense. As a consequence, she was found innocent and acquitted. Confronted with societal situations such as these, the Korean Sexual Violence Relief Center was established in 1991. (Hyung Ki Choi and colleagues)]

Rape   HUSO YI

In one study, almost half (45.5 percent) of female high school students reported having been sexually harassed by being touched on the breast, hips, and genital areas and, among them, 99.3 percent had been harassed by their male friends (Kim et al. 1997). The victims' responses were: 70.8 percent tried to avoid the situation, 11.3 percent showed no resistance, 10.1 percent confronted the harasser with shouting, and only 0.8 percent looked for help. After being raped, 29.2 percent did nothing, 25.8 percent talked to friends, 14.6 percent told their mother, 2.2 percent reported the assault to the police, and 1.1 percent spoke to a teacher. Having no education about rape and a very low reporting rate does nothing to reduce the incidence of rape, and may well promote it. [The law dealing with rape used to be categorized under the title "Crime Against Chastity." This divided the victims of rape into two groups, respectable women who deserve legal protection and those (fallen women) who do not. Therefore, it was irrelevant to the court decision whether or not the victim resisted. Also irrelevant was the victim's sexual history (Chang 2000). The myths of rape were still prevalent among males at that time: "Rape occurs because of men's uncontrollable sexual urge" (69.0 percent), "a sexy female's looks provoke rape" (93.9 percent), "the best prevention is women's caution" (66.2 percent), and "rape cannot occur if women persistently refuse" (52.6 percent) (Byun et al. 2000) (Huso Yi)]

B. Industrial Prostitution
WHASOON BYUN AND JUNGIM HWANG (SUMMARIZED BY HUSO YI)
Overview of Industrial Prostitution

The entertainment industry in Korean society began to grow in the 1970s, based upon the material wealth of capitalism. Amidst a materialistic social environment, a great change occurred in the form of prostitution. Rather than being confined in certain districts, industrial prostitution began spreading rapidly as a form of secondary service available in new entertainment establishments that provided a primary service. Unlike traditional prostitution, industrial prostitution involves establishments centered mainly on the tertiary service industry, in which sex can be provided legally on the side. The tertiary service industry includes the restaurant and hotel/motel business, entertainment and cultural services, and individual and household services provided by individuals and by companies. The number of women employed in these businesses rose steadily from 21.2 percent in 1983, to 22.9 percent in 1986, and 23.3 percent in 1989. [According to Our Society Research Center (1994), around 1.5 millions are engaged in the prostitution industry. That number was one fifth of the population aged 15 to 29 (6.2 million). Over 91 percent of the female prostitutes had run away from home, and more than 90 percent had experiences of incest and/or had been sexually abused by members of their family. (Huso Yi)] These businesses hire women who then provide sex as an additional service paid for at the end by the consumer.

Establishments that incorporate "industrial prostitution" in their services include restaurants, singing-room (karaoke) salons, room salons (adults bars with private rooms served by escort women), ticket coffee shops, steambaths, (adult) barbershops, and massage parlors. According to data from the Ministry of Health and Welfare (1998), there were 40,123 so-called singing-room and room salons under the category of liquor parlors, about 3,000 steambaths, barber shops (under the category of sanitary parlors), and 535 massage parlors, bringing the total number of such establishments to 43,658. This is just the official count; the unofficial count is expected to be much higher than this. The prostitution at these facilities is called "second stops," and according to the specific type of establishment, sexual activities are conducted either at the same place or at another location. According to the Korea Anti-AIDS Federation's specialized analysis in 1997, 24.5 percent of the respondents experienced sex in singing-room salons and room salons. Other places were in the red-light district at 24 percent, massage parlors at 19.9 percent, barbershops at 17.2 percent, hotels and motels at 13.8 percent, and others at 0.6 percent. A survey by the Korean Research Institute on Sexuality and Culture (Kim et al. 1997) of female high school students' awareness of sex and factual findings showed 2.1 percent of the 773 respondents said they had part-time experience working at singing-room salons and room salons. Especially, with the economically hard times, dubbed "the IMF (International Monetary Fund) era," a number of women are likely to be lured into places where industrial prostitution is possible.

Types of Facilities

1. Ticket Coffee Shop: In these shops, the customer pays for tickets sold by the hour and takes the woman out for sex. The money paid for the tickets make up for the woman's absent time from the coffee shop, whether the time is spent drinking wine, socializing, in prostitution,

or other activities. When sex is provided as a service, the woman gets to keep that fee which is over and above the shop ticket.

2. Room Salon: Room salons and regular bars are allowed by law to hire female employees and hostesses. According to Article 6 of the eighth provision of the Food and Sanitation Law, a hostess refers to a woman, single or married, who drinks, sings, and dances with a customer to promote merrymaking. These women usually move to another place with the customer when he decides to engage in prostitution. Unlike women at ticket coffee shops, these women do not get paid for the time they lose at the shops, but go out for prostitution after reporting to their madams. The hostess gets to keep the money.

3. Singing-Room Salon: By law, it is illegal for singing-room salons to hire female employees. Although waitresses may be allowed, hiring a hostess is forbidden. Reality does not follow the law, and a lot of pubs have female hostesses catering to customers. The types of prostitution being conducted in these singing-room salons is identical to that at regular room salons, the only difference being that the hostesses have to report to the owner, not to the madams.

4. Barbershops, steambaths, and massage parlors: The female employees at barbershops, steambaths, and massage parlors provide shaving, massaging, and bathing services prior to prostitution. At barbershops, the female employees provide shaves and massages to the customers, and at steambaths, the women bathe the customers and provide massages, during which they incite sexual desires and then provide prostitution. At massage parlors, blind masseuses and female workers are employed, with the latter providing prostitution. When there were no female employees available, the blind women used to provide sex, but with the introduction of female employees, prostitution at massage parlors came into full swing. At most of these parlors, the cost for prostitution is included in the overall charge. The women take their share from the prostitution and the owners take the remainder. Prostitution is much more likely to occur in the barber shops, steambaths, and massage parlors than in the other facilities listed above.

Each facility has slightly different characteristics on the basis of its own type of services. But regardless of the type, prostitution is an important factor that maintains these facilities where both the main service and prostitution are being conducted under the protection of the facility.

Analysis of Industrial Prostitution

Many sociocultural, economic, and institutional factors draw women into industrial prostitution. From the perspective of sociocultural factors, a lot of women surveyed were exposed to the adult-entertainment industry at an early age because they had either run away from home or indulged in delinquency. They tended to run away because they did not want to study or because they were reared in an unfavorable home environment. More often than not, if the woman is a breadwinner for the family, albeit single or married, she usually selects the service industry after a divorce or separation to make a living. The service industry is an easy way to make a lot of money in a short period of time. Women who choose this service industry may do so because they do not have much education, have no special skills, or do not want to work in a factory. Most of the women had experience working in a legitimate company before they turned to the prostitution service industry. But, they either failed or worked at low-paying jobs. Sometimes, they had no other choice but to quit their jobs to escape a hostile work environment in which a supervisor pressured them for sex. Meanwhile, with the nationwide economic crisis of the "IMF era," women have been observed moonlighting in the sex trade because they did not make enough money.

From the institutional perspective, all work facilities have health permits, but if a woman contracts venereal disease, she tends to it on her own. That is why a health permit becomes useless in solving the problem. Also, there are no social services that prostitutes can utilize, and they do not even look for them. The health permits are taken care of by the owner. Normally, establishments involved in industrial prostitution receive permits from the government. Therefore, the exploitation link is not as conspicuous as in the case of traditional prostitution. But despite that fact, many parts of the management structure are distributed among the women, those involved in the trade and related agencies, all of whom together collude in whatever corruption is needed.

[In a report by the Seoul Metropolitan Police Agency, among 222 teenage female prostitutes,

- 67 (30.2 percent) were 16 years old, 48 (21.6 percent) were 18 years old, 38 (17.1 percent) were 15 years old, 35 (15.8 percent) were 17 years old, 26 (11.7 percent) were 14 years old, and 8 girls were under the age of 13.
- 47.3 percent of the girls attended school and the rest were suspended.
- 23 had been sentenced to probation.

As for 282 adult male partners,

- 123 (43.6 percent) were in their 30s, 115 (40.8 percent) were in their 20s, 36 (12.7 percent) were in their 40s, 5 (1.5 percent) were in their teen years, and 3 (1.1 percent) were over 50.
- 137 of them had been sentenced to prison and 145 were on probation.
- Half (53.5 percent) of the men met the women on the Internet, 62 (22.2 percent) met them through "telephone rooms," 38 (13.5 percent) met them by voicemail, 18 (6.4 percent) met them through friends, and 13 (4.6 percent) worked on the street. (Report Center of Cyber Sexual Violence 2000. (Telephone rooms are telephone booths located in private space where someone can call another person to arrange for sex or call a sex worker for phone sex. Telephone calls in a private home can be easily traced and show up on the telephone bill so Koreans are more likely to use the private telephone room. (Huso Yi)]

B. Pornography

Historically, the earliest documented erotica can be found in the Koryo period (918-1392). Since the seventeenth century, erotica has been freely imported from China for the enjoyment of ordinary people. Compared to China and Japan, Korea was somewhat late in developing a taste for pornography because of the unique characteristics of conservatism in the Chosun dynasty. Later in the eighteenth century, erotica was created and produced by Koreans and widely distributed. However, the Korean erotica was not as explicit as much of that from China and Japan. After the industrialization of the 1970s, various kinds of pornography were developed as in other countries. Before the Internet was created, the main source for accessing pornography was at lodging houses and late-night coffee shops that served the role of adult theaters. Today, access to pornography has been much easier via Internet adult television, adult magazines, video purchases and rentals, and computer programs.

In a study of 1,976 male and 3,134 female high school students, 60.5 percent of the male students had seen all kinds of pornographic materials, such as magazines, adult videos, and computer-related materials, 28.1 percent had experience only with magazines, 27.4 percent only with adult videos, and 3.6 percent only with computer programs. Just under 2 percent had not seen any adult erotica. Meanwhile, 52.2 percent of the female students had never seen adult magazines, 36.3 percent no adult movies, and 93.9 percent no computer-related adult materials (Kim et al. 1997). Considering the lack of adequate sexuality education for Korean adolescents, the impact of their exposure to pornography remains to be studied. In 1997, for example, three 17-year-old male students and a 15-year-old female student recorded their sexual intercourse on videotape and sold it. The tape was spread nationwide. After conviction, one male was sentenced to six months in a juvenile prison, the other males were sentenced to work in social welfare, and the female student received two years of guidance. They said that they just wanted to make a tape like adults do.

9. Contraception, Abortion, and Population Planning

A. Contraception   HYUNG KI CHOI AND COLLEAGUES

After 1961, when most active contraceptive programs were started, married women who practiced contraception increased from 44.2 percent in 1976 to 80.5 percent in 1997 (see Table 6). The most common method of contraception in 1976 was vasectomy, followed by the intrauterine device (IUD), oral pills, condoms, and fallopian tubal ligation. In 1988, the most common form became tubal ligation (37.2 percent). In 1997, the most common form of contraception was still tubal ligation (24.1 percent), followed by condoms, vasectomy, the IUD, and oral pills. The usage of the IUD and oral pill is considerably low in Korea.

B. Teenage (Unmarried) Pregnancies   HUSO YI

As noted earlier, premarital sexual experience is still prohibited, and there is a strong denial of adolescents' sexual relationships. Besides, adolescent

Table 6

Contraceptive-Practice Rate of Married Women, Aged 15-44

Year	Total	Tubectomy	Vasectomy	IUD	Pills	Condom	Others
1976	44.2%	4.1%	10.5%	7.8%	7.8%	6.3%	11.3%
1979	54.5	14.5	9.6	7.2	7.2	5.2	12.1
1982	57.7	23.0	6.7	5.4	5.4	7.2	10.3
1985	70.4	31.6	7.4	4.3	4.3	7.2	11.0
1988	77.1	37.2	6.7	2.8	2.8	10.2	9.2
1991	79.4	35.3	9.0	3.0	3.0	10.2	9.9
1994	77.4	28.6	10.5	1.8	1.8	14.3	10.6
1997	80.5	24.1	13.2	1.8	1.8	15.1	13.6

Source: Korea Institute for Health and Social Affairs 1998

pregnancy and abortion are another serious problem. It is estimated that around one third of all abortions might be performed among unmarried adolescents (Youn 1995). However, no official report has been published on adolescent pregnancy and abortion. Given the fact that being a teenage mother is most undesirable, adolescents may have two choices, abortion or adoption: "Most adolescent mothers who carry their pregnancies to term surrender their babies to adoption agencies" (Youn 1996:630). According to the Korean Ministry of Health and Welfare, the number of babies given up by adolescent mothers was 1,904 in 1993, 1,781 in 1994 (Youn 1995) and 1,802 in 1999 (Ministry of Health and Welfare, MOHW 2000) In summary, one third of the abortion cases were performed on pregnant teens and one third of the adopted babies were surrendered by teens (see Table 7).

Table 7

Number of Adopted Children, 1995-1999

	Total	Domestic	Overseas
1995	3,205	1,025	2,180
1996	3,309	1,229	2,080
1997	3,469	1,412	2,057
1998	3,675	1,426	2,249
1999	(1,802)[a]/4,135	(645)/1,726	(1,157)/2,409

[a]Numbers in parentheses are the number of adopted children surrendered by adolescent mothers the number following the / is the total number of adopted children.
Source: Ministry of Health and Welfare 2000: Child Health

C. Abortion   HYUNG KI CHOI AND COLLEAGUES (REDACTED BY HUSO YI)

In Korean law, an induced abortion, defined as the removing of a fetus before the twenty-eighth week of gestation, is allowed in cases of genetically inherited diseases, transmitted diseases, incest, rape, and those cases that may greatly harm maternal health. However, it has been used as a form of contraception in Korea, and the number of induced abortions runs between 1.5 to 2 million cases annually. There are 600,000 newborns in Korea each year, and the number of abortions is nearly three times the number of deliveries. The total number of abortions in Korea is the second highest in the world. One-out-of-two married women has experienced an abortion. Eighty percent of abortions are done for gender-selection purposes, using an ultrasound scan to ascertain the gender and then selectively abort female fetuses. Those who seek abortions for reasons defined by the law account for only 20 percent of all abortions. Unmarried women have 18.5 percent of the induced abortions; 26.5 percent of these women were between ages 16 and 20. The overwhelming majority of women who had an abortion, 77.9 percent of married women and 71.3 percent of unmarried women, reported satisfaction with the results of the abortion. This reflects, perhaps, the fact that abortion has become commonplace in Korea (PPFK 1996).

D. Cesarean Operations   HUSO YI

Korea's frequency of cesarean (c-) section delivery is the highest in the world. According to the National Health Insurance Corporation (NHIC), almost half (43 percent) of the Korean women who had a baby in 1999 delivered by the cesarean operation. The rate of increase has been surprisingly rapid: from 6.0 percent in 1985, to 13.3 percent in 1990, to 21.3 percent in 1995, and most recently, in 1999, to 43 percent.

By age-cohort group, 29.4 percent of mothers under 19 years old delivered by c-section, with 37.0 percent of mothers between ages 20 and 24, 40.7 percent between ages 25 and 29, 46.5 percent between 30 and 34, 58.4 percent between 35 and 39, and 68.7 percent over 40 years old (see the NHIC Web site: http://www.nhic.or.kr, in Korean).

The highest c-section frequency rate among hospitals was 75.6 percent of all deliveries. Even the lowest hospital rate (16.1 percent) exceeded the World Health Organization (WHO) recommendation of 10 percent. The 1999 rates for the United States was 20 percent and for Japan, 15 percent. A survey showed that 80 percent of the participants were recommended by doctors for caesareans without detailed benefits and risks (Kim 2000). The main reason of the highest rate comes from the insurance policy. Natural delivery costs about US$40 for outpatients and US$330 for inpatients, whereas the operation costs US$180 for outpatients and US$860 for inpatients. In addition, in cases of natural delivery, women need to be taken care of for at least 12 hours, but caesarean operations only take 40 minutes. Lawsuit cases regarding vaginal delivery accidents ranks the first. Thus, doctors prefer the high-profit and low-risk caesarean operation. The issue received public attention right after NHIC announced the annual report on caesarean operations in July of 2000. Since then, women's rights groups have worked to promote the "right of choice" for women's bodies, together with the issue of abortion.

E. Population Programs   HYUNG KI CHOI AND COLLEAGUES

Family planning started in Korea in 1961 with the slogan of "Two children whether they are a boy or a girl." The population-increase rate has diminished from 2.32 in 1970 to 1.54 in 1980 to 1.02 in 1997. The total fertility rate has also decreased from 4.5 in 1970 to 2.8 in 1980 to 1.6 in 1997 (see

Tables 8 and 9). Korea's population-increase rate and fertility rate decreased only after considerable effort. Although the trend and current rates are encouraging, this trend has not become solid. The reasons for this uncertainty are as follows: First, the strong preference toward boys is worsening the male-to-female ratio. Second, late deliveries for women in their later 30s are increasing. There are also significant increases in the reversal of tubal ligations and vasectomies. Third, there still exists a high rate of unwanted pregnancies, which corresponds to the high rate of induced abortion. Fourth, the number of emigrants has decreased considerably, but immigrants into Korea have increased recently. Fifth, the rapid decrease in the death ratio is producing significant increases in the adult and elderly populations.

Table 8

Natural Population Increase Rate

Year	1970	1980	1985	1990	1991	1992	1993	1994	1995	1996	1997
Rate	2.32	1.54	1.02	9.5	1.08	1.13	1.08	1.06	1.04	0.99	1.02

Source: National Statistical Office 1999b

Table 9

Total Fertility Rate

Year	1970	1980	1985	1990	1991	1992	1993	1994	1995	1996	1997
Rate	4.5	2.8	1.7	1.6	1.7	1.8	1.7	1.7	1.7	1.6	1.6

Source: National Statistical Office 1999b

10. Sexually Transmitted Diseases

A. Incidence, Patterns, and Trends   HYUNG KI CHOI AND COLLEAGUES

Korean law lists syphilis, gonorrhea, chlamydia, herpes, candida, chancre, cancroids, nongonococcal urethritis, and lymphogranuloma venereum as sexually transmitted diseases. The number of STDs steadily declined from 145,802 cases in 1985, to 121,585 in 1990, and to 120,320 in 1995, but it increased to 127,389 in 1996 and 134,726 in 1997. Beginning in 1984, a law mandated that those who are employed in situations with a high risk of STDs must have regular screenings. There are 324 centers designated to prevent, diagnose, and treat sexually transmitted diseases (see Table 10).

11. HIV/AIDS

A. Incidence, Patterns, and Trends
                    HYUNG KI CHOI AND COLLEAGUES (REDACTED BY HUSO YI)

The first report of an HIV-positive foreigner in Korea came in June 1985, followed by the first report of a Korean HIV-positive case (contracted abroad) December 1985. The first AIDS patient was diagnosed in February 1987 following an unsafe transfusion in Kenya. As of the end of 1998, the total number of HIV-positive cases in Korea was 876 and the number of

Table 10

STD Screening Criteria and Required Frequency of Tests

	Frequency of Tests	
	Serologic Test	**STD Test**
Waitresses and Dancers at Foreign Amusement Restaurants	Once every 3 months	Once a week
Waitresses and Dancers at Amusement Restaurants	Once every 3 months	Once a month
Service Girls at Lodging Houses/Love Motels	Once every 6 months	Once every 6 months
Service Girls at Massage Rooms	Once every 3 months	Once every 3 months

Source: Ministry of Health and Welfare 1999

AIDS patients was 131 (see Table 11). The estimated number of HIV-positive cases as of the end of 2000 is around 5,000, most of them being in their 20s and 30s. [According to a recent report by the Ministry of Health and Welfare (2001), as of the end of 2000, Korea had 1,280 HIV-positive cases; 219 new cases were reported and 52 died of AIDS in 2000. The annual-increase rate from 1994 to 1998 was 12.8 percent. However, in 1999, the increase was 44 percent compared to the previous five years and, in 2000, a 17.7-percent increase occurred. The reasons for this significant increase can be found in the increase in voluntary testing, increased awareness of HIV/AIDS prevention, and the need for HIV treatment. (Huso Yi)]

Table 11

HIV/AIDS Cases in Korea, 1985-1998

	1985-91	1992	1993	1994	1995	1996	1997	1998	Total
HIV Infected	169	76	78	90	108	102	124	129	876
AIDS Patients	8	2	6	11	14	22	33	35	131

Source: Ministry of Health and Welfare 1999

In the epidemiology of HIV infection in Korea, heterosexual contact accounted for 339 cases, and heterosexual contact abroad for 236 cases. Homosexual contact was the modality in 191 cases, and 38 cases contracted HIV via blood products (see Table 12).

B. Availability of Treatment, Prevention Programs, and Government Policies

HYUNG KI CHOI AND COLLEAGUES (REDACTED BY HUSO YI)

With the initial report of an HIV-positive case in 1985, the Korean government enacted a strict law to deal with this threat. Mandatory screening of all blood products was instituted in July 1985 and expanded in July 1987. AIDS-prevention legislation was enacted in November to prevent rapid transmission of this deadly disease. In 1991, a professional health care education conference on AIDS prevention was offered by the Korean Institute of Health. Semiannual screening programs are designed to find

Table 12
Route of Infection

Route of Infection	Cases	Route of Infection	Cases
Sexual Contact		Blood Products	17
Korean Heterosexual	339	Maternal	1
Foreign Heterosexual	236	Intravenous Drug Use	0
Homosexual	191	Others	42
Blood Transfusion			
Domestic	10	Total	876
Abroad	11		

Source: Ministry of Health and Welfare 1999

and treat HIV/AIDS patients among waitresses and dancers at foreign amusement restaurants, service girls at lodging houses and massage parlors, and waitresses at tearooms. This program includes informing the spouse and friends of HIV/AIDS-infected persons and close surveillance, with financial support from both the local and central governments.

[People with HIV are required to receive HIV-prevention training and counseling at local health centers, as well as to report to a government office when moving. The government provides medication for HIV/AIDS for free. The problem, however, is that these patients with HIV/AIDS first have to pay for medications at the hospital and then request reimbursement. Thus, if they do not have enough money for treatment in the first 3 months, they cannot get medication. With respect to the HIV test, voluntary tests rarely occurred because of the mandatory law for reporting. Only targeted groups in the sex industry get mandatory testing. The current policy does not consider the rights of people with HIV. Once notified that they are HIV-positive, they are listed under the permanent control of the government, so they cannot guarantee their privacy. It is reported that people with HIV suffer more from government surveillance than from illness and/or the fact of HIV infection. The AIDS-related law states that if people with HIV refuse to report regularly, government officers, designated by the state governor or the Ministry of Health department, can visit them in their living places without notification and take them to separate places for treatment. In case they refuse the officer's acts, they will be sentenced for one year in prison or a US$1,000 fine. People with HIV cannot work in the mandatory testing places. As shown, unlike those of developed countries, the AIDS-prevention law is primarily to enforce punishment and not to protect those with HIV, so that it certainly violates human rights (Chung 1999). In order to ensure their rights, actual name reporting at government offices, mandatory testing, separation for treatment, and excessive criminal law enforcement should be revised. (Huso Yi)]

[Meanwhile, awareness about the importance of HIV testing may be different issue. A study reported that, among 507 college students, only 5 male students and 1 female student had taken the HIV test (Kang 1994). (Huso Yi)]

12. *Sexual Dysfunctions, Counseling, and Therapies*

A. Sexual Dysfunctions and Attitudes

HUSO YI

Erectile dysfunction in males and inhibited female orgasm were the most frequently reported dysfunctions (Yoo et al. 1989). Male expectation anxiety and female orgasmic disorder were highly related to morality by repressing sexual desire. In terms of morality, it was also pointed out that masturbation and sexual fantasy were effective therapy for single adults, but little research had been done with married couples. In their study, more than 90 percent of the 120 married-couple respondents had sexual fantasies. With respect to the content of the sexual fantasies, the female showed more various content than those of the males: replacement of the partner (52.6 percent of males and 38.5 percent of females); unusual positions (21.1 percent of males and 13.2 percent of females); unusual sexual activity (15.8 percent of males and 3.8 percent of females); group-sex experiences (7.9 percent of males and 1.9 percent of females), and the use of sex toys (2.6 percent of males and 3.8 percent of females). The following things were only fantasized by the females: forced sexual encounters, sadistic imagery, observation of sexual activity, and sexual activities with animals. Thirty percent of the females gave no response. The findings suggested conflicts between the females' sexual desires and their activities, which results in sexual dysfunction.

B. The Availability of Diagnosis and Treatment

HYUNG KI CHOI AND COLLEAGUES (REDACTED BY HUSO YI)

[Sex therapy was first offered by a few psychiatrists in the 1970s, and until the early 1980s, only partial analyses through case studies were available (Yoo et al. 1990). Later in the 1980s, as Korean society became more Westernized, the issue of sexual dysfunctions received attention. The first sex therapy clinic was established in April 1986 at Yonsei Medical Center. The clinic developed a Korean version of the Self-Evaluation of Sexual Behavior & Gratification (Lief 1981) and DSFI: Derogatis Sexual Functioning Inventory (Derogatis & Melisoratos 1979). These Korean translations were evaluated for reliability and validity and have been effective in sex therapy settings (Lee et al. 1989). In a review of the 231 patients who visited the sex therapy clinic from its opening to April 1995, 75.8 percent were male and 24.2 percent were female. The most prevalent sexual disorders were male erectile dysfunction (40.1 percent), premature ejaculation (20.3 percent) and inhibited female orgasm (10.6 percent). Those who underwent sex therapy with their partners were 11. 5 percent where the male had the problem and 20.0 percent where it was the female, which were significantly lower than those in Western countries (Yoo 1999) (Huso Yi)]

Since the 1980s, there has been a rapid increase in the number of publications associated with sexual dysfunction and andrology. In the *Journal of Urology*, there were 13 papers published by Koreans researchers and clinicians in 1983. This increased to 33 in 1988, and to 52 in 1993. In an effort to accommodate this increase, the *Korean Journal of Andrology* began publishing in 1989. *Andrology*, a textbook on sexual dysfunction and infertility, was authored by Hee-young Lee, and in 1995, Sae-chul Kim published

Diagnosis and Treatment of Male Sexual Dysfunction. Hyung-ki Choi also published the experiences of a sexual dysfunction clinic to further the knowledge of the general public.

Male sexual dysfunction includes a decrease in libido, erectile dysfunction, and ejaculatory abnormality. It is estimated that there are 1.2 million such patients in Korea. This number is ever increasing because of prolonged life expectancy, stress, and various traffic and industrial accidents. Since penile prosthesis implantation was introduced by Professor Hyung-ki Choi and Sae-chul Kim in Korea in 1983, some 800 cases were performed as of 1995. Professor Hee-young Lee introduced triple pharmacologic agents for corporal injection in patients with erectile dysfunction, and vascular reconstruction for arteriogenic impotence was first performed in 1989. Sildenafil sulfate (Viagra) has been available to Korean patients since October 1999. In Korea, patients over 21 can purchase a monthly allowance of 8 sildenafil pills (Viagra) with written proof from a physician that they are free from any cardiovascular diseases.

No nationwide data on the clinical profiles of sexual dysfunctions are yet available in Korea. In 1998, Hyung-ki Choi from Yonsei University reported the results of 2,000 consecutive patients visiting a sexual dysfunction clinic from September 1995 to March 1997. Patients in their 40s were most common at 29.4 percent, and unmarried patients comprised 11.5 percent. The most common complaint was erectile dysfunction with 61.8 percent, premature ejaculation with 15.0 percent, and those with both diseases at 11.7 percent; 40.4 percent of patients had a previous experience of counseling or treatment with health care professionals, 70.3 percent being non-physician care. The most common associated diseases were diabetes (17.3 percent) and cardiovascular abnormality (13.8 percent). Medical treatment was offered in 64.7 percent of the patients, and among them, 21.5 percent gained erectile ability capable of intromission.

[Another well-known sex therapy clinic is the Seoul-Cornell Clinic for Human Sexuality, with Dr. Hyun Uk Seol, who is a member of the Society for Scientific Study of Sexuality and was trained in sex therapy by Dr. Helen Singer Kaplan at Cornell Medical School in New York City. His clinic opened in 1995 and he has published a dozen books about sexuality from his own publisher, Sex-Academy. His sex therapy Web site (http://www.sex-academy.com; contact: seolhu@nuri.net) has good resources with online sex counseling. (Huso Yi)]

C. Therapist Training and Certification   HUSO YI

There is no organization offering a certificate for sex therapy, nor is there any institutional training program for sex therapy in Korea. Usually, medical doctors, who are trained in psychiatry, obstetrics and gynecology, urology, andrology, and its related fields, practice sex therapy. In the medical school, the need for courses about sexuality has been discussed, but the problem remains as to which department should be responsible for the curricula (Hong et al. 1993). For sexuality counseling, several organizations, such as the Sexual Violence Relief Center, the Planned Parenthood Federation of Korea (PPFK), the Young Women's Christian Association

(YWCA), and other social welfare organizations have developed their own programs on sexuality counselor certification, so that no official criteria or guidelines have yet been established.

13. Research and Advanced Education

A. Graduate Programs and Sexological Research   HUSO YI

The Korean Research Institute for Culture and Sexuality was founded in July 1996 under the supervision of the Planned Parenthood Federation of Korea with funding from the Korean government. The tasks of this Institute are to resolve the problems of male preference and the imbalance of sex-ratio at birth, prevent abortion by promoting contraceptive use, and establish effective sexuality education. The Institute has conducted not only nationwide studies about the issues of adolescent and adult sexuality, but also investigated sexuality education and counseling centers all over the country. The Institute has been very successful in developing resources for sexuality education, with more than 200 visual materials and a guidebook of sexuality education. Especially, the major achievement is that the Institute has offered training programs in sexuality education and counseling for the officers at local health centers and school teachers since 1997. The training is composed of three courses. The trainees first attend lectures and a field study at a sexuality education center, and then attend 20 sessions of sexuality education and 50 sessions of a counseling internship. In the last course, they participate in the discussion of case studies, sexuality counseling supervision, and psychological testing. Those who pass the course receive the certificate of sexuality educator/counseling specialist (PPFK 2000). For information, see http://www.yline.re.kr; contact: sjoon@ppfk.re.kr.

The Korean Society of Human Sexuality (KSHS) was founded in 1988 and lasted until 1995. Composed mainly of scholars in medical science, KSHS also included social scientists, psychologists, relationship counselors, and other professionals. The Society published the *Journal of the Korean Society for Human Sexuality,* as well as held monthly colloquia on sexual issues and topics, such as sex therapy, sexuality and religion, sexuality education, sexual physiology, sex and art, transsexualism, homosexuality, psychosexual development, and so on. All abstracts of the journal (1989-1994) are available in English. Efforts are underway in 2001 to revive the organization.

In 1997, Ewha Woman's University* opened the Korean Women's Institute and offered women's studies courses at the undergraduate level. The Department of Women's Studies was established in the graduate school in 1982 and expanded to offer Ph.D. degrees in 1990. Through such achievements, Ewha Woman's University has led in the development of women's studies in Korea. The Asian Center for Women's Studies (ACWS) was established in May 1995 for the purpose of fostering an understanding of

---

[*"Woman's" represents the university's founding with just one student; it further symbolizes its high respect for the individuality of her wonderful women. Therefore, Ewha is not a "women's" university, but "Woman's university," keeping each woman's distinctive being intact in its name" (Quoted from the Ewha Woman's University Web site: http://www.ewha.ac.kr/ewhaeng/index.html). (Huso Yi)]

women's issues in Asia through extensive research, educational programs, and international exchanges (ACWS 2000). Since then, the ACWS has conducted the "Asian Women's Studies Curriculum Development Project" and English lectures/workshops on "Women in Korea," held an international conference on women's studies, and published the *Asian Journal of Women's Studies* For information, see http://home.ewha.ac.kr/~ewsadmin/ www_page/eng/ (in English); contact: acwsewha@mm.ehwa.ac.kr.

The Korean Women's Development Institute (KWDI) is not focused mainly on sexological research itself, yet the KWDI, funded by Korean government, implements numerous research activities and projects in relation to gender and sexuality, with Departments of Law and Politics, Education, Labor and Statistics, Family Health and Welfare, Social Culture, and Information Development. The Institute publishes an annual report comparing statistics for women and men, conducts research on sexual abuse, sexuality education, and prostitution, and produces visual materials on these topics (KWDI 1999). For information: http://kwdi.re.kr; contact: S4KWDI@unitel.or.kr.

B. Sexological Organization and Publications

HYUNG KI CHOI AND COLLEAGUES

In January 1982, at a World Health Organization meeting, the Korean Society of Andrology was formed with plans to publish a journal. The second meeting was held in September 1983. The interest in this new field of medicine was amplified by the first Korean implantation of a penile prosthesis in December 1983. The Korean Society enrolled as a member of the International Society of Andrology in 1985. The Asia-Pacific Society for Impotence Research (APSIR) was organized in November 1987 in Hong Kong, and the founding delegates from Korea included Hyung-ki Choi, first author of this chapter, Sae-chul Kim, and Jun-kyu Seo. Hyung-ki Choi was elected president at this meeting for the second meeting of Asia-Pacific Society for Impotence Research held in Seoul in November 1989, with 239 scientists and physicians attending. In June 1994, the Korean Society for Andrology held a meeting to update private physicians on erectile dysfunction.

References and Suggested Readings

Asian Center for Women's Studies (ACWS). 2000. *Asian Center for Women's Studies: Activity report 1995-2000. 2* (in English). Seoul, Korea: Asian Center for Women's Studies, Ewha Woman's University.

Byun, W., & Hwang, J. 1999. A study of industrial prostitution. *Women's Studies Forum* [Korean Women's Development Institute], *15*:211-230.

Byun, W., Won, Y., & Chung, S. 2000. *Study of sexual consciousness and violence against women* (abstract in English). Seoul: Korean Women's Development Institute.

Chang, P. 1998. Korean mothers, daughters, and wives. In: *Korean culture through women's eyes: Lectures in English* (in English). Seoul: Asian Center for Women's Studies, Ewha Woman's University.

Chang, P. 2000. Women and sexuality. In: *Women of Korea: Lectures in English* (in English). Seoul: Asian Center for Women's Studies, Ewha Woman's University.

Chang, S. B., Lee, Y. J., Park, S. J., Song, E. I., Suh, J. A., & Oh, Y. K. 1998. A study on college students' sexual behaviors. *Korea Research Institute for Culture and Sexuality Report* [Seoul], 98-03 (abstract in English).

Chang, Y. A. 1996. A study on reformation of the head of household law. *Korean Women's Development Institute Research Report*, 200-4. Seoul: KWDI.

Chin, K. N., Lee, Y. J., Park, S. J., Song, E. I., & Kim, S. R. 1997. A study of married adults' sexuality consciousness and attitudes. *Korea Research Institute for Culture and Sexuality Report* [Seoul], 97-01 (abstract in English).

Cho, D. H. 1993. Legal problems in operation for transsexualism. *Journal of Korean Society for Human Sexuality,* 4(1):16-20.

Choi, Y. A. 1996. *Reality and problems in sexual violence.* Presentation at 8th Symposium of Social-Ethics, Seoul.

Chung, D. C. 1990. A survey on sexual violence of adolescents at the urban area. *Journal of Korean Society of Human Sexuality,* 2(1):33-62 (abstract in English).

Chung, H. M. 1999. *Criminal legal problems of AIDS and prevention strategy. Annual report,* 98-12 (abstract in German). Seoul: Korean Institute of Criminology.

Chung, S. H. 1998. *Sexual customs in the Chosun Dynasty: The view of women and sexual culture.* Seoul: Garam Kihuk.

Citizens for Abolition of the Family Headship (*Hoju*) System. 2000. Available: http://antihoju.jinbo.net/ (in Korean).

Committee of Korean Genealogy. 2000. Available: http://www.koreafamily.com (in Korean).

Derogatis, L. R., & Melisoratos, N. 1979. The DSFI: A multidimensional measure of sexual functions. *Journal of Sex and Marital Therapy,* 5:244-281.

Fellows, W. J. 1979. *Religions east and west.* New York: Holt, Rinehart and Winston.

Gregersen, E. 1994. *The world of human sexuality: Behaviors, customs and beliefs.* New York: Irvington Publishers.

Hankyere. 1996 (September 19). Analysis about prevalence of 'son-bearing treatment' and its problem. *Hanhyere 21* [Seoul].

Headquarter of the Family Headship Law Abolition. 2000. Available: http://no-hoju.women21.or.kr/ (in Korean).

Hong, K. E. 1996. Sexual problems in adolescence. *Journal of Korean Medical Association,* 39(12):1514-1518.

Hong, K. E., Cho, D. Y., & Shin, H. C. 1993. Need of human sexuality course. *Journal of Korean Society for Human Sexuality,* 4(1):45-53.

Jung, K. M. 1971. A study on the foreskin and circumcision of the penis of Korean male. *Korean Journal of Public Health,* 8:369.

Kang, B. W. 1994. A study of the university students' consciousness about sex and AIDS. *Journal of Korean Society for Health Education,* 11(1):43-56.

Kendall, L. 1996. *Getting married in Korea.* Berkeley: University of California Press.

Kim, D. S., Lee, J. Y., & Pang, M. G. 1999. Male circumcision: A South Korean perspective. *British Journal of Urology International, 83,* Supplement; *1*:28-33.

Kim, D. S., & Yoon, Y. S. 1997. *Sexual stone of Korea.* Seoul: Blue Forrest Publisher.

Kim, E. 1992. Reformed family law and movement for reforming family law. *Korean Women's Development Institute research report,* 200-3 (in English). Seoul: KWDI.

Kim, E. 1996. The current laws on women in Korea. *Women's Studies Forum* [Korean Women's Development Institute, Seoul] (in English), *12*:33-49.

Kim, E., Yoon, D., & Park, H. 2000. *Acts on violence against women: Enforcement status and tasks* (abstract in English). Seoul: Korean Women's Development Institute.

Kim, H. J. 2001 (January 18). Prosecution to arrest Internet adult TV operators for showing porn. *Korea Herald* [Seoul] (available in English at http://www.koreaherald.co.kr/SITE/data/html_dir/2001/01/19/200101190034.asp).

Kim. H. W. 1996. *Effects of sexual satisfaction in marital adjustments.* Unpublished master's thesis, Seoul: Yonsei University.

Kim, J. H., Lee, Y. J., Park, S. J., Song, E.I., Suh, J. A., & Oh, Y. J. 1998. A study on unmarried working adults' sexuality consciousness and sexual behaviors. *Korea Research Institute for Culture and Sexuality Report* [Seoul], 98-104 (abstract in English).

Kim, J. R. 1993. *Study of male preference and reproductive health.* Unpublished master's thesis, Taegu: Kyemyung University.

Kim, S. W., Lee, Y. J., Park, S. J., Kim, S. R., & Song, E. I. 1997. *A study of high school girls' sexuality consciousness: Their sexual behaviors and problems of sexuality* (vol. 97, no. 102, abstract in English). Seoul: The Korea Research Institute for Culture and Sexuality.

Kim, S. W., Shin, D. J., Song, I. S., & Park, S. J. 1996. *A study of high school boys' sexuality consciousness.* Seoul: Korea Research Institute for Culture and Sexuality.

Kim, U. N. 2000. Protest to regain the right of delivery choice. *Sisa Journal* [Seoul], 561.

Kim, Y. C. 1976. *Women of Korea: A history from ancient times to 1945* (in English). Seoul: Ewha Woman's University Press.

King Y.-J. 1736. *Woman's four book* (trans. by J.-K. Kim in 1987). Seoul: Myung Moon Dang.

Korea Anti-AIDS Federation. 1997. *Annual report on AIDS specialized counseling.* Seoul: Korea Anti-AIDS Federation.

Korea Herald. 2001 (January 18). Koreans spend much time on Net. *Korea Herald* [Seoul] (available in English at http://www.koreaherald.co.kr/SITE/data/html_dir/ 2001/ 01/18/200101180033.asp).

Korean Council for Women Drafted into Military Sexual Slavery by Japan. 2000. Available: http://witness.peacenet.or.kr/kindex.htm (in English).

Korean Government Homepage. 2000. Available: http://www.korea.net; for demographic information, see http://www.korea.net/menu/koreainfo/kitspeople.htm (in English).

Korea Institute for Health and Social Affairs. 1998. *National fertility and family health survey report.*

Korean Institute for Health and Social Welfare. 1991. *Sex preference for children and gender discrimination.* Seoul: Korean Institute for Health and Social Welfare.

Korean Institute for Health and Social Welfare. 1999. *Study of Korean sexual violence problems.* Seoul: Korean Institute for Health and Social Welfare.

Korean Institute of Criminology. 1998. *Investigation on sexual violence.* Seoul: Korean Institute of Criminology.

Korean Sexuality Counseling Center. 1997. *Sexuality counseling activity report.* Seoul: Planned Parenthood Federation of Korea.

Korean Sexual Violence Relief Center. 1999. Case report on sexual violence. *Nanumte* [*Sharing Place,* Seoul], 29.

Korean Women's Development Institute (KWDI). 2000a. *Study of sexual consciousness and violence against women.*

Korean Women's Development Institute (KWDI). 2000b. *Women's statistical yearbook* [women's social indicator information]. Available at: http://www.kwdi.re.kr (English).

Korean Women's Development Institute (KWDI). 1999. Korean women today. *KWDI Newsletter* [Seoul], 65 (in English).

Lee, B. S., & Chung, H. S. 2000. *Guidebook of sexual rehabilitation for the spinal cord injured.* Seoul: The National Rehabilitation Center.

Lee, C. 1996. *Study of Korean women's sexual attitudes.* Unpublished master's thesis, Pusan: Pusan University.

Lee, H. S. 1997. Birth of Korean gay community and its future. *Another World,* 5. Seoul: Kiri Kiri.

Lee, H. S., Oh, B. H., Yoo, K. J., Lee, M. S., & Kim, M. K. 1989. DSFI characteristics between normal and male sexual dysfunction. *Journal of Korean Society for Human Sexuality,* 1(1):83-93 (abstract in English).

Lee, J. S. 1993. Social aspects in transsexualism. *Journal of Korean Society for Human Sexuality,* 4(1):21-29 (abstract in English).

Lee, Y. J., Kim, S. R., & Song, I. E. 1998. A study of factors influenced to high school girl's experiences of having sex and attitudes on premarital intercourse. *Korea Research Institute for Culture and Sexuality Report* [Seoul], 98-102 (abstract in English).

Leupp, G. P. 1995. *Male colors: The construction of homosexuality in Tokugawa, Japan.* Berkeley: University of California Press.

Lief, H. I. 1981. *Sexual problem in medical practice: Sexual performance evaluation.* New York: American Medical Association.

Martin, F., & Berry, C. 1998. QueerNAsian on the Net: Syncretic sexualities in Taiwan and Korean cyberspaces. *Critical in Queeries,* 2(1):67-93.

Ministry of Health and Welfare (MOHW). 1998. *Statistical annual report.* Seoul: Ministry of Health and Welfare.

Ministry of Health and Welfare (MOHW). 1999. *Statistical annual report.* Seoul: Communicable Disease Control Division, Ministry of Health and Welfare.

Ministry of Health and Welfare (MOHW). 2000. *Statistical annual report.* Seoul: Ministry of Health and Welfare.

Moon. H. S. 1993. *Study of types about spousal relationships by marital and sexual satisfaction.* Unpublished doctoral dissertation, Seoul: Dongguk University.

Murray, S. 1992. *Oceanic homosexualities.* New York: Garland.

Murray, S. 2000. *Homosexualities.* Chicago: The University of Chicago Press.

National Statistical Office (NSO). 1985. *Census of surname and family origin.* Seoul: National Statistical Office.

National Statistical Office (NSO). 1998. *1997 annual report on the economically active population survey.* Seoul: National Statistical Office.

National Statistical Office (NSO). 1999a. *Annual report on the economically active population survey (1996-1999).* Seoul: National Statistical Office.

National Statistical Office (NSO). 1999b. *Annual report on the vital statistics.* Seoul: National Statistical Office (available in English at http://www.nso.go.kr/eindex .html).

NHCROK. 2001. *National history compilation of the Republic of Korea.* Available: http://kuksa.nhcc.go.kr/english/index.html (in English).

Noss, D. S., & Noss, J. B. 1990. *A history of the world's religions.* New York: Macmillan.

Oh, B. H., Yoo, K. J., Lee, H. S., Lee, H. Y., & Moon, J. H. 1990. A study on the sexual behavior of spinal cord injured men. *Journal of Korean Society for Human Sexuality,* 2(1):92-105 (abstract in English).

Oh, C. S. 1997. History of son-wish-stone. In: D. S. Kim & Y. S. Yoon, *Sexual stone of Korea* (pp. 216-220). Seoul: Blue Forrest Publisher.

Our Society Research Center. 1994. *Sexuality and modern society.* Seoul: Blue Land Publisher.

Park, J. I. 1994 (August 25). Compensation for hymen lost: Not lost of virginity but a medical accident. *Chosun Daily* [Seoul].

Planned Parenthood Federation of Korea (PPFK). 1996. *Study of abortion cases in the major 20 hospitals.* Seoul: Planned Parenthood Federation of Korea.

Planned Parenthood Federation of Korea. 2000 (PPFK). *The annual report of family health.* Seoul: Planned Parenthood Federation of Korea.

Presidential Commission on Women's Affairs. 2000. Available: http://www.pcwa .go.kr/w-en/home.htm (in English).

Report Center of Cyber Sexual Violence. 2000. *Survey about cyber sexual violence* (cited January 23, 2001; available: http://www.gender.co.kr, in Korean).

Seol, H. U. 2000. *Dr. Hyun Uk Seol's sexology Q&A volume 3.* Seoul: Sex-Academy.

Shong, S., & Icard, L. D. 1996. A Korean gay man in the United States: Toward a cultural context for social service practice. *Journal of Gay and Lesbian Social Services,* 5(2/3):115-137.

Yi, H. 1998. *History of homosexuality and gay movements in Korea.* Paper presented at the 5th Congress of Asian Sexology, Seoul.

Yi, H. 2000. *Coming out: 300 Q&A about gay and lesbian people* (trans. of E. Marcus's *Is it a choice?* with added Q&A about Korean gays). Seoul: Park Young-Yul Publisher.

Yoo, K. J. 1993. Psychiatric aspects in transsexualism. *Journal of Korean Society for Human Sexuality,* 4(1):5-11 (abstract in English).

Yoo, K. J., Namkoong, K., Lee, H. Y., Lee, H. S., Oh, B. H., & Lee, B. Y. 1990. Clinical study of patients who visited a sex clinic. *Journal of Korean Society for Human Sexuality,* 2(1):77-91 (abstract in English).

Yoo, K. J., Oh, B. H., Lee, H. S., Kim, M. K., & Yoon, K. S. 1989. Sexual fantasies in married couple. *Journal of Koran Society for Human Sexuality,* 1(1):71-82 (abstract in English).

Yoo, K. J., Oh, B. H., & Soh, E. H. 1990. Parents' attitude toward masturbation. *Journal of Korean Society for Human Sexuality,* 2(1):63-76 (abstract in English).

Youn, G. 1995 (March). Adolescent sexuality: A speculation on the abortion debate. *Jisung Paegee,* 27:122-125.

Youn, G. 1996. Sexual activities and attitudes of adolescent Koreans. *Archives of Sexual Behavior,* 25(6):629-643.

Turkey
(*Türkiye Cumhuriyeti*)
(The Republic of Turkey)

Hamdullah Aydin, M.D.*, and Zeynep Gülçat, Ph.D.**

Contents

Demographics and a Historical Perspective

A. Demographics

Turkey is located at the intersection of two continents, with the small region of Thrace and the ancient city of Istanbul in Europe, and the larger part of the country, Anatolia, in Asia Minor. Turkey is twice the size of the state of California, with an area of 301,382 square miles (780,580 square kilometers). Anatolia (Asia Minor) is surrounded by the Black Sea, the Aegean Sea, and the Mediterranean. An inland sea, the Marmara, separates Anatolia from Thrace and Istanbul to the northwest. Turkey has 4,471 miles (8,333 kilometers) of coastline. Rectangular in shape, Turkey stretches 1,565 kilometers east to west, and 650 kilometers north to south. Its neighbors are Greece and Bulgaria to the west, the Black Sea, Georgia, and Armenia on the

*Communications: Hamdullah Aydn, M.D., S. Adem Yavuz Sok 9/11, 06440 Kizilay, Ankara, Turkey; hAydn@gata.edu.tr.

**Zeynep Gülçat, Ph.D., Fevzi Çakmak Sok 41/A-5, 06440 Kizilay, Ankara, Turkey; zeygul@Superonline.com.

northeast, Azerbaijan and Iran to the east, and Iraq and Syria on the south. Mid Anatolia and the eastern regions are typically hot and dry during the summer and cold and rainy during winter. The coastline along the north, west, and south of Turkey has a milder climate throughout the year.

Turkey's agricultural production is, on the whole, self-sufficient, but the country is not rich in the natural resources. A radical transition toward industrial development has occurred in Turkey's economy, which was based on agriculture in the past. State intervention in the economy has gradually diminished since the 1980s, and at present, the economy relies on free-market rules. Turkey possesses a wealth of historical and tourist sites, with a rich potential for summer as well as winter tourism.

Many ancient cultures of Anatolia, including the Mesopotamian, Sumerian, and Hittite, constitute Turkey's basic cultural heritage. An Islamic culture is woven into this background.

Ankara, the capital of Turkey, with 2.7 million people, is in the center of Anatolia. Turkey's largest city, Istanbul, has a population of 7.3 million. Located in the northwest, along the shores of the Bosphorus, the point where East and West meet, Istanbul and its environs are the most densely populated, urbanized, and developed part of the country. The city is a center of trade, large and small-scale industry, as well as a center of arts and historical places.

The age distribution of Turkey's 1999 estimated 65.6 million population was 30.9 percent below age 15, 63.4 percent between ages 15 and 65, and 5.7 percent over age 65. Turkey has a young population, with more than half under age 24. Eighty percent of the population is Turkish and 20 percent are Kurds; 99.8 percent are Muslim, mostly Sunni.

Turkey's total life expectancy at birth in 1999 was 70.8 years for males and 75.9 years for females. The 1999 birthrate was 20.9 per 1,000 persons and declining, and the death rate 5.27 per 1,000, giving Turkey an annual natural increase of 1.57 percent. The infant mortality rate was 35.8 per 1,000 live births in 1999 and is expected to drop to 3.5 by the year 2000. The mean family population is 4.75 people. In 1997, Turkey's Total Fertility Rate (TFR) was 2.5 births per fertile woman, placing it 128 among the 227 nations of the world. In 1997, Turkey had one hospital bed per 450 persons and one physician per 1,200 persons. The 1995 literacy rate was 82 percent, with 95 percent attendance for free and compulsory school between ages 6 and 14. The per capita gross domestic product in 1997 was $6,100.

Turkey, like many countries, has experienced a huge population shift in the past fifty years. The percentage of the population living in the cities has doubled in 35 years, from 25 percent in 1950 to 53 percent in 1985. Now, in 2000, it is between 65 and 70 percent. Istanbul is one of the most densely populated cities in Europe, with 9.5 million inhabitants. Ankara, the capital, has 2.8 million. This dramatic population shift is almost entirely attributed to the massive departure of people from the rural areas of central, eastern, and southeastern regions of Anatolia. This population shift facilitates changes in the family structure from the patriarchal to the nuclear model. This rapid transformation and urbanization has also created difficulties in religious, moral, and sociocultural adaptation. Housing problems in urban areas induced migrants into building shanty houses, called *gecekondu* ("built overnight"), in the vicinity of big cities. These *gecekondu* are lacking in municipal services and facilities. As a result, a whole new subculture has emerged with its own lifestyle, bringing with it many social and economic problems. *Gecekondu* families are employed in small-scale or marginal jobs. Although they have now become permanent and essential factors in the urban economy, they are not yet fully integrated into the urban culture, because of their low education levels, limited income, and cultural differences reflecting the traditional lifestyles.

Another important social phenomenon has been the out-migration of labor from the rural parts of Turkey to the countries of Western Europe, beginning in the early 1960s. It is estimated that two to three million Turkish workers currently reside in western European countries. The so-called "second generation" born in these countries are subject to ethnic identity problems. They call themselves "European Turks," while they are labeled as "Almancilar" (Germaners) in Turkey. A considerable number of workers have migrated back to Turkey in the last decade, bringing back Western values, which have affected male and female roles, as well as relations between men and women. The response to this process depends on many factors, including environmental support, family background, and individual characteristics. It remains to be seen how this out-migration and back-migration will affect overall sexual attitudes and behavior in Turkey.

Thus, as Kagitçibasi (1982a) has noted, Turkish society presents a highly complex, heterogeneous picture, with diverse ethnic, cultural, and religious influences, which differentiate along social class, rural-urban, and regional development dimensions. From the historical point of view, various cultural influences, which include the nomadic-Turkish, ancient Anatolian, Islamic-Middle Eastern, the Mediterranean, and contemporary Western attitudes and values, have shaped and are still shaping Turkish society today.

B. A Brief Historical Perspective

The ancient inhabitants of Turkey were among the world's first agriculturalists. The Hittite, an Indo-European people, created an empire in Anatolia over four thousand years ago and controlled much of what is modern-day Turkey for a thousand years. Phyrgian and Lydian cultures also flourished in Asiatic Turkey. The rise of Greek civilization, with city-states like Troy on the coast of Asia Minor, and expansion of the Assyrian empire led to the collapse of the Hittites about 900 B.C.E. In the early centuries, among the ancient Turkish tribes in central Asia, both sexes were considered as equals in a society where men and women took equal share of responsibility in affairs of the country, although there has been a dominance of patriarchal or matriarchal family structures in different Turkish tribes throughout history. Records of ancient Turkish families reveal that monogamy was the basic model, although some tribes were polygynous. In some tribes, the marital union only became valid after the birth of the first child (Tezcan 1998). There are also records indicating that there was an annual tradition of freedom, in terms of social and sexual interaction, which could be an ancient model of contemporary *carnivals* or *mardi gras* in Western countries.

In the sixth century B.C.E., Anatolia, except for some city-states on the Aegean coast, was incorporated into the Persian Empire. Alexander the Great conquered the area, but it returned to Persian rule when his empire collapsed around 300 B.C.E. By the end of the first century of the Common Era, Thrace and Anatolia were incorporated into the Roman Empire. Constantine the Great founded the city of Constantinople on the site of ancient Byzantium in 330 as the empire's eastern capital. Following the decline of the Roman Empire in the west, Constantinople became the capital of the independent Eastern Roman (Byzantine) Empire in the seventh century and retained this role for a thousand years. Repeated attacks by Arab Islamic forces were fought off in the seventh and eighth centuries, but the empire lost control of central Anatolia to the Seljuk Turkish rulers of Persia after 1038. The thirteenth century Mongul invasions left Turkey mainly untouched, but they weakened both Byzantine and Seljuk power.

In 1453, the Byzantine Empire fell to the Ottoman Turks, who established a vast empire that lasted until the end of World War I. After embracing the Muslim religion, the social life of Turkish women became restricted, and they lost most of the rights of their ancestors. In the six centuries of Islamic influence and Ottoman control prior to the twentieth century, discrimination between the sexes grew and women were forced to live as a separate group. The harem life was introduced, and in the fifteenth century, the palace of the sultan was divided into a *Harem* (women's section) and a *Selamlik* (men's section). Soon, harem life and polygyny became customary throughout the state. According to the Islamic family laws adopted by the Ottomans, women could not choose their husbands, marriages were arranged by the older members of the family, a woman was not supposed to be seen by her husband before or during the marriage ceremony, and a wife could be easily divorced by her husband, who alone could decide to do so.

Towards the end of the nineteenth century, with the penetration of Western ideas into Ottoman society, women were allowed some education, and their status began to improve. Turkey's independence war under the leadership of Mustafa Kemal Atatürk resulted in the fall of the sultanate and abolishment of the religious authority and spiritual leadership of the caliphate. Thus, the religiously based system of the Ottoman Empire was ended. The Turkish Republic was declared in 1923 and a sudden break was made with old values and concepts. Secularism, Statism, Nationalism, Reformism, Populism, and Republicanism were declared the ideologies of the new state. Turkish civil law was accepted in 1926, triggering a wave of rapid change in social life throughout the country. Polygyny was ended and religious marriages were rendered legally (but not always socially) invalid. Women gained equal rights with men, including the rights of inheritance, divorce, and owning property. In 1934, Turkey was among the first nations to give women the political rights to vote and hold elected office. At the beginning, however, these radical changes could not be assimilated equally in all parts of the country. Thus, for example, polygyny can still be seen today in the less developed regions of Turkey, though it is relatively rare. Many uneducated women are still not aware of their civil rights. Also, for many women, legal rights may have little practical value if social and economic pressures do not allow them to use these rights.

In summary, with the declaration of the Turkish Republic and the adoption of Western values and lifestyle in the first quarter of the twentieth century, a major break or even a social split has occurred in the community, which has a rich and complex background. Such an abrupt change undoubtedly affected concepts and experiences in sexuality in contradictory ways. While liberating women and mitigating segregation between male and female roles, it has at the same time created gaps between generations and various social structures that are difficult to bridge.

1. Basic Sexological Premises

A. Character of Gender Roles

The Effects of Social Change

At the beginning of the twentieth century, a movement against Ottoman marriage customs and concerned with the plight of Turkish women began. The protesters were mostly upper- and middle-class men who were allowed by Islamic rules to marry up to four wives, supplement them by concubines, repudiate them at will, and exercise strict control over their mobility outside the household. These protesters were against arranged marriages; they desired educated wives with whom they could have intellectual as well as emotional communication, and a social life where the sexes could mingle freely (Kandiyoti 1995).

In this period, the Turkish nationalist movement also introduced new elements into the debate between Western ideologies and Islam. The ideologues of the Turkish nationalism asserted that ancient Turkish customs in Central Asia involved total equality between conjugal partners in a monogamous and democratic family. In 1917, the Family Code was accepted, and represented the first intervention of the central state into the family, which had previously been under the control of the religious authorities. With the establishment of the Turkish Republic in 1923, a major break had taken place; the caliphate was abolished, the new constitution was based on secularism, and measures were taken to heighten Turkey's national consciousness in place of an Islamic identification. Revolutionary changes in the new state included the romanization of the alphabet, the new dress code, and an interpretation of Turkish history stressing its pre-Islamic cultural heritage. Laws were passed for compulsory and standard primary education throughout the country. The state and parents were made responsible for the education of each child. The modern woman of the Turkish Republic experienced a kind of metamorphosis, becoming a prominent figure, dressed in the Western style or in a school or military uniform, and wearing evening dresses for ballroom dances. In the male-oriented society where son preference was the main attitude, Atatürk, the founder of the Turkish Republic, set a new tone by adopting daughters. Highly trained professional women started working in the republican offices. However, as members of a strictly segregated society in which male honor was dependent on the behavior of their womenfolk, women could only enter the public arena by emphasizing their respectability and non-availability as sexual objects (Kandiyoti 1995).

Initially, these changes affected only a small urban layer. The spread of schooling and health services throughout the country proceeded gradually. Marriage alliances remained firmly under the control of local communities and followed customary practices, which were now denounced as "traditional" or even "backward" by the enlightened technocrats of the republic. Turkey was assumed to be moving from tradition to modernity, and the idealized model of the "modern" nuclear family involved companionate marriage, role-sharing between spouses, and child orientation. The ideology of the modern nuclear family was a radical departure from the pressures and control of older kin characteristic of Muslim societies. However, Kagitçibasi (1982b) argued that the "modern" Turkish family was not based on the autonomy of its members, which modernization theory implied, and that emotional interdependence between family members persisted. Ayata (1988) has commented that tradition and modernity are being lived concretely in Turkish households as a literal "split" between the styles of consumption, formal dress, and conduct displayed in the guest room; and those adopted in the intimate inner space of the rest of the house, which is a place of informality and closeness.

Social change is almost an everyday matter for people in Turkey. Technological innovation and a new monetary economic base for agriculture, land fragmentation and shifts in income distribution, the growth of industry, cultural diffusion, education, and the mass media have all helped precipitate this social change, along with internal and international migration. This unceasing mobility has caused people to change.

The Turkish state, through family legislation and the inclusion of women in the definition of full citizenship, has brought about a decrease in the legitimacy of patriarchy. On the other hand, discriminatory practices in many areas, such as employment, education, and social welfare, have not ended, and women's basic role as caretaker within the family has not changed substantially. Meanwhile, women's monetary contributions have become necessary for the survival of households, leading to some conflict in the sexual division of labor within the family.

Family, Kinship, and Community

In traditional Turkey, members of a whole village are often related to each other through marriages and blood relations. Thus, kinship forms the basis of social relations in the rural setting. Brothers and nephews stand together in disputes and are called upon for help, support, defense, or even revenge.

With economic change, out-migration from the village took place, and accordingly, the pattern of daily contact, mutual services, and solidarity has been weakening. Still, in times of need and crisis, family and kin are called upon for help. Whenever the husband has to leave the village for long periods to work in the city or abroad, he may leave his wife with his or her parents, as she is accepted as a member of her husband's core family when she marries. When this is not possible, other kin take over this function. Similarly, kinship ties are functional in shared agricultural work, house building, child-care, etc., and this function continues even in the urban *gecekondu* context.

If, as a result of migration, kinship bonds weaken, the neighborhood assumes greater importance as a support system, because public services are still insufficient in rural areas. Thus, as family extends into kin, so kinship extends into neighborhood and community in terms of networks of bonds involving duties, responsibilities, common concerns, support, and help.

It seems that male power is more prominent in lower-class families, where males have less resources in terms of income and occupation than in the middle classes. Kuyas (1982) found that middle-class women perceive mutuality or sharing between spouses, and think this is how it should be, whereas lower-class women perceive almost total male control, but again feel this is how it should be. Despite the overwhelming prevalence of nuclear-family residences, extended family and wider kinship ties have not decreased in importance in the city.

Sex Roles

Although Turkey is in the process of rapid social change, it can safely be claimed that the general family pattern is predominantly patriarchal. While there are powerful crosscurrents acting both to reinforce and to mitigate male dominance in different contexts, the second-class status of women in the Middle East still prevails in Turkey. Clearly defined sex roles, division of labor, and separate social networks both help the women endure the status difference, and yet at the same time serve to reinforce and perpetuate this difference. Supportive same-sex friendship/kinship networks further contribute to this separation (Kagitçibasi 1982a).

The concept of honor, referring to the sexual modesty of a woman, implies that men control the sexuality of women. Honor is largely dependent on others' evaluations, and an insult to honor results in disputes, fights, or even blood feuds. The ties among the family members, kin, and community are so close that sometimes the honor of a whole village or community is affected by the honor of one man.

Within the family, young women are controlled and their status is low. The young bride, in particular, is expected to serve all adults within the patrilocal household. Once she bears a son, however, her status improves, especially when the son grows up and brings in a bride and the cycle thus repeats itself. Hence, every woman in the traditional rural society prefers a son as a child; if she does not bear one, her marriage may be threatened (Kagitçibasi 1982a).

The preference for sons does not only depend on an economic basis. The son, especially the eldest one, is responsible for all women in the family, including his mother in the absence of his father. In contrast to the central role of the son in the patrilocal family, a daughter leaves the household to get married when she reaches an age to be "useful." However, Kiray (1976) noted the changing value placed on daughters, who now often replace sons as the "dependable" child.

In the traditional Turkish family, the mother's relationship to her son is intimate and affectionate, in contrast with that of the father who is authoritative and distant. In some ethnic groups, the father is such an authority figure that his son cannot even talk to his own wife or show affection to his own children in the presence of his father. In fact, the mother often protects the son from the father's disciplinary acts. The mother–son relationship is generally stronger than the husband–wife relationship in the traditional family, where any public show of affection between spouses is disapproved of. A man does not even talk about his wife in the company of others, and if he has to, often he uses the word "family" to mean "wife." Communication and role sharing between spouses is limited, and sex roles are well differentiated and non-overlapping. Males are the decision-makers in the family.

Özgür and Sunar (1982), who examined the problem of homicide in Turkey, attributed the high rates of homicide to a traditional system of norms that condone and require a violent response to violations of personal honor. Male homicide was found to stem from more normatively approved motives, such as self-defense, property defense, or honor, whereas a greater proportion of female homicides stemmed from domestic quarrels, jealousy, and similar motives.

Status of Women as Laborers and Professionals

The effect of introducing modern technology into agriculture, and the resultant economic-structural change for rural women, has been a general reduction in their workload. With farm mechanization and the monopoly of such farming by men, women's farming decreased. With the introduction of ready-made goods, such as clothing and food, women's domestic chores have also decreased. This change has been considered to have a positive effect on women's well being, relieving them from some of their heavy burdens. However, it can also be claimed that decreased workload has alienated women from production and has stressed their reproductive role (Kagitçibasi 1982a).

In some areas, with the participation of men in factory work, an opposite outcome of economic-structural change has taken place, with women again being disadvantaged, just as they are completely tied down in agricultural and domestic work and do not have access to education and mobility. Most "unskilled" women in the rural areas are engaged in production of handicrafts, such as embroidery and carpetmaking, which is also considered a part of women's duties and responsibilities for her home. Years before they marry, young girls and their mothers begin preparing *çehiz*, handmade carpets, rugs, quilts, tablecloths, and scarves, which will be needed when they establish their own homes. These handicrafts constitute a major part of the folk arts, and during the past few decades, they have become a source of income for the households, because they have gained monetary value as well.

Women's work in the rural economy is often not considered "work," for it is, rather, a total lifestyle. It is not differentiated as to locality or time, and different types of work may be done in the same place and at the same time, such as food production, housework, and childcare. Neither does it involve specialization or formal training.

Underestimation of women's work also derives from social values, which assign the provider role to men. In the idealized image of the affluent family, the woman does not have to work, an image that is especially prevalent in urban and small-town culture and that is spreading among *gecekondu* dwellers and villagers, who emulate townspeople (Kagitçibasi 1982a).

Kandiyoti (1982) noted that urban Turkish women do not in any way challenge the male role. Lower-class urban women may retreat into domesticity, or if they have to work, it is considered unimportant or temporary. In the case of lower- and middle-class women, subordination is reflected in their very limited access to the outside world. In the case of professional women, husbands are still reluctant to take over roles traditionally accepted as belonging to women, such as taking care of children or sharing housework.

In rural areas, a negative relationship pertains between socioeconomic development and women's labor participation. Özbay (1982) points to the fact that women's labor force participation is decreasing, though it is still high; and women's literacy is increasing, though it is still low. In urban areas, on the other hand, the substantial percentage of professional, highly educated, highly skilled women is notable in view of the low overall female education and skills in Turkey. The overall figures show that the proportion of working women has been declining in Turkey. According to the 1997 figures of the State Institute of Statistics (SIS), women's labor-force participation was 34.7 percent in 1990, 31.4 percent in 1992, and 25.2 percent in 1997 (Aydin 1998).

Erkut (1982) addressed the fact that, "despite the low levels of educational attainment for women in general, substantial numbers of Turkish women obtain professional degrees and practice in what are considered to be male-dominated occupations in the West." She explained that this has happened as women have been able to pursue professional careers without posing a threat to the male sex role and its privileged status. Highly educated women have had access to the support and services of other women, from the extended family and kin or from among the less advantaged, so that their professional roles have not had to hinge upon their husband's help in carrying out their domestic chores. Men have thus enjoyed the enhanced family prestige and income provided by career women, without themselves changing their status or incurring more work. Erkut points out that men are the real beneficiaries of "the rise of a few women made possible by the exploitation of many." Thus, positive attitudes toward professional education of elite women exist side by side with negative attitudes toward women's universal education deriving from traditional culture.

Fertility and the Value of Children

As a result of high fertility rates in the past, the population of Turkey is young. Government policy changed from a pronatalist to an antinatalist one during the 1960s and, accordingly, fertility rates started to decline.

In the face-to-face interpersonal relations of the small community, every one is a "significant other," and no one can be ignored; thus, other-directed behavior tendencies develop from childhood on. In the village setting, the child is socialized not only in a family, but also in a kinship–community system characterized by mutual obligations. Expectations from the child, accordingly, are not only individual and familial, but communal as well.

Kagitçibasi (1982b) noted that with development and especially with education, the perceived economic value of children decreases, but their perceived psychological value increases, at least in relative terms. When the economic value of children is high, the number of children increases, whereas when a low economic value is coupled with a high psychological value, the result is lowered fertility. Thus, the value of children forms an explanatory link, at the individual level, between the level of development and fertility rates. The economic value of children goes hand in hand with son preference, as sons are more dependable sources of economic benefits, especially in old age. This is of key importance in the sociocultural economic context, where patriarchal traditions are strong and institutional support of the elderly is lacking. The dependent, inferior status of the uneducated woman is crucial in this context. It is apparent in widespread male decision-making and low levels of communication and role sharing between spouses. It is an inherent part of a general pattern of interdependent relationships, appearing first as the dependency of the child on the parents and then as the reversal of this relationship. Socioeconomic development, and especially women's education and professionalization, are the key precipitators of change in this pattern.

The traditional Turkish way of adopting a child, which was also prevalent during the Ottoman Empire, is significant in some aspects. Wealthy traditional families usually adopt a child who is in economic or social need. Moreover, it is usually a girl, which seems to reflect the inclination to protect the weak. The child, called an *evlatlik*, is sometimes of an age when she (or he) is well aware that she is adopted and has a different position in the family. The *evlatlik* is well-cared for, is educated like other children, and is provided for until she marries. On the other hand, she is expected to help with the housework, which constitutes her different role in the household. This tradition, which, partly because of economic and social changes, is on the decline, may be considered as an informal social support system to protect the child where state supports are lacking. The *evlatlik* tradition does not exclude the more contemporary legal adoption system. Couples who wish to legally adopt a child must meet specific strict rules and usually have to wait for long periods. The couples (on the whole, those without children) usually prefer a newborn child as they wish the child to think that he or she is their biological offspring.

Another way of adoption is seen in infertile couples in highly traditional Turkish communities in which one child of a relative (who is usually a brother or sister of one of the spouses) is adopted. The purpose of choosing a close relative's child seems to be related to the wish to keep the family ties together.

B. Sociolegal Status of Males and Females

Today, civil marriage is generally practiced with or without an additional religious ceremony. However, the practice of religious marriage alone has not disappeared. Polygyny was prohibited in 1926, with the acceptance of the Civil Code. Nevertheless, it is still possible to see it in some regions, though it is rare and was not very common even before 1926.

According to the Constitution of the Republic of Turkey, citizens cannot be discriminated against on the basis of their gender, and all individuals have personal, inviolable, non-transferable, vested basic rights and liberties. In spite of this legal foundation for equality between the sexes, there are articles in laws that contradict this principle. For example, according to the Civil Code, the husband is the head of the marital union and is in charge of the choice of residence. The Civil Code states that the husband speaks for and represents the marital union; the woman only has the right to represent the union for the permanent needs of the house. Nevertheless, a Draft Amendment of the Civil Code has been submitted to the Parliament, and if the draft is ratified, a number of inequalities will be eliminated (Ergöçmen 1997).

Equality between the sexes was introduced in the legal structure through the reforms implemented following the declaration of the Republic, and opportunities were provided for effective participation of women in public life. One of the most important steps in this respect was recognizing women's right to vote and eligibility to be elected as early as 1934. In spite of this relatively early access to participation in the political decision-making process, women in Turkey have limited political involvement in terms of representation in the Parliament.

Even though under the Civil Code women have inheritance rights equal to men's, in some rural areas, women still get either nothing or much less than what men get, and inheritance issues are resolved informally within the family or the village. This practice is, however, on the decline, and equal sharing is the rule for urban people.

On the other hand, there are two types of regulations with regard to women in the labor force. The first set of regulations prevents women from undertaking dangerous work, while the second set relates to protective measures regarding maternal functions of women.

Since the foundation of the Turkish Republic in 1923, the basic principles in education have been the universality of services and the equality of opportunities. There are also principles like coeducation and the right of all to education. Primary education, which had been five years but was recently raised to eight years after much debate, is compulsory for every Turkish child and is free in public schools.

Almost all boys and girls attend primary education, although the dropout rate at later stages of education is higher for girls. For instance, whereas 91 percent of boys and 87 percent of girls attended primary school in the 1994-1995 academic year, 78 percent of the boys continued on to secondary school while only 53 percent of the girls continued into secondary schools. Women thus still lag behind men in literacy and level of education (Ergöçmen 1997).

The legal age of marriage, which had been 15 for females and 17 for males until recently, has been raised to 18 for both sexes. To secure the family unit is both a part of the main Turkish traditional approach and the official policy of the state. Thus, for example, if both the husband and the wife are government employees appointed in different cities, they have the right to demand to be employed in the same town to maintain the family union. In 1989, the State Department of Family Research was established as an independent branch under the Prime Ministry to develop national policies for the maintenance and welfare of the Turkish family.

In the Turkish Civil Code, punishment for adultery for women constituted the husband's right to divorce her, while the woman was also sentenced to imprisonment. For men, the same behavior was not punished as severely. Recent regulations in the Civil Code abolished this inequality for both sexes. Indeed, adultery is currently not considered a criminal act for either men or women.

On the other hand, adultery (*zina*) is severely punished by religious tradition and by society. In Islam, adultery must be witnessed by four adult Muslim males. A woman who commits the crime of adultery is supposed to be stoned to death, whereas no such strict punishment exists for adulterous men. Interestingly, there has been no recorded case of punishment for adultery during the whole history of the Ottoman Empire, which implies that religious rules were less harshly practiced during the Ottoman reign.

The civil law of Turkey accepts the absolute divorce of couples. Moreover, judges have the right to decide a legal separation of couples for a certain time period before absolute divorce. Turkish divorce law has been reviewed as a result of changes in social life, and the new regulations of 1988 make attaining a divorce much easier. For example, if one of the spouses does not agree to a divorce, a three-year period of separation is sufficient to grant a divorce.

Divorce rates showed an increase in 1988 because of the enactment of the new law, but have stabilized and remained constant during subsequent years. The most commonly cited cause of divorce is incompatibility between spouses, with willful desertion and adultery following (SIS 1995). As far as women are concerned, the causes of divorce are adultery (81.3 percent), intrafamilial violence (65.5 percent), and alcoholism (59 percent).

C. General Concepts of Sexuality and Love

Reflections of the Oedipal theme can be traced in the Anatolian culture and folklore. The colloquial Turkish language and Turkish slang is full of examples of male sexual aggression toward the mother, sister, and wife, or threats of castration directed toward boys and men. In rural Turkey, the custom of firing guns during the wedding ceremony, sometimes with fatal consequences, can also be regarded as an example of the Oedipal theme.

Physical contact between same-sex people is common in Turkey. It is socially acceptable for women and men to embrace, kiss, and walk hand-in-hand with others of the same sex in public. However, physical closeness and any show of affection between the sexes in public are generally not condoned, even between husband and wife.

In Turkish folklore and legends (such as those of Yusuf and Züleyha, Ferhat and Sirin, Kerem and Asli, and Leyla and Mecnun), the main theme is longing for the loved one. Love and passion, almost devoid of bodily senses and sexuality, is experienced as a search for the mystical, a way to reach God.

Ancient Turkish verses, tales, and music reflect the mystical quality of love. In traditional Turkish arts, such as carpet-making, which is usually woven by women, decorations and ornaments carry messages for the loved one.

Turkish melodrama represents the woman by her changing status in society as well as by the split in her identity. Films present prudent, poor, but highly talented women who are exploited in the patriarchal household and become very famous and rich by the help of a man who is financially and socially in a higher position. However, fame and fortune do not help her to form a stable identity; she is abused again, because she cannot attain the idealized love and security she has aspired to.

With few exceptions, Turkish media serve to accentuate traditional gender roles. Imamoglu (1996), in her review of newspapers, noted that, whether representing leftist, rightist, or liberal viewpoints in the political spectrum, Turkish papers share the ideology of perpetuating gender stereotypes in a subtle but consistent way. She concludes that, similar to Western papers, women seem to be defined in terms of their relationship to men. Women's maternal and marital roles and sex-object images are emphasized while their femininity is defined from a male perspective.

It is not easy to reach a conclusion regarding the basic concepts of sexuality, love, and sexual attitudes of people in modern Turkey. Besides the media, which carry Western values into the very homes of the most isolated, many ancient cultures and civilizations have contributed to the present, as well as Islamic, Arabic, and Persian influences. These effects can be traced in Turkish legends and folk tales, while common themes can be observed with other cultures in the Middle East.

2. Religious and Ethnic Factors Affecting Sexuality

A. Source and Character of Religious Values

Turkey is a secular state according to the Constitution. Although the community is predominantly Muslim, mostly Sunni with a considerable proportion in the Alevi tradition, Turkish people are unique in their mild interpretation of Islam. A number of varieties of Islamic interpretation exist, as well as non-Muslim groups. In the past decade, radical religious movements in the Middle East have found supporters in Turkey, and these fundamentalist religious groups have been exerting pressure in favor of a return to Sharia (laws according to the Koran). Their political party was closed down in early 1998 by the legal authorities, because their activities were against the Constitution. More recently, a new party with a much milder religious discourse was established and is now represented in the Turkish Parliament.

The Turkish Constitution is based on secularity and does not permit any religious ideology to control the political system. Although contemporary interpreters of the Koran believe in the equality of males and females in the Western sense, fundamentalists refrain from any interpretation of the Koran other than the original form of the Koran.

On the other hand, the effects of Islam on many sexual behavior patterns of Turkish men and women can be discerned, except among a highly educated minority residing in major metropolitan areas. There are significant differences in the sexual lifestyles of people from rural and urban areas. In terms of sexual behavior, Turkey manifests a very complex picture, because the Turkish cultural mosaic is made up of many different value systems. There are insufficient data to support a conclusion. Along with ancient Turkish traditions and Islamic influences, elements of secular Western culture, atheistic socialism, and various regional cultures interact with each other to create an extremely rich and complex whole (Tekeli 1995). This mix gives Turkish citizens their distinctive, more liberal characteristic.

During the Ottoman Empire, the presence of two witnesses who testified that the woman and the man (or their representatives) had decided to marry was the sufficient condition to marry. Marriages were not recorded officially until the establishment of the Turkish Republic. The marital union was basically a contract between the two partners. Thus, no official approval was considered necessary. Later, this ceremony took place in the presence of an imam, a religious leader, and this practice was called *imam nikahi*, a religious marriage.

More legendary than real, a man who intended to marry was supposed to present the bride with the amount of gold which equaled her body weight. A man could marry four wives, but he had to treat them all equally. Contemporary authorities of Islam in Turkey do not regard polygamy as a valid norm of religion in modern times, and they mostly approve only of monogamy. In spite of this, most couples prefer a religious ceremony in addition to the official marriage, as it is accepted rather as a declaration of the marital union before God and society.

On the other hand, the religious marital union could easily be broken if the husband alone so desired. This marital arrangement rested on the absolute fidelity of the woman, while permitting the man much sexual freedom. The woman could not divorce her husband and marry again under any circumstance, except when her husband divorced her. The most she could do was to leave home if her husband brought in a new wife.

According to religious rules, a man could marry again as soon as he divorced his wife, whereas a woman had to wait for at least three months if she wished to marry another man, because of possible pregnancy from the former husband. However, if the man divorced his wife more than twice, he could not marry her again if the woman did not marry and had sexual intercourse with another man. This Islamic custom, called *hülle*, has, in a way, a protective function for women, although in modern Turkey, which interprets Islam in a very mild manner, it is never seen.

A kind of Islamic marriage contract called *mut'a*, which is valid for a short period of time or under certain conditions, is not prevalent in Turkey, although in some fundamentalist religious groups, it is sometimes resorted to, presumably with the purpose of justifying sexual involvement. (See discussion of *mut'a* in the chapter on Iran, pp. 637-638, Section 5C, Interpersonal Heterosexual Behaviors, Adults, Marriage and the Family, in Volume 2 of this *International Encyclopedia of Sexuality*.)

An old custom called *mehir* (a kind of dowry), which involved paying a certain amount of money to the bride's parents has been known from ancient times. This custom probably originated during the process of transition from the matriarchal to the patriarchal social order, when women began to be regarded as commodities, with a price that could be paid for. Starting with the early years of Islam, this custom took the form of a payment made directly to the woman for her security. Thus, while the woman was withdrawn from social life and productivity, a certain means of security were provided for her. This practice, which could be regarded as progressive centuries ago, is maintained today as a tradition. Today, in rural areas, this custom prevails as a *baslik* (bride price or dowry), an amount of money paid by the groom to the girl's family. *Baslik* is an indication of social and economic power for both sides, although this practice is declining with urbanization and the nuclearization of the family.

Only 1.6 percent of all married women are or once were in religion-based polygynous marriages, according to a nationwide survey in 1988 (Hacet-tepe-HIPS 1989a). Thus, it is obvious that polygynous marriages are not widespread. However, there are some variations by rural/urban, geographical, socioeconomic, and sociocultural characteristics. For example, polygynous marriages are more widespread in the east, in rural areas, and among those who have no education.

On the other hand, while marriages with religious ceremonies are socially recognized, they have no legal standing. Surveys imply that the prevalence of such marriages is of a sizable magnitude. Among all marital unions in Turkey, 8.3 percent are based only on religious ceremonies, whereas 80.5 percent of the officially married couples have chosen to have both a civil and a religious ceremony (Hacettepe-HIPS 1989b). Since marital unions based only on religious ceremonies are not legally recognized, the partners are deprived of their institutional rights within the family, such as inheritance or parental rights on the education of their children. Whereas 4 percent of urban women live in religious unions, three times as many do so in rural areas.

B. Character of Ethnic Values

The family as a valued social system has always been important for Turkish people. According to the traditions of ancient Turkish states, such as Hun Turks and Göktürks, which serve to keep the family secure and united, males married their stepmothers or their brother's wife if their husbands died.

Since the acceptance of Islam, religious and ethnic factors have become so mingled with each other through the centuries that it is not always possible to distinguish their separate effects on sexual attitudes and behavior. Although ethnic minorities exist, they are not recognized by the state, which accepts everyone as Turkish citizens, and statistical data are not available for these groups as separate entities.

If the traditional Turkish agrarian society—the core society—and its values are taken as a reference point, modifications in outlooks and ways of life can be better understood. The family system in the small agricultural community is generally assumed to be patriarchal with close kin and family relations. However, surveys have shown that the majority of families are nuclear and probably have always been. Kagitçibasi (1982a) noted that the extended family is an ideal, especially in rural areas.

This extended-family ideal involves expectations of living in old age with the adult son's family and being supported by him. Underlying this ideal is, on the one hand, economic necessity, mainly lack of institutional support or other means of old-age security, resulting in dependence on children and a consequently high value put on children's loyalty to the parents and the family. On the other hand, idealization of the extended family is partly the continuation of a tradition or a sign of longing for the past, as well as a sort of status aspiration. Generally, rural patriarchal extended families have been the rich families, which could afford to keep all the family members under the same roof, as they had large land holdings to live on. Consequently, in the eyes of the poor peasant, the extended family has been identified with wealth, thus symbolizing an ideal.

The dynamic nature of the family undergoes modifications in the face of changing socioeconomic conditions in Turkey. A typical pattern of change through the life cycle of the rural family involves first, the newly married couple living with the husband's parents as a valued pattern and because of economic necessities—the patriarchal extended family—then moving out as the young man gains more income and autonomy—the nuclear family—and then later on, the aged parent(s) moving in again for protection in old age—a "transient extended family."

Even when conjugal families live in separate households, the functions of an extended family are served by them, in that they are called upon to provide material support when needed, forming what might be called the "functionally extended family." Thus, close family ties extending into kinship relations serve an important function of security in times of crises and conflicts, which are often faced by the families undergoing change in both the rural and the marginal urban context (Kagitçibasi (1982a).

The spatial proximity of the separate family and kin households, even in urban areas, symbolizes and may even strengthen the close mutual bonds of family and kin. Mutual support within the family is the rule. Thus, for example, older brothers are expected to finance younger siblings' education and be available for assistance for their parents in old age. Family relations are mostly patriarchal, with men having authority over their wives and children. Brides in rural areas often have to live within their husband's family, which can cause many interpersonal and role problems between her and the in-laws. This extended-family type contains three generations, with the grandfather and grandmother having authority to manage the family income and take care of grandchildren. After the bride has a child, particularly if it is a boy, she ascends to a higher status in the family. Usually, men work outside the home whereas women do the housework and take care of the children. Relations with the relatives are still very close in Turkey.

Endogamous marriage—marriage within one's own religion, ethnic, or kinship group—which is still commonly practiced in some regions, has various social functions, such as maintaining local cohesiveness, control over land, and protection of the family from "strangers." Twenty-one percent of marriages were found to be consanguineous. This rate increases to 31 percent in eastern Anatolia and decreases to 13 percent in western Anatolia. Educational level of the women seems to be an important determinant, and the proportion of consanguineous marriages drops with increased education (Hacettepe-HIPS 1989b).

Marriage in the rural context appears to assume more of a social than an individual or conjugal character, as a means of establishing economic and social ties. It is especially instrumental in strengthening existing kinship relations or extending them outside the village to similar ethnic groups or in forming neighborhood and territorial ties, and in increasing the number of relations and friends who are potential sources of aid. Thus, arranged marriages are common in rural parts of Turkey and not rare in small towns and cities.

Related to the social function of marriage, a widespread custom is "asking for the girl." The elderly, respectable, usually male family members of the groom candidate visit the girl's parents at home and ask for their permission for the young couple to get married. This visit is usually accompanied with presents, such as flowers or sweets in a silver plate, which may show variations according to regional custom. This custom has been modified throughout the modernization process. In transitional families, mostly in small towns and *gecekondu* areas, families of both parties bargain on the household needs for the young couple. Sometimes this may take months.

In the peasant culture, although abduction and elopement still exist, they are not condoned; only 1.3 percent of marriages in 1989 involved elopement. The responses to such action range from tolerance to strong disapproval, and even vengeance and strife between the families involved. It is also seen as a breach of the proper standards for formal marriage and the financial contract, namely, the dowry.

During the marriage ceremony, relatives present the couple with household needs, jewelry, and gold. Jewelry and gold belong to the woman and constitute a kind of security for her. If later it has to be exchanged for money, the husband is obliged to ask his wife's permission to sell them. Valuable presents given during the engagement period are supposed to be returned if the engagement is broken.

In arranged marriages, the man is not supposed to see the bride until the wedding night. After the wedding ceremonies, the husband presents his wife a gold coin as a gift in exchange for seeing her in person. This is called *yüz görümlülügü* (price for seeing the bride's face).

The dowry has traditional functions, such as the economic gains it brings in exchange for the loss of the labor of the girl and providing security for the wife if the husband dies. However, if the man is unable to pay the dowry, abduction may provide a solution. Another function of the dowry is providing support for the wife in case of divorce, yet divorce is quite rare in rural Turkey as it is not condoned and is resorted to only under extreme conditions. Since endogamy is more prevalent in rural areas, or, at least because people are tied in close kinship bonds with patriarchal, authoritarian relations, this social structure limits individual acts, such as divorce. One acceptable reason for divorce may be suspicions about the wife's infidelity. Divorcing an officially married wife for special reasons, such as her infertility or failure to give birth to a son, may lead the man to a religious marital union with another woman. Divorce, in this case, does not result in separation from the first wife, because the man behaves as a responsible husband for both women.

Although some groups organize their life according to Islam, it cannot be generalized to the whole community. Ancient Turkish influences and Anatolian civilizations constitute the main background, while Islamic and Western effects are woven into this pattern. It can be claimed that traditional institutions, such as marriage and kinship relations, serve both individual and social functions. Such ceremonial relationship patterns help people perceive themselves both as individuals and as a part of the community.

3. Sexual Knowledge and Education

A. Government Policies and Programs

In the last fifteen years, sexual education has been a topic of debate in Turkey. In the past, even in medical schools, sexual education was limited to courses on the anatomy and physiology of the sexual organs. Recently, in medical schools and in some psychology undergraduate programs, human sexuality, sexual functions, and dysfunctions have become a part of the curriculum. However, it remains to be decided what sort of a sexual education program should be given in primary and high schools. In elementary education and high schools, there was no formal sexual education programs, while biology courses included only information about reproduction in various life forms, including humans. In a study of 13,000 female high school students, it was found that 75 percent had some information on sexuality, including contraceptive methods and sexually transmitted diseases, although on the whole, the level of sexual knowledge was low in this group (Vicdan 1993). On the other hand, students in the 12- to 15-year-old age cohort reported that sexual education should be included in the school curriculum (Basgül 1997).

In the 1999-2000 academic year, a sexual education project was put into practice by the Ministry of Education. The education program covers topics such as physical growth, development, and maturation, male and female reproductive systems, adolescence, sexuality and sexual identity, contraception, and sexually transmitted diseases (Ministry of Education, 2000).

A number of non-governmental organizations, among them the Family Planning Association and various women associations, provide educational programs on family planning and contraceptive methods in rural and *gecekondu* areas.

B. Informal Sources of Sexual Knowledge

A conservative attitude in discussing sexual matters with children is apparent in Turkish families. Moreover, parents may not possess an idea about how and what kind of information and experience they should share with their children. Thus, the majority of young people do not have much opportunity to consult with their parents about sexuality. On the other hand, former generations probably lack objective, scientific information with which they can supply their children. In such a situation where the young group cannot obtain information from their trusted elders, they turn to popular publications they can obtain or share experiences with each other. Unnecessary fears and anxieties arise from tales about, for example, the first night in which girls are led to expect to suffer great pain and face excessive bleeding during coitus. Many young men are worried about the size of their penis or their performance or whether they will be able to satisfy their partner.

Various studies indicate that the main sources of sexual information are peers and publications. A study of adolescents revealed that for 15 percent, the source of sexual knowledge was the family, for 35 percent peers, for 20 percent the media, for 8 percent the school, and for 12 percent other sources. A quarter of adolescents reported that they had no information about sexual matters before puberty. Negative feelings toward changes in puberty were much more prominent in girls. On the other hand, 7 percent of college students reported that their most important problem area was sexuality, among various psychosocial problems (Eksi 1982). In another study, the adolescents' same-sex peer group seemed to be the main source of information about sexuality, followed by the mother for girls and the father for boys. Within same-sex friend groups, sex is a frequently talked about topic. Younger members learn about sex in these intimate groups. The media was again another important source of sexual information for both male and female students (Basgül 1997).

In rural communities, the elders traditionally supply the adolescents with information about sexuality. Rural youth also learn by watching the copulation of animals.

Every adolescent is personally responsible for his (or her) own thoughts and behavior in the name of God and obliged to follow the Islamic rules when he or she reaches puberty. When a child reaches puberty, he (or she) has to regulate his (or her) own life and start to pray regularly according to the Koran. Parents are responsible to provide religious information for their children. As a part of this, a Muslim is obliged to follow religious rules and perform rituals. One of the rituals is called *abdest*, which involves washing parts of the body in a predetermined order before prayers and after any type of sexual activity whether intentional or spontaneous. Parents warn their children to wash whenever they have a "wet dream." This tradition implies that nocturnal ejaculations are not provoked by erotic stimuli alone, and sexual content in dreams may occur without any experience or information about sexuality.

Another traditional attitude is a religion-based responsibility of the family members to provide sexual information for the adolescent before marriage. An elder male member of the family, the *sagdiç* (best man), gives sexual information to the boy, while *yenge* (chaperon), a female family member, informs the girl about sexual matters.

In summary, while there are still no governmental policies to regulate sex education, in rural areas, at least, the traditional Turkish family system supplies some information about sex and sexuality to children and adolescents.

4. Autoerotic Behaviors and Patterns

A large-scale population survey on autoerotic activity in Turkey does not exist. Studies in student populations show that for 50 percent, the main sexual activity was masturbation (Çok et al. 1998). In another study, 11.5 percent of female and 87.2 percent of male university students admitted to having masturbated, while 21 percent of the females and 26 percent of the males reported that masturbation was unhealthy (Erkmen et al. 1990). Similarly, Eksi (1990) reported that male students regarded masturbation as a "problematic" issue, particularly those whose fathers were less educated. These studies imply that while autoerotic activities are not rare among unmarried young males and females, nevertheless they are not very comfortable with such activities. Even the most highly educated people still do not regard masturbation as an acceptable sexual outlet.

Clinical observations and ongoing studies with sexually dysfunctional patient groups imply that masturbation is more common in Turkish males than females. Sexual fantasies and autoerotic activities seem to be reported rarely by Turkish females. However, these observations rest on clinical samples and may not reflect patterns of sexual behavior in the normal population. Attempts to study sexual behavior in the normal population are hindered by a reluctance on the part of the respondents, because sexuality is still considered as a taboo topic of discussion by the larger part of the population.

Masturbation is commonly regarded as a kind of sin in Islam, as it is in most other religions. Although there is no written rule in the Koran that prohibits masturbation, most people who refrain from autoerotic activities believe that such behavior is sinful.

5. Interpersonal Heterosexual Behaviors

A. Children

According to Islam, puberty is a stage when a child is ready to take on some adult responsibilities. As a part of this, while adolescent girls are expected to behave and dress as mature women, every male child should be circumcised before he reaches puberty as a step into manhood. In the traditional context, *sünnet* (circumcision) is usually performed by a "*sünnetçi*," always a male, who has been trained and is experienced in circumcision but does not have a medical degree. During the operation, which usually takes place at home, the *kirve* (a close friend of the father or a male relative) holds the child, and the *sünnetçi* conducts the operation, usually without any anesthetics if performed in the traditional way.

Great importance is attached to this ritual in traditional Turkey, as it is accepted as a step into manhood. A special feast is prepared, and the child is dressed in a white gown and a cap adorned with decorations. Following the operation, he is laid down in a decorated bed while prayers are said and visitors bring in presents and are offered food and sherbet. *Sünnet* is a religious rule, although many people believe that it is also a requirement for healthy sexuality, both in the medical and functional sense. As a result of this, if the child is born in a hospital, many parents now prefer the operation to take place in the hospital setting, a few days after birth, out of hygienic as well as economic concerns.

Although circumcision is an obligation for males according to Islamic rules, it is also seen in many pre-Islamic cultures and religious practices. The age of circumcision in Islam varies from birth to adolescence, while Turkish boys are mostly circumcised between 3 and 6 years of age (Öztürk 1963). As is well known, this period has been regarded as a critical stage in terms of psychosexual development, and circumcision at this age might be deleterious for later stages of development. Öztürk, who studied this phenomenon in Turkish males, found no evidence to support the hypothesis that circumcision at an early age (or during the phallic stage) might have a negative effect later on.

B. Adolescents

The primary and secondary sexual characteristics in Turkish male adolescents develop at roughly the same age as in Europeans, whereas the rate of physical development of females is closer to that of the Mediterranean region, where they enter adolescence at an earlier age compared to northern countries. Along with the development of secondary sex characteristics, menarche and first nocturnal ejaculation are accepted as an indication to start sex education in the traditional sense.

Girls and boys have attended school together during primary education since the establishment of the Turkish Republic. In the past, they were separated after completing primary school. During the Ottoman Empire, private teachers educated young girls in special subjects, such as music, literature, and the arts. During the past few decades, sexual segregation in schools has been totally abolished.

Studies of the sexual activities of Turkish students indicate that about half of unmarried male college students report that they have had sexual relations with the opposite sex, whereas the percentage drops to between 4 and 19 percent for college girls (Çok et al. 1998; Eksi 1990). This great difference probably reflects male's experiencing sexual intercourse with prostitutes. Overall, 66.2 percent of male and 8.5 percent of female university students reported having had premarital sexual intercourse (Erkmen et al. 1990).

C. Adults

Marriage

About 92 percent of the Turkish population get married to establish a family. In rural areas, the age of marriage is quite low, although it is customary for young men to complete their compulsory military service before they can be accepted as candidates who can support a family. For urban men and women, because of the longer time spent in education, the age of marriage is higher.

Marriages are highly concentrated in the 15- to 24-year-olds for females and the 20- to 29-year age group for males. Medical screening is obligatory for men and women before marriage, according to the law enacted in 1930.

As a preventive measure, the aim was to recognize and cure people with contagious diseases. The law was passed in the period between the two World Wars, when serious economic and social problems had to be overcome. At that time, one of the main concerns of the newly established Turkish Republic was to prevent epidemics of tuberculosis, syphilis, malaria, etc.

Hamams (Turkish baths) had been a major locus of social interaction until modern facilities supplied hot water to houses. There were separate sections or days for men and women in *hamams*. Children of both sexes were accepted into the women's section. Women went to the *hamams* with their female friends and kin and spent long hours bathing, chatting, gossiping, singing, dancing, and sharing the food they prepared for these occasions. Older women looked for young girls whom they could choose as wives for their sons. Hamams are still a social factor in Turkish life.

Weddings, Virginity, and Childbirth

Traditional wedding ceremonies in Anatolia last for four to seven days. The ceremony starts with music played on local instruments and a flag hung over the groom's house. Men and women entertain themselves separately until the *gerdek* (first night of the wedding). Some traditional activities common during the ceremonies are: the *hamam* (Turkish bath) custom lasting for hours, during which food is served, and the *kina gecesi* (henna night), during which the hands and feet of the bride are colored with henna. Visitors sing and dance and are served food and drinks. During the wedding day proper, a group of men and women take the bride from her home. She rides on horseback to the groom's house with the crowd while everyone sings and dances. When the bride enters the house, coins (or gold, if the groom is wealthy) are spread over her. The groom's friends punch him before the couple is left alone as a symbol of their rejecting him as a bachelor. The ceremonies end with prayers.

As a symbol of passing from virginity to womanhood, a lock of the bride's hair is cut the day after the wedding. Magical practices, such as holding a mirror to the bride's face and spilling water as the bride leaves her home for the wedding ceremony, are believed to facilitate the bride's adaptation to marriage.

Virginity is still a much-treasured value for women in most parts of Turkey. Even among the higher educated young people, who flirt and make love with each other like their Western contemporaries, most reserve sexual intercourse for the first night of marriage. In traditional regions, parents or older members of the family wait outside the newly married couples' room for the realization of the sexual act. Tradition dictates that a blood-stain on the bedsheet caused by the perforation of the hymen proves that nothing is wrong, dishonorable, or shameful with the man or his wife. This bloodstain is then displayed to the waiting members of the family and is taken as proof of chastity on the part of the woman as well as the honor of the man who has successfully performed the sexual act. This custom inevitably exerts a great deal of pressure on the young couple. The bride is expected to have no sexual experience, and for many young men also, the first night of the marriage is the first time he experiences sexual intercourse. There are many cases of erectile or intromission difficulties that can be attributed to this stressful situation on the wedding night and a general lack of sexual knowledge. Tragic consequences may ensue if the girl is not a virgin or if it is a case of a penetrable hymen, often mistaken for previous loss of virginity. However, it is not unheard of that the couple escapes the forces of tradition by showing their parents or family members red paint or some bloodstain caused by other means.

The *lohusa* period is the forty days after childbirth, during which it is believed that both the mother and the child require special care. The mother is usually confined to bed in the first ten days, after which she gets up, but does not go out of the house. She is helped by female members of her family or by other female relatives. A special bed adorned with ornaments is prepared for her. She puts on her best traditional dress and jewelry, accepting visitors in her bedroom during the first ten days. She is fed with sweets and dishes believed to make her stronger and to increase her milk. Visitors bring presents, such as gold coins or clothes for the child. Prayers are said and visitors are offered a special sweet sherbet. In the *lohusa* period, the woman is also restricted in her sexual activities.

Divorce and Widowhood

The crude divorce rate of Turkey, less than one in a thousand marriages per year, is low compared to divorce rates in many other countries. Reasons for this can be the country's strong religious and family ties, and the traditional nature of Turkish society. However, it should be noted that statistics do not reflect the divorces among religious marriages in the rural areas. (See also earlier comments about divorce in Section 2B, Religious and Ethnic Factors Affecting Sexuality, Character of Ethnic Values.)

In Turkey, 49 percent of all divorces occur in the first five years of marriage and 45 percent occur in childless couples—an indication that children help to keep the continuity of marriage (SIS 1995). In other words, not having children may be considered as a social implication and probably a reason for divorce.

Levine (1982), who investigated the nature of divorce in Turkey, considered divorce as a "barometer of social change," "a struggle against conservatism," and "an act of female emancipation." Reviewing national divorce statistics, he noted that divorce is associated more with urbanism and urban occupations, with a higher level of development, with changing women's roles, with developed agriculture rather than with full-scale industry, and with being barely literate (especially among women). Thus, it is the people "caught in the middle" of economic and structural change who are most vulnerable to divorce, as they are subject to the most stress. In effect, the urban poor who are dislocated and economically vulnerable are more likely to get divorced. Levine views the patriarchal family as a hindrance to individual autonomy and initiative, in which the needs of the family hold primacy over those of individual members. In this family type, divorce can be seen as a liberating act, although it brings with it serious problems of readjustment, especially for the woman, in a society which does not condone it.

If the husband dies, it used to be the duty of one of his brothers to marry the widow. This tradition, which was functional in providing security for the woman, as well as for the children of the deceased man in the rural context, is rare at present.

Potency and Fertility Potions

Sexual potency and fertility have been important aspects of the Turkish male's sexual identity throughout history. Thus, methods to enhance sexual potency, such as *kuvvet macunu* (herbal pastes) and potions were invented, and selected foods were recommended, to enhance potency and fertility. Pastes and potions are still prepared today and handed out freely in some regions on special feasts. The preparations may take days, and large amounts of herbs are boiled in huge pots during festival days. These annual ceremonies are local celebrations led by townsmen dressed in traditional Anatolian costumes for the occasion. *Kuvvet macunu* are handed out with prayers to everyone. These potions are believed to protect the user from diseases, make people sexually potent, and guarantee the health of children born that year.

6. Homoerotic, Homosexual, and Ambisexual Behaviors

A. Children and Adolescents

Case histories of psychiatric patients sometimes reveal homoerotic activity during childhood, although empirical studies for this period are not available. On the other hand, a number of retrospective studies with late adolescent male homosexuals and transsexuals imply that, in both groups, the first sexual experience occurs at an early age. Most transsexuals and about a third of homosexuals reported that they had their first sexual experience before age 12 (Gülçat et al. 1988; Inci 1993). These studies also show that sexual intercourse is mostly initiated by the youths, that is, without being forced, which seems particularly to be the case for transsexuals.

Most homosexuals and transsexuals came from families with more than three children, had pathological relations with parents, and traumatic childhood experiences. Based on their study using the MMPI with subjects in the 20- to 25-year-old age group, Battal et al. (1989) argued that transsexuals were characterized by the existence of early infantile conflicts and fixations, while homosexuals showed pathological resolutions for identification processes. Inci (1993) found that the self-esteem and self-image of homosexuals were lower than in transsexuals in the late adolescent group. Anxiety, depression, and over-sensitivity were also characteristic of homosexuals, while suicide attempts seemed to be common in both groups.

B. Adults

Males who play the "active" role in homosexual relations are not socially regarded as homosexuals in the Turkish culture. The active homosexual role is more likely to be assumed as a variety of sexuality experienced by a heterosexual male. That is, homosexuality is rather restricted in meaning and covers almost exclusively effeminacy and the "passive" homosexual role. This attitude is even apparent in some legal and official practices of establishments like the armed forces. Homosexuals are not accepted in the army and if such acts are witnessed during the military service, which is compulsory for every Turkish male citizen, the effeminate, passive partner is sent for medical evaluation and eventually discharged from the army.

Little is known about lesbians in present-day Turkey. Legends about females who lived and fought like brigands are still told, without their sexual orientation being directly mentioned or alluded to.

7. Gender Conflicted Persons

Sex-reassignment operations have been occasionally performed in Turkey in recent years, along with debates centering around ethical issues about the incompleteness of evaluation processes of such cases. It is legally accepted that transsexuals can obtain an identity in accordance with their acquired sex; they can change their name with a court order and they can officially marry.

It can be claimed that there is a double standard concerning attitudes toward male homosexuals and transsexuals in Turkey. On the one hand, they are alienated, ridiculed, and even persecuted by the society in general and by the police, as they are regarded as a threat to social values. On the other hand, they are condoned, especially those in show business, who usually claim that God willed them to be as they are. Although rare, female-to-male sex-reassignment operations have been performed in Turkey.

8. Significant Unconventional Sexual Behaviors

A. Coercive Sex

Child Sexual Abuse and Incest

Statistical data about child sexual abuse are almost nonexistent in Turkey. During the last decade, several initiatives have been started to prevent child sexual abuse with the support of international organizations. Several associations, such as *Çocuk Ihmali ve Istismarini Önleme Dernegi* (The Association for the Prevention of Child Neglect and Abuse), were founded to help abused children and to conduct studies in this area (TC Hükümeti ve UNICEF 1991).

Although no statistical data are available, child sexual abuse does not seem to be rare in Turkey. Occasional news in the media indicates that child sexual abuse, including incest, occurs. However, such acts are not condoned, and child molesters, whether homosexual or heterosexual, are strongly disapproved of in the community. Indeed, prisoners convicted of such acts are usually punished further and alienated or even killed by other prisoners.

Among cases of child abuse, sexual abuse seems to be the most frequent type. It is estimated that child sexual abuse is involved in approximately 50 percent of all kinds of child abuse, including unreported and unregistered cases. According to forensic medical records, 350 to 400 cases of child sexual abuse are documented each year. These figures are not conclusive though, because Turkish society is sensitive in sexual matters, and a considerable proportion of cases may not even come to the attention of legal authorities because families are concerned about the protection of children and the honor of the family from publicity. On the other hand, because scandalous news sells, the media may also be exaggerating the news and figures to increase their sales (Kozcu 1991).

Child sexual abuse rehabilitation services have been established in a number of university and state hospitals in Turkey. Victims of abuse are generally referred to these centers by legal authorities.

Although incest is defined in all cultures, the boundaries of definitions may vary. The Turkish culture does not consider sexual relations and marriage between cousins as incestuous behavior. Thus, it is not uncommon for daughters and sons of brothers and sisters to marry. In fact, in arranged marriages, it is often regarded as a preferred way of marital union, especially in the eastern parts of Turkey, if it serves to keep the unity of land and power.

Other Unconventional Sexual Outlets

Although there is no recorded case, it is claimed that males occasionally use animals (such as sheep) as a sex object in rural areas. Especially in isolated villages, where sexual outlets for unmarried adolescents are lacking, sexual intercourse with animals may provide experience and can be viewed as educative more than perversion.

B. Prostitution

Commercial sex is legal in Turkey, and registered prostitutes are under periodic medical control. There is also illegal prostitution, which stems mostly from immigrants coming from neighboring countries. Many unregistered male and female prostitutes constitute a threat for public health, because they are not subject to routine medical check-ups. Prostitutes may play a special role for male adolescents in their first sexual experience. An older male kin may facilitate the adolescent relative's first experience by offering to take him to the prostitute who is usually informed on the matter beforehand.

C. Pornography and Erotica

Many publications on sexuality can be found in Turkish bookstores and newsstands. A number of popular magazines frequently publish articles on sexuality, mostly focusing on ways to enhance sexual satisfaction. Serious books on sexuality, including an encyclopedia on sexuality and books on human sexuality written for children and adolescents, have been published in recent years.

Although there is no strict control over them, pornographic publications are not distributed freely. Sale of these publications to persons under the age of 18 is illegal. In one 1990 study by Erkmen at al. (1990), 26 percent of the females and 48 percent of males reported that pornographic material should be allowed to be freely published. However, many social organizations have campaigns against pornography and violence, particularly to protect children and moral values.

9. Contraception, Abortion, and Population Planning

A. Contraception

The shift from a pronatalist to an antinatalist policy during the 1960s influenced contraceptive use by the introduction of modern methods to the public. In the early 1960s, only one fifth of Turkish women used any method of contraception and traditional methods were more common. The proportion of users was 38 percent in 1978, rose to 51 percent in 1983, and to 64 percent in 1988. By 1988, modern methods accounted for almost half of all contraceptive use, which shows that there were significant changes in contraceptive methods as well (Hancioglu 1997). Turkish women usually breastfeed their children, and many believe that lactation prevents pregnancy. The Family Planning Project began functioning by the end of the 1960s.

Almost all women, 99.1 percent, in the 15-to-49 age group have some idea about contraceptive methods, and 62.6 percent of women are currently using a method of contraception. The most common method is the IUD (18.8 percent), followed by condoms (6.6 percent), and contraceptive pills (4.9 percent). Regional differences in terms of contraception are very high. In the east, 42 percent use a contraceptive, whereas in the west the proportion is 72 percent (Hacettepe-HIPS 1989a).

Among the reasons for non-use of contraceptives, the most common one was health concerns related to the method. Other reasons were the husband's opposition, lack of knowledge, difficulty in availability, and religious beliefs (Hacettepe-HIPS 1989a).

The preferred method of contraception for Turkish males seems to be withdrawal before ejaculation. More than one quarter of sexually active males report using the withdrawal method, while 6.6 percent use condoms, and 1 percent refrain from intercourse during the ovulation period (Hacettepe-HIPS 1989a).

There is a strong positive correlation between education and use of modern contraceptives such as the pill, the diaphragm, and IUDs. In urban areas, the main source of obtaining IUDs is private doctors, whereas in rural areas, the majority of women obtain IUDs from health centers (Hacettepe-HIPS 1989a).

A majority of college students claim that they would refrain from unsafe sexual activities that might expose them to AIDS, and most are willing to use condoms during sex (Çok et al. 2000). The media has played an important role in campaigns for condom use in the prevention of HIV/AIDS, which has also promoted indirectly their use as a contraceptive.

Turkey also has some interesting traditional methods of contraception. These include taking herbal preparations made with boiled selected local plants and vegetable skins, and homemade or readymade materials, such as soap inserted into the vagina. There is also a local belief that if a woman is able to pass a kitten over the saddle of a horse while riding, she will be protected from pregnancy.

B. Teenage (Unmarried) Pregnancies

Statistical data are not available for unmarried teenage pregnancies. Since pregnancy out of wedlock is traumatic for both parties involved, these incidents are covered up and are not referred to state hospitals, where the signed consent of the parent is required before any medical intervention. Those who can afford to do so seek abortion in the private offices of gynecologists. In small towns or rural areas, where there is a risk of scandal or where private gynecologic services are not available, traditional methods of abortion are resorted to. On the other hand, pregnancy in the married adolescent presents a more common problem for Turkey, because the age of marriage is low in rural areas. In 1991 to 1992, 4 percent of all pregnancies were to teenagers. These pregnancies are usually unplanned and antenatal follow-up is lacking. Risks of pregnancy increase with low education and younger age of the mother, where symptoms may not be understood and spontaneous abortions may occur. However, if the pregnant adolescent is living in the traditional household with elder members of the family, there is a good chance that she is well cared for, even if medical care is not sought. In 1995, the State Department of Social Services started a project for teenage mothers.

C. Abortion

Until 1983, induced abortion in Turkey was prohibited except for eugenic reasons and when the life of the pregnant woman was in danger. In May 1983, the law on population planning was liberalized to provide abortion in a legal and safe manner. At present, women may obtain an abortion on request up to the tenth week of pregnancy for medical or social reasons. In 1988, it was found that 23.6 percent of pregnancies were terminated by induced abortion, 8.2 percent by spontaneous miscarriages, and 1.0 percent by stillbirths (Hacettepe-HIPS 1989b). The number of abortions induced for legal and medical indications was 15,571, while there were 49,655 abortions for unspecified causes, with 121 deaths in 1995.

Traditional methods of abortion, such as pushing sticks or long bird feathers into the uterus are still resorted to in rural areas. To induce abortion, some women take herbal preparations, such as boiled onions or aspirin, to trigger bleeding in the uterus. Carrying heavy loads and being exposed to heavy massage on the lower back area are other traditional methods believed to cause abortion (Hacettepe-HIPS 1989b).

D. Population Programs

Following the loss of males during the War of Independence (1918-1924), a shortage of manpower and a high mortality rate led the Turkish state toward a pronatalist policy to increase fertility and population growth until the mid 1960s. As a part of this policy, the government provided its employees financial support for each child. During the late 1950s, public opinion began to change, and the adverse effects of rapid population growth were gradually accepted. An antinatalist population planning law was enacted in 1965, legalizing contraception and promoting avoidance of unwanted pregnancies by public education.

Illegal abortion under unhealthy conditions was a cause behind high maternal mortality rates until 1983. The population planning law was revised, and abortions up to the tenth week of pregnancy and voluntary surgical contraception were legalized, while midwives were permitted to insert IUDs (Hanciogu 1997). In 1996, there were 274 Mother–Child Health and Family Planning Centers throughout Turkey, while the number of units giving exclusively family planning services was 5,328.

10. Sexually Transmitted Diseases

Syphilis is one of the diseases for which there is compulsory reporting to the Ministry of Health. The disease was considered a primary health problem in the years following the establishment of the Turkish Republic in the 1920s. Because of its high incidence, it had been a major health problem in Turkey. Thus, information on syphilis and other sexually transmitted diseases was an important part of the curricula of medical schools in the past. At present, each case of syphilis is followed up until the treatment is completed. According to figures of the Ministry of Health, 2,870 recorded and 196 new cases of syphilis were diagnosed in 1994. Syphilis does not now constitute a major health problem; its prevalence rate has decreased from 7.1 per 100,000 to 5.1 in the ten years between 1987 and 1997.

A. Incidence, Patterns, and Trends of STD

The Ministry of Health declared that the number of cases with gonococcal infections was 1,071 and cases of hepatitis B was 2,435 in 1996. Out of 3,267 prostitutes screened in 1997, 1,136 were infected with gonorrhea, 36 with syphilis, and 27 with hepatitis. Only a small percentage of college students reported gonorrhea (1.3 percent) and hepatitis B (3 percent), whereas none reported having a history of syphilis (Çok et al. 1998).

B. Availability of Treatment and Prevention Efforts

There are twelve venereal disease dispensaries in Turkey, in addition to services for sexually transmitted diseases in most public hospitals. The Ministry of Health has organized courses and conferences, and prepared brochures and booklets for the public and professionals, in accordance with the World Health Organization (WHO) for the control, prevention, and care of STD and HIV infections.

11. HIV/AIDS

The number of diagnosed HIV/AIDS cases was 753 by the end of 1997 in a population of about 63 million in Turkey. Regarding the 1997 Turkish HIV/AIDS statistics, the Ministry of Health stated that 84.6 percent of HIV/AIDS cases were Turkish citizens, while 15.4 percent were foreigners. Nine percent of HIV cases were infected by homosexual contact, 11.2 percent by intravenous injections, 6.4 percent by blood transfusions, 44.2 percent by heterosexual contact, 0.9 percent by infected mothers, and 28.3 percent by unknown causes.

Because of low public awareness of HIV/AIDS, the prevalence of commercial sex, the lack of educational campaigns, and immigration patterns, tourism, and returning workers from Europe, HIV/AIDS is considered as a potentially serious health problem in Turkey.

While the majority of college students are aware of the disease, 30 percent reported that they had never discussed HIV/AIDS with anyone. Students learn about AIDS from a variety of sources, including the media, books, and peers. Only a small percentage of the students obtain information from health professionals, family members, or at school (Çok et al. 2000). This study revealed that Turkish students had a moderate level of knowledge about the transmission, symptoms, and prevention of HIV/AIDS. A majority of students believed that they were not at risk for getting AIDS or that the risk was very low. Six percent stated that AIDS does not concern them. About half of the students stated that they would avoid people with AIDS, whereas 23 percent were willing to open their houses to anyone with AIDS.

12. Sexual Dysfunctions, Counseling, and Therapies

A. Concepts of Sexual Dysfunction

Because having children is socially regarded as a natural consequence of marriage in Turkey, there is a strong expectation of a child almost immediately after marriage on the part of the parents, relatives, neighbors, and friends of the couple. Indeed, most young couples themselves expect to have a baby and are almost impatient to do so. In unconsummated marriages as a result of sexual dysfunction, the couple faces the additional burden of explaining to inquisitive relatives and friends why they do not yet have a baby. Thus, for the majority of these couples, to make conception possible is the main reason they offer for seeking sex therapy. In childless couples, the blame is usually attributed to the women. In such cases, couples often seek help from traditional healers. Traditional healers generally supply the couple with charms, prayers, or sacred objects. Visits to the tombs of holy persons (*türbe*) are another traditional way to deal with various social and health problems, especially for women. During the *türbe* visit, the usual practice is to pray to the spirit of the holy person and ask for his or her help. Sometimes pieces of rags or colored strings are tied to the branches of trees or just left over the tombs. Whereas young girls may pray for husbands, childless women pray for a child.

Various magical beliefs and customs are still seen in some parts of Turkey as a remedy for sexual problems, childbearing, or infertility. One of these beliefs is a vow or a promise to God that if the woman can give birth to a son, they will not cut his hair, will dress him as a girl, and give sacrifices to God every year until his seventh birthday (Soylu et al. 1997).

Traditionally, sexual dysfunctions and infertility, along with many other health problems and diseases, were explained by folkloric beliefs, some of them based in Islam and others apparently unrelated to religion. There are still many people, even in cities, who believe that erectile dysfunction, vaginismus, or lack of sexual desire are consequences of evil forces, such as *büyü*, or magical procedures conducted by those who mean to destroy the happiness of the couple. In other cases, the supposed cause is the *nazar*, or the evil eye, or the *djins*, spirits described in the Koran, which sometimes reveal themselves to human beings. One example of such a *djin* is *alkarisi*, a witch-woman who visits women who have just given birth to a child. *Alkarisi* is believed to inflict a disease called *albasmasi*, characterized by the woman seeing everything in red, turning hot, getting cramps, and choking. If the cause of the sexual dysfunction or infertility is attributed to magical forces, treatment is usually sought from traditional healers called *hoca, medyum, falci,* etc., rather than medical doctors. Although prohibited by law, such para-medical healers provide their clients with preventive or curative measures, such as charms, prayers, and specific rituals. Doctors and psychologists have observed that many young couples with sexual problems, while claiming that they do not believe in supernatural phenomena, were pressed by their older relatives to seek a solution for their problems from traditional healers.

A study of patients at a primary health care clinic revealed that one in thirteen patients had a symptom of sexual dysfunction during the last month and one in twenty had a sexual dysfunction sometime in the past. Lack of sexual desire is the most prevalent symptom, occurring in 3.9 percent of all patients.

In a survey of 15- to 65-year-old men and women by Sagduyu (1997), 32.1 percent refused to participate in a study related to sexuality, 11.8 percent reported having no sexual experiences, while 92.8 percent of males and 54.0 percent of females valued sexuality positively. Negative feelings about sexuality were prominent in the older age group. Among patients with sexual dysfunction, 25 percent of females and 5 percent of males have suffered from lack of sexual desire.

Sexual dysfunctions are most commonly perceived as a failure of men. Therapists usually have difficulty in getting in contact with wives even as a part of therapy. It is not socially appropriate for a woman to have a sexual problem, because she is not even expected to desire sex. On the other hand, sometimes men resist participating in sex therapy if they think the problem belongs exclusively to the wife.

Kayir (1990) reported that among women with sexual dysfunctions, vaginismus was diagnosed in 52 percent, low sexual desire in 25 percent, anorgasmia in 15 percent, and painful intercourse (dyspareunia) in 2 percent. Among male sexual dysfunction patients, 48 percent experienced erectile dysfunction, 20 percent had premature ejaculation, 22 percent were mixed sexual dysfunction, 5 percent had low sexual desire, and 2 percent experienced inhibited ejaculation. Özkan (1981) has reported similar find-ings in a psychiatric population, with 49 percent of male patients having erectile dysfunction. He found that 52.9 percent complained of premature ejaculation, whereas 35.5 percent of female psychiatric patients complained of dyspareunia, 53.3 percent of vaginismus, 66.6 percent of anorgasmia, 60 percent of sexual arousal problems, and 84.4 percent of low sexual desire.

The figures and clinical observations imply that vaginismus is seen relatively frequently in Turkey, compared to Western countries. Five to ten percent of patients with sexual dysfunctions suffer from vaginismus. Many of these can be traced to a lack of sexual education and conservative attitudes, which, in turn, lead women to see sexual intercourse as an activity to be feared and avoided. During the evaluation process, it is observed that the majority of sexually dysfunctional couples' problems are initially related to mild or moderate cases of vaginismus-like complaints, which on further interview turn out not to be true vaginismus cases. Rather, the vaginismus-like symptoms are the result of the wife consciously or otherwise taking over the sexual problem (or, in other words, she assumes the blame for the husband's lack of desire, or erectile or ejaculation problem). Thus, the problem becomes more complicated, where tactful and original approaches on the part of the therapist may be needed.

B. Availability of Diagnosis and Treatment

Centers for treatment of sexual dysfunctions have been established in Turkey's university-associated hospitals during the past twenty years. In these units, patients are fully screened upon admission. The screening covers psychological and physical examinations. Methods such as Doppler ultrasonography and endocrinological and neurological examinations are available in most centers. In some sexual dysfunction units, more detailed examinations, such as neurophysiological evaluation and nocturnal penile tumescence (NPT), can be made if necessary.

Kayir (1995) argued that this improvement in diagnostic and therapeutic services has encouraged people with sexual dysfunctions to refer to these units, while perhaps also leading to the idea that each sexual problem is an illness that can be treated by doctors.

Many couples who seek treatment for their sexual problem are not highly motivated for sex therapy, because they expect the therapist to almost magically "cure" the problem by a simple intervention such as by prescribing a drug (Sungur 1998).

Treatment is available according to the etiology of the sexual problem and the specific needs of the patient. Couple therapy based on Masters and Johnson's techniques is the main approach if the etiology is psychological and both partners are willing to attend therapy sessions. Individual therapy and group therapy for men and women with similar sexual problems are also available in some centers. However, traditional values may sometimes hinder the man or his wife from taking part in therapeutic attempts to solve problems that prevail in the sexual area.

Generally, professional help is not sought when the couple is first faced with a sexual problem, especially if it is a case of female sexual dysfunction. The typical Turkish couple at first communicates the problem to their families and tries to tackle the problem within the family or with the help of traditional healers. In some cases, suggestions, reassurances, and para-psychological approaches work and the presenting problem is solved. In many cases, as expected, the difficulties persist and the relationship of the couple is threatened. The couple and families begin to split and blame each other. Usually, it is only then that the couple is referred for sex therapy. This delay and the introduction of other variables, such as the couple's blaming attitude and the families' concern and even intrusion are factors, which make the therapeutic process more difficult and complicated. The sexual problem of the couple can easily become a problem of the whole family, including the parents, siblings, and even relatives, which places an additional burden on patients and therapists. When incomplete sexual knowledge, erroneous expectations, lack of sexual experience, fears, and false beliefs are added to the picture, therapists are faced with multifaceted problems, which they have to deal with even though the couple is initially referred with a sexual dysfunction problem. Thus, the therapy proceeds on several levels at the same time, which may range from a teaching process to marital counseling and even to an insight-oriented approach. Thus, as Sungur (1994) has pointed out, formal training in sex therapy in Turkey is not sufficient for sex therapists who must also have experience in handling marital problems, as well as giving special attention to cultural factors that may necessitate modifications in treatment programs.

In some cases with organic etiology, the psychotherapeutic approach is also utilized to help the adaptation of the patients before or after organic interventions. Penile prosthesis is the most common method for male organic sexual dysfunctions. A penile revascularization operation is made for selected patients.

Sildenafil (Viagra) has become very popular. It was approved by the Ministry of Health and became available in the market in May 1999. Although strict regulations on the prescription were imposed in the beginning, these were shortly changed, and specialists, such as cardiologists, psychiatrists, and endocrinologists can now freely prescribe the medication.

13. Research and Advanced Education

Two main lines of sexual research can be delineated in Turkey. The first consists of surveys in student populations, which cover mainly the sexual attitudes, knowledge, and experience of this group. Some of these studies have been reviewed elsewhere in this chapter. The other area in which sexual research is conducted is in the clinical population, mainly in those who apply with sexual problems. A series of studies have focused on psychological factors involved in sexual dysfunctions: Igikli (1993) found that sexually dysfunctional couples' problems in the relationship accumulated in emotional, cognitive, and communication areas.

Bozkurt (1996) found that patients with psychogenic erectile problems were significantly more anxious and depressed when compared to organogenic patients. In the psychogenic impotence group, 19.4 percent had mood disorders, 5.6 percent had anxiety disorders, and 22.2 percent had mixed mood and anxiety disorders, whereas in the organically impotent group, no pathology in the mood and anxiety disorders spectrum was found.

The MMPI profiles of psychogenic impotence subjects had more similarity to neurotics than normal controls. The personality patterns of psychogenic erectile dysfunction patients revealed by the MMPI suggested that while they have no problems with the sexual role, they have depressive tendencies with difficulty in implementing activities and an inclination to introversion (Aydin 1991).

Özgen et al.'s (1993) study indicated that organic causes more commonly underlie sexual dysfunctions in the older age group, whereas psychological factors predominate in younger patients. If a dysfunction appears in one area of sexuality, it tends to spread to other areas, causing problems in experiencing sexuality. As a result, it was claimed that the person's perception of and being in the sexual sphere are distorted.

In a recent large-scale population survey on the prevalence of erectile dysfunction, in the sample comprised of 1,982 men, 64.3 percent of the men over 40 years of age reported some degree of erectile dysfunction (35.7 percent minimal, 23 percent moderate, and 5.6 percent complete). The prevalence of erectile dysfunction increased by age, with diabetes, and cardiovascular and prostatic diseases contributing to the increase (Akkus et al. 1999).

Gülçat (1995) found that 30 percent of non-clinical male subjects had a sexual problem. While this finding is in accordance with surveys in Western countries, it also implies the need for further studies in the area of sexuality and sexual problems in Turkey.

Advanced education in sexual dysfunctions, evaluation methods, and treatment has been offered in some university hospitals for the last ten to fifteen years. There has been growing interest and data accumulation in this area in the last decade. Since 1988, several congresses and symposia were organized on issues in sexual dysfunctions and treatment. The main aim has been to adopt a multidisciplinary approach in which psychiatrists, psychologists, urologists, and gynecologists work together in the assessment and treatment of patients. In late 1999, a Sexual Education, Treatment, and Research Association was founded to integrate the studies of various disciplines, prepare educational programs for the layman as well as for professionals, conduct research, and set ethical standards in the patient-therapist relationship.

The Turkish Family Health and Planning Foundation, located at Sitesi A Blok D, 3-4, 80660 Etiler, Istanbul, Turkey, is the main organization dealing with sexuality issues, family planning, and sexual health.

A Final Remark

Social change involving modifications in social structure, attitudes, beliefs, and norms is rapidly altering Turkish society. Shifts in the demographic composition of rural and urban areas, industrial growth, and related changes in the economy and social structure precipitate modifications in family structure, functions, and dynamics, as well as in traditional male and female roles.

The Turkish panorama of sexuality reveals that modern and traditional attitudes exist side by side, and this fact, while contributing to the richness of the Turkish culture, is also fertile ground for social, interpersonal, and intrapsychic conflicts.

References and Suggested Readings

Akkus, E., Kadioglu, A., Esen, A., et al. 1999. Prevalence of erectile dysfunction in Turkey. Unpublished data.
Ayata, S. 1988. Statü yarismasi ve salon kullanimi [Status competition and life in the living room]. *Toplum ve Bilim*, 42:5-25.

Aydin, H. 1991. Psikojen empotansta kisilik yapisinin arastirilmasi [A study of the personality pattern in patients with psychogenic impotency]. *GATA Bülteni, 33*:187-194.

Aydin, O. 1998 (October). *Çalisma yasminda kadin is isçlerin kotunmasi [Protective measures for women laborers]*. Paper presented at the Symposium on Legal Regulations for Women Laborers (Ministry of Social Security), Ankara.

Badran, M. 1995. *Feminists, Islam, and nation: Gender and the making of modern Egypt.* Princeton, NJ: Princeton University Press.

Basgül, F. U. 1997. *12-15 yas grubu ergenlerin cinsel egitim konusundaki görüsleri [Opinions of adolescents in the 12-15 age group on sexual education]*. Unpublished thesis at Ankara Universitesi Sosyal Bilimler Enstitüsü, Ankara.

Battal, S., Aydin, H., & Gülçat, Z. 1989. Cinsel kimlik ve cinsel davranis bozukluklarinda kisilik özellikeri [Personality structures of subjects with gender identity and sexual behavior disorders]. *GATA Bülteni, 31*:651-660.

Beck, L. G., & Keddie, N., eds. 1978. *Women in the Muslim world.* Cambridge, MA: Harvard University Press.

Bouhdiba, A. 1985. *Sexuality in Islam* (A. Sheridan, trans.). London: Rutledge and Kegan Paul.

Bozkurt, A. 1996. *Erkek cinsel islev bozukluklarnda psikopaolojinin arastirilmasi [A study on psychopathology in male sexual dysfunction]*. Unpublished dissertation, GATA, Ankara.

Brooks, G. 1995. *Nine parts of desire: The hidden world of Islamic women.* New York: Anchor Books/Doubleday.

Çok, F. 2000 (April/May). Reflections on an adolescent sexuality education program in Turkey. *SIECUS Report, 28*(4):5-7.

Çok, F., Ersever, H., & Gray, L. A. 1998. Bir grup üniversite ögrencisinde cinsel ödafvranis [Sexual behavior in a group of university students]. *HIV/AIDS, 1*:23-29.

Çok, F., Gray, L. A., & Ersever, H. 2001. Turkish university students' sexual behavior, knowledge, attitudes and perceptions about HIV/AIDS. *Culture, Health and Sexuality* (accepted for publication).

Eksi, A. 1982. *Gençlerimiz ve sorunlari [Turkish youth and their problems]*. Istanbul: University Publications, #2790.

Eksi, A. 1990. *Çocuk genç, anababalar [Children, teenagers, parents]*. Istanbul: Bilgi Publications.

Ergöçmen, B. A. 1997. Women's status and fertility in Turkey. In: Hacettepe University Institute of Population Studies (HIPS) and Macro International Inc. (MI), *Fertility trends, women's status and reproductive expectations in Turkey: Results of further analysis of the 1993 Turkish Demographic and Health Survey.* Calverton, Maryland: HIPS MI.

Erkmen, H., Dilbaz, N., Deber, G. S., et al. 1990. Sexual attitudes of Turkish university students. *Journal Sex Education and Therapy, 16*:251-261.

Erkut, S. 1982. Dualism in values toward education of Turkish women. In: Ç. Kagitçibasi, ed., *Sex roles, family and community in Turkey. Turkish studies 3.* Bloomington, IN: Indiana University Press.

Fernea, E. W. 1998. Turkey. In: *In search of feminism: One woman's global journey* (pp. 200-239). New York: Doubleday.

Gülçat, Z. 1995. *Cinsel lev bozukluklarndan empotansn psikolojik boyutlar üzerine bir aratrma [A study on the psychology of impotence]*. Unpublished dissertation, University of Ankara, Turkey.

Gülçat, Z., Aydin, H., Battal, S., et al. 1988. *Transseküel ve homoseksüeller üzerine psikosyal bir çalisma [A psychosocial study on transsexuals and homosexuals]*. Proceedings of papers presented at the 24th National Congress of Psychiatry and Neurological Sciences in Ankara (pp. 638-649).

Hacettepe University Institute of Population Studies (HIPS). 1989a. *1988 Turkish fertility and health survey.* Ankara: HIPS.

Hacettepe University Institute of Population Studies (HIPS). 1989b. *1983 Turkish population and health survey.* Ankara: HIPS.

Hancolu, A. 1997. Fertility Trends in Turkey: 1978-1993. In: Hacettepe University Institute of Population Studies (HIPS) and Macro International Inc. (MI), Fertility Trends, Women's Status and Reproductive Expectations in Turkey: Results of Further Analysis of the 1993 Turkish Demographic and Health Survey. Calverton, Maryland: HIPS MI.

İmamoglu, O. 1996. The perpetuation of gender stereotypes through the media: The case of Turkish newspapers. In: N. Dacovic, D. Derman, & K. Ross, eds., *Gender and media*. Ankara: Medi-Campus Project #A 126 Publications, Mediation.

İnci, Y. 1993. *Homoseksel ve transseksellerde kendilik kavrami* [*Self concept in homosexuals and transsexuals*]. Unpublished dissertation, GATA, Ankara.

Ikl, H. 1993. *Cinsel fonksiyon bozukluklarinda e likilerinin deerlendirilmesi.* [*Evaluation of marital relationship in sexually dysfunctional couples*]. Unpublished dissertation, Gulhane Military Medical Academy, Ankara.

Kagitçibasi, Ç. 1982a. Introduction. In: Ç. Kagitçibasi, ed., *Sex roles, family and community in Turkey. Turkish studies 3.* Bloomington, IN: Indiana University Press.

Kagitçibasi, Ç. 1982b. Sex roles, value of children and fertility. In: Ç. Kagitçibasi, ed., *Sex roles, family and community in Turkey. Turkish studies 3.* Bloomington, IN: Indiana University Press.

Kandiyoti, D. 1982. Urban change and women's roles in Turkey: An overview and evaluation. In: Ç. Kagitçibasi, ed., *Sex roles, family and community in Turkey. Turkish studies 3.* Bloomington, IN: Indiana University Press.

Kandiyoti, D. 1995. Patterns of patriarchy: Notes for an analysis of male dominance in Turkish society. In: S. Tekeli, ed., *Women in modern Turkish society: A reader.* London and New Jersey: Zed Books.

Kayir, A. 1995. Women and their sexual problems in Turkey. In: S. Tekeli, ed., *Women in modern Turkish society: A reader.* London and New Jersey: Zed Books

Kayir, A., Geyran, P., Tükel, R., & Kiziltug, A. 1990. *Cinsel sorunlarda basvuri özellikleri ve tedavi seçimi* [*Patient referrals and treatment choice in sexual problems*]. Paper presented at the 26th National Psychiatric Congress, Turkey.

Kiray, M. 1976. The new role of mothers: Changing intra-familial relationships in a small town in Turkey. In: J. G. Peristiany, ed., *Mediterranean family structures.* London: Cambridge University Press.

Kozcu, S. 1991. Çocuk istismari ve ihmali aile yazilari III [Child abuse and neglect III]. *Türkiye aile yilligi, TC basbakanlik aile arastirma kurumu baskanligi.* Ankara: MN Ofset.

Kuyas, N. 1982. Female labor power relations in the urban Turkish family. In: Ç. Kagitçibasi, ed., *Sex roles, family and community in Turkey. Turkish studies 3.* Bloomington, IN: Indiana University Press.

Levine, N. 1982. Social Change and Family Crisis: The nature of Turkish divorce. In: Ç. Kagitçibasi, ed., *Sex roles, family and community in Turkey. Turkish studies 3.* Bloomington, IN: Indiana University Press.

Mernissi, F. 1991. *The veil and the male elite: A feminist interpretation of women's rights in Islam.* Reading, MA: Addison-Wesley.

Mernissi, F. 1993. *Islam and democracy: Fear of the modern world.* Reading, MA: Addison-Wesley.

Ministry of Education (Republic of Turkey). 2000. *Ergenlik döneminde degisim* [*Changes during adolescence*]. Ankara: MEB.

Ministry of Health (Republic of Turkey). 1996. *Health statistics 1995* (Publication No. 579). Ankara: Ministry of Health.

Murray, S. O. 1997a. Homosexuality among slave elites in Ottoman Turkey. In: S. O. Murray & W. Roscoe, eds., *Islamic homosexualities: Culture, history, and literature.* New York/London: New York University Press.

Murray, S. O. 1997b. The will not to know: Islamic accommodations of male homosexuality. In: S. O. Murray & W. Roscoe, eds., *Islamic homosexualities: Culture, history, and literature.* New York/London: New York University Press.

Murray, S. O. 1997c. Woman–woman love in Islamic societies. In: S. O. Murray & W. Roscoe, eds., *Islamic homosexualities: Culture, history, and literature.* New York/London: New York University Press.

Murray, S. O., & Roscoe, W., eds. 1997. *Islamic homosexualities: Culture, history, and literature.* New York/London: New York University Press.

Naipaul, V. S. 1998. *Beyond belief: Islamic excursions among the converted peoples.* New York: Random House.

Özbay, F. 1982. "Women's Education in Rural Turkey." In: Ç. Kagitçibasi, ed., *Sex roles, family and community in Turkey. Turkish studies 3.* Bloomington, IN: Indiana University Press.

Özgren, F., et al. 1993. Erkek cinsel fonksiyon bozukluklarinda sorun alanlari üzerine bir arastirma [A study of problem areas in male sexual dysfunctions]. *GATA Bülteni, 35*:701-710.

Özgür, S., & Sunar, D. 1982. Social psychological patterns of homicide in Turkey: A comparison of male and female convicted murderers. In: Ç. Kagitçibasi, ed., *Sex roles, family and community in Turkey. Turkish studies 3.* Bloomington, IN: Indiana University Press.

Öztürk, O. 1963. Psychological effects of circumcision practiced in Turkey. *Turkish Journal of Pediatrics, 5*:66-69.

Parrinder, G. 1980. *Sex in the world's great religions.* Don Mills, Ontario, Canada: General Publishing Company.

Sagduyu, A., et al. 1997. Saglik ocagina basvuran hastalarda cinsel sorrunlar [Sexual problems in patients at a primary health care clinic]. *Türk Psikiyatry Dergisi, 8*(2):102-109.

Soylu, L. M., Tamam, L., & Avci, A. 1997. Bir adagin cinsel kimlik ve islevlere olasi etkileri: Bir olgu sunumu [Possible influence of a vow on gender identity and sexual function: A case report]. *3 P, 5*(2):146-149.

SIS (State Institute of Statistics, Prime Ministry, Republic of Turkey). 1995. *Divorce statistics—1993.* Ankara: SIS.

Sungur, M. Z. 1994. Evaluation of couples referred to a sexual dysfunction unit and prognostic factors in sexual and marital therapy. *Sex and Marital Therapy, 9*:251-265.

Sungur, M. Z. 1998. Difficulties encountered during the assessment and treatment of sexual dysfunction—A Turkish perspective. *Sex and Marital Therapy, 13*:71-81.

TC Hükümeti ve UNICEF (Turkish Government and UNICEF). 1991. *Türkiye'de anne ve çokoklarin durum analizi.* Ankara: Yeniçag Matbassi.

Tekeli, S. 1995. Introduction: Women in Turkey in the 1980s. In: S. Tekeli, ed., *Women in modern Turkish society: A reader.* London and New Jersey: Zed Books.

Tezcan, M. 1998. Islam öncesi ve sonras eski Türk ailesinin sosoyokültürei nitelikleri [Sociocultural characteristics of pre-Islamic and Islamic Turkish family]. *Türk Düinyasi, 15*:12-23.

Vicdan, K. 1993. *Ülkemizde adolesanlarin demograpfik ve epidemiyolojik özellikleri: Mevcut problemler ve çözüm önerileri* [Demographic and epidemiologic characteristics of Turkish adolescents: Problems and proposals].Unpublished dissertation. Ankara: Dr. Zekai Tahir Burak Kadin Hastanesi.

Yüksel, S., et al. 1988. *Marital relationship in women with and without sexual dysfunction.* Paper presented at the 3rd World Congress on Behavior Therapy, Edinborough, Scotland.

Zilfi, M. C. 1997. *Women in the Ottoman Empire: Middle Eastern women in the early modern era.* Leiden: Brill and New York: Köln.

Vietnam
(*Công Hoa Xa Hôi Chú Nghia Viêt Nam*)
Socialist Republic of Vietnam

Jakob Pastoetter, M.A.*

Contents

Demographics and a Historical Perspective

A. Demographics

Vietnam is the second largest country in Southeast Asia after Indonesia. With 127,200 square miles (330,363 square km), it is twice the size of the state of Arizona, slightly larger than Malaysia (including East Malaysia), and about 15 percent smaller than Japan. Vietnam is bordered on the north by China, on the east by the Gulf of Tonkin and the South China Sea, and on the west by Cambodia, Laos, and the Gulf of Thailand. The country extends some 1,000 miles (1,700 km) from north to south. Its widest east-to-west point is 372 miles (600 km), whereas in some places it is only 31 miles (50 km) wide. The capital, Hanoi (2.194 million), is situated in

Communications: Jakob Pastoetter, M.A., Eichborndamm 38 D-13403, Berlin, Germany; jmpastoetter@compuserve.de.

the northern region, while the largest city, Ho Chi Minh City (4.392 million), the former Saigon, is in the south.

In 1999, Vietnam had a population of more than 76 million, up from only 47 million in 1975. Almost 40 percent of the population are under 15 years of age, about 80 percent are under 40, and 5.3 percent are 65 or older. Life expectancy at birth in 1995 was 62.9 years for males and 67.3 years for females. The population is still almost 80 percent rural and is concentrated in the two main rice-growing deltas: the Red River in the north and the Mekong in the south. In the Red River Delta (excluding Hanoi), population density averages 1,170 per square kilometer, and in Thai Binh it rises to 1,230 per square kilometer, among the highest rural densities in the world. The Mekong Delta, which is over twice as large as the Red River Delta, has a far lower population density (400 per square kilometer) and is the source of the rice surpluses that Vietnam exports.

Traditionally, education has been of great importance to the Vietnamese, and the State has always set aside a significant portion of its budget for education. Although access to higher levels of education has been limited, the introduction of near-universal primary education has produced a high literacy rate. According to the 1999 World Bank figures, 83 percent of the population over 15 years old was literate. [The meaning of "literate" is not specified, whether this means able to write one's name, or able to read a newspaper. (Editor)] In rural areas, the education system has been nearly as well developed as in urban areas, particularly in the north: 87 percent of the rural population was literate in 1989 compared with 95 percent of the urban population.

Vietnam has a good record in providing health care, as measured by such indicators as life expectancy, infant mortality, and the number of doctors per citizen. After 1954, the government set up a public-health infrastructure, which reached down to hamlet level. This system was extended to the south after reunification in 1976. In the late 1980s, a combination of reform factors, budgetary constraints, the decision to shift more responsibility for health care financing to the provinces, the reduced social role of agricultural cooperatives in 1988, and the introduction of fees in 1989, began to affect the quality of health care. By 1996, the government was devoting only 1 percent of the gross domestic product to health spending, and 85 percent of all spending on health services came from private sources.

Vietnam has one of the most complex ethnolinguistic patterns in Asia. About 50 different ethnic minorities make up more than 10 percent of the population, while approximately 87 percent of the population is ethnic Vietnamese (Kinh). The Vietnamese were significantly Sinicized during a millennium of Chinese rule. Vietnamese, one of the Mon-Khmer languages of the Austro-Asiatic language family, exhibits strong Chinese influence. Diverse cultural traditions, geographic variations, and historical events have created distinct traditional regions within the country. The general topographic dichotomy of highland and lowland regions also has ethnolinguistic significance: The lowlands generally have been occupied by ethnic Vietnamese, while the highlands have been home to numerous smaller ethnic groups that differ culturally and linguistically from the Vietnamese.

The highland peoples can be divided into the northern ethnic groups, with affinities to peoples in southern China, and the southern highland populations, with ties to the Mon-Khmer and Austronesian peoples of Cambodia, Indonesia, and elsewhere in Southeast Asia (see Section 14, Sexual Attitudes and Behaviors Among Ethnic Minorities).

A north-south variation also evolved among the ethnic Vietnamese as they expanded southward from the Red River Delta along the coastal plain and into the Mekong River Delta. The Vietnamese themselves have long made a distinction between the northern region, with Hanoi as its cultural center, the central region, with the traditional royal capital of Hue, and the southern region, with Saigon (Ho Chi Minh City) as its urban center. The French also divided Vietnam into three parts: the northern Tonkin, the central Annam, and Cochinchina in the south. Official efforts to move families from the densely populated areas to the "new economic zones" in the Central Highlands have tended to marginalize the minority groups living there, in addition to causing ecological stress.

The once sizeable overseas Chinese community, which was largely concentrated in the south, was depleted after many decided to leave the country as "boat people" when the government closed down private businesses in 1978. The 1989 census counted 962,000 Chinese, barely changed from the 949,000 recorded in the 1979 census. But as elsewhere in Southeast Asia, the Chinese minority wields great influence in the economy. Ho Chi Minh City alone is estimated to have about half a million Cantonese-speaking ethnic Chinese residents.

Vietnamese is the official language. Although the Vietnamese language is distinct, it nevertheless can be described as a fusion of Mon-Khmer, Tai, and Chinese elements. The minorities have languages of their own, and the Constitution guarantees their right to use these languages before the courts. English is gaining popularity as a second language, whereas many people still speak French, Russian, and German. In the early seventeenth century, Catholic missionaries introduced *chu quôc ngu* ("national written language") using an adapted form of the Western alphabet. The four letters, *f*, *j*, *w*, and *z*, are omitted, and accents are added. The resultant *chu quôc ngu* was made popular by the French and has been used officially since 1918. In Vietnamese, quite a few words are spelled in the same way. Differences in meaning result through pronunciation: e.g., *ca* (to sing), *cà* (eggplant), and *cá* (fish).

The names of the authors, researchers, institutions, titles of books, and locations occurring in this chapter are written in the form in which they were used in the international research literature. In order to facilitate literature searches, Vietnamese authors are referred to in exactly the writing of their names in the quoted articles and books. To avoid confusion for the non-Vietnamese users of the *International Encyclopedia of Sexuality*, who might not know what the family, middle, and first names are, we did also not alter the order of the three parts of the names but used the form we found.

B. A Brief Historical Perspective

The two most characteristic features of Vietnam's history are the country's struggle against foreign occupation and intervention, which has been going on for a good part of the last two thousand years, and the ability of the Vietnamese people to learn from their occupants and finally overcome the foreign rule. The invaders were mostly, but not exclusively the Han Chinese, who ruled Vietnam for over one thousand years from 111 B.C.E. to the fifteenth century. The Chinese were also in power during the wars between the Monguls and the Cham state, from 1428 to 1672, when Le Loi expelled the Chinese and was crowned emperor. In the middle of the nineteenth century, the French began intervening in the country's affairs on a large scale. Within ten years of seizing Saigon, they had taken control of the whole country, which they governed as a colony and incorporated into French Indochina in spite of resistance from the Vietnamese.

After 1940, when France surrendered to Germany in World War II, the Vichy government had to accept the presence of Japanese troops in Vietnam, although the Vichy government continued to govern the colony. During this period, Ho Chi Minh founded the Viet Minh, a nationalist liberation movement inspired by communist ideals, whose aim was to free Vietnam from foreign rule. A few months before the Japanese were defeated and finally surrendered to the Allied forces in September 1945, the Viet Minh took direct control from the French, and Ho Chi Minh declared the Democratic Republic of Vietnam independent on 2 September 1945.

After the end of World War II, the French deployed a substantial number of troops and fought the Viet Minh, led again by Ho Chi Minh, in order to regain control over Vietnam. The French were defeated decisively in 1954 at Dien Bien Phu and were forced to withdraw after they had dominated Vietnam for almost one hundred years. However, the Viet Minh controlled only the northern part of Vietnam. The establishment of a second government, led by Ngo Dinh Diem in Saigon, led to the separation of the country into North and South Vietnam along the seventeenth parallel, the latter backed by the United States. Under the influence of the Korean War and the so-called Domino theory, the United States gave South Vietnam political and military support against North Vietnamese attempts to take over the south. The United States' involvement gradually grew from a few advisers to hundreds of thousands of ground troops to fight the National Liberation Front, otherwise known as Vietcong. Nevertheless, the Vietcong and the North Vietnamese prevailed. In 1973, the United States signed a treaty with North Vietnam that provided for withdrawal of all American ground troops and aimed at restoring peace. After the American withdrawal, the government of South Vietnam crumbled rapidly and the North took control in 1975, ending a war that had lasted nearly thirty years. In July 1976, the nation was reunited, and the Socialist Republic of Vietnam was established.

Important events since the reunification of the country include a border war with China in 1979 and Vietnam's invasion of Cambodia the year before. Vietnam finally withdrew its troops from Cambodia in 1989. Perhaps the key feature, though, was the country's economic deterioration and its dire position by the mid 1980s. The breakthrough came at the end of 1986 with the introduction of the *doi moi*, or renovation policy. The aim was to move from a centrally planned to a market economy while still retaining the socialist political structure. The introduction of the new foreign investment law in December 1987, allowing and encouraging foreign investment, was a major step from which all the current excitement in the international business community has stemmed. Parallels have been drawn to China's experience. Such has been the rapidity and the strength of the process, that the near-total withdrawal of Soviet aid 1991 and the collapse of the COMECON trading bloc, which should in theory have cut away the great majority of Vietnam's trade, had little effect.

There is now far greater openness towards foreign countries in general, and improved relations with other Southeast Asian and Western nations in particular. Vietnam became a full member of the Association of Southeast Asian Nations (ASEAN) at the meeting in Brunei in July 1995. Full diplomatic relations with the United States were reestablished in July 1995, some 20 years after the fall of Saigon.

Nevertheless, Vietnam is in desperate need of foreign investors. Over the last six years, the inflow of foreign capital dwindled from US$3 billion to little more than US$500 million since Vietnam lost its privileged position as favorite of Western investors because of the multiple domestic and external trading restrictions and widespread corruption. Many foreign investors have left the country in frustration, according to the *Neue Züricher Zeitung* (7/14/2000). The situation might change as a result of normalization of trade relations between the U.S. and Vietnam in 2000, which opened the Vietnamese market for American investors in such important key sectors as telecommunications and financial services. Still, Vietnam is one of the world's poorest countries. Its average per capita gross domestic product is estimated to be about US$150 per year; the statutory minimum wage is US$35 per month in Ho Chi Minh City and Hanoi and US$30 elsewhere for local employees employed by foreign invested enterprises. The economic reforms during the last few years have permitted some people to fare better in the private sector, but overall living standards still remain low. Viewed in this light, it is evident that, even with an inflation rate decreased from almost 400 percent in 1988 to 17 percent in 1995, it will be many years before Vietnam comes close to reaching the financial strength attributed to some of its Asian neighbors—especially since the growth rate for 1999 dwindled to 3 percent from an official estimate of 5.8 percent in 1998.

Real household income per head rose by 5 percent in 1995 and 4.2 percent in 1996. The percentage of people living in poverty (as defined by the World Bank) has fallen from almost 55 percent in 1992 to less than 30 percent by 1998. The poorest quintile of the population does not appear to have fared so well. Between 1994 and 1996, its income per head rose by just 0.5 percent annually, far less than the annual growth of 6.8 percent experienced by the top quintile.

Official figures obtained by Reuters show less than 600,000 foreign tourists visited Vietnam in 1998, down from 690,000 the previous year, a drop the government blamed on Asia's economic crisis. Hanoi lumps tourist figures with total arrivals, including business and official visitors, ending up with a figure of 1.5 million in 1998, down from 1.7 million in 1997. Its goal in 2000 was two million total visitors, compared with nearby Thailand, which expected to attract 8.2 million tourists during the same period.

1. Basic Sexological Premises

Authors' Note: Because of the specific difficulties of doing sex research in a communist and Neo-Confucian country like Vietnam, we could not do field research on our own and instead had to rely on the published papers and books about Vietnam. The challenge we faced in preparing this chapter was confirmed early on by Professor Frank Proschan, an expert on Vietnamese culture at the Folklore Institute at Indiana University (Bloomington) who told us that no Vietnamese scholar would be able to write such a chapter, because the Vietnamese have just started walking the path of independent science after many years of Confucian and communist censorship. The Vietnamese resources we subsequently found and incorporated into this chapter supported this thesis. Since the resources came from many different fields of research—history, medicine, ethnology, anthropology, sociology, religious studies, sexology, and sociology—we thought it best to leave them as much unchanged as possible to prevent misinterpretation (compare Gammeltoft 1999, and Elizabeth Amaya-Fernandez's chapter on Cuba in this volume). At the same time, we also tried to make the text as readable as possible without too many direct quotations or heavy use of indirect speech. Nevertheless the chapter should be transparent enough to track all the sources down to find more in-depth information if necessary.

What information we have on contemporary sexuality in Vietnam had to be gleaned on the one hand from the Vietnamese and international anthropological and ethnological literature, as well as AIDS, STD, and family planning research (compare Sections 9, Contraception, Abortion, and Population Planning, 10, Sexually Transmitted Diseases, and 11, HIV/AIDS). On the other hand, there exists the domestic social science research, which is focused mainly on "gender and development," and more recently on the nature of the Vietnamese family. For the French period, the late 1800s and the first half of the twentieth century, we used mainly the works of Jacobus X. (1898, writing as "A French Army-Surgeon") and Annick Guénel (1997). For the Vietnam War period, a major resource was *Saigon After Dark* by Philip Marnais (1967). We emphasize that neither Jacobus X. nor Philip Marnais are acknowledged anthropologists or ethnologists. Although their writings are quite sensationalistic and written from the point of view of a so-called ethnoerotologist and an American journalist, respectively, the facts they provide are regarded as reliable, even if they reveal more about the colonial fantasies and fears connected with "alien" sexuality, than they do about the perception and feelings of the native Vietnamese. Last but not least, Professor Frank Proschan of Indiana University, an expert on Vietnamese culture at the Folklore Institute, provided us not only with his own findings, but also books and articles about other subjects only available in Vietnam. We cannot stress the fact enough that without him we would not have been able to include reliable information about the Vietnamese homosexual culture. Additional information, as well as confirmation, was acquired by interviewing Vietnamese students at Indiana University and the Kinsey Institute and author Robert Taylor (1997), who served as an officer in the U.S. Army during the Vietnam War.

A. Character of Gender Roles

Reality and Fantasy

The character of Vietnamese gender roles reflects the over two-thousand-year influence of Confucianism, which is still the most important single influence on gender roles. Vietnamese women were comparably less degraded by the "three submissions" (to father, husband, and eldest son) and the four virtues (skill with her hands, an agreeable appearance, prudence in speech, and exemplary conduct) than women in China (see Section 2, Religious and Ethnic Factors Affecting Sexuality). Gender roles in Vietnam are changing rapidly, though with different speeds in different social layers. Although men are still more visible in society, it is not necessarily a sign of their also having more power. Far from a clear picture, the one sure statement is that Vietnamese gender roles are loaded with contradictions.

There is still a continuity of Vietnamese ideas of the power of women within the household ("the general of the interior"), and the way in which state socialism splits men and women. For example, the Peasant Union represents men and the Women's Union only women, thereby encouraging a popular public view that women are not farmers and need not be directly involved in economic change, although up to 80 percent of the field work is done by them. Also, the psychological dimensions of male–female relationships within the family and community are unrepresented and unidentified in the State bureaucracy, and new contradictions begin to emerge between the power of women in family and culture and their empowerment by the state. As Wazir Jahan Karim observed in 1995, "This seems to be a repeat of a typical Southeast Asian model of change and development: that women continue to experience contradictory statements of their usefulness and power, and that the public view usually contradicts the popular."

Unlike the prevalence of male domination in neighboring cultures, the earliest legend about the founding of Vietnam claims equality among the spouses. The mythic founders of Vietnam were a couple, Au Co, the wife, and Lac Long Quan, the husband. The husband was a dragon, suited to live on the coastal plains; the wife was a fairy who wanted to live in the mountains. As they agreed to part, fifty sons followed their mother and governed the northern part of Vietnam, while fifty sons followed their father and reigned over the kingdom bordering the South China Sea. Before separating, they pledged mutual respect and aid in time of crisis.

Vietnamese folklore, female buddhas, goddesses, and proverbs seem to show that Vietnamese women have some influence in society. Goddesses commonly presided over the cultivation of rice and other food crops. Streets and districts are named after female cult heroes, such as the Trung sisters (40 C.E.), who led a revolt of independence, and Trieu Thi Trinh, who took up a similar warrior role in the third century. She is described as nine feet tall, with three-foot-long breasts and a voice like a temple bell, able to eat a bushel of rice and walk 1,500 miles in a single day. Vietnamese nationalists have also resurrected the poetry of Ho Xuan Huong, a female poet who was critical of gender inequality more than fifty years before French colonization.

Gender and Economic Control

Nearly all the country's market stalls today are run by women. Though they are more often small merchants, it is interesting that the richest private capitalist in Vietnam today is also a woman. Not only do women form the overwhelming majority of all active merchants in the country, they constitute the majority of the customers as well. As O'Harrow (1995) points out, in spite of the male role of provider, which is implicit in the Confucian paradigm, Vietnamese mothers raise their daughters to understand, if not explicitly, then by example, that they should always have their own money and cannot depend on men.

The most commonly acquired commodity for this kind of female protective investment is jewelry, preferably in unalloyed gold or with recognizable gems. Young girls quietly watch their mother's elaborate systems of boxes, jars, purses, hidden floor boards, and furtive containers of every kind and dimension, never opened in the father's presence. They observe and learn. The extraordinary interest Vietnamese women appear to take in jewelry is commonly misunderstood by outsiders as simple vanity. But in fact the precious contents are considered the mother's property and will stay with her should she leave.

Relationships Between (Married) Women and Men

Acccording to O'Harrow (1995), the polite term for a wife is *noi tro* ("interior helper"), the common, not-so-polite epithet is *Noi Ttoung* or "general of the interior." The women of Ha Dong in particular have a reputation for being fierce spouses that has gained them the nickname of *Su Tu Ha Dong* or "Ha Dong Lionesses." It is said about their husbands that they belong to a very ancient club, the *Hoi So Vo* or "Society of Men Who Fear Their Wives." Folk humor aside, it is a strategy to survive that motivates women to gain control of the family finances. Because the wife is in fact the backbone of the family, many families get into deep trouble or even break up when the wife/mother dies. The social system in Southeast Asia is based on a system of moral debts and balances. The relationship between (married) women and men is not one between two individuals, but between two life projects, which depend on one another. Break one side away and the whole system crumbles.

Contrary to Western notions, where feelings of guilt support freedom before marriage but faithfulness afterwards, in societies where shame and the notion of virgin marriage is operative, extramarital affairs outnumber premarital ones. If a Vietnamese woman takes a lover and can keep the fact secret and so avoid shame, she can maintain an upper hand. The man, on the other hand, while much less bound by problems of public shame for having a girlfriend, is more likely to be worried about surrendering self-control and so losing his face. As O'Harrow (1995) points out, Vietnamese women seldom have male friends, per se, because they have very few social mechanisms for dealing with men on an equal footing. Men are always patrons or clients, fathers, sons, husbands, or lovers. A wife deals with her husband with the same mechanisms that a mother uses to deal with her son, and a lover is usually treated as a daughter treats her father. So one can understand why tales of female sexual insatiability also attach to the Ha Dong lioness myth: It is the woman who controls the man, and he is the one who loses face.

Relationships Between (Unmarried) Women and Men

It seems that at least in the urban centers of Vietnam, women are behaving in quite the same way as in the Western world: They have boyfriends and they have sexual intercourse with them, but are still anxious to pretend that the current boyfriend is the first and only one. Over 95 percent of the 279 unmarried women in the Hanoi sample of Bélanger and Hong (1998) had a boyfriend at the time of the survey, and they defined a boyfriend as a male friend with whom they had a committed relationship, and in most cases, a person with whom they had sexual intercourse. Once dating was initiated, one third of the women had had their first sexual experience in less than a year. After a year, two thirds had had sexual intercourse. The average duration between the two events was about 15 months. Most of the women did not engage in sex unless they knew their boyfriend for some time. Nevertheless, all the women but one said that their boyfriend took the initiative to engage in sexual relations. It was also not possible for them to introduce the subject of birth control, or to reveal that they had boyfriends before him. The women were afraid that, if they revealed their previous experiences to their current boyfriends, they might lose his respect and thus damage the relationship. They may obtain an abortion if they do not want to marry him (at least at the moment).

Proper Work for Women

According to the Confucian cultural norms, women in pre-revolutionary Vietnam were supposed to have little or no authority in any sphere—political, economic, educational, or familial. There were no women in the "council of notables" that governed the village, nor were they part of the village political community that met in the communal hall. Because a woman was always incorporated within a family and subject to male authority within the family, a woman's economic management and enterprise was always subject to male control and therefore not "real" authority.

Under Communist rule a new social role for women in the countryside has opened up: *co giao*, "Miss Teacher," who teaches her pupils norms and behaviors, which may conflict with those of the parents. Vietnamese studies cite with approval cases where rural students admonish their parents on the grounds that "Miss Teacher would not like it," "it" being, for example, not boiling water before drinking, or quarreling. However, women's present leading role in primary-level education, as well as in health, is conceptualized as an extension of women's traditional role in the family: teaching children and caring for the sick.

As Pelzer White (1987) further points out, women are seen as making good cooperative accountants only as an extension of their traditional role as the keeper of the household budget. On the other hand, young men would never be allowed to train for careers as caretakers of very young children and infants. Only during the war was there a policy, expressed in a 1967 law, to promote women to leading positions in the countryside. The percentage of women acting as cooperative chairmen and other management posts shot up. After demobilization, however, the roles changed again. Even today, women face hostility from their husbands, and especially from their mother-in-laws, if they have higher status jobs.

The "New" Vietnamese Middle-Class Woman

As Fahey (1998) observed, over the past ten years, Vietnam has witnessed a dramatic change in the images of women. The globalization process has drawn many urban women into the commercial sphere, as consumers of products as well as models with which to advertise products.

Nevertheless, the images of the women visible in the streets remain contradictory. The communist ideal for women was equality with men, to be achieved through the demise of private property and women's domestic role. Interestingly, women were also highly praised by the Communist Party as freedom fighters and war heroes; however, they are underrepresented in the political hierarchy. Female members of the National Assembly and of the Vietnamese Communist Central Committee do exist, but they represent an infinitesimal portion of the whole, and exercise almost no real decision-making power. The Politburo has never had a female member, and the female representation in the National Assembly began to decline immediately after the war from 27 percent in 1976, to 22 percent in 1981, and to 18 percent in 1987 (Fahey 1998). By 1992, the proportion had increased only marginally, but it was expected to decline as the quota that required proportional female representation of 18 percent was eliminated before the last election. Such data suggest that the recent changes in women's position may have less to do with economic renovation as such, and more to do with restoration of certain aspects of pre-war gender practices. However, as Vietnamese women told Fahey (1998), they regard the decline in representation as irrelevant, because the National Assembly is losing authority and ambitious women can use their time more productively in private enterprise.

On the other hand, Vietnamese women are flooded with more and more Western images of how up-to-date women live. Beauty contests, fashion clubs, and magazines exert the strongest influence. Fahey (1998) reported that fashion clubs appeared in the early 1990s, with members including fashion designers, models, and companies eager to establish a fashion industry. The first modeling agency, CATD, begun by a young overseas Vietnamese woman, was licensed in Vietnam in 1995. Vietnam now has two locally produced fashion magazines: one for women in general (*Thoi Trang*) and the other for younger women (*Thoi Trang Tre*). Another magazine called *Thoi Trang Dien Anh* (*Movie Fashion*) reproduces sections from international fashion magazines, including French and American fashions, and appears to be more popular in the South. These magazines also have small sections for men, perhaps indicating that the commercialization of beauty is not entirely limited to women. Most newspapers now have a women's section that covers topics from how to pluck eyebrows to Japanese-sponsored parades.

A popular activity for middle-class women, especially those with substantial independent incomes, is attending the gym before work. The membership fee is about US$10 per month or 5 to 10 percent of these women's monthly income. Interviews with these women reveal that they attend them both for social interaction and to improve their body shape. Although they are conscious of maintaining a shapely body, and coyly admit this, they inevitably refer to both inner and outer beauty when asked open-ended questions about the definition of a beautiful woman.

The Male Gender Image

Proschan (1998) observed that traditional Vietnamese society was strongly shaped by Neo-Confucian conceptions and practices of ancestral veneration and filial responsibility (*hieu*):

> A man's most important duty is to reproduce a male child to carry on the ancestral line: "The Annamite* loathes dying without being assured of male dependants. One can say that there exists a veritable obligation, of the religious or at least mystical order, to give birth as early as possible to the cult's heir" (Khèrian 1937:29). Ethnologist Nguyen Van Huyen noted in 1939 that "male celibacy is always in complete disfavor. It continues to be considered as an act of filial impiety," with bachelors prohibited from participating in certain family and village rituals (Nguyen Van Huyen, 1944/1939:41). The tenacity of this traditional stricture is evident from current census data: of Vietnamese males over the age of 40, barely 1 percent has never married (Vietnam Population Census, 1989).

That Vietnamese men are as imbued with the work ethic as are the women can be attested to by any observer of the economic activity of the Vietnamese refugee communities in the West, where Vietnamese men commonly hold two or sometimes three jobs at a time to support their families. But the popular notion persists, commonly abetted by male authors, such as the nineteenth-century libertine and poet, Tran Te Xoung (1890), that the height of machismo is not some Mediterranean predilection to physical abuse of women, but rather a gentlemanly idleness at their expense: "Drink and gamble 'til you're in over your head, but even if you are out of money, your kid's mother is still out there selling her wares."

It is interesting to note that during the Vietnam War, men envied the American soldiers. Vietnamese men have little or no body hair, but hairiness is regarded as a strong symbol of masculinity. It seems to have put men into a state of constant humiliation to watch hairy GIs being admired by Vietnamese women. The body image of men was changing a lot in the 1990s. The bodybuilding industry began to boom. Today, street posters of bodybuilders, often with Western faces, advertise gymnasiums; national competitions are held; and magazines are available for those who wish to know more. The body shape acquired by bodybuilders is significantly different from that of the majority of Vietnamese men, and there appears to be no precedent for such a practice. As to how Vietnamese men will be

---

*Annamite(s) is the term used for the Vietnamese during the periods of the Kingdom and French Protectorate.

able to deal with this strong influence, and how it will change their attitudes toward their bodies are important questions.

B. Sociolegal Status of Males and Females

Children and Adolescents

Over a hundred years ago, Jacobus X. (1898), whose observations as "A French Army-Surgeon" are regarded as quite reliable "although embed with racist and colonialist attitudes of superiority" (Proschan letter, 2000), observed that children were breastfed until they were 3 or 4 years old if a boy; and even longer if it was a girl. When the Vietnamese child could walk alone, he was allowed to run free, almost or quite naked, or roll in the dust, or wallow in the mire. After he was 12, he wore a ragged pair of pants and an old coat, the cast-off garments of his father, and then went to work, minding the buffaloes, helping his parents cultivate the rice field, or steering the sampan or junk. Children born to concubines had the same rights as the children of the legitimate wife. There was no distinction between "natural" and "adulterine" children in Cochin China. Girls and boys mingled promiscuously, "with the result that might be expected. That is why it is rare to find an Annamite girl, of more than ten years of age, a virgin." But that was a hundred years ago.

Adults

Although the Vietnamese adopted the Confucian principle of male superiority, they still granted women some rights. Except for some restrictions concerning properties reserved for ancestor worship, daughters shared in the inheritance of parental properties on the same basis as their brothers. Divorced women and widows who remarried after their husband's death remained the owners of properties acquired during their marriage (*Le Code*, Codex Juris), arts. 388, 374, 375, 376; Nguyen & Ta 1987).

The full and complete equality of Vietnamese women was enshrined in the first Constitution of the Democratic Republic of Vietnam of 1946: "Women enjoy equal rights with men in all spheres." The 1980 Constitution guarantees equal rights for men and women in all respects, although a resolution passed by the Council of Ministers in December 1984 highlighted problems involved in promoting female status. Women are still a minority at the executive level. On the other hand, Vietnam has an official matriarchal heritage.

C. General Concepts of Sexuality and Love

Grammar makes clear how important marriage is in Vietnamese society. Proschan (1998) provides this example: "When Vietnamese ask one another about their marital status they do not ask 'Are you married?' but 'Have you married yet?' A proper response is not a yes-or-no answer but the answer 'Already' or 'Not yet'." Although the minimum legal age at marriage is 18 years for women, postponing marriage until age 22 is strongly recommended. Up to and through the French Colonial period, Vietnamese women were not regarded as nubile until about their 16th or 17th year. However, according to the *Ly-Ky* ("The Book of Rites"), girls might marry after 14 years and men at 16. Any marriages prior to those ages were not accepted.

According to Proschan (1998), if men feared that marriage might complicate their lives, they tried to find a girl who did not see in them as the focus of her desires and demands. In fact, many Vietnamese men believed that women were perfectly satisfied with something like a companionate marriage, which involved sufficient ardor to produce offspring, but was not complicated by passionate desire. A hundred years earlier, Jacobus X. (1898) confirmed this rather unromantic view of marriage:

> Marriage is for the Annamite a question of business and the procreation of descendants, rather than of sentimental love. On her side, the woman has not generally a very great affection for her husband, but concentrates all her love on her children.

Proschan (1998) writes that before colonial and revolutionary legal reforms made monogamy the only acceptable form of marriage, polygamy (specifically, polygyny) had been equally legitimate. When polygyny lost its legal sanction, it nevertheless continued outside the law, and women in polygynous relationships lost the protections and rights that the older legal codes had afforded their predecessors—i.e., those of second wives or concubines. Indications are that extramarital heterosexual relations were frequent enough among married men that most people—male or female—assumed that they were the norm. There were numerous available partners—female or male—for men whose wives "fail[ed] to provide proper attention and stimulation" (Khuat Thu Hong 1998), as one researcher characterized the common rationale.

2. Religious and Ethnic Factors Affecting Sexuality

A. Source and Character of Religious Values

Religious and Social Factors Present in Vietnam

The traditional Vietnamese religion includes elements of Hinduism and all three Chinese religions: Mahayana Buddhism, Daoism, and Confucianism. Although Confucianism (i.e., Neo-Confucianism in its rather value-conservative form) is without doubt the most influential and deeply rooted of these influences, to say that the Vietnamese are "Confucian" is to oversimplify their social and personal realities. The most widespread feature of Vietnamese Confucianism is the cult of ancestors, practiced in individual households and clan temples. As such, it is strongly tied to folk religion.

There is also a wide variety of Buddhist sects, sects belonging to the "new" religions of Cadoaism and Hoa Hao, and the Protestant and Roman Catholic Churches. The number of Christian adherents in 1991 constituted an estimated 7 percent of the total population: 180,000 Protestants and five million Roman Catholics. The Catholic Church has been active in Vietnam since the seventeenth century, and since 1933 has been led mainly by Vietnamese priests. The number of Muslims is estimated at 50,000.

While the Vietnamese government guarantees freedom of religion, other factors influencing (and changing) the character of social values can be observed in communist ideology and Western ideas. The latter, first introduced during the French occupation followed by the Vietnam War, has been given fresh impetus since 1986 through *doi moi* economic reforms.

Ancestor Worship

Ancestor worship, which originated with Confucianism, holds that the soul of the dead person does disappear from sight but stays around to look after the family. Emperors and kings built imperial temples where they worshipped the late emperors whose achievements and exploits were recorded on ancestral tablets and steles. Wealthy people have their family temples for the whole family to worship their ancestors. Poor people, who have no temple of their own, set up an altar in the best part of their home to show gratitude and respect for their ancestors. Because of the war, which produced a serious shortage of dwelling places, most houses are now too small, and very few family temples or permanent ancestors' altars can be set up.

It is the responsibility of the eldest son to take care of the various anniversaries during the year. For this, he receives income from a number of rice fields or land as a hereditary state. The eldest son records the ancestor's date of death in a family register.

On the day of the anniversary, the chief of the family, properly attired, stands solemnly before the altar, with three sticks of incense in his hands, held to the level of his forehead, and says the pseudonym, the real name, and the date of death, and invites the ancestor to the feast. At the same time, he will pray to the dead to protect the members of his family. Various dishes have to be prepared for display before the altar on each ancestor's anniversary.

Nowadays, probably 70 percent of the Vietnamese are followers of ancestor worship.

Buddhism

The origins of Buddhism in Vietnam can be traced to the second century. For the Buddhist, life is seen as a vast sea of suffering. Wisdom lies in the suppression of desires: desires for life, happiness, riches, power, etc., which are believed to be the roots of human suffering. The very essence of Buddhism is the Law of Karma, which states that man is reincarnated and rewarded in the next life for his good deeds in this life, and punished for his bad ones. The present existence is conditioned by earlier existence and will condition those to follow. Desire must first be overcome; a pure heart is necessary to break the chains binding man to his earthly existence.

In 1920, an organized movement for the restoration of Buddhism began throughout the country. Starting in 1931, Associations of Buddhist Studies were established in the South, the Center, and North Vietnam. Many translations of both Greater and Lesser Vehicle Buddhist Texts were distributed. Finally, after many assemblies of monks and National Delegate Congresses, the Buddhist Institute for the Propagation of the Faith, the *Viean Houa Naio*, was established.

The most important Buddhist sect is Cadoaism. Formally inaugurated in 1926, this syncretic religion is based on spiritualist seances with a predominantly ethical content, but sometimes with political overtones. Several other sects exist, like the Tien Thien and the Tay Ninh. It is estimated that these Buddhist sects have two million adherents. Another influential sect is Hoa Hao. Founded in 1939, it has one and a half million adherents.

Through Buddhist-nun monasteries, Buddhism exerted a strong influence for the equality of men and women. Although the monasteries were skeptically regarded by the Confucianist elite—one of the common defamations being that the nuns were involved in lesbian sexual practices—Buddhism gave women another role model besides that of wife and mother. This was especially true for elderly widows who were entering Buddhist orders. On the other hand, their influence on the priesthood seems to be difficult to detect.

Daoism

Vietnamese Daoism, derived from the doctrine of Lao Tzu, is based essentially on the participation of man in the universal order. This order depends on the equilibrium of the two elements Yin and Yang, which represent the constant duality of nature: rest and motion, liquid and solid, light and darkness, concentration and expansion, and material and spiritual. The material world being imbued with these two principles, the Daoist believes that whoever is able to act according to these principles could become the master of the world. This belief, in turn, has promoted a kind of mysticism, reflected in the magical practices of certain sorcerers who claim to possess the secret of the universe.

The Daoist refrains from troubling the natural order of things; on the contrary, he conforms to it in every circumstance. He considers the taking of initiatives to be a waste of time and energy. In respecting the basic Daoist doctrines of passivity and absence of care, he avoids the active life. These doctrines, which were adopted by many Confucian scholars as well, are summed up in the Daoist maxim: "Do nothing and everything will be accomplished simultaneously." The supreme divinity of Daoism is the Emperor of Jade. With his ministers of Death and Birth, he controls the destiny of men. The cult is replete with incantations, charms, and amulets, which once made for prosperous trade, with the sorcerers intervening in every possible occasion in life.

In the context of sexuality, *yang* is identified with semen or seminal essence (*jing, yin*), which is why Daoists are encouraged to have intercourse often but without ejaculating. The aim is to build up *jing* but retain *yang* through not ejaculating, but at the same time enabling the woman to reach orgasm and give off her *yin* essence, which additionally strengthens the man. Another Daoist practice is to get a young man and woman together and to gather up their sexual secretions and swallow them—a practice that is believed to prolong life for the Daoist. Jacobus X. (1898) reported that it was still very common at the end of the 1800s, although he did put it strongly as a "strange freak of eroticism":

The old Celadon is accompanied by a servant or strong coolie, who copulates with a woman in his presence, and then retires . . . When once the agent is retired, well and duly paid, the old debauchee is left alone with the woman, who is still resting upon the field of battle. Then the man approaches, and eagerly receives in *bucca sua*, the liquid which runs *ex vulva feminae*.

Confucianism

Confucianism, a generic Western term, is a *Weltanschauung*, i.e., a social ethic, a political ideology, a scholarly tradition, and a way of life, but it is not an organized religion. Chinese governors introduced Confucianism to Vietnam from 939 to 1407. The doctrine of Confucius is set forth in four classical texts and in five canonical books. By rigid rules, it determines the attitude the every man in society should adopt to guide his relationships as an individual with his superiors, with his wife and friends, and with his inferiors. The philosophy suggests a moral code, which advocates the Middle Way for the worthy man's behavior. According to Mencius, the most distinguished disciple of Confucius, man is inherently good. To preserve his goodness, he needs to check his passions. The wise man improves himself through study; he knows himself and is the master of his passions.

There are four rules for a man to achieve self-perfection: to cultivate himself, to run his family, to rule the country, and pacify the world. The three important sets of social interaction are between king and citizen, between father and son (*hieu*—filial piety or responsibility), and between husband and wife. Five cardinal virtues have to be achieved in order to become a man of virtue: humanity, equity, urbanity, intelligence, and honesty. As for the woman, Confucius teaches four virtues: skill with her hands, agreeable appearance, prudence in speech, and exemplary conduct, and three submissions or obediences: to the father until she is married, to the husband after she leaves her parents' house, and to the eldest son when her husband dies. Interestingly, the real order as seen by most Vietnamese, and also by the French, is a different one: the Vietnamese woman was inferior to her father but just about equal to her husband, provisionally superior to her minor brothers, and always superior to her sons.

In sexual matters, Confucianism is quite "puritanic." A "good" young girl is not only expected to keep her virginity until she gets married and to get married only once in her life, she is not supposed to make herself attractive, even to her own husband. Confucianism does not consider sexual activity as wrong, but love and tenderness are treated with mistrust, and physical displays of them are considered at least questionable. This rule applies not only to showing affection in public, but also to its display in the privacy of the home. As early as in the seventeenth century, male and female poets protested against it.

"Popular Religion"

As Thien Do (1997) showed, there exists also a very specific Vietnamese "popular religion" characterized by the propitiation of spirits and deities of a certain typology:

1. The tutelary or guardian spirits, either originally worshipped by the villagers or historically instituted by Vietnamese or Chinese rulers. They include the nation-founding patriarch, past male and female heroes, and able ministers;
2. The nature spirits of the grottos, rocks and trees, and rivers and oceans;
3. Immortals (*tien*) and holy sages (*thanh*), in the Daoist tradition, together with Lady Lieu Hanh and her affiliates, including the Mandarin Snakes and the Five Tigers (Agents), forming the *chu vi* (divine ensemble) in the belief systems of sorcerers and mediums;
4. Deities of Cham and Khmer origin, such as Po Yan Inu Nagar, the Whale Spirit, and the Neak Ta (Ong Ta); and
5. Consecrated to a lesser extent are founding patriarchs of the arts and crafts (including the martial arts), the domestic deities, marginal demonic spirits, and lonely ghosts.

The places of veneration and features of spiritual practices are divided between the village communal house or *dinh*, where local participants emulate the court elite in Daoist-Confucian formats, the private Buddhist-Daoist temple or *chua*, where a three-religion pattern of Chinese origin has been practiced and modified to suit Vietnamese adherents, the trance mediumship, with the special importance of the Earth God and of female deities, and finally the practice of self-cultivation, mainly practiced by Daoists (*ong dao*).

Of importance for gender images is the fact that many of the Vietnamese deities were thought of as female and sometimes even worshipped exclusively by women. This behavior has not stopped with communism or *doi moi*. Since the late 1980s, village pagodas have undergone a frenzy of refurbishment. As Stephanie Fahey (1998) reports, in a pagoda in a village near Hanoi, a local woman pharmacist of two hundred years ago is revered for the birth of the prosperous traditional craft of pharmaceutical production, and a temple on West Lake features Ba Chua Lieu, supposedly a princess who developed a prosperous silk industry. The young, as well as the prosperous, patronize these pagodas to implore the appropriate female deities with such different petitions as economic success and the birth of a son. It seems that with the demise of the Communist moral code, the Vietnamese are searching their past for more traditional values.

Among the religions in Vietnam, the "Popular Religion" seems to be the most liberal in sexual aspects. Khuat Thu Hong (1998) presents dozens of examples that show this liberal attitude from ancient times to the present. Lingam and yoni worship is the most obvious. But there is also the worship of the god No Nuong (*No* meaning a bamboo phallus, and *Nuong*, a vulva, made of a spathe from an areca tree). This worship centers on the ritual striking together of these genital symbols by the village head and deputy village head, while the young boys and girls called out, *tung tung, dap* (onomatopoeia of a drumbeat in Vietnamese) according to the beat. There is also the game of grabbing eels from a jar: In this game, each team of a young man and a woman observed the following rule: While trying to catch the eel in the jar, neither the young man nor the woman could look into the jar, and the young man had to keep one hand on the young women's breast. At the same time, a committee of judges closely watched, along with fellow villagers who called out and teased them.

Communism

Communist ideology expects all men to behave according to the principles of a "new society" founded on a Marxist-Leninist base. Regarding gender issues, it implies equality of men and women. Because Engels depicted traditional child-rearing practices as the main impediment for achieving gender equality, communist societies tended to socialize childcare and education to enable women to work for the society as men do. The institutions of marriage and the family were considered to be the key to the reproduction of social inequality, because the practices that evolve within these institutions obviously preserved the underlying system of private property and its inheritance. Thus, communist thought was suspicious of devotion to family and treated this as "unsocialist" in a man, especially a Party member. In its first two decades, the Communist government in Vietnam made specific efforts to destroy all Confucian traces in Vietnamese society. To break the strong ties binding members of Vietnamese families that had been molded by Confucian principles, the Communists even encouraged betrayal among family members. Over the years, the anti-Confucian policy has changed Vietnamese family structure considerably. The government has acquired most of the authority and influence attributed to Confucian scholars, especially regarding questions of sexual morality and behavior.

Interestingly, communist gender ideas changed dramatically during the war with the South and after the reunification. The typical functionary now clearly resembled the ideal authoritarian Confucian gentlemen. Women are supposed to care for the family and especially the husband. The few state-honored female revolutionists and freedom fighters fell into oblivion.

At the same time, it was the Communist government, which set up the Central Committee for Mother and Infant Welfare in 1971. The committee's responsibility was to guide and unify the organization of *crèches* (day nurseries). About one third of all children were raised in such facilities. Further support was given to women to separate themselves from domestic duties according to the 1980 State Constitution Article 63, requiring the state and society to ensure the development of maternity homes, *crèches*, kindergartens, community dining halls, and other social amenities to create favorable conditions for women to work, study, and rest. Even men were asked to share household tasks. But these efforts remained rather at cultural and ideological levels. Vietnamese Communists were keen to maintain the family as a social, but not necessarily an economic unit. For that reason, they argued that it was necessary for women to handle both employment and domestic duties.

Communism brought improvement for women by reducing early forced marriages, publicly condemning wife-beating, providing free childcare, and recognizing the economic value of housework. Legislation, together with women's prolonged contribution to the war effort, assisted in dismantling the absolute authority of the Confucian "three submissions." But with *doi moi*, it seems that the Communist Party has withdrawn from social engineering. Membership figures indicate that the Party is losing women's support, with a drop in membership from 34 percent women in 1960 to only 16 percent today. Most women enjoy the rediscovered freedom of wearing nice and individual clothes and putting on make-up. In the heydays of Communist rule, these fashions were badly received, as this newspaper excerpt shows:

> You young people, I know you need make-up to be beautiful . . . but you should also keep the Vietnamese manner; simplicity, purity and wholesomeness are beauty. It is advisable not to imitate the alien "styles" imported from the European capitalist counties, and you see, these styles could really reflect only the lowly liking and crazy, carefree and pessimistic moods. A girl living in such a wholesome social situation as you are in now is advised not to wear such a queer and carefree hairstyle. And such thin, tight and revealing clothes as you are wearing now, in our North, all the decent, cultured women have never cared to wear (*Vietnamese Woman* No. 293, May 1972:6)

War and the Influence of Western Civilization

In the northern areas controlled by the non-Communist side prior to 1975, the authorities did not carry out a policy systematically hostile to Confucianism. But disruption of the old social framework because of war, which forced people to abandon their villages for urban areas, as well as the impact of new living conditions and broader contact with Western civilization, also loosened traditional family ties. Children became more independent from their parents and the former strict obedience to the elders diminished.

Since 1986, the same changes were occurring in the Socialist Republic of Vietnam because of the influence of the official policy of a free-market economy. The ideals of consuming and having fun through buying goods are especially attractive to the younger generation, which is also the vast majority of the Vietnamese, 80 percent of whom are under 40 years of age. Pelzer White (1993) concluded that the beauty contests and calendars now sanctioned by the Communist state as a signal to the international business community that Vietnam is open for business, also convey a visual message supporting social change.

B. Character of Ethnic Values

The Concept of "Phuc Duc"

The single most specific Vietnamese concept that exerts influence on the gender roles of men and women seems to be the concept of *phuc duc* or "merit-virtue," a kind of karma concept. It refers to the merit that, in a former life, oneself and/or an ancestor acquired through virtuous deeds that is then passed on to succeeding generations, and the merit that a member of the present generation passes to future generations as yet unborn. It is "quantifiable," as in "a lot of *phuc duc*."

Based on the manner in which one lives one's life, it can be an evil force (*vo phuc*) as well as a benevolent one. It is considered influential over a span of five generations. Thus, the nature of one's *phuc duc*, together with the horoscope and geomancy, which reads the composition of *am* (*yin*) and *dong* (*yang*) in the earth, determines the course of life. The individual can exert only a limited personal influence. The definition of what is regarded as a virtuous life follows the Buddhist-Confucian code. The specific Vietnamese interpretation goes back at least to the fifteenth century and can be found in the poem, *Gia Huan Ca*. It is interesting to note that the primary determinant is not the act itself but the motivation beneath the act.

Slote (1998) presented an example of how *phuc duc* works with *Kieu*, the hero in the epic poem, *Kim Van Kieu*:

> She is a girl of particular charm, beauty, accomplishment, and morality, who sells herself as a minor wife to an unscrupulous scholar in order to redeem her father who has been beset by ill fortune. The scholar, a man devoid of virtue, turns out to be the husband of the madame of a brothel and Kieu is forced into prostitution. Under these circumstances, Kieu's sacrificial act brings much *phuc duc*. On the other hand, were she to have become a prostitute for profit alone, she would have been condemned, her family would have suffered, and future generations would have borne the penalties. In a parallel sense Kieu's misfortune inasmuch as her life had been thoroughly virtuous, could be ascribed to bad *phuc duc* visited upon her because of transgressions of some ancestor.
>
> Coupled with the nature of the motivation that serves to precipitate the act is the issue of sacrifice. An act that is performed easily brings far less reward than an equivalent action that is difficult and involves suffering. Since it was very difficult to bear the life in a brothel for Kieu, she was finally reunited with the man she loved, to whom she had originally been betrothed.

Based on the belief that "merit virtue is caused by the maternal," women can create destiny. Deserving women of good conduct bring felicity to their descendants, just as tragedy, poverty, and other incidents of bad fortune can be blamed on one's wife, mother, or grandmother. So important was (and still is) this concept, that although the wealth and status of a bride's family matters, it is secondary to her *phuc duc*. A poor but virtuous woman of good heritage and blessed at birth by the heavens, who would increase the family's fortune and ultimate destiny, would be a most desirable bride. And when a marriage is arranged between a poor but virtuous girl and the son of a wealthy family, the girl's family also usually benefits. To a great extent, *phuc duc* has been influential in making the class system less stringent than in other cultures.

With the responsibility of acquiring *phuc duc*, a double standard has been created: Men, if they chose, were relatively free to act in ways that are scarcely designed to build *phuc duc*. Examples are gambling, cheating, and whoring. On the other hand, there were also the elderly men referred to as living saints, a position that carried great esteem because it contributes to the building of *phuc duc* for the family. As Slote (1998) observed, the very concept of *phuc duc* may lead to manipulation, because it can be used as a metaphor in the service of many emotions: hostility, competitiveness, defiance, self-sacrifice, guilt, and control. It is also a justification when all else fails, when the children misbehave, or when one is beset by misfortune.

Astrology and the Influence of the "Thay Boi"

Another very strong influence on sexual behavior is the belief that the specific constellation of stars at the time of one's birth can reveal one's destiny. The *thay boi* (the mostly female fortune teller) is the first resource to consult if something goes wrong. A good example of *thay boi* influence is the following statement of a 30-year-old transvestite (Bao, Long, & Taylor 1998:20):

> In my childhood when my father was alive, he forced me to wear shorts, but I did not and he fought me. My mother resorted to the fortune teller and knew that was my fate. It means that she must have such a child, no one expected that. My father who was a government officer felt shy and did not agree and said "the male should be male and the female should be female." My mother could not stand it and said to my father you could not fight me any more. If you fight him I will leave. She said to my father you can not prevent him from that and finally he accepted me. I have always been like this when I was growing up. All my relatives did not accept me. I think that is my fate. What problems I suffer because I can't wear male clothes. I only wanted to be a girl.

One might suggest that the astrologer seems to be as important for Vietnamese society as sex therapists, psychologists, and marriage counselors are for Western societies. Even today, nearly two thirds of the couples in the south and (because of the stronger influence of communism in the north) a smaller part in the north have their horoscopes matched before marriage (Goodkind 1996). Since geomancy is believed to reveal if the location of one's house is the reason for quarreling in the family or even for sterility, asking a geomancer is also regarded as helpful. According to Young (1998), the third precise way to measure the energy believed to cause change in the fortune of any individual is to study the shape of the person's face. Although it cannot be changed by reading the face of others, one gains intimate knowledge about them.

Alteration of the Genitals

Khuat Thu Hong (1998) mentions that some men, especially male prostitutes, are undergoing the surgery of "putting pellets" (small, metal balls— usually two or three at a time, but some men have as many as nine or ten) or "swords" (the sword-like plastic pieces are punched through the penis) into their penis. The men argue that the altered penis creates special pleasure for women.

3. Sexual Knowledge and Education

Although Vietnam can be regarded as a fairly liberal society when it comes to sexual behavior, talking or writing about sexuality is a totally different matter. Vietnam never produced sex education books like the Indian *Kama Sutra* or the Chinese and Japanese pillow books. Most young people get married without the least elementary knowledge, as a collection of interviews in Khuat Thu Hong's (1998) book shows:

> On our wedding night, neither of us knew anything—meaning that we slept together as friends. We even tried to do something, but we didn't know what we were doing (born 1959).

> On my wedding day, I didn't understand why when we slept with another, one person laid atop another. . . . I thought we were only supposed to lie side by side (born 1957).

After 1950, a few books on sexuality and sex education were published. Most prominent was Dr. Nguyen Manh Bong's book, *What Lovers Should Know*, published by Huong Son Publishers in Hanoi in 1949. Similar publications appeared in the south of Vietnam during the succeeding years. In 1970, one Saigon newspaper ran a column called "Replying to Your Questions on Sexuality," which was written by two psychologists. In the North, prior to *doi moi*, there were almost no publications on sexuality. In the 1970s, the sole publication on sex education was *Girl's Hygiene*, which included quite sketchy information on female sexual organs, menstruation, and how to maintain personal hygiene. In 1988, David Reuben's book, *Answering Those Questions You Don't Dare Ask*, was translated from English and attracted much attention, but was banned from official circulation until 1989. Other books were translated from German, including Rudolf Neubert's *Marital Relations*, published in 1989. In 1991, David Elia and Genevieve Doucet's book, *1000 Questions and Answers About Women and Their Bodies*, was translated from French and published in Vietnam.

In recent years, many books by Vietnamese on sex and sexuality have begun to appear in bookstores. Ho Ngoc Dai's 1991 book, *Chuyen Ay (That Conversation)*, which talked about sexuality within a philosophical and psychological framework, drew much attention. Books based on scientific knowledge are more common and include Doan Van Thong's book, *Nhung Thac Mac Tham kin Cua Ban Tre (The Secret Questions of Young Friends)* published by Tien Giang Publishers in 1991, and Minh Phuong's book, *Hoi Dap ve Gioi Tinh va Tinh Duc (Questions and Answers About Sex and Sexuality)*, edited by Dr. Le Van Tri, published by Medical Publishers in 1995. Psychologist Dr. Pham Con Son has also written about love, sexuality, marriage, and family in books such as *Nhung Thu Dich Cua Hanh Phuc Lua Doi (The Foes of a Couple's Happiness)*, published by Dong Thap Publishers in 1996. The Research Center for Gender, Family, and Environmental Development is the first social science research institute to begin writing books on sex and sexuality, including Dr. Dao Xuan Dung's book, *Gia Duc Tinh Duc (Sex Education)*, published in 1996 by Youth Publishing House. In addition, there are series of other books written by local and foreign authors mainly from Russia, the Czech Republic, and Poland (Khuat Thu Hong 1998).

As Gammeltoft (1999) points out, many aspects of everyday life in Vietnam are politicized through governmental mass education and mass mobilization campaigns. In fields as diverse as diet, marriage, religion, and pregnancy, there are politically right and wrong answers to any question, and everyone knows precisely what is politically correct and socially desirable and what is not. This is particularly true for family planning issues, which have been given a very high priority on the government agenda since the late 1980s. There are efforts to educate people about sexual issues, as may be exemplified by this report:

> One morning at the shrimp factory I watched as 700 women in identical white smocks cleaned the shrimp. Suddenly their work was interrupted—all had to stand and watch a video on AIDS prevention. Some cases had appeared in town, a manager told me. That night the scenes were the same in boomtown Nam Can. AIDS is just another risk of frontier living. (*National Geographic*, February 1993:35)

Sex education has been limited because of Vietnam's traditional bias against the public mention of anything sexual. Although this situation may seem similar to other countries, in Vietnam much of the opposition to "sex education" comes from administrators and teachers, of whom many are reportedly too embarrassed to discuss intimate sexual matters with the students. Faced with an increasing HIV-infection rate and an abortion rate thought to be among the highest in the world, Hanoi health officials opened the city's first sex education café in November 1999. The café fills a void in sex education, as the subject is not taught in schools, and many parents admit they are too embarrassed to raise the issue with teenage children who are becoming increasingly sexually active. The idea for the Hanoi café stemmed from a study that detailed how young people spend their time. It is also modeled on a similar initiative in Ho Chi Minh City. The café offers a place where young people can spend time talking with their friends and freely ask for information about sex and AIDS. Although the café will not distribute condoms, a female physician specializing in reproductive health, and an HIV/AIDS counselor are on hand to answer questions. On average, about 50 customers, ages 16 to 24, have visited the café on a daily basis (Watkin, *South China Morning Post*, December 20, 1999).

In 2000, a pilot project sponsored by the United Nations Fund for Population Activities was started that allows high schools in eight of Vietnam's 61 provinces to offer advice on obtaining contraceptives at government clinics and pharmacies. Three thousand pharmacists in five provinces are being trained to provide customers with better information on contraceptives, and state-run radio airs a weekly show answering youths' sex-related queries (Cohen, *Far Eastern Economic Review*, 6/29).

As far as homosexuality is concerned, only in the last three years has a grassroots group emerged with the aim of reducing the spread of HIV/AIDS among gay and bisexual men in Ho Chi Minh City. The Nguyen Friendship Society consists of about fifty volunteers who prepare and print leaflets about sex education to be handed out to patrons in bars and clubs.

4. Autoerotic Behaviors and Patterns

No information about autoerotic practices exists except for the French period. According to Jacobus X. (1898), masturbation occurred very often:

"Nearly all the boys practice masturbation from the age of fourteen or fifteen years," but it seemed to him that it was practiced only by males:

> This, no doubt, results from the ease with which the girl or woman can satisfy her natural desires; moreover, the great frequency of the "flowers" [an STD, probably gonorrhea] must help to limit this special form of vice. I never met but two cases, and both of these were the mistresses of Europeans (Jacobus X. 1898).

5. Interpersonal Heterosexual Behaviors

A. Talking About Sexuality

The Vietnamese prefer a flowery, euphemistic vocabulary when they speak about sexuality. For example, a man having sexual desires might say, "I am going to buy a tree." Food is also heavily connected with sexual activity. Words like "crisp, sticky, spicy" are used to describe food as well as women and are frequent in erotic fantasies. Many dishes are identified with female figures or organs: The white rice flour cake is the image of a virgin; the pulpy interior of a breadfruit with its sticky juice is associated with the vagina; the eating of a rice flour pancake is similar to the defloration rite; the sucking of the honey flambéed banana and the scooping of water in the rice field are symbols of having sex. As in many Asian countries, this type of language helps people to speak about sexual matters without using the terms that would embarrass them.

B. Sexual Behaviors

Kissing and Sex Positions

In traditional Vietnam, kissing in the "Western" sense was forbidden. Instead, nose sniffing or rubbing, comparable with Inuit customs, was practiced. The preferred position for sexual intercourse among the Vietnamese was both partners lying face to face, side by side, or the rear-entry position. The reason for these preferences, Jacobus X. (1898) suggests, is the structure of the Vietnamese bed, which is made of bamboo slates. In the missionary position, which he calls *la position de l'amour classique,* a man would scrape the skin off his knees.

Premarital Relations, Courtship, and Dating

The information one can gather about the beliefs and practices of young people regarding premarital relations and the role of sexuality are quite contradictory and are evidence that sex research is still underdeveloped in Vietnam. For example, the Departments of Psychology and Sociology of Hanoi University conducted research in 1992 on the sexual relations of university and high school students in Hanoi (Hoang Ba Thinh 1992). About 72.4 percent of female students in their fourth year of university had sexual relations, with only 17.6 percent having had one (usually their first) partner, whereas the others had between two and four partners. Yet, after graduating, only 8.2 percent of respondents had married one of these partners. Among those female students who had boyfriends, it was quite common for them to live together in the dormitories. An early 1990s' survey by CARE (Cooperative for American Relief Everywhere) found that just over half of Vietnamese men had had two or more sexual partners in the previous two weeks (Franklin 1993).

In a recent survey, only 34 percent of students in Ho Chi Minh City responded that they found premarital sex "acceptable." Although not considered high by international standards, the statistic was shocking to most Vietnamese. A socially more acceptable figure was that only 10.3 percent of men and 1.4 percent of women had had sexual intercourse before their marriage, and 57.5 percent said they did not plan to have sex before marriage, whereas only 14.7 percent replied that they did plan to have sex before marriage (Chittick 1997).

O'Harrow (1995) reports that premarital intercourse is quite common in Vietnamese villages, but also that there is still an obligation on the man's part to marry the girl he has deflowered, and she reminds him of this fact in the strongest possible terms. Young couples in Hanoi, even married couples, face great difficulty in finding a place for private encounters. The evening stroller through the city's lakeside public parks must step carefully to avoid interrupting lovers hard at work.

Marriage and Family

In the past Vietnamese marriages were arranged through matrimonial agents (*mai-dongs*) who brought the two families together and arranged the question of the wedding portion (bride price). Interestingly, the woman did not bring any marriage portion, and it was the groom who paid for the wedding presents, brought to the common lot his fortune of rice fields and cattle, and often had to pay money to the wife's family. In return, his compensation was comparatively small: a tobacco jar, for example, a box for betel nuts, or a cigarette case. The wedding ceremony was quite simple: The future husband and wife met, mutually offered themselves to each other, and chewed betel nut together. Though Confucian tradition permits the husband to take lesser wives (theoretically to be chosen for him by the first wife), economic realities (and relatively innocuous modern laws) would force him to be content with one at a time. O'Harrow (1995) reports also that to give a woman a piece of fine jewelry in Vietnamese tradition is to help confirm her independence as a human being, and for a mother to hand over a piece of her jewelry to her daughter is a universally understood gesture, for which the subtext is "may this protect you from misery." Nowadays, divorce is increasingly easy to obtain.

Adultery

A quite questionable story found in different sources dating back to the nineteenth century is that a woman found guilty of adultery would be thrown to a specially trained elephant, which in turn threw her into the air with his trunk and trampled her to death when she landed. Quite telling is the gusto with which this story was spread by European authors.

The early *Annamite Code* contained the following article: "An adulteress shall receive ninety blows of the rattan upon her buttocks, and her husband may afterwards marry her to another, or sell her if he pleases, or keep her in his house." Jacobus X. (1898) quotes the *Le Code*: "Shop men who commit adultery with the wife of their master shall be treated as servitors or slaves, and punished by strangulation."

As O'Harrow (1995) shows, moral values in Vietnamese society are enforced by constraints of shame rather than guilt. A Vietnamese woman can cheat (in the Western sense) on her husband without regret, as long as it is not known. The following saying illustrates the point: "Flirtations with desire, I wore a wedding ring for protection; I lost my wedding ring, but my desire remains." Vietnamese men, in their turn, know the "rules of the game" and have less of a tendency than women to brag publicly about their conquests.

It seems that the younger generation in particular, which grew up during *doi moi*, tends to excuse adultery. Unhappiness in marriage, being sexually unfulfilled, or just being attracted by another person are now regarded as legitimate reasons to have sexual contact with another person other than one's partner (Khuat Thu Hong 1998).

According to Fahey (1998), middle-class urban women often confide during informal interviews that their husbands have a mistress or entertain several girlfriends. Because women are still responsible for family finances and the welfare of children, it is common for them to have secret savings as a buffer against their husband's indiscretions with other women.

Incidence of Oral and Anal Sex

Jacobus X. (1898) described oral sex as a way to avoid infection with a venereal disease. Apparently, it is not a very successful method, as he later writes: "I have found eruptions, ulcerations, and the scars of chancres, on the lips and tongue of the unhappy victims of this form of debauchery. When once they are affected, they in turn help to spread the syphilitic virus, by a law of reciprocity which it would be very difficult to repress." This was confirmed by the French surgeon Joyeux (1930).

Anal sex seems to have been far more common as a homosexual practice than among heterosexual couples. Jacobus X. (1898) suggests that it was a phenomenon that only occurred between prostitutes and their customers: "The woman is old when she takes to sodomy, which she does rather from economic motives, on account of the money it brings, than from natural taste."

6. Homoerotic, Homosexual, and Ambisexual Behaviors

A. Contemporary Practices

In Vietnam, there has historically been relatively little male homosexuality, although a few of the emperors of the sixteenth and seventeenth centuries did maintain male concubines. In present-day Vietnam, homosexuality is still regarded as being a foreign problem, and, as in other socialist countries, there is a lack of official research on homosexual behavior. In fact, homosexuality is quite a common sexual behavior. It may well be that the Communist state is reluctant to recognize its existence. As long as it is not practiced "openly," state officials will not interfere. This is evident in the 1998 case of a lesbian couple who married in public. Because of the public ceremony, Vietnamese authorities were forced to act, even though they did not know how to deal with the couple:

Two women were wed in Vinh Long province (about 70 kilometers from Ho Chi Minh City). Hundreds of people, including friends, family members and a number of curious onlookers attended the ceremony on Saturday to celebrate the marriage of a 30-year-old woman to another woman aged about 20. Local authorities did not know how to react to the marriage (*Lao Dong* [Newspaper] March 8, 1998).

Two months later, the government reacted:

Government officials have broken up the country's first known lesbian marriage and extracted a promise from the lovers they will never live together. Twenty officials from various Communist Party groups met the couple for three hours at their home in the Mekong Delta town of Vinh Long. They were acting on instructions of the Justice Ministry in Hanoi "to put an end to the marriage," the *Thanh Nien* newspaper reported. It is unclear what kind of persuasion was used to get the couple's agreement or what punishment they could face if they change their minds, but they signed a document promising not to live together, the justice official said. "They would have had no trouble with their relationship if they had not chosen to have a public wedding," a member of the provincial justice department said. The issue was raised at the most recent session of the National Assembly during debate on amendments to the law. There were many other homosexual women living together in the province but Hong Kim Huong, 30, and Cao Tien Duyen, 23, were the only ones who were married publicly, he said. He said the wedding was an unwelcome challenge to traditional sensibilities and public morality but added: "As long as they don't wed publicly they are left in peace." (Reuters May 23, 1998).

In 1997, the same newspaper launched a virulent critique of a marriage between two men in Ho Chi Minh City. The apparently lavish ceremony held in a big Saigon hotel provoked an avalanche of protests from residents. Other homosexual marriages have taken place in Vietnam in discrete ceremonies, but homosexuality remains taboo in the country, although it is not officially illegal.

Vietnam's first gay wedding took place in Ho Chi Minh City. The two men celebrated their union at a local restaurant with over one hundred guests. Some authorities, however, were not in the mood to congratulate the grooms. "It should be publicly condemned," said Nguyen Thi Thuong, vice-director of the city's state-run Consulting Center for Love, Marriage and Families. "Public opinion does not support this." The police are reported as saying that no laws exist which would enable them to punish the happy couple. The honeymooners could not be reached for comment (Reuters April 7, 1997).

Sexual encounters between male adolescents may be facilitated by socially sanctioned close physical contacts considered "normal" between males, such as holding hands and resting or sleeping close together in the same bed. As far as the prevailing sexual activities, mutual masturbation and fellatio, are concerned, there does not appear to be any strongly developed sense of playing a masculine or feminine sexual role of the kind as is often found in other societies where anal intercourse is more prevalent and the ultimate objective of homosexual encounters.

Proschan (1998) has reported that although "gay" might be the only English word some of his informants had known, they had embraced it as their own and imbued it with meanings that diverge from those of English-speakers elsewhere:

> Vietnamese men today are fashioning diverse ways of living as men-who-love-men, drawing variously on endogenous traditions and identities as well as exogenous concepts and practices, combining and recombining them, and at the same time contesting both cultural conventions that would condemn homosexuality as incompatible with filial piety and metropolitan notions that would insist there is only one way to be authentically gay.

B. Homosexuality Under French Rule

Jacobus X. (1898) interpreted homosexuality as a questionable behavior resulting from the Chinese cultural influence, and a sign of decadence that disappeared after the French influence gained influence. If it was practiced by the French, he claimed, it was only to escape the dangers of syphilitic female prostitutes. Interestingly, he does not discuss the interdependency between male prostitution and homosexuality. According to him, the customers in this era were Chinese and French, and the prostitutes Annamite boys:

> It is only the nays and the boys who come in direct and permanent contact with the Europeans. Nay signifies "basket." The nays are children of from seven to fifteen years, who are provided with round baskets. They are found on the quays, in the market, and in front of the shops, waiting for a customer to make a purchase of any kind. . . . It is from these baskets that the class of boys is recruited. These latter are from fifteen to twenty-five years of age [acting as valet]. . . . When once he [the nay with his basket in which he carries the goods] gets to your house, if he should suspect that you have depraved tastes, he will soon offer you his services: "Captain" (everybody was a captain in 1860) "me much know chewchew banana," and if the client appeared to hesitate, "Me know ablic." That is sabir (patois). The nay and the boy are generally, to use the Tardieu's expression, "suckers of the dart." . . . Whilst the European lies at full length on a long chair, or on his bed, the boy—kneeling or stooping—*inguina osculatur, sugit, emissumque semen in bucca recipit, usque ad ultimam guttam* [a kiss between the thighs, rise, ejaculate in the mouth of recipient, even to the ultimate].
>
> Although by preference a "sucker of the dart," the nay, or the boy, will not refuse sodomy, but he is not enthusiastic about it. It is not any moral reason which stops him, for he is above prejudices of that sort. It is simply the disproportion, which exists between the anus of a lad of ten or twelve years, and the penis of an adult European, for two nays have no objection to committing the act with one another. (Jacobus X. 1898)

C. Homosexuality During the Vietnam War

Lesbianism

According to Marnais (1967), who describes in detail male and female homosexuality, lesbianism could be found at all levels of society during the Vietnam War. There were three bars catering exclusively to lesbians, and lesbian marriages were also not uncommon in Saigon, obviously tolerated by a society that referred to such couples as "friends." He interpreted lesbianism in Saigon as particularly rife among the city's prostitutes. The so-called "bull dyke" lesbian did not exist, but there was a role division between the "Sugar Mommy" and the young girl who lived at her expense. In the late 1960s, the *Saigon Daily* news reported a case about a major lesbian "call-girl" operation catering mainly to wealthy female tourists from the West and to jaded Saigon society women. The organization was disbanded when there was proof of the involvement of girls under 15.

Male Homosexuality

During the Vietnam War, much of Saigon's organized homosexual activity revolved around the city's "gay" bars. According to Marnais (1967), there were a total of eighteen such establishments in existence during the late 1960s. Many of the customers could be found among middle-aged Saigon businessmen and teenage students. Only a small minority displayed the slightest effeminate trait. There were also homosexual steam baths, night-clubs, and coffee shops, and young boys, impoverished and orphaned by the war, sold themselves openly on street corners to passersby. There were at least four "call-boy" operations, catering mainly to wealthy Chinese businessmen and foreign (primarily French) residents. For American soldiers, it was risky to be involved in homosexual activity, because the army did not tolerate it, and suspected homosexuals were immediately given a dishonorable discharge (Taylor 1997).

The only hint that the long years of living in the jungle and tunnels of the Ho Chi Minh Trail left traces in the specific sexual preferences of the Viet Cong can be found in the reports of journalists. According to Scholl-Latour (2000), most of the Viet Cong were so uninterested in women when Saigon finally fell that the female prostitutes did not appeal to them. But it seems far more probable that it was the strict discipline of the Viet Cong that prevented them from "fraternizing" with prostitutes.

D. Homosexuality and Vietnamese Law

Proschan (Aronson 1999; "Frank" 2000) writes that neither homosexual identity nor behaviors had ever been explicitly illegal in Vietnam. The ancient legal codes of the Le Dynasty (1428-1787) and the Nguyen Dynasty (1802-1945) detailed the penalties for crimes such as heterosexual rape, assault, adultery, and incest, but left homosexuality unmentioned. The only provisions in the codes that might refer to deviant sexuality were the prohibition against "men who wear weird or sorceress garments" (*Le Code*, Article 640; Nguyen & Ta 1987), and a prohibition of castration and self-castration (*Le Code*, Article 305; *Nguyen Code*, Article 344). Both provisions were not found in earlier Chinese codes. On the few occasions when homosexual activities seem to have been punished, they had been treated as rape or as adultery (disregarding the fact that both partners were the same sex, and concentrating instead on the fact that one or both were married to other partners). Vietnamese legal codes had always been strongly influenced by the Chinese codes of the same eras. In 1740, when the Ching Dynasty in China elaborated for the first time in Chinese history punishment for sodomy between consenting adults, the Vietnamese did not follow suit, once again omitting any such prohibitions in the Nguyen Code that was promulgated soon after. Nor did the French colonials institute explicit prohibitions against sodomy or pederasty in their colonies, because under the Code Napoléon, these acts did not fall under the purview of the legal system.

Although homosexuality or sodomy was not specifically referred to anywhere in modern Vietnamese criminal law, "sex buying and selling in any form" was prohibited, as were more general and vague crimes such as "undermining public morality." In the latest Law on Marriage and Family (1986), no article mentioned the State attitude or any guidelines for public opinion about homosexual behavior. The Penal Code did not mention homosexuality either in its articles on incest, rape, prostitution, sexual assault, or child marriage. But Vietnamese authorities could find legal basis for punishing homosexual behavior if they chose, because crimes such as "undermining public morality" could be used (as similar crimes of "public indecency" or "soliciting" are in the U.S.) to prosecute homosexuality.

E. Language and Homosexuality

The Vietnamese use more than one expression for the Western neologism *homosexuality*, although all have the same underlying meaning of "half man and half woman." For example, *Dong Tinh Luyen Ai* is a literal translation via Chinese of "homosexuality," which dates back to 1869. Its entry date into the Vietnamese language is not very clear. It did not appear in Dao Duy Anh's *Han Viet Tu Dien* of 1931, but it did appear in his *Phap Viet Tu Dien* of 1936, and might have had limited currency in the journalistic vocabulary of the 1930s.

The concept of homosexuality only came into greater use with the introduction of Western psychology and sexology in so-called hygiene manuals in the 1950s and 1960s. *Ai Nam Ai Nu* is the closest descriptive approximation to what is meant ontologically and behaviorally by the Western term *homosexuality*, though, if one takes *Ai* as a verb, the term comes closer to "bisexual" behavior. It did not come into use before the 1940s. Another variation on this term, which is more common in the biological and medical vocabulary, is *Ban Nam Ban Nu. Pe De,* for the French *pederaste,* is probably the most common byword for a gay person in Vietnam. It is urban in origin and can be dated to the French usage of the word. From the Chinese is borrowed *Ke Gian,* which is mostly used to depict anal intercourse, being thus is not limited to same-sex practice ("Vinh N." 1999).

F. Sex Tourism

As publications like *The Men of Viet Nam: A Travel Guide to Gay Viet Nam* and Web sites like www.utopia-asia.com suggest, foreign homosexual sex tourism is on the rise. Many Western visitors, who are called "Rice Queens," leave behind everything they know about safe sex practices when they come to Vietnam. According to an estimate of the Nguyen Friendship Society, one third of Vietnamese men who have sex with foreigners do not use a condom, and may have never used a condom before.

7. Gender Conflicted Persons

Bao, Long, & Taylor (1998) report that a transgendered person in Vietnam is mainly a "man" who wears female clothes and presents himself as a female. *Bong cai* is the common term in the south and is translated literally as "female shadow," whereas *dong co* is the common term in the north and is translated as "woman goes into a trance," revealing its origin from the shamanistic tradition: The male *ong dong* or the female *ba dong* are shamanic mediums who incarnate a pantheon of spirits, both male and female, during the course of a *len dong* performance in one of the fortune teller's temples. They take on, in succession, the costume and comportment of the numerous spirits invoked, in what can be a daylong show of elaborate costumery. It seems that Vietnamese transgendered males only have sex with men, never with women or with other transgendered persons. Transgendered males refer to one another as "sisters" (*chi em*).

There are quite a few transvestites in Saigon who are trying to earn a living through prostitution. They look for customers in certain nightclubs and bars as well as on the streets. Being a transvestite seems not to be something that is displayed in public, and the search for customers is done in an aggressive though feminine way.

Jacobus X. (1898) mentions transvestitism in connection with prostitution during the French period of Vietnam:

> I cannot, however, pass over in silence, one eccentric form of the *lusus amoris*. The Chinese actors who play the women's parts, come in their costumes [to the brothel], and assume the character of a modest virgin, afraid of losing her virginity, a refinement of vice which is much appreciated. In the presence of a number of old men, not very particular, the scenes of the first night of wedded life are represented without any shame.

Commenting on transvestite singers and transvestite striptease in the homosexual nightclubs of Saigon catering to male homosexual transvestites during the Vietnamese-American War, Marnais (1967) reported that transvestite prostitutes would congregate daily on the terrace of the Continental Hotel in Saigon. They were reported to have disappeared from view after the Communist takeover of South Vietnam in 1975, but recent reports from the informants of Carrier, Nguyen, and Su (1997) returning from Saigon show that male transvestites can be seen on the streets once again, and some are again earning their income as prostitutes.

They may also make a living by joining a lottery team (*lo to*), often during adolescence, as singers. "Lottery team" refers to a mobile lottery team, who sell tickets and then spin for a prize at that establishment. The teams use singing to advertise (Bao, Long, & Taylor 1998).

8. Significant Unconventional Sexual Behaviors

A. Coercive Sex

Coercive sex is prohibited in Vietnam. Article 112 of the Vietnamese Penal Code says:

1. Any person who uses force or any other means to have sexual intercourse with another person against his will shall be sentenced to imprisonment from 1 to 5 years. Any person who commits rape of a minor aged from 13 upward or a girl to whom he has the responsibility to give care and education or to provide medical treatment shall be sentenced to imprisonment from 2 to 7 years.
2. Any person who commits a crime in one of the following cases shall be sentenced to imprisonment from 5 to 15 years:
   a. Organized rape or rape that does serious harms to the victim's health
   b. Rape of many persons or creation of serious harms to the victim's health
   c. Relapse into former crime with more severity.
3. Any person who commits a crime which causes the death or the suicide of the victim or commits a crime in a specially serious circumstance shall be sentenced to imprisonment from 12 to 20 years, to life imprisonment or to death penalty.
4. Any cases of having sex with a child aged under 13 shall be regarded as committing a rape and the person in question shall be sentenced to imprisonment from 7 to 15 years. Any person who commits a crime belonging to one of the cases stipulated in items 2 and 3 of this article shall be sentenced to imprisonment from 12 to 20 years, to life imprisonment or to death penalty.

Child Sexual Abuse and Pedophilia

Incestuous relations and child marriages, as well as early marriages, are prohibited by the Penal Code in Articles 112, 146, and 145. Although reliable statistical data are not available, it seems quite certain that the number of juvenile prostitutes has increased rather quickly in recent years. Based on the ratio of age range of prostitutes provided by the Nam Ha province, it is known that among 164 prostitutes, 17.6 percent of them are in the 13-to-16-year age group and 19.5 percent are in the 16-to-18-year age group. Together, there are 37.4 percent in the 13-to-19-year age group. Another research document on prostitution in Ho Chi Minh City shows that in 1989, juvenile prostitutes accounted for 2.1 percent of the total number of prostitutes; in 1990, the rate was 5.2 percent, and in 1995, it was as high as 15 percent (Hoang Ba & Pham Kim Ngoc 1996). The United Nations Children's Fund (UNICEF) had a 1995 estimate that there were 40,000 child sex workers throughout Vietnam.

Jacobus X. (1898) records a variety of proverbial sayings common in French-dominated Vietnam of the nineteenth century: "For a girl to be still a virgin at ten years old, she must have neither brothers nor fathers." The same author reports on pedophilia:

> . . . whilst he is a *nay* [a boy who is carrying a "basket" for a customer], he has not usually reached the age of puberty. As may easily be imagined, these poor little wretches fall into the hands of "active" pederasts, who are not remarkable for gentleness and kindness, and who brutally assuage their lewd passions without caring what may be the result. I have often found, in these unfortunate *nays*, marks of attempts that have been committed almost by violence, the fact being that a lad not yet arrived at puberty, and frail and weak, is incapable of making any serious resistance to brutal attempts at sodomy on the part of an adult European or Asiatic. (Jacobus X. 1898)

During the Vietnam War, sex with children and incestuous sex was frequently connected with prostitution. Marnais (1967) reported that it was possible to watch live sex shows with teenage twins and also hire them for sex. In a Saigon brothel called the "Doll House," over fifty girls, none older than 12, served the clients for sadomasochistic games. In the "House of Pain," very young girls got injections of heroin to make them physically and psychologically dependent.

Rape

There exist few statistics about sexual abuse, and they are not very reliable. It is, for instance, quite questionable when Hoang Ba and Pham Kim Ngoc (1996) state that before the 1990s, only 400 cases of rape of women and children had occurred in the whole country in one year:

> From January 1993 to July 1995, 1,685 cases of rape (324 cases being of children) occurred. Compared with the years prior to 1990, cases of child raping only accounted for 4 to 6 percent of the total, but in the past three years, this rate has increased. Concretely speaking, in 1993 rapes of children accounted for 14.6 percent, in 1994 16.6 percent and in the first months of 1995, the rate reached as high as 30 percent. The victims were young girls in the age group 10-13 but there were also cases of raping little girls aged only 4-5. In Ho Chi Minh City in 1994, 55 rapes of children occurred out of a total of 107 cases. 43 of them were under 13 (Hoang Ba & Pham Kim Ngoc 1996).

Incest

As O'Harrow (1995) remarked, the vocative system of the Vietnamese language is largely devoid of pronouns and uses, relying instead on static kinship terms. Thus, in Vietnamese, a husband and wife enjoy a fictive incest. The husband speaks to his wife using the same terms he has always used towards his real younger sisters, referring to himself as "older brother" (*anh*) and calling his wife "little sister" (*em*). Also, a very peculiar incest taboo is found in Vietnam: It is forbidden for a Buddhist student to marry the widow of his teacher (Gregersen 1996). The traditional punishment for incest was strangulation of the offender.

B. Prostitution

Prostitution in the Pre-Colonial Era

Jacobus X. (1898) reported that prostitution was very common during the nineteenth century. He distinguished between the Annamite "Bamboo," the Chinese brothel, and the "Flower Boats," the Annamite "Daylight Whore" and the Annamite "Mistress of the European." These girls were either sold by their poor parents or even kidnapped by professional girl traders. It seems that the Annamite "Bamboo" was the brothel for the natives and the lower social layers of the French colonials. The prostitutes were Vietnamese girls who had to wait for customers in bamboo huts, hence the name. The infection rate with STDs was high, and the standard of hygiene quite low. Jacobus X. (1898) mentioned black lacquered teeth (a Chinese fashion) and hairless pubes as ethnic peculiarities. The girls had to sell themselves for very little money, and most of the money went to the pimp.

He also described the style of living of Chinese prostitutes, who first came from Singapore. They resided in big houses and waited on the verandas for clients. An elder women acted as "mama." On the first floor were a lot of Chinese beds with dark-colored mosquito curtains to conceal the couples. For waiting opium-smokers, there would be a pipe. Although few of the girls smoked, they were instructed in preparing the pipes. The owners of the brothels and flower boats, which are houseboats in the channels, worked without license, and were free to carry on their trade. However, they had to put up with the extortion of the Mandarins. Under the most trivial presumption of harboring criminals, their inhabitants might be mercilessly driven out. Interestingly, the Chinese prostitutes had a chance to become a concubine of a man of reputation, and then rise to a more honored position. The houses of prostitution of Cholon were almost exclusively reserved for the Chinese and resembled the "society houses" in Europe. They were quite luxurious, with salons, divans, sofas, mirrors, and pictures.

Besides these brothels, there also existed the so-called "Daylight Whore" and the system of the mistress. Apparently, the first was formerly in the bamboo but left because of her age. She also had a *souteneur*, who protected her from the police officers. They lingered in the streets and around restaurants, waiting to contact some possible client. After the initial contact was made, they followed the client to his house, ready to suggest sodomy and the kneeling instead of the horizontal position.

The mistress of the European were often bought directly from the parents "for some twenty piasters," a young girl of 15 or 16, selected from those whose fate it would ultimately be to be sent to the "bamboo." It was quite common, though, to take the mistress of some friend or colleague who was leaving the colony, and thus get a woman "who has had some training, requires no outfit, and understands a little French." To prevent the mistress from "going wrong," Jacobus X. (1898) suggested setting his own Annamite boy over her as bodyguard.

Official French Policy Towards Prostitution

According to Troung (1990) who quoted the report of the Commission of Enquiry of the League of Nations (1933), French colonial policy adhered to the International Convention for the Suppression of the White Slave Traffic of 1910, but did not accede to the International Convention for the Suppression of the Traffic in Women and Children of 1921. The general policy pursued by the French government in Indochina was regulation, i.e., control through registration and supervision of brothels and women who were already prostitutes, and safeguarding women and girls from being induced by force or deceit into prostitution. The control of prostitution was entrusted to municipal and provincial authorities. The age of consent for registered prostitution was established at 18 years for Asians and 21 years for Europeans. The police registered a prostitute if she was found soliciting in the streets or if a person complained of having been "contaminated" by her. In 1926, about 24 licensed brothels paid taxes every month to the Hanoi city administration in addition to the hotels and lodging houses that secretly harbored prostitution. In 1935, H. Virgitti, mayor of Hanoi, disclosed that there were about 4,000 people working in the sex industry, not including geishas and dancers (Khuat Thu Hong 1998).

It is interesting to note that traffic in women was considered by the French colonial administration a problem solely connected with Asian traditions and customs. The 1929 report of the police prosecutor at the Court of Appeal in Saigon cited the following example of this quite hypocritical attitude towards the Vietnamese and the belief in the colonial authorities' own superiority:

> It may be that the supervision exercised, the severe sentences by the courts and the administrative measures taken against foreign Asiatics sentenced for offences of this nature, have warned delinquent people against the consequences of this shameful commerce; it may be that the mental attitude modified through French influence and through contact with our civilization, so respectful of the rights of women and children, has brought about an almost complete change of the native customs (Commission of Enquiry of the League of Nations, 1933:218).

The French believed that licensed brothels were a far more humane and civilized treatment of prostitutes who were assumed to have entered the profession deliberately, even though the conditions were quite unbearable because of extreme exploitation. Medical officers sometimes sent girls to hospital not because of venereal diseases, but because they were in a state of "very great exhaustion, having been obliged by the keepers of the house to receive an excessive number of customers" (Commission of Enquiry of the League of Nations, 1933:217).

As in other colonies, Vietnam had a double standard. The few white prostitutes possessed certain rights; they could, for example, institute legal procedures against *souteneurs* of French nationality, and the men were invariably punished and expelled (Commission of Enquiry of the League of Nations (1933:215-217). Because of the ideas of the Social Purity movement, prostitution was regarded as evil. Because the aim was not to analyze the social and economic reasons for prostitution, prostitutes became criminalized, in contrast to their customers.

The French also used *Bordels Mobile de Campagne*, huge trailer trucks converted into mobile field brothels with ten women to each truck. The *Bordels Mobile* traveled to every fighting front. When on leave in Hanoi or Saigon, the French soldiers preferred non-military-organized establishments.

Vietnam War Period

According to Khuat Thu Hong (1998), archive materials indicate that in 1954 in Hanoi alone, there were around 12,000 professional prostitutes working in 45 brothels and 55 cabaret houses of whom over 6,000 were licensed. After 1954, in northern Vietnam, prostitution was theoretically eliminated. Article 202 of the Criminal Code states that any sheltering, enticement, or inducement of prostitutes is an illegal act, and punishment will vary by degree of violation. Yet, every year, about 300 to 400 persons were discovered working in this trade.

Between 1959 and 1962, organized prostitution in the South was almost totally crushed by Madame Nhu, who closed down every brothel and heavily fined the owners. This changed after the Ngo Dinh Diem regime was overthrown in 1963. During the late 1960s, about thirty-two establishments in Saigon were houses of prostitution, ranging from modest apartments to elegant three-story establishments. A good deal of the sex business was in the hands of the Vietnamese underworld, like the "Yellow Pang Society." In the French as well as in the American period, the "Flower Boats" or sampans plied their trade. They were frequently family operations, with the daughter(s) working as prostitute(s) while the brothers pimped on dry land. Some of the larger junks, however, were professionally run, often by the Saigon underworld. Prior to 1975, statistics from the Ministry of Society of the Saigon government reported about 200,000 professional prostitutes. In Saigon alone in 1968, there were about 10,000 professional prostitutes. By 1974, the figure had reached 100,000.

During the Vietnam War, one million soldiers from the United States were stationed throughout Southeast Asia. Most of these host countries signed agreements to provide their services as "Rest and Recreation" centers for United States military and aid personnel. Their presence contributed to the proliferation of commercial sexual intercourse. Although the U.S. Army was not officially involved in providing sex workers to cover itself against congressional reaction at home, it is known that some of the brothels kept by the Vietnamese Government and the ARVIN (Army of Vietnam) were exclusively reserved for GIs. The first military brothel opened in 1966 in Pleiku in the central highlands. According to Marnais (1967), it was to be the model for other "recreation centers," including several within the Saigon area:

> The Pleiku brothel has twenty rooms, whitewashed and pleasantly furnished. The girls are all carefully selected on the basis of good looks, personality and knowledge of English. (U.S. Army Intelligence also runs a security check on each girl to make sure she is not a Viet Cong agent out to pick up useful information from her trusting bedmates.) The girls are closely supervised by a matron under contract to the Pleiku

Administrative Council. An American GI pays 300 piastres ($2.50) for a ticket, allowing him up to three hours with any given girl. (Twosomes and other exotic sexual ménages are out.) Between 100 and 300 GIs visit the house each day, passing through a sandbagged guard post where they are required to show their ticket and have it stamped by a Vietnamese soldier. Fifteen percent of the girl's earnings are deducted to pay for expenses at the center, but a hard-working and a popular prostitute can earn between 8000 to 15,000 piastres ($66 to $125) a month, a good salary in today's Vietnam.

The main reason for the U.S. Army to provide those establishments was the alarmingly high venereal disease rate among U.S. enlisted men. However, most of the soldiers preferred to look for prostitutes themselves in bars catering to GIs.

A prostitute earned as much as $180 per month. The average government civil servant earned roughly $30 a month, and even cabinet ministers and Assembly members had fixed salaries of $120. A special form of prostitution was the "mistress," i.e., a paid steady girlfriend. GIs considered this a "safer" alternative to the brothels and bar girls. There existed rumors about an incurable strain of syphilis, called "Black Clap," and Viet Cong girls who were able to put razor blades into their vaginas to castrate or even kill clients (Gulzow & Mitchell 1980). The latter rumor is without doubt a reflection of the ability of some trained girls to use their vaginas to smoke cigarettes, shoot arrows, or to put razor blades or other sharp materials in them without getting hurt.

While under French rule, marriages of French soldiers and Vietnamese women were prohibited. American soldiers, on the other hand, could marry. A U.S. Army study of sixty-four GIs who had filed applications to marry Vietnamese girls between June 1964 and November 1966 concluded that a high proportion of GIs who married Vietnamese women were divorced, sexually inhibited, fearful of American women, or disenchanted with some aspects of American life (Marnais 1967).

The Present

After the Viet Cong occupation of Saigon, the new government tried to eliminate prostitution by closing brothels and sending prostitutes to work or to so-called reeducation centers. Between 1975 and 1985, 14,304 prostitutes in Ho Chi Minh City were sent to those centers. The Government claimed that prostitution was eradicated in the South by 1985. But as Stephanie Fahey (1998) remarked: "In a country where the Communist Party attempted to eradicate prostitution and pornography, prostitutes are now found in almost every bar, restaurant and hotel whether private or state-owned." According to statistics from the Department of Criminal Police, Ministry of the Interior, in the first six months of 1990, Vietnam had 40,000 prostitutes and 1,000 brothels. By the first six months of 1993, there were 200,000 prostitutes and 2,000 brothels. A report prepared by SCF (Save the Children Fund) in 1995 estimated that there were 149 brothels in Ho Chi Minh City alone. Many of the establishments are, officially, bars selling beer to Vietnamese clients. According to one recent unofficial estimate (Khuat Thu Hong 1998), there may be half a million sex workers in all of Vietnam, not including the increasing number of male prostitutes in the southern provinces and the big northern cities. Government Resolutions 53, 87, and 88, passed in 1994 and 1995, strengthen management over cultural activities and monitor the struggle against the so-called social evils, including prostitution, gambling, and drug use.

The reasons for women to become sex workers remain the same as during the Vietnam War and in other developing countries where there are few opportunities in rural areas and low wages in the jobs open for uneducated girls. Poverty is not the sole reason pushing women into prostitution. Family conflicts and their feeling of hopelessness about their husbands or boyfriends are also important reasons. The women interviewed by Cooper and Hanson (1998) stated that they were much better off now than in their villages. Although prostitution is illegal in Vietnam, because of economic problems it is again becoming the booming business it was during the Vietnam War. But tourists report that because of corruption, the interpretation of the law is quite broad. Some of the girls who are looking for customers and are talking to tourists are agent provocateurs for corrupt policemen who force the foreigner to pay large sums to "avoid an incident." On the other hand, there are also police actions to clean up streets and districts with known prostitution, as Cooper and Hanson (1998) were told by a madam.

Prostitutes can be found on the street, sometimes with a pimp in the background, in massage parlors, and nightclubs. Two types of social networks are most common in the sex workers: peer and friend relations. They often work together in groups of two to five at a site, and this site remains fixed for a number of prostitutes for an extended period of time, from several months to a year or two. Many prostitutes are organized in groups for protection, or they may become friends. As a result of these social groupings, newcomers may be bullied by older prostitutes. They often make friends with a man who is referred to as their "boyfriend" (*bo ruot*). He may be a familiar client or a man who lives with the prostitute in a hired room and can protect her during work. Prostitutes have sexual relations with clients, boyfriends, and husbands. The average number of sexual contacts of the ten prostitutes interviewed by Bao, Long, and Taylor (1998) was twenty-three per month, some having forty or fifty.

Clients of Prostitutes

Clients of sex workers are called *Khach lang choi* in Vietnamese. According to the study by Bao, Long, and Taylor (1998), all social classes, with the exception of farmers, can be found among them: workers, truck drivers, students, engineers, married, and unmarried men. The clients often start off going to a *beer hug bar* or restaurant to drink beer where they end up negotiating sex with one of the beer hug girls. Or they drink beer or alcohol first at one place and then go to another place to seek sex.

As in other developing countries, sex tourism is a growing business. Although reliable statistics are not available, such indicators as Web sites with advice for international tourists show a tremendous increase of travelers interested in sex, especially because Vietnam wrongly has the reputation of being "safer" with regard to STDs and AIDS than other countries in Southeast Asia. Because by law, Vietnamese citizens are prohibited from going into a hotel room of a tourist unless they are registered guests, prostitutes and customers meet at small Vietnamese-owned mini-hotels that cater to the locals and tolerate prostitution.

Health Care

Since the early 1990s, the New Zealand Prostitutes Collective has worked together with the Save the Children Fund in providing peer-training workshops for sex workers. According to the SCF official report of 1995:

> Peer educators and peer counselors serve as credible and impactful disseminators of preventive/protective knowledge and behavior skills, and as positively reinforcing role models and change agents in the referent target populations (including sex workers). (p. 4)

On the street, an outreach worker reported to Cooper and Hanson (1998) that there is at the start always some mistrust when they try to bring women for an STD checkup, but with developing relationships, the women are glad that someone looks after them.

Sexual Slavery

According to Article 115 of the Penal Code, any person who buys and sells women shall be sentenced to imprisonment from 5 to 7 years. Any person who engages in this kind of behavior with an organization, takes the woman abroad, buys or sells many women, or relapses into this crime shall be sentenced to 5 to 20 years in prison.

According to news in the *South China Morning Post* (July 29, 1999), domestic sexual slavery is increasing, with an estimated 20 percent of Vietnam's commercial sex workers held in brothels against their will. In Vietnam, women can be sold to brothels for two million dong (HK$1,120), but according to the Ministry of Labor, brothels in Taiwan and China pay up to US$7,000 (HK$54,250) for young Vietnamese women. Therefore, it is no wonder that Vietnam is becoming an important source of women destined for sexual slavery in Hong Kong, Macao, and Southeast Asia. Many victims are lured into marriages with foreigners and migrate with their new husbands before being sold to brothels.

C. Pornography and Erotica

Jacobus X. (1898) reported that in the second half of the nineteenth century, Chinese merchants were famous for selling Chinese and Japanese phalli (dildoes) and the colored albums of Chinese erotica. At first, the merchants had quite a bad reputation, but this changed gradually, with the merchants becoming esteemed for their business.

During the Vietnam War, the main sources for pornographic photographs were the black market moneychangers who always had some pictures to sell to GIs. The Tu Do Street was the main center to purchase pornographic material, according to Marnais (1967). During the early

1960s, the only pornographic pictures and books available in the city were imports from Hong Kong and Bangkok, where little cartoon folios, pornographic poems, and photographs were turned out by the hundreds of thousands. By 1967, with the influx of GIs, the market had grown, and a group of domestic entrepreneurs has sprung up to take advantage of it. Pornographic paperbacks, featuring young Vietnamese girls and boys sold along the "Rue Cat," were printed on Saigon's presses.

The "blue" movie houses were located on the same street in little rooms above shops or bars, and the locations fluctuated frequently to keep the authorities away. The windows were painted black or covered with heavy curtains. The movies usually showed a young women waking up in her small room, taking off her few clothes, starting to masturbate with some kind of dildo or fruit, and ending with a male or female visitor to her room having intercourse with her. As in the 1960s, they were usually short 16-mm films, mostly in black and white and without sound; some were more expensively produced in color, some with threesomes or bestiality. In the background of the rooms were prostitutes waiting for potential customers, most of whom were Westerners. Prostitutes also used pornographic pictures and movies to get their clients "in the mood." European pornographic films existed for homosexuals. Although pornography is forbidden today, according to Stephanie Fahey (1998), government research institutes are known to import pornographic magazines for resale.

9. Contraception, Abortion, and Population Planning

A. Vietnam's Family Planning Policy

The Vietnamese family planning program has its roots in the early 1960s, when some contraceptive methods became available in both the southern and northern regions on a limited basis. Beginning in 1962 in the northern province, the government planning policy was directed to reducing the rate of population growth, and the use of certain relatively permanent contraceptive methods, such as the IUD, was promoted. Until the 1970s, however, a governmental policy was not formally implemented. The family planning program in the southern province began in the late 1960s, largely in response to concern over maternal and infant mortality and the increasing number of illegal abortions. In the mid-1970s, the Government of the Republic of the South Vietnam stated that family planning had been adopted as an official policy, but inadequate medical facilities made it impossible to implement an effective family planning program.

The Committee for Population and Family Planning (CPFP) was established during the early 1980s, and a one- or two-child policy was formally initiated in late 1988. At about the same time, Vietnam introduced comprehensive free-market reforms, which increased the effectiveness of the population program. The program included an extensive media campaign, free provision of contraceptive services and devices, and the creation of incentives and disincentives to encourage compliance. With a government target to reduce the total fertility rate to 3.0 births per woman by the year 2000, the fertility rate had already fallen to 3.1 by 1994. The sharp drop in

Vietnam's fertility over the past several years, which has attracted global attention, can be linked to the general context of how family planning is delivered—including penalties for family planning violation, and to the widespread use of modern contraceptive methods and abortion. The intrauterine device (IUD) is by far the most popular contraceptive method, followed by traditional methods (withdrawal, "rhythm," and breastfeeding), increasing use of the condom, and the pill a distant last place.

B. Increasing Condom Use

The condom was rarely used in Vietnam until recently, but both knowledge and use of the condom have increased significantly over the past ten years. Among married women aged 15 to 49, knowledge of the condom rose from 45 percent in 1988 to 76 percent in 1994, and the use of the condom more than tripled from 1 percent in 1988 to 4 percent in 1994. The predominant contraceptive method, however, has been the IUD: in 1988, 33 percent of the respondents relied on the IUD (with neither a decrease nor increase in 1994). But the IUD is nevertheless known and feared for its side effects: heavy bleeding, infection of the ovaries, and severe abdominal pains, as well as very likely infection of the cervix, ectopic pregnancies, and a low effectiveness rate in general (Goodkind & Anh 1997). As Gammeltoft (1999) was told by a woman: "You know, in the old days, heaven decided how many children one would have. Today we have the IUD, so heaven still decides." One reason for failure and health problems may be that for a long time, the only IUDs available were used IUDs from Communist East Block countries. Some health providers also complain that the IUDs, which today are imported from the U.S., are too large for the uteruses of Vietnamese women. Most improbable seems to be the opinion of Women's Union cadres that "it is a disease of the mind," and that women simply blame all their troubles in life on the IUD.

According to Goodkind (1997), primary reliance on the IUD and abortion is typical of former Marxist states, which have tended to discourage supply-based methods, thus reflecting an indifference to consumer choice and an inability to afford these methods, or to keep tight reins on their distribution and use. Within Asia, Vietnam is distinguished by having the highest levels of IUD and abortion use in the region, perhaps partly because policymakers see this strategy as the most effective way to meet current fertility targets.

One reason for the rise in condom use is the increased availability of the product because of free-market reforms introduced in the mid-1980s. In combination with family planning promotion in the late 1980s, these reforms allowed for two channels of condom distribution: through the public health sector and sales through private pharmacies and family-owned roadside stalls. There are drawbacks, however, to obtaining condoms through public sector centers, namely, the necessity to travel some distance to reach a center, the need to register one's name to receive supplies, and the necessity to use whatever brand of condom is being offered. But because condoms are offered free of charge, a growing number of condom users seems to prefer going through the private sector. In recent years, the growth of social marketing programs has increased the number of brands available and also competition, which has kept prices low.

The condom is more popular than the pill, both for spacing births and for preventing them. One reason for the greater popularity of the condom may be its greater compatibility with traditional methods, such as withdrawal. Data from the 1994 national Vietnam Inter-Censal Demographic Survey (VICDS), being both an inter-census demographic survey and a family planning survey, indicated that 31 percent of married women of reproductive age who switched from the condom to another method did prefer one or both traditional methods, rhythm or withdrawal, compared with only 24 percent of those women who switched from the pill. Given the high prevalence of traditional-method use in Vietnam—22 percent in 1994—these attitudinal dynamics seem to favor use of the condom over the pill. As Goodkind (1997) pointed out, the preference for condoms cannot be fully accounted for only by conventional explanations like the lesser compatibility of the pill with traditional methods, monetary concerns, or problems in pill supplies. In addition to these reasons, one might speculate that the national family planning leaders discouraged pill use, because they were skeptical that rural women could use it effectively. Also, the IUD and sterilization, even abortion, are being looked at much more favorably, because they reflect the socialist legacy of de-emphasizing consumer choice and ensuring compliance with the one- or two-child policy. Goodkind argued that enduring cultural factors, including its Confucian heritage, may also contribute to a preference for condoms over the pill. Vietnam exhibits the same family-formation characteristics as many other Confucian societies in East Asia: patrilineal family organization, son preference, lunar birth timing, and high rates of abortion. Preference of the condom may stem from traditional Chinese medical beliefs, which are intertwined with Confucian, Buddhist, and Daoist religious philosophies. These beliefs often emphasize the importance of maintaining a balance of natural body rhythms. The pill may thus be perceived as interfering with the menstrual cycle and disturbing the proper balance between "hot and cold" food intake.

C. Socioeconomic Characteristics and Contraceptive Methods

The condom is the only method with a higher preference among urban users and among those with higher levels of educational and occupational status. In 1994, 10 percent of urban residents used condoms, compared with 4 percent of rural residents. However, women of all occupational statuses and educational levels overwhelmingly prefer the IUD and traditional methods, with the pill coming in a distant last place.

Goodkind (1997) suggested that because Vietnam is currently developing very rapidly, its population is becoming better educated, more affluent, and more urbanized. Economic reforms have contributed to a rising standard of living as well as to a growing disparity between rich and poor. These conditions have also increased the numbers of commercial sex workers and their patrons. Because of these social and demographic developments, one can expect the use of condoms to increase both for pregnancy and STD prevention outside marriage.

According to a recent but undated United Nations study, 40 percent of Vietnamese married men have had extramarital sex. Another survey conducted in 1993 showed that 69 percent of homosexual men and 38 percent of urban heterosexual men used condoms during their sexual encounters. Half of sex workers had not used a condom during their most recent sexual encounters (Goodkind 1997).

The decision to use condoms is partly a question of government efforts to improve knowledge and awareness of HIV and other STDs and how to prevent them. There are influential political groups, however, who assume that condoms encourage people to engage in premarital or extramarital sex; these groups object to the discussion and distribution of condoms. Others, like the Vietnam Women's Union, hold a more pragmatic view. They have recently prepared a publication about AIDS prevention that is targeted to young people.

Condom use will very likely continue to increase because:

- Family-size desires are still declining;
- Economic reforms and increased personal income have made condoms more accessible;
- Condoms are suitable to use with traditional methods;
- Current social mobility and migratory patterns are redistributing more Vietnamese into better educated, wealthier social groups; and
- Recent increases in adolescent and extramarital sexual activity, coupled with a growing concern over STD/AIDS prevention.

D. The 1994 Vietnam Inter-Censal Demographic Survey (VICDS)

North Vietnam was among the first countries in the developing world to adopt an official policy to reduce population growth. Following reunification, policies to reduce population growth received increasing political attention from the national government. In January 1993, the Communist Party Central Committee identified population growth as contributing to a wide range of social, economic, and ecological problems. A resolution endorsed the recommendation that each family should have only one or two children, so that fertility could be lowered and population stabilization achieved. In June 1993, the prime minister approved the "Population and Family Planning Strategy to the Year 2000," a comprehensive plan to guide the implementation of the resolution.

The 1994 Vietnam Inter-Censal Demographic Survey (VICDS) was conducted from April through June 1994 in a nationwide effort to obtain information about fertility, investigate the prior trend of fertility decline, and determine whether the decline is likely to continue. [An intercensal survey is a national survey conducted to obtain information not gathered in the regular national censuses.] Results revealed a substantial change over recent years in reproductive attitudes and behavior. Fertility has continued to decline to a level not far above three children per woman. Compared with the late 1980s, contraceptive knowledge has broadened and contraceptive use has increased. Stated family-size preferences have shifted noticeably downward. The findings also confirmed that urban women are characterized by far lower fertility than rural women, that the Red River Delta (which includes Hanoi) followed by the Southeast (Ho Chi Minh City) show the lowest fertility levels, and that the Central Highlands show the highest fertility rates. Finally, the survey documented that there is an inverse association between fertility levels and educational attainment: The fertility rate for each successively higher educational grouping is lower than for the previous grouping.

E. Knowledge of Contraceptive Methods

By 1988, 94 percent of all married Vietnamese women were familiar with at least some methods of contraception, including at least one modern method; 90 percent of the married women were familiar with the IUD (Goodkind 1997). By 1994, a marked increase in familiarity with specific methods, both modern and traditional, was evident. About 75 percent of the women surveyed indicated awareness of the condom and both male and female sterilization, whereas 68 percent said they had heard about the pill. Reported contraceptive use was substantial and, according to the VICDS (1994), continued to increase between 1988 and 1994. About 73 percent of married women reported ever having practiced some form of contraception, compared with 60 percent in 1988. In 1997, according to the most recent Demographic and Health Survey of Vietnam (VN-DHS II), more than 84 percent of currently married women aged 15 to 49 have ever used a contraceptive method. The contraceptive prevalence rate (CPR) is 75 percent, and 56 percent of ever-married women are currently using a modern method. The total CPR is up by 10 percent over the level of the 1994 survey, and the use of modern methods rose by 12 percent, with traditional-method use falling by about 2 percent owing to less frequent use of periodic abstinence. Compared with the 1988 DHS NCPFP, Vietnam Demographic and Halth Survey, 1988 (Hanoie, 1990) and 1994 VICDS, the contraceptive mix has not changed very much. About half of the reported increase was attributed to use of modern methods and half to increased use of traditional methods. As far as the "method mix" is concerned, two features stand out: the dominance of the IUD among modern methods, and the relatively high share of traditional methods. Current use of oral contraceptives is still very low, being used by 2 percent of married women.

F. Abortion

In North Vietnam, since 1962, abortion on request (with the husband's consent) was available during the first trimester of pregnancy and was usually performed by vacuum curettage. Because of the 1933 decree enforcing a French law prohibiting abortion and the use of contraception in the Republic of South Vietnam, abortions could be performed only for narrowly interpreted indications. Between the late 1960s and the early 1970s, family planning clinics offered services only to women with at least five living children. Even when family planning clinics were later expanded to include women with one living child, a marriage or cohabitation certificate was required to obtain an abortion.

Abortion on request has been available in North Vietnam since at least 1971, and in the entire country since its unification in 1975. The Law on the Protection of Public Health (30 June 1989) states that "women shall be entitled to have an abortion if they so desire." According to Decision No. 162 of the Council of Ministers in January 1989, the State will supply, free of charge, birth control devices and public-health services, including induced abortion, to eligible persons that register to practice family planning. As mentioned earlier, it is typical of former Marxist states to primarily rely on abortion, together with the IUD, for population control. Henceforth, all possible grounds for abortion are permitted as long as the abortion is performed by a physician.

The proportion of single women among all women seeking abortion has increased to 20-to-30 percent in 1995 (compared with 7 percent in 1991), suggesting an increase in premarital sexual activity. Attitudes toward informal dating have become more tolerant, especially in urban areas. The availability of Western videos, TV programs, and other media have brought specific images of sex and romance to young people, and these are slowly changing the norms of acceptable behavior in Vietnamese culture.

According to the United Nations, Vietnam had 59 abortions per 1,000 women in 1987, 71 per 1,000 in 1988, and 70 per 1,000 in 1989. The Alan Guttmacher Institute reported in 1998 reported that Vietnam had the highest abortion rate of any nation in 1996, with 83 abortions per 1,000 women between the ages of 15 to 44. This number covers only abortions performed at state clinics; and when private clinics are included, the abortion rate was 111 per 1,000 women, or a total of roughly two million abortions. In 1999, the state-run media reported that the abortion rate in Hanoi continues to rise. In the first six months of 1999, 33,215 abortions were performed at Hanoi city hospitals, a 3-percent increase over the previous year, and nearly double the number of reported births. Although the government does not espouse abortion as a preferred family planning method, the procedure is heavily subsidized by the government, and many published family planning campaigns still list abortion as a method of birth control after IUDs, condoms, and the pill, according to the *Deutsche Presse-Agentur* (7/1999).

10. Sexually Transmitted Diseases

There is no information on venereal diseases in the early days of what is now Vietnam, although some descriptions of Sino-Annamese medicine suggest that this "scholarly" medicine did already know a distinction between the early and late symptoms of syphilis. Altogether, the frequencies of STDs were apparently only high in those regions that had a close contact with Europeans. Figures for the early French period are also difficult to obtain. The first French colonial physicians were largely concerned with malaria and dysentery, since these were responsible for decimating the troops. However, as rates of morbidity for sexually transmitted diseases (STDs) in the colonial army increased to one in ten in 1887, the French colony of 1890 reached first place, along with Madagascar, in all reports on venereal diseases. The situation did not improve at the beginning of the twentieth century. Between 1903 and 1911, morbidity attributed to syphilis increased among the French troops to account for 23 to 40 hospital admissions per 1000 men. In a division stationed in Tonkin, the medical officer noted that in 1902, venereal diseases accounted for 8.4 percent of total morbidity (508 admissions), of which 1.1 percent were for syphilis, 3.7 percent for gonorrhea, and 3.5 percent for chancroid and its complications. In 1904, out of 607 admissions, the total percentage of venereal diseases went up to 19.1 percent, with percentages for each of the three conditions at 3.7 percent, 9.7 percent, and 5.7 percent, respectively. For the medical officer, the spectacular rise coincided with the 1901-1902 expedition to China, which had mobilized contingents from Tonkin (Guénel 1997).

According to Assistance Médicale d'Indochine, founded in 1904, STDs became the second most common reason for hospitalization after malaria in the 1910s. The first statistics regarding STDs in the Vietnamese population are available through the maternity hospital in Cholon: During the first quarter of 1927, out of 2,500 births, 40 percent of the children had congenital syphilis. Guénel (1997) suggests this accounted for a large part of the perinatal mortality of 38 percent. In the North, at Hanoi, one in four children was estimated to die of syphilis during the first year. But one has to keep in mind that even in 1930, not more than 10 percent of the population in the big cities was accessing the services of the Assistance Médicale, and hardly any of the rural population did. All over Indochina, 92 percent of the prostitutes were infected with STDs compared with 10 percent in France.

Although hospital admissions because of syphilis infections decreased slightly during the 1930s, from 61 percent in 1930 to 21 percent in 1938, gonorrhea increased from 49 percent in 1930 to 70 percent in 1938. The two Indochina wars reactivated the problem of infected servicemen: Between 1945 and 1954, 12 percent of the 1.6 million men (700,000 of whom were Indochinese) were suffering from one of the four STDs then diagnosed. In 1975, the South Vietnamese government estimated that 10 percent of the population, or one million people, were infected, compared with a paltry 350 STD-infected American soldiers in 1963 (Greenberg 1972). In North Vietnam, as well as later in the unified country, the existence of venereal diseases was denied.

According to the WHO (1993), in 1991, gonorrhea still accounted for the highest percentage among STDs with 11 cases per 100,000 inhabitants. The Ho Chi Minh City Dermato-Venereology Institute, reorganized in 1975, reported a certain stabilization of STDs since 1985, representing, on average, 10 percent of all consultations (13,700 in 1993 for STDs alone), with a still marked prevalence of syphilis and gonorrhea, 25 percent and 17 percent, respectively, of STDs in 1993) according to Guénel (1997). The National Institute situated in Hanoi assesses the prevalence of syphilis at 10,000 cases per annum. But as Guénel points out, the incidence of STDs in Vietnam elude national statistics, much more so than in industrialized countries.

11. HIV/AIDS

Epidemiological and laboratory data indicate that epidemic spread of the HIV virus, the cause of AIDS, did not occur in any large human population until the mid-to-late 1970s. During the early to mid-1980s, extensive spread was documented for sub-Saharan Africa, the industrialized Western countries of North America, Europe, and Oceania, and many countries of Latin America, including the Caribbean. Although a few HIV infections and AIDS cases were detected in Asia during that period, there was no evidence of an epidemic spread, leading to speculation that AIDS would not become a major global health problem. Since the late 1980s, however, when explosive epidemics of HIV were documented in several South and Southeast Asian countries, the general complacency about AIDS has given way to alarm over the virus's potentially devastating impact on individual lives, as well as on the economies of the region.

In Vietnam, the first AIDS case was identified in 1990. It is safe to say that the epidemic will continue to spread, although the prevalence and distribution of AIDS, as well as the future of other STDs such as syphilis and gonorrhea, will vary widely among Asian countries. Countries with low STD-prevalence rates should not expect to have high rates of HIV and AIDS, but countries and populations with high STD rates are at high risk of developing high HIV/AIDS rates in the future, the reason being that syphilis and other STDs are spread through the same routes as HIV.

A study conducted by Franklin on HIV/AIDS in late 1993 found that 54 percent of the men interviewed in cafés, restaurants, nightclubs, parks, and the streets where sex was sold or where dates for sex could be made, had had two or more sexual partners in the previous two weeks (as cited by Goodkind 1997). Within three years, from 1996 to 1999, the number of reported HIV cases doubled. By late 1999, approximately 15,800 Vietnamese were reported HIV-positive, and approximately 1,500 had died of AIDS. The actual number of infections, however, could be ten times that number. Most cases go undetected because HIV testing is only done selectively. The actual number of people infected with HIV by the end of 1999 was expected to exceed 129,000. Vietnam's biggest city, Ho Chi Minh City, claimed the highest number with 2,600 cases. The disease is expected to have an especially harmful effect, not only on individual lives, but also on the economy, because 50 percent of those infected are between 15 and 24 years old.

HIV cases among Vietnam's prison inmates have tripled since 1998, now comprising one fifth of all infections in the country, according to a government newspaper. A total of 22,161 inmates had tested HIV-positive as of July 20, 1999, with 3,621 AIDS cases and 1,895 inmate deaths from AIDS since the first case detection in 1990. A National AIDS Committee official said that the actual number of HIV infections in Vietnam's prisons could be 10 times higher. Infected inmates remain in the general prison population until they develop AIDS, when they are transferred to the prison's clinic. Hoping to curb the spread of the virus, the Ministry of Public Security launched an HIV/AIDS-awareness campaign in prisons and correctional institutions in 1999 (Associated Press, 7/28/99).

The Vietnamese government has launched nationwide campaigns to raise people's awareness. Using mass media and other avenues, the campaigns are designed to provide Vietnamese students and 90 percent of people between ages 15 and 50 with general knowledge of the epidemic and how to protect themselves. However, cultural taboos have proven to be a hindrance to tackling the issue. An estimated 200,000 intravenous drug users and 100,000 prostitutes are blamed for the spread of AIDS.

12. Sexual Dysfunctions, Counseling, and Therapies

As O'Harrow (1995) pointed out, Vietnamese men tend to think of lovemaking in almost medical terms, concerned about the maintenance of their potency, psychological as well as physical. The main "sex therapy" for impotence is Chinese medicine. On the side of women, giving birth only to daughters is still regarded as the only noteworthy female "sexual dysfunction." But she can rely on her confidante, the soothsayer, fortune-teller, or *thay boi*. The *thay boi* is nearly always herself female, and although men also come to learn the future from her, the majority of her clients are women, with whom she maintains a semi-psychic relationship. The ability to be of help depends on the *thay boi*'s combined knowledge of and sensitivity to the predictable psychological concerns of her women clients, the range going from faithless husbands to vicious mother-in-laws, prying sister-in-laws, and rebellious children. She controls the commonly accepted cultural signs and knows the symbols that are needed to interpret these phenomena in a manner acceptable to her clients. The fortune-teller is the only credible yet disinterested female confidante available to Vietnamese women suffering psychological pain.

13. Research and Advanced Education

A. The Nature of Vietnamese Sex Research and Resources

According to Fahey (1998), very little social science research of any sort—in the Western meaning of the word—has been conducted in the country after the reunification of Vietnam in 1976. The Communist Party's approach to social issues has been prescriptive rather than analytic. It was not until the mid-1980s that social research centers were established. Most contemporary Vietnamese research on women's issues is generated through these centers, including the Center for Research on Gender in Hanoi and the Center for Scientific Study of Women and the Family in Ho Chi Minh City. As Fahey (1998) further observes, the Women's Union and women's branches of organizations like the Vietnam General Confederation of Labor have a much longer history, with the responsibility of lobbying for women's rights and conflict resolution. Although they have generated some information on women's position, more recently they have been co-opted by international organizations for the administration of aid and have lost much of their lobbying role. At the same time, the Women's Union, a national organization of over 11 million members and 7,000 employees, has shifted from an organization responsible for protecting women's rights to an implementation agency for programs of immunization, family planning, credit, and nutrition education for international funding organizations.

Fahey (1998) points out that, for political reasons, the social science research by Vietnamese scholars largely plays down the importance of divisions other than those stemming from Confucianism or the cult of the ancestors cutting across the nature of the family-like class and regional differences. Research is concentrated rather on politically relevant issues, like female employment, access to birth control, and prostitution and other so-called "social evils," like drug addiction, alcoholism, and gambling. Concerns with no immediate policy relevance, such as the commodification of women, have hardly been considered as yet. But in 1996, a very interesting survey was conducted by the Hanoi Institute of Sociology in cooperation with the Population Council to gain understanding of the participants' views toward sexuality and sexual activity, including differences across the pre-*doi moi* and *doi moi*-era generation (Khuat Thu Hong 1998).

B. Institutes for Sexological Research

There is no independent institute for sexological research in Vietnam. The main Vietnamese organizations involved in sexological research are strictly regulated by the government and its ministries. The more recent research projects were conducted by the Research Center of Gender, Family and Environment in Development (CGFED) and by the Center for Women and Family Studies (CWFS). The Institute of Sociology and the Institute of Educational Psychology of Hanoi University are leading in surveys dealing with sexual related topics. The Committee for Population and Family Planning (CPFP) and the Women's Union, as well as the Youth Union of Vietnam, both in Hanoi, have also conducted some sexological research. There is also the Vietnam Family Planning Association (VINAFPA). The Population Council Hanoi supports these institutions and single researchers, as well as conducts its own studies. The Population Council assists the Vietnamese government in testing reproductive health interventions and incorporating them into current maternal and child health and family planning policies, programs, and research.

The reproductive health program objectives are to develop intervention research and training and to provide research results to individuals at all levels in the public and private sectors. The current agenda addresses a broad range of reproductive concerns, including youth reproductive health, male involvement, reproductive tract infections (RTIs), sexuality, violence, and sexual harassment. The Save the Children Fund (SCF) is very active in conducting studies about child prostitution.

Summary

Vietnam is a country with a long and complex history and cultural traditions that vary a good deal in the different regions. We hope this heterogeneous character is clear in our chapter. As in other Southeast Asian countries, Vietnamese society is in rapid transformation because of the enormous influx of "modern" thinking as presented by commercials, international women's and men's magazines, and the introduction of Western economic system rules. The Vietnamese people are trying to find, at least in privacy, some stability and security, especially for the traditional values of the national ethic system of Confucianism. From a sexological viewpoint, this is, literally, a deadly mixture. It involves a tension between sexual hedonism and the perception of sex as something to buy or sell on one side, and the customs and traditions demanding a strict separation between sexual pleasures and ordinary life on the other side. Talking about sexuality, be it in public or in intimate partnership, is a Vietnamese taboo. This makes for an ideal breeding ground for AIDS and other STDs. But it also means that a neutral and unprejudiced approach to sexual habits is hardly possible, not just for the people but also for the state representatives and researchers. Foreign researchers, in particular, are not seen as neutral and nonjudgmental, but as outsiders. The perceived threat of the etic (outside) researcher calls into play the most important rule of Confucianism, "save face."

Our chapter is a direct result of this cultural rule, and it is not accidental that most of the historic and culturally relevant materials we drew on reflect a strong subjective coloring. This material was gathered by foreigners, who reported (and often exaggerated) only what was interesting from their etic viewpoint, with little objectivity and considerable sensational flavoring to create French or American public interest in their books. Unfortunately, we have no other resources. Sex research in Vietnam is still, even today, only legitimate if it serves public health issues like STD and AIDS research, family planning and abortion-related issues, or elimination of the victimization of women and children. Even then, it is difficult to decide which survey results are accurate and which are only political correct. Gammeltoft (1999) reports this problem most insistently, and our experience with Vietnamese students and Vietnamese research confirmed this. To all these difficulties, one has to add that Vietnam is a nation with many different regional traditions. Without substantial funding and government cooperation, sexological field research in Vietnam will not be possible. Sexological research in Vietnam still awaits the arrival of a Vietnamese "Kinsey," much as sexological research was not possible in China until Dalin Liu obtained government cooperation and support for a Kinsey-like nationwide survey of 20,000 Chinese men and women (see M. L. Lau's summary of Dalin Liu's research in the chapter on China in volume 1 of this *International Encyclopedia of Sexuality*).

A long ignored but promising approach to Vietnamese sexuality might be a survey of U.S. Vietnam War veterans. Unfortunately, the U.S. Army did not care enough about the Vietnamese people or their own soldiers to gather data on what was going on in thousands of brothels and in the provinces during the war. Insights and perspectives provided by Robert Taylor (1997) suggest that this kind of retrospective research would still be possible in the U.S.A., as well as in Vietnam. It would be extremely useful to have data regarding how the military and civil societies deal with sexuality under the circumstances of war.

Vietnam won the war against the United States 25 years ago, but now it seems the U.S.A. will win the cultural war. At least, such is the perception of many people in Vietnam and the United States. This is only partly true, and then mainly for the young people. As for effective countermeasures against the rising tide of AIDS and other STDs, and more so for a healthy and even joyful sexuality, neither traditional Vietnamese values nor American pop culture offers any solutions for these challenges. In fact, they may make effective solutions more difficult. What Vietnam needs is an extended understanding of its own sexual heritage, neutral scientific sex surveys, and a broad public embracing of sex education. With these, Vietnam should be able to win the war against sexual ignorance.

Acknowledgments

The author wishes to acknowledge the staff and Library of the Archive of Sexology, Berlin, especially its Director, Prof. Dr. Erwin Haeberle, for assistance and use of its holdings, and the staff and Library of Indiana University, Bloomington, and of the Kinsey Institute for Research in Sex, Gender, and Reproduction for assistance and use of their libraries and collections. The author also thanks Professor Frank Proschan, an expert on Vietnamese culture at the Folklore Institute at Indiana University (Bloomington)

References and Suggested Readings*

Aronson, J. 1999. Homosex in Hanoi? In: W. L. Leap, ed., *Sex, the public sphere, and public sex. Public sex/Gay space* (pp. 203-221). New York: Columbia University Press.

Bao, V. N., Long, L. D., & Taylor, Y. 1998 (November). *"Suffered lives": Assessment of social and behavioral practices for HIV/AIDS prevention in Can Tho.* A report prepared for Family Health International and the National AIDS Committee. The Population Council, Vietnam Office.

Bélanger, Danièle, & Khuat, Thu Hong. 1998 (June). Young single women using abortion in Hanoi, Viet Nam. *Asia-Pacific Population Journal, 13*(2):3-26. (Bangkok, Thailand).

Carrier, J., Nguyen, B., & Su, S. 1997. Sexual relations between migrating populations (Vietnamese with Mexican and Anglo) and HIV/STD infections in southern California. In: G. Herdt, ed., *Sexual cultures and migration in the era of AIDS: Anthropological and demographic perspectives* (pp. 225-250). Oxford: Clarendon Press.

Chittick, J. B. 1997. *The threat of HIV/AIDS on Viet Nam's youth: Meeting the challenge of prevention* (A report on the 1996 Viet Nam Youth Union Conference with additional commentary on the Government's approach to the teen AIDS epidemic in 1997). Boston: (Unpublished).

Commission of Enquiry of the League of Nations, 1933.

Cooper, M., & Hanson, J. 1998. Where there are no tourists . . . yet: A visit to the slum brothels in Ho Chi Minh City, Vietnam. In: M. Oppermann, ed., *Sex tourism and prostitution: Aspects of leisure, recreation, and work* (pp. 144-152). New York: Cognizant Communication.

Cultural Information Analysis Center, American University. 1966. *Minority groups in the Republic of Vietnam.* Washington, DC: Headquarters, Dept. of the Army.

Do, T. 1997. Popular Religion in contemporary southern Vietnam: A personal approach. *Sojourn, 12*(1):64-91.

---

*Non-Vietnamese scholars follow no standardized format for listing the author(s). The common practice of adding a comma after the first or second name leaves the reader without a clue as to which of the three names is the family name. Citations here follow the format used in our sources.

Fahey, S. 1998. Vietnam's women in the Renovation Era. In: K. Sen & M. Stivens, eds., *Gender and power in affluent Asia* (pp. 222-249). London/New York: Routledge.

"Frank." 2000. *On the legality of homosexuality in Vietnam.* [WWW document] http://www.utopia-asia.com/vietterm.htm (The VN-GBLF E-Mail Forum).

Franklin, B. 1993. *The risk of AIDS in Vietnam* (Monograph Series 1). Hanoi: Care International in Vietnam.

Gammeltoft, T. 1999. *Women's bodies, women's worries. Health and family planning in a Vietnamese rural community.* Richmond, VA: Curzon Press.

Goodkind, D. 1994 (November/December). Abortion in Vietnam: Measurements, puzzles, and concerns (Pt. 1). *Studies in Family Planning, 25*(6):342-352.

Goodkind, D. M. 1995 (March). Vietnam's one-or-two-child policy in action. *Population and Development Review, 21*(1):85-111, 217-218, 220.

Goodkind, D. 1996. State agendas, local sentiments: Vietnamese wedding practices amidst socialist transformations. *Social Forces, 75*(2):717-742.

Goodkind, D. 1997 (Spring). The Vietnamese double marriage squeeze. *International Migration Review, 31*(1):108-27.

Goodkind, D., & Anh, P. T. 1997 (December). Reasons for rising condom use in Vietnam. *International Family Planning Perspectives, 23*(4):173-178.

Greenberg, J. H. 1972. Venereal disease in the armed forces. *Medical Clinics of North America, 56*(5):1087-1100.

Gregersen, E. 1996. *The world of human sexuality.* New York: Irvington Publishers.

Guénel, A. 1997. Sexually transmitted diseases in Vietnam and Cambodia since the French Colonial Period. In: M. Lewis, S. Bamber, & M. Waugh, eds., *Sex, disease, and society. A comparative history of sexually transmitted diseases and HIV/AIDS in Asia and the Pacific* (pp. 139-153). Westport, CT/London: Greenwood Press.

Gulzow, M. & Mitchell, C. 1980 (October). "Vagina dentate" and "incurable venereal disease" legends from the Vietnam war. *Western Folklore.* 39:306-316.

Hickey, G. C. 1982a. *Sons of the mountains: Ethnohistory of the Vietnamese Central Highlands to 1954.* New Haven, CT: Yale University Press.

Hickey, G. C. 1982b. *Free in the forest: Ethnohistory of the Vietnamese Central Highlands, 1954-1976.* New Haven, CT: Yale University Press.

Hoang Ba Thinh. 1992. *Œsai Lech Trong Quan He Tinh Cam Khac Gioi Trong Sinh Vien: Bieu Hien, Nguyen Nhan Va Kien Nghi. Ky Yeu Hoi Thao Khoa Hoc "Doi Moi Cac Chinh Sach Xa Hoi Nham Khac Phuc Te Nam Xa Hoi Trong Dieu Kien Kinh Te Thi Truong."* Bo Noi Vu [Hanoi University].

Hoang, B. T. 1999. *Sexual exploitation of children.* Hanoi: The Gioi Publishers.

Hoang, B. & Ngoc, P. K. 1996. Teen-age sexuality in Vietnam. *Vietnam Social Sciences, 6*(56):57-69.

Joyeux, B. 1930. *Le péril vénérien et la prostitution a Hanoi.* Hanoi: Imprimerie d'Extrême-Orient.

Karim, W. J. 1995. Bilaterism and gender in Southeast Asia. In: W. J. Karim, ed., *"Male" and "female" in developing Southeast Asia* (pp. 35-74). Oxford/Washington, DC: Berg Publishers.

Khuat Thu Hong. 1998. *Study on sexuality in Vietnam: The known and unknown issues* (South & East Asia Regional Working Papers No. 11). Hanoi: Population Council.

Lebar, F. M., Hickey, G. C., & Musgrave, J. K. 1964. *Ethnic groups of mainland Southeast Asia.* New Haven, CT: Human Relations Area Files Press.

Mackay, J. 2000. *The Penguin atlas of human sexual behavior. Sexuality and sexual practice around the world.* New York/London: Penguin Group.

Marnais, P. 1967. *Saigon after dark.* New York: MacFadden-Bartell.

Mole, R. L. 1970. *The Montagnards of South Vietnam: A study of nine tribes.* Rutland Vermont: C. E. Tuttle Co.

Nguyen Huu Minh. 1997 (June). Age at first marriage in Viet Nam: Patterns and determinants. *Asia-Pacific Population Journal, 12*(2):49-74.

Nguyen Ngoc Huy and Ta Van Tai. 1987. *Le Code: Law in traditional Vietnam: A comparative Sino-Vietnamese legal study with historical-juridical analysis and annotations.* Athens, OH: Ohio University Press.

O'Harrow, S. 1995. Vietnamese women and Confucianism: Creating spaces from patriarchy. In: W. J. Karim, ed., *"Male" and "female" in developing Southeast Asia* (pp. 161-180). Oxford/Washington, DC: Berg Publishers.

Pelzer White, C. 1987. State, culture and gender: Continuity and change in women's position in rural Vietnam. In: H. Afshar, ed., *Women, state, and ideology: Studies from Africa and Asia* (pp. 226-234). Albany: State University of New York Press.

Proschan, F. 1998. *Filial piety and non-procreative male-to-male sex among Vietnamese.* Unpublished paper presented at the Annual meeting of the American Anthropological Association.

Proschan, F. 1999. *"Syphilis, opiomania, and pederasty": Colonial constructions of Vietnamese (and French) genders, sexualities, and social diseases.* Unpublished article.

Scholl-Latour, P. 2000. *Der tod im reisfeld. Dreißig jahre krieg in Indochina.* Muenchen, Germany: DTV.

Slote, W. H., & DeVos, G. A., eds. 1998. *Confucianism and the family.* Albany, NY: State University of New York Press.

Taylor, R. 1997. *The innocent.* Santa Barbara, CA: Fithian Press.

Truong, T. D. 1990. *Sex, money, and morality: Prostitution and tourism in Southeast Asia.* London: Atlantic Highlands; New York: Zed Books.

"Vinh N." 1999. *Vietnamese terms for homosexuality.* [WWW document] http://www.utopia-asia.com/vietterm.htm (The VN-GBLF E-Mail Forum).

WHO (World Health Organization), Western Pacific Regional Office. 1993. *Le SIDA dans la région du Pacifique occidental.* Manila: WHO.

Wijeyewardene, G., ed. 1990. *Ethnic groups across national boundaries in mainland Southeast Asia.* Singapore: Institute of Southeast Asian Studies.

X., Jacobus [as "A French Army-Surgeon"]. 1898. *Untrodden Fields of Anthropology by a French Army Surgeon; Observations on the Esoteric Manners and Customs of Semi-Civilized Peoples; Being a Record of Thirty Years Experience in Asia, Africa, America and Oceania* (Two volumes). Paris: Librairie de Médicine, Folklore et Anthropologie. [Second, enlarged English edition of *L'Amour aux colonies*, 1893; a facsimile edition was published by Robert F. Krieger Publishing Company, Huntington, NY, in 1972].

Young, S. B. 1998. The Orthodox Chinese Confucian social paradigm versus Vietnamese individualism (pp. 137-161). In: W. H. Slote & G. A. DeVos, eds., *Confucianism and the family.* Albany, NY: State University of New York Press.

Contributors

ROBERT T. FRANCOEUR, PH.D., A.C.S. (General Editor) Trained in embryology, evolution, theology, and the humanities, Dr. Francoeur's main work has been to synthesize and integrate the findings of primary sexological researchers. He is the author of twenty-two books, contributor to seventy-eight textbooks, handbooks, and encyclopedias, and the author of fifty-eight technical papers on various aspects of sexuality. His books include *The Scent of Eros: Mysteries of Odor in Human Sexuality* (1995), *Becoming a Sexual Person* (1982, 1984, 1991) and *Taking Sides: Clashing Views on Controversial Issues in Human Sexuality* (1987, 1989, 1991, 1993, 1995, 1997, 1999)—two college textbooks, *Utopian Motherhood: New Trends in Human Reproduction* (1970, 1974, 1977), *Eve's New Rib: 20 Faces of Sex, Marriage, and Family* (1972), *Hot and Cool Sex: Cultures in Conflict* (1974), and *The Future of Sexual Relations* (1974). He is editor-in-chief of *The Complete Dictionary of Sexology* (1991, 1995). A fellow of the Society for the Scientific Study of Sexuality and past president of the Society's Eastern Region, he is also a charter member of the American College of Sexology. He is currently professor of biological and allied health sciences at Fairleigh Dickinson University, Madison, New Jersey, U.S.A., adjunct professor in the doctoral Program in Human Sexuality at New York University, and professor in the New York University "Sexuality in Two Cultures" program in Copenhagen.

RAYMOND J. NOONAN, PH.D. (Associate Editor), is an instructor of human sexuality and health education and acting chairperson of the Health and Physical Education Department at the Fashion Institute of Technology of the State University of New York (FIT-SUNY) in Manhattan. He is also director of SexQuest/The Sex Institute, providing educational consulting in human sexuality and educational content for the World Wide Web, http://www.SexQuest.com/, on which he manages and edits *IES on the Web: Updates to the International Encyclopedia of Sexuality*. He is coeditor and author of *Does Anyone Still Remember When Sex Was Fun? Positive Sexuality in the Age of AIDS* (3rd edition, 1996). He has written and presented on sexuality in the environment of space, sexuality and the Internet, philosophy and sex, heterophobia and sex negativity in American culture, and sexual expression in musical lyrics. He contributed articles on sex surrogates and the impact of AIDS on our perception of sexuality to Robert T. Francoeur's *Sexuality in America: Understanding Our Sexual Values and Behavior* (1998), and to the *International Encyclopedia of Sexuality* (1997), which also included comments in its chapter on Brazil. In this volume of *IES*, he translated (with Sandra Almeida) the chapter on Morocco. Sex in space was the subject of his doctoral dissertation in the Human Sexuality Program at New York University.

Authors of Individual Chapters

Austria:

DR. ROTRAUD PERNER, L.L.D., is founder and director of the Training Program for Sexual and Social Life Counselors (GAMED), Vienna Academy for Holistic Medicine, and director of the training program for sexual and social counselors at the Verein fuer Prophylaktisches Gesundheitsarbeit (Association for Prophylactic Health Work), Linz. Following her graduate education and professional training/certification, Dr. Perner received her doctorate in law from the University of Vienna in 1967. She holds diplomas in psychoanalysis (1984) and systematic sexual therapy (1987), plus five other psychotherapeutic-related diplomas. In 1966, Dr. Perner became the first woman to be awarded the Paracelsus Ring for work in therapeutic communication, sexual therapy, and violence prevention. In addition to many publications and important affiliations, she is currently first chairperson of the Austrian Society for Sexology and a member of the University of Vienna Department of Education. Her main research focuses on the exercise and balance of power in gender relationships.

Colombia:

JOSÉ MANUEL GONZÁLEZ, M.A., is director of *Revista Latinoamericana de Sexologia*, graduate director for sexual education at Simón Bolivar University and director of the González Clinique, the latter two in Barranquilla, Colombia. He has a bachelor's degree in psychology from the University del Norte (1975), a master's degree from the University del Valle de Guatmala (1977), and his doctorate from the University of Habana (Cuba) in 2000. He is the author of *Educacion de la Sexualidad* (Barranquilla: Club del Libro, 1994).

RUBÉN ARDILA, PH.D., a practicing psychologist, is director of the *Revista Latinoamericana de Psicologia*, president of the *Fundacion para el Avance de la Psicologia*, a professor and researcher at the National University of Colombia, and author of various books on human behavior

PEDRO GUERRERO, M.D., a psychiatrist and sexual therapist, is director of the National Project of Sexual Education in the Colombian National Ministry of Education. He is the author of various books on human sexuality.

GLORIA PENAGOS, M.D., a gynecologist and sexual educator, teaches and does research at the University of Antioquia. She is also a member of the board of directors of the Colombian Society of Sexologists.

BERNARDO USECHE, PH.D., is a psychologist, sexual therapist, director of the graduate program in sexual education at the University of Caldas, and author of various investigations and books about human sexuality.

Croatia:

ALEKSANDAR ŠTULHOFER, PH.D., is chair and assistant professor of sociology at the University of Zagreb. The author of *The Invisible Hand of Transition* (2000), editor or co-editor of *Sociology and War* (1992), *Sociology of Everyday Life* (1993), and *Social Capital and Transition in Croatia* (1998), he currently teaches Sociology of Sexuality and Sociology of Culture at the University of Zagreb. His latest research projects are a rapid assessment study on trafficking in women in Croatia and a quantitative cross-cultural study of adolescent sexuality.

GORDAN BOSANAC. A physicist at the R. Boskovic Institute, he also teaches a course on culture, technology, and communications at the Peace Studies in Zagreb. He is an active member of the Anti-War Campaign Croatia.

GORDANA BULJAN-FLANDER, M.A., holds a master's degree in psychology from the University of Zagreb and in integrative psychotherapy from the Sherwood Training Institute and University of Derby, U.K.. Ms. Buljan-Flander is a psychologist/psychotherapist at Psycho-trauma Center, Children's Hospital Zagreb since 1981, coordinator, educator, and supervisor on the Prevention and Intervention in the Field of Child Abuse project and head of the hotline for abused and neglected children. She also provides clinical training for the Department of Psychology and Medical School for Nurses (University of Zagreb), and lectures at postgraduate studies in domestic violence, Police Academy. She is the author of *Hyperactive Child* (1997).

VLASTA HIRŠL-HECEJ, M.D., M.A., is consultant epidemiologist, the head of the Department of Reproductive Health, and chief of the Division of Epidemiology and Health Statistics in Children's Hospital Zagreb, University of Zagreb Medical School. She has published over thirty scientific and professional papers on the health problems of children and adolescents, as well as reproductive health and family planning in Croatia. Her research interests include public health and preventive programs promoting adolescents' general and reproductive health, sexual behavior, and sex education. During the last decade, Dr Hiršl-Hecej's department has authored several publications educating Croatian adolescents about responsible sexuality.

PETRA HOBLAJ recently graduated in sociology (University of Zagreb). Aside from her research activities on prostitution and trafficking in Croatia, she works as a journalist and a program supervisor at a county radio station.

IVANKA IVKANEC holds a B.A. in ethnology and sociology from the University of Zagreb. She works as an expert adviser with the Museum of Ethnology in Zagreb, where she has organized 18 exhibitions, two of which explored sexual mores and relevant folk traditions in Croatia. Her work has been the inspiration for a documentary TV sequel titled *Folk Intimacy*.

ALEKSANDRA KORAC, PH.D., assistant professor of family law at the Faculty of Law, University of Zagreb, is a member of the working committee of the Ministry of Labor and Social Welfare for the Proposal of the Family Act (enacted in 1999), a member of the working committee of the Ministry of Health for the proposal of the laws concerning human procreation (assisted procreation, abortion, sterilization, and educational measurements), and a member of the working group of the Government of the Republic of Croatia for the implementation of the European Convention for the Protection of Human Rights and Fundamental Freedoms (1996-1998).

MAJA MAMULA, M.A., works at the Center for Women War Victims as counselor, trainer, and coordinator of the Women's Counseling Center. Ms. Mamula has been training and supervising women's groups and SOS lines on the issues of domestic violence and sexual violence for years. She has authored several manuals: *Violence Against Women* (Society for Psychological Assistance, 1999); *Self-Help Groups* (Center for Women War Victims, 2000); and *Sexual Violence* (Center for Women War Victims, 2000) and a book, *Overcome Your Shyness* (1998).

ZELJKO MRKŠIC studied sociology and works as a publisher and NGO activist.

SANJA SAGASTA, a graduate student at the University of Zagreb, Department of Croatian Language and Literature, is a poet and a lesbian human rights activist, as well as a co-founder of numerous lesbian projects and initiatives in Croatia.

HRVOJE TILJAK, M.D., PH.D., completed his training in general practice/family medicine at the University of Zagreb and the University of Antwerp (Belgium). Presently, he is a senior lecturer at the Department of Family Medicine, University of Zagreb Medical School, and works part time as a family medicine practitioner. In 1996, he was one of the organizers of the continuing medical education course *Sexual Problems in Family Practice*, the first of its kind at the University of Zagreb Medical School.

Cyprus:

GEORGE JOHN GEORGIOU, PH.D., the only certified sexologist on the island of Cyprus, is director of the Natural Therapy Center in Larnaca. He earned his bachelor of science degree in biology and psychology at Oxford (U.K.), a master of science degree in clinical psychology at Surrey (U.K.), and a doctorate in clinical sexology from the Institute for the Advanced Study of Human Sexuality in San Francisco, with extensive training in homeopathic medicine in London. He is also a fellow of the American Academy of Clinical Sexologists, and a diplomate of the American Board of Sexology and Sex Therapists. He was the main researcher for two WHO studies on HIV/AIDS and on drugs. Other research has dealt with sex and religion, herbal medicine, and nutrition. He is the author of a 1995 book in Greek on *Premature Ejaculation.*

ALECOS F. MODINOS, B.Arch., A.R.I.B.A., is cofounder and president of the Gay Liberation Movement of Cyprus, founder and member of the AIDS Solidarity Movement of Cyprus, and contact person for Cyprus to the European Council of AIDS Service Organizations (EUROCASO). A chartered architect, he earned his degree from the University of Strathclyde, Glascow, Scotland.

NATHANIEL PAPAGEORGIOU, a career police officer with more than 35 years field experience, is assistant chief of police (Support Services) in Nicosia.

LAURA PAPANTONIOU, M.Sc.(epidemiology), M.D., is Senior Medical Officer, Department of Medical and Public Health Services, the Ministry of Health, Nicosia. She is also editor of *Health for All,* a public service journal published by the Ministry of Health. Trained in medicine in Lille, France, she is the focal point for women's affairs in the Ministry.

NICOS PERISTIANIS, PH.D.(hon.), is executive dean of Intercollege and president of the Cyprus Sociological Association. With graduate studies in the United Kingdom and United States, his main research interest is in the sociology of social change, social institutions, and ethnic and cultural identity.

Egypt:

BAHIRA SHERIF, PH.D. A cultural anthropologist who has done fieldwork in Egypt, Dr. Sherif is an assistant professor of Individual and Family Studies at the University of Delaware. After receiving a bachelor's degree from Yale University, she did her doctoral studies at the University of Pennsylvania. Her research has dealt with aspects of ethnically diverse families, Islam, gender issues in the Middle East, intergenerational relations, and women's employment. Her publications include "Islamic Families in America: Diversity and Uniformity in the Family Experience" for Harriette Pipes' *Family Ethnicity: Strength in Diversity* (1999), "Treat Your Elders with Respect and Kindness: The Islamic Model." in *Aging in Africa: Colonial and Post-Colonial Representations,* edited by Mario Aguilar (1999), and "Understanding the Rights of Women: The Egyptian Example," in *Women's Rights in an International Perspective* (L. Walters, ed. 1999). She also authored "The Prayer of a Married Man Is Equivalent to Seventy Prayers of a Single Man: The Significance of Marriage to Muslim Egyptians" in *Journal of Family Issues* (1999) and "When a Father Goes to Jail: Legal Latitude and the Implications of Cross-Cultural Issues" in *Practicing Anthropology* (1999).

Hong Kong:

EMIL MAN-LUN NG, M.D., is a professor in the Department of Psychiatry at the University of Hong Kong. He is vice-president of the Hong Kong Sex Education Association and served as president of the Fourteenth World Congress of Sexology held in Hong Kong in August 1999. A member of the Royal College of Psychiatrists (U.K.) since 1976, he received his M.D. from the University of Hong Kong in 1992. He is a fellow of the Hong Kong College of Psychiatrists, the Royal College of Psychiatrists (U.K.), the American College of Sexologists, the Hong Kong Academy of Medicine (Psychiatry), and the Royal Australian and New Zealand College of Psychiatrists. Dr. Ng's main areas of research are Chinese sexual attitudes and culture and sex education and therapy for the Chinese. He is coeditor with D. L. Liu of *A Dictionary of Sexology* (Taipei: Wen-He, 1996) and with M. Y. Deng, D. Ming, and E. H. W. Yen, coeditor of *Practical Sexual Medicine,* published by the International Association of Chinese Medical Specialists and Psychologists (New York, 1998), both in Chinese. Dr. Ng is also a coeditor of *Chung-Kuo Tang Tai Hsing Wen Hua,* and coeditor with E. Haeberle of the English-language edition, *Sexual Behavior in Modern China: Report of the Nationwide Survey of 20,000 Men and Women* (New York:

Continuum, 1997). (Contact: Queen Mary Hospital, University of Hong Kong, Psychiatry Dept., Hong Kong; nml@i.am.)

JOYCE L. C. MA, PH.D., is a senior lecturer and associate professor in the Department of Social Work at the Chinese University of Hong Kong. She is also a faculty member of Family Studies, Hong Kong, a branch of Family Studies, New York, and a social work member of the Gender Identity Team, Sex Clinic, Department of Psychiatry, the University of Hong Kong. She obtained a bachelor's and a master's degree in social sciences, the latter with distinction, and a doctorate in 1995, all from the University of Hong Kong. Since 1994, she has trained as a family therapist with Dr. Salvador Minuchin, founder of structural family therapy. Focusing her clinical and research interests on couple and family therapy, she has published 21 journal papers and contributed chapters to eleven books. (Contact: joycelai@cuhk.edu.hk.)

Iceland:

SÓLEY S. BENDER, R.N., B.S.N., M.S., coordinator and main author of the Iceland chapter, is assistant professor of nursing at the University of Iceland. She is currently helping to develop clinical guidelines for emergency contraception and chairing a working group of the Icelandic Association for Sexual and Reproductive Health developing a sex education curriculum for young people 16 to 20 years old. As a nurse specialist for the Icelandic Association for Sexual and Reproductive Health, she coordinates sexual and reproductive counseling for young people and does educational and counseling work. She holds a bachelor of science degree in nursing from the University of Iceland (1973), a master of science degree in Family Planning Administration from the University of Minnesota (1983), and is a doctoral candidate at the Department of Medicine at the University of Iceland. She has edited, co-authored, and authored several articles and major reports on her main research interest, the sexual and reproductive health of Iceland's young people.

GUDRÚN JÓNSDÓTTIR, PH.D., a retired professor of social work, earned his doctorate in social work at the University of Sheffield in the U.K. His main research interest is sexual violence against women and children, and studies of incest survivors' experiences of abuse in Iceland and Britain.

SIGRÚN JÚLÍIUSDÓTTIR, PH.D., is professor and chief of social work education at the University of Iceland. She graduated from the School of Social Work, University of Lund, Sweden (1970) and completed a Phil. Cand. degree in social sciences, Department of Sociology, University of Stockholm. She holds a master's degree in Social Work from the University of Michigan (1978) and a Ph.D. in social work, University of Gothenburg, Sweden (1993). A licensed psychotherapist in private practice, Dr. Juliusdottir is a member of the American Family Therapy Academy, the Swedish Association of Supervisors, and the Icelandic Association of Sexology. Her main area of research is family matters, intimate interaction, and divorce issues.

THORVALDUR KRISTINSSON is a leading figure in the Icelandic gay movement and presently the chairman of Samtökin 78, the Lesbian and Gay Association of Iceland.

Indonesia:

RAMSEY ELKHOLY, PH.D. (cand.) is completing his doctoral studies in ecological anthropology at the University of Manchester in the U.K. His main area of research focuses on hunter-gatherers, with an emphasis on Sumatran groups, their sociality, and environmental perceptions. His main fieldwork has been with the Orang-Rimba indigenous forest people of Indonesia. His paper on "Hunter-Gatherers, Native Ecologies and Human Sociality" is forthcoming in the *Journal of the Royal Anthropological Institute* (U.K.).

WIMPIE PANGKAHILA, M.D., PH.D., a lecturer in the Medical School and secretary of the Study Group on Human Reproduction of Udayana University (Bali, Indonesia), is also chairperson of the Indonesian Society of Andrology in Bali. As an andrologist and sexologist, he specializes in infertility, adolescent sexuality, and sexual dysfunctions. He is author of *What You Should Know About Sex* (1981), *About the Sexual Problem in the Family* (1988), *Discussing Sexual Problems in the Family* (1991), *We and Sex* (1991), and *Some Sexual Problems in the Female* (1991).

Italy:

BRUNO P. F. WANROOIJ, PH.D., is professor of history and social sciences at Syracuse University in Italy and at Georgetown University at Villa Le Balze. After a cum laude degree in history from the University of Amsterdam, the Netherlands, he received his doctorate in history and civilization from the European University Institute, Florence, Italy. His main interests are in the history of sexuality, family, and mentalities (ideas). He is the author of *Storia del Pudore: La Questione Sessuale in Italia (1860-1940)* (Venezia: Marsilio, 1990). Among his many recent articles are: "Italy. Sexuality, Morality, and Public Authority in Italy," "Universalismo Versus Cosmopolitismo. I Cattolici Italiani e Hollywood," "Back to the Future. Gender, Morality and Modernization in Twentieth Century Italy," "Impariamo ad Amare'. L'Avvio della Consulenza Matrimoniale in Italia (1948-1975)," "Soyez des Hommes'. Appunti sulla Crisi della Virilità 1930-1960," and "La Passione Svelata. Sessualità, Crimine ed Educazione in Italia tra '800 e '900."

Morocco:

NADIA KADIRI, M.D., is a psychiatrist in the University Psychiatric Center in Casablanca and a member of the Scientific Committee of the Moroccan Society of Sexology.

ABDERRAZAK MOUSSAÏD, M.D., founded the Moroccan Society of Sexology. A medical doctor at the University of Casablanca, he specializes in psychosomatic medicine and sexology. He also holds a díplome-inter-universitaire de sexologie from the Faculté de Médicine de Paris XIII-Boigny.

ABDELKRIM TIRRAF, M.D., a specialist in male erectile problems, sterility, and sexual maladies, Dr. Tirraf holds a diplomé in andrology from the Université de Paris. A member of the Moroccan Society of Sexology, he maintains a private medical practice in Casablanca.

Nigeria:

UWEM EDIMO ESIET, M.B., M.P.H., a public health physician, has spent over ten years promoting sexual health in Nigeria. He has served on the task force on producing the *National Guidelines for Sexuality Education in Nigeria* and on the committee responsible for producing the Sexuality Education Curriculum for use in Nigerian schools. A leading commentator on sexuality in Nigeria, he is an alternate member of the National Working Group on adolescent health in Nigeria and is co-founder, chapter coordinator, and medical director of Action Health Incorporated (AHI) in Lagos, one of Nigeria's largest and most effective NGOs working for adolescent reproductive health. In 1996, AHI helped to coordinate the first Nigerian National Conference on Adolescent Reproductive Health and, as follow up to that meeting, successfully lobbied the Nigerian Ministry of Education to approve the integration of sexuality education into the Nigerian secondary school curriculum and the adoption of the sexuality education guidelines for Nigerian schools.

CHRISTINE OLUNFINKE ADEBAJO, PH.D., is deputy general secretary of the National Association of Nigerian Nurses and Midwives (NANNM), director of the Health Services Consultancy, president of the Federation of Female Nurses and Midwives of Nigeria (FENAM), and vice president of Nigeria's National Council for Population Activities. She has authored two books on female circumcision and strategies for its eradication, as well as co-authoring *Women's Health Issues in Nigeria* (1992) and *Traditional Practices of Child Marriage, Teenage Pregnancy, and Nutritional Taboos* (1989).

IBIRONKE AKINSETE. Professor Akinsete is president of the Society for Women and AIDS in Africa Nigerian Chapter (SWAAN).

MAIRO VICTORIA BELLO is project director and coordinator for the Adolescent Health and Information Project in Tarauni, Kano, Nigeria. An officer of Women for Independence, Self-Sufficiency, and Economic Advancement (WISSEA), her research has focused on adolescent sexuality and socialization, sexual violence and abuse, and women's health and reproductive track infections, as well as on broader women's issues in politics and economics.

RAKIYA BOOTH, M.B.B.S., is director of primary health care services of the Christian Health Association of Nigeria in Jos. A diplomate of dermatology and fellow of the East African College of Physicians, her specialization is in STD and AIDS education.

IMO I. ESIET, ESQ., B.SC.(HONS), L.L.B.(HONS), B.L., is a member of the Nigerian Bar Association and a counselor and legal advisor involved in women's rights.

NIKE ESIET, B.SC., M.H.P (Harvard), a journalist and former public relations officer for the Society for Women and AIDS, Nigeria Chapter (SWAAN), Mrs. Esiet was educated in Nigeria and Harvard. She is now the project director and co-founder of Lagos-based Action Health Incorporated (AHI), one of Nigeria's largest and most effective NGOs working for adolescent reproductive health. Since 1989, she has built AHI from an idea into a vibrant organization that combines community education, a reproductive health clinic, and a multifaceted youth center with in-school programs and work at the policy level, to change the way that adolescent health and sexuality is thought of, communicated, and taught throughout Nigeria. Her work has been supported by a three-year "social entrepreneur" fellowship from the U.S.-based Ashoka: Innovators for the Public and support from the MacArthur Foundation.

MRS. FOYIN OYEBOLA earned her B.Sc. in nursing and an M.A. in family planning and program administration. She is currently program officer at the Planned Parenthood Federation of Nigeria National Headquarters in Lagos, and a member of the Campaign Against Unwanted Pregnancy (C.A.U.P.) in Lagos.

BILKISU YUSUF, a journalist, media administrator, and social activist, received his master of arts degree from the University of Wisconsin and an advanced diploma in journalism from the Moscow Institute of Journalism. He has contributed to various books, with chapters on such topics as "Challenges of the Muslim Women," "Hausa Fulani Women: The State of the Struggle," "Challenges Facing Muslim Women in Secular States," and "The Impact of Islam and Culture on Marriage Age in Hausa Society."

Norway:

ELSA ALMÅS, Cand. Psychol. at the University of Bergen, is a specialist in clinical psychology in private practice. She is president of both the Norwegian Society for Clinical Sexology and the Nordic Association for Clinical Sexology, a member of the Harry Benjamin International Gender Dysphoria Association, and member of the Resource and Reference Group for Sexual Dysfunctions in Norway. Almås's clinical and research interests include psychotherapy, sex and family therapy, education in sexology, health politics, gender issues, and public sex education. She authored *Den Skjulte Lyst* (*The Hidden Desire*) (Oslow: Faktum Forlag, 1987), and with Esben Esther Pirelli Benestad, co-authored *Sexologi i Praksis* (*Sexology in Practice*) (Oslo: Tano Ascehoug, 1997). Almås has authored and co-authored many professional research papers. (Contact: Grimstad MPAT-Institute, Storgaten 42, 4876 Grimstad, Norway; elsa.almas@sexologi.com.)

ESBEN ESTHER PIRELLI BENESTAD, M.D., a general practitioner (University of Oslo) and family therapist in private practice, is a board member of the Norwegian Society for Clinical Sexology and a member of the Harry Benjamin International Gender Dysphoria Association and the Nordic Group for Developing Sexological Education and Authorisation. Benestad's main research and clinical work is in general health service, family and sex therapy, psychotherapy, education, and supervision in sexology, public sex education, and counseling in gender issues. Among his many publications, Benestad has authored several articles on transvestism. (Contact: Grimstad MPAT-Institute, Storgaten 42, 4876 Grimstad, Norway; esben.benestad@sexologi.com or esther.pirelli@sexologi.com.)

Outer Space:

RAYMOND J. NOONAN, PH.D. worked with Robert T. Francoeur on the four-volume *International Encyclopedia of Sexuality* (1997, 2001), on this fourth volume as associate editor. Since 1987, he has presented his ideas and research on the need for sex research in space at numerous conferences, including those of the Aerospace Medical Association (AsMA), the Society for the Scientific Study of Sexuality (SSSS), the National Space Society (NSS), and the American Association of Sex Educators, Counselors, and Therapists (AASECT). A recent article, "Sexuality and Space: Theoretical Considerations for Extended Spaceflight," is under review by the AsMA journal, *Aviation, Space, and Environmental Medicine*. Sex in space was the subject of his doctoral dissertation in 1998 in the Human Sexuality Program at New York University. His fuller biographical sketch appears at the beginning of this Contributors' section.

Papua New Guinea:

SHIRLEY OLIVER-MILLER. As Senior Program Officer II, Margaret Sanger Center International, Planned Parenthood of New York City, since 1980, Shirley Oliver-Miller has been responsible for managing government and non-government projects, and developing and implementing program strategies around reproductive and sexual health issues. She has worked in 37 countries, developing programs for government and non-governmental agencies around population health. Author of more than a dozen training manuals, she has trained thousands of professionals, with support from the United States Agency for International Development (USAID), United Nations Funds for Population Activities (UNFPA), International Planned Parenthood Federation (IPPF), Family Health International, Planned Parenthood Federation of America (PPFA), Johns Hopkins University, Population Council, Pathfinder International, and the World Health Organization (WHO). Her work has focused on sexuality, family life education, AIDS/STDs, traditional practices, adolescent health, women's empowerment, gender roles, male involvement, parent education, and more.

The Philippines:

JOSE FLORANTE J. LEYSON, M.S., M.D., F.A.C.S., FACCS, FABFM, is director of the Sexual Dysfunction Center, Spinal Cord Injury Service, Department of Veterans Affairs, New Jersey Health Care Systems, East Orange. Chairman of the American College of Clinical Sexologists for Licensure in New Jersey State, he edited *Sexual Rehabilitation of the Spinal-Cord-Injured Patient* (Humana Press 1991). He is a member of the Medical Expert Advisory Panel (Sexology and Urology), New Jersey Board of Medical Examiners, and medical director of the North Jersey Impotence Center, Jersey City, New Jersey. In 1988, he was the recipient of the Most Outstanding Filipino Overseas Award (National Sex Institute, Washington, DC) and the 1986 Filipino Physician of the Year Award from the Department of Veterans Affairs, East Orange, New Jersey.

Portugal:

NUNO NODIN, M.A., is a counsellor at the Associação para o Planeamento Familiar (Portuguese Family Planning Association) and the Sexualidade em Linha (telephone help-line for adolescents), both in Lisboa (Lisbon). He also teaches at the Instituto Superior de Psicologia Aplicada, Lisboa. He holds a certificate as a psychologist and a master's degree in health psychology, both from the Instituto Superior de Psicologia Aplicada, Lisbon. He has trained in sexuality and counselling with the Associação para o Planeamento da Família and in the psychological and social aspects of AIDS with the Instituto Superior de Psicologia Aplicada. A member of the Sociedade Portuguesa de Psicologia da Saúde (Portuguese Society of Health Psychology), the Associação Portuguesa de Análise Bio Energética (Portuguese Bio-Energetic Analysis Association), and the International Institute for Bioenergetic Analysis, his main areas of interest are human sexuality, sexuality education, sexual and reproductive health, psychotherapy, and counselling. His chapter, "Do Desejo Homossexual à Identidade Sexual: A Invenção de uma Diferença" ("From the Homosexual Desire to the Homosexual Identity: The Invention of a Difference"), appeared in a book edited by I. Leal (Lisbon: Instituto Superior de Psicologia Aplicada, 1997).

SARA MOREIRA is a sex education counsellor at the Associação para o Planeamento da Família (Portuguese Family Planning Association) and a counsellor at Sexualidade em Linha (telephone help-line for adolescents). In additional to training in international relations at the Instituto Superior de Ciências do Trabalho e da Empresa, Lisbon, Ms. Moreira trained in sexuality and counselling at the Associação para o Planeamento da Família, and in pregnancy and maternity psychology. Her main work has been in youth counselling at the Family Planning Association and sexuality help-line, peer-education youth training in sexuality projects, the Family Planning Association Project on Child and Adolescents Sexual Abuse, and the Family Planning Association Co-operation Project with Portuguese-speaking countries.

ANA MARGARIDA OURÔ is a clinical psychologist in a military rest home for adult men with severe disabilities. Her clinical and research interests include women's psychology, rape and battered women, domestic violence, and handicaps and disability. Her graduate education and professional training includes certification as a psychologist by the Instituto Superior de Psicologia Aplicada in Lisbon, post-graduate training in health psychology at the same institute, education in psychopharmacology, pregnancy and maternity psychology, and certification in couple relationships and human sexuality. Among her recent publications are a study of the psychology of pregnant HIV-positive women (2000), and "O Ventre Sacia-Se, Os Olhos Não: O Suporte Social em Adolescentes Que Prosseguiram a Gravidez e Mulheres Que Recorreram à Interrupção Voluntária de Gravidez na Adolescência" ("The Womb Is Satisfied, the Eyes Are Not: Social Support in Adolescents Who Carried Their Pregnancy to Term and Women Who Interrupted Their Pregnancy") (*Análise Psicológica*, Lisbon, 1998).

South Korea:

HYUNG-KI CHOI, M.D., PH.D. Dr. Choi is currently the director of the Sex Clinic at Yonsei Medical Center and the president of the Asian Federation of Sexology. He is one of the founders of the Asia-Pacific Society for Impotence Research (APSIR) and served the president for the APSIR. Since the 1980s, he has been actively involved in the field of erectile dysfunction research and has published numerous articles in that area. He is one of the leading scholars and therapists in the world in sexual impotence.

HUSO YI is a doctoral candidate in the Professional Program in Human Sexuality of the Department of Health Studies at New York University. His main interest is the area of sexual orientation and East Asian sexualities. He has given a number of professional presentations about East Asian gay men, published books about gay issues in Korea, and reviewed the HIV-patient's guide of Asian Pacific Islander Coalition on HIV/AIDS in the U.S. He is now preparing his doctoral dissertation about sexuality identity of Korean lesbians, gay men, and bisexuals.

WHASON BYUN is the director of the Family, Health, and Welfare Division of the Korean Women's Development Institute (KWDI) and lecturer on women's policy at Seong-Sin Women's University. She graduated from Yonsei University and has a doctoral degree from the University of V, Rene Descartes, Paris, in demography and sociology of family. She has published on women's and family issues.

PILWHA CHANG has played a key role in the development of women's studies and is affiliated with various women's organizations. She is a graduate of Ewha Woman's University and earned a Ph.D. from Sussex University. She was the commissioner for the Presidential Commission of Women's Affairs in 1998, founder of the Asian Center for Women's Studies in 1995, and a professor of the Department of Women's Studies, Graduate School of Ewha University from 1984 to the present. In addition, she is the director for the Korean Women's Institute and Asian Center for Women's Studies and the chair for the Som Adhoc Committee for Gender Integration of APEC (Asia Pacific Economic Cooperation).

KI-NAM CHIN is an associate professor of health administration at Yonsei University.

JUNGIM HWANG is a research fellow at Korean Women's Development Institute.

YUNG-CHUNG KIM has been actively involved in academics, politics, and non-governmental organizations. A graduate from Ewha Woman's University with a master of arts degree from the University of Toronto and a Ph.D. from Indiana University, she was a professor of history and dean of the Graduate School at Ewha Woman's University. From 1977 to 1983, she served as the director of the Korean Women's Institute. In the mid-1980s, she was president of the Korean Women's Development Institute, the Minister of Political Affairs II, and the vice president of the Korean National Red Cross. Currently, she is on the United Nations Committee for the Convention on the Elimination of All Forms of Discrimination Against Women.

Turkey:

HAMDULLAH AYDIN, M.D., is a professor of psychiatry at the Gulhane Military Medical Academy and Faculty of Medicine in Ankara, Turkey. Following a residency in psychiatry, he pursued postdoctoral study and research at Baylor College of Medicine in Houston, Texas, in 1983 and 1984. Although his main research interest is in sleep disorders, much of his clinical work and education focuses on sexual dysfunctions, neuropsychology, and neurophysiology. Among his recent professional articles (in Turkish) are *Sexuality and Sexual Function* (1998) and *Psychopharmacological Treatment in Sexual Dysfunctions* (1998). He serves on the editorial board of various scientific journals in Turkey.

ZEYNEP GÜLÇAT, PH.D., completed her doctorate in clinical psychology in Ankara in 1995. She is currently a clinical psychologist at the Gulhane Military Medical Academy and Faculty of Medicine in Ankara, Turkey. Her main interest is in sexual dysfunctions and neuropsychology. Among her recent professional publications (in Turkish) are *A Study on the Psychology of Impotence* (1995), *Paraphilias and Incest* (1998), and *Sexual Identity and Sexual Orientation Disorders* (1998).

Vietnam:

JAKOB PASTOETTER, M.A., PH.D. (cand.) a 1998-2000 Visiting Scholar at the Kinsey Institute for Research in Sex, Gender, and Reproduction in Bloomington, Indiana, holds a master of arts degree in cultural anthropology and is a doctoral student in human ontogenetics at Humboldt University, Berlin. A member of Deutsche Gesellschaft für Sozialwissenschaftliche Sexualforschung (DGSS), his main research interests lie in the historical and contemporary social and cultural aspects of sexuality. He recently published an article on "Pornography as Academic Field of Research" (*Pornographie als akademisches Forschungsfeld*) in *Sexualmedizin* (September, 2000; *22*:247-250).

Brief Identifications for Contributors of Supplemental Notes:

Brazil: Luciane Raibin, M.A., a native of Brazil and young sexologist at Fairleigh Dickinson University (Madison, NJ); e-mail: Raibin@usa.net.

China: Fang-fu Ruan, M.D., Ph.D., co-author of the China chapter, *IES* volume 1, and chairperson of Oriental studies at the Institute for the Advanced Study of Human Sexuality, San Francisco; e-mail: ruanff@yahoo.com.

Germany: Jakob Pastoetter, M.A., cultural anthropologist and doctoral student in human ontogenetics at Humboldt University, Berlin; e-mail: jmpastoetter@crosswinds.net.

India: Karen Pechilis-Prentiss, Ph.D., professor of religion at Drew University (Madison, NJ), does fieldwork and researches gender roles and women in India; e-mail: kpechili@drew.edu.

Iran: Paul Drew, Ph.D., cultural anthropologist and author of Iran chapter, *IES* volume 2; e-mail: spid@nac.net.

Israel: Ronny A. Shtarkshall, Ph.D., co-author of the Israel chapter, *IES* volume 2, and professor of social medicine at Hebrew University; e-mail: ronys@md2.huji.ac.il.

Japan: Yoshimi Kaji, M.A., contributor to the Japan chapter, *IES* volume 2, now working for the Japanese Association for Sex Education; e-mail: ykaji@crocus.ocn.ne.jp.

Polynesia: Anne Bolin, Ph.D., author of the French Polynesia chapter, *IES* volume 2, and professor of cultural anthropology at Elon College in North Carolina; e-mail: Anne.Bolin@elon.edu.

Russia: Igor S. Kon, Ph.D., author of the Russia chapter, *IES* volume 2, and chief researcher at the Institute for Ethnography and Anthropology, the Russian Academy of Sciences; e-mail: igor_kon@mail.ru.

South Africa: Lionel John Nicholas, Ph.D., co-author of South Africa, *IES* volume 3, and senior psychologist/lecturer at the University of the Western Cape, Bellville, South Africa; e-mail: lnicholas@chs.uwc.ac.za.

United Kingdom: Kevan R. Wylie, M.B., coordinator and author of several sections of the United Kingdom chapter in *IES* volume 3, and a specialist in sexual medicine at the Clinic in Sheffield; e-mail: k.r.wylie@sheffield.ac.uk.

Also contributing to the U.K. chapter and Supplemental Notes: Anthony Bains, B.A., gay men's community worker; Dinesh Bhugra; Mary Griffin, M.Sc., coordinator of couple relationship and sexual dysfunction at London's Institute of Psychiatry; Margot Huish, B.A., sexual relationship therapist at Barnet General Hospital; George Kinghorn, M.D., clinical director for communicable diseases at Central Sheffield University Hospitals; Jane Morgan; Helen Mott, Ph.D., sexual harassment specialist; Fran Reader, consultant in family planning and reproductive health at Ipswich Hospital; Jose von Buhler, specialist in human sexuality and relationship psychotherapy at the Cardinal Clinic, Berkshire; Stephen Whittle, Ph.D., lecturer in law at Manchester Metropolitan University.

Index

This index is designed to help the reader quickly locate parallel discussions of specific topics in the 51 countries contained in the first three volumes of *The International Encyclopedia of Sexuality*, this fourth volume, and the countries and Supplemental Notes on our SexQuest Web site. This Index enables the reader to compare an issue, such as "sexuality education" or "contraception," in 51 countries. It also provides a more conventional guide to issues and topics, which are peculiar to certain cultures or countries. Sexual harassment, for instance, is a major issue in Europe and North America, but hardly or not at all recognized in some South American, African, Eastern European, and Asian societies. Similarly, female circumcision, woman-woman, and leviratate marriages are issues in a few countries, but not in others. Although this Index is a handy guide to all major issues, it is not comprehensive because of space limitations. This Index can be used in conjunction with the outline of the main topics provided on the first page of all chapters. A familiarity with the detailed content outline given in the section "Using This Encyclopedia," on pages 15 and 16 of volume 1, will also help the reader pursue specific information, because all chapters are structured on this detailed outline.

References to topics in **volumes 1-3** include the country name and page number.

References to topics in **volume 4** include the country name, "iv:" and page number; Outer Space iv: indicates the chapter on Outer Space; Philippines iv: indicates The Philippines.

References to **Hong Kong** and **Norway** include the country name, "sq:" and the page number on www.SexQuest.com.

References to **Supplemental Notes**, which update countries covered in volumes 1-3, include the country name and "sqsp" indicating the Supplemental Notes on www.SexQuest.com.

aboriginal peoples Argentina 35; Australia 107-13; Brazil 217-9; Canada 226, 325-6; Indonesia iv:301-22; Papua iv:493-513

abortion Argentina 69-70; Australia 102-3, 112; Austria iv:37; Bahrain 168; Brazil 210-11; Canada 231-306-9; China 371, 388; Colombia iv:72-7; Croatia iv:111; Cyprus iv:130, 166-8; Czech/Slovakia 413; Egypt iv:210; Finland 47304; Germany 513-4; Ghana 541-2; Greece 561-2; Hong Kong sq:236; Iceland iv:237; India 600; Indonesia 617, iv:265, 290; Iran 644; Ireland 667-8; Israel 723-7; Italy iv:318-20; Japan 832-3; Kenya 863-4; Mexico 886-7; Morocco iv:342; Netherlands 944-5; Nigeria iv:405; Norway sq:465; Outer Space iv:426; Papua iv:392; Philippines iv:491; Poland 977-9; Portugal iv:532; Puerto Rico 1037; Russia 1070-1; S.Africa 1109-10, 1125-6; S.Korea iv:557, 590; Spain 1162-3; Sweden 1187-8; Thailand 1252-3; Turkey iv:629; Ukraine 1297; United Kingdom 1352-5; USA 1382, 1414, 1422, 1606-11; Vietnam iv:682

abstinence, sexual India sqsp

acquired immune deficiency syndrome (AIDS) See: HIV/AIDS

adolescents, sexual activities of Argentina 44-8; Australia 93-4; Austria iv:20, 26; Bahrain 134-5, 139-40, 150; Brazil 195-6, 217-9; Canada 251-6, 275-7, 322-5; China 356-7, 381-5; Colombia iv:58, 63; Croatia iv:94, 100-5; Cyprus iv:142, 152-61; Czech/Slovakia 404-5, 407; Egypt iv:196, 206; Finland 433, 436-42; Germany 498-502; Ghana 526-8; Greece 553; Hong Kong sq:225; Iceland iv:227; India 588-9; Indonesia 611-13, iv:255, 260, 282, 288; Iran 636-7; Ireland 656-7; Israel 676-7, 691-99, 717-8, 756-8; sqsp; Italy iv:30; Japan 787-810; Kenya 851-3, 857-8; Mexico 876-7, 881; Morocco iv:337-8; Netherlands 905-6, 909-12, 924-5, 940; Nigeria iv:369-75, 384; Norway sq:453; Outer Space iv:421; Papua iv:443, 448; Philippines iv:467-72; Pland 967, 969-70; Polynesia 998-99, 1000-04, 1010; Portugal iv:512-3; Puerto Rico 1031-2: Russia 1058, 1121-2; S.Africa sqsp: S.Korea iv:568, 570-2, 580; Spain 1149-50, 1151-2; Sweden 1177; Thailand 1214-18; Turkey iv:621-22, 625; Ukraine 1276-82, 1286-87; United Kingdom 1325; USA 1420, 1429-30, 1462-3, 1479-98, explanations of 1489-98, homosexual 1520-22. See also: children, sexual activities of; premarital sex, sexarche; teenage pregnancy

adultery See: extramarital sex

adults, sexual activities of Argentina 48-50; Australia 94-5; Austria iv:20, 23-6; Bahrain 140-52; Brazil 199-204, 218-19; Canada 256-73; China 357-66, 387-94; Colombia iv:58-63; Croatia iv:94-101; Cyprus iv:143-52; Czech/Slovakia 405-8; Egypt iv:197-207; Finland 434-6, 442-64; Germany 501-09; Ghana 528-36; Greece553-57; Hong Kong sq:225-9; Iceland iv:227-61; India